Building Web Applications with C# and .NET

A Complete Reference

Building Web Applications with C# and .NET

A Complete Reference

Dudley W. Gill

CRC Press
Taylor & Francis Group
Boca Raton London New York

CRC Press is an imprint of the
Taylor & Francis Group, an **informa** business

CRC Press
Taylor & Francis Group
6000 Broken Sound Parkway NW, Suite 300
Boca Raton, FL 33487-2742

© 2003 by Taylor & Francis Group, LLC
CRC Press is an imprint of Taylor & Francis Group, an Informa business

No claim to original U.S. Government works

ISBN 13: 978-0-8493-1250-2 (pbk)
ISBN 13: 978-1-138-46855-9 (hbk)

Visit the Taylor & Francis Web site at
http://www.taylorandfrancis.com

and the CRC Press Web site at
http://www.crcpress.com

Library of Congress Cataloging-in-Publication Data

Gill, Dudley W.
    Building Web applications with C# and .NET : a complete reference / Dudley W. Gill.
        p. cm.
    ISBN 0-8493-1250-7
        1. Web site development. 2. Application software—Development. 3. C# (Computer program language) 4. Microsoft .NET. I. Title.

    TK5105.888 .G54 2002
    005.2'76—dc21   2002034915

Library of Congress Card Number 2002034915

About This Book

Building Web Applications with C# and .NET: A Complete Reference presents the basic knowledge and illustrative examples needed to build dynamic and robust Web applications using the .NET Framework technology. This book stresses the use of code-behind procedural coding.

Who Should Read This Book

This book is intended for people interested in Web application development using the .NET Framework technology. It promotes the use of code-behind file programming; thus, it should be extremely attractive to Visual Basic programmers familiar with the separation of visual and procedural components.

No prior experience with Web-page or Web-server development, HTML or XML is required because the Appendices provide an introduction to these Web standards. Consequently, this book should be useful to newcomers who need a basic understanding of these standards as well as "technical gurus" needing to research an obscure facet of these standards.

Familiarity with a procedural programming language is an asset but is not required. The Appendix contains an introduction to C# that will provide the knowledge and skill required to develop Web applications using .NET Framework. For this reason, the book is ideal for beginning programmers, as well as for C++ programmers transitioning to .NET.

This book is also intended for developers needing knowledge and skill with the Visual Studio.NET integrated development environment. Familiarity with the Microsoft Windows operating system and Windows-based applications is assumed.

Conventions Used

The following conventions are used throughout the book:

- Important terms are first introduced in **bold typeface**.
- Throughout the text, references to code variables, references, delegates and methods are in `Courier New` typeface.
- In the Hands-On exercises, user-entered data are presented in **`Courier New` bold typeface**.
- Standards, reference materials and code examples are set off from the rest of the text.

Organization

The book is divided into four parts:

1. Fundamentals: creating Web Forms using the **Web Forms Server Controls**.
2. Implementing Services: creation and consumption of **Web Services** including the use of HTTP, XML and SOAP to move messages across firewalls.

3. Accessing Data: accessing relational databases including **ADO** architecture and datasets.
4. Implementing Web Applications: techniques and concepts underlying Web applications including navigation, data search, retrieval, presentation and management.

Throughout, the book contains hands-on examples illustrating the development of client and server applications using Visual Studio.NET, which is an Integrated Development Environment complementing .NET Framework. It includes a suite of rapid application development tools addressing the development requirements of client–server application and distributed computing development. The examples also illustrate the use of .NET Frameworks classes, a comprehensive collection of object-oriented classes encapsulating the functionality common to application development.

The following appendices in the book provide tutorial and reference material regarding associated technologies:

C#: C# is a language targeted to the .NET Framework's Common Language Runtime. C# is an object-oriented programming language built from the ground up that provides the robustness of C++ but without its shortfalls. It has been estimated that most C++ programmers will migrate to C# in the next 5 years.

Industry Standards: Industry standards comprising the underpinnings of Web Services include the following:

XML:	Extensible Markup Language defines the way information is described in a Web Service.
WSDL:	Web Services Description Language defines an XML-based document that describes a Web Service.
SOAP:	Simple Object Access Protocol is the core protocol for Web Service communications.
HTML:	Hypertext Markup Language is the language of Web Pages. HTML concepts, elements and attributes are needed to develop Web Pages incorporating ASP Web Controls.
Database:	An introduction to relational databases including hands-on Access examples.

Documentation

Documentation based on documentation provided with the .NET Framework SDK is set apart from the rest of the text. The documentation presents summaries reflecting the more important and most used features. In general, inherited members are not shown. As the reader becomes comfortable with .NET Framework technology, reference to the online documentation will reveal its full capability. A hands-on exercise in Chapter 1 illustrates several online documentation access modes.

Downloadable Files

Sample code for all hands-on exercises and applications developed in the text are available for downloading at the CRC Press Web site: http://www.crcpress.com. This saves the reader from typing the code and enables faster mastery of .NET Framework technology.

Acknowledgments

It is always a pleasure to acknowledge efforts made by others on your behalf. I was fortunate to be able to work with a wonderful CRC Press team. Their enthusiasm, dedication and tolerance have enabled me to do my best. Thanks!

Special thanks are due to my family for their support and encouragement.

About the Author

Dudley W. Gill, Sc.D., has more than 40 years experience in application development. Dr. Gill earned his B.S.E.E. from Howard University, his M.S.E.E. from the University of Pennsylvania and his Sc.D. from George Washington University. He has developed applications for federal, state and city agencies; Fortune 500 companies; and educational institutions. He takes great pleasure in sharing his knowledge of computer science and technology by teaching community college through graduate level courses.

He enjoys the West Florida and New Jersey coasts.

Dr. Gill can be reached at **www.BuildingWebApplications.com**.

* * *

Welcome to Application Development with C# and .NET Framework!

Dedication

Dedicated to visionaries:

Dean Lewis K. Downing
Dean Stephen S. Davis
Chairman Ernest R. Welch
Chairman Walter T. Daniels
Chairman Darnley M. Howard
Professor Lee J. Purnell

and
to those who continued their work:

Dean M. Lucius Walker
Dean Eugene M. DeLoach
Professor Woolsey Semple

Contents

Appendices

List of Figures

Part 1

Fundamentals

1

.NET Framework

The **.NET Framework** provides the technology to develop and implement Web-based applications and services efficiently. The .NET Framework's core consists of the following:

- A runtime environment called the common language runtime. Code developed on compilers that target the common language runtime can be compiled once and run on any platform that supports the common-language runtime.
- A collection of reusable classes, interfaces, structures, enumerations and delegates called the class library.

The .NET Framework architecture is characterized in Figure 1.1.

The .NET Framework supports ASP.NET applications. ASP.NET Web Services are built on top of ASP.NET. The Microsoft.NET Framework SDK is supported on the following operating systems: Windows 2000, Windows NT 4 with Service Pack 6a, Windows ME, Windows 98, Windows SE and Windows 95.

Complementing the .NET Framework is **Visual Studio.NET**, an integrated development environment. Visual Studio.NET addresses the development requirements of client-server application and distributed computing development with a suite of rapid application development tools including a WYSIWYG (What You See Is What You Get) form designer and prompted code development.

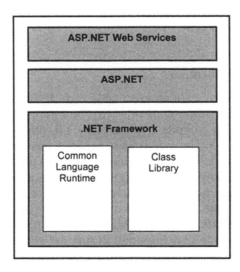

FIGURE 1.1
.NET Framework architecture and relationship to ASP.NET and ASP.NET Web Services.

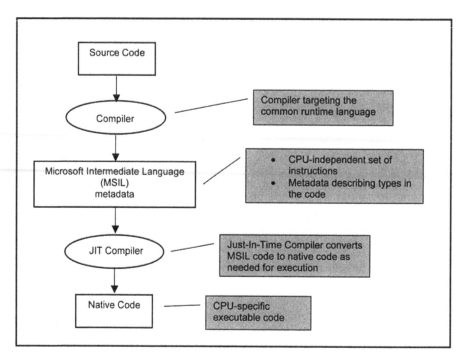

FIGURE 1.2
Compilation steps in the transition from source code to executable code.

Common Language Runtime

The **common language runtime (CLR)** provides an execution environment that incorporates features such as memory management, security management, code verification and compilation. Code that targets the runtime is known as **managed code** and code that does not is known as **unmanaged code**.

Compilation and Code Verification

The compilation from source code to executable code is summarized in Figure 1.2. To obtain the CLR benefits, the source code must first be compiled with a compiler targeting CLR. C# is a language with compiler that targets CLR; other languages include Visual Basic, Jscript and Visual C++. These compilers export types and features of the common language specification (CLS). The CLS defines general characteristics such as visibility; naming (including casing), keywords and signatures; types including primitive, reference array and enumeration; and type members, methods, properties and events.

The compiler translates the source code into a CPU-independent set of instructions called **Microsoft Intermediate Language (MSIL)**. The compiler also produces metadata along with the compiled code that provide information about the types, members and references in the code. These metadata are stored along with the code and used by the runtime to manage code execution. The metadata provide a description of the code, thereby eliminating the need for Type Libraries and Interface Definition Language.

The **just-in-time compiler (JIT compiler)** converts the MSIL code to native code. A JIT compiler is supplied for each CPU and thus generates CPU-specific code, called **native code**.

Each method is JIT-compiled the first time it is called and stored. The stored code is executed during subsequent calls.

Code verification is performed as part of the MSIL to native code compilation to ensure the code is type safe, i.e.:

- Types are only referenced by compatible type reference.
- Access and subsequent invocation are appropriate.
- Identities are valid.

Note!

A major feature of CLR is the ability to compile once and run on any platform that supports the CLR.

Memory Management

Memory management eliminates the two most common memory management problems: memory leaks and invalid memory references. This is accomplished by managing the references to objects and releasing them when they are no longer used. C# is targeted to CLR. A **garbage collector** implements memory management. The garbage collector maintains information about the object and its use. The memory management life cycle consists of the following phases:

- Memory is allocated for newly created objects and appropriately located in memory. When the new operator is used, the runtime allocates memory for the object from the managed heap. Space is allocated as long as memory exists.
- The managed heap is monitored and and eligibility for garbage collection is established by the garbarge collector's optimizing engine, which takes into account the memory allocations made.
- Applicable destructors are executed during garbage collection and memory is released.

GC class methods influence when an object is subject to garbage collection and the resources used are released. The GC class derives directly from the object class and is in the system namespace. Invoking GC class methods should be avoided because excessive use can lead to performance problems and offset the benefits of the garbage collection's optimizing engine.

This automatic memory management relieves developers of the time-consuming task of manual memory management, a task which often fails to prevent memory leaks that bring down a system at the most inopportune time.

Note!

Memory management eliminates the two common problems associated with manual memory management: memory leaks and invalid references.

Security

The .NET Framework provides for code access security and role-based security. Code-access security relies on the type-safe nature of managed code and permissions. Permissions are used to control the operations that code can perform and are determined by the runtime. Role-based security is an integral part of the managed code runtime environment. Typically, access to a resource is based on information supplied by the user. Role-based security is automatically available to managed code or can be application-defined.

Class Library

The .NET Framework class library is a library of classes, interfaces, structures, enumerations and delegates intended to provide the foundation for .NET applications, components, services and controls. The .NET Framework uses the dot syntax naming convention. The system namespace is the root namespace for the .NET Framework and has secondary namespaces. Figure 1.3 summarizes namespaces commonly referenced in the development of distributed applications.

Library classes, interfaces, structures, enumerations and delegates are grouped into **namespaces**. A name consists of two parts. The last part, that is, the part to the right of

Namespace	Description
System	Classes, interfaces, structures, delegates and enumerations including definition of the data types and data conversion, events and event handlers, common mathematical functions and environment management.
System.Collections	Classes and interfaces describing collections such as lists, arrays, tables, queues and dictionaries.
System.ComponentModel	Classes, interfaces, delegates and enumerations used to implement components and controls including implementation of attributes, type converters and data source binding.
System.Data	Classes, interfaces, delegates and enumerations that constitute the ADO.NET architecture enabling access and management of multiple data sources.
System.Drawing	Classes, structures, delegates and enumerations providing basic graphic functionality.
System.Web	Classes, interfaces, delegates and enumerations enabling browser/server communications including the HTTPRequest class representing the current HTTP request from the client and the HTTPResponse class representing HTTP output directed to the client.
System.Web.UI	Classes, interfaces, delegates and ennumerations that enable creation of controls and pages used as Web pages in Web applications.
System.Web.UI.WebControls	Classes, interfaces, structures, delegates and enumerations enabling the creation of Web server controls on a Web page including form controls such as labels, text boxes buttons and lists. Web controls are more abstract than HtmlControls and provide for robust server-side programming.
System.Web.UI.HtmlControls	Classes enabling the creation of HTML server controls on a Web page. The HTML server controls map directly to the industry standard HTML tags supported by browsers.

FIGURE 1.3
Namespaces commonly referenced in distributed application development.

the right-most dot, is the name of the class, interface, structure, enumeration or delegate. The first part, i.e., the part to the left of the rightmost dot, is the namespace name. For example, the name

```
System.Data.DataTable
```

represents an in-memory data table of DataTable type that belongs to the System.Data namespace.

The standard naming convention reduces learning time and difficulty in researching and finding resources that can be used in application development.

Data Types

Data types supported by .NET Framework are summarized in Figure 1.4.

Type	Description
Boolean	Represents the primitive Boolean type.
Byte	8-bit unsigned integer value ranging from 0 to 255.
Char	Represents Unicode characters with values ranging from hexadecimal 0x0000 to 0xFFFF.
DateTime	Structure representing date and time with values ranging from 12:00:00 AM, 1/1/0001 to 11:59:59 PM, 12/31/9999 CE. CE stands for Common Era, which is equivalent to the AD, for "Anno Domini" which means "in the year of our Lord".
Decimal	Represents a decimal value ranging from positive 79,228,162,514,264,337,593,543,950,335 to negative 79,228,162,514,264,337,593,543,950,335 suitable for financial calculations.
Double	A double-precision floating point 64-bit number with values ranging from negative 1.79769313486232e308 to positive 1.79769313486232e308 as well as positive or negative zero, positive infinity, negative infinity and Not-a-Number.
Int16	A 16-bit signed integer with values ranging from negative 32768 to positive 32767.
Int32	A 32-bit signed integer with values ranging from negative 2,147,483,648 to positive 2,147,483,647.
Int64	A 64-bit signed integer with values ranging from negative 9,223,372,036,854,775,808 to positive 9,223,372,036,854,775,807.
SByte	An 8-bit signed integer with values ranging from negative 128 to positive 127.
Single	A single-precision 32-bit floating point number with values ranging from negative 3.402823e38 to positive 3.402823e38 as well as positive or negative zero, positive infinity, negative infinity and Not-a-Number.
String	An immutable string of characters including the empty string ("").
TimeSpan	A period of time valued in ticks, that is the smallest unit of time that can be specified: 100 nanoseconds.
UInt16	A 16-bit unsigned integer with values ranging from 0 to 65,535.
UInt32	A 32-bit unsigned integer with values ranging from 0 to 4,294,967,295.
UInt64	A 64-bit unsigned integer with values ranging from 0 to 18,446,744,073,709,551,615.

FIGURE 1.4
Data types supported by .NET Framework.

Hands-On Exercise 1: Accessing .NET Framework Documentation

Documentation included as part of the .NET Framework SDK is a complete reference for developers utilizing .NET framework technologies in their applications. Included are complete descriptions of all the classes, interfaces, structures, delegates and enumerations in the class library. Examples are included with many references.

The following Hands-On describes how to navigate to documentation regarding System Namespace in the Documentation's Table of Contents, access documentation regarding the Object class using the Index, and search for information regarding ASP control syntax using the Search window. Note that the Object class is the root class of all classes included in the Framework's Class Library.

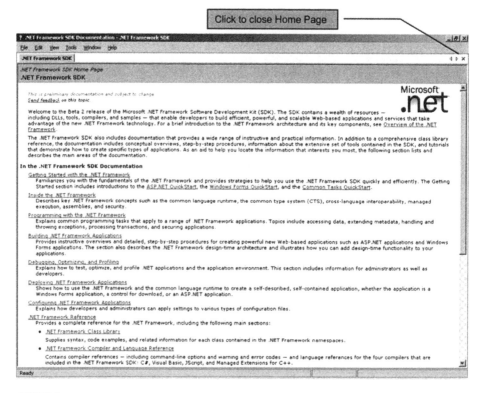

Figure HO1.1–1
.NET Framework SDK Documentation Home Page.

Step 1: Open the Documentation

1. Start → Programs → Microsoft.NET Framework SDK → Documentation. The Document Explorer opens with the .NET Framework SDK Home Page.

2. Review the available documentation, noting the following:

   - .NET Framework Compiler and Language Reference

   - .NET Framework Class Library

   - ASP.NET Syntax

3. Click the X icon on the .NET Framework SDK tab's title bar to close the Home Page.

Step 2: Managing the Help Dialog Boxes

The dialog boxes displaying the Documentation's content and index and facilitating a search are dockable and can be automatically hidden in the side margins when not in use.

1. In the Help menu, click the Contents... command. Alternately, press the Ctrl+Alt+F1 keys. The Contents dialog window is opened in the docked state. Note that the page shown in the bottom half of the window is the Home Page that was displayed when the Contents dialog box window was opened.

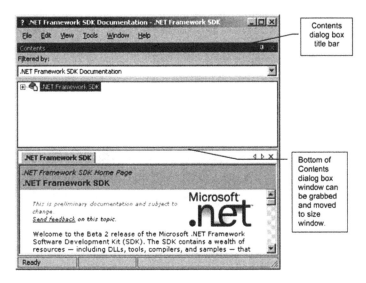

FIGURE HO1.1–2
Contents dialog box docked at window top.

2. Right-click the Contents dialog box title bar to display the options menu:

   Dockable: The dialog box is toggled between a docked window and a tab window. When docked, the dialog box can be set to hide in the margin when not in use by checking the Auto-Hide option.

   Hide: The dialog box window is closed.

   Floating: The dialog box is toggled in and out of a floating window status. When floating, the dialog box can be moved anywhere in the desktop.

   Auto-Hide: The dialog box is toggled in and out of the automatic hide state. When hidden, the window is represented by a tab in the Documentation window.

   Clicking the Floating option sets the dialog box in the Floating state. A dialog box in this state can be moved about the desktop.

4. Right-click the Contents dialog box title bar to expose the Options submenu. Select the Dockable option. Grab the dialog box's title bar and dock the dialog box window at the top of the Framework's Documentation window. Note that the dialog window is pinned open, i.e., the pin icon is poised to pin the window.

5. Click the pin to set the dialog to Auto-Hide. Alternately, right click the dialog's tab and set the option to Auto-Hide. The dialog window closes and is simply represented by a tab in the top margin of the Documentation window when the cursor is moved off the dialog window.

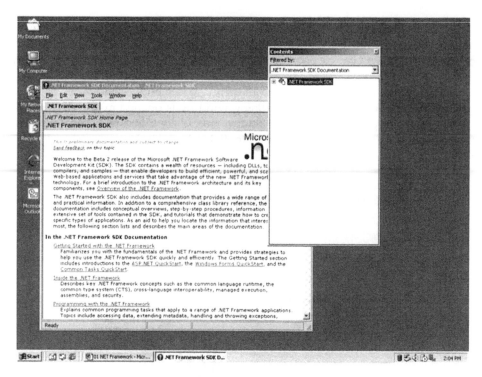

FIGURE HO1.1–3
Contents dialog box floating in window.

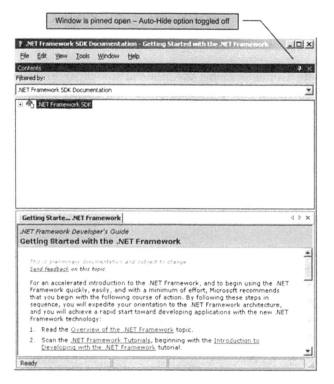

FIGURE HO1.1–4
Contents dialog box docked and pinned open.

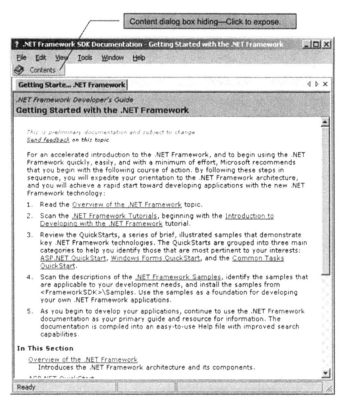

FIGURE HO1.1–5
Contents dialog box hiding.

6. To expose the dialog window, simply click its tab. The dialog box window is opened. Note that the pin is set not to pin the dialog window open.

The dialog window remains open as long as the focus is on the window; when the Documentation window is opened, the dialog box closes.

Step 3: Navigating the Table of Contents

1. In the Help menu, click the Contents... command or press the Ctrl+Alt+F1 keys. The Contents dialog box window opens. (See Figure HO1–6.)
2. Click the plus sign (+) to the right of the root element, .NET Framework SDK, to expand the Table of Contents. (Clicking the minus sign (–) will contract the topic's contents table.) (See Figures HO1–7 and HO1–8.)
3. Expand the Content to expose the System namespace by subsequently expanding the following topics:
   - .NET Framework Reference
   - .NET Framework Class Library
   - System
4. Scroll down until the Object class title is displayed in the Table of Contents. (See Figure HO1–9.)
5. Click the Object class to display the documentation.

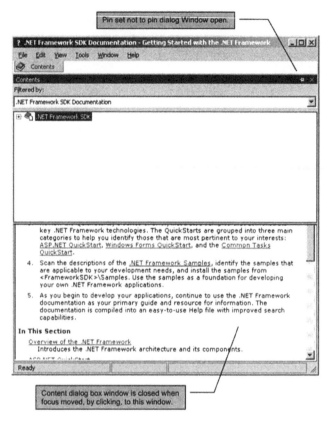

FIGURE HO1.1–6
Pin set not to pin Contents dialog Window open.

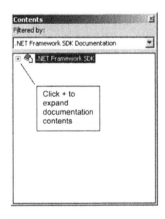

FIGURE HO1.1–7
Click plus sign "+" to expand Table of Contents.

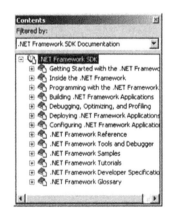

FIGURE HO1.1–8
Expanded Table of Contents.

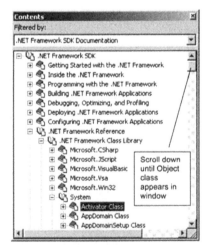

FIGURE HO1.1–9
Scrolling and expanding subcontent tables.

6. Unpin the Content dialog box window and move the focus to the window with Object class documentation. The Content dialog box window closes.

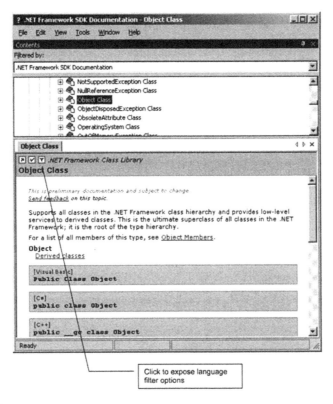

Click to expose language filter options

FIGURE HO1.1–10
Click Object Class topic to access documentation.

7. Click the Language Filter icon, a funnel symbol, at the top of the Documentation window. The documentation is displayed for several languages. The following language options are displayed: C#, C++, Jscript, Visual Basic and Show All. Select the C# option. The documentation displayed pertains to the C# language only. Links throughout the page point to detailed information regarding the class.

Step 4: Using the Help Index

1. In the Help menu, click the Index... command. Alternately, press the Ctrl+Alt+F2 keys. The Index dialog box is opened.

2. Enter a keyword describing the subject for which documentation is desired in the "Look for:" textbox — in this case, "object." The index automatically scrolls to the best match for the entered keyword.

3. Click the topic in the Index that best meets a description of the information desired — in this case, Object class. The index references Object class more than once. The multiple listings are displayed in an Index Results dialog box.

4. Note that the Index Results window can also be managed in terms of its display mode. Click on the title bar to expose the options.

5. Click the Index Results window pin to toggle the window to Auto-Hide. Similarly, click the Index window pin to toggle the Index window to Auto-Hide.

6. Select the Object class reference in the Index Results window.

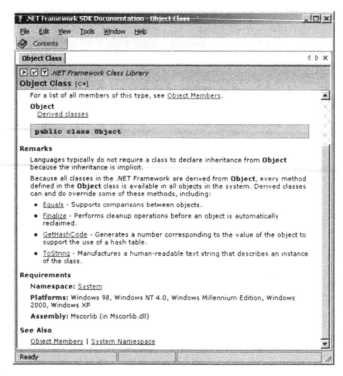

FIGURE HO1.1–11
Click Object Class documentation to close dialog and expose documentation.

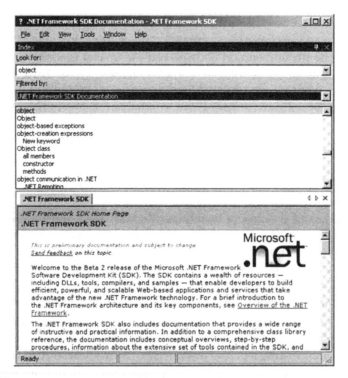

FIGURE HO1.1–12
Index dialog.

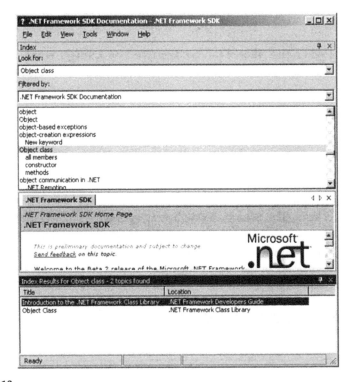

FIGURE HO1.1–13
Multiple references are listed in an Index Results dialog box.

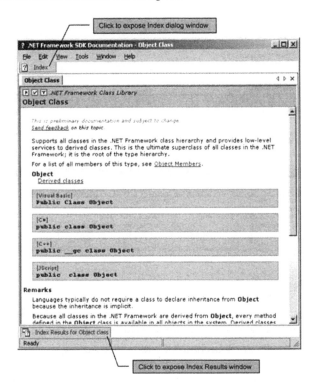

FIGURE HO1.1–14
Click hiding Index tab to expose dialog box.

Tip!

Use the Index when the subject can be described by a single word.

Step 5: Using the Search Dialog Window

The Search dialog window can be very helpful when a specific keyword describing the subject is not known but several keywords describing the subject area are known: for example, asp controls syntax.

1. In the Help menu, click the Search... command. Alternately, press the Ctrl+Alt+F3 keys. The Search dialog box is opened.

2. Enter a keyword describing the subject for which documentation is desired in the "Look for:" textbox — in this case, asp. Click the Search button. The search results are displayed in the Search Results window. Note that 500 topics relating to asp were found.

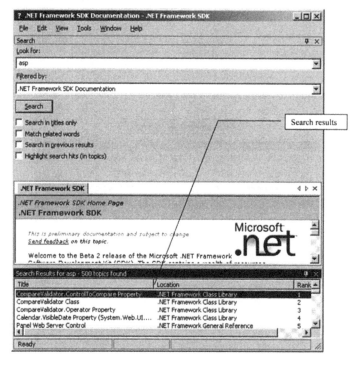

FIGURE HO1.1–15
Search and Search Results dialog boxes.

3. Enter a second search criterion (in this case, syntax) in the "Look For" textbox. Check the Search in previous results checkbox. Click the Search button.

4. The previous results are searched for topics pertaining to syntax. The results are displayed in the Search Results window. Double click the third item in the Search Results window to display documentation entitled ASP.NET Syntax.

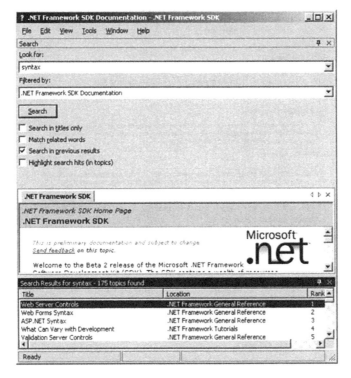

FIGURE HO1.1–16
Search previous results to narrow results.

5. Unpin the Search and Search Results windows. The documentation contains links and descriptions regarding ASP.NET Syntax documentation.

Step 6: Synchronizing Contents

When reading a specific topic, the need for more background in the area is often uncovered. Identification of the general area in the Table of Contents provides for identification of the topics needed to develop the topic in an orderly manner. For example, consider the documentation resulting from the search regarding asp syntax.

1. In the View menu, select the Toolbars command. Check the Standard option in the submenu to display the Standard Toolbar.
2. To show this documentation topic in the Table of Contents, click the Synchronization Button in the Standard Toolbar. The Contents window automatically opens with the topic of the currently displayed page highlighted.

Tip!

Commands for opening the Contents, Index and Search dialog boxes are also in the View menu's Navigation submenu.

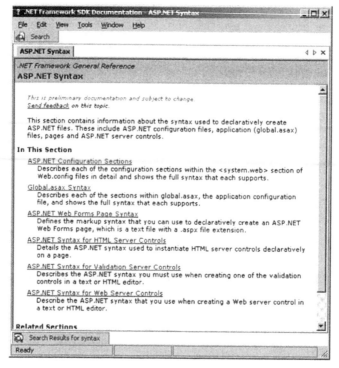

FIGURE HO1.1–17
Documentation is linked to Search topics.

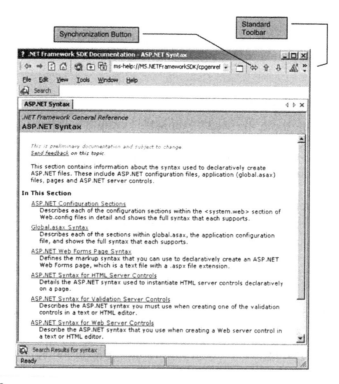

FIGURE HO1.1–18
Synchronizing current topic and Table of Contents.

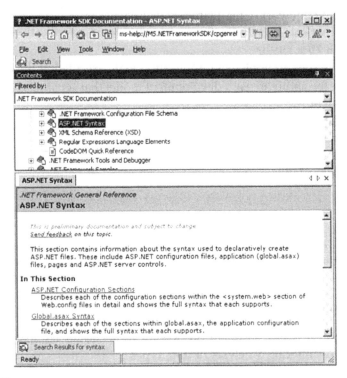

FIGURE HO1.1–19
Table of Contents synchronized to current topic.

ASP.NET Applications

ASP.NET is a development platform that provides for the development of enterprise level Web-based applications. An ASP.NET application consists of Web Forms and Web Services residing on and invoked from a virtual directory and its subdirectories on a Web application server. For the most part, ASP.NET is compatible with **Active Server Pages (ASP)**.

ASP.NET is supported on the following platforms: Windows 2000 and Windows NT 4 with Service Pack 6a with the exception of using Web Services. Using Web Services is supported on the following platforms: Windows 2000 and Windows NT 4 with Service Pack 6a, Windows ME, Windows 98 and Windows SE.

Web Forms

Web Forms are Web pages developed with ASP.NET technology; they have many features essential to the development of enterprise-level applications:

- They are able to run on any browser and to be custom tailored to take advantage of feature-rich browsers.
- They effectively display information using markup language and Web Server Controls. Web Server Controls are robust user-interface controls enabling the display of static information, data input, selection with buttons and checkboxes, and data manipulation with lists and grids.

- The .NET Framework CLR features include programming in C# and Class Libraries that can be effectively used in developing application functionality supporting Web Forms.
- They utilize code to implement application logic executed at the server.
- They have the ability to use a development model that separates code from page visual content.
- The availability of Visual Studio.NET provides for the efficient design and development of Web Forms.
- Automatic state management that preserves state properties between client requests is available.

Web Services

A **Web Service** provides an application or system function that is accessible to disparate applications through industry Internet standards. That is, Web Services can be called from different programming languages, different operating systems and different processing units.

Underlying industry standards include the following:

- **Simple Object Access Protocol (SOAP)** — an emerging standard for invoking Web Services offering a rich set of data types
- **Web Services Description Language (WSDL)** — the language used to describe the Web Service's methods, thereby informing clients how to invoke the method
- **XML** — markup for data returned from a Web Service using all methods of invocations and the parameters sent to the Web Service when invoked with SOAP

Services can be used by Web applications internally or exposed over the Internet to all sorts of applications, including other Web Services.

Hands-On Exercise 2: Running an Existing .NET Framework Application

Step 1: Deploy Application

Files for all examples and Hands-on exercises are available at the CRC Press Web site: http://www.crcpress.com/e-products/downloads/default.asp.

1. Click on the title to navigate to download instructions.
2. Download the files. Unzip the files in a local directory, for example, BWA.
3. Locate the NETFrameworkApplication folder containing the files:
   - WelcomeForm.aspx
   - NetFrameworkApplication.dll
4. In the default home directory, C:\Internet\wwwroot, paste a copy of the downloaded NETFrameworkApplication folder.

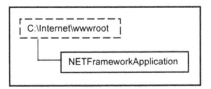

FIGURE HO1.2–1
Locating the application.

Step 2: Execute Application

1. Open Internet Explorer, offline.
2. Enter the address of the Web page (in this case, a Web form) to be displayed:

   http://lajolla/NETFrameworkApplication/WelcomeForm.aspx
3. Click the Go button. The Web form welcome.aspx is displayed. This page contains three Web Form controls: Label, TextBox and Button.
4. Enter your name in the text box.

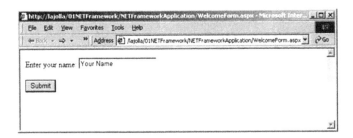

FIGURE HO1.2–2
Browser rendering of Web page WelcomeForm.aspx.

5. Click the Submit button. The Web Form is submitted to the Server and programming associated with the form is executed:

   - The name is retrieved from the text box and parsed into a message that will be displayed on the page in previously empty label controls.
   - The textbox and button controls are made invisible.
   - The revised page is returned to the client and displayed in the browser.

The browser rendering of the returned page is shown below (Figure HO1.2–3).

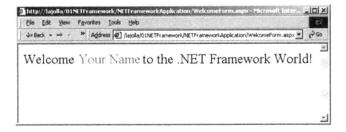

FIGURE HO1.2–3
Browser rendering of the returned Web page.

2

Web Forms

World Wide Web Basics

The Web started with a 1960s U.S. Department of Defense project, ARPANET, to provide a reliable, secure and robust communications network that could still operate even if a part failed. Throughout the 1970s and 1980s the network grew as universities not involved in the original project linked onto the network. To overcome system disparities, the network adopted communication protocols. A **protocol** specifies how systems or computers will treat information resources. By adhering to the protocol, diverse computer systems can communicate. These protocols have evolved over time and are now widely used. Several widely used protocols are summarized in Figure 2.1. Other protocols provide for services such as email transmission and group access.

Protocol	Use
HTTP	Requesting and sending Web documents.
FTP	File transfer from one system to another
Telnet	Remote login and use of server resources
File	Local system file access

FIGURE 2.1
Widely used protocols.

Hypertext Transfer Protocol

In 1989, Tim Berners-Lee at the European Particle Physics Laboratory (CERN) proposed a new protocol for hypertext documents. **Hypertext** documents are text documents that contain links to other documents. By simply clicking on the hypertext link, the reader retrieves the related document. This capability marks the beginning of the World Wide Web known today.

The basis of Berners-Lee's concept is a **client program** called a browser and a **server program**. All servers running on an Internet host respond to client requests. The requests specify a document using a unique address called a uniform resource location.

The first Web browser with a graphical interface, called Mosaic, was developed by Marc Andreessen and an associate, Eric Bina, in 1993. The rest is history!

Internet Protocol Number

Every machine connected to the Internet has a unique address called the **Internet Protocol (IP)** number. This address is not user friendly in that it is composed of four 8-bit numbers separated by periods. A typical IP address is 111.222.001.255. Additionally, a TCP/IP (Transfer Control Protocol/Internet Protocol) port number can be added to the address.

The IP address has an alias that can be used in its place — the **host name**. Technically, the host name consists of two parts: a host name and a domain name. The domain name is an extension identifying country or type of organization. For example, government organizations belong to **.gov**, educational institutions to **.edu**, and business organizations to **.com**. Note that the use of the term *host name* is used to identify the name part of the IP address as well as the name part and domain part combination.

Uniform Resource Locators

Network resources, such as files or directories, are uniquely named and located on the World Wide Web with a **Universal Resource Locator** (URL). A typical URL is shown in Figure 2.2.

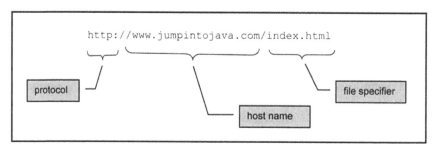

FIGURE 2.2
Typical URL.

The URL indicates that the document is to be handled with the **HTTP protocol**. Thus, both the client system and the server system are able to communicate and transfer this file by using the HTTP protocol. The URL also specifies the machine on which the file is located with the **host name**. The host name begins with double slashes (//). Finally, the specific file on the machine is specified with the URL **file specifier**. The file specifier follows the host name separated by a slash (/). URLs specify the machine on which the file is located, how the file is handled, and the file's name.

Hypertext Markup Language

Web pages are created with a computer language **HTML**. A simple text file not requiring compilation, the language prescribes tags that are placed within the text. These tags specify how the text is to be displayed. For example, a tag can specify that text be displayed as a title or as a hyperlink. Web pages are stored on computers continuously connected to the Internet, commonly called servers. These files are retrieved by Web clients and displayed using a Web browser. The browser uses these tags to create the image displayed.

Web Page

A **Web page** is a file with Hypertext Markup Language (HTML)-notated content and .html or .htm extension. Notation is performed with HTML elements such as <H1>, <BR> and <HR> that denote the largest heading size, line break and horizontal rule, respectively. A Web page, also referred to as an HTML document, with basic HTML elements is illustrated in Figure 2.3.

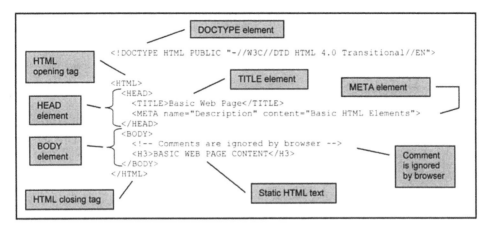

FIGURE 2.3
HTML document with basic elements, basicwebpage.html.

DOCTYPE Element

The **DOCTYPE element** defines the document type and goes before the HTML start tag. For example, within HTML 4.0 there are three Document Type Definitions (DTDs): Strict DTD, Transitional DTD and Frameset DTD. For example,

```
<!DOCTYPE HTML PUBLIC "-//W3C//DTD HTML 4.0 Transitional//EN">
```

describes a document using Transitional DTD that includes presentation attributes and elements that W3C expects to move to a style sheet. Note that an exclamation point is required after the opening bracket. The DOCTYPE element does not have any attributes.

HEAD Element

The **HEAD element** contains meta-information about the document. Note that meta means "information about" and thus the HEAD element contains information about the information in the document. Valid elements within the HEAD element include the following:

Element	Description
TITLE	Defines the document's title and is displayed in the browser's title bar.

META	Facilitates provision of meta-information about the document. Some search engines use keywords defined in a META element, for example:
	`<META name = "keywords" content = "HTML, HEAD, BODY, META>`
	Similarly, the META element can contain a description of the page, for example:
	`<META name = "description" content = "BASIC HTML elements">`

Note the use of the name and content attributes within the META element. Additionally, META attributes can be unique to the site or author.

BODY Element

The **BODY element** defines the part of the document that contains document content, such as text, links to other documents and images. The BODY element provides for selected elements including the **MS_POSITIONING** attribute that characterizes the layout of elements within the body. Valid values for the MS_POSITIONING attribute are the following:

Value	Description
FlowLayout	Elements are added to the page without absolute positioning attributes, i.e., x and y positioning values. The elements are displayed by browsers in the order that they occur on the page.
GridLayout	Elements are added to the page with absolute positioning attributes, i.e., x and y positioning values.

The MS_POSITIONING attribute is related to the pageLayoutProperty that determines whether components added to the document in design view are positioned in-line or with absolute locations.

The BODY element in Figure 2.3 contains the following:

Element/Content	Description
Heading element	Heading elements are defined with the <H1>, <H2>, <H3>, <H4>, <H5>, <H6>, where <H1> defines the largest heading and <H6> defines the smallest heading. The content between the start and end tag is rendered with the defined weight. Note that HTML automatically adds an extra blank line before and after the heading.
Static HTML text	An example of static HTML text is the following: `BASIC WEB PAGE CONTENT` Although the text is expressed in the default weight, it is included between heading tags and thus is rendered as heading <H3>.
Comment	The <!--> element defines an HTML source code comment. The browser ignores comments. For example, `<!-- Comments are ignored by browser -->`

Note that an exclamation point is included after the opening bracket, but not before the closing one. Comments are a useful way of documenting code.

Other HTML elements used to specify content layout include those in the following table.

Element	Description
 	Inserts a single line break. The break element ends a line but does not start a new paragraph.
<HR>	Defines a horizontal rule. The horizontal rule can be used to separate sections of a document.
<P>	Defines a paragraph. The <P> element should not be used to insert blank lines; the element should be used to create blank lines. An extra blank line is added before and after a paragraph.

Note that the layout displayed can vary from browser to browser and can change every time the browser's window is resized. Additionally, spaces in static text are truncated.

Today's browsers are forgiving and poorly constructed pages are rendered correctly by some browsers (see Figure 2.4).

```
<TITLE>Basic Web Page</TITLE>
<META name="Description" content="Basic HTML Elements">

<!-- Comments are ignored by browser -->
<H3>BASIC WEB PAGE CONTENT</H3>
Without HTML, HEAD and BODY elements
```

FIGURE 2.4
Browsers can correctly render this file.

Form Element

The **Form element** defines an area that can contain elements that allow a user to enter information. In some cases, the user will enter keywords that will be used to retrieve information returned to the user. In other cases, the user enters information that is saved in a database. In all cases, the manipulation of the data is performed at the server. The user's interface is through a form rendered at the user's browser. The Web page in Figure 2.5A illustrates the typical Form element included in a Web page, basicform.html.

```
<!DOCTYPE HTML PUBLIC "-//W3C//DTD HTML 4.0 Transitional//EN">
<HTML>
  <HEAD>
    <TITLE>Basic Form</TITLE>
    <META name="Description" content="Basic HTML Elements">
  </HEAD>
  <BODY>
    <FORM action="TargetPage.html">
      Name:
      <INPUT type="text" name="nameInput">
      <BR>
      <INPUT type="submit" value="Press To Submit">
    </FORM>
  </BODY>
</HTML>
```

FORM element opening tag

FORM element closing tag

Textbox input element

Button element

FIGURE 2.5A
Typical Web page with a Form element, basicform.html.

A Form element is defined with the <FORM> tag. The form's content typically includes elements that enable a user to enter information, such as text fields, drop-down lists, check boxes and radio buttons. In the example shown, the form includes a textbox and a button.

The input element, defined with the <INPUT> tag, provides for a variety of input configurations. The particular rendering of the input element depends on the value of the type of attribute:

Value	Description
Checkbox	User is able to select and unselect multiple choices.
Radio	User is able to select one of a number of choices. Selection of a new choice automatically unselects the previously selected choice.
Submit	Button. Note that a value attribute provides for specifying the button's caption.
Text	Text field in which the user can type characters.

A name attribute provides for identifying a specific element. The page's browser rendering is shown in Figure 2.5B.

FIGURE 2.5B
Browser rendering of the typical Web page with a Form element.

The user is able to enter text in the textbox. When the user clicks on the "Press To Submit" button, the content of the form is sent to the file specified in the form's action attribute. In this case, the file specified is `TargetPage.html`.

```
<FORM action = "TargetPage.html">
```

Typically, the file prescribes what is to be done with the information received.

Web Forms Page

An ASP.NET feature used to create a user interface for Web applications, a **Web Forms page** is a file with the ".aspx" extension. The file is referred to commonly as "page" or "Web page." The file consists of HTML markup, including a form element plus Web-form-specific elements called Web controls. The file illustrating a Web Forms page — basicwebformspage.aspx — is shown in Figure 2.6A. The browser rendering of the page is shown in Figure 2.6B.

```
<!DOCTYPE HTML PUBLIC "-//W3C//DTD HTML 4.0 Transitional//EN">
<%@ Page Language="C#" %>                    ┌─────────────────┐
                                             │  Page directive │
<HTML>                                       └─────────────────┘
  <HEAD>
    <TITLE>Basic Web Forms Page</TITLE>
  </HEAD>
  <BODY>                                              ┌──────────────┐
    <FORM id="BasicWebForm" method="post" runat="server">  │ HTMLForm     │
        <H3>Form Content</H3>                          │ control with id,
    </FORM>                                            │ method and
  </BODY>                                              │ runat attributes
</HTML>                                                └──────────────┘
```

FIGURE 2.6A
Web Forms page file, basicwebformspage.aspx.

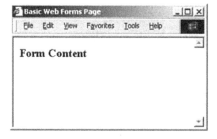

FIGURE 2.6B
Browser rendering of Web Forms page file, basicwebformspage.aspx.

HTMLForm Control

The Web Forms page includes the **HTMLForm control**, which enables programming against the HTML <FORM> element. The HTMLForm control can be placed anywhere between the <BODY> and </BODY> tags. Only one HTMLForm control can be placed on a Web Forms page because the Framework will throw an exception if more than one is included on a page. The syntax for the HTMLForm control is summarized in Figure 2.7.

The HTMLForm control includes an identification attribute **id** that, in terms of the page, uniquely names the form control. This identifier can be used to access the control programmatically. The HTMLForm control also includes the **action** attribute that specifies the name of the .aspx page that processes the data in the form. Additionally, the **runat = server** attribute and value identify the control as an ASP.NET Server Control.

```
<form
    runat="server"
    id="programID"
    method=POST | GET
    action="sourcercpageURL"
>
    Other controls
</form>
```

Attribute	Description
runat	A required attribute, specifies that the form is to be processed at the server.
id	A required attribute, specifies a unique control identifier.
method	POST by default.
action	URL of the page that will be processed using data contained in the form. Default is the URL of the source page.

Content	Description
Other controls	Server controls, including both HTMLServer and Web Forms.

FIGURE 2.7
HTMLForm control syntax for Web forms pages.

Page Directive

Page compilation and parsing directives are defined by the @ **Page** directive attributes. Only one @ Page directive can be included in an .aspx file. The @ Page syntax is shown in Figure 2.8.

```
<%@ Page attribute=value [attribute=value ...] %>
```

Attributes are declared as a space-separated attribute-value list with no space around the equal sign.

Attribute	
Inherits	Name of the code-behind class to inherit, that is the class file from which the .aspx file is derived.
Language	Language for <% %> and <%= %> blocks in the page. Valid values are C#, Visual Basic and Jscript.NET.
Codebehind	The name of the code-behind file.
AutoEventWireup	If false, event handlers are wired-up explicitly by the Web Forms designer; true otherwise. Note: events are considered in Chapter 4.

FIGURE 2.8
Selected @ Page directive syntax.

The Web Forms page created by Visual Studio is shown in Figure 2.9A.

The file is created in a developer-created namespace, in this case WebFormsBasics. The file is BasicWebForm.aspx. The directive

```
<%@ Page language = "c#" Codebehind = " BasicWebForm.aspx.cs "
AutoEventWireup = "false"
Inherits = "WebFormsBasic.BasicWebForm"%>
```

indicates that C# is the code language, BasicWebForm.aspx.cs is the code-behind file and WebFormsBasic.BasicWebForm is the code-behind class inherited .

Code-Behind File

Visual Studio automatically creates BasicWebForm.aspx.cs, the code-behind file that contains the form's code component (see Figure 2.9b). The **using** keyword is used to expose

```
<%@ Page language="c#" Codebehind="BasicWebForm.aspx.cs"
        AutoEventWireup="false" Inherits="WebFormsBasics.BasicWebForm" %>
<!DOCTYPE HTML PUBLIC "-//W3C//DTD HTML 4.0 Transitional//EN" >

<html>
  <head>                                    ┌─────────────────────────────┐
    <title>Basic Web Form</title>      ───┤ Manually added title element │
    <meta name="GENERATOR" Content="Microsoft Visual Studio 7.0">
    <meta name="CODE_LANGUAGE" Content="C#">
    <meta name=vs_defaultClientScript content="JavaScript (ECMAScript)">
    <meta name=vs_targetSchema
          content="http://schemas.microsoft.com/intellisense/ie5">
  </head>
  <body MS_POSITIONING="GridLayout">

    <form id="BasicWebForm"  method="post" runat="server"  >

    </form>

  </body>
</html>
```

FIGURE 2.9A
Web Forms page BasicWebForm.aspx created by Visual Studio.

types in namespaces typically used in application development. As such, the types can be referenced without qualification.

The application is developed in a namespace — in this case, WebFormsBasics.

Note that the class BasicWebForm is derived from the Page class:

```
public class BasicWebForm : System.Web.UI.Page
```

The class BasicWebForm is the class referenced in the file BasicWebForm.aspx with the Inherits attribute. The class inherits the functionality of the Page class. The Page class is summarized in Figure 2.13.

The BasicWebForm class constructor contains the statement

```
Page.Init + = new System.EventHandler(Page_Init);
```

which wires the Page class Init event inherited from the Control class, with the Page_Init event handler defined in the class. Thus, the class Page_Init method is invoked when the control is first initialized in the page's life cycle.

Event handling is explained in Appendix A.11 of the appendices.

The Init event is handled by the Page_Init method, defined by the statements

```
private void Page_Init(object sender, EventArgs e)
{
    InitializeComponent();
}
```

The method InitializeComponent is invoked in the Page_Init method. The Initialize-Component method is defined with the statements

```
private void InitializeComponent()
{
    this.Load + = new System.EventHandler(this.Page_Load);
}
```

```
    using System;
    using System.Collections;
    using System.ComponentModel;
    using System.Data;
    using System.Drawing;                          Namespaces typically
    using System.Web;                              used are automatically
    using System.Web.SessionState;                 imported
    using System.Web.UI;
    using System.Web.UI.WebControls;
    using System.Web.UI.HtmlControls;

    namespace WebFormsBasics
    {
        /// <summary>
        /// Summary description for BasicWebForm.
        /// </summary>
        public class BasicWebForm : System.Web.UI.Page
        {
            public BasicWebForm()
            {
                Page.Init += new System.EventHandler(Page_Init);
            }

            private void Page_Load(object sender, System.EventArgs e)
            {
                // Put user code to initialize the page here
            }

            private void Page_Init(object sender, EventArgs e)
            {
                //
                // CODEGEN: This call is required by the
                // ASP.NET Web Form Designer
                //
                InitializeComponent();
            }

            #region Web Form Designer generated code
            /// <summary>
            /// Required method for Designer support - do not modify
            /// the contents of this method with the code editor.
            /// </summary>
            private void InitializeComponent()
            {
                this.Load += new System.EventHandler(this.Page_Load);
            }
            #endregion
        }
    }
```

Called by Framework when page is loaded

FIGURE 2.9B
Code-behind for Web Forms page BasicWebForm.aspx.

In the skeletal class created by Visual Studio, this method is managed entirely by the Web form designer. The contents of the InitializeComponent function should not be modified with the code editor. In this case, the method defines a handler for the Load event. The Load event, inherited from the Control class, is raised whenever a control is loaded into the Page object. As such, the handler Page_Load is called every time the page is loaded.

Page_Load class is defined with the statements

```
protected void Page_Load(object sender, EventArgs e)
{
}
```

As indicated, this function is called when the page, which is a Control, is first loaded.

The IsPostBack property of the page can be tested in the Page_Load method to determine if the page is being loaded for the first time or in response to a user postback. The following code can be included in the Page_Load function to examine the IsPostBack property of the Page class. When the property is *not* true, i.e., the page is being loaded for the first time, the function's body is executed. This capability can be used to modify the form based on whether it is being loaded for the first time or as the result of a user postback.

```
if (!IsPostBack)
{
}
```

The Framework provides for the automatic wiring of the following methods:

- Page_Init
- Page_Load
- Page_DataBind
- Page_PreRender
- Page_Dispose
- Page_Error

A browser rendering of the page is shown in Figure 2.9C. Note the Title bar and page HTML text content.

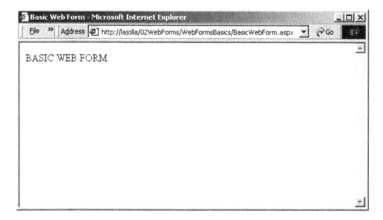

FIGURE 2.9C
Browser rendering of Web Forms page BasicWebForm.aspx.

Code Model

The **Code Model** is illustrated in Figure 2.10. The project's code-behind class files are compiled into a dynamic link library (.dll) file. The first time a user browses the .aspx page, ASP.NET generates a .NET class file representing the page and compiles it into a second .dll file. This file inherits the code-behind class functionality represented by the project .dll file.

The resultant .dll file, representing the page, is run at the server whenever the page is requested. The .dll file processes the incoming request from the browser and produces the response sent back to the browser.

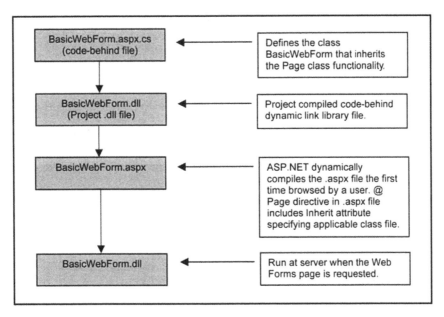

FIGURE 2.10
Page code model.

Page Class

The **Page** class defines the properties, methods and events common to all Web Form pages. Page class objects are compiled and cached in memory. The class used in the code-behind is derived from the Page class. The Page class is inherited from the TemplateControl class, which is inherited from the Control class, which is inherited from the Object class.

Class	Description
Object	The class from which all classes in the .NET Framework are derived.
Control	Defines the properties, methods and events common to all ASP.NET server controls. The Control class is examined in Chapter 3.
TemplateControl	Provides the Page class with basic control functionality including the following:
Method	Description
InstantiateIn	Builds a control tree for a page at runtime.
LoadControl	Loads a user control, in contrast to the .NET Framework controls
ParseControl	Parses an input string that contains control content

The Page class also inherits the **IHttpHandler** interface in the System.Web namespace. The IHttpHandler interface defines the contract that must be implemented to process HTTP Web requests synchronously. The interface defines the ProcessRequest method that drives Web-processing execution. An IsReusable method is defined and indicates if a request can be recycled and used by another request.

Several enumerations are used in the characterization of a page. The TraceMode enumeration, shown in Figure 2.11, specifies how trace statements are output to a page.

Members of the TransactionOption enumeration, Figure 2.12, characterize the type of automatic transaction requested by the component.

public enum **TraceMode**	
Namespace: System.Web	
Member Name	**Output Mode Description**
SortByCategory	Alphabetically by category.
SortByTime	Order processed.

FIGURE 2.11
TraceMode enumeration.

public enum **TransactionOption**	
Namespace: System.EnterpriseServices	
Member Name	**Description**
Disable	Ignore any transaction in the current context.
NotSupported	Create the component in a context with no governing transaction.
Required	Share a transaction if existing, create a new transaction otherwise.
RequiresNew	Create the component with a new transaction always.
Supported	Share an existing transaction.

FIGURE 2.12
TransactionOption enumeration.

Supporting classes include the following:

Class	Description
HttpRequest	Enables access to the HTTP values, such as client browser information, form variables, HTTP type and query string variables, sent by the client during a Web request.
HttpResponse	Encapsulates the HTTP response from an ASP.NET operation such as buffering, caching policy and HTTP status.
HttpContext	Encapsulates HTTP-specific request information such as application state, cache object, HttpRequest and HttpResponse objects.
HttpSessionState	Provides information about the current request session including the state mode, whether the session is managed by a cookie and session state information.
HttpServerUtility	Provides methods and properties for managing Web requests including server name and URL information.

These classes are accessed by properties of the Page class.

Coding the Load Event Handler: Page_Load

The Load event, inherited from the Control class, is raised whenever a control is loaded into the Page object. As such, the handler Page_Load is called every time the page is loaded. In Figure 2.14, the Page_Load method has been coded to illustrate use of the following property values:

Property	Value
Response	HttpResponse
Request	Http Request
Session	HttpSessionState
Server	HttpServerUtility

```
public class Page : TemplateControl, IHttpHandler

Hierarchy
Object
  Control
    TemplateControl
      Page

Namespace: System.Web.UI
```

Public Instance Constructors	
public **Page**( );	Initializes a new instance of the class.

Public Instance Properties	
public HttpApplicationState **Application**{get;};	Gets the HttpApplicationState object for the current request.
public Cache **Cache**{get;};	Gets the Cache object for storing the page's data for subsequent requests.
public stringe **ClientTarget**{get; set;};	Gets and sets a string value specifing browser capabilities override.
public override bool **EnableViewState**{get; set;}	Gets and sets the value true if the page maintains its view state; false otherwise. The default is true. The value is extended to any controls the page contains.
public string **ErrorPage**{get; set;};	Gets and sets the error page to which the browser is redirected when a page exception is raised.
public override string **ID**{get; set;};	Gets and sets page's ID.
public bool **IsPostBack**{get;};	Gets the value true if the page is being loaded in response to a client postback; false otherwise.
public bool **IsValid**{get;};	Gets the value true if the page validation succeeded; false otherwise, that is the page is being loaded for the first time.
public HttpRequest **Request**{get;}	Gets the HttpRequest object enabling accessing of data from incoming HTTP requests, that is, data elements supplied by the client.
public HttpResponse **Reponse**{get;}	Gets the HttpResponse object, provided by the HTTP Runtime, enabling sending HTTP data to a client.
public HttpServerUtility **Server**{get;}	Gets the current Server, HttpServerUtility, object.
public virtual HttpSessionState **Session**{get;}	Gets the current HttpSessionState, object providing information regarding the current request's session.
public bool **SmartNavigation**{get; set;};	Gets the value true if smart navigation is enabled; false otherwise.
public TraceContext **Trace**{get;};	Gets the TraceContext object for the current Web request.
public IPrincipal **User**{get;};	Gets the IPrincipal object describing the user requesting the page.
public ValidationCollection **Validators**{get;};	Gets the collection of validation controls on the requested page.
public override bool **Visible**{get; set;};	Gets and sets the value true if the page is rendered visible; false otherwise.

FIGURE 2.13
Page class summary. (Inherited members are not shown.)

The Response property value is the HTTP Runtime-provided object, HttpResponse, that enables sending response data to the client browser. The object is also known as the Response object. For example, the HttpResponse class Write method provides for sending character, object, string and character array content to the HTTP output stream. In the example, the statement

```
this.Response.Write(message);
```

sends the string message to the HTTP output content stream. The string is displayed at the client's browser (see Figure 2.15).

Protected Instance Properties	
bool **AspCompatMode** {set;};	When true the page can be executed on a single-threaded apartment (STA) thread; false otherwise. The default is false.
bool **Buffer** {set;};	When true the page output is buffered; false otherwise. The default is true.
int **CodePage** {set;};	An integer representing the code page identifier for the current Page object.
string **ContentType** {set;};	The HTTP MIME type associated with the current page.
override HttpContext **Context** {get;}	HttpContext object containing information about the current page request.
string **Culture** {set;};	The current Web request's cultural information.
bool **EnableViewStateMac** {get; set;}	True if the view state should be MAC checked; false otherwise. The default is false.
ArrayList **FileDependencies** {set;}	Array of files the current HttpResponse object is dependent upon.
int **LCID** {set;}	Locale identifier for the page to the cultural information provided by the current Web request's thread.
string **ResponseEncoding** {set;};	Encoding language for the current HttpResponse object.
bool **TraceEnabled** {set;}	True if tracing is enabled; false otherwise. The default is false.
TraceMode **TraceModeValue** {set;}	Trace mode enumeration member indicating display mode of trace statements on the page.
int **TransactionMode** {set;}	Integer value, TransactionOption enumeration member, representing level of transaction support for the page.
string **UICulture** {set;};	Representation of the current cultural information provided by the current thread object.

FIGURE 2.13 (CONTINUED)
Page class summary.

The Response property accesses the HTTP Runtime-provided HttpRequest object, also known as the request object. HttpRequest class property values include the following:

Property	Description
Browser	HttpBrowserCapabilities object that encapsulates the client's browser including browser type `this.Request.Browser.Browser` and browser version `this.Request.Browser.Version`
FilePath	Virtual path of the current request `this.Request.FilePath`
HttpMethod	HTTP data transfer method, for example, GET and POST `this.Request.HttpMethod`
UserHostAddress	Client IP host address `this.Request.UserHostAddress`
UserHostName	Client DNS name `this.Request.UserHostName`
QueryString	Collection of HTTP query string variables. The collection is represented by the NameValueCollection class with Count property, GetKey and Get methods. The QueryString variables are ampersand (&)-separated name = value elements appended to the address of the Web page and separated from the address by a question mark (?). For example: `http://lajolla/02WebForms/WebFormsBasics/BasicWebForm.aspx?name = Dudley&password = V2105`

Public Instance Methods	
public void **DesignerInitialize**( );	Performs page initialization required by Rapid Application Development designers.
public string **GetPostBackClientEvent** (Control *control*, String *argument*);	Returns a string representing the client event for selected browsers where *control* is the server control receiving the client event postback and *argument* is the script passed to the server control.
public string **GetPostBackClientHyperlink** (Control *control*, String *argument*);	Returns a string enabling hyperlink postback processing where *control* is the server control receiving the client event postback and *argument* is the script passed to the server control.
public string **GetPostBackEventReference** (Control *control*);	Returns a reference to the server control, *control*, that will process the postback.
public string **GetPostBackEventReference** (Control *control*, String *argument*);	Returns a reference to the server control, *control*, that will process the postback and *argument* is the parameter passed to the control.
public virtual int **getTypeHashCode**( );	Returns a unique hash code generated at run time. The default is 0.
public bool **IsClientScriptBlockRegistered** (string *key*);	Returns true if the client script with index value *key* is registered with the page; false otherwise.
public bool **IsStartupScriptRegistered** (string *key*);	Returns true if the client startup script with index value *key* is registered with the page; false otherwise.
public string **MapPath** (string *virtualPath*);	Assigns a virtual path, represented by *virtualPath* to a physical path. The virtual path can be absolute or relative.
public void **RegisterArrayDeclaration** (string *arrayName*, string *arrayValue*);	Registers the value *arrayValue* in the array *arrayName* for controls that utilize ECMAScript (Jscript and JavaScript) event architecture.
public virtual void **RegisterClientScriptBlock** (string *key*, string *script*);	Registers the value *arrayValue* in the array *arrayName* for controls that utilize ECMAScript (Jscript and JavaScript) event architecture.
public virtual void **RegisterHiddenField** (string *hiddenFieldName*, string *hiddenFieldInitialValue*);	Registers a hidden field, *hiddenFieldName*, on the form with initial value *hiddenFieldInitialValue*.
public void **RegisterOnSubmitStatement** (string *key*, string *script*);	Enables a control to access the client onsubmit event where *key* uniquely identifies the script block and *script* represents the content sent to the client.
public void **RegisterRequiresPostBack** (Control *control*);	Registers the control, *control*, as one that requires postback handling.
public void **RegisterRequiresRaiseEvent** (IPostBackEventHandler *control*);	Registers the control, *control*, as one that requires an event to be raised when it is processed.
public virtual void **RegisterStartupScript** (string *key*, string *script*);	Registers a script, represented by *script*, with key value, *key*, that will be sent to the client.
public void **RegisterViewStateHandler** ( );	Registers the view state handler.
public virtual void **Validate** ( );	Effects the validation of content by validation controls on the page.

FIGURE 2.13 (CONTINUED)
Page class summary.

Property	Description
	defines a QueryString name variable with value "Dudley" and password variable with value "V2105." The number of elements in the collection is accessed with the collection's Count property
`this.Request.QueryString.Count`
The collection's keys, i.e., variable names, are accessed with the GetKey method, where the zero-based index represents the element's position in the collection
`this.Request.QueryString.GetKey(i)`
Similarly, the collection's values are accessed with the Get method
`this.Request.QueryString.Get(i)`
Form	Collection of HTTP form variables

Protected Instance Methods	
protected IAsyncResult **AspCompatBeginProcessRequest (** HttpContext *context*, AsyncCallback *cb*, object *extraData*);	Initiates a request for Active Server Pages (ASP) resources where *context* is an HttpContext object representing current request information, *cd* is the callback method and data associated associated with the request are represented by the object *extraData*.
protected void **AspCompatEndProcessRequest (** IAsyncResult *result*);	Terminates a request for Active Server Pages (ASP) resources where *result* is the ASP page generated by the request
protected virtual HtlTextWriter **CreateHtmlTextWriter (** TextWriter *tw*);	Creates an HtmltextWriter object to render the page's content where *tw* is a TextWriter object intended for character output.
protected virtual NameValueCollection **DeterminePostBackMode ( );**	Returns the form information if the postback used the POST method and Querystring information if the postback used the GET method. The null reference is returned the first time the page is requested.
protected virtual void **InitOutputCache (** int *duration*, string *varyByHeader*, string *varyByCustom*, OutputCacheLocation location, String *varyByParam*);	Initializes the output cache for the current page request. The length of storage time is specified by *duration*. *varyByHeader* is semi-colon-separated list of headers by which the output cache content will vary. *varyByCustom* represents the Vary HTTP header. The location of the output cache is specified by the OutputCacheLocation object *location*. *varyByParam* is a semi-colon-separated list of parameters, received from the GET orPOST method, by which output cache content will vary.
protected virtual object **LoadPageStateFromPersistanceMedium ( );**	Loads the saved view state information for the page. The method returns the saved view state.
protected virtual void **RaisePostBackEvent (** IPostBackEventHandler *sourceControl*, string *eventArgument*);	Raises the PostBackEvent.

FIGURE 2.13 (CONTINUED)
Page class summary.

```
private void Page_Load(object sender, System.EventArgs e)
{
    string message = "REQUEST OBJECT PROPERTIES <BR> ";
    message += "Browser Type: " + this.Request.Browser.Browser + "<BR>";
    message += "Browser: " + this.Request.Browser.Version + "<BR>";
    message += "File Path: " + this.Request.FilePath + "<BR>";
    message += "Http Method: " + this.Request.HttpMethod + "<BR>";
    message += "User Host Address: " + this.Request.UserHostAddress + "<BR>";
    message += "User Host Name: " + this.Request.UserHostName + "<BR>";

    message += "QUERY STRING <BR> ";
    message += "Count: " + this.Request.QueryString.Count + "<BR>";
    for (int i=0;i < this.Request.QueryString.Count; i++)
    {
        message += this.Request.QueryString.GetKey(i) + ": "
                 + this.Request.QueryString.Get(i) +  "<BR>";
    }

    message += "SESSION OBJECT PROPERTIES <BR> ";
    message += "Mode: " + this.Session.Mode+ "<BR>";
    message += "Session ID: " + this.Session.SessionID + "<BR>";
    message += "Timeout: " + this.Session.Timeout + "<BR>";

    message += "SERVER OBJECT PROPERTIES <BR> ";
    message += "Machine Name: " + this.Server.MachineName + "<BR>";
    message += "Type: " + this.Server.GetType() + "<BR>";

    this.Response.Write(message);
}
```

FIGURE 2.14
Page_Load method of completed BasicWebForm.aspx.cs file.

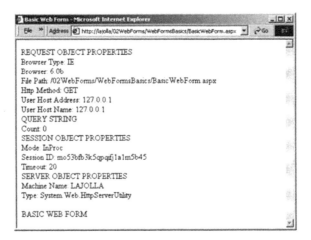

FIGURE 2.15
Browser rendering of BasicWebForm.aspx.

The Session property exposes the ASP.NET-provided HttpSessionState object, also known as the Session object, representing the current session. HttpSessionState property values include the following:

Property	Description
Mode	SessionStateMode enumeration member specifying the session state mode
	`this.Session.Mode`
SessionID	Unique ID identifying the session
	`this.Session.SessionID`
Timeout	Period between requests, in minutes, before the session terminates
	`this.Session.Timeout`

The Server property exposes the HttpServerUtility object, also known as the Server object, representing the server. HttpServerUtility class includes the following members:

Member	Description
MachineName	Property representing the server's machine name
	`this.Server.MachineName`
GetType	Method inherited from object class that represents the type of the current instance
	`this.Server.GetType()`
	`this.Server.GetType()`

Note!

An ASP.NET Web form consists of a visual component and a code component. These components can be contained in the same .aspx file or they can be maintained in separate files. Separation of the visual and code components is generally preferred, in which case the visual component, including the HTML elements and the Web controls, is contained in the .aspx file and the code is contained in the code-behind file.

Hands-On Exercise: Creating a Basic Web Form

Step 1: Launch Visual Studio.NET

In the Taskbar, click Start, point to Programs in the Start menu, point to Microsoft Visual Studio.Net 7.0 in the submenu. Click Microsoft Visual Studio.Net 7.0.

Step 2: Create the Application

1. In the File menu, place the cursor over New and select the Project... option. Alternately, press the Ctrl+Shift+N key combination. The New Project dialog opens, as seen in Figure HO2.1.

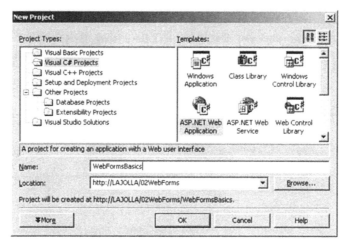

FIGURE HO2.1
New Project dialog.

2. Select and enter the following:

Project Types:	**Visual C# Projects**
Templates:	**ASP.NET Web Application**
Name:	**WebFormsBasics**
Location:	**http://LAJOLLA/02WebForms**

     Note: LAJOLLA is the machine name and 02WebForms is a subdirectory created in the path C:/Inetpub/wwwroot directory.

3. Click the OK button to create the project. The Web Designer opens in Design View (Figure HO2.2).

Step 3: Delete WebForm1.aspx and Create the Web Page BasicWebForm

1. In the View menu, select the Solution Explorer option. Alternately, press the Ctrl+Alt+L key combination. The Solution Explorer is opened.

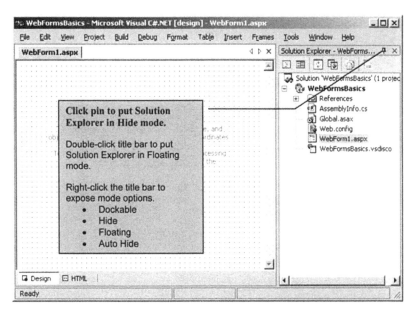

FIGURE HO2.2
New Project dialog.

2. In Solution Explorer, right-click WebForm1.aspx and select the Delete option. Confirm deletion.

3. In the Solution Explorer, right-click WebFormsBasics. Position the cursor over the Add option in the submenu. Select the Add Web Form... option. The Add New Item dialog opens (Figure HO2.3), with Web form selected in the Templates pane. Enter **BasicWebForm.aspx** in the Name textbox.

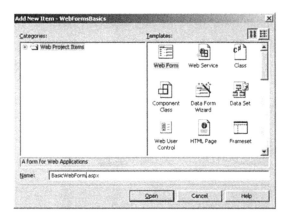

FIGURE HO2.3
Add new Item dialog.

4. Click OK. The dialog box closes. The web Forms page, named BasicWebForm, is created. The page is displayed in the Web Forms Designer in Design view (Figure HO2.4).

New pages are added to a project in the grid layout mode. In this mode, objects are arranged on the page with absolute x and y coordinates.

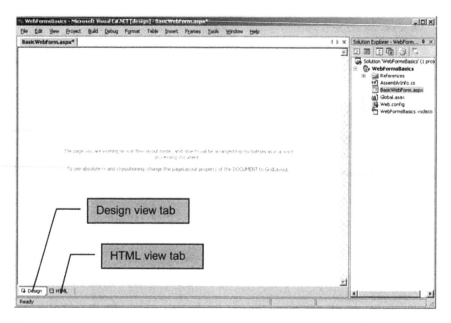

FIGURE HO2.4
BasicWebForm.aspx displayed in Design View.

5. Click the HTML tab to change to the HTML view. The HTML BODY element is defined with the following code:

```
<body ms_positioning = "GridLayout">
<form id = "BasicWebForm" method = "post" runat = "server">;
</form>
</body>
```

The body ms_positioning attribute has the "GridLayout" value.

6. Click the Design View tab to change to the design view.

7. Right-click the page and select the Properties option to open the Document Property Pages dialog (Figure HO2.5).

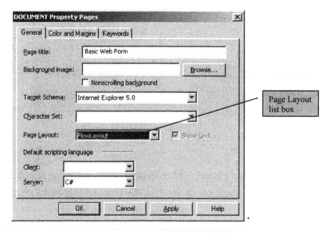

FIGURE HO2.5
DOCUMENT Property Pages dialog.

8. Select the FlowLayout item in the PageLayout list box to change the layout to FlowLayout mode. In the FlowLayout mode, objects are added to the page, one after another, from left to right. When the row is filled, another row is started with objects added from left to right. The number of items displayed on a row varies as the user resizes the browser window.

Step 4: Formatting the Web Page

1. In the Design View position the cursor over the text editor. Right click and select the Properties option in the menu to expose the DOCUMENT Property Pages. Click the Colors and Margin tab in the DOCUMENT Property Pages dialog. Click the ellipses next to the Background color box. The Color Picker opens. In the Web Pallette, select a Yellow-like color. Click OK. The Color Picker dialog closes.

2. Click the Apply button in the Document Property Pages dialog. Note the background color of the page in the Design view changes to Yellow. Click OK to close the Document Property Pages dialog. Note that, in the HTML view, the markup is as follows:

```
<body bgColor = #ffff66>
<form id = "BasicWebForm" method = "post" runat = "server">
</form>
</body>
```

Note that the BODY tag no longer has the ms_positioning attribute; the page is in FlowLayout mode. Note also the background color attribute–value combination.

3. Switch to Design View. Type the following text directly on the page:

```
BASIC Web FORM
```

4. Switch to HTML view; the BODY markup is as follows:

```
<body bgColor = #ffff66>
<form id = "BasicWebForm" method = "post" runat = "server">
<P>BASIC WEB FORM </P>
</form>
</body>
```

5. Add a TITLE element to the HEAD element:

```
<title>Basic Web Form</title>
```

6. Switch to the Design View.

7. In the View menu, position the cursor over the Toolbars option, and then select the Formatting option in the submenu. The Formatting toolbar opens.

8. Select the text: "BASIC WEB FORM." Use the Font Size dropdown list, Foreground Color and Background Color buttons to set the font size to 6 and the text color to Light Green and the background of the selected text to Dark Green. The formatted page is shown in Figure HO2.6.

9. Switch to HTML view and note that the BODY markup reflects the presentation changes. The markup has been indented to promote readability.

```
<body bgColor = #ffff66>
<form id = BasicWebForm method = post runat = "server">
```

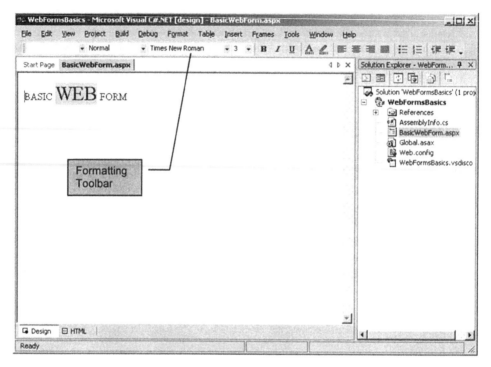

FIGURE HO2.6
Formatted document in Design View.

```
<P>BASIC <FONT style = "BACKGROUND-COLOR: #66ff33"
color = #003300 size = 6>WEB</FONT> FORM</P>
</FORM>
</body>
```

Step 5: Building and Running the Web Forms Page in Debug Mode

The Web forms Page class file must be compiled before the Web page is run.

1. In Solution Explorer, right-click the BasicWebForm.aspx. Select the Build and Browse option. Alternately, press the CTRL+F8 key combination. Visual Studio automatically runs the page in the debugger. The page is displayed in the Browse tab, as seen in Figure HO2.7.
2. Close the Browse tab to stop running the Web page.

Step 6: Building and Running the Application in Internet Explorer

1. In the Solution Explorer, right-click the BasicwebForm.aspx. Select the Start As Start Page option in the submenu.
2. In the Debug menu, select the Start Without Debugging option. Alternately, press the CTRL+F5 key combination. Internet Explorer displays the page; see Figure HO2.8.
3. To stop running the application, close Internet Explorer.

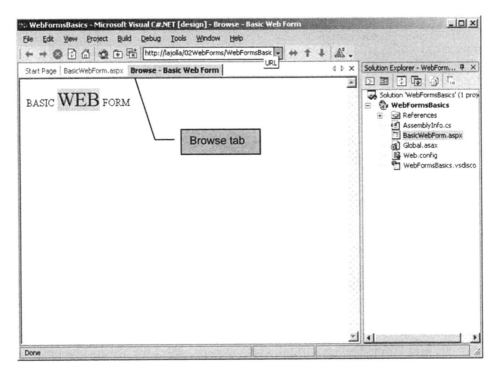

FIGURE HO2.7
Web page running in debugger and shown in Browse tab.

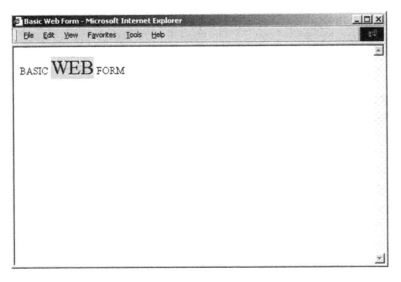

FIGURE HO2.8
Application running in Internet Explorer.

Step 7: Code-Behind File

1. The code-behind file can be exposed in many ways, including the following:
   - In Solution Explorer, click the Show Code icon (Figure HO2.9).

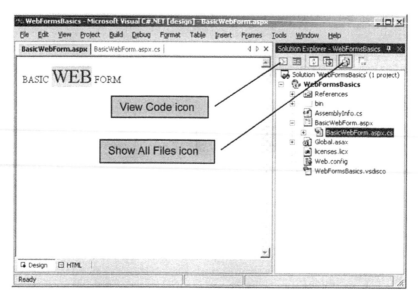

FIGURE HO2.9
Accessing the code-behind file.

- In Web Forms Designer, right-click the page, select the View Code option.
- In the View menu, select the Code option.
- Press the F7 key. Press the Shift+F7 key combination to show the page in the Web Form Designer.
- In Solution Explorer, click the Show All Files icon. Click the + sign at BasicWeb-Form.aspx to expand the list. Double-click the BasicWebForm.aspx.cs entry.

The code-behind file is displayed in the Code Editor (Figure HO2.10).

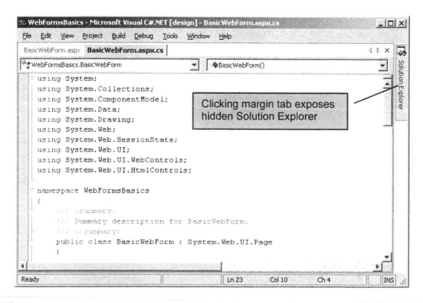

FIGURE HO2.10
Code-behind file in Code Editor.

2. Close Solution Explorer. Alternately, hide Solution Explorer by clicking the pin. Solution Explorer hides in the margin when focus is transferred to the web Form Designer. Clicking its tab in the margin exposes a hidden Solution Explorer.

3. In the Page_Load method, add the bold code shown below:

```
private void Page_Load(object sender, System.EventArgs e)
{
    string message = "REQUEST OBJECT PROPERTIES <BR> ";
    message + = "Browser Type: "" + this.Request.Browser.Browser
        + "<BR>";
    message + = "Browser: " + this.Request.Browser.Version +
        "<BR>";
    message + = "File Path: " + this.Request.FilePath + "<BR>";
    message + = "Http Method: " + this.Request.HttpMethod + "<BR>";
    message + = "User Host Address: "
    this.Request.UserHostAddress + "<BR>";
    message + = "User Host Name: " + this.Request.UserHostName
        + "<BR>";
    message + = "QUERY STRING <BR> ;" message + = "Count: " +
        this.Request.QueryString.Count + "<BR>;" for (int i = 0;
        i < this.Request.QueryString.Count; i++)
    {
    message + = this.Request.QueryString.GetKey(i) + ": "
    this.Request.QueryString.Get(i) + "<BR>";
    }
    message + = "SESSION OBJECT PROPERTIES <BR> ";
    message + = "Mode: " + this.Session.Mode+ "<BR>";
    message + = "Session ID: " + this.Session.SessionID + "<BR>";
    message + = "Timeout: " + this.Session.Timeout + "<BR>";
    message + = "SERVER OBJECT PROPERTIES <BR> ;" message + =
        "Machine Name: " + this.Server.MachineName + "<BR>;"
        message + = "Type: " + this.Server.GetType() + "<BR>";
    this.Response.Write(message));
}
```

Note that HTML markup, in the example "<BR>", is included in the string.

4. In the View menu, select the Build option. Alternately, press the Ctrl+Shift+B key combination. In this case, Build errors result and are listed in the Task List, Figure HO2.11.

!	Description	File	Line
	Click here to add a new task		
!	; expected	C:\Documents and....aspx.cs	53
!	Invalid expression term ')'	C:\Documents and....aspx.cs	53

Task List – 2 Build Error tasks shown (filtered)

FIGURE HO2.11
Task List of errors.

5. Double click the first task; the syntax error is highlighted in the Code Editor. Correct the error by removing the extra parenthesis. In this case, the remaining tasks disappear from the list. In other cases, continue to correct the remaining tasks.

6. Build the application. The resultant Output window, Figure HO2.12, indicates a successful build.

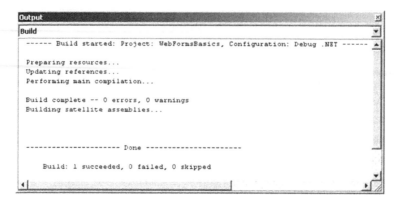

FIGURE HO2.12
Output window for a successful build: 0 errors.

Step 8: Browse Web Forms Page WebFormsBasics.aspx.

1. Start Internet Explorer.
2. In the address box, enter the following page address:

   http://lajolla/02WebForms/WebFormsBasics/BasicWebForm.aspx?name = Dudley&password = V2105

3. Click Go or press the Enter key. The browsed page BasicWebForm is displayed. The Response object's Write method is used to pass a string containing Request, Session and Server object properties. Note that the number of variables contained in the QueryString property object of the Request object, as well as the variable names and values, are also included in the string output.

Note!

Typically, output will be contained in HTML and Web Server controls and not as the Http output content stream. Its use in this case is intended to illustrate functionality of the Page class and its supporting classes.

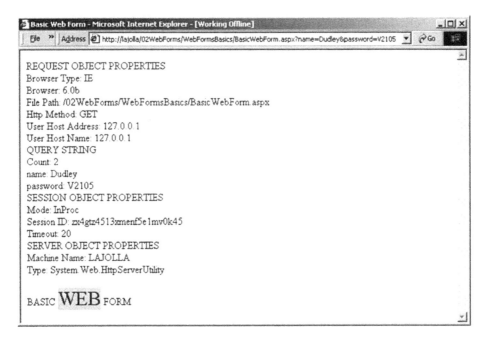

FIGURE HO2.13
Browsing the page BasicWebForm.aspx with appended QueryString.

3

Form Controls

Form controls, also known simply as **controls,** are Web page elements such as labels, textboxes, buttons and lists that enable user interaction. Additionally, controls are exposed to the server as programmable objects. Controls fall into four major groups:

Control Type	Description
HTML server controls	Controls that map closely to the HTML elements and reflect the HTML syntax.
ASP.NET server controls	Feature-rich controls with robustness and abstraction beyond the HTML server controls.
Validation controls	Controls incorporating logic enabling editing (that is, "testing") of user input. Typical tests implemented with validation controls include testing for specific values, patterns and ranges.
User Controls	Controls created as Web Form pages. User controls can be incorporated in other pages and are reusable. Typical user controls are menus and toolboxes.

HTML server controls enabling programming against HTML elements are summarized in Figure 3.1. Additionally, regular HTML tags as well as text can be included in the form.

Control	Enables Programming Against HTML Element
HtmlAnchor	<a>
HtmlButton	<button
HtmlForm	<form>
HtmlGenericControl	<span>, <body> and <font>.
HtmlImage	<img>
HtmlInputButton(Button)	<input type=button>
HtmlInputButton(Reset)	<input type=reset>
HtmlInputButton(Submit)	<input type=submit>
HtmlInputCheckBox	<input type=checkbox>
HtmlInputFile	<input type=file>
HtmlInputHidden	<input type=hidden>
HtmlInputImage	<input type=image>
HtmlInputRadioButton	<input type=radio>
HtmlInputText(Password)	<input type=password>
HtmlInputText(Text)	<input type=text>
HtmlSelect	<select>
HtmlTable	<table>
HtmlTableCell	<td> and <th>
HtmlTableRow	<tr>
HtmlTextArea	<textarea>

FIGURE 3.1
HTML server controls.

ASP.NET server controls also affect the user interface and provide functionality and programmability not available in the HTML controls. ASP.NET server control robustness is reflected in the following features:

Extension and variety: Functionality over and above that available in HTML controls plus additional controls such as calendar control.

Browser awareness: Controls are able to detect the browser's capabilities and modify rendering.

Customizable: Templates can be used to customize style as well as items in data presentation controls such as grids.

Postable: Events created by user interaction can result in immediate posting or can be stored for use when the form is submitted to the server.

Basic Web Forms server controls are summarized in Figure 3.2.

Control	Description
Button	Posts the form to the server for processing.
CheckBox	Displays a box that can be toggled on or off, enabling users to select or not select.
CheckBoxList	Groups check boxes in which multiple boxes in the group can be selected.
DropDownList	Enables users to select from a list.
HyperLink	Creates a Web navigation link.
Image	Displays an image.
ImageButton	A button with an image in place of the text.
Label	Displays text that cannot be edited by users but can be manipulated programmatically
LinkButton	A button with the appearance of a hyperlink.
ListBox	Enables users to select from a list.
Panel	Creates a borderless container for controls on the form.
PlaceHolder	Used as a container for other controls added during page processing.
RadioButton	Displays a single button that can be toggled on or off, enabling the user to select or not select.
RadioButtonList	Groups radio buttons in which only one button in the group can be selected.
Table	Creates a table.
TableCell	Creates a cell in a table row.
TableRow	Creates a row in a table
TextBox	Displays text that can be edited by either the user or programmatically.
XML	Displays an XML document.

FIGURE 3.2
Basic ASP.NET Web Forms controls.

Repeater, DataList and DataGrid controls are also available for displaying data. Other controls are provided for specialized functionality, for example, an AdRotator control that displays a predefined sequence of images, and a Calendar control that enables the user to select a date. Controls enabling data validation include the following: CompareValidator, CustomValidator, RangeValidator, RegularExpressionValidator, RequiredFieldValidator and ValidationSummary.

Declaring Server Controls

The syntax for declaring controls, i.e., adding controls to Web forms, is summarized in Figure 3.3. The exact syntax depends on the control. Basic attributes or properties that apply to all controls are summarized in Figure 3.4. Note that some properties do not work in some browsers.

```
Beginning tag and closing tag

<asp:control
        runat="server"
        id = identifier
        attributes
></ asp:control>

Self closing tag

<asp:control
        runat="server"
        id = identifier
        attributes
/>

Beginning and closing tags for controls with subcontrol elements

<asp:control runat="server" id=identifier attributes >
        <asp:subcontrol runat="server" id=identifier attributes >value</asp:subcontrol>
        <asp:subcontrol runat="server" id=identifier attributes >value</asp:subcontrol>
        <asp:subcontrol runat="server" id=identifier attributes >value</asp:subcontrol>
</ asp:control>

General Guidelines

Controls are declared with an XML tag that references the asp namespace.
Controls must include the runat attribute with value "server".
The id attribute should be set unless the control is a component of a complex control. The id
attribute value identifier must uniquely page-wise identify the control. The DataGrid control,
used to display data in a tabular form, is an example of a complex control.
Applicable attributes, characterizing the control, are included as attribute/value pairs.
Control declarations must be closed.
```

FIGURE 3.3
ASP.NET control syntax.

The color value for the background color and the text color can be specified with the standard HTML color identifiers — for example, the name of a color such as "red" or an RGB value expressed in hex such as "#ffffff." The Height and Width attribute values are specified in pixels. The Width attribute value can also be specified as a percentage, for example, 25%.

Note!

Attributes characterizing a control are referred to as properties of objects representing the control.

Declaring Label, TextBox and Button Controls

The Label, TextBox and Button controls are the Web page "work horses."

Label Control

The ASP.NET Server **Label Control** is rendered as static text, i.e., the user cannot change the text. However, the properties of the label can be changed programmatically. A label is placed on a page with the syntax summarized in Figure 3.5.

Attribute/Property	Description
AccessKey	The controls accelerator key.
Attributes	Complete set of the attributes for the control's persistence. This attribute can only be set programmatically.
BackColor	Background color of the control.
BorderWidth	Size of the control's border in pixels.
BorderStyle	Style of the control's border. Valid values are the following: • NotSet • None • Dotted • Dashed • Solid • Double • Groove • Ridge • Inset • Outset
CCSClass	CCS style class assigned to the control.
CCSStyle	A collection of text attributes that are rendered as a CCS style. This attribute can only be set programmatically.
Enable	Enables the control if set to true, disables the control if set to false. The default value is false.
Font-Bold	Text is rendered bold if set true. The default is false.
ForeColor	Color of the controls text.
Height	Height of the control in pixels.
Font-Italic	Text is rendered italicized if true, not italicized if false. The default is false.
Font-Name	Font face in which the control's text is displayed. Some browsers do not support settings for individual controls.
Font-Names	A list of font faces, in order of precedence, in which the control's text is displayed. Some browsers do not support settings for individual controls.
Font-Overline	Text is rendered with a line above if true, not overlined if false. The default is false.
Font-Size	Size of the font user to render the text. Valid values are the HTML sizes: 1 to 7. Note, some browsers do not support settings for individual controls.
Font-Strikeout	Text is rendered with a line through it if true and with no line through it if false. The default is false.
Font-Underline	Text is rendered underlined if true, not underlined if false. The default is false.
TabIndex	The order in which the controls receive focus when the user tabs. The default value is zero. Controls with the same value are ordered, with respect to tab order, in the order of their declaration.
Tooltip	Text that appears when the mouse pointer is over the controls. Tool tips are not supported in all browsers.
Width	Width of the control in pixels.

FIGURE 3.4
Attributes and properties shared by all Web controls.

The Text property of the label control can be, and often is, set programmatically.

The Web page defined in Figure 3.6A illustrates declaration of a Label control. When browsed, the page appears as shown in Figure 3.6B.

TextBox Control

The ASP.NET **TextBox** control represents a text box for displaying or user entry of text. The syntax for creating the TextBox control is shown in Figure 3.7.

The Text property is the primary means of enabling user input and displaying output to the user.

The Web page defined in Figure 3.8A illustrates declaration of a TextBox control. When browsed, the page appears as shown in Figure 3.8B.

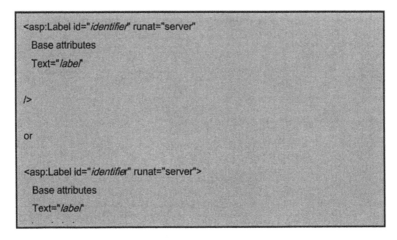

FIGURE 3.5
Label control syntax.

```
<HTML>
<HEAD>
  <TITLE>Label Control</TITLE>
</HEAD>
<BODY>
  <FORM method="post" runat="server">
    <asp:label id=labelID runat=server text="Enter Name:">
    </asp:label>
  </FORM>
</BODY>
</HTML>
```

FIGURE 3.6A
Declaration of a Label control (03WebControls/LabelControl.aspx).

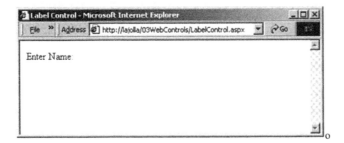

FIGURE 3.6B
Browser rendering of Web page declaring a Label control (03WebControls/LabelControl.aspx).

Note that the text attribute value is displayed in the text box. The user can enter information in the text box; the text property value can be, and generally is, programmatically managed at the server.

Button Control

The ASP.NET Server **Button control** button is rendered as an HTML submit button. Clicking the button posts the page back to the server. The page's data and events åre posted. A button is placed on a page with the **<asp:button .../>** element. The syntax for creating the Button control is shown in Figure 3.9.

```
<asp:TextBox id="identifier" runat="SERVER"
    Base Properties
    AutoPostBack="True|False"
    Columns="nocharacters"
    MaxLength="maxnocharacters"
    Rows="rows"
    Text="text"
    TextMode="Single | Multiline | Password"
    Wrap="True|False"
    OnTextChanged="OnTextChangedMethod"
>
</asp:TextBox>
```

Properties	Description
Base properties	Properties common to all controls.
AutoPostBack	Client-side changes automatically cause postback if true and do not automatically cause postback if false. The default is false.
Columns	Control width in terms of characters.
MaxLength	Maximum number of characters that can be contained in the text box if the TextMode property is set to SingleLine or Password. The property has no effect otherwise.
Rows	Number of rows in the text box. This property is only in effect if the TextMode is set to MultiLine.
Text	Text content of the text box.
TextMode	Indicates the text mode of the box. Valid values are the following: • Single • MultiLine • Password
p	Text wraps within the text box if set to true and does not wrap within the box if set to false. The default is true. The Wrap property is only in effect if the TextMode property is set to MultiLine.

Event	Description
OnTextChanged (Object *sender*, EventArgs *e*)	Raised on the server when the content of the text box changes if the AutoPostBack property is set to true. The parameters are the following: • *sender* is the object raising the event, the button clicked. • *e*, the event argument object

FIGURE 3.7
ASP.NET TextBox control syntax.

The Text property captions the button.

The Web page defined in Figure 3.10A illustrates declaration of a Button control. The button element does not have content and thus "/>"can close it. When browsed, the page appears as shown in Figure 3.10B.

Note that the text attribute value is displayed as the button's caption.

Web Page with Multiple Controls

Typically, a Web page contains multiple controls, HTML text and markup. The browser rendering of Web page Login.aspx, shown in Figure 3.11A, illustrates an often seen combination of HTML Web server controls, HTML text and markup.

The page's control declarations and HTML text and markup are shown in Figure 3.11B. Note the use of HTML <table>, <tr> and <td> elements to lay out the controls. In this case, the Document's pageLayout property value is FlowLayout. Note also the use of static text, in this case "Name:" and "Password:", in lieu of the Web server Label control. In general, static text can be used whenever programmatic reference is not required.

```
            <HTML>
              <HEAD>
                <TITLE>TextBox Control</TITLE>
              </HEAD>
              <BODY>
                <FORM method="post" runat="server">
                  <asp:TextBox id=name runat=server text="Initial value">
                  </asp:TextBox>
                </FORM>
              </BODY>
            </HTML>
```

TextBox control

FIGURE 3.8A
Declaration of a TextBox control (03WebControls/TextBoxControl.aspx).

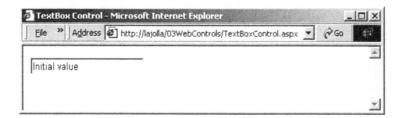

FIGURE 3.8B
Browser rendering of Web page declaring a TextBox control (03WebControls/TextBoxControl.aspx).

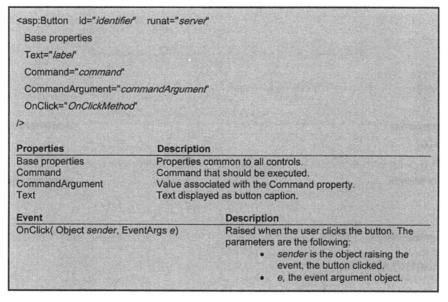

FIGURE 3.9
ASP.NET Button control syntax.

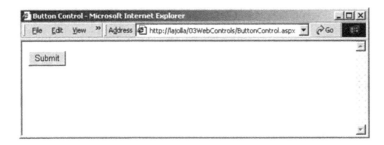

```
          <HTML>
            <HEAD>
              <TITLE>Button Control</TITLE>
            </HEAD>
            <BODY>
              <FORM method="post" runat="server">
                <asp:Button id=submitButton runat=server text=Submit/>
              </FORM>
            </BODY>
          </HTML>
```

FIGURE 3.10A
Declaration of a Button control (03WebControls/ButtonControl.aspx).

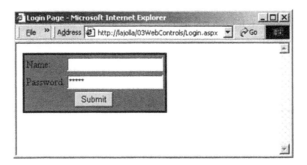

FIGURE 3.10B
Browser rendering of Web page declaring a Button control (03WebControls/ButtonControl.aspx).

FIGURE 3.11A
Browser rendering of Web page with multiple controls and HTML markup (03WebControls/Login.aspx).

Note!

HTML text and elements can be mixed with Web server controls.

Web Control Classes

Classes model the ASP.NET Web Controls. The hierarchy of the Button, Label and TextBox control classes is shown in Figure 3.12.

```
<HTML>
  <HEAD>
    <TITLE>Login Page</TITLE>
  </HEAD>
  <BODY>
    <FORM method="post" runat="server">
      <table bgcolor="Gray"
             style="border-color:black;border-style:solid;border-width:3;">
        <tr>
          <td>
            Name:
          </td>
          <td>
            <asp:TextBox id=name runat=server text=""/>
          </td>
        </tr>
        <tr>
          <td>
            Password:
          </td>
          <td>
            <asp:TextBox id=password runat=server text="*****"/>
          </td>
        </tr>
        <tr>
          <td colspan=2 align=center>
              <asp:Button id=submitButton runat=server text=Submit/>
          </td>
        <tr>
      </table>
    </FORM>
  </BODY>
</HTML>
```

FIGURE 3.11B
Web page with multiple controls and HTML markup (03WebControls/Login.aspx).

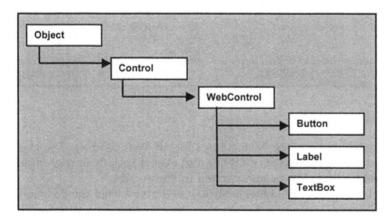

FIGURE 3.12
Control class hierarchy.

The ASP.NET server controls are exposed to the server as objects. The ASP.NET server controls are derived from the Control class. The **Control class** defines the properties, methods and events common to all controls used, is derived directly from the Object class and is in the **System.Web.UI** Namespace. The Control class properties and methods are summarized in Figure 3.13.

public class **Control** : IComponent, IDisposable, IParserAccessor, IDaataBindingsAccessor	
Namespace: System.Web.UI	
Hierarchy	
Object Control	
Selected Public Instance Properties	
public string **ID** {virtual get; virtual set;}	Gets or sets a unique identifier for the control. An identifier is required to reference the control programatically.
public bool **Visible** {virtual get; virtual set;}	Gets or sets a value indicating if the control should be rendered visible. A true value indicates the control should be rendered and false indicates not rendered.
Public Instance Methods	
public virtual void **DataBind**();	Causes data binding on the invoked control and its child controls.
public virtual void **Dispose**();	Enables final cleanup in a control.
Protected Instance Methods	
protected virtual void **OnDataBinding**(EventArgs *e*);	Raises the DataBinding event. The EventArgs object *e* contains the event data.
protected virtual void **OnInit**(EventArgs *e*);	Raises the Init event. The EventArgs object *e* contains the event data.
protected virtual void **OnLoad**(EventArgs *e*);	Raises the Load event. The EventArgs object *e* contains the event data.
protected virtual void **OnPreRender**();	Raises the PreRender event.
protected virtual void **OnPreRender**(EventArgs *e*);	Raises the PreRender event. The EventArgs object *e* contains the event data.
protected virtual void **OnUnLoad**(EventArgs *e*);	Raises the UnLoad event. The EventArgs object *e* contains the event data.
public virtual void **Dispose**();	Enables final cleanup in a control.
Public Instance Events	
public event EventHandler **DataBinding**;	Occurs when the control binds to a data source.
public event EventHandler **Init**;	Occurs when the control is initialized.
public event EventHandler **Load**;	Occurs when the control is loaded to the Page object. The Load event occurs on each page request.
public event EventHandler **PreRender**;	Occurs when the control is about to render.
public event EventHandler **UnLoad**;	Occurs when the control is unloaded from memory.

FIGURE 3.13
Control class summary.

The **WebControl** class is the base control for all Web controls. The class extends the Control class defining properties, methods and events specific to user interface representation. The WebControl class is summarized in Figure 3.14.

The **Label class** represents a label control; it is derived from the WebControl class. The Label control differs from static text in that the text property of the control can be set programmatically. The Label control is summarized in Figure 3.15.

Sample markup adding a Web server control Label element is as follows:

```
<asp:label id = "labelID" runat = "Server"
    font-size = "18"
    text = "Enter name:"
/>
```

The **TextBox** class represents a text box and is derived from the WebControl class. The TextBox control provides for the display of information as well as user entry of information.

public class **WebControl** : Control, IAttributeAccessor	
Namespace: System.Web.UI.WebControls	
Hierarchy	
Object Control WebControl	
Public Instance Constructors	
WebControl (HtmlTextWriterTag *tag*)	Initializes a new instance of the class where *tag* is the HtmlTextWriterTag enumeration member defining the HTML tag passed to the output stream.
Public Instance Properties	
virtual string **AccessKey** {get; set;}	Keyboard key that transfers focus to the Web control when pressed in combination with the ALT key. (Not HTML 4.0. Works in IE 4 or higher.)
AttributeCollection **Attributes** {get;}	Collection of arbitrary attributes that do not correspond to the control's properties.
virtual Color **Backcolor** {get; set;}	Background color. The default is Color.Empty.
virtual Color **BorderColor** {get; set;}	Border color. The default is Color.Empty.
virtual BorderStyle **BorderStyle** {get; set;}	Border style. The default is BorderStyle.NotSet.
virtual Unit **BorderWidth** {get; set;}	Border width. The default is Unit.Empty.
Style **ControlStyle** {get;}	Web control style.
bool **ControlStyleCreated** {get;}	True if the control style is created; false otherwise.
virtual string **CssClass** {get;}	CSS class rendered by the Web control.
virtual bool **Enabled** {get; set;}	True if the control is enabled; false otherwise. The default is true.
virtual FontInfo **Font** {get;}	Font information.
virtual Color **ForeColor** {get; set;}	Foreground color. The default is Color.Empty. The foreground is generally the text.
virtual Unit **Height** {get; set;}	Control height. The default is Unit.Empty.
CssStyleCollection **Style** {get;}	Collection of text attributes that will be rendered as a style attribute on the outer tag of the control.
virtual short **TabIndex** {get; set;}	Tab index of the control. The default is 0. When multiple controls share the same TabIndex value their tab order is determined by order of declaration.
virtual string **ToolTip** {get; set;}	Tool tip displayed when the cursor is positioned over the control. Default is String.Empty. Not applicable to all browsers.
virtual Unit **Width** {get; set;}	Control width. The default is Unit.Empty.

FIGURE 3.14
WebControl class summary.

public class **Label** : WebControl	
Public Instance Constructors	
public Label()	Creates and initializes a new instance of the Label control.
public Label(string *tag*)	Creates and initializes a new instance of the Label control and renders it as a *tag* element. For example, if tag is <Button> the label will be rendered as a button. On the other hand, if the tag is <TextArea> the label will be rendered as a text area.
Public Instance Properties	
Text	Gets or sets the Label control's text content.

Note: Inherited properties, methods and events are not listed

FIGURE 3.15
Label control constructors and properties.

public class **TextBox** : WebControl, IpostBackDataHandler	
Constructor	
public **TextBox**()	Initializes a new instance of the TextBox class.
Properties	
public bool **AutoPostBack** {virtual get; virtual set;}	Gets or sets a value indicating if automatic postback will occur if the user changes the textbox content. The value is true if automatic postback will occur, false otherwise. The default value is false.
public int **Columns** {virtual get; virtual set;}	Gets or sets width of the textbox in terms of the number of characters that will be displayed. The default value is zero.
public int **MaxLength** {virtual get; virtual set;}	Gets or sets the maximum number of characters the textbox will contain. The default value is zero.
public int **Rows** {virtual get; virtual set;}	Gets or sets the height of a multiline textbox. The default value is zero.
protected string **TagName** {override get;}	Gets the HTML tag for the textbox control. Valid values are the following: <ul><li>"textarea" if the TextBox is multiline.</li><li>"input" if the TextBox is not multiline.</li></ul>
public string **Text** {virtual get; virtual set;}	Gets or sets the text content of the textbox. The default value is a constant representing the empty string.
public enum **TextBoxMode** {virtual get; virtual set;}	Gets or sets the text mode of the textbox. The valid values are TextBoxMode enum values: <ul><li>"Multiline" — allows multiple lines in the textbox.</li><li>"NotSet" — TextMode not set.</li><li>"Password" — asterisks are displayed instead of the actual characters.</li><li>"SingleLine" — allows a single line of text.</li></ul>
public bool **Wrap** {virtual get; virtual set;}	Gets or sets the value indicating if the text is wrapped. The text is wrapped if the value is true, false otherwise. The default value is true. The Wrap property is only applicable when the TextMode value is TextBoxMode.Multiline.
Method	
protected virtual void **OnTextChanged**(EventArgs e);	Raises the TextChanged event.
Event	
protected event EventHandler **OnTextChanged**;	Occurs, on postback, when the content of the textbox is changed.

FIGURE 3.16
TextBox class summary.

Selected members of the TextBox class are presented in Figure 3.16. The **Button** class represents a push button. Selected members of the Button class are shown in Figure 3.17.

Representing Control Property Values

Control property values are represented by classes, structures and enumerations, including the following:

public class **Button** : WebControl, IPostBackEventHandler, IPostBackDataHandler	
Properties	
public string **CommandArgument** {get; set;}	Gets or sets the argument passed to the handler of the Command event. The default value is the constant representing the empty string.
public string **CommandName** {get; set;}	Gets or sets the name of the command to perform when the button is clicked, that is, the Command event is raised. The default value is the constant representing the empty string.
public string **Text** {get; set;}	Gets or sets the button's text caption.
Methods	
protected virtual void **OnClick**(EventArgs *e*);	Raises the Button Click event. *e* is the EventArgs object containing data regarding the event.
protected virtual void **OnCommand**(CommandEventArgs *e*)	Raises the Button Command event. *e* is the CommandEventArgs object containing data regarding the event.
Events	
public event EventHandler **Click**;	Occurs when a Button is clicked. The event causes the page to be posted back to the server. This event is used when no command is associated with the Button.
public eventCommandEventHandler **Command**;	Occurs when a Button is clicked. The event causes the page to be posted back to the server. This event is used when a command is associated with the Button.

FIGURE 3.17
Button class summary.

Colors: Colors are represented by a three-component model referred to as the three-component RBG model. The model is represented by the Color structure.

Border Styles: The edges of the rectangular area surrounding a control can be set off with various style lines including solid, dashed and inset.

Units: Various measurement types including centimeters, picas and pixels are supported. The types are represented by members of the UnitTypes enumeration. A Unit structure encapsulates the notion of measurement type.

Fonts: Fonts rendered are characterized by family name, size, style and color. Size is characterized by FontSize enumeration members and FontUnit structure. Additionally, the FontInfo class encapsulates font representation attributes.

Style: A Style class encapsulates control object representation attributes.

Colors

The **Color** structure represents an ARBG color. In this model, colors are represented as a combination of components. An alpha component represents the transparency of the color, i.e., the extent to which the color blends with the background color. Alpha values range from 0, representing a fully transparent color, to a value of 255, which corresponds to fully opaque color. The color is a blend of red, green and blue color components. The contribution of each component is specified with a value ranging from 0 to 255. A value of 0 indicates absence of the component, whereas a value of 255 implies the component is represented at full intensity. Fields, properties and methods of the Color structure are shown in Figure 3.18.

public struct Color	
Hierarchy	
Object	
ValueType	
Color	
Namespace: System.Drawing	
Public Static Fields	
public static readonly Color **Empty**;	Represents a null color.
Public Static Properties	
public static Color AliceBlue {get;}	System-defined color.
. . .	
public static Color YellowGreen {get;}	System-defined color.
Public Instance Properties *(Selected)*	
public byte A {get;}	Gets the Color's alpha component value.
public byte B {get;}	Gets the Color's blue component value.
public byte G {get;}	Gets the Color's green component value.
public string Name {get;}	Gets the name of the color. The name returned is either the system-defined name or the user-defined name. The RGB value is returned for custom colors.
public byte R {get;}	Gets the Color's red component value.
Public Static Methods *(Selected Methods)*	
public static Color FromArgb(int *argbValue*)	Creates a Color from the integral *argbValue* specifying the components of the color. The 32-bit argbValue represents the byte values of the alpha, red, blue and green components.
public static Color FromArgb(int *red*, int *green*, int *blue*)	Creates a Color from the specified *red*, *green* and *blue* component values. Component values range from 0 to 255.
public static Color FromArgb(int *alpha*, int *red*, int *green*, int *blue*)	Creates a Color from the specified *alpha*, *red*, *green*, and *blue* component values. Component values range from 0 to 155.
public static Color FromName(string *name*)	Creates a Color from the specified *name*.

FIGURE 3.18
Color structure summary.

The following example illustrates creation of a Color, named errorColor, that is blue and opaque.

```
int alpha = 255;
int red = 0;
int green = 0;
int blue = 255;
Color errorColor = Color.FromARGB(alpha, red, green, blue);
```

Figure 3.19 lists several colors and their RGB components.

Border Styles

The **BorderStyle** enumeration represents the different control border styles. This enumeration is summarized in Figure 3.20. Note that the Double style of border requires a minimum width of 3 pixels to accommodate lines and the spaces between the lines.

Color	Red Component	Green Component	Blue Component
Black	0	0	0
White	255	255	255
Red	255	0	0
Green	0	255	0
Blue	0	0	255
Brown	165	42	42
Aqua	0	255	255
Orange	255	165	0
Purple	128	0	128
Yellow	255	255	0

FIGURE 3.19
Selected colors and their RGB component values.

public enum BorderStyle

Namespace: System.Web.UI.WebControls

Member Name	Description
Dashed	Dashed line border
Dotted	Dotted line border
Double	Double solid line border
Groove	Grooved border for sunken border appearance
Inset	Inset border for a sunken control appearance
None	No border
NotSet	No set border style
Outset	Outset border for a raised control appearance
Ridge	Ridged border for a raised border appearance
Solid	Solid line border

FIGURE 3.20
BorderStyle enumeration summary.

A Web page illustrating the various options available for control border styles is shown in Figure 3.21A. The rendering of these border styles is shown in Figure 3.21B. Note the insert and outsert styles that give the effect of raised and sunken controls. The groove and ridge enclose the control within a groove and ridge, respectively. The solid border is the most used border style; the double style provides for offsetting a control. Similarly, the dashed and dotted styles provide for minimizing the prominence of controls.

Units

The **UnitType** enumeration shown in Figure 3.22 represents different measurement units — for example, pixel, point and inch. The **Unit** structure enables specification of values for measurement-related properties such as height and width. The Unit structure is summarized in Figure 3.23.

Fonts

Many typefaces, sizes and styles are available for rendering text. Figure 3.24A illustrates several popular fonts: Arial, Courier New, Times New Roman, Tahoma and Verdana. Also illustrated are various sizes measured in points and styles, including underline, italic, bold and strikethrough. The HTML markup illustrating the typefaces, sizes and styles is shown in Figure 3.24B.

```
<html>
  <head>
    <TITLE>Border Styles</TITLE>
  </head>
  <body >

    <form id="Form1" method="post" runat="server">
        <asp:Label ID=dashed Runat=server BorderStyle=Dashed>Dashed
Border</asp:Label>
        <asp:Label ID=dotted Runat=server BorderStyle=Dotted>Dotted
Border</asp:Label>
        <asp:Label ID=Double Runat=server BorderStyle=Double>Double
Border</asp:Label>
        <BR><BR>
        <asp:Label ID=groove Runat=server BorderStyle=Groove>Groove
Border</asp:Label>
        <asp:Label ID=inset Runat=server BorderStyle=Inset>Inset
Border</asp:Label>
        <asp:Label ID=Outset Runat=server BorderStyle=Outset>Outset
Border</asp:Label>
        <BR><BR>
      <asp:Label ID=Ridge Runat=server BorderStyle=Ridge>Ridge
Border</asp:Label>
      <asp:Label ID=Solid Runat=server BorderStyle=Solid>Solid
Border</asp:Label>
    </form>

  </body>
</html>
```

FIGURE 3.21A
Page with examples of border style options (03WebControls/BorderStyles.aspx).

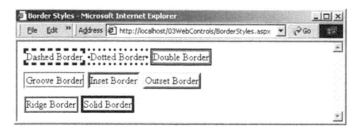

FIGURE 3.21B
Browser rendering of Web page illustrating border styles.

public enum UnitType	
Namespace: System.Web.UI.WebControls	
Member Name	**Measurement Description**
Cm	Centimeters
Em	Relative to height of parent element's font
Ex	Relative to height of lowercase letter x of parent element's font
Inch	Inches
Mm	Millimeters
Percentage	Percentage of parent element
Pica	Picas (a pica represents 12 points)
Pixel	Pixels
Point	Points (a point represents 1/72 of an inch)

FIGURE 3.22
UnitType enumeration.

public struct Unit	
Hierarchy	
Object	
ValueType	
Unit	
Namespace: System.Web.UI.WebControls	
Public Static Fields	
readonly Unit **Empty**;	Represents an empty unit.
Public Static Methods	
static Unit **Percentage** (double *n*);	Creates a Unit of type Percentage from value *n*. The Unit created is returned.
static Unit **Pixel** (int *n*);	Creates a Unit of type Pixel from value *n*. The Unit created is returned.
static Unit **Point** (int *n*);	Creates a Unit of type Point from value *n*. The Unit created is returned.
Public Instance Constructors	
Unit (double *n*);	Creates a new instance of Unit structure representing the value *n* as Pixel unit type.
Unit (int *n*);	Creates a new instance of Unit structure representing the value *n* as Pixel unit type.
Unit (string *stg*);	Creates a new instance of Unit structure representing the type and value specifed by the string. The type is Pixel if not specified.
Public Instance Properties	
bool **IsEmpty** {get;}	True if the Unit is empty; false otherwise.
UnitType **Type** {get;}	UnitType enumeration member representing the type of the Unit. The default is UnitType.Pixel.
double **Value** {get;}	Numerical representation of the value of the Unit.

FIGURE 3.23
Unit structure selected member summary.

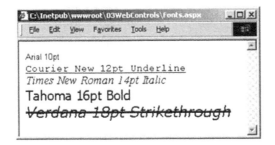

FIGURE 3.24A
Typical fonts and styles.

Note the specification of font size in terms of points: pt. A point is 1/72 of an inch. The **FontSize** enumeration, defined by HTML 4.0, also represents font sizes; it is summarized in Figure 3.25. Also, note that some browsers do not recognize the relative font sizes Smaller and Larger.

A Web page illustrating use of the FontSize enumeration members in specifying font size is shown in Figure 3.26A. The page's rendering is shown in Figure 3.26B.

```
<html>
  <body>
    <span style="font-family:Arial;
                 font-size:10pt;">
       Arial 10pt
    </span>
    <br>
    <span style="font-family:Courier New;
                 font-size:12pt;
                 Text-Decoration:underline; ">
       Courier New 12pt Underline
    </span>
    <br>
    <span style="font-family:Times New Roman;
                 font-size:14pt;
                 font-style:italic;">
       Times New Roman 14pt Italic
    </span>
    <br>
    <span style="font-family:Tahoma;
                 font-size:16pt;
                 font-style:bold;">
       Tahoma 16pt Bold
    </span>
    <br>
    <span style="font-family:Verdana;
                 font-size:18pt;
                 font-style:italic;
                 Text-Decoration:line-through;">
      Verdana 18pt Strikethrough
    </span>
  </body>
</html>
```

FIGURE 3.24B
Markup illustrating typical fonts and styles.

public enum FontSize	
Namespace: System.Web.UI.WebControls	
Member Name	**Font Size Determinate**
AsUnit	Point value.
Large	Two sizes larger than base font size.
Larger	One size larger than parent element.
Medium	One size larger than default font size.
NotSet	Font size not set.
Small	Determined by browser.
Smaller	One size smaller than parent element.
XLarge	Three sizes larger than base font size.
XSmall	One size smaller than base font size.
XXLarge	Four sizes larger than base font size.
XXSmall	Two sizes smaller than base font size.

FIGURE 3.25
FontSize enumeration summary.

The **FontUnit** structure represents font size and is summarized in Figure 3.27. The **FontInfo** class encapsulates font properties of text, for example, name and size. The FontInfo class is summarized in Figure 3.28.

Style

The **Style** class encapsulates the style of a Web Forms control; it is summarized in Figure 3.29.

```
<HTML>
  <HEAD>
    <TITLE>Font Basics</TITLE>
  </HEAD>
  <body>
    <form id="FormID" method="post" runat="server">
      <asp:Label ID=label1 Runat=server Font-Bold=True
                 Font-Size="Smaller" Font-Overline=True
                 Font-Names="Arial">Arial Bold 12 Point Overline
      </asp:Label>
      <p></p>
      <asp:Label ID=label2 Runat=server Font-Italic=True
                 Font-Size="X-Large" Font-Underline=True
                 Font-Name="Courier New" >Courier New X-Large Italic Underline
      </asp:Label>
    </form>
  </body>
</HTML>
```

FIGURE 3.26A
Web page illustrating use of FontSize enumeration members (03WebControls/FontBasics.aspx).

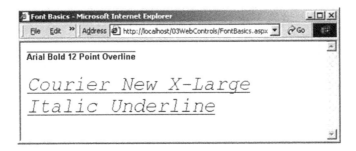

FIGURE 3.26B
Rendering of page illustrating use of FontSize enumeration members (03WebControls/FontBasics.aspx).

Hands-On Exercise: Declaring Controls

Most Web Forms pages include multiple HTML text, elements and Web Forms server controls. An example is a page that enables user Login, as seen in Figure HO3.1.
This page includes the following:

Gray Panel	HTML <DIV> element
"Login Name:" and "Password:"	HTML <DIV> elements and text
Login and password text boxes	Web Forms Server TextBox control
Login button	Web Forms Server Button control
Message area	Web Forms Server Label control

Typically, the page is presented to a user browsing a secure Web site to ascertain the user's access rights. The user firsts enters a login name and password and then presses the button to send the page, with the entered name and password, back to the server. The entered name and password are verified at the server. If they are valid, a page representing the application's functionality is returned to the user. If the name and password are invalid, the page is returned to the user with an appropriate message in the message area.

public struct FontUnit	
Hierarchy	
Object ValueType FontInfo	
Namespace: System.Web.UI.WebControls	
Public Instance Constructors	
FontUnit (FontSize *size*);	Initializes a new instance of the class with the FontSize object *size*.
FontUnit (int *size*);	Initializes a new instance of the class with the size of the font specified by *size*.
FontUnit (string *size*);	Initializes a new instance of the class with the string representation *size* of the font size.
FontUnit (Unit *size*);	Initializes a new instance of the class with the Unit object, *size*, representation of the font size.
Public Instance Properties	
bool **IsEmpty** {get;}	True if the font size has not been set; false otherwise.
FontSize **Type** {get;}	FontSize object that represents the font size.
Unit **Unit** {get;}	Unit object that represents the font size.
Public Static Fields	
readonly FontUnit **Empty**;	Represents an empty FontUnit object.
readonly FontUnit **Large**;	Type property set to FontUnit.Large font.
readonly FontUnit **Larger**;	Type property set to FontUnit.Larger font.
readonly FontUnit **Medium**;	Type property set to FontUnit.Medium font.
readonly FontUnit **Small**;	Type property set to FontUnit.Small font.
readonly FontUnit **Smaller**;	Type property set to FontUnit.Smaller font.
readonly FontUnit **XLarge**;	Type property set to FontUnit.XLarge font.
readonly FontUnit **XSmall**;	Type property set to FontUnit.XSmall font.
readonly FontUnit **XXLarge**;	Type property set to FontUnit.XXLarge font.
readonly FontUnit **XXSmall**;	Type property set to FontUnit.XXSmall font.
Public Static Method	
FontUnit **Parse** (string *size*);	Converts the string *size* to its FontUnit equivalent.

FIGURE 3.27
FontUnit structure summary.

Step 1: Create Project — DeclaringControls

1. Create a Visual Studio.NET project:

   Project type: **Visual C# Project**

   Template: **ASP.NET Web Application**

   Name: **DeclaringControls**

   Location: **http://LAJOLLA/03WebControls**

2. In Solution Explorer, delete WebForm1.aspx.

3. Add Web Form page Login.aspx. The Web Form page is opened in the Design View. The page opens in the default page layout mode: GridLayout. In this mode, controls are added to the page using absolute coordinates, i.e., the x and y coordinates of the control are specified.

4. Switch to the HTML View and enter the <TITLE> element:

   <title>Login</title>

Public sealed class FontInfo	
Hierarchy	
Object FontInfo	
Namespace: System.Web.UI.WebControls	
Public Instance Properties	
bool **Bold** {get; set;}	True if the font is bold; false otherwise. The default is false.
bool **Italic** {get; set;}	True if the font is italic; false otherwise. The default is false.
string **Name** {get; set;}	Font name. The default is String.Empty.
string [ ] **Names** {get; set;}	Array of font names.
bool **Overline** {get; set;}	True if the font is overlined; false otherwise. The default is false.
FontUnit **Size** {get; set;}	Font size represented by FontUnit object.
bool **Strikeout** {get; set;}	True if the font is striked out, that is contains a line through the center of the text; false otherwise. The default is false.
bool **Underline** {get; set;}	True if the font is underlined; false otherwise. The default is false.
Public Instance Methods	
void **MergeWith** (FontInfo *info*);	Combines the properties of the FontInfo object *info* with the font properties of the invoking FontInfo object.

FIGURE 3.28
FontInfo class summary.

public class Style : Component, IStateManager	
Hierarchy	
Object MarshallByRefObject Component Style	
Namespace: System.Web.UI.WebControls	
Public Instance Constructors	
Style ( );	Initializes a new instance of the class.
Style (StateBag *bag*);	Initializes a new instance of the class with the view state information represented by *bag*.
Public Instance Properties	
Color **BackColor** {get; set;}	Background color property. The default is Color.Empty.
Color **BorderColor** {get; set;}	Border color property. The default is Color.Empty.
BorderStyle **BorderStyle** {get; set;}	Border style property. The default is BorderStyle.NotSet.
Unit **BorderWidth** {get; set;}	Border width property. The default is Unit.Empty.
string **CssClass** {get; set;}	CSS class property. The default is String.Empty.
FontInfo **Font** {get;}	Font properties.
Color **ForeColor** {get; set;}	Foreground color, for example text or caption, property. The default is Color.Empty.
Unit **Height** {get; set;}	Height property. The default is Unit.Empty.
Unit **Width** {get; set;}	Width property. The default is Unit.Empty.

FIGURE 3.29
Style class summary.

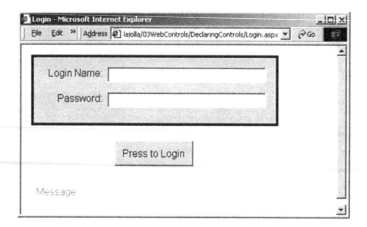

FIGURE HO3.1
Login page.

Tip!

In practice, each page should be uniquely titled, thereby enabling the Help Desk to ascertain the user's difficulty.

---

5. Additionally, in Solution Explorer, right-click the page Login.aspx. Select Set As Start Page in the submenu.
6. Return to the Design View.

Step 2: Configure the Design Environment

1. Expose the Design toolbar by selecting Design in the View menu Toolbars option submenu (Figure HO3.2). The toolbar provides for setting the following design options:

   Display Borders: Display of borders around objects that normally do not have visible borders, such as the Grid Layout Panel.

   Show Detail: Display of opening and closing tags for all elements.

   Lock Element: Locked objects cannot be resized or moved.

   Show Grid: Positioning grid displayed in the Design View.

   Snap to Grid: Moved object borders automatically align with the nearest grid points when the mouse is released.

2. Select Options... in the Tools menu to open the Options dialog. Select the HTML Designer folder. The Options dialog opens with General settings (Figure HO3.3A). Note specification of the starting view.
3. Click Display to display the HTML designer display options (Figure HO3.3B).
4. Check the Snap to grid box. Note that the horizontal and vertical spacing of the grid can be set. The default values are 8 pixels. Click OK.
5. Open the Toolbox. In the View menu, select the Toolbox option. Alternately, press the Ctrl+Alt+X key combination. The Toolbox opens in the Dockable mode. Right-click the Toolbox title bar and select the Auto-Hide option.

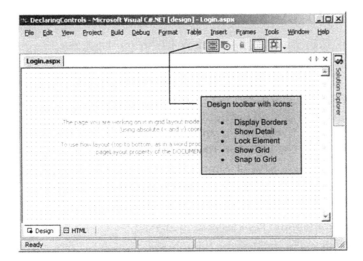

FIGURE HO3.2
Exposed Design toolbar.

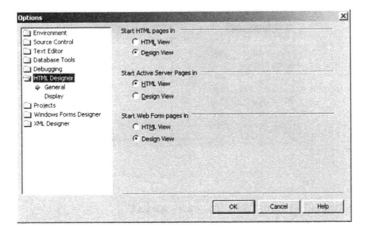

FIGURE HO3.3A
General options of HTML Designer.

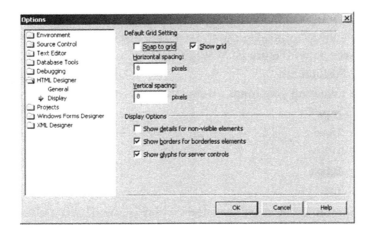

FIGURE HO3.3B
Display options of HTML Designer.

Step 3: Add Grid Layout Panel

1. Position the cursor over the Toolbox tab in the Designer margin to open the Toolbox.
2. Click the HTML tab in the Toolbox to expose the HTML components.
3. Select the GridLayout Panel and drag it to the desired position on the Designer editing window. The Grid Layout Panel inserts a <DIV> element that includes the ms_positioning = "GridLayout" attribute–value pair. The <DIV> element encloses a block of HTML elements and enables application of CSS attributes to them.
4. Select the GridLayout Panel component.
5. Press the F4 key to open the Properties window.
6. Click the ellipses in the style box to open the Style Builder.
7. Click the Font tab; the Font page is displayed.
8. Click the ellipses to display the Font Picker.

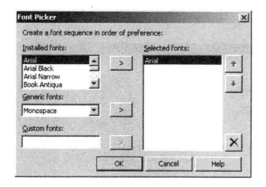

FIGURE HO3.4
Font Picker dialog.

9. Select an "Installed fonts:"; in this case, **Arial**.
10. Click the "**>**" button to move the selected font to the "Selected fonts:" area.
11. Click the OK button; the Font Picker closes. The Style Builder regains the focus with font selected (Figure HO3.5A).
12. Click the Background tab; the Background page is then displayed.
13. Click the ellipses to display the Color Picker. Select the color Light Gray in the named color pallet (Figure HO3.5B).
14. Click the Position tab.
15. Enter the following positional values:

    Top: **16px**
    Left: **16px**
    Height: **112px**
    Width: **400px**
    Z-Index: **101**

    The Z-Index or Z-Order controls the display of overlapping elements. Higher Z-Order values are displayed in front of lower Z-Order values (Figure HO3.5C).

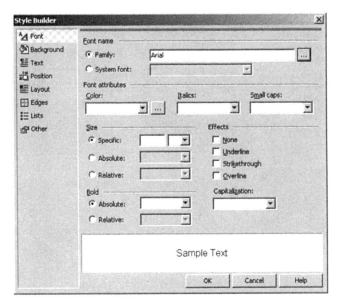

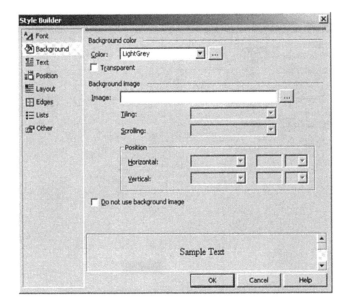

FIGURE HO3.5B
Style Builder Background page.

16. Click the Edges tab.
17. Enter the following edge parameter values (Figure HO3.5D):
    Select the edge to be changed: **All**
    Style: **Solid Line**
    Width: **Medium**
    Black is the default color.

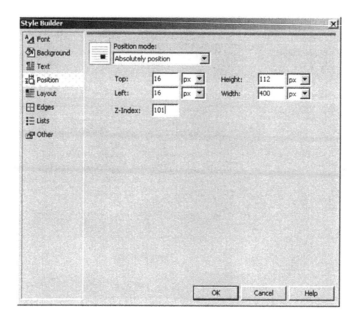

FIGURE HO3.5C
Style Builder Position page.

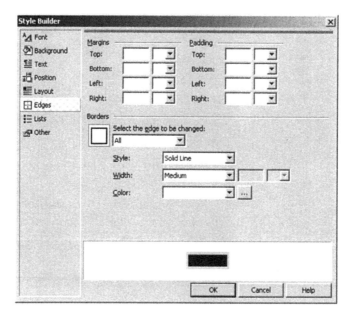

FIGURE HO3.5D
Style Builder Edges page.

18. Click OK. The GridLayout Panel is prominently displayed in the Designer (Figure HO3.6).

19. Switch to HTML view. The following element has been added to the page.

```
<DIV style = "BORDER-RIGHT: solid;
BORDER-TOP: solid;
Z-INDEX: 101;
```

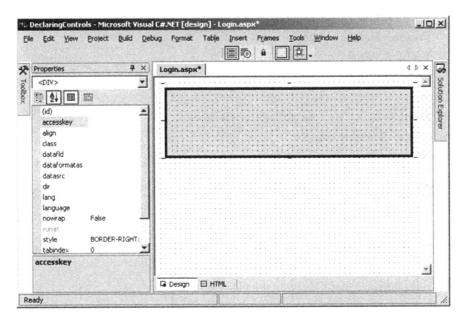

FIGURE HO3.6
Configured Grid Layout Panel in Design View.

```
LEFT: 16px;
BORDER-LEFT: solid;
WIDTH: 400px;
BORDER-BOTTOM: solid;
POSITION: absolute;
TOP: 16px;
HEIGHT: 112px;
BACKGROUND-COLOR: lightgray"
ms_positioning = "GridLayout">
</DIV>
```

20. Close or hide Properties window.

Step 4: Add HTML Label Element

1. Drag an HTML Label element onto the page. Position the label in the upper-left corner of the GridLayout Panel.
2. Select the HTML Label element and open the Properties window.
3. Enter the following property values:

Align	**Right**
Style	
Font Family	**Arial**
Font Size	**Small**
Position Top	**16px**

Position Left	**16px**
Position Height	**20px**
Position Width	**96px**
Position Z-Index	**101**

Layout

Display   **As an inflow element**

4. Select the elements content.
5. Enter **Login Name:**.

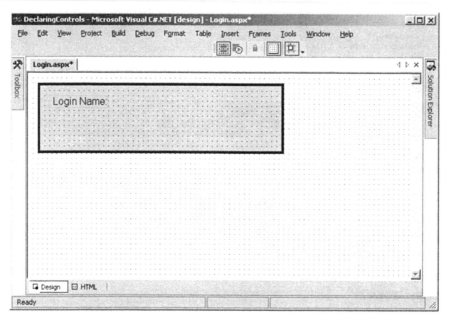

FIGURE HO3.7
HTML Label component added to panel.

6. Switch to HTML view. The following <DIV> element has been added as content to the <DIV> element representing the GridLayout Panel.

```
<DIV style = "DISPLAY: inline;
   FONT-SIZE: small;
   Z-INDEX: 101;
   LEFT: 16px;
   WIDTH: 96px;
   FONT-FAMILY: Arial;
   POSITION: absolute;
   TOP: 16px;
   HEIGHT: 20px"
align = right
ms_positioning = "FlowLayout">Login Name:
</DIV>
```

Step 5: Add Web Forms TextBox Control

1. Click the Web Forms tab in the Toolbox to expose the Web Forms server controls.
2. Drag a TextBox control onto the page.
3. Position the TextBox control to the left of the HTML Label component.
4. Select the TextBox and open the Properties window.
5. Enter the following property values:

   (ID)   **nameTextBox**

   Height   **24px**

   Width   **256px**

   The small green icon in the upper-left corner of the control indicates that the control is a server control.

Tip!

Most "shops" and all productive developers have naming standards. Most control names include a component reflecting the control's context and a component reflecting the control type. Alternative names for the text box include the following:

nameTxt
LoginNameTB
tbName

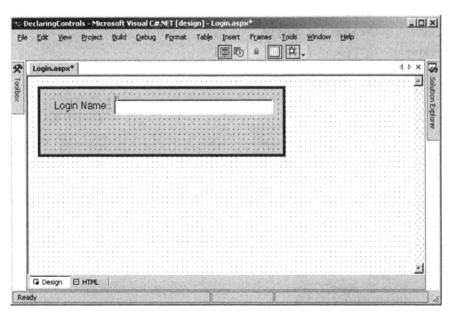

FIGURE HO3.8
Web Server ToolBox control added to panel.

6. Switch to HTML view. The following <asp:TextBox> element is added as content of the <DIV> element representing the GridLayout Panel:

```
<asp:TextBox id = nameTextBox
style = "Z-INDEX: 102;
LEFT: 120px;
POSITION: absolute;
TOP: 16px"
runat = "server"
Width = "256px"
Height = "24px">
</asp:TextBox>
```

Step 6: Add Web Forms Button Control

1. Click the Web Forms tab in the Toolbox to expose the Web Forms server controls.
2. Drag a Button control onto the page.
3. Center the Button control under the Grid Layout Panel.
4. Select the Button and open the Properties window.
5. Enter the following property values:

   (ID)   **loginButton**

   Font

      Name   **Arial**

      Size   **Small**

   Height   **40px**

   Text   **Press to Login**

   Width   **128px**

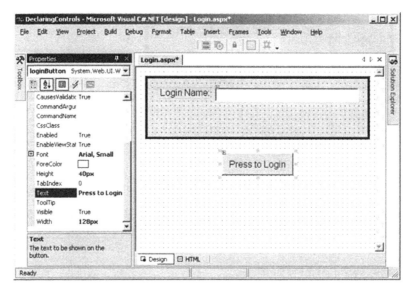

FIGURE HO3.9
Web Server Button control added to page.

6. Switch to HTML view. The following <asp:Button> element is added to the page:

```
<asp:Button id = loginButton
style = "Z-INDEX: 102;
   LEFT: 152px;
   POSITION: absolute;
   TOP: 152px"
runat = "server"
Width = "128px"
Height = "40px"
Text = "Press to Login"
Font-Size = "Small"
Font-Name = "Arial">
</asp:Button>
```

Step 7: Add Web Forms Label Control

1. Click the Web Forms tab in the Toolbox to expose the Web Forms server controls.
2. Drag a Label control onto the page.
3. Center the Label control under the Button control.
4. Select the Label and open the Properties window.
5. Enter the following property values:

(ID)		**messageLabel**
Font		
	Name	**Arial**
	Size	**Small**
ForeColor		**Red**
Height		**56px**
Text		**Message:**
Width		**388px**

6. Switch to HTML view. The following <asp:Label> element is added to the page:

```
<asp:Label id = messageLabel
style = "Z-INDEX: 103;
LEFT: 24px;
POSITION: absolute;
TOP: 224px"
runat = "server"
Width = "388px"
Height = "56px"
ForeColor = "Red"
Font-Size = "Small"
```

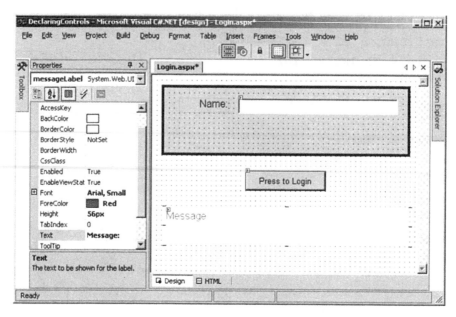

FIGURE HO3.10
Web Server Label control added to page.

```
Font-Names = "Arial">
Message
</asp:Label>
```

Step 8: Build and Run the Application

1. In the Debug menu, select the Start Without Debugging option.

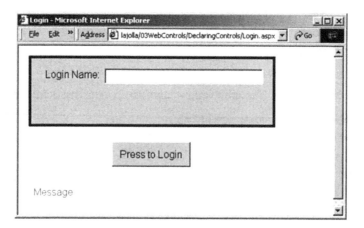

FIGURE HO3.11
Browsed page.

Step 9: Complete the Application

1. Add Password Label and TextBox.
2. Add and position an HTML Label component under the Login Name Label.
3. Enter the following property values:

Align   **Right**

Style

  Font Family   **Arial**

  Font Size   **Small**

  Position Top   **56px**

  Position Left   **16px**

  Position Height **24px**

  Position Width   **96px**

  Position Z-Index **103**

Layout

  Display   **As an inflow element**

4. Enter the element content: **Password:**
5. Add and position a web Forms TextBox server control component under the Login Name TextBox.
6. Enter the following property values:

(ID)   **passwordTextBox**

Height **24px**

Width   **256px**

Step 10: Build and Run the Completed Application

4

Client–Server Relationship

The following scenario depicts the elements of a Web-based application.

1. A user interacts with a browsed Web page. For example, most applications start with a user entering a login name and password. In the example of the ubiquitous Web store, the user selects an item for purchase. In another example, a reservation system, a user enters the destination airport, boarding airport and date of travel.

2. The user sends the page to the server. The page sent to the server is referred to as **posted**. Posting is generally initiated when the user clicks a submit button; however, it can also be initiated by selection of a choice. When posting is initiated, the page and the information entered by the user are electronically submitted to the server.

3. At the server, the data transmitted are processed. Processing at the server is referred to as **server-side processing.** Processing includes the retrieval and updating of database information, validation of data input, various computations, and generation of results and findings.

4. The findings and results are rendered as a page that is sent back to the browser. The returned page is loaded at the browser.

5. The user reviews the results and findings. Typically, more user interaction is undertaken.

The passage from browser to server and back to browser is referred to as a **round trip**. Note that some processing, such as user input validation, can be performed at the client side, but client-side processing does not interact with server-side components such as databases. A typical round trip is illustrated in Figure 4.1.

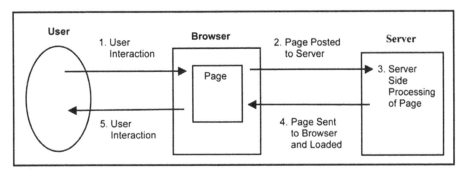

FIGURE 4.1
Elements of a Web page round trip.

User interaction with the page is enabled by form controls, for example, text boxes and labels. Information regarding the page's controls is not saved at the server. Every time a page is posted to the server, processing starts anew. For this reason, pages are said to be **stateless** because their state is not preserved from trip to trip. This situation is mediated by several Framework capabilities:

- Preservation of control values and properties in a **view state**
- Possibility of identification of pages with prior posting
- Storage of application data

Note that the page is also loaded at the server when requested, i.e., browsed, by the user. This scenario is depicted in Figure 4.2.

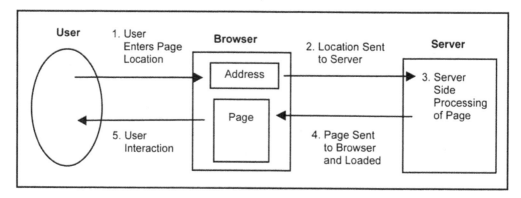

FIGURE 4.2
Elements of a Web page life that does not reflect a round trip.

In this case, the page is not posted. Steps involved in retrieving a page are as follows:

1. A user enters the location of a page, for example, the Web address of an airline or Web address of an online store.
2. The user sends the address to the server, typically by pressing the Enter key or clicking a go button.
3. At the server, the page at the address is loaded. Pages loaded in this manner are not posted pages. As before, server-side processing defined for the page is performed. Typically, processing includes data retrieval and computations.
4. The retrieved data and computational results are rendered as a page that is sent back to the browser. The returned page is loaded at the browser.
5. The user reviews page content. Typically, more user interaction is undertaken.

Note!

Pages returned to the server are posted.

Server-Side Processing

Appropriately defined methods in the page's code-behind file are automatically invoked during server-side processing. Consider the page lifecycle.aspx shown in Figure 4.3A. Note that the identification attributes of the controls are assigned. For example, the label is assigned the identification value "msgID" and the button is assigned the identification value "buttonID".

The code-behind file is shown in Figure 4.3B. Note the method Page_Load. This method is invoked as a result of the Load event automatically raised at the server whenever a control is loaded. Remember, a Page object is a Control object.

```
protected void Page_Load(object sender, EventArgs e)
{
}
```

The Framework passes to the method two arguments that represent information regarding the event leading to invocation of the method. The first argument, sender, represents the source of the event. The second argument, e, represents information regarding the event. Note that the source, sender, is an object type and the event information, e, is an EventArgs type. The statement

```
using Systems;
```

is required to access the class EventArgs without full name qualification.

As indicated, the Page_Load method is called every time the page is loaded. The page's IsPostBack property is tested with the expression

```
if (!IsPostBack).
```

When the page is loaded at the server in response to user browsing, the IsPostBack property is false. In this case, the label msgID is assigned the textual content "Not Postback." Additional processing is not defined; consequently, the page is sent to the user. The browser rendering of the page is shown in Figure 4.3C. Note that the label is rendered at the browser with the assigned text property "Not Postback."

```
<%@ Page language="c#" Codebehind="lifecycle1.cs"
    AutoEventWireup="false" Inherits="LifeCycle.LifeCycle1" %>

<html>
  <head>
  </head>
  <body>
    <form method="post" runat="server">
          <h3>Life Cycle</h3>

          <asp:label id="msgID" runat="Server"/>
          <p>
          <asp:button id="buttonID" runat="Server"
               text="Submit"
               font-bold="True"/>
    </form>
  </body>
</html>
```

FIGURE 4.3A
Page with label and button (lifecycle.aspx).

```
namespace LifeCycle
{
    using System;

    public class LifeCycle1 : System.Web.UI.Page
    {
            protected System.Web.UI.WebControls.Button buttonID;
            protected System.Web.UI.WebControls.Label msgID;

            public LifeCycle1()
            {
                    Page.Init += new System.EventHandler(Page_Init);
            }
                                                    ┌─────────────────────────┐
                                                    │ Automatically invoked whenever │
                                                    │ page is loaded at server │
                                                    └─────────────────────────┘

        protected void Page_Load(object sender, EventArgs e)
        {
            if (!IsPostBack) ────────────────       ┌─────────────────┐
            {                                        │ Testing value of │
                msgID.Text = "Not Postback";         │ postback property │
            }                                        └─────────────────┘
            else
            {
                msgID.Text = "Postback";
            }
        }

        protected void Page_Init(object sender, EventArgs e)
        {
            InitializeComponent();
        }

        private void InitializeComponent()
        {
            this.Load += new System.EventHandler (this.Page_Load);
        }
    }
}
```

FIGURE 4.3B
Page with label and button code-behind file (lifecycle.aspx.cs).

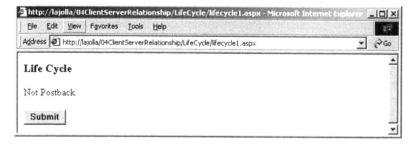

FIGURE 4.3C
Page rendering when first loaded (lifecycle.aspx.cs).

The page is posted to the server when the user clicks the Submit button. At the server, the Page_Load method is called when the page is loaded. This time, however, the IsPostBack property has the value true and the label msgID is assigned the textual content "Postback." The browser rendering of the page is shown in Figure 4.3D. Processing at the server consists of stages, as generally summarized in Figure 4.4. At each stage, the Framework raises events that can be connected to methods defining processing.

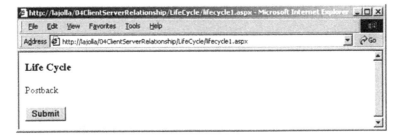

FIGURE 4.3D
Page rendering after user causes postback by clicking Submit button (lifecycle.aspx.cs).

Stage	Description
Configuration	The page is loaded. Processing activities typically include the following: • Test IsPostBack page property to determine first or subsequent posting. • Bind control values to specified sources, referred to as data binding. • Read the control values, perform computations and update the control properties.
Event Handling	Events initially raised at the client are raised at the server. Processing is handled by event-handling methods defined in the code-behind file. Processing includes reading control values and the status of validation controls (described below), database access, computation and finally the updating of control properties. Additionally, processing typically includes the management of page variables.
Configuration	Rendering of the page is completed and ready for unloading and return to the browser. Processing typically includes the following: • Closing files and database connections. • Discarding of unused objects preventing tying up resources that may not be released for some time by the garbage collector.

FIGURE 4.4
Summary of server-side processing stages.

Events Model

Server-side processing is brought about with events. An **event** provides notification to clients of a class, called **listeners**, that a change has happened to an object of the class. Classes representing user interface controls define events; for example, the Click event is raised when the user clicks a control. Events are not restricted to user interface controls. For example, the framework raises the Load event when a control is loaded. Additionally, an event can be triggered by program logic. In fact, events provide a general method for objects to notify (often referred to as signal) other objects that they have changed in some way.

The event sender does not know what object or method will receive the event. The Framework defines the **delegate** type that serves to connect the sender to the receiver. Delegates hold a reference to a method, have a signature, and can only hold references to methods that match the signature. Delegates provide a pointer-like mechanism relating events to methods that handle the event. Moreover, delegates are not sensitive to the class of the object referenced. On this basis, delegates are said to facilitate **"anonymous" invocation**.

Reference

Delegates are explained in Appendix A.11.

```
namespace EventBasics
{
    using System;

    public class ProcessAccount
    {
        public static int Main(string[] args)
        {
            NotifyCustomer notifyCustomer = new NotifyCustomer();

            Account information is made available and processing initiated.
            Assume account number 711, type 'R' new balance of –101.99.

            BalanceMonitor balanceMonitor =
                new BalanceMonitor(711, 'R', -101.99m);

            balanceMonitor.NegativeBalance +=
            new NegativeBalanceEventHandler(notifyCustomer.SendMessage);

            balanceMonitor.ExamineBalance();

            Account processing completed.

            return 0;
        }
    }

    public class NotifyCustomer
    {
        public void SendMessage(object sender,
            NegativeBalanceEventArgs e)
        {
            Console.WriteLine("Customer Notification");
            Console.WriteLine(" Account:   " + e.AccountNo);
            Console.WriteLine(" Amount:    " + e.Amount);
            Console.WriteLine(" Message:   " + e.Message);
        }
    }
}
```

FIGURE 4.5
Banking application illustrating the event model (EventBasics.cs).

The keys to understanding events are the following: declaring events, wiring or hooking up events, invoking events and handling events. These concepts are illustrated in an accounting application, shown in Figure 4.5, that represents the processing of banking transactions. Of special interest are those transactions that result in a negative balance; in such a case, notification is sent to the customer.

The class ProcessAccount contains the Main method that is called on application execution. Input of information regarding the account is assumed. First, an instance of the NotifyCustomer class is created with the statement

```
NotifyCustomer notifyCustomer = new NotifyCustomer();
```

The NotifyCustomer class brings about notification to the customer of the account status. The object is created just in case some form of notification must be sent to the customer.

Processing of the account begins. The program assumes account information has been made available and that the processing results in a new account balance of –$101.99.

Typically, an account's balance is monitored. In this application, balance monitoring is encapsulated in the BalanceMonitor class, which represents the various business rules related to account balance and account type. For example, an account with overdraft protection is treated differently than an account without overdraft protection. An instance of the BalanceMonitor class is created and initialized with the account information.

```
public class NegativeBalanceEventArgs : EventArgs
{
    public readonly int no;
    public readonly char type;
    public readonly decimal amt;
    public readonly string msg;

    public NegativeBalanceEventArgs(
    int n, char t, decimal a, string m)
    {
        no = n;
        type = t;
        amt = a;
        msg = m;
    }

    public int AccountNo
    {
        get { return no; }
    }
    public char Type
    {
        get { return type; }
    }
    public decimal Amount
    {
        get { return amt; }
    }
        public string Message
    {
        get { return msg; }
    }
}

public delegate void
    NegativeBalanceEventHandler(object sender,
                        NegativeBalanceEventArgs e);
```

Class encapsulating information about the NegativeBalance event

Delegate declaration

FIGURE 4.5 (CONTINUED)
Banking application illustrating the event model (EventBasics.cs).

```
BalanceMonitor balanceMonitor =
new BalanceMonitor(711, 'R', -101.99m);
```

Typically, the BalanceMonitor object will signal other objects regarding account conditions by raising events. For example, the BalanceMonitor object will raise a Negative-Balance event when it encounters a negative balance condition.

The SendMessage method in the NotifyCustomer class instance is "wired" to the NegativeBalance event with the statement

```
balanceMonitor.NegativeBalance + =
    new NegativeBalanceEventHandler(notifyCustomer.SendMessage);
```

That is, the NotifyCustomer class listens for the NegativeBalance event and its Send-Message event is invoked when the event is raised.

Note!

The SendMessage method is a handler for the NegativeBalance event.

```
    public class BalanceMonitor
    {
        private int no;
        private char type;
        private decimal amt;

        public BalanceMonitor(int n, char t, decimal a)
        {
            no = n;
            type = t;
            amt = a;
        }

        public event NegativeBalanceEventHandler NegativeBalance;

        protected virtual void
            OnNegativeBalance(NegativeBalanceEventArgs e)
        {
            if (NegativeBalance != null)
            {
                NegativeBalance(this, e);
            }
        }

        public void ExamineBalance()
        {
            if (amt < 0 && type == 'R')
            {
                NegativeBalanceEventArgs e = new
                    NegativeBalanceEventArgs( no, type, amt,
                                              "Overdrawn");
                OnNegativeBalance(e);
            }
        }
    }
}
```

FIGURE 4.5 (CONTINUED)
Banking application illustrating the event model (EventBasics.cs).

Examination of the account balance is performed in the ExamineBalance method of the BalanceMonitor instance

```
balanceMonitor.ExamineBalance();
```

Because the account type is 'R' and the balance is negative, the NegativeBalance event is raised in the ExamineBalance method of the BalanceMonitor class. The delegates are invoked and the SendMethod of the NotifyCustomer class is invoked.

The program output displayed at the console is as follows:

```
Customer Notification
Account: 711
Amount: -101.99
Message: Overdrawn
```

The SendMessage method, wired to the NegativeBalance event, has two arguments. The first represents an object raising the event and the second represents information about the event.

The class NegativeBalanceEventArgs provides this functionality. It defines four variables: account number, account type, account balance and a message. Properties for accessing these variables are defined as well as a constructor that initializes new instances of the class. The class NegativeBalanceEventArgs inherits from the EventsArgs class. The EventArgs class shown in Figure 4.6 is the base class for event data and derives directly from the Object class.

public class **EventArgs**	
Hierarchy	
Object	
EventArgs	
Namespace: System	
Public Static Fields	
readonly EventArgs **Empty**;	Represents an event with no data.
Public Instance Constructors	
EventArgs( );	Initializes a new instance of the class. This constructor is only called by the Common Language Runtime.

FIGURE 4.6
EventArgs class summary.

The delegate NegativeBalanceEventHandler is declared with the statement:

```
public delegate void
NegativeBalanceEventHandler(object sender,
    NegativeBalanceEventArgs e);
```

The delegate takes a parameter, in this case called NegativeBalanceEventArgs, that provides the handlers with information required to process the negative balance condition properly, for example, the account number; account type, e.g., 'R' for regular and 'P' for overdraft-protected; account amount; and a message. Note that the signature of the delegate perfectly matches the signature of the NotifyCustomer class SendMessage method.

The BalanceMonitor class encapsulates the business rules relevant to examining account balance. The BalanceMonitor class contains a constructor that initializes instances of the class with information regarding the account, i.e., the account number, type and balance. The class also declares the event NegativeBalance.

The **event** keyword enables the declaration of a delegate that will be called whenever an event occurs. The syntax for declaring an event is shown in Figure 4.7.

[attributes] [modifiers] **event** type declarator ; [attributes] [modifiers] **event** type member-name {accessor-declarations}	
attributes	Custom optional declarative information.
modifiers	Optional modifiers including abstract, new, override, static virtual and access modifiers: public, protected, internal or private.
type	The delegate associated with the event.
declarator	Name of the event.
member-name	Name of the event property.
accessor-declarations	Optional declaration of accessors used to add and remove event handlers. Although optional, if one is defined both must be defined.

FIGURE 4.7
Event declaration syntax.

Note that the event declaration presumes the existence of a delegate. For example, the statement

```
public event NegativeBalanceEventHandler NegativeBalance;
```

declares an event NegativeBalance associated with the NegativeBalanceEventHandler delegate type. The negative balance condition is uncovered in the ExamineBalance method, which is a member of the MonitorBalance class, resulting in the following:

- A NegativeBalanceEventArgs object is created representing the account, balance, type of account and message "Overdrawn."
- The class's OnNegativeBalance method is invoked.

The NegativeBalance event is raised in the OnNegativeBalance method with the statement

```
NegativeBalance(this, e);
```

Note that a reference to the invoking method is passed as the first argument and that the NegativeBalanceEventArgs object representing the event information is passed as the second argument. Remember that the SendMessage method of the NotifyCustomer is wired to the NegativeBalance event and thus is invoked.

The method SendMethod has a signature matching the signature required to be encapsulated by the NegativeBalanceEventHandler type delegate. Typically, the Notify-Customer class would be used by many applications. The class uses information in the NegativeBalanceEventArgs object, passed as a parameter in the method call, to notify the customer regarding the negative balance condition.

.NET Web Events

With Web Forms, events are raised at the client and handled at the server. This differs from client-based applications in which the event is handled at the client. Information regarding the event is transmitted to the server with an HTTP protocol.

HTTP Post

HTTP Post is an open protocol based on the underlying HTTP protocol. In the transmission of form-related information, the name–value pairs are transmitted inside the HTTP request message. This is in contrast to the HTTP-Get protocol in which parameters are passed as a coded text appended to the URL.

The .NET Framework interprets the transmitted information to determine the event raised and then calls the associated method. The designer is responsible for defining the event handler functionality. The server controls support a limited set of events. For example, Button control supports the Click event and the TextBox control supports the TextChanged event. However, most of the events raised invisibly by the user, such as the mouseover event, are not supported by the server controls.

The events governing a control's life cycle are defined in the **System.Web.UI.Control** class and summarized in Figure 4.8.

The .NET Framework event model requires a class derived from EventArgs to hold the event data and a delegate that points to the method defining the event response. The **EventArgs** class inherits the functionality of the Object class and is the base class for all event data, as shown in Figure 4.9.

EventHandler delegates handle these events. The EventHandler delegate represents a method that handles an event that has no event data; it is summarized in Figure 4.10.

Name	Argument	Description
public event EventHandler **DataBinding**;		Notifies server controls to perform defined data binding.
public event EventHandler **Disposed**		Raised in the last stage of the server control lifecycle. Used to release resources.
public event EventHandler **Init**;		Raised in the first stage fo the server control life cycle. Used to create and initialize resources.
public event EventHandler **Load**;		Raised when the server control is loaded into a Page object. Used to initiate processing related to the page request.
public event EventHandler **PreRender**;		Raised when the server control is about to be rendered on its Page object. Used to initiate updates prior to rendering. Changes made are not saved.
public event EventHandler **Unload**;		Raised when the server control is unloaded from memory. Used to initiate final cleanup before the control instance is unloaded.

FIGURE 4.8
Events in a server control life cycle.

```
public class EventArgs

Hierarchy
Object
    EventArgs

Namespace: System

Public Static Fields
readonly EventArgs Empty ;              Represents an event with no data.

Public Instance Constructors
public EventArgs ( );                   Called only by the common language runtime, the
                                        constructor initializes a new instance of the class.
```

FIGURE 4.9
EventArgs class summary.

```
public delegate void EventHandler (
    object sender,
    EventArgs e
)

sender              Source of the event.
e                   Argument object containing the event data.
```

FIGURE 4.10
EventHandler delegate summary.

Overriding Inherited Events

The inherited events are handled by overriding the inherited method associated with the event.

Event	Method To Override
Init	OnInit
Load	OnLoad
DataBinding	OnDataBinding
PreRender	OnPreRender
UnLoad	OnUnLoad

The inherited method of the base class should be called in the overriding method to ensure that the delegates associated with the event are invoked. For example, the Control class defines the override method OnLoad as shown below:

```
protected virtual void OnLoad(EventArgs);
```

An example of an override of the OnLoad method inherited from the Control class is shown in Figure 4.11.

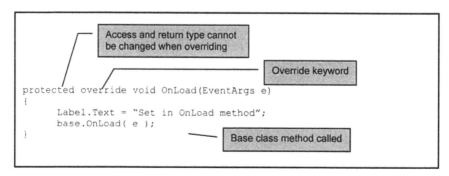

FIGURE 4.11
Overriding the inherited method OnLoad.

When the label control is loaded, the overriding method will be invoked and the text will be set to the string "Set in OnLoad method," which will be displayed when the control is rendered. Note that the base class OnLoad method is also called with the statement

```
base.OnLoad(e);
```

The EventsArgs argument e is passed as an argument to the base class method. A page with a label control is shown in Figure 4.12A.

```
<%@ Page language="c#" Codebehind="WebForm1.cs" AutoEventWireup="false"
    Inherits="Override.WebForm1" %>

<html>
  <head>
    <meta name="GENERATOR" Content="Microsoft Visual Studio 7.0">
    <meta name="CODE_LANGUAGE" Content="C#">
  </head>
  <body>

    <form method="post" runat="server">

      <asp:label id="labelID" runat="Server">Label Text</asp:label>

    </form>
  </body>
</html>
```

FIGURE 4.12A
HTML page with a label control.

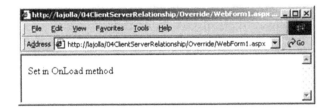

FIGURE 4.12B
Browser rendering of page with OnLoad override that changes the label's text.

```
using System.Collections;
using System.ComponentModel;
using System.Data;
using System.Drawing;
using System.Web;
using System.Web.SessionState;
using System.Web.UI;
using System.Web.UI.WebControls;
using System.Web.UI.HtmlControls;

 public class WebForm1 : System.Web.UI.Page
 {
    protected System.Web.UI.WebControls.Label labelID;

    public WebForm1()
    {
        Page.Init += new System.EventHandler(Page_Init);
    }

    protected void Page_Load(object sender, EventArgs e)
    {

    }

    protected void Page_Init(object sender, EventArgs e)
    {
        InitializeComponent();
    }

    private void InitializeComponent()
    {
        this.Load += new System.EventHandler (this.Page_Load);
    }

    protected override void OnLoad(EventArgs e)
    {
        labelID.Text = "Set in OnLoad method";
        base.OnLoad( e );
    }
 }
}
```

FIGURE 4.12C
Code-behind file of page with OnLoad override that changes the label's text.

Note that label's text is set to "Label Text." The code-behind file contains an override of the OnLoad method in which the label's text is set to "Set in OnLoad method." The page is rendered at the browser as shown in Figure 4.12B.

The code-behind file containing the OnLoad override is shown in Figure 4.12C. The overridden OnLoad method is invoked in response to the Load event raised when the page is processed at the server. The code-behind file in Figure 4.12C contains imports and methods reflecting the requirements of Visual Studio.NET Designer and presumptions regarding the requirements of typical Web applications.

Validation Controls

The Validation controls provided by the .NET Framework enable the validation of data input by users and are able to test the values of selected input controls. Applicable Web Forms input controls are listed in Figure 4.13.

Control	Property Validated
TextBox	Text
ListBox	SelectedItem.Value
DropDownList	SelectedItem.Value
RadioButtonList	SelectedItem.Value

FIGURE 4.13
Web Forms controls that can be validated.

Additionally, the Value property of the HTML InputText, TextArea, Select and InputFile controls is also applicable to validation. The validation controls are summarized below:

Control Name	Valid Condition Description
RequiredFieldValidator	The control validated has an input, text or selected value.
RangeValidator	The value of the input control is within the boundary specified by minimum and maximum values.
RegularExpressionValidator	The value of the input control matches a regular expression pattern.
CompareValidator	Using a specified comparison operator, the value of the input control compares favorably with a specified constant or another control's value.
CustomValidator	The value of the input control is validated with custom code.
ValidationSummary	Error messages of validation control are displayed on the page.

A major benefit of the validation controls is their ability to perform the validation on the client side in validation-supporting browsers. Typically, validation of a control's value is performed when the focus is moved from the control. If the control's value is not valid, an error message is displayed. Validation of all controls is performed when the page is posted; posting is cancelled if the validation fails.

Server-side validation is initiated whenever the user clicks a button with its Cause-Validation property set to "true." The .NET FrameworkButton, ImageButton and LinkButton have this property and its default value is true. The HtmlInputButton, HtmlInputImage and HtmlButton also have this property. At the server, the Page's Validate method is invoked, resulting in iteration through the Page's validation control and processing the validation procedure. The Page's ValidationCollection object, accessed through the Page's Validator property, is the collection of the Page's validation controls.

Note!

Client-side validation of user input data saves the cost of a round trip.

public enum ValidatorDisplay	
Namespace: System.Web.UI.WebControls	
Member Name	**Comparison**
Dynamic	Space for the validation content, error message, is allocated dynamically when validation fails. (Multiple validators can share the same space.) Page layout change can be avoided by placing the validators in an element large enough to accommodate the largest validator.
None	The error message is only displayed in a ValidationSummary control. (The error message does not display in the area of the page occupied by the validation control.)
Static	The error message is displayed in the area of the page occupied by the validation control. The layout of the page does not change when error messages are displayed. (Multiple validators for the same input control must occupy different areas of the page.)

FIGURE 4.14
ValidatorDisplay enumeration.

When validation fails, the validator's error message is displayed. Members of the Validator-Display enumeration, seen in Figure 4.14, characterize the display of the error message when validation is not successful.

The **BaseValidator** class provides validation functionality common to all validation controls; it is summarized in Figure 4.15. The **RequiredFieldValidator** is used to ensure that an entry is made. A field in which an entry is required is said to be a **required field**. The RequiredFieldValidator control syntax is summarized in Figure 4.16A.

A RequiredFieldValidator control is created with the following markup:

```
<asp:requiredfieldvalidator id = firstRFV runat = "server"
    style = "Z-INDEX: 110;
        LEFT: 312px;
        POSITION: absolute;
        TOP: 16px"
    Height = "24px"
    Width = "8px"
    Font-Size = "Small"
    Font-Names = "Arial"
    ControlToValidate = "firstTB"
    ErrorMessage = "First Name" >
*
</asp:requiredfieldvalidator>
```

The control's content, in this case an asterisk, is displayed when validation fails. Validation is performed when focus is moved from the input control, as well as when the form is posted. Posting is cancelled if validation fails. The RequiredFieldValidator is represented by the RequiredFieldValidator class shown Figure 4.16B.

The InitialValue property can be used to ensure that a value is entered. For example, assume the input control contains the prompt "Enter name here." If the InitialValue is also "Enter name here," the validation will fail when focus leaves the input control. Note that the Text property, inherited from the Label control, is used to specify the control's text content.

```
public abstract class BaseValidator : Label, IValidator

Hierarchy
Object
   Control
      WebControl
         Label
            BaseValidator

Namespace: System.Web.UI.WebControls
```

Public Static Methods	
propertyDescriptor **GetValidationProperty** (object *component*);	Returns the validation property of the control, *component*, if it exists.

Public Instance Properties	
string **ControlToValidate** {get; set;}	Identification of the input conrol to validate. The default value is String.Empty.
ValidatorDisplay **Display** {get; set;}	ValidatorDisplay enumeration member specifying the display behavior of error messages. The default value is Static.
bool **EnableClientScript** {get; set;}	True if client-side validation is enabled; false otherwise. The default value is true.
override bool **Enabled** {get; set;}	True if validation control is enabled; false otherwise. The default value is true.
override Color **ForeColor** {get; set;}	Color of the error messages displayed when input data is invalid. The default value is Red.
bool **IsValid** {get; set;}	True if validation of the input control is successful; false otherwise. The default value is true.

Public Instance Methods	
void **Validate** ( );	Performs validation of the input control specified in the ControlToValidate property and updates the IsValid property with the validation results.

FIGURE 4.15
BaseValidator class summary.

```
<asp:RequiredFieldValidator id=controlID runat=server
                ControlToValidate=controlToValidateID
                InitalValue=initial
                ErrorMessage="errorMsg" ... >
</asp:CompareValidator>
```

controlToValidateID	Identification of the input control to compare with the input control being validated. The default value is String.Empty.
initial	Validation fails if the validated control's value matches this value when the focus moves to another control. The default value is String.Empty.
errorMsg	String representing the error message, inherited from the BaseValidator class, that is displayed when the validation fails.

FIGURE 4.16A
RequiredFieldValidator control syntax.

The **ValidationSummary** control enables summarization of validation error messages. A page typically contains multiple validation controls; each has an ErrorMessage property. The validation summary control displays the error messages of all validation controls associated with invalid data. The error messages can be shown in several formats: bullet list, list and single paragraph. The ValidationSummaryDisplayMode enumeration (Figure 4.17) represents the different ValidationSummary controls' display modes. The ValidationSummary control syntax is summarized in Figure 4.18A.

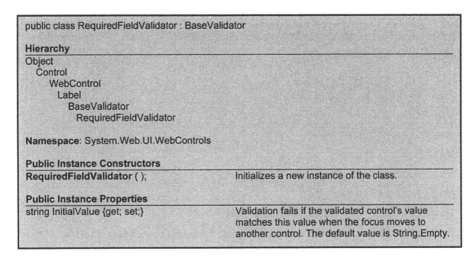

FIGURE 4.16B
RequiredFieldValidator class.

```
public enum ValidationSummaryDisplayMode

Namespace: System.Web.UI.WebControls
```

Member Name	Error Message Display Mode
BulletList	Bulleted list.
List	List
SingleParagraph	Single paragraph with messages separated by a space.

FIGURE 4.17
ValidationSummaryDisplayMode enumeration.

```
<asp:ValidationSummary id=controlID runat=server
                DisplayMode=mode
                EnabelClientScript=script
                ShowSummary=summary
                ShowMessageBox=box
                HeaderText=header ... >
</asp: ValidationSummary >
```

mode	ValidationSummaryDisplayMode enumeration member specifying the summary display mode. The default is BulletList.
script	true if client side validation is to be performed on supporting browsers; false otherwise. The default is true.
summary	True if the validation summary is shown inline; false otherwise. The default is false. Only applied when EnableClientScript is true.
box	True if the message summary is shown inside a box; false otherwise. The default is false. Only applied when EnableClientScript is true.
header	Text displayed at the top of the summary. The default value is String.Empty.

FIGURE 4.18A
ValidationSummary control syntax.

A ValidationSummary control is created with the following markup:

```
<asp:validationsummary id = addBioDataVS runat = "server"
    style = "Z-INDEX: 114;
        LEFT: 152px;
        POSITION: absolute;
        TOP: 152px"
    Height = "56px"
    Width = "376px"
    Font-Size = "Small"
    Font-Names = "Arial"
    DisplayMode = "SingleParagraph"
    HeaderText = "A valid value in the following fields is
        required:">
</asp:validationsummary>
```

In this case, the error messages are displayed as a single paragraph following the Header-Text string. The messages are displayed in the control's default ForeColor property: Color.Red. The ValidationSummary control is represented by the ValidationSummary class shown in Figure 4.18B.

public class ValidationSummary : WebControl	
Hierarchy	
Object	
Control	
WebControl	
ValidationSummary	
Namespace: System.Web.UI.WebControls	
Public Instance Constructors	
ValidationSummary ( );	Initializes a new instance of the class.
Public Instance Properties	
string **InitialValue** {get; set;}	Validation fails if the validated control's value matches this value when the focus moves to another control. The default value is String.Empty.
ValidationSummaryDisplayMode **DisplayMode** {get; set;}	ValidationSummaryDisplayMode enumeration member specifying the summary display mode. The default is BulletList.
bool **EnableClientScript** {get; set;}	true if client side validation is to be performed on supporting browsers; false otherwise. The default is true.
override Color **ForeColor** {get; set;}	Color of the control. The default is Red.
string **HeaderText** {get; set;}	Text displayed at the top of the summary. The default value is String.Empty.
bool **ShowMessageBox** {get; set;}	true if the message summary is shown inside a box; false otherwise. The default is false. Only applied when EnableClientScript is true.
bool **ShowSummary** {get; set;}	true if the validation summary is shown inline; false otherwise. The default is false. Only applied when EnableClientScript is true.

FIGURE 4.18B
ValidationSummary class.

When the ShowMessageBox property value is set "true," the error messages are also displayed in a Message Box (Figure 4.18C).

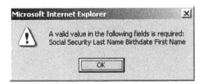

FIGURE 4.18C
Message Box with error messages.

The **RangeValidator** enables verifying that an input control value is between a lower and upper bound. The validation is applicable to numbers, strings and dates. The ValidationDataType enumeration (see Figure 4.19) represents the data types that the RangeValidator, and also the CompareValidator, can validate. Values are converted to the specified type before comparison. The RangeValidator control syntax is summarized in Figure 4.20A.

public enum ValidationDataType	
Namespace: System.Web.UI.WebControls	
Member Name	**Data Type**
Currency	Currency
Date	Date
Double	Double
Integer	Integer
String	String

FIGURE 4.19
ValidationDataType enumeration.

```
<asp:RangeValidator id=controlID runat=server
                ControlToValidate=controlToValidateID
                MinimumValue=min
                MaximumValue=max
                Type=dataType
                ErrorMessage= errorMsg ... >
</asp:RangeValidator>
```

controlToValidateID	Identification of the input control to compare with the input control being validated. The default value is String.Empty.
min	Minimum value of the validation range. The default value is String.Empty.
max	Maximum value of the validation range. The default value is String.Empty.
dataType	ValidationDataType enumeration member specifying the data types of the values compared. The default value is String.
errorMsg	String representing the error message, inherited from the BaseValidator class, that is displayed when the validation fails.

FIGURE 4.20A
RangeValidator control syntax.

The following markup creates a RangeValidator:

```
<asp:RangeValidator id = birthdateRV runat = "server"
    style = "Z-INDEX: 115;
        LEFT: 336px;
        POSITION: absolute;
        TOP: 112px"
    Height = "16px"
    Width = "193px"
    Font-Size = "Small"
    Font-Names = "Arial"
    ControlToValidate = "birthdateTB"
    ErrorMessage = "Date"
    Type = "Date"
    MaximumValue = "12/31/1997"
    MinimumValue = "1/1/1995">
1/1/1995 - 1/1/1997
</asp:RangeValidator>
```

The control being validated is birthdateRV. The control's value, converted to Date data type, is compared with the MinimumValue and MaximumValue. If the control's value falls outside the range, the validation fails and the ErrorMessage is displayed. The Range-Validator class depicted in Figure 4.20B represents the RangeValidator control.

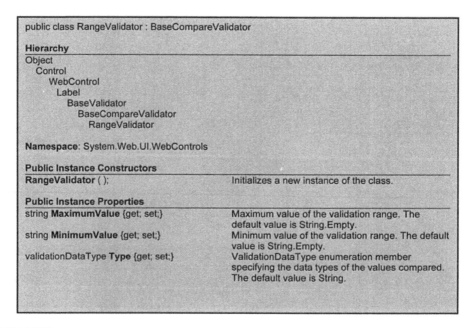

FIGURE 4.20B
RangeValidator class.

```
<asp:RegularExpressionValidator id=controlID runat=server
                ControlToValidate=controlToValidateID
                ValidationExpression=expression
                ErrorMessage="errorMsg" >
</asp: RegularExpressionValidator >

controlToValidateID                Identification of the input control to validate. The
                                   default value is String.Empty.
expression                         Regular expression used to match with input
                                   controls value. The default value is String.Empty.
                                   Data conversion is performed before validation.
ErrorMsg                           String representing the error message, inherited
                                   from the BaseValidator class, that is displayed
                                   when the validation fails.
```

FIGURE 4.21A
RegularExpressionValidator control syntax.

The **RegularExpressionValidator** control tests whether the input control's value matches a pattern defined by a regular expression. Figure 4.21A summarizes control syntax of the RegularExpressionValidator.

The following markup creates a RegularExpressionValidator:

```
<asp:RegularExpressionValidator id = socialSecurityREV
    runat = "server"
    style = "Z-INDEX: 114;
        LEFT: 336px;
        POSITION: absolute;
        TOP: 80px"
    Font-Size = "Small"
    Font-Names = "Arial"
    ControlToValidate = "socialSecurityTB"
    ErrorMessage = "Social Security"
    ValidationExpression = "\d{3}-\d{2}-\d{4}">
  nnn-nn-nnnn format required
</asp:RegularExpressionValidator>
```

In this case, the input control validated is socialSecurityTB. The ValidationExpression is

```
\d{3}-\d{2}-\d{4}
```

that matches exactly three digits, a hyphen, two digits, a hyphen and four digits. The message displayed in the validation control is

```
nnn-nn-nnnn format required
```

The message displayed in the ValidationSummary control is

```
Social Security
```

The RegularExpressionValidator control is represented by the RegularExpression class, Figure 4.21B.

The **CompareValidator** enables the comparison of an input control value against a constant value or the value of another control. The types of valid comparisons are represented by members of the **ValidationCompareOperator** enumeration, shown in Figure 4.22. The CompareValidator control syntax is summarized in Figure 4.23A.

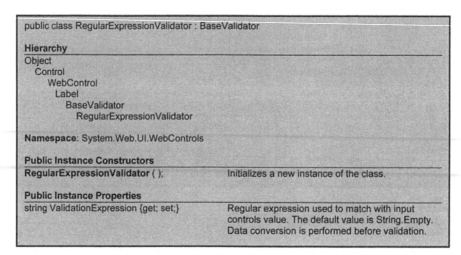

```
public class RegularExpressionValidator : BaseValidator

Hierarchy
Object
   Control
      WebControl
         Label
            BaseValidator
               RegularExpressionValidator

Namespace: System.Web.UI.WebControls

Public Instance Constructors
```

RegularExpressionValidator ( );	Initializes a new instance of the class.

Public Instance Properties

string ValidationExpression {get; set;}	Regular expression used to match with input controls value. The default value is String.Empty. Data conversion is performed before validation.

FIGURE 4.21B
RegularExpressionValidator class.

```
public enum ValidationCompareOperator

Namespace: System.Web.UI.WebControls
```

Member Name	Comparison
DataTypeCheck	Data type only
Equal	Equality
GreaterThan	Greater than
GreaterThanEqual	Greater than or equal to
LessThan	Less than
LessThanEqual	Less than or equal to
NotEqual	Inequality

FIGURE 4.22
ValidationCompareOperator enumeration.

```
<asp:CompareValidator id=controlID runat=server
            ControlToValidate=controlToValidateID
            ValueToCompare=valueToCompare
            Type=dataType
            Operator=operation
            ErrorMessage="errorMsg" ... >
</asp:CompareValidator>
```

controlToValidateID	Identification of the input control to compare with the input control being validated. The default value is String.Empty. ControlToCompare and ValueToCompare cannot be set at the same time.
valueToCompare	Constant value to compare with the input control being validated. The default value is String.Empty. ControlToCompare and ValueToCompare cannot be set at the same time.
dataType	ValidationDataType enumeration member specifying the data type compared.
operation	ValidationCompareOperator enumeration specifying the comparison.
ErrorMsg	String representing the error message, inherited from the BaseValidator class, that is displayed when the validation fails.

FIGURE 4.23A
CompareValidator control syntax.

A page collecting medical data in which birth date and inoculation date are input is an example of an instance in which two input controls should be compared. When the inoculation date is not greater than the birth date, an error is probable. A CompareValidator control enabling the required validation is created with the following markup:

```
<asp:CompareValidator id = CompareValidator1 runat = "server"
    style = "Z-INDEX: 118;
        LEFT: 200px;
        POSITION: absolute;
        TOP: 247px"
    Width = "257px"
    Height = "25px" ErrorMessage = "CompareValidator"
        ControlToValidate = "birthdateTB"
    Type = "Date"
    Operator = "LessThan"
    ControlToCompare = "inoculationTB">
Inoculation date should be greater than birth date
</asp:CompareValidator>
```

In this case, the input control birth date, birthdateTB, is compared with another input control, inoculationTB. The data type to be compared is specified with the Type attribute value as "Date." The comparison is specified as "LessThan." When the comparison fails, the error message "Inoculation date should be greater than birth date" is displayed. The CompareValidator class (Figure 4.23B) represents the CompareValidator control.

public class CompareValidator : BaseCompareValidator	
Hierarchy	
Object	
Control	
WebControl	
Label	
BaseValidator	
BaseCompareValidator	
CompareValidator	
Namespace: System.Web.UI.WebControls	
Public Instance Constructors	
CompareValidator ( );	Initializes a new instance of the class.
Public Instance Properties	
string ControlToCompare {get; set;}	Identification of the input control to compare with the input control being validated. The default value is String.Empty. ControlToCompare and ValueToCompare cannot be set at the same time.
string ValueToCompare {get; set;}	Constant value to compare with the input control being validated. The default value is String.Empty. ControlToCompare and ValueToCompare cannot be set at the same time.

FIGURE 4.23B
CompareValidator class.

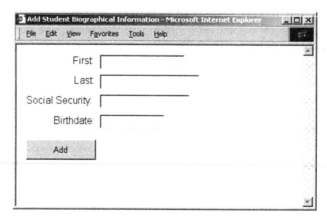

FIGURE HO4.1
Student biographical data entry page.

Hands-On Exercise: Using Validators

All applications have a data entry requirement. For example, Figure HO4.1 illustrates the page used to enter student biographical data.

Validation control can be used to ensure that required data are entered and to verify appropriateness of selected data elements such as Social Security, date and telephone numbers.

Step 1: Create Project UsingValidationControls

1. Create a Visual Studio.NET project:

   Project Type: **Visual C# Project**

   Template: **ASP.NET Web Application**

   Name: **UsingValidationControls**

   Location: **http://LAJOLLA/04ClientServerRelationship**

2. In Solution Explorer, delete WebForm1.aspx.
3. Add Web Form page AddBioData.aspx. The Web Form page is opened in the Design view.
4. Switch to the HTML View and enter the <TITLE> element:

   <title>Add Student Biographical Information</title>

5. Additionally, in Solution Explorer, right-click the page AddBioData.aspx. Select Set as start Page in the submenu.
6. Return to the Design View.

Step 2: Add Label, TextBox and Button Controls

1. Add controls to implement the page shown in Figure HO4.1. The controls, property values and content are specified below.

Control Type		Properties Values/Content
HTML Label	Align	**Right**
Style		
Font Family		**Arial**
Font Size		**Small**
Position Top		**16px**
Position Left		**16px**
Position Height		**24px**
Position Width		**112px**
Content		**First:**
HTML Label	Align	**Right**
Style		
Font Family		**Arial**
Font Size		**Small**
Position Top		**48px**
Position Left		**16px**
Position Height		**24px**
Position Width		**112px**
Position Z-Index		**101**
Content		**Last:**
HTML Label	Align	**Right**
Style		
Font Family		**Arial**
Font Size		**Small**
Position Top		**80px**
Position Left		**16px**
Position Height		**24px**
Position Width		**112px**
Position Z-Index		**101**
Content		**Social Security:**
HTML Label	Align	**Right**
Style		
Font Family		**Arial**
Font Size		**Small**
Position Top		**112px**
Position Left		**16px**
Position Height		**24px**
Position Width		**112px**
Position Z-Index		**101**
Content		**Birthdate:**
Web Forms TextBox (ID)		**firstTB**
Height		**24px**
Width		**136px**
Web Forms TextBox (ID)		**lastTB**
Height		**24px**
Width		**160px**
Web Forms TextBox (ID)		**socialSecurityTB**
Height		**24px**
Width		**144px**
Web Forms TextBox (ID)		**birthdateTB**
Height		**24px**
Width		**104px**
Web Forms Button (ID)		**addB**
Height		**32px**
Width		**114px**
Text		**Add**

Step 3: Add Required Field Validation Controls

1. In Design view, drag Web Forms toolbox tab RequiredFieldValidator controls onto the page. Position the controls to the left of the text boxes. The controls, property values and content are specified below.

Web Forms Control Type	Properties/Values Content
RequiredFieldValidator (ID)	**firstRFV**
ControlToValidate	**firstTB**
ErrorMessage	**First name is required**
Font	
Name	**Arial**
Size	**Small**
Forecolor	**Red**
Height	**24px**
Width	**192px**
RequiredFieldValidator (ID)	**lastRFV**
ControlToValidate	**lastTB**
ErrorMessage	**Last name is required**
Font	
Name	**Arial**
Size	**Small**
Forecolor	**Red**
Height	**24px**
Width	**192px**
RequiredFieldValidator (ID)	**socialSecurityRFV**
ControlToValidate	**socialSecurityTB**
ErrorMessage	**Social Security is required**
Font	
Name	**Arial**
Size	**Small**
Forecolor	**Red**
Height	**24px**
Width	**192px**
RequiredFieldValidator (ID)	**birthdateRFV**
ControlToValidate	**birthdateTB**
ErrorMessage	**Birthdate is required**
Font	
Name	**Arial**
Size	**Small**
Forecolor	**Red**
Height	**24px**
Width	**192px**

Step 4: Add Code To Display Messages When Page Is Initially Loaded

1. In the code-behind file Page-Load method, add the following:

```
if (!IsPostBack) Validate();
```

to display the validation messages when the page is first loaded.

Step 5: Execute the Application

1. In the Debug menu, select the Start Without Debugging option. The page is displayed with the validation messages.

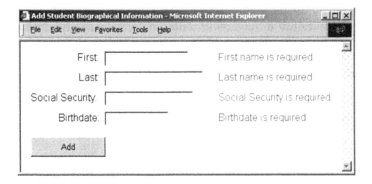

FIGURE HO4.2
Error messages reflect invalid data entry.

2. Enter a last name.
3. Click the Last name text box to remove the focus from the First name text box. Note that the First name text box content is validated.

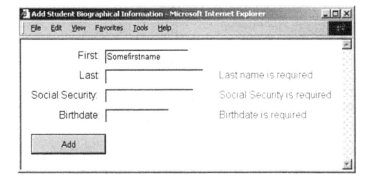

FIGURE HO4.3
Validation reflects valid First name when focus moves from control.

4. Remove the First name entry.
5. Click the Add button. Validation is performed. Validation is also performed when the form is posted to the server. Posting is cancelled if validation fails.

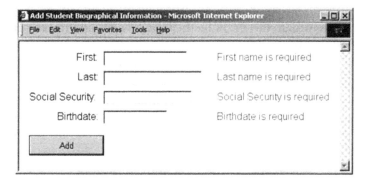

FIGURE HO4.4
Validation is performed on posting.

6. Enter data in all the fields and click the Add button. Validation is performed and all controls are found to have valid data. The page is posted on the server.

Step 6: Summarize Validation Messages

1. Put the "*" between the opening and closing tags of the RequiredFieldValidator controls. For example,

```
<asp:RequiredFieldValidator id = firstRFV runat = "server"
    style = "Z-INDEX: 110;
        LEFT: 312px;
        POSITION: absolute;
        TOP: 16px"
    Width = "8px"
    Height = "24px"
    ErrorMessage = "First name is required"
    ControlToValidate = "firstTB"
    Font-Names = "Arial"
    Font-Size = "Small" >
*
</asp:RequiredFieldValidator>
```

2. Reduce the width of the required field validator control to display the asterisk only and revise the error message as indicated:

Web Forms Control ID		Property Values
firstRFV	ErrorMessage	**First Name**
Width		**8px**
lastRFV	ErrorMessage	**Last Name**
Width		**8px**
socialSecurityRFV	ErrorMessage	**Social Security**
Width		**8px**
birthdateRFV	ErrorMessage	**Birthdate**
Width		**8px**

3. From the Web Forms Toolbox, drag a ValidationSummary control onto the page. Position the control to the left of the RequiredFieldValidation controls. Enter the following property values:

Web Forms Control Type	Property Values/Content
ValidationSummary (ID)	**addBioDataVS**
DisplayMode	**SingleParagraph**
Font	
Name	**Arial**
Size	**Small**
Forecolor	**Red**
HeaderText	**Correct the following:**
Height	**56px**
Width	**192px**

4. Remove the following statement in the code-behind file:

```
if (!IsPostBack) Validate();
```

Step 7: Execute the Application

1. Without entering any data, click the Add button. The validation messages are displayed.

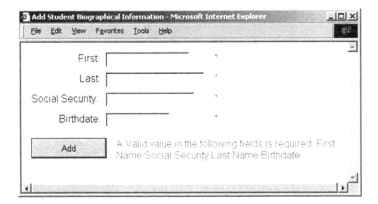

FIGURE HO4.5
Validation summary control lists all validation errors.

2. Vary the fields with data entered and click the Add button. Note the following:

- RequiredFieldValidator content, in this case an asterisk character, is displayed and reflects validation performed when focus moves from the control.
- The ValidationSummary reflects invalid status compiled when the page is posted. Posting is cancelled if any of the controls polled are invalid.

Step 8: Validate Social Security Number Format

1. From the Web Forms Toolbox, drag a RegularExpressionValidator control onto the page. Position the control to the right of the Social Security required field validation controls. Enter the following property values:

Web Forms Control Type	Property Values/Content
RegularExpressionValidator (ID)	**socialSecurityREV**
ControlToValidate	**socialSecurityTB**
ErrorMessage	**Social Security**
Height	**56px**
Font	
Name	**Arial**
Size	**Small**
Forecolor	**Red**
Text	**nnn–nn–nnnn format required**
Width	**192px**

2. In the Properties window, for the RegularExpressionValidator socialSecurityREV, click the ellipses at the right side of the ValidationExpression box. The Regular Expression Editor opens.

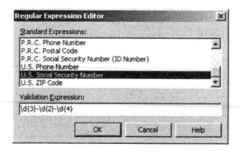

FIGURE HO4.6
Regular Expression Editor dialog.

3. Select the U.S. Social Security Number list item. Click the OK button. The following regular expression is entered for the ValidationExpression property value:

```
\d{3}-\d{2}-\d{4}
```

Step 9: Execute the Application

Note that the RegularExpressionValidator displays an error message if it contains an invalid expression when the focus is moved. In this case, the entered data lack the required hyphens: 123-45-6789. Note that the error message, "Social Security," is also included in the summary when the Add button is clicked.

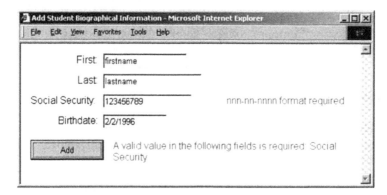

FIGURE HO4.7
Invalid Social Security format validation error.

Step 10: Validate Date

Birth dates of new students are between 1/1/95 and 12/31/97. The RangeValidator enables range validation.

1. From the Web Forms Toolbox, drag a RangeValidator control onto the page. Position the control to the right of the Birthdate required field validation controls. Enter the following property values:

Web Forms Control Type	Property Values/Content
RangeValidator (ID)	**birthdateRV**
ControlToValidate	**birthdateTB**
ErrorMessage	**Date**
Font	
Name	**Arial**
Size	**Small**
Forecolor	**Red**
Height	**16px**
MaximumValue	**12/31/1997**
MinimumValue	**1/1/1995**
Text	**1/1/1995 – 12/31/1997**
Type	**Date**
Width	**192px**

Step 11: Execute the Application

Note that the RegularExpressionValidator displays an error message if it contains an invalid birthdate when the focus is moved. In this case, the entered date, 4/19/02, is not in the required range. Note that the "Date" error message is also included in the summary when the Add button is clicked.

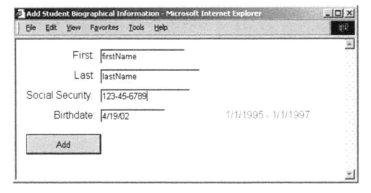

FIGURE HO4.8
Invalid birthdate message displayed when focus moves from control.

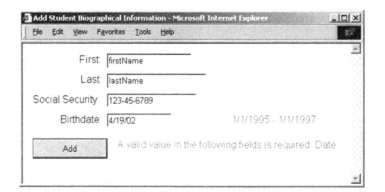

FIGURE HO4.9
Invalid birthdate message displayed in summary when posting is attempted.

Part 2

Implementing Services

5

Web Services

Few new applications today, and even fewer tomorrow, will be developed without concern and consideration given to the leveraging of Web technology. Moreover, the integration of legacy applications, built into a single enterprise application with a myriad of outdated technologies, including programming techniques, programming languages and operating systems, raises the need to consider the communication capabilities offered by Web technologies. Additionally, as the worldwide nature of business continues to evolve, the need to communicate across company, and even national, boundaries becomes a primary imperative in any business information-related solution. Web Services provides a technological tool for addressing these requirements.

A Web Service is a component that provides functionality accessible through Internet standards. Because access is through Internet standards XML and HTTP, the functionality is available to highly disparate clients. As such, if the client can speak the Internet standards, the client can access and use the components' functionality. Platform is not a constraint, programming language is not a constraint, and distance is not a constraint. Legacy applications can make use of the functionality by simply expressing their conversation in the standard language of the Internet.

Note!

The only knowledge required of a Web Service client is the service's input, output and location and the client's ability to communicate using Internet standards.

The ASP.NET Web Services are built on top of ASP.NET. In turn, ASP.NET is built on top of the .NET Framework, as Figure 5.1 illustrates. As such, Web Services can take advantage of the capabilities of these foundation elements. For example, the .NET Framework provides a common language runtime and ASP.NET provides for state management.

ASP.NET Web Services
ASP.NET
.NET Framework

FIGURE 5.1
ASP.NET Web Service foundation.

The ASP.NET Web Services infrastructure consists of industry standards SOAP, XML and WSDL:

XML — XML has emerged as the industry-accepted standard for data exchange. XML provides a standardized language for information exchange just as TCP/IP provides for universal connectivity, HTML provides a standard for displaying information and HTTP for network information transport. XML enables a computer to send and receive data independent of technology factors such as operating system and programming language. XML fundamentals are presented in Appendix C.

SOAP — **Simple Object Access Protocol** passes data to and from a Web Service using XML. Using XSD schemas, complex data types can be defined in XML. Definition of complex data types is automatically handled as ASP.NET converts classes into an XSD schema to facilitate passing the data types over the Internet. SOAP fundamentals are presented in Appendix D.

WSDL — **Web Services Description Language** is an XML grammar for describing network services as a collection of communication end points, or ports, capable of exchanging messages. A WSDL document describes these services. WSDL fundamentals are presented in Appendix E.

An example of a business operation that can be expressed as a Web Service is the service fee charged to accounts by financial institutions. The amount of the fee is often based on characteristics of the account. For example, service fees for major accounts, often characterized as "gold" are typically waived. In the same fashion, the service fee for regular accounts with a large balance is often waived. These business rules are reflected in the following decision table:

	Fee	
	Account Type	
Balance	**Gold**	**Other**
Less than $500	$0.00	$5.50
$500 and greater	$0.00	$0.00

In the real world, the decision rules are more complicated. However, this example typifies the type of functionality applicable to implementation as a Web Service. In most cases, this computation would be widely performed throughout the financial institution. Encapsulating the computation as an ASP.NET Web Service makes the functionality accessible throughout the institution. Any client application that can format a request in SOAP and send it across the Internet can call the Web Service regardless of the client's platform. ASP.NET Web Services automatically support clients using the SOAP, HTTP-GET or HTTP-POST protocols to invoke Web Service methods. An additional advantage of expressing the fee computation as a Web Service is that the maintenance of the business rules, which are probably always changing, is reduced to one point. This contrasts favorably with current practice in which the business rules are embedded within every application used, resulting in the maintenance of multiple applications.

Note!

Web Services are used by Web Service Clients. These Clients are typically Web Applications such as Web Forms or other Web Services. Web Service Clients can also be Windows-based applications.

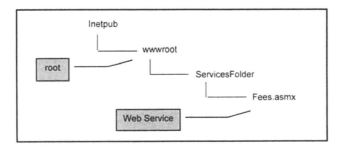

FIGURE 5.2
Directory hierarchy of the exposed Web Service Fees.asmx.

Discovering Web Services

A **Web Service** is exposed as a text file with an **.asmx** extension in the virtual path of an ASP.NET Web Application. For example, the directory hierarchy shown in Figure 5.2 illustrates the exposure of the Web Service Fees.asmx.

Clients can utilize the service by simply issuing the HTTP request:

```
http://localhost/servicesfolder/fees.asmx
```

Discovery of the service by developers is facilitated by the page rendered when the service is browsed (see Figure 5.3).

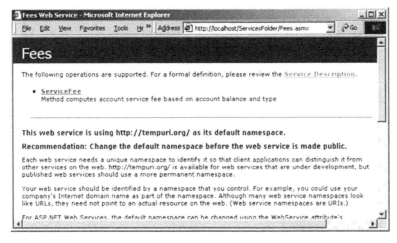

FIGURE 5.3
Discovery page rendered when Fees.asmx is browsed.

Clicking the ServiceFee link results in the rendering of a page, enabling execution of the service's method ServiceFee shown in Figure 5.4. Sample values for balance, $250.00, and account type, R, have been entered. Pressing the invoke button posts the page to the server and invokes the method Fees. The computed value is returned to the client, as shown in Figure 5.5.

The computed value is returned as an XML document. Note that the namespace `http://tempuri.org/` is a temporary namespace used during development. A unique namespace is used for published services. Typically, the namespace includes the company URI, thereby ensuring uniqueness.

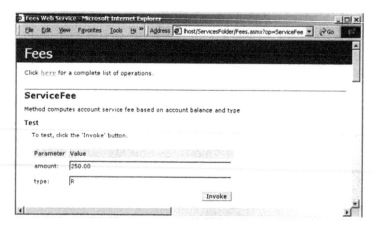

FIGURE 5.4
Discovery page enabling invocation of ServiceFee with sample data.

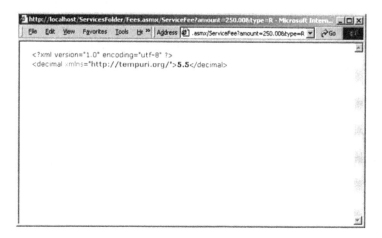

FIGURE 5.5
Fee computed by ServiceFee.

The .asmx file references classes that contain the functionality of the service. These references exist in two forms:

- In-line code in the .asmx file that is dynamically compiled and cached the first time the file is accessed
- External precompiled assemblies

A file implementing the ServiceFee Web Service is shown in Figure 5.6.

The business rules are implemented with the statements

```
if (type = = 'G')
    return 0m;
else
    if (amount > 500)
        return 0m;
    else
        return 5.5m;
```

```
<%@ WebService Language="C#" Class="Fees" %>

using System;
using System.Web.Services;

public class Fees : WebService
{
        [WebMethod] public decimal ServiceFee(decimal amount, char type)
        {
                if ( type == 'G' )
                        return 0m;
                else
                        if ( amount > 500 )
                                return 0m;
                        else
                                return 5.5m;
        }
}
```

FIGURE 5.6
Web Service declaration Fee.asmx.

If the type of the account is "G," i.e., gold, the service fee is zero. In other cases, the service fee depends upon the amount of the balance. If the amount is greater than $500, then the service fee is again zero; otherwise, the service fee is $5.50.

@WebService Directive

An **@WebService** directive defines Web Service (.asmx file) attributes. An @WebService directive is required at the top of a file defining a Web Service. In the example, the @WebService directive is the following:

```
<%@ WebService Language = "C#" Class = "Fees"%>
```

The directive specifies the language used in implementing the Web Service — in the above example, C#. The directive also specifies the class implementing the Web Service, in the example, Fees. Note that the class declaration must reside in the same file or in a separate file. If the class definition is in a separate file it must be placed in the \Bin directory underneath the folder in which the Web Service is located. In the example, the Web Service resides in the same file. The @WebService directive syntax is summarized in Figure 5.7.

<%@ WebService Language="*language*" Class="*className*" Codebehind="*code*" %>	
language	Programming language used in implementing the Web Service. Valid values are C#, VB and JS, corresponding to the languages C#, Visual Basic.NET and Jscript.NET.
className	Name of the class implementing the Web Service. Any valid class name can be used.
code	Code behind file.

FIGURE 5.7
@WebService directive syntax.

The file must reside in the home directory IIS folder, e.g., c:\inetpub\wwwroot. In the example, the file Fees.asmx is placed in a folder named ServicesFolders within the folder wwwroot. Typically, the folder's name would represent the nature of the services residing within.

Declaring Exposed Methods

Methods to be exposed within a Web Service are declared by placing the Web Method **[Web Method]** attribute before the method's declaration. Such methods are called **Web Methods**. Methods within the Web Service file that do not have the WebMethod attribute will not be exposed as Web Methods. In the example, the method ServiceFee is declared as a Web Method.

```
[WebMethod] public decimal ServiceFee(decimal amount, char type)
{
//method definition
}
```

Note the following:

- The method takes two parameters, a decimal identified as amount and a char identified as type. These parameters are also exposed in Discovery.
- The method to which the Web Method attribute is associated must be public.
- The class in which the method is declared must also be public.

Web Services can run within automatic transaction. The type of automatic transaction support provided the TransactionOption enumeration members (Figure 5.8) characterizes an instance. The WebMethodAttribute is represented by the WebMethodAttribute class illustrated in Figure 5.9. The class inherits the Attribute class functionality, i.e., methods to access and test custom attributes.

The Web Method attribute description property is set with the following statement:

```
[WebMethod (Description = "Method computes account service fee
based on account balance and type")]
public decimal ServiceFee(decimal amount, char type)
{
//method definition
}
```

The description appears in the discovery, Figure 5.10, and is useful because it can provide a general description of the service's method.

WebService Class

The **WebService** class, seen in Figure 5.11, is the optional base class for WebServices. Classes derived from the WebService class have direct access to ASP.NET objects such as the application and session state objects.

public enum TransactionOption	
Namespace: System.EnterpriseServices	
Member Name	**Description**
Disabled	Ignore automatic transaction object control.
NotSupported	Object does not require transaction. Process the component in a context with no governing transactions.
Required	Object requires a transaction. Share a transaction if one exists, create a new transaction if necessary. Required is the default.
RequiresNew	Object requires a transaction; create a new transaction for each request.
Supported	Share a transaction if one exists, without if one does not exist.

FIGURE 5.8
TransactionOption enumeration.

public sealed class WebMethodAttribute : Attribute	
Hierarchy	
Object Attribute WebMethodAttribute	
Namespace: System.Web.Services	
Public Instance Constructors	
WebMethodAttribute( );	Initializes a new instance of the class. Overloaded versions provide for initializing selected properties.
Public Instance Properties	
bool **BufferResponse** {get; set;}	True when the service's response is buffered until the response is completely serialized or the buffer is full; false otherwise. The default is true.
int **CacheDuration** {get; set;}	Time in seconds the response should be held in the cache. The default is 0, indicating the response is not cached.
string **Description** {get; set;}	Descriptive message describing the service method displayed during discovery. The default is String.Empty.
bool **EnableSession** {get; set;}	True when session state is enabled for the method; false otherwise. The default is false.
string **MessageName** {get; set;}	Name used within the Web Service request and response. Can be used to uniquely identify overloaded methods. The default is the name of the Web Service method.
TransactionOption **TransactionOption** {get; set;}	TransactionEnumeration member specifying the transaction support provided the Web Service method. The default is Disabled.

FIGURE 5.9
WebMethodAttribute class summary.

A web service class does not need to inherit the WebService class, but when it does, it gains access to the following ASP.NET objects:

Application: Application object for the current request. The application spans all sessions accessing the Web Service and enables storing and receiving state information over the lifetime of the application.

Context: Context object encapsulating the HTTP server context used to process the request.

Server: Server object containing methods used in processing the request.

Session: Session object encapsulates the specific user session and enables storing and receiving session-specific state information over the lifetime of the session.

User: User object that enables user authentication.

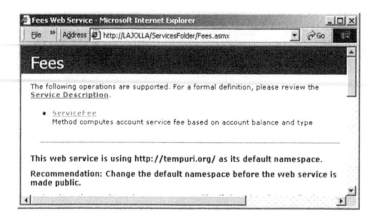

FIGURE 5.10
WebMethod Description property displayed in discovery.

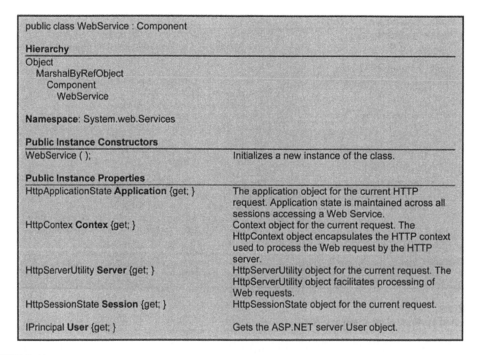

FIGURE 5.11
WebService class summary.

These objects provide access to information often needed in processing Web Requests.

The Server object has a MachineName property set to the name of the server. For example,

```
return Server.MachineName;
```

returns the server name. This provides an example of access to the HttpServerUtility object and its server management functionality.

Access is also provided to the HttpContext object. The Context object has a Timestamp property that accesses a DateTime object set to the time of the current request. The DateTime class has a variety of properties enabling direct access to the Year, Month, Day, Hour, Minute and TimeOfDay for the current request. The following statement evaluates the date and time of the current request:

```
Context.TimeStamp.Date.ToString();
```

This type of information is useful in time-sensitive financial computations like interest and penalties.

Additionally, the Context object also provides access to other objects, including the Request and Response objects. The Request object encapsulates the HTTP values of the client request such as browser information, path, request type, URL and user information. For example, the statement

```
return Context.Request.UserHostAddress;
```

returns the IP host address of the client. Similarly, the statement

```
return Context.Request.RequestType;
```

returns the request type.

WebServiceAttribute

The **WebServiceAttribute** is used to provide meta-information regarding a Web Service: Description, Name and Namespace.

- The **Description** property provides for a descriptive message that is displayed during Web Service discovery.
- The **Name** property specifies the name of the Web Service. The default name is the name of the class implementing the Web Service. The name is displayed during discovery of the Web Service and comprises the local part of the XML-qualified Web Service name.
- The **Namespace** property of the attribute manages the default XML namespace for the Web Service. A temporary XML namespace is used during development: http://www.tempuri.org. This namespace should be changed to a unique namespace to avoid confusion before the Web Service is published. The Namespace property provides for assigning the default namespace. XML namespaces enable the creation of Uniform Resource Identifier (URI) names in an XML document. Using a proprietary URI enables the unique identification of the elements and attributes in the XML document.

The WebServiceAttribute class is summarized in Figure 5.12.

A revised version of the Fees Web Service incorporating WebServiceAttribute properties to provide meta-information is shown in Figure 5.13A. When the page Fees.asmx is browsed, the service's Service Help Page is displayed, enabling discovery (Figure 5.13B). Clicking Service Description links to a help page that displays the XML namespace, as shown in Figure 5.13C.

public sealed class WebServiceAttribute : Attribute	
Hierarchy	
Object　　Attribute　　　　WebServiceAttribute	
Namespace: System.Web.Services	
Public Instance Constructors	
WebServiceAttribute ( );	Initializes a new instance of the class.
Public Instance Properties	
string **Description** {get; set; }	Descriptive message describing the service displayed during discovery. The default is String.Empty.
string **Name** {get; set; }	Name of the Web Service. The name is displayed during discovery. The default name is the name of the class.
string **Namespace** {get; set; }	The default XML namespace. The development default name is http://tempuri.org/.

FIGURE 5.12
WebServiceAttribute class summary.

```
<%@ WebService Language="C#" Class="Fees" %>

using System;
using System.Web.Services;

[WebService ( Description="Fee computation utility", Name="Fee Utility",
            Namespace="htt://www.BuildingWebApplications.com/" )]
public class Fees : WebService
{
      [WebMethod ( Description="Method computes account service fee based
                             on account balance and type")]
      public decimal ServiceFee(decimal amount, char type)
      {
            if ( type == 'G' )
                  return 0m;
            else
                  if ( amount > 500m )
                        return 0m;
                  else
                        return 5.5m;
      }
}
```

FIGURE 5.13A
WebServiceAttribute class summary.

Web Service Development Summary

Elements underlying development of classes that provide Web Services are:

    .asmx File — Web Services are saved as .asmx extension files.

    @WebService — A Web Service directive is required at the top of every Web Service file.

[WebMethod] — The [WebMethod] attribute is required on methods that are to be exposed.

WebService class — Derivation from the WebService class is optional but provides access to the ASP.NET application and session state objects. (Note that the .NET creates a new object with every Web method invocation and destroys the object when the method returns. Consequently, Web Service objects must retrieve their state as well as save it in each and every call.)

[WebService] — The [WebService] attribute is optional. Use of the attribute enables the specification of a namespace that contains the method and specification of other meta-information.

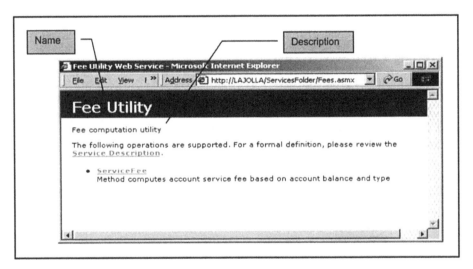

FIGURE 5.13B
Fees Web Service Help page.

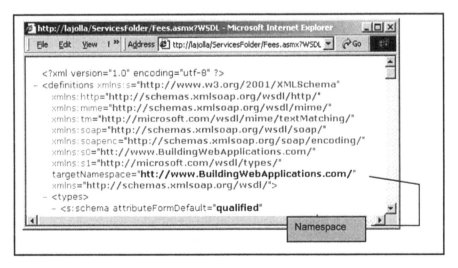

FIGURE 5.13C
Fees Web Service Help page displaying namespace name.

Hands-On Exercise: Creating a Web Service

This hands-on exercise creates a Web Service, using the Visual Studio development environment that implements a service fee application fulfilling the business rules:

| | Fee | |
| | Account Type | |
Balance	Gold	Other
Less than $500	$0.00	$5.50
$500 and greater	$0.00	$0.00

Step 1: Creating a Web Service Project

Web projects are created on a Web server as contrasted with applications created on a local computer. These projects provide for Web site elements including web forms, HTML pages, and Web Services. The URL of the project's location is specified when the project is created or opened. All the project files are stored in that location. Temporary copies of the files are maintained in a cache location for use when working offline from the Web server.

1. Click the Project option in the File menu's New option submenu. The New Project dialog box is displayed (see Figure HO5.1).

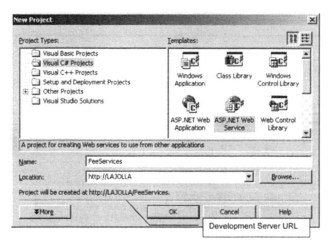

FIGURE HO5.1
New Project Dialog box.

2. Select Visual C# Projects in the Project Types window.

3. Select the ASP.NET Web Service icon in the Templates window.

4. Change the Name to **FeeServices**. The Location defaults to the name of the **Development Server**, the machine on which Visual Studio is installed and development will take place. Web Service project files, by default, must be located under the IIS Home Directory, which is usually c://inetpub/wwwroot. (Typically, the application will be created in a subdirectory in the IIS Home Directory and

the subdirectory name will reflect a business operation.) This location is also known as a virtual directory, i.e., a disk location that has a URL associated with it.

5. Click OK. Visual Studio creates the necessary files.

Step 2: Delete the Skeletal Service Automatically Created

1. Click the Solution Explorer in the View menu, or the Toolbar icon, to open the Solution Explorer, shown in Figure HO5.2.

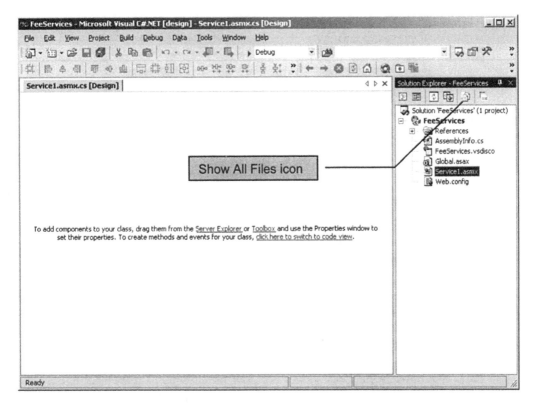

FIGURE HO5.2
Design view with Solution Explorer pinned open.

2. VS.NET creates a skeletal WebService called Service1 in the Service1.asmx file. Right-click this file and select the Delete command.

Step 3: Add the ServiceFee Service

1. In the Solution Explorer, right-click on FeeServices, select the Add option from the popup context menu and select Add New Item. The Add New Item dialog box is displayed (see Figure HO5.3). Alternately, select the Add Web Service... in the Project menu.

2. Under the Web Project Items in the Categories pane, open Default and select the Web Services icon in the Templates pane.

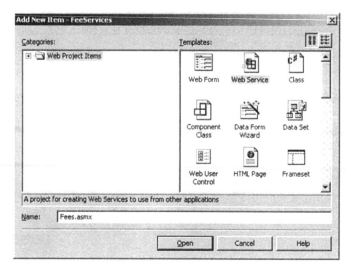

FIGURE HO5.3
Add New Item dialog.

3. Enter the name: **Fees.aspx**

4. Click Open.

5. A skeletal Service file Fees.asmx is created that contains the following directive:

   %@ WebService Language = "c#" Codebehind = "Fees.asmx.cs"
   Class = "FeeServices.Fees"%>

   Note the reference to the code-behind file, Fees.asmx.cs, and the class declared in the file, Fees.

6. Code is placed in a code-behind file associated with the .asmx. The code-behind file has a .cs extension and is hidden by default. To expose the code-behind file, click the Show All Files in the Solution Explorer or select the Show All Files command in the Project menu (see Figure HO5.2).

7. Right-click the Fees.asmx file and select the View Code command. The Fees.asmx.cs file is displayed in the Code Editor window, as shown in Figure HO5.4.

8. Alternately, select Fees.asmx in the Solution Explorer and press F7 to display the code-behind file.

9. Click the plus sign next to the References icon in the Solution Explorer to expand the References (Figure HO5.5).

10. By default, the project is created without a reference to System.Xml.Serialization namespace. In the Solution Explorer, select and right-click the project and select the Add Reference option. The Add Reference dialog opens, as illustrated in Figure HO5.6.

11. Select the.Net Framework tab.

12. Scroll to and select the reference System.Xml.Serialization

13. Click the Select button. The selected reference is displayed in the bottom window.

14. Click the OK button. Note that the System.Xml.Serialization is referenced in the Solution Explorer window.

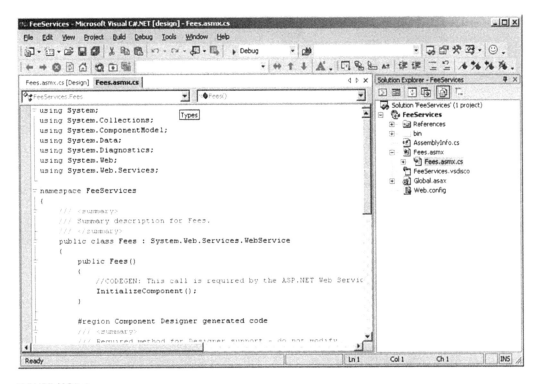

FIGURE HO5.4
File Fees.asmx.cs opened in the Code Editor.

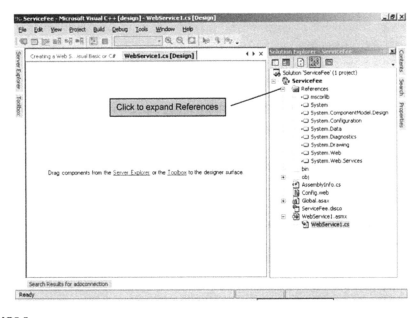

FIGURE HO5.5
Solution Explorer with References expanded.

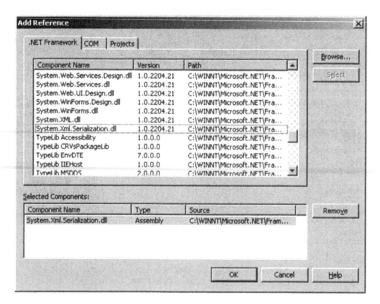

FIGURE HO5.6
Add Reference dialog.

Step 4: Implement the Fee Service

1. The skeletal file contains a "commented-out" method exposed as a Web Service, HelloWorld(), at the end of the file. Scroll down to the HelloWorld Web Service example in the code and replace with the following:

```
[WebMethod] public decimal ServiceFee(decimal amount, char type)
    {
        if (type =  = 'G')
            return 0m;
        else
            if (amount > 500m)
                return 0m;
            else
                return 5.50m;
    }
```

Note the following:

- [WebMethod] attribute is declared.
- The method ServiceFee is defined with public access.
- The class Fees is defined with public access and inherits the System.Web.Services.WebService class.

Programming Tip!

0.0. is not a decimal type; 0.0m is a decimal type.

Step 5: Build the Web Service

1. In the Build menu, click Build. Alternately, press the Ctrl + Shift + B key combination. Results of the Build are displayed.

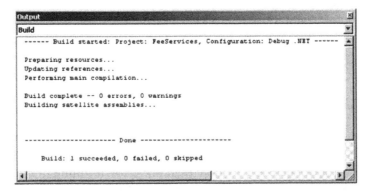

FIGURE HO5.7
Build results displayed in Output Window.

If the code has errors such as:

```
[WebMethod] public decimal ServiceFee(decimal amount, char type)
    {
        if (type =  = 'G')
            return 0m;
        else
            if (amount > 500)
                return 0m;
            else
                return 5.50;//line returns type double
    }
```

note that 5.50 is type double and cannot be implicitly converted to decimal, i.e., 5.50m. The build summary reflects the detection of errors and resultant build failure (see Figure HO5.8).

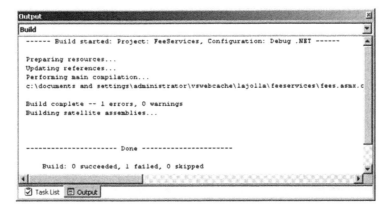

FIGURE HO5.8
Build results with error and Task List in Dockable mode.

2. Detected errors that must be corrected are shown in a Task List. Click the Task List tab to see details regarding build errors (Figure HO5.9).

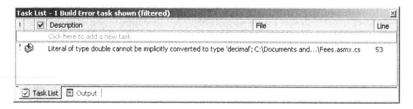

FIGURE HO5.9
Detected errors displayed in Task List.

Note that all detected errors are underlined in the Code Editor. The error's description is shown as a tool tip when the cursor is placed over the underlined code.

Often an error can give rise to more than one error, resulting in multiple entries in the Task List. Another wrinkle is added to the debugging process because the actual error often does not occur at the line in which the error is reported but in preceding code lines. For example, a missing statement-terminating semicolon often results in a Task List item pointing to the following line. In this example, the error is reported without ambiguity. Double-clicking the item in the Task List will shift the focus to the problem area in the Code Editor with the presumed error highlighted, as shown in Figure HO5.10.

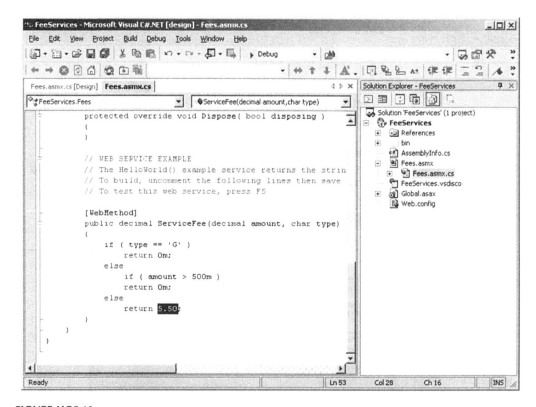

FIGURE HO5.10
Code Editor with problem highlighted.

3. Insert the decimal type suffix "m".

4. Build the Web Service. Note that all the errors may not be shown initially. Repeat building and code correction until the build is error free.

5. Close the Task List and Output windows by clicking the "X" in the window's upper right corner.

Note!

The attribute [WebMethod] is required to expose a method as a Web Service.

Step 6: Browse the ServiceFee Web Service

1. Select the Fees.asmx file in the Solution Explorer and right click.

2. Select Set As Start Page.

3. In the File menu, select View In Browser. The ServiceFee method is exposed (Figure HO5.11).

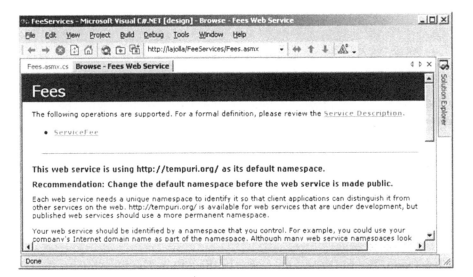

FIGURE HO5.11
ServiceFee method exposed.

4. Alternately, right-click Fees.asmx in the Solution Explorer and select the View In Browser option.

5. Press F5 to browse the file Fees.asmx in Internet Explorer (see Figure HO5.12).

6. Click the CalculateServiceFee link or scroll down.

7. Enter 300 in the Balance text box and click Invoke. The result is displayed in an XML document:

```
<?xml version = "1.0" ?>
<double xmlns = "http://tempuri.org/">0.3</double>
```

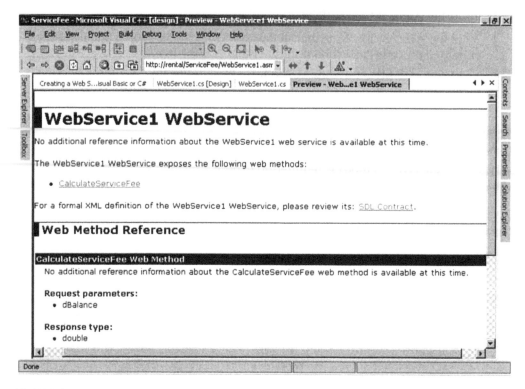

FIGURE HO5.12
Fees.asmx browsed.

8. Close the results window and enter another value, perhaps 501. The service fee associated with a $500.00 balance is displayed.

Step 7: Viewing the .asmx File

1. In Solution Explorer, right-click Fees.asmx and select Open With... in the menu. The Open With dialog opens.

2. Select the Source Code (Text) Editor option.

3. Click Open. The file Fees.asmx opens in the editor. The file contains the @Web-Service directive. The directive specifies C# as the language and Fees.asmx.cs as the code-behind file.

```
<%@ WebService Language = "c#"
Codebehind = "Fees.asmx.cs"
Class = "FeeServices.Fees"
%>
```

6

Web Services Framework

HTTP Protocol

The **Hypertext Transfer Protocol (HTTP)** is the primary protocol for data transfer across the Web. The HTTP has been in use since 1990 and was developed by Tim Berners-Lee, Roy Fielding and Henrik Frystyk Nielsen. HTTP operates on top of the TCP/IP and is used to request and retrieve URI named resources. In operation, the client establishes a connection with a remote server and then issues a request. The server processes the request, returns a response and finally closes the connection. The server does not keep track of the client's attributes and thus views the next request by the client without any knowledge of the client's previous request. The servers are stateless, i.e., the clients and servers establish their data representations anew every time a connection is made. The client request and server response are guided by a formal syntax described in the protocol.

Reference

Information regarding the Hypertext Transfer Protocol can be obtained at www.w3c.org.

Examples are based on the application "ApplyFees" that invokes the method ServiceFee developed in the Hands-On Exercises.

HTTP GET Request

GET is the most common HTTP method. In general, the **GET** method simply requests that the server send a copy of the specified resource to the client. The HTTP GET request syntax and example are illustrated in Figure 6.1.

The first line of the HTTP GET request is the request line, which consists of three fields. The first field specifies the method — GET — which must be uppercase. The second parameter, called the request URI, specifies the target resource, specifically the URI without the protocol and server domain name, and the request parameters. The request parameters are appended to the path as name-value pairs separated by the ampersand character. The question mark character separates the path and parameters. For example:

```
/FeeServices/Fees.asmx/ServiceFee?amount = 321.58&type = R
```

In this case, the target is the method ServiceFee in the resource Fees.asmx residing in the folder ServiceFee in the server's virtual root directory. The third field specifies, in uppercase, the protocol version used by the client, for example:

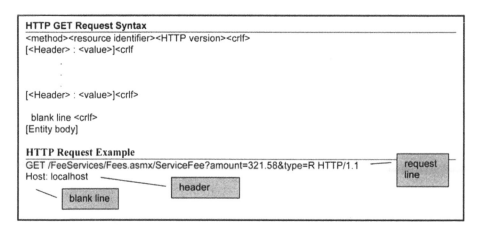

FIGURE 6.1
HTTP GET request.

HTTP/1.1. The request lines fields are separated by white space and the line is ended with a carriage-return–line-feed combination: <crlf>.

Header lines that provide information about the request and the client follow the request line. Each header field consists of a name followed by a colon (:) and header field value. The header field name is not case sensitive, although the header field value may be. Spaces or tabs may separate the colon and the field value. Header lines beginning with space or tabs are part of the previous header line and end with a carriage-return–line-feed combination. For example,

```
Host: localhost
```

The header Host is required; the other headers specified in HTTP 1.1 are not. A required blank line, also terminated with a carriage-return–line-feed combination, follows the headers. An optional entity body, or message, can be used to pass information. The example, HTTP GET request, does not have a message.

HTTP Response

The HTTP response consists of a status line, one or more optional header fields and an optional entity body or message. The syntax and example of an HTTP response are shown in Figure 6.2.

The status line has three parts separated by spaces. The first is the HTTP version and the second is a status code that indicates the status of the request. The third part is a "readable and understandable" description of the status. For example,

```
HTTP/1.1 200 OK
```

indicating HTTP version 1.1, status code 200 (the code for a successful request) and the phrase "OK," summarizing the status code meaning.

Status codes are three-digit integers and the first digit indicates the category of the response. The response code categories are summarized in Figure 6.3. The status line ends with a carriage-return–line-feed character combination.

Header lines follow the request line. Each header field consists of a name followed by a colon (:) and header field value. The header field name is not case sensitive although the header field value may be. Spaces or tabs may separate the colon and the field value.

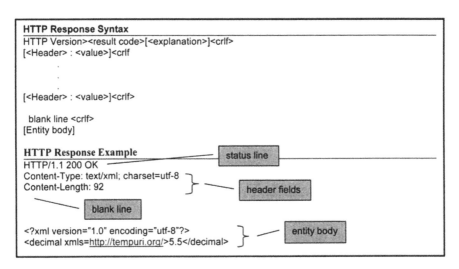

```
HTTP Response Syntax
HTTP Version><result code>[<explanation>]<crlf>
[<Header> : <value>]<crlf


[<Header> : <value>]<crlf>

 blank line <crlf>
[Entity body]
```

HTTP Response Example
HTTP/1.1 200 OK — status line
Content-Type: text/xml; charset=utf-8 ⎤
Content-Length: 92   ⎦ header fields

blank line

```
<?xml version="1.0" encoding="utf-8"?>  ⎤ entity body
<decimal xmls=http://tempuri.org/>5.5</decimal> ⎦
```

FIGURE 6.2
HTTP response.

Code	Category	Example
1xx	Informational	
2xx	Success	200 OK
		The request succeeded and the response is returned in the message body
3xx	Redirection to another URL	301 Moved permanently
4xx	Client error	404 Not found
		The resource could not be located; that is, it doesn't exist
5xx	Server error	500 Server Error
		The server code cannot be executed correctly

FIGURE 6.3
HTTP Status code categories and examples.

Header lines beginning with space or tabs are part of the previous header line and end with a carriage-return–line-feed combination. For example,

```
Content-Type: text/xml; charset = utf-8
Content-Length: 92
```

The Content-Type header specifies the MINE-type of the entity or message body, for example, text/xml. The Content-Length header field specifies the length, i.e., number of bytes, of the message body. A blank line also terminated by a carriage return follows the header-fields–line-feed combination. The message body follows. For example, for an xml document:

```
<?xml version = "1.0" encoding = "utf-8"?>
<decimal xmls = http://tempuri.org/>5.5</decimal>
```

The document describes a decimal number with value 5.5.

HTTP POST Request

The POST method is used to send data to a server to be processed. This method differs from the GET method in several ways. First, the data are sent in the message body as

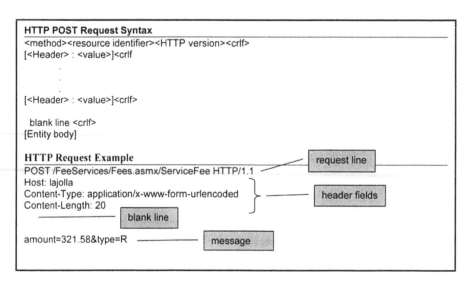

FIGURE 6.4
HTTP POST request.

opposed to being appended to the URI. Second, the request URI specifies a procedure to be performed as opposed to a resource to be returned. Third, the response is program output as opposed to a static file. The POST syntax and an example are shown in Figure 6.4.

The first line of the HTTP POST request is the request line, which consists of three fields. The first field specifies the method — POST — which must be uppercase. The second parameter, called the request URI, specifies the target resource, specifically the URI without the protocol and server domain name. Note that the request parameters are not appended to the path. For example:

```
/FeeServices/Fees.asmx/ServiceFee
```

In this case, the target is the method ServiceFee in the resource Fees.asmx residing in the folder ServiceFee in the server's virtual root directory. The third field specifies the protocol version used by the client in uppercase, for example: HTTP/1.1. The request lines fields are separated by white space and the line is ended with a carriage-return–line-feed combination: <crlf>.

Header lines follow the request line. Each header field consists of a name followed by a colon (:) and header field value. The header field name is not case sensitive, although the header field value may be. Spaces or tabs may separate the colon and the field value. Header lines beginning with space or tabs are part of the previous header line and end with a carriage-return–line-feed combination. For example,

```
Host: localhost

Content-Type: application/x-www-form-urlencoded

Content-Length: 20
```

The header Host is required; the other headers specified in HTTP 1.1 are not. In this case, the header Content-Type specifies the body type and the Content-Length specifies the length of the body. A required blank line also terminated with a carriage-return–line-feed combination follows the headers.

The message body contains the data submitted. For example,

```
amount = 321.58&type = R
```

describes an amount datum with value 321.58 and a type datum with value R. Typically, the data are the content of fields on a form submitted as parameters regarding a process. Note that the data are name-value pairs separated by the ampersand character.

Note

Only a limited set of data types are supported by the HTTP GET and HTTP POST. These messaging methodologies are thus limited with regard to passing parameters to a Web Service.

```
POST /FeeServices/Fees.asmx HTTP/1.1
Host: lajolla
Content-Type: text/xml; charset=utf-8          SOAP request body
Content-Length: 334
SOAPAction: "http://tempuri.org/ServiceFee"

<?xml version="1.0" encoding="utf-8"?>
<soap:Envelope xmlns:xsi="http://www.w3.org/2001/XMLSchema-instance"
   xmlns:xsd="http://www.w3.org/2001/XMLSchema"
   xmlns:soap="http://schemas.xmlsoap.org/soap/envelope/">
   <soap:Body>
      <ServiceFee xmlns="http://tempuri.org/">
         <amount>321.58</amount>
         <type>R</type>
      </ServiceFee>
   </soap:Body>
</soap:Envelope>
```

FIGURE 6.5
SOAP request.

SOAP

Simple Object Access Protocol (SOAP) is an XML-based protocol for exchanging structure and type information across the Web. As such, SOAP provides the means for passing complex data types as parameters to a Web Service. A SOAP document included as the body of an HTTP POST request is shown in Figure 6.5.

The SOAP document is the body of an HTTP request. Note the inclusion of the SOAPAction header. Additionally, note that the SOAP document specifies two parameters: an amount parameter with value 321.58 and a type parameter with value R. A SOAP-based response is shown in Figure 6.6. Note that the SOAP document describes a result with value 5.5.

Web Service Consumption

Clients throughout the Web automatically treat Microsoft.NET server object methods declared with a WebMethod attribute as if they were local clients. Consumption of a Web Service by a foreign client is summarized in Figure 6.7.

```
HTTP/1.1 200 OK
Content-Type: text/xml; charset=utf-8          SOAP response body
Content-Length: 355

<?xml version="1.0" encoding="utf-8"?>
<soap:Envelope xmlns:xsi=http://www.w3.org/2001/XMLSchema-instance
  xmlns:xsd="http://www.w3.org/2001/XMLSchema"
  xmlns:soap="http://schemas.xmlsoap.org/soap/envelope/">
  <soap:Body>
    <ServiceFeeResponse xmlns="http://tempuri.org/">
      <ServiceFeeResult>5.5</ServiceFeeResult>
    </ServiceFeeResponse>
  </soap:Body>
</soap:Envelope>
```

FIGURE 6.6
SOAP response.

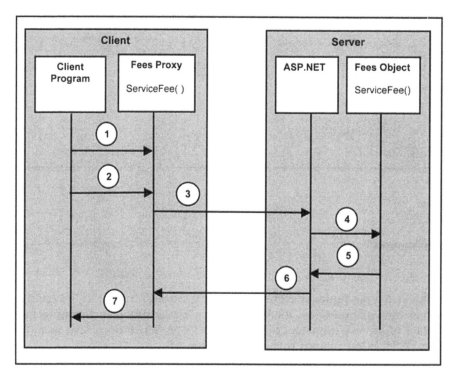

FIGURE 6.7
Web Service consumption.

1. At runtime, the client program creates a proxy based on a description of the Web Service. In the example, the proxy is of the class Fees. Developer tools included in ASP.NET produce the description.

2. When the client calls a Web Service method, for example, ServiceFee, the call is directed to the proxy class.

3. The proxy class automatically generates an HTTP request and sends it to the server. Parameters associated with the method call are encoded as part of the URI or as a separate XML document, as in Figure 6.4.

4. ASP.NET automatically connects the incoming HTTP request to the Web Service object containing the called method, in this case Fees.ServiceFee().

5. The Web Service, Fees.ServiceFee method, returns the computational result to ASP.NET.

6. ASP.NET automatically converts the results to XML and returns the result to the client proxy as an HTTP response (Figure 6.6).

7. The client proxy receives the result, parses the XML and returns the result to the calling program.

Note!

The Web Services objects are available to any application able to communicate with HTTP and XML. The infrastructure required for implementing the communication requirements — for example, creating HTTP requests and responses — is performed automatically by ASP.NET. Additionally, the creation of an XML document describing the parameter values passed to the method and creation of the XML document describing the result data values are also automatically performed by ASP.NET.

Describing Web Services

ASP.NET provides a description of the Web Service that lists the protocols supported by the service, the methods included in the service and the parameters required. The description is XML encoded, using a vocabulary and structure called the **Web Service Description Language (WSDL)**. Note that WSDL is pronounced "Wiz Dull." The WSDL for a web Service can be obtained by appending "?WSDL" to the service's URI. For example, the URI

```
http://localhost/FeeServices/Fees.asmx?wsdl
```

retrieves the description of the Web Service called Fees that resides in the folder FeeService. The service description for the Web Service Fees is shown in Figure 6.8.

```
<?xml version="1.0" encoding="utf-8" ?>
<definitions xmlns:s="http://www.w3.org/2001/XMLSchema"
    xmlns:http="http://schemas.xmlsoap.org/wsdl/http/"
    xmlns:mime="http://schemas.xmlsoap.org/wsdl/mime/"
    xmlns:tm="http://microsoft.com/wsdl/mime/textMatching/"
    xmlns:soap="http://schemas.xmlsoap.org/wsdl/soap/"
    xmlns:soapenc="http://schemas.xmlsoap.org/soap/encoding/"
    xmlns:s0="http://tempuri.org/"
    xmlns:s1="http://microsoft.com/wsdl/types/"
    targetNamespace="http://tempuri.org/"
    xmlns="http://schemas.xmlsoap.org/wsdl/">
```

FIGURE 6.8
Service description of the Web Service Fees.

```xml
- <types>
  - <s:schema attributeFormDefault="qualified"
      elementFormDefault="qualified"
      targetNamespace="http://tempuri.org/">
    - <s:element name="ServiceFee">
      - <s:complexType>
        - <s:sequence>
            <s:element minOccurs="1" maxOccurs="1"
              name="amount" type="s:decimal" />
            <s:element minOccurs="1" maxOccurs="1"
              name="type" type="s1:char" />
          </s:sequence>
        </s:complexType>
      </s:element>
    - <s:element name="ServiceFeeResponse">
      - <s:complexType>
        - <s:sequence>
            <s:element minOccurs="1" maxOccurs="1"
              name="ServiceFeeResult"
              type="s:decimal" />
          </s:sequence>
        </s:complexType>
      </s:element>
        <s:element name="decimal" type="s:decimal" />
    </s:schema>
  - <s:schema attributeFormDefault="qualified"
      elementFormDefault="qualified"
      targetNamespace="http://microsoft.com/wsdl/types/">
    - <s:simpleType name="char">
        <s:restriction base="s:unsignedShort" />
      </s:simpleType>
    </s:schema>
  </types>
- <message name="ServiceFeeSoapIn">
    <part name="parameters" element="s0:ServiceFee" />
  </message>
- <message name="ServiceFeeSoapOut">
    <part name="parameters" element="s0:ServiceFeeResponse"
      />
  </message>
- <message name="ServiceFeeHttpGetIn">
    <part name="amount" type="s:string" />
    <part name="type" type="s:string" />
  </message>
- <message name="ServiceFeeHttpGetOut">
    <part name="Body" element="s0:decimal" />
  </message>
- <message name="ServiceFeeHttpPostIn">
    <part name="amount" type="s:string" />
    <part name="type" type="s:string" />
  </message>
- <message name="ServiceFeeHttpPostOut">
    <part name="Body" element="s0:decimal" />
  </message>
- <portType name="FeesSoap">
  - <operation name="ServiceFee">
      <input message="s0:ServiceFeeSoapIn" />
      <output message="s0:ServiceFeeSoapOut" />
    </operation>
  </portType>
```

FIGURE 6.8 (CONTINUED)
Service description of the Web Service Fees.

```
- <portType name="FeesHttpGet">
  - <operation name="ServiceFee">
      <input message="s0:ServiceFeeHttpGetIn" />
      <output message="s0:ServiceFeeHttpGetOut" />
    </operation>
  </portType>
- <portType name="FeesHttpPost">
  - <operation name="ServiceFee">
      <input message="s0:ServiceFeeHttpPostIn" />
      <output message="s0:ServiceFeeHttpPostOut" />
    </operation>
  </portType>
- <binding name="FeesSoap" type="s0:FeesSoap">
    <soap:binding
      transport="http://schemas.xmlsoap.org/soap/http"
      style="document" />
  - <operation name="ServiceFee">
      <soap:operation
        soapAction="http://tempuri.org/ServiceFee"
        style="document" />
    - <input>
        <soap:body use="literal" />
      </input>
    - <output>
        <soap:body use="literal" />
      </output>
    </operation>
  </binding>
- <binding name="FeesHttpGet" type="s0:FeesHttpGet">
    <http:binding verb="GET" />
  - <operation name="ServiceFee">
      <http:operation location="/ServiceFee" />
    - <input>
        <http:urlEncoded />
      </input>
    - <output>
        <mime:mimeXml part="Body" />
      </output>
    </operation>
  </binding>
- <binding name="FeesHttpPost" type="s0:FeesHttpPost">
    <http:binding verb="POST" />
  - <operation name="ServiceFee">
      <http:operation location="/ServiceFee" />
    - <input>
        <mime:content type="application/x-www-form-
          urlencoded" />
      </input>
    - <output>
        <mime:mimeXml part="Body" />
      </output>
    </operation>
  </binding>
- <binding name="FeesSoap" type="s0:FeesSoap">
    <soap:binding
      transport="http://schemas.xmlsoap.org/soap/http"
      style="document" />
```

FIGURE 6.8 (CONTINUED)
Service description of the Web Service Fees.

```
    - <operation name="ServiceFee">
        <soap:operation
          soapAction="http://tempuri.org/ServiceFee"
          style="document" />
      - <input>
          <soap:body use="literal" />
        </input>
      - <output>
          <soap:body use="literal" />
        </output>
      </operation>
    </binding>
  - <binding name="FeesHttpGet" type="s0:FeesHttpGet">
      <http:binding verb="GET" />
    - <operation name="ServiceFee">
        <http:operation location="/ServiceFee" />
      - <input>
          <http:urlEncoded />
        </input>
      - <output>
          <mime:mimeXml part="Body" />
        </output>
      </operation>
    </binding>
  - <binding name="FeesHttpPost" type="s0:FeesHttpPost">
      <http:binding verb="POST" />
    - <operation name="ServiceFee">
        <http:operation location="/ServiceFee" />
      - <input>
          <mime:content type="application/x-www-form-
            urlencoded" />
        </input>
      - <output>
          <mime:mimeXml part="Body" />
        </output>
      </operation>
    </binding>
  - <service name="Fees">
    - <port name="FeesSoap" binding="s0:FeesSoap">
        <soap:address
          location="http://localhost/FeeServices/Fees.asmx" />
      </port>
    - <port name="FeesHttpGet" binding="s0:FeesHttpGet">
        <http:address
          location="http://localhost/FeeServices/Fees.asmx" />
      </port>
    - <port name="FeesHttpPost" binding="s0:FeesHttpPost">
        <http:address
          location="http://localhost/FeeServices/Fees.asmx" />
      </port>
    </service>
  </definitions>
```

FIGURE 6.8 (CONTINUED)
Service description of the Web Service Fees.

Hands-On Exercise: Using a Web Service

The application Apply Fees invokes the Web Service method ServiceFee.

Step 1: Create a Client Application — ApplyFees

1. Launch Visual Studio.NET and create a new project.
2. Select and enter the following:

    Project Type: **Visual C# Projects**

    Templates: **ASP.NET Web Application**

    Name: **ApplyFees**

    Location: **http://LAJOLLA/06UsingWebServices**
3. Click the OK button to create the project. The Web Designer opens in Design View.

Step 2: Create a Proxy

1. Right-click the Project or References icon in the Solution Explorer. Select the Add Web Reference.... The Add Web Reference dialog is displayed (Figure HO6.1). Typically, the Web address of the service desired would be entered in the address box. In this case, the Web Service is located on the same machine.

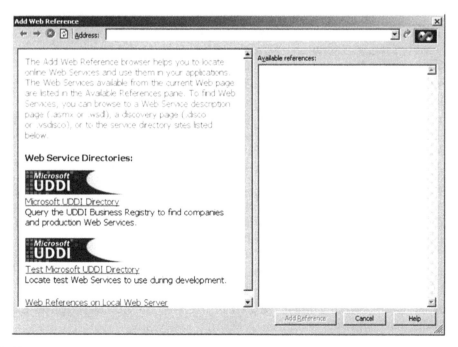

FIGURE HO6.1
Add Web Reference dialog.

2. Click the Web References on Local Web Server link in the left pane. Local services are discovered (see Figure HO6.2).

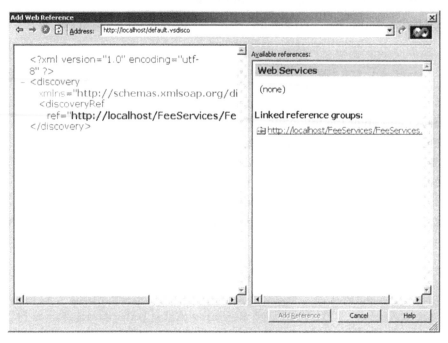

FIGURE HO6.2
Discovery of local Web Services.

3. Select the FeeServices link in the right pane. The service discovery continues (Figure HO6.3). Initial left pane contents speak to the name of the contract (Figure HO6.4).

4. When the View Contract link in the right pane is clicked, the contract is displayed in the left pane, as shown in Figure HO6.5.

5. When the View Document link is clicked, the Web Service Help Page is displayed in the left pane (Figure HO6.6). The Help Page enables invocation of the service with sample data. **Discovery is complete**.

6. Click Add Reference button. The Add Web Reference dialog closes.

7. Expand the Web References in the Solution Explorer by clicking the plus sign. Note the references to the FeeServices Web Service located on the local machine (localhost), Figure HO6.7. Visual Studio.NET has added Web References. These files are located in the VSWebCache.

Step 3: Fees.wsdl File

A .**wsdl** file is an XML document written in the **Web Service Description Language (WSDL)** describing the following:

- Web Service behavior
- Client interaction

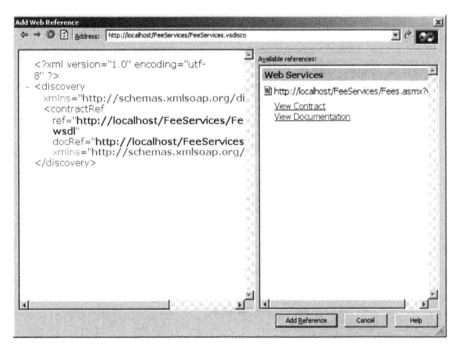

FIGURE HO6.3
Discovery of local Web Services continues.

```xml
<?xml version="1.0" encoding="utf-8" ?>
- <discovery xmlns="http://schemas.xmlsoap.org/disco/">
    <contractRef ref="http://localhost/FeeServices/Fees.asmx?wsdl"
        docRef="http://localhost/FeeServices/Fees.asmx"
        xmlns="http://schemas.xmlsoap.org/disco/scl/" />
  </discovery>
```

FIGURE HO6.4
Contract name.

The .NET Framework provides a Web Services Description Language Tool (Wsdl.exe) that generates WSDL contract files (.wsdl), XSD schemas (.xsd) and .discomap discovery documents. The wsdl.exe syntax is listed in Figure HO6.8. A .wsdl file in the C# language is created with the following command:

```
Wsdl http://LAJOLLA/WebServiceRoot/WebServiceName.asmx?wsdl
```

Step 4: Create a Client

1. Add the controls listed in Figure HO6.9 to the form WebForm1.aspx. (In most cases, the controls would be added to a page with a name reflecting the page's consequence.)
2. Arrange the controls as shown in Figure HO6.10.
3. Add the following method to the class webForm1:

```
public void SubmitBtn_Click(Object sender, EventArgs e)
```

```xml
<?xml version="1.0" encoding="utf-8" ?>
<definitions xmlns:s="http://www.w3.org/2001/XMLSchema"
    xmlns:http="http://schemas.xmlsoap.org/wsdl/http/"
    xmlns:mime="http://schemas.xmlsoap.org/wsdl/mime/"
    xmlns:tm="http://microsoft.com/wsdl/mime/textMatching/"
    xmlns:soap="http://schemas.xmlsoap.org/wsdl/soap/"
    xmlns:soapenc="http://schemas.xmlsoap.org/soap/encoding/"
    xmlns:s0="http://tempuri.org/"
    xmlns:s1="http://microsoft.com/wsdl/types/"
    targetNamespace="http://tempuri.org/"
    xmlns="http://schemas.xmlsoap.org/wsdl/">
  <types>
    <s:schema attributeFormDefault="qualified"
        elementFormDefault="qualified"
        targetNamespace="http://tempuri.org/">
      <s:import namespace="http://microsoft.com/wsdl/types/"
          />
      <s:element name="ServiceFee">
        <s:complexType>
          <s:sequence>
            <s:element minOccurs="1" maxOccurs="1"
              name="amount" type="s:decimal" />
            <s:element minOccurs="1" maxOccurs="1"
              name="type" type="s1:char" />
          </s:sequence>
        </s:complexType>
      </s:element>
      <s:element name="ServiceFeeResponse">
        <s:complexType>
          <s:sequence>
            <s:element minOccurs="1" maxOccurs="1"
              name="ServiceFeeResult" type="s:decimal"
              />
          </s:sequence>
        </s:complexType>
      </s:element>
      <s:element name="decimal" type="s:decimal" />
    </s:schema>
    <s:schema attributeFormDefault="qualified"
        elementFormDefault="qualified"
        targetNamespace="http://microsoft.com/wsdl/types/">
      <s:simpleType name="char">
        <s:restriction base="s:unsignedShort" />
      </s:simpleType>
    </s:schema>
  </types>
```

FIGURE HO6.5
Contract.

```csharp
        {
decimal amount = Convert.ToDecimal(Amount.Text);
char type = Convert.ToChar(Type.Text);
localhost.Fees fees = new localhost.Fees();
decimal serviceFee = fees.ServiceFee(amount, type);
Fee.Text = serviceFee.ToString();
        }
```

```
- <message name="ServiceFeeSoapIn">
    <part name="parameters" element="s0:ServiceFee" />
  </message>
- <message name="ServiceFeeSoapOut">
    <part name="parameters" element="s0:ServiceFeeResponse" />
  </message>
- <message name="ServiceFeeHttpGetIn">
    <part name="amount" type="s:string" />
    <part name="type" type="s:string" />
  </message>
- <message name="ServiceFeeHttpGetOut">
    <part name="Body" element="s0:decimal" />
  </message>
- <message name="ServiceFeeHttpPostIn">
    <part name="amount" type="s:string" />
    <part name="type" type="s:string" />
  </message>
- <message name="ServiceFeeHttpPostOut">
    <part name="Body" element="s0:decimal" />
  </message>
- <portType name="FeesSoap">
  - <operation name="ServiceFee">
      <documentation>Computes service fee based on account
        balance and type</documentation>
      <input message="s0:ServiceFeeSoapIn" />
      <output message="s0:ServiceFeeSoapOut" />
    </operation>
  </portType>
- <portType name="FeesHttpGet">
  - <operation name="ServiceFee">
      <documentation>Computes service fee based on account
        balance and type</documentation>
      <input message="s0:ServiceFeeHttpGetIn" />
      <output message="s0:ServiceFeeHttpGetOut" />
    </operation>
  </portType>
- <portType name="FeesHttpPost">
  - <operation name="ServiceFee">
      <documentation>Computes service fee based on account
        balance and type</documentation>
      <input message="s0:ServiceFeeHttpPostIn" />
      <output message="s0:ServiceFeeHttpPostOut" />
    </operation>
  </portType>
```

FIGURE HO6.5 (CONTINUED)
Contract.

4. Modify the Page_Load method to simulate a form initialized to display an account number:

```
private void Page_Load(object sender, System.EventArgs e)

{

AccountNo.Text = "711";

}
```

```xml
- <binding name="FeesSoap" type="s0:FeesSoap">
    <soap:binding
      transport="http://schemas.xmlsoap.org/soap/http"
      style="document" />
  - <operation name="ServiceFee">
      <soap:operation soapAction="http://tempuri.org/ServiceFee"
        style="document" />
    - <input>
        <soap:body use="literal" />
      </input>
    - <output>
        <soap:body use="literal" />
      </output>
    </operation>
  </binding>
- <binding name="FeesHttpGet" type="s0:FeesHttpGet">
    <http:binding verb="GET" />
  - <operation name="ServiceFee">
      <http:operation location="/ServiceFee" />
    - <input>
        <http:urlEncoded />
      </input>
    - <output>
        <mime:mimeXml part="Body" />
      </output>
    </operation>
  </binding>
- <binding name="FeesHttpPost" type="s0:FeesHttpPost">
    <http:binding verb="POST" />
  - <operation name="ServiceFee">
      <http:operation location="/ServiceFee" />
    - <input>
        <mime:content type="application/x-www-form-
          urlencoded" />
      </input>
    - <output>
        <mime:mimeXml part="Body" />
      </output>
    </operation>
  </binding>
- <service name="Fees">
  - <port name="FeesSoap" binding="s0:FeesSoap">
      <soap:address
        location="http://localhost/FeeServices/Fees.asmx" />
    </port>
  - <port name="FeesHttpGet" binding="s0:FeesHttpGet">
      <http:address
        location="http://localhost/FeeServices/Fees.asmx" />
    </port>
  - <port name="FeesHttpPost" binding="s0:FeesHttpPost">
      <http:address
        location="http://localhost/FeeServices/Fees.asmx" />
    </port>
  </service>
  </definitions>
```

FIGURE HO6.5 (CONTINUED)
Contract.

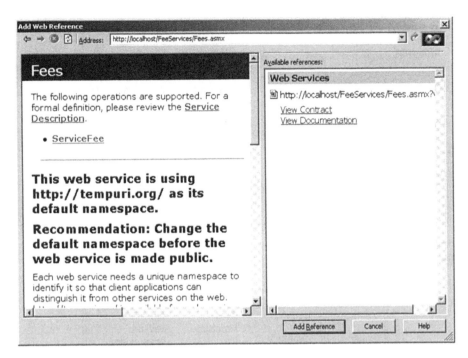

FIGURE HO6.6
Web Service Help Page.

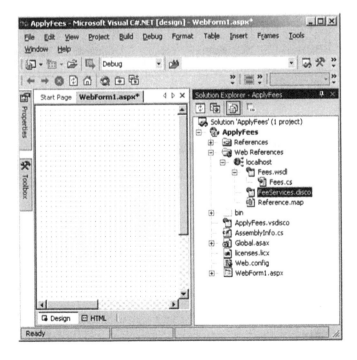

FIGURE HO6.7
Web References.

wsdl [*options*] { *URL* | *path* }

Argument	Description
URL	The URL to the WSDL contract file, XSD schema and discovery document.
Path	Path to a local WSDL contract file, XSD schema and discovery document.

Selected Options	Description
/l[anguage]:*language*	Specifies the language for the generated proxy class. Valid values are CS, VB and JS. The default is CS.
/protocol:*protocol*	Specifies the protocol implemented. Valid values are SOAP, HttpGet, HttpPost or custom protocol. The default is SOAP.
/?	Help, displays the command syntax.

FIGURE HO6.8
wsdl.exe syntax.

Type	ID	Attribute	Description
Label	Label1	Text	Apply Fee
		Font Size	Medium
Label	Label2	Text	Account No.
TextBox	AccountNo		
Label	Label3	Text	Type
TextBox	Type		
Label	Label4	Text	Amount
TextBox	Amount		
Label	Label5	Text	Fee
TextBox	Fee		
Button	SubmitBtn	Text	Submit
		OnClick	

FIGURE HO6.9
Client page's controls.

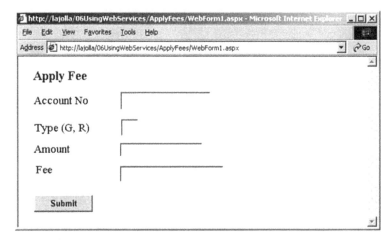

FIGURE HO6.10
Layout of client page's controls.

Step 5: Run the Application

1. Set a breakpoint at the following statement by clicking the left margin opposite the statement:

```
decimal serviceFee = fees.ServiceFee(amount, type);
```

A colorized circle represents the breakpoint.

2. Run the application; click Start in the Debug menu. The Apply Fee form is displayed in Internet Explorer (Figure HO6.11).

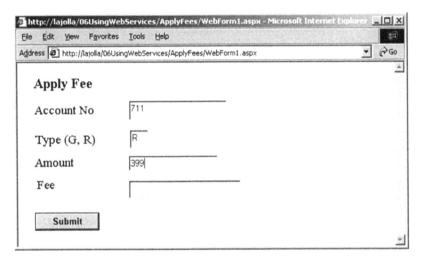

FIGURE HO6.11
Client application's start page is displayed with initial Account No. value.

3. Enter the following values:

Type: **R**

Amount: **399**

4. Click the **Submit** button. The Visual Studio.NET Code Window gains focus with program execution stopped at the breakpoint. The breakpoint is opposite the statement invoking the Web Service method (Figure HO6.12). The arrow in the left margin indicates the next statement to be executed.

5. In the Debug menu, select the Step Into option. The next statement is executed. Note that pressing the F5 key will also result in execution of the next statement. Visual Studio.Net regains the focus with the Code Editor opened to the first statement in the body of the method ServiceFee, as shown in Figure HO6.13.

6. Select the QuickWatch in the Debug menu to open the QuickWatch window (Figure HO6.14).

7. Enter in the Expression textbox: **amount**.

8. Press the **Recalculate** button. The QuickWatch window displays the current value of amount. Pressing the Ctrl+Alt+Q key combination also opens the QuickWatch Window.

9. Note the value 399. Enter in the Expression textbox: **type**.

FIGURE HO6.12
Execution stopped at breakpoint.

FIGURE HO6.13
File Fees.asmx.cs open in Code Editor with cursor at first statement in ServiceFee method.

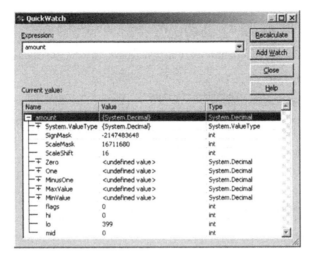

FIGURE HO6.14
QuickWatch window with amount value.

10. Press the **Recalculate** button. The window reflects the current value of type (Figure HO6.15). Note the value R.

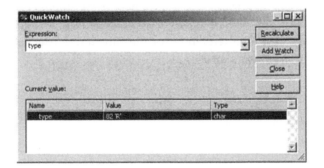

FIGURE HO6.15
QuickWatch window with type value.

11. Click Close to close the QuickWatch window.
12. Click Continue in the Debug menu. Alternately, press the F5 key. The Web Service method returns a value that is displayed in the Fee textbox; see Figure HO6.16. Note that the Fee is 5.5.

Try other combinations of Type and Amount.

Selected Debug Features
Clicking the breakpoint toggles off breakpoints.

Key Combination Action

F5 — Program execution continues until the next breakpoint.
Shift+F5 — Program execution stops.

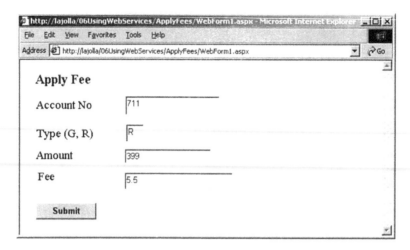

FIGURE HO6.16
Computed Fee is displayed.

F11 — Step Into. The next statement is executed; if the statement is a function call, execution stops at the first statement of the called function. Step Into enables examination of the function's internal workings.

F10 — Stepover. The next statement is executed; if the statement is a function, the entire function is executed. Step Over avoids stepping through a function.

Shift+F11 — Step Out. The remainder of the function is executed and execution stops after the function's return.

Part 3

Accessing Data

7

Connected DataBase Access

OLE DB supports data access from any source for which an OLE DB provider is available. For example, data can be accessed from Microsoft Access, Oracle and Microsoft SQL Server databases, as well as from other formats such as spreadsheets and text files. The classes used to implement OLE DB data access are contained in the System.Data.OleDb namespace. The following classes enable data access:

- OleDbConnection represents a unique connection to a data source.
- OleDbCommand represents an SQL statement of stored procedure executed at the data source.
- OleDbDataReader enables the forward-only iteration through the rows of a result set and read-only access of the row's column values.

Use of the data reader is viewed as a connected data access process because the connection cannot be used for any other purpose until the reader is closed. The components of connected OLE DB data access are shown in Figure 7.1.

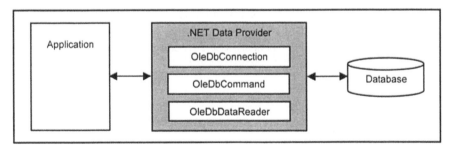

FIGURE 7.1
Connected OLE DB Access.

Connected access to an SQLServer database, defined in the System.Data.SqlClient namespace, is similarly affected with a provider containing the following classes:

- SqlConnection represents a connection to a SQL Server database.
- SqlCommand represents a TRANSACT-SQL statement or stored procedure to execute on an SQL Server database.
- SqlDataReader affects access to returned rows from an SQL Server database in a read-only and forward-only manner.

The techniques required to implement an OLE DB data access, including creating and configuring the connection, creating and defining the command and using a data reader, are presented in this section.

Connection

ConnectionState Enumeration

The **ConnectionState** enumeration members classify the state of the connection to the data source. Figure 7.2 summarizes the ConnectionState enumeration. Only the OleDbConnection and SqlConnection classes use the Closed and Open states. Note that the only valid state changes are from Closed to Open initiated by the Open method of a connection object and the Open to Closed initiated by the Close and Dispose methods of a connection object.

public enum ConnectionState	
Namespace: System.Data	
Members	
Name	**Description**
Broken	A previously opened connection is broken. A broken connection can be closed and then reopened. This state is not supported by the OleDbConnection and SqlConnection classes.
Closed	The connection is closed.
Connecting	The connection is in process. This state is not supported by the OleDbConnection and SqlConnection classes.
Executing	The connection is executing a command. This state is not supported by the OleDbConnection and SqlConnection classes.
Fetching	The connection is returning results. This state is not supported by the OleDbConnection and SqlConnection classes.
Open	The connection is opened.
Valid Changes	
Change	**Initiated By**
Closed to Open	Open method of a connection object.
Open to Closed	Close and Dispose methods of a connection object.

FIGURE 7.2
ConnectionState enumeration.

OleDbConnection Class

The **OleDbConnection** class (Figure 7.3) object represents a unique connection to a data source. When an OleDbConnection is created, the properties of the connection are set to values specified by keywords in a connection string or their default values. These properties include the name of the database, name of the data source and connection timeout, as well as the connection string. Once created, a connection is opened by calling its Open method.

When the OleDbConnection object goes out of scope, it is not automatically closed; therefore, the Close or Dispose methods must be explicitly called to close the connection. Note that a closed connection can be reopened.

The Web page part of an application illustrating use of the OleDbConnection class is shown in Figure 7.4A. The Web page contains a form with a single ASP.Label control msg. The code-behind file contains the statement

public sealed class **OleDbConnection** : Component, IClonable, IDbConnection	
Hierarchy	
Object MarshalByRefObject Component OleDbConnection	
Namespace: System.Data.OleDb	
Constructors	
public **OleDbConnection**();	Initializes a new instance of the OleDbConnection class.
public **OleDbConnection**(string *connectionString*);	Initializes a new instance of the OleDbConnection class. The *connectionString* contains values that are assigned to OleDbConnection properties used to establish a connection.
Public Instance Properties	
public string **ConnectionString** {get; set;}	Gets and sets the string containing the properties used to establish a connection.
public int **ConnectionTimeout** {get;}	Gets the time, in seconds, to wait for a connection to open before terminating the attempt and raising an exception. The default value is 15 seconds. A value of 0 indicates no limit and should be avoided in practice.
public string **Database** {get;}	Gets the name of the current database or the name of the database to be opened. The default is an empty string.
public string **DataSource** {get;}	Gets the location and file name of the data source. The default is an empty string.
public string **Provider** {get;}	Gets the name of the provider. The default is an empty string.
public string **ServerVersion** {get;}	Gets the version of the server the client is connected to.
public ConnectionState **State** {get;}	Gets the current connection state.

FIGURE 7.3
OleDbConnection class.

```
using System.Data.OleDb;
```

to expose the classes, delegates and enumerations of the System.Data.OleDb namespace. In this case, the connection with the database is established in the Page_Load method. Figure 7.4B shows the Page_Load method of the code-behind file. The database connection, conn, is created with the statement

```
OleDbConnection conn = new OleDbConnection(connectStg);
```

The initial values of the connection are specified in the "keyword = value" pairs in the connection string connectStg. The Provider property and Data Source property values are set with the following strings:

```
string provider = "Provider = Microsoft.Jet.OLEDB.4.0";
string dataSource = "Data Source =
    C:\\DB\\StudentAdministratorDB.mdb";
```

The provider string and dataSource string are combined in connection string connectStg; a semicolon separates the two strings.

```
string connectStg = provider + ";" + dataSource;
```

The connection string is parsed when the OleDbConnection object is created. Parsing is based on the use of keywords corresponding to the names of the connection properties. In this case, the string's Provider keyword is associated with the value Microsoft.Jet.OLEDB.4.0.

Public Instance Methods	
public OleDdTransaction **BeginTransaction** ( );	Begins a database transaction.
public OleDdTransaction **BeginTransaction** (IsolationLevel *isoLevel*);	Begins a database transaction with isolation level *isoLevel*.
public void **ChangeDatabase** (string *dbName*) ;	Changes the current database for an open connection to the database *dbName*. Note that *dbName* must be a valid name, cannot be an empty string or a string with only blank values.
public void **Close** ( );	Closes the connection to the data source. Pending transactions are rolled back when the Close method is called and the connection is released to the connection pool. If connection pooling is not enabled, the connection closes. No exception is thrown if Close is called more than once.
public OleDbCommand **CreateCommand** ( );	Creates and returns a command object associated with the connection object.
public DataTable **GetOleDbSchemaTable** (Guide *schema*, object[ ] *restrictions*);	Returns a data table containing a list of schema restrictions where *schema*, a globally unique identifier (Guid), specifies the schema table to be returned and *restrictions* is an array of filter value objects corresponding to a DataColumn in the returned table.
public void **Open** ( );	Opens a database connection with property values specified in the ConnectionString object. An available connection in the connection pool is used if one is available. A new connection is created if one is not available.
Public Instance Events	
public event OleDbInfoMessageEventHandler **InfoMessage** ;	Raised when the provider sends a message.
public event StateChangedEventHandler **StateChange** ;	Raised when the connection's state changes.
Protected Instance Methods	
protected override void **Dispose** (bool *allResource*);	Releases both managed and unmanaged resources if *allResource* is true and only unmanaged resources if false.

FIGURE 7.3 (CONTINUED)
OleDbConnection class.

```
<%@ Page language="c#" Codebehind="ConnectionProperties.aspx.cs"
         AutoEventWireup="false" Inherits="DBConnection.ConnectionProperties" %>
<HTML>
  <HEAD>
  </HEAD>
  <body>
    <form id="ConnectionProperties" method="post" runat="server">
      <asp:Label ID=msg Runat=server></asp:Label>
    </form>
  </body>
</HTML>
```

FIGURE 7.4A
Web page of OleDbConnection application (DBConnection\ConnectionProperties.aspx) .

This value is assigned to the connection object's Provider property. Similarly, the string's Data Source keyword is associated with the value C:\\DB\\StudentAdministratorDB.mdb, which is assigned to the connection object's Data Source property. OleDbConnection object properties not specified in the connection string are set to their default values.

The connection is changed to the Open state with the statement

```
conn.Open();
```

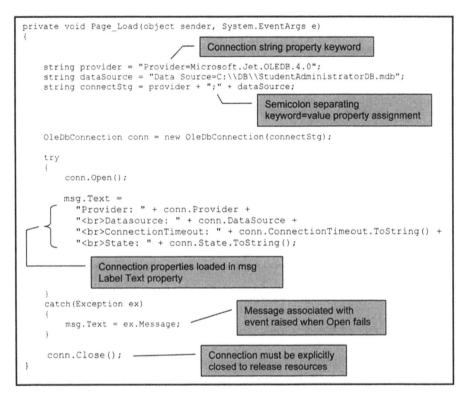

```
private void Page_Load(object sender, System.EventArgs e)
{
                                    ┌─ Connection string property keyword
    string provider = "Provider=Microsoft.Jet.OLEDB.4.0";
    string dataSource = "Data Source=C:\\DB\\StudentAdministratorDB.mdb";
    string connectStg = provider + ";" + dataSource;
                                    └─ Semicolon separating
                                       keyword=value property assignment

    OleDbConnection conn = new OleDbConnection(connectStg);

    try
    {
        conn.Open();

        msg.Text =
            "Provider: " + conn.Provider +
            "<br>Datasource: " + conn.DataSource +
            "<br>ConnectionTimeout: " + conn.ConnectionTimeout.ToString() +
            "<br>State: " + conn.State.ToString();
                     ┌─ Connection properties loaded in msg
                     │  Label Text property
    }
    catch(Exception ex)
    {                              ┌─ Message associated with
        msg.Text = ex.Message;     │  event raised when Open fails
    }

    conn.Close();  ──────────  Connection must be explicitly
}                              closed to release resources
```

FIGURE 7.4B
Page_Load method of OleDbConnection application (DBConnection\ConnectionProperties.aspx.cs).

An open connection is drawn from the connection pool that is automatically maintained by .NET. If a connection is not available, a new connection to the data source is created. The connection object properties are accessed and loaded into the msg Label's Text property with the statement

```
msg.Text =
"Provider: " + conn.Provider +
"<br>Datasource: " + conn.DataSource +
"<br>ConnectionTimeout: " + conn.ConnectionTimeout.ToString() +
"<br>State: " + conn.State.ToString();
```

The Open method is called within a try block. If the Open method raises an exception, control is transferred to the catch block and the message associated with the exception is loaded in the msg Text property. For example, if the Data Source property value specifying the path is incorrect, i.e., specifies a nonexisting file C\DB\BadData.mdb, an exception is raised and the msg Text property is set to **"Could not find file 'C:\DB\BadData.mdb'."** Similarly, if the Provider value is not valid, as in Microsoft.Access.OLEDB, an exception is raised. The message associated with the exception contains information pertaining to the Provider value submitted, in this case, **"The provider is unavailable for the 'Provider = Microsoft.Jet.OLEDB.4.0X;Data Source = C:\DB\StudentAdministratorDB.mdb' connection string."**

Finally, calling the Close method closes the connection.

```
conn.Close();
```

If connection pooling is enabled, the connection is released to the pool. If connection pooling is disabled, the connection is closed. The Close method must be called because the OleDbConnection object is not automatically closed when the object goes out of scope.

When the connection is successfully opened, the values of selected properties are loaded in the page's msg Label text property. These values are displayed at the user browser when the page is returned, as shown in Figure 7.4C. Note, that the OLE DB Data Provider manages connection pooling automatically.

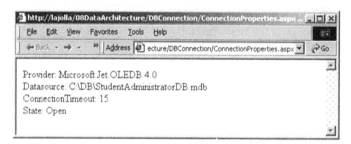

FIGURE 7.4C
Returned Web page of OleDbConnection application (DBConnection\ConnectionProperties.aspx.cs).

The Dispose method can also be called. This method calls the Close method and removes the OleDbConnection object from the connection pool and releases both managed and unmanaged resources. A version of the Dispose method provides for a Boolean parameter, in which case both managed and unmanaged resources are released if the parameter value is true. If the parameter value is false, only the unmanaged resources are released.

Command

Manipulation of the data in a database is specified with commands. The members of the **CommandType** enumeration (Figure 7.5) classify the types of commands. Accessibility of a database is characterized by the transaction's isolation level, which is characterized by the IsolationLevel enumeration shown in Figure 7.6. The IsolationLevel can be changed at any time and remains in effect until explicitly changed. A changed isolation level takes effect at execution time, not parse time, and applies to all remaining statements.

public enum **CommandType**	
Namespace: System.Data	
Members	
Name	**Description**
StoredProcedure	Name of a procedure stored in the Database.
TableDirect	A table name, all of the columns are returned.
Text	SQL statement.

FIGURE 7.5
CommandType enumeration.

Name	Description
Chaos	Pending changes from more highly isolated transactions cannot be overwritten.
ReadCommitted	Dirty reads are avoided while data is being read by holding shared locks. Data can be changed before the end of the transaction. Note that the reads may be non-repeatable and phantom data is possible.
ReadUncommitted	Shared locks are not instituted and exclusive locks are not honored. Note that dirty reads are possible.
RepeatableRead	Locks are placed preventing other users from updating the data. Note that dirty reads are prevented but phantom data is possible.
Serializable	A lock is placed on a DataSet preventing other users from inserting or updating until the transaction is complete.
Unspecified	The isolation level is not the level specified and cannot be determined.

public enum IsolationLevel

Namespace: System.Data

Members

FIGURE 7.6
IsolationLevel enumeration.

Many database transactions require multiple operations. For example, the transaction might have insert operations related to entry of items to an order, updating operations reflecting changes in customer account balance and selection operations to prepare shipping and invoice advices.

A method of processing known as transaction processing ensures that the databases involved are not updated unless all of the events involved are successfully completed. That is, the database operations involved are treated as a logical group. The **OleDbTransaction** class, summarized in Figure 7.7, provides for enabling transaction processing. The OleDb-Transaction class represents SQL transactions made at the data source. Invoking the Begin-Transaction method on the OldDbConnection object creates an OleDbTransaction object.

public sealed class **OleDbTransaction** : MarshalByRefObject, IdbTransaction, IDisposable

Hierarchy

Object
   MarshalByRefObject
      OleDbTransaction

Namespace: System.Data.OleDb

Public Instance Property

public IsolationLevel **IsolationLevel** {get;}	Gets the isolation level of the entire transaction.

Public Instance Methods

public OleDbTransaction **Begin** ( );	Initiates a new transaction nested within the current transaction.
public OleDbTransaction **Begin** (IsolationLevel *isolevel*);	Initiates a new nested transaction with isolation level specified by *isolevel*.
public void **Commit** ( );	Completes database actions initiated with the Begin method.
public void **Rollback** ( );	Rolls back transactions initiated after the Begin method but before the Commit method is invoked.

FIGURE 7.7
OleDbTransaction class.

OleDbCommand Class

The **OleDbCommand** class represents a database operation, including returning, inserting, updating and deleting information. The OleDbCommand object's properties characterize the operation:

- CommandText specifies the operation, for example, an SQL statement describing a database operation or the name of a stored procedure to be performed. For example,

  ```
  SELECT LastName, FirstName FROM Students;
  ```

  is an SQL statement that returns the FirstName and LastName attribute values for every row in the Student table. Execution of the command presumes that a connection to a data source containing the tables is established.
- Connection specifies the database that will be affected by the database operations. A connection is represented by an OleDbConnection object. Again, execution of the command presumes that a connection to a data source containing the tables is established.
- Command Type is a characterization of the command, for example, a stored procedure or SQL text. The CommandType is represented by a member of the CommandType enumeration.

The CommandType, Connection and CommandText properties of the OleDbCommand object cannot be set if the connection is performing an operation.

Additional properties characterizing the operation include the following:

- CommandTimeout is the time allowed for the command to execute before the attempt is terminated.
- DesignTimeVisible is a true or false value used by Windows Forms developers to facilitate design.
- Parameters are parameters of an SQL statement or stored procedure represented as an OleDbParameterCollection.
- Transaction specifies the transaction in which the commands execute, enabling the grouping of commands into a logical unit. An OleDbTransaction object represents the value.
- UpdatedRowSource describes how the command results are applied to the data row being updated and is applicable to disconnected data access. Members of the UpdateRowSource enumeration represent the values.

The OleDbCommand class is summarized in Figure 7.8.

Key methods implemented in the OleDbCommand class provide command execution:

- ExecuteNonQuery executes nonquery SQL statements, such as insert, update and delete.
- ExecuteReader executes a query command and returns an OleDbDataReader object containing the results.
- ExecuteScaler executes queries returning a single value, for example, number of rows in the table.

The Web page part of an application illustrating use of the OleDbCommand class is shown in Figure 7.9A. The Web page contains a form with a single ASP.Label control msg.

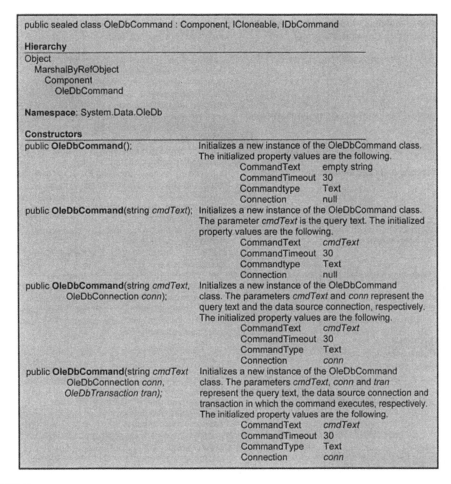

public sealed class OleDbCommand : Component, ICloneable, IDbCommand

Hierarchy

Object
  MarshalByRefObject
    Component
      OleDbCommand

Namespace: System.Data.OleDb

Constructors

public **OleDbCommand**();	Initializes a new instance of the OleDbCommand class. The initialized property values are the following. CommandText empty string CommandTimeout 30 Commandtype Text Connection null
public **OleDbCommand**(string *cmdText*);	Initializes a new instance of the OleDbCommand class. The parameter *cmdText* is the query text. The initialized property values are the following. CommandText *cmdText* CommandTimeout 30 Commandtype Text Connection null
public **OleDbCommand**(string *cmdText*, OleDbConnection *conn*);	Initializes a new instance of the OleDbCommand class. The parameters *cmdText* and *conn* represent the query text and the data source connection, respectively. The initialized property values are the following. CommandText *cmdText* CommandTimeout 30 CommandType Text Connection *conn*
public **OleDbCommand**(string *cmdText* OleDbConnection *conn*, OleDbTransaction *tran*);	Initializes a new instance of the OleDbCommand class. The parameters *cmdText*, *conn* and *tran* represent the query text, the data source connection and transaction in which the command executes, respectively. The initialized property values are the following. CommandText *cmdText* CommandTimeout 30 CommandType Text Connection *conn*

FIGURE 7.8
OleDbCommand class.

Note that the control is sized to provide for long lines and multiple lines. The code-behind file contains the statement

```
using System.Data.OleDb;
```

to expose the classes, delegates and enumerations of the System.Data.OleDb namespace.

In this case, the connection with the database is established and the command is created and executed in the Page_Load method. Figure 7.9B shows the Page_Load method of the code-behind file. AnOleDbCommand object is created with the statement

```
OleDbCommand command = new OleDbCommand();
```

The command object is created with the default property values. The default values for the CommandText, CommandTimeout and CommandType properties are accessed and loaded into the msg Label's Text property with the statement.

```
msg.Text =
    "INITIAL COMMAND VALUES" +
    "<br>CommandText: " + command.CommandText +
    "<br>CommandTimeout: " + command.CommandTimeout.ToString() +
    "<br>CommandType: " + command.CommandType.ToString() ;
```

Public Instance Properties	
public string **CommandText** {get; set;}	Gets and sets the SQL statement or stored procedure to be executed.
public int **CommandTimeout** {get; set;}	Gets the time, in seconds, to wait for a command to execute before terminating the attempt and raising an exception. The default value is 30 seconds. A value of 0 indicates no limit and should be avoided in practice.
public CommandType **CommandType** {get;}	Gets the name of the current database or the name of the database to be opened. The default is an empty string.
public OleDbConnection **Connection** {get; set;}	Gets and sets the connection to the data source used by this command object instance.
public bool **DesignTimeVisible** {get; set;}	Gets or sets a value indicating the visibility of the command object in a customized Windows Forms Designer control. The command object is visible if true and not visible if the value is false. The default is false.
public OleDbParameterCollection **Parameters** {get;}	Gets the parameters of an SQL statement or stored procedure as an OleDbParameterCollection. The default is an empty collection.
public OleDbTransaction **Transaction** {get; set;}	Gets and sets the transaction in which the commands, represented by the OleDbCommand object, execute. The default is a null reference.
public UpdateRowSource **UpdatedRowSource** {get; set;}	Gets or sets how the query command results are applied to the data row being updated. The default value is None.
Public Instance Methods	
public void **Cancel** ( );	Cancels execution of the OleDbCommand.
public OleDbParameter **CreateParameter** ( );	Creates a new instance of an OleDbParameter object.
public int **ExecuteNonQuery** ( );	Executes a nonquery sql statement, such as insert, update and delete, and returns the number of rows affected.
public OleDbDataReader **ExecuteReader** ( );	Creates a new instance of an OleDbDataReader object.
public OleDbDataReader **ExecuterReader** (CommandBehavior *behavior*);	Returns an instance of the OleDbDataReader reflecting the command and the command behavior *behavior*.
public object **ExecuteScaler** ( );	Executes a query used to retrieve a single value, for example, an aggregate value.
public void **Prepare** ( );	Creates a prepared version of command at data source.
public void **ResetCommandTimeout** ( );	Resets the CommandTimeout property to the default value of 30 seconds.

FIGURE 7.8 (CONTINUED)
OleDbCommand class.

```
<%@ Page language="c#" Codebehind="CreateCommand.aspx.cs"
        AutoEventWireup="false" Inherits="DBCommand.CreateCommand" %>
<HTML>
  <HEAD>
  </HEAD>
  <body >
    <form id="CreateCommand" method="post" runat="server">
      <asp:Label ID=msg Runat=server Width="100%" Height="25%"></asp:Label>
    </form>
  </body>
</HTML>
```

FIGURE 7.9A
Web page of OleDbCommand application (DBCommand\CreateCommand.aspx) .

```
private void Page_Load(object sender, System.EventArgs e)
{
    string provider = "Provider=Microsoft.Jet.OLEDB.4.0";
    string dataSource = "Data Source=C:\\DB\\StudentAdministratorDB.mdb";
    string connectStg = provider + ";" + dataSource;

    OleDbConnection connection = new OleDbConnection(connectStg);

    OleDbCommand command = new OleDbCommand();        [Command object created]

    msg.Text =                                        [Get command object properties]
        "INITAIL COMMAND VALUES" +
        "<br>CommandText: " + command.CommandText +
        "<br>CommandTimeout: " + command.CommandTimeout.ToString() +
        "<br>CommandType: " + command.CommandType.ToString() ;

    command.CommandText = "SELECT Count(*) AS RecordCount FROM Student";
    command.CommandTimeout = 15;
    command.Connection = connection;                  [Set command object properties]

    msg.Text = msg.Text +
        "<br>REVISED COMMAND PROPERTY VALUES" +
        "<br>CommandText: " + command.CommandText +
        "<br>CommandTimeout: " + command.CommandTimeout.ToString() +
        "<br>CommandType: " + command.CommandType.ToString() +
        "<br>Connection.ConnectionString: " +
                command.Connection.ConnectionString;

    try
    {
        connection.Open();
        msg.Text = msg.Text +
            "<br>SCALER QUERY RESULTS" +
            "<br>ExecuteScaler: " + command.ExecuteScalar().ToString();
    }
    catch(Exception ex)
    {
        msg.Text = ex.Message;
    }

    connection.Close();                               [Command execution]
}
```

FIGURE 7.9B
Page_Load method of OleDbCommand application (DBCommand\CreateCommand.aspx.cs).

The command object's CommandText property is set with the statement

```
command.CommandText = "SELECT Count(*) AS RecordCount FROM
    Student";
```

which is an aggregate type command returning a single value describing the number of rows in the Student table. Similarly, the CommandTimeout and Connection properties are set with the statements

```
command.CommandTimeout = 15;

command.Connection = connection;
```

Note that the Connection property value is an OleDbConnection object that specifies a connection to a specific data source.

The revised command object properties are added to the text of the msg Label control with the statements

```
msg.Text = msg.Text +

    "<br>REVISED COMMAND PROPERTY VALUES" +

    "<br>CommandText: " + command.CommandText +

    "<br>CommandTimeout: " + command.CommandTimeout.ToString() +
```

```
"<br>CommandType: " + command.CommandType.ToString() +
"<br>Connection.ConnectionString: " +
command.Connection.ConnectionString;
```

The expression

```
command.Connection
```

returns an OleDbConnection object representing the connection to the data source. The ConnectionString property of this object is subsequently accessed.

The expression

```
command.ExecuteScalar()
```

invokes the ExecuteScaler method of the command OleDbCommand type object. The ExecuteScaler returns an Object type that, in this case, is an integral data type describing the number of rows in the Student table. The integral value is converted to an equivalent string expression by the ToString method:

```
command.ExecuteScalar().ToString();
```

The ExecuteScalar method is invoked and the returned value appended to the msg Text property with the statement:

```
msg.Text = msg.Text +
    "<br>SCALER QUERY RESULTS" +
    "<br>ExecuteScaler: " + command.ExecuteScalar().ToString();
```

Figure 7.9C shows how the msg Label Text property value is displayed at the user's browser when the page is returned.

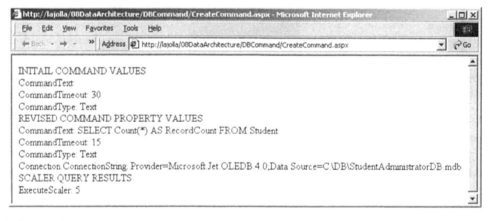

FIGURE 7.9C
Returned Web page of OleDbCommand application (DBCommand\CreateCommand.aspx).

DataReader

The data reader contains a result set and has the key capabilities of accessing the rows of the resultset one after another and accessing each column value in a row. The **OleDb-DataReader** class represents a data reader and is summarized in Figure 7.10.

public sealed class OleDbDataReader : MarshalByRefObject, IdataReader, IdataRecord, IEnumerable, IDisposable	
Hierarchy	
Object MarshalByRefObject OleDbDataReader	
Namespace: System.Data.OleDb	
Public Instance Properties	
public int **Depth** {get;};	Gets a value specifying the nesting depth of the current row. The outermost table has depth zero.
public int **FieldCount** {get;};	Gets the number of columns in the current row. The value is 0 when not positioned on a valid row. The default value is −1.
public bool **IsClosed** {get;};	Gets the status of the data reader. The value is true if the data reader is closed; false otherwise.
public object **this**[string *name*]{get;}	Gets the value of the column specified by *name*.
public object **this**[int *index*]{get;}	Gets the value of the column specified by the column ordinal *index*.
public int **RecordsAffected**{get;}	Gets the number of rows changed, inserted or deleted by execution of an SQL statement. A value of −1 indicates no rows were affected or the statement failed. The RecordsAffected property is set after all the rows are read and the data reader is closed.

FIGURE 7.10
OleDbDataReader class.

The Web page part of an application illustrating use of the OleDbDataReader class is shown in Figure 7.11A. This page contains a form with a single ASP.Label control msg. Note that the control is sized to provide for long lines and multiple lines. The code-behind file contains the statement

```
using System.Data.OleDb;
```

to expose the classes, delegates and enumerations of the System.Data.OleDb namespace.

In this application, the connection with the database is established and data reader implemented in the Page_Load method. Figure 7.11B shows the Page_Load method of the code-behind file. A reference, reader, to an OleDbDataReader object is declared with the statement

```
OleDbDataReader reader;
```

An OleDbDataReader object is returned by the OleDbCommand class's ExecuteReader method:

```
reader = command.ExecuteReader();
```

Note that the ExecuteReader method is invoked by an OleDbCommand object whose properties include:

- CommandText property value describing an SQL statement or stored procedure returning results — in this case, the "SELECT LastName, FirstName, Birthdate, EnglishProficiencyCd FROM Student," which returns the LastName, FirstName, Birthdate and EnglishProficiencyCd fields from the Student table
- Connection property value specifying the data source from which the results will be extracted — in this case, the data source named "C:\\DB\\Student-AdministratorDB.mdb"

Public Instance Methods	
public void **Close** ();	Closes the OleDbDataReader object. The Close method must be explicitly called when the reader is no longer needed.
public bool **GetBoolean** (int *ordinal*);	Gets the value of the column specified by the zero-based column *ordinal* as a boolean.
public byte **GetByte** (int *ordinal*);	Gets the value of the column specified by the zero-based column *ordinal* as a byte.
public long **GetBytes** (int *ordinal*, long *dataIndex*, char[] *buffer*, int *bufferIndex*, int *length*)	Reads *length* number of bytes starting from column *ordinal* starting at *dataIndex* in the field into the byte array *buffer* starting at buffer position *bufferIndex*. The return value is the actual number of bytes read.
public char **GetChar** (int *ordinal*);	Gets the value of the column specified by the zero-based column *ordinal* as a character.
public long **GetChars** (int *ordinal*, long *dataIndex*, char[] *buffer*, int *bufferIndex*, int *length*)	Reads *length* number of characters starting from column *ordinal* starting at *dataIndex* in the field into the byte array *buffer* starting at buffer position *bufferIndex*. The return value is the actual number of characters read.
public string **GetDataTypeName** (int *ordinal*);	Gets the name of the data type of the column specified by the zero-based column *ordinal*.
public DateTime **GetDateTime** (int *ordinal*);	Gets the value of the column specified by the zero-based column *ordinal* as a DateTime object.
public decimal **GetDecimal** (int *ordinal*);	Gets the value of the column specified by the zero-based column *ordinal* as a decimal.
public double **GetDouble** (int *ordinal*);	Gets the value of the column specified by the zero-based column *ordinal* as a double-precision floating point number.
public Type **GetFieldType** (int *ordinal*);	Gets the data type of the column specified by the zero-based column *ordinal*.
public float **GetFloat** (int *ordinal*);	Gets the value of the column specified by the zero-based column *ordinal* as a single-precision floating point number.
public Guid **GetGuid** (int *ordinal*);	Gets the value of the column specified by the zero-based column *ordinal* as a globally unique identifier (GUID).
public short **GetInt16** (int *ordinal*);	Gets the value of the column specified by the zero-based column *ordinal* as a 16-bit signed integer.
public int **GetInt32** (int *ordinal*);	Gets the value of the column specified by the zero-based column *ordinal* as a 32-bit signed integer.
public long **GetInt64** (int *ordinal*);	Gets the value of the column specified by the zero-based column *ordinal* as a 64-bit signed integer.
public string **GetName** (int *ordinal*);	Gets the name of the column specified by the zero-based column.
public int **GetOrdinal** (string *name*);	Gets the column ordinal value of the *name* column.

FIGURE 7.10 (CONTINUED)
OleDbDataReader class.

When the ExecuteReader method is invoked, the command is enacted through the connection, resulting in returned rows. The ExecuteReader method returns an OleDbData-Reader object, which accesses a row in the returned results. The returned data reader object is assigned to the reference reader. The returned data reader is automatically opened and positioned in front of the first row of the returned results.

Key methods implemented in the OleDbDataReader class include the following:

- Close closes the OleDbDataReader object. While the data reader object is opened, the connection cannot be used for any other operations with the exception of closing. Thus, the data reader must be explicitly closed. The IsClosed property can be used while the data reader is open or closed to test if the reader is closed.

- Read advances the reader to the next row in the returned results. The method returns true as long as additional rows remain in the returned results.

Public Instance Methods	
public DataTable **GetSchemaTable** ();	Returns a DataTable object describing the column metadata of the data reader.
public string **GetString** (int *ordinal*);	Gets the value of the column specified by the zero-based column *ordinal* as a string.
public TimeSpan **GetTimeSpan** (int *ordinal*);	Gets the value of the column specified by the zero-based column *ordinal* as a TimeSpan object.
public object **GetValue** (int *ordinal*);	Gets the value of the column specified by the zero-based column *ordinal* as an object.
public int **GetValues** (object[] *values*);	Gets all the column values in the current row as elements of an object array *values*. The method returns the number of array elements.
public bool **IsDBNull** (int *ordinal*);	Gets a boolean value, true indicating if the column specified by the zero-based column *ordinal* has missing or non-existing value; false otherwise.
public bool **NextResult** (int *ordinal*);	Advances the data reader to the result when the results represent a batch of SQL statements. The value true is returned if there are more rows and false otherwise.
public bool **Read** ( );	Advances the data reader to the next row. The value true is returned if there are more rows and false otherwise.
Protected Instance Methods	
~OleDbDatareader( )	The Finalize method frees resources before the OleDbDataReader is reclaimed by the garbage collector.

FIGURE 7.10 (CONTINUED)
OleDbDataReader class.

```
<%@ Page language="c#" Codebehind="RetrieveData.aspx.cs" AutoEventWireup="false"
        Inherits="UsingDataReader.RetrieveData" %>
<!DOCTYPE HTML PUBLIC "-//W3C//DTD HTML 4.0 Transitional//EN" >
<HTML>
  <HEAD>
  </HEAD>
  <body >
    <form id="RetrieveData" method="post" runat="server">
      <asp:Label ID=msg Runat=server Width="100%" Height="50%"></asp:Label>
    </form>
  </body>
</HTML>
```

FIGURE 7.11A
Web page of OleDbDataReader application (UsingDataReader\RetrieveData.aspx).

A "while" loop can be used to iterate through the returned results accessed by a data reader:

```
while (reader.Read())
{
}
```

Because the "while" statement evaluates the test condition first, the data reader is moved to the first row of the returned results in the first iteration. The iterations continue until there is no next row and the read method returns the value false.

The data reader returns a row from the returned results and provides methods to access the values of the columns of the row. These methods take the ordinal position of the column as a parameter and include the following:

- GetBoolean gets the value of the specified column as a Boolean.
- GetDateTime gets the value of the specified column as a DateTime object. Methods of the DateTime object provide for extracting the elements of the date and time

```
private void Page_Load(object sender, System.EventArgs e)
{
    string cmdText =
        "SELECT LastName, FirstName, Birthdate, EnglishProficiencyCd FROM Student";

    string provider = "Provider=Microsoft.Jet.OLEDB.4.0";
    string dataSource = "Data Source=C:\\DB\\StudentAdministratorDB.mdb";
    string connectStg = provider + ";" + dataSource;

    OleDbConnection connection = new OleDbConnection(connectStg);

    OleDbCommand command = new OleDbCommand(cmdText, connection);

    connection.Open();                      ┌─ Declare reference to DataReader object

    OleDbDataReader reader;
                                            ┌─ ExecuteReader method of
    reader = command.ExecuteReader( );      │  OleDbCommand object returns
                                            └─ DataReader with query results

    while (reader.Read() )  ─────────  Read next DataReader row
    {
        msg.Text =
                                            ┌─ Get value of first column
            reader.GetString(0) + ", " +    └─ as String data type

            reader.GetString(1) + ", " +
                                            ┌─ Get value of third column
            reader.GetDateTime(2).Date + ", " +  └─ as DateTime data type

            reader.GetValue(3).ToString() +
            "<br>";                         ┌─ Get value of fourth column as
    }                                       └─ Object data type
    reader.Close();

    connection.Close();
}
```

FIGURE 7.11B
Code-behind OleDbDataReader application (UsingDataReader\RetrieveData.aspx.cs).

such as Day, Month, Year, Hour, Minute and Second as well as other elements such as DayOfWeek and DayOfYear.

- GetInt32 gets the value of the specified column as a 32-bit signed integer.
- GetValue gets the value of the specified column in its native format represented as an object type.
- GetString gets the value of the specified column as a string.

No conversions are performed by these methods; thus, the data value must already be in the specified type or an exception will be raised. For example, the first column is LastName, is a string type and is accessed with the expression

```
reader.GetString(0)
```

Similarly, the second column, which contains FirstName, also a string, is accessed with the expression

```
reader.GetString(1)
```

The third column contains a DateTime value, the birthdate, and is accessed with the expression

```
reader.GetDateTime(2)
```

The Date property of the DateTime object is used to get the date and time value of the object. The Day property can be used to get the day, the Month property to get the month and the Year property to get the year.

The fourth column contains a 32-bit integral property. The GetValue method returns the value in its native type. The ToString method converts integral values to their string equivalent.

```
reader.GetValue(3).ToString()
```

This value can also be accessed with the expression

```
reader.GetInt32(3)
```

Note that the returned rows can be accessed in a forward-only path.

The data reader is closed with the statement

```
reader.Close();
```

After the reader is closed, the connection is available for other operations. The returned Web page is shown in Figure 7.11C.

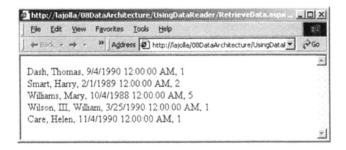

FIGURE 7.11C
Returned Web page of UsingDataReader application (UsingDataReader\RetrieveData.aspx).

Transactions

The **OleDbTransaction** class provides for grouping database operations into a group or transaction in which all are executed successfully or none is executed. The Web page part of an application illustrating transaction processing class is shown in Figure 7.12A. The Web page contains a form with a single ASP.Label control msg. Note that the control is sized to provide for long lines and multiple lines.

```
<%@ Page language="c#" Codebehind="ExecuteTransaction.aspx.cs"
AutoEventWireup="false" Inherits="Transactions.ExecuteTransaction" %>
<HTML>
  <HEAD>
  </HEAD>
  <body MS_POSITIONING="GridLayout">
    <form id="ExecuteTransaction" method="post" runat="server">
      <asp:Label ID=msg Runat=server Width="75%" Height="50%"></asp:Label>
    </form>
  </body>
</HTML>
```

FIGURE 7.12A
Web page of application using transaction processing (Transactions\ExecuteTransaction.aspx).

The code-behind file contains the statement

```
using System.Data.OleDb;
```

to expose the classes, delegates and enumerations of the System.Data.OleDb namespace. The code-behind file contains a Page_Load method, shown in Figure 7.12B.

```
private void Page_Load(object sender, System.EventArgs e)
{
        string provider = "Provider=Microsoft.Jet.OLEDB.4.0";
        string dataSource = "Data Source=C:\\DB\\StudentAdministratorDB.mdb";
        string connectStg = provider + ";" + dataSource;
        OleDbConnection connection = new OleDbConnection(connectStg);
        connection.Open();
        OleDbCommand command = new OleDbCommand();        Declare Transaction object
        command.Connection = connection;

        OleDbTransaction transaction;
                                              BeginTransaction method of OleDbConnecton
                                              object returns OleDbTransaction object

        transaction = connection.BeginTransaction(IsolationLevel.ReadCommitted);
        command.Transaction = transaction;

        try                                   Build command text
        {
                command.CommandText =
                        "INSERT INTO Contact (StudentID, Name, Telephone) ";
                command.CommandText = command.CommandText +
                        "VALUES ( 5, 'Virgil Blue', '732 774 7172')";

                command.ExecuteNonQuery();
                                              Execute command inside
                                              transaction
                command.CommandText =
                        "INSERT INTO Contact (StudentID, Name, Telephone) ";
                command.CommandText = command.CommandText +
                        VALUES ( 5, 'Sandra Blue', '732 774 7172')";
                command.ExecuteNonQuery();
                                              Commit all operations in
                                              transaction if all successful
                transaction.Commit();
                msg.Text = "Database operations completed sucessfully!";
        }
        catch(Exception ex)
        {                                     Rollback transaction
                                              operations if an
                transaction.Rollback();       operation fails
                msg.Text = "EXCEPTION: " + ex.Message;
        }

        connection.Close();
}
```

FIGURE 7.12B

Page_Load method in code-behind Web page of application using transaction processing (Transactions\Execute-Transaction.aspx).

A reference to an OleDbTransaction object, transaction, is declared with the statement

```
OleDbTransaction transaction;
```

An OleDbTransaction object is returned by the OleDbConnection BeginTransaction method and assigned to the transaction reference:

```
transaction =
    connection.BeginTransaction(IsolationLevel.ReadCommitted);
```

The object referenced by transaction represents a transaction associated with the connection object that represents a unique connection to a data source. A command is made a part of the transaction by setting its Transaction property to the value of the transaction object:

```
command.Transaction = transaction;
```

A command operation is defined and executed with the following statement; in this case, a row is inserted into a Contact table with an SQL INSERT INTO statement:

```
command.CommandText =
    "INSERT INTO Contact (StudentID, Name, Telephone) ";
command.CommandText = command.CommandText +
    "VALUES (5, 'Virgil Blue', '732 774 7172')";
```

The SQL Statement does not return any rows and thus the command is executed with the OleDbCommand method ExecuteNonQuery method:

```
command.ExecuteNonQuery();
```

The OleDbCommand object referenced by command is associated with the OleDbTransaction object referenced by transaction. As such, the operation specified by the command is performed but the changes to the data source are not made permanent. Another row is similarly added to the Contact table with the statements:

```
command.CommandText =
    "INSERT INTO Contact (StudentID, Name, Telephone) ";
command.CommandText = command.CommandText +
    "VALUES (5, 'Sandra Blue', '732 774 7172')";
command.ExecuteNonQuery();
```

Note that the statements are contained within a "try" block. If any of the statements raise an exception, control transfers out of the try block and passes to the following catch block. If all of the operations are completed successfully, control remains in the try block and the data source changes prescribed by the operations are made permanent with the statement:

```
transaction.Commit();
```

On the other hand, if any of the operations raises an exception, control passes to the catch block and the operations are reversed with the statement

```
transaction.Rollback();
```

All commands with the same transaction property are treated as a unit. The changes to the data source are made permanent when the transaction's Commit method is invoked. Conversely, data source changes associated with the transaction are reversed with the transaction's Rollback method.

Hands-On Exercise: Implementing Connected Data Access

Step 1: Create the Application

1. Create and open an ASP.NET Web application named ConnectedAccess in location http://LAJOLLA/09ConnectedDataAccess.

2. In the Solution Explorer, delete WebForm1.aspx. and add Web form Access-Data.aspx.

3. In the View menu, select the Toolbox command. Alternately, press the Ctrl+Alt+X key combination.

4. In the View menu, select the Properties Window command. Alternately, press the F4 key.

Step 2: Create and Configure the Connection

1. Click the Data tab in the Toolbox window to open the Data objects pane.
2. From the Data tab in the Toolbox, drag an OleDbConnection onto the Access-Data.aspx page in the Designer window.
3. Click the OleDbConnection in the Designer to shift the focus to the object.
4. In the properties window, change the Name to connection.
5. Click the button at the right end of the Connection property to display a list of the available connections. Select one, if appropriate, or select <New Connection...> to open the Data Link Properties window.
6. Click the Provider tab and choose Microsoft Jet 4.0 OLE DB Provider.

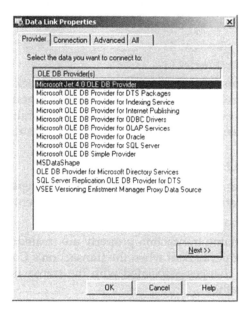

FIGURE HO7.1
Data Link Properties dialog, Provider tab.

7. Click the Next button. The Connection tab is opened.
8. Enter the name or browse and select the StudentAdministratorDB.mdb database file.
9. Click the Test Connection button to test the connection. The results are displayed in Figure HO7.3.
10. Click OK to close the Microsoft Data Link message box.
11. Click OK to close the Data Link Properties box. Visual Studio.NET adds the following code automatically. The OleDbConnection object is declared when the object is added to the page in the Designer.

```
protected System.Data.OleDb.OleDbConnection connection;
```

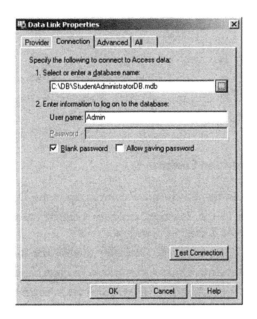

FIGURE HO7.2
Data Link Properties dialog, Connection tab.

FIGURE HO7.3
Data Link test results.

An OleDbConnection object is created in the InitializeComponent method with
the statement

```
this.connection = new System.Data.OleDb.OleDbConnection();
```

The connection properties are set, with the following statement in the Initialize-
Component method, when the Connection property is defined in the properties
window:

```
this.connection.ConnectionString =
@"Provider = Microsoft.Jet.OLEDB.4.0;Password = """";
User ID = Admin;
Data Source = C:\DB\StudentAdministratorDB.mdb;
Mode = Share Deny None;Extended Properties = """";
Jet OLEDB:System database = """";
Jet OLEDB:Registry Path = """";
Jet OLEDB:Database Password = """";
Jet OLEDB:Engine Type = 5;Jet OLEDB:Database Locking Mode = 1;
Jet OLEDB:Global Partial Bulk Ops = 2;
Jet OLEDB:Global Bulk Transactions = 1;
```

```
Jet OLEDB:New Database Password = """";
Jet OLEDB:Create System Database = False;
Jet OLEDB:Encrypt Database = False;
Jet OLEDB:Don't Copy Locale on Compact = False;
Jet OLEDB:Compact Without Replica Repair = False;
Jet OLEDB:SFP = False";
```

Step 3: Create and Specify the Command

1. Click the Data tab in the Toolbox window to open the Data objects pane.
2. From the Data tab in the Toolbox, drag an OleDbCommand onto the Access-Data.aspx page in the Designer window.
3. Click the OleDbCommand in the Designer to shift the focus to the object.
4. In the Properties window, change the Name to command.
5. Click the button at the right end of the Connection property to display a diagram listing available connections. Click the + symbol to expand the list of Existing connections; connections on the page are displayed. Select connection. Note that the Connection property must be defined before the CommandText property can be defined.
6. Click the button at the left of the Command property. The Query Builder is opened with the Add Table window opened, as illustrated in Figure HO7.4.

FIGURE HO7.4
Add Table dialog.

7. Select the Student table.
8. Click Add to add the Student table to the Query Designer (Figure HO7.5).
9. Click Close to close the Add Table window.
10. Click the fields desired in the results table.
11. Click the LastName field. Click the FirstName field. The fields are added to the columns table in the order clicked.
12. Click the Sort Order element in the first row; select 1. The results will be sorted first by LastName.

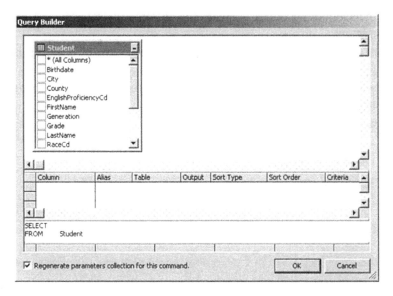

FIGURE HO7.5
Query Builder dialog with Student table added.

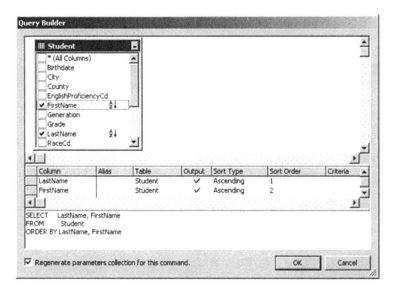

FIGURE HO7.6
Query Builder dialog with SELECT statement.

13. Click the Sort Order element in the second row; select 2. The results will be sorted first by FirstName and next by FirstName within LastName order. The SQL statement text is shown in the lower pane of the Query Builder window (see Figure HO7.6).

14. Click OK to close the Query builder and set CommandText to the SQL Statement defined. Visual Studio.NET adds the following code automatically. The OleDb-Command object is declared when the object is added to the page in the Designer:

```
protected System.Data.OleDb.OleDbCommand command;
```

An OleDbCommand object is created in the InitializeComponent method with the statement

```
this.command = new System.Data.OleDb.OleDbCommand();
```

The CommandText property is set to the SQL Statement defined in the Query Builder, with the following statement in the InitializeComponent method, when the Query Builder is closed:

```
this.command.CommandText =
    "SELECT LastName, FirstName
    FROM Student
    ORDER BY LastName, FirstName";
```

Step 4: Add Label Control to Display Data

1. Click the Web Forms tab in the Toolbox to display the Web Form controls.
2. Drag a Label control object onto the Web page AccessData.aspx.
3. Grab the object's handles to size the control to contain a list of the results.
4. In the Properties window, change the ID value to **names** (see Figure HO7.7). The Label control is shown on the page. The OleDbConnection and OleDbCommand objects, associated with the page, are displayed at the bottom of the designer. Visual Studio.NET automatically adds a reference to the Label control object names to the code-behind file.

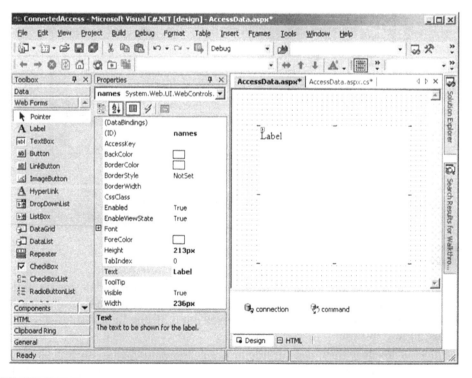

FIGURE HO7.7
AccessData.aspx with Label control added.

5. Manually add the following to the Page_Load method of the file Access-Data.aspx.cs:

```
connection.Open();
System.Data.OleDb.OleDbDataReader reader;
reader = command.ExecuteReader();
while (reader.Read())
{
    names.Text = names.Text +
        reader.GetString(0) + ," " +
        reader.GetString(1) + "<br>" ;
}
reader.Close();
connection.Close();
```

Note that the Open method of the connection object is called to open the connection. A data reader is declared and created by invoking the ExecuteReader method of the command object. The Read method is called in a "while" loop to iterate through the result rows. The reader objects' accessors are used to get the values of each row, which are added to the Text property of the names control. The close method is invoked for both reader and connection objects. The Web page sent to the browser is shown in Figure HO7.8.

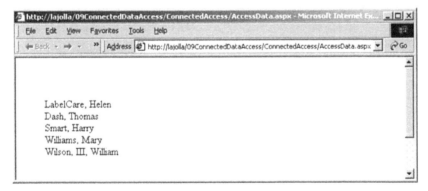

FIGURE HO7.8
AccessData.aspx page sent to browser.

Note!

A .NET data provider is a collection of classes facilitating data access in a managed space.

8

Data Tables

Tables are an effective structure for data arrangement and management. Student identification number, last name, first name and birth date are efficiently handled in a table, as shown in Figure 8.1. The .NET Framework provides support for utilization of tabular data structures.

ID	Last Name	First Name	Birth Date
1001	Vbaby	Ann	1/1/1952
1002	Ormand	Bergen	3/25/1935
1003	Alenda	Denna	7/7/1985

FIGURE 8.1
Student data arranged in a tabular format.

Data Table Architecture

The DataTable class represents one tabular data structure in memory. Figure 8.2 shows the DataTable object model. Properties providing access to the objects are shown in parentheses. Objects used to define a DataTable are summarized below:

- DataRowCollection — Collection of DataRow objects representing the rows of the table
- DataColumnCollection — Collection of DataColumn objects defining the columns of the table
- DataColumn — Array of DataColumn objects that specify the columns comprising the table's primary key
- DataView — Collection of Row objects defining the rows of the table
- ChildRelationCollection — Collection of DataRelation objects defining the relationship with other tables
- ParentRelationCollection — Collection of DataRelation objects defining the parent relationship with other table
- ConstraintCollection — Collection of Constraint objects defining restraints imposed on column values
- PropertyCollection — Collection of custom information values stored in a Hashtable

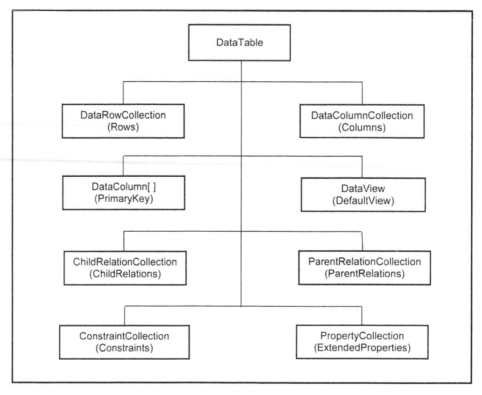

FIGURE 8.2
DataTable object model with associated properties and ChildRelations.

Data Columns

DataColumn objects are used to define the schema or structure of the table. The Data-Column objects are added to the DataColumnCollection object of the table. Selected members of the DataColumn class are listed in Figure 8.3.

The DataColumnCollection (Figure 8.4) represents the DataTable schema. Each of the collection elements represents a data column with a DataColumn object. A DataColumn element is required for each column in a table. The Add and Remove methods are used to insert and delete DataColumn objects to and from the collection. The Count property, inherited from the InternalDataCollectionBase class, gets the total number of DataColumn objects in the collection.

Data Rows

DataRow objects represent the data stored in the table.

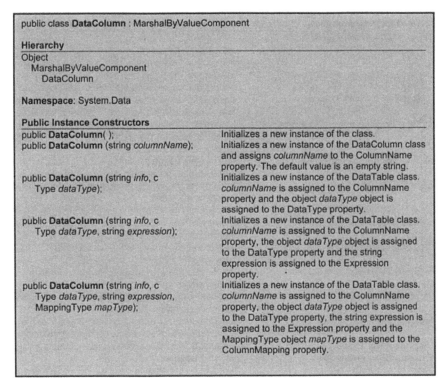

```
public class DataColumn : MarshalByValueComponent

Hierarchy
Object
   MarshalByValueComponent
      DataColumn

Namespace: System.Data

Public Instance Constructors
```

public **DataColumn**( );	Initializes a new instance of the class.
public **DataColumn** (string *columnName*);	Initializes a new instance of the DataColumn class and assigns *columnName* to the ColumnName property. The default value is an empty string.
public **DataColumn** (string *info*, c Type *dataType*);	Initializes a new instance of the DataTable class. *columnName* is assigned to the ColumnName property and the object *dataType* object is assigned to the DataType property.
public **DataColumn** (string *info*, c Type *dataType*, string *expression*);	Initializes a new instance of the DataTable class. *columnName* is assigned to the ColumnName property, the object *dataType* object is assigned to the DataType property and the string expression is assigned to the Expression property.
public **DataColumn** (string *info*, c Type *dataType*, string *expression*, MappingType *mapType*);	Initializes a new instance of the DataTable class. *columnName* is assigned to the ColumnName property, the object *dataType* object is assigned to the DataType property, the string expression is assigned to the Expression property and the MappingType object *mapType* is assigned to the ColumnMapping property.

FIGURE 8.3
Selected DataColumn members.

DataRowState Enumeration

The DataRowState enumeration members specify the state of a data row; these members are listed in Figure 8.5. The state of the row is changed as the row is created, added to the collection, changed, removed from a collection or deleted.

DataRowVersion Enumeration

The DataRowVersion enumeration members specify the state of a row's version if versions exist. Members of the enumeration are listed in Figure 8.6.

Both the current and proposed values become available after the row's BeginEdit method is invoked. The Proposed value becomes the Current value when the EndEdit method is invoked The Proposed value is deleted when the CancelEdit method is invoked. When the AcceptChanges method is invoked, the Proposed value becomes current and the Original value becomes identical to the current value. When the RejectChanges method is invoked, the Proposed value is discarded.

DataRow Objects

DataRow objects are added to the table's DataRowCollection object of the table. Selected members of the DataRow class are listed in Figure 8.7. A DataRow object is created by invoking the NewRow method of the DataTable object to which the row will belong.

Public Instance Properties	
public bool **AllowDBNull** {get; set;}	Gets or sets the value indicating if null values are allowed in the column. If null values are allowed the value is true; false otherwise. The default is true.
public bool **AutoIncrement** {get; set;}	Gets or sets the value indicating if the column's value is automatically incremented when new rows are added to the table. If null values are automatically incremented; false otherwise. The default is false.
public long **AutoIncrementSeed** {get; set;}	Gets or sets the starting value, the value for the first row added to the table, if the column's AutoIncrement property is set true.
public long **AutoIncrementStep** {get; set;}	Gets or sets the incrementing value if the column's AutoIncrement property is set true. The default is 1.
public string **Caption** {get; set;}	Gets or sets the column's caption. The default is the ColumnName value.
public virtual MappingType **ColumnMapping** {get; set;}	Gets or sets the MappingType object that determines how a DataColumn is mapped when a DataSet is saved as an XML document.
public string **ColumnName** {get; set;}	Gets or sets the name of the column in the DataColumnCollection.
public Type **DataType** {get; set;}	Gets or sets the Type object that represents the column's data type.
public object **DefaultValue** {get; set;}	Gets or sets the default value for the column when new rows are added to the table.
public sring **Expression** {get; set;}	Gets or sets the expression used to calculate the value of the column or create an aggregate column.
public PropertyCollection **ExtendedProperties** {get;}	Gets the PropertyCollection object containing custom properties.
public int **MaxLength** {get; set;}	Gets or sets the maximum length of a text column. The default value, indicating no maximum length, is –1.
public string **Namespace** {get; set;}	Gets or sets the namespace of the DataColumn.
public int **Ordinal** {get;;}	Gets the position of the column in the DataColumnCollection object.
public string **Prefix** {get; set;}	Gets or sets the XML prefix that aliases the namespace.
public bool **ReadOnly** {get; set;}	Gets or sets the value indicating whether the column allows changes. If changes are not allowed the value is true; false otherwise. The default is false.
public DataTable **Table** {get;}	Gets the DataTable to which the column belongs.
public bool **Unique** {get; set;}	Gets or sets the value indicating whether the column's values must be unique. If unique values are required the value is true; false otherwise. The default is false.

FIGURE 8.3 (CONTINUED)
Selected DataColumn members.

While the row is in the edit mode, the DataRow object stores the original version of the row as well as the edited version. Until the EndEdit method is called, either the original or edited version of the row can be retrieved with the DataRowVersion. Original or DataRowVersion.Proposed for the version parameter of the Item property (dataRow indexer).

Changes to the row are committed with the EndEdit method. A deleted row can be undeleted by invoking the RejectChanges method. When the RejectChanges method is called, the CancelEdit method is implicitly called, thus cancelling any edits. The consequences of the RejectChanges method depend on the RowState value. If the RowState is Deleted or Modified, the row reverts to its previous values and the RowState becomes Unchanged. If the RowState is Added, the row is removed.

public class **DataColumnCollection** : InternalDataCollectionBase	
Hierarchy	

Object
  InternalDataCollectionBase
    DataColumnCollection	

Namespace: System.Data	
Public Instance Properties	
public virtual **DataColumn** this[int *index*] {get;}	Gets the DataColumn object from the collection at the position specified by the zero-based *index*.
public virtual **DataColumn** this[string *columnName*] {get;}	Gets the DataColumn object from the collection with the ColumnName property value *columnName*.
Public Instance Methods	
public virtual DataColumn **Add** ( );	Creates and adds a DataColumn object to the DataColumnCollection. The default name "Column*n*", where *n* is incremented for subsequent DataColumn objects, is assigned to the ColumnName property. The method returns the DataColumn object added.
public void **Add** (DataColumn *dataColumn*);	Adds the DataColumn object *dataColumn* to the DataColumnCollection.
public virtual DataColumn **Add** (string *columnName*);	Creates and adds a DataColumn object to the DataColumnCollection with *columnName* value assigned to the DataColumn's ColumnName property value. The method returns the DataColumn object added.
public virtual DataColumn **Add** (string *columnName*, Type *type*);	Creates and adds a DataColumn object to the DataColumnCollection with *columnName* and *type* object values assigned to the DataColumn's ColumnName and DataType property values. The method returns the DataColumn object added.

public virtual DataColumn **Add** (
  string *columnName*, Type *type*,
  string *expression*);
	Creates and adds a DataColumn object to the DataColumnCollection with *columnName*, *type* object and *expression* values assigned to the DataColumn's ColumnName, DataType and Expression property values. The method returns the DataColumn object added.

public void **AddRange** (DataColumn[ ] *columns*);	Copies the elements of the DataColumn array *columns* to the end of the collection.
public bool **CanRemove** (DataColumn *columns*);	Returns true if the DataColumn *columns* can be removed from the collection; false otherwise.
public void **Clear** ( );	Clears the collection of any columns.
public bool **Contains** (string *name*);	Returns true if the collection contains a DataColumn with the Name property *name*.
public intl **IndexOf** (string *columnName*);	Returns the index of the DataColumn object with the Name property *columnName*. If the specified DataColumn object is not found the returned value is −1. The column name search is not case-sensitive.
public void **Remove** (DataColumn *column*);	Removes the DataColumn object *column* from the collection.
public void **Remove** (string *name*);	Removes the DataColumn object with the Name property value *name* from the collection.
public void **RemoveAt** (int *index*);	Removes the DataColumn object at the position *index* from the collection.
Protected Instance Property	
protected override ArrayList **List** {get;};	Gets an ArrayList that represents the collection items.

FIGURE 8.4
Selected DataColumnCollection members.

public enum DataRowState	
Namespace: System.Data	
Members	
Name	**Description**
Added	The row has been added to the row collection and the AcceptChanges method of the DataRow object has not been invoked.
Deleted	The row was deleted using the Delete method of the DataRow object.
Detached	The row has been created but has not been added to or has been removed from a DataRowCollection.
Modified	The row has been modified and the AcceptChanges method of the DataRow object has not been invoked.
Unchanged	The row has not been modified since the AcceptChanges method of the DataRow object was last invoked.

FIGURE 8.5
DataRowState enumeration.

public enum DataRowState	
Namespace: System.Data	
Members	
Name	**Description**
Current	The row contains current values.
Default	The row contains default values.
Original	The row contains original values.
Proposed	The row contains a proposed value.

FIGURE 8.6
DataRowVersion enumeration.

public class **DataRow**	
Hierarchy	
Object DataColumn	
Namespace: System.Data	
Public Instance Properties	
public bool **HasErrors** {get;}	Gets a value indicating if there are errors in the row's columns. If any DataColumn in the row contains an error the value is true; false otherwise.
public object **this** [string *columnName*] {get; set;}	Gets or sets the object representing the value in the column named *columnName*.
public object **this** [DataColumn *column*] {get; set;}	Gets or sets the object representing the value in the DataColumn object referenced by *column*.
public object **this** [int *columnIndex*] {get; set;}	Gets or sets the object representing the value in the DataColumn object specified by the index value *columnIndex*.
public object[ ] **ItemArray** [ ] {get; set;}	Gets or sets a row's column values with the elements in the array.
public string **RowError** {get; set;}	Gets or sets the row's custom error description text.
public DataRowState **RowState** {get;}	Gets the DataRowState ennumeration member describing the current state of the row.
public DataTable **Table** {get;}	Gets the DataTable object with the row's schema.

FIGURE 8.7
Selected DataRow members.

Public Instance Methods	
public void **AcceptChanges** ( );	Commits all changes to the row since AcceptChanges was last invoked.
public void **BeginEdit** ( );	Places the row in edit mode in which events are suspended until the EndEdit or CancelEdit method is invoked.
public void **CancelEdit** ( );	Cancels the current row's edit status.
public void **ClearErrors** ( );	Clears the row's errors.
public void **Delete** ( );	The row is removed from the table.
public void **EndEdit** ( );	Ends the current row's edit status.
public DataRow[ ] **GetChildRows** (DataRelation *relation*);	Gets the child rows of the DataRow using the DataRelation object *relation* as a DataRow array.
public DataRow[ ] **GetChildRows** (string *relationName*);	Gets the child rows of the DataRow, using the DataRelation object specified by *relationName*, as a DataRow array.
public string **GetColumnError** (DataColumn *column*);	Gets the child error description of the DataColumn specified by the object reference *column*.
public string **GetColumnError** (int *columnIndex*);	Gets the child error description of the DataColumn at index position specified by *columnIndex*.
public string **GetColumnError** (string *columnName*);	Gets the child error description of the DataColumn specified by the name *columnName*.
public DataColumn[ ] **GetColumnsInError** ( );	Gets DataColumn objects that have an error as an array.
public DataRow **GetParentRow** (DataRelation *relation*);	Gets the parent row using the DataRelation object specified by *relation*.
public DataRow **GetParentRow** (string *relationName*);	Gets the parent row using the DataRelation object with the name *relationName*.
public DataRow[ ] **GetParentRows** (DataRelation *relation*);	Gets the parent rows of the current row, as an array of DataRow objects, specified by the DataRelation object reference *relation*.
public DataRow[ ] **GetParentRows** (string *relationName*);	Gets the parent rows of the current row, as an array of DataRow objects, specified by the DataRelation object named *relationName*.
public bool **HasVersion** (DataRowVersion *version*);	Gets a value indicating the existence of the version specified by the DataRowVersion member *version*.
public bool **IsNull** (DataColumn *column*);	Gets a value indicating a null value in the DataColumn *column*. The value returned is true if the value is null; false otherwise.
public bool **IsNull** (int *columnIndex*);	Gets a value indicating a null value in the DataColumn at the position *columnIndex*. The value returned is true if the value is null; false otherwise.
public bool **IsNull** (string *columnName*);	Gets a value indicating a null value in the DataColumn with the name *columnName*. The value returned is true if the value is null; false otherwise.
public void **RejectChanges** ( );	Rejects all changes made since the AcceptChanges method was invoked.
public void **SetColumnError** (DataColumn *column* string *errorMsg*);	Sets the error message description text *errorMsg* for the DataRow object referenced by *column*.
public void **SetColumnError** (int *columnIndex* string *errorMsg*);	Sets the error message description text *errorMsg* for the DataRow object at the index position *columnIndex*.
public void **SetColumnError** (sting *columnName* string *errorMsg*);	Sets the error message description text *errorMsg* for the DataRow object with the name *columnName*.
public void **SetParentRow** (DataRow *parentRow*);	Sets the parent rows of the current row with the parent DataRow *parentRow*.
public void **SetParentRow** (DataRow *parentRow* DataRelation *relation*);	Sets the parent rows of the current row with the new parent DataRow *parentRow* and DataRelation relation object *relation*.
public void **SetUnspecified** (DataColumn *column*);	Sets the value of the DataColumn object *column* unspecified.
Protected Instance Methods	
protected void **SetNull** (DataColumn *column*);	Sets the value of the DataColumn object referenced by *column* to a null value.

FIGURE 8.7 (CONTINUED)
Selected DataRow public and protected instance methods.

public class **DataRowCollection**	
Hierarchy	

Object
   InternalDataCollectionBase
      DataRowCollection	

Namespace: System.Data	
Public Instance Properties	
public DataRow **this** [int *index*] {get; set;}	Gets TheDataRow object at the position specified by the index value *index*.
Public Instance Methods	
public void **Add** (DataRow *row*);	Adds the specified DataRow object referenced by *row* to the collection.
public virtual DataRow **Add** (object[ ] *values*);	Creates a new row with the values of the array *values* and adds the row to the tables row collection. The method returns the DataRow created and added to the collection.
public void **Clear** ();	Clears the table's row collection of all DataRow objects.
public bool **Contains** (object *key*);	Returns a true value if the collection contains a DataRow object with primary key value of *key*; false otherwise.
public bool **Contains** (object[ ] *keys*);	Returns a true value if the collection contains a multiple column primary key DataRow object with primary key values matching the array of values *keys*; false otherwise.
public DataRow **Find** (object *key*);	Returns the DataRow object with primary key value of *key*. If the DataRow does not exist a null value is returned.
public DataRow **Find** (object[ ] *keys*);	Returns the DataRow object with multiple column primary key values matching the array of values *keys*. A null value is returned if the DataRow does not exist.
public void **InsertAt** (DataRow *row*, int *index*);	Inserts the DataRow object *row* into the collection at the index position *index*.
public void **Remove** (DataRow row);	Removes the DataRow object *row* from the collection.
public void **RemoveAt** (int *index*);	Removes the DataRow object *row* from the collection at the index position *index*.

FIGURE 8.8
Selected DataRowCollection members.

Data Row Collection

The DataRowCollection objects are the collection of DataRow objects that represent the table's data. Selected members of the DataRowCollection class are listed in Figure 8.8.

Using the table's schema, a new row is created by invoking the table's NewRow method. The new row is added to the table's row collection with the DataRowCollection's Add method. Prior to insertion in the table, the row's column values are assigned to their initial value. The Contains method is used to ascertain if a row with the specified primary key value exists in the collection. A row with a specific primary key value can be accessed with the Find method.

The Remove and RemoveAt methods remove the specified row from the collection; the removed row is lost. This contrasts with the Delete method that only marks a row for removal. The actual removal of a marked row does not occur until the AcceptChanges method is invoked.

Data Table

The DataTable class represents a table including row, column, relation and constraint collections. The DataTable class is summarized in Figure 8.9.

DataTable class functionality includes the following:

- When the DataTable is contained within a DataSet, the default values of many of the DataTable's properties are the DataSet's values for the property.
- The rules for forming a DisplayExpression expression string are contained in the DataColumn.Expression property.
- When the AcceptChanges method is invoked, all DataRow objects in the edit mode end the edit mode and change the DataRowState. All Added and Modified state rows change to the Unchanged state. All Deleted state rows are removed from the table.
- After the AcceptChanges method is called, all rows in the Added, Modified or Deleted state are viewed as original. If the Dataset has not been updated using the DbDataAdapter.Update method, the additions, changes and deletions are lost because the Dataset cannot ascertain which rows must be sent to the database management system to reconcile the data source.
- The BeginLoadData method is used in conjunction with the LoadDataRow and EndLoadData methods.
- When the Clear method is called, an exception is raised if the table has "child" relations that would result in "orphaned child" rows.
- The table created with the Clone method does not include any rows, i.e., the row count is zero.
- The AcceptChanges method should not be called until all errors have been resolved. The rows with errors can be accessed with the GetErrors method. That is, the GetErrors method returns a DataRow array with all rows that have errors.
- When the RejectChanges method is called, DataRow objects in the edit mode cancel their edits; new rows are removed. Rows with the DataRowState set to Modified or Deleted states are returned to their original states.

The Web page part of an application illustrating use of the DataTable class is shown in Figure 8.10A. The Web page contains a form with a single ASP.Label control msg. Note that the control is sized to provide for long lines and multiple lines. The code-behind file contains the statement

```
using System.Data.OleDb;
```

to expose the classes, delegates and enumerations of the System.Data.OleDb namespace.

In this case, the connection with the database is established and the command is created and executed in the Page_Load method. The Page_Load method of the code-behind file is shown in Figure 8.10B.

A DataTable named studentTable is created with the statement

```
DataTable studentTable = new DataTable("Student");
```

The DataTable constructor is overloaded; this version initializes a new DataTable object and sets its TableName property to the string value passed as the method's parameter. A DataColumn object, named studentIDColumn, is declared and created with the statement

```
DataColumn studentIDColumn = new DataColumn();
```

```
public class DataTable : MarshalByValueComponent, IListSource, ISupportInitialize, ISerializable
```

Hierarchy

Object
  MarshalByValueComponent
    DataTable

Namespace: System.Data

Constructors

public **DataTable**( );	Initializes a new instance of the DataTable class.
public **DataTable** (string *tableName*);	Initializes a new instance of the DataTable class and assigns *tableName* to the TableName property or system default.
public **DataTable** (SerializationInfo *info*, StreamingContex *context*);	Initializes a new instance of the DataTable class. Information to serialize or deserialize an object is specified by the SerializationInfo object *info*. The source and destination of the serialized stream are specified by the StreamingContex object *context*.

Public Instance Properties

public bool **CaseSensitive**{get; set;};	Gets or sets a value indicating whether string comparisons in sorting, searching and filtering are false otherwise. The default value is false.
public DataRelationCollection **ChildRelations** {get;};	Gets the DataRelationCollection object containing the child relations for the table. If no data relation exists the value is null.
public DataColumnCollection **Columns** {get;};	Gets the DataColumnCollection object containing the DataColumn objects for the table. If no DataColumn exists the value is null.
public ConstraintCollection **Columns** {get;};	Gets the ConstraintCollection object containing the Constraint objects for the table. If no Constraint exists the value is null.
public DataSet **DataSet** {get;};	Gets the DataSet object the table belongs to.
public DataView **DefaultView** {get;};	Gets the DataView object associated with the table. The DataView object can be used to sort, search and filter the table.
public string **DisplayExpression**{get; se};	Gets or sets the expression that will return a value used to represent the table in user interface.
public PropertyCollection **ExtendedProperties** {get;};	Gets the PropertyCollection object containing custom user information, for example a password, for the table.
public bool **HasErrors** {get;};	Gets a value indicating whether there are any errors in any row in any table in the DataSet to which the table belongs. The value true indicates errors; false otherwise.
public CultureInfo **Local** {get; set;}	Gets or sets a CultureInfo object that contains information about the user's machine locale that is used to compare strings during sorting. The default is a null reference.
public int **MinimumCapacity** {get; set;}	Gets or sets the initial size for the table. The default value is 25 rows.
public string **Namespace** {get; set;}	Gets or sets the namespace of the XML representation of the table's data.
public DataRelationCollection **ParentRelations** {get;};	Gets the DataRelationCollection object containing DataRelation objects describing parent relationships. The value is null if no DataRelation object exists.
public string **Prefix** {get; set;}	Gets or sets the prefix that aliases the table's namespace.
public DataColumn[ ] **PrimaryKey** {get; set;};	Gets or sets an array of columns that act as the table's primary key.
public DataRowCollection **Rows** {get;}	Gets the DataRowCollection that contains the table's DataRow objects. If there is no DataRow the value is null.
public override ISite **Site** {get; set;}	Gets or sets the ISite object for the DataTable that binds a component and container enabling communication between them and enabling management of the container's components.
public string **TableName** {get; set;}	Gets or sets the table's name.

FIGURE 8.9
DataTable.

Public Instance Methods	
public void **AcceptChanges** ( );	Commits all changes to the table since the AcceptChanges method was previously called.
public void **BeginInit** ( );	The Visual Studio.NET design environment uses the method to start initialization of a DataTable object at run time.
public void **BeginLoadData** ( );	Turns off notification, index maintenance and constraints enabling the unfettered loading of data.
public void **Clear** ( );	Removes all rows in the table.
public DataTable **Clone** ( );	Creates a new table with the schema, relations and constraints of the invoking table.
public object **Compute** (string *expression*, string *filter*);	Computes an aggregate such as Count or Sum defined by *expression* for all rows satisfying the filter criteria *filter*.
public DataTable **Copy** ( );	Creates a new table with the data, schema, relations and constraints of the invoking table.
public void **EndInit** ( );	The Visual Studio.NET design environment uses the method to end initialization of a DataTable object at run time.
public void **EndLoadData** ( );	Turns on notification, index maintenance and constraints that were turned off to enable data loading. Beta 2 documentation indicates this method "Turns off notifications, index maintenance and constraints while loading data".
public DataTable **GetChanges** ( );	Returns a copy of the table with all changes made since it was last loaded or the AcceptChanges method was last called. A null reference is returned if none is found.
public DataTable **GetChanges** (DataRowState *rowState*);	Returns a copy of the table with all changes made since it was last loaded or the AcceptChanges method was last called filtered by the dataRowState object *rowState*. A null reference is returned if none are found.
public DataRow[ ] **GetErrors** ( );	Returns an array of DataRow objects that have errors.
public void **ImportRow** (DataRow *row*);	Copies a DataRow referenced by *row* into the DataTable. Original values, current values, DataRowState values and errors are imported into the DataTable.
public DataRow **LoadDataRow** (object[ ] *values*, bool *acceptChangesFlag*);	Finds the row with the same primary key values as specified in the object array *values*. If the row is found the values are used to update the row. If the row is not found a new row is created. If the *acceptChangesFlag* is true the new data is added and the AcceptChanges method is called; otherwise the newly added row is marked as insertion. The new DataRow is returned.

FIGURE 8.9 (CONTINUED)
DataTable public instance methods.

The property values of the object studentIDColumn are set to reflect the characteristics of the table column represented by the object, in this case the StudentID column, that uniquely identifies the student. For example, the statement

```
studentIDColumn.ColumnName = "StudentIDColumn";
```

sets the ColumnName property value to "StudentIDColumn".

The value of the DataType property is set with the statement

```
studentIDColumn.DataType = System.Type.GetType("System.Int32");
```

The DataType property value is a Type class object. The Type class represents type declarations and contains the static method GetType that returns the Type object with the specified name, in this case "System.Int32."

Typically, a column that uniquely represents the row is used as the table's primary key. Most database management systems have an autoincrement column property in which each row is assigned an integral value that is automatically incremented every time a row

Public Instance Methods	
public DataRow **NewRow** ( );	Creates a new DataRow with the same schema as the table.
public void **RejectChanges** ( );	Rolls back all changes made to table since it was loaded or AcceptChanges was last called.
public DataRow[ ] **Select** ( );	Returns an array of current rows in order of the primary key if the key exists or in order of addition if the primary key does not exist.
public DataRow[ ] **Select** (string *filterExpression*);	Returns an array of current rows, in order of the primary key if the key exists or in order of addition if the primary key does not exist, for DataRow objects that match the criteria *filterExpression*.
public DataRow[ ] **Select** (string *filterExpression* string *sort*);	Returns an array of current rows, in order of the primary key if the key exists or in order of addition if the primary key does not exist, for DataRow objects that match the criteria *filterExpression*. The rows are sorted in the order specified by *sort*.
public DataRow[ ] **Select** (string *filterExpression* string *sort* DataViewRowState *rowState*);	Returns an array of current rows, in order of the primary key if the key exists or in order of addition if the primary key does not exist, for DataRow objects that match the criterion *filterExpression*. The rows are sorted in the order specified by *sort*. Only rows with the DataViewRowStatte value *rowState* are included.
public override string **ToString** ( );	Returns the TableName and DisplayExpression property values in a string.

FIGURE 8.9 (CONTINUED)
DataTable public instance methods.

```
<%@ Page language="c#" Codebehind="BasicTable.aspx.cs" AutoEventWireup="false"
         Inherits="DataTableBasics.BasicTable" %>
<HTML>
  <HEAD>
  </HEAD>
  <body MS_POSITIONING="GridLayout">
    <form id="BasicTable" method="post" runat="server">
        <asp:Label ID=msg Runat=server Width="75%" Height="50%"></asp:Label>
    </form>
  </body>
</HTML>
```

FIGURE 8.10A
Web page of DataTable application (DataTableBasics\BasicTable.aspx).

is added to the table. The column studentIDColumn's AutoIncrement property is set to enable autoincrementation with the statement

```
studentIDColumn.AutoIncrement = true;
```

Most systems provide for setting the first value assigned to an autoincrementing value in the first row entered. This value, referred to as the seed value, is assigned with the statement

```
studentIDColumn.AutoIncrementSeed = 1001;
```

which results in the first row entered being assigned the value 1001. Subsequent rows are assigned the values 10002, 1003, 1004 and so forth. An AutoIncrementStep property sets the increment value. The default value is 1, which is assigned in this case because the property value is not explicitly set.

A Unique property can be set to ensure that the values in each row are unique. The default value is false, so the values need not be unique and the rows cannot be uniquely identified. Therefore, the Unique property is set true with the statement

```
studentIDColumn.Unique = true;
```

```
private void Page_Load(object sender, System.EventArgs e)
{
                                                        ┌─────────────────────┐
     DataTable studentTable = new DataTable("Student");  │  Create DataTable   │
                                                        └─────────────────────┘
                                                        ┌─────────────────────┐
     DataColumn studentIDColumn = new DataColumn( );     │ Create DataColumn   │
                                                        └─────────────────────┘
     studentIDColumn.ColumnName = "StudentIDColumn";
     studentIDColumn.DataType = System.Type.GetType("System.Int32");
     studentIDColumn.AutoIncrement = true;
     studentIDColumn.AutoIncrementSeed = 1001;
     studentIDColumn.Unique = true;
     studentIDColumn.Caption = "ID";
                                            ┌─────────────────────┐
                                            │  Configure column   │
                                            └─────────────────────┘
                                                      ┌─────────────────────┐
     studentTable.Columns.Add(studentIDColumn);        │ Add column to table's│
                                                      │  column collection  │
                                                      └─────────────────────┘
     DataColumn lastNameColumn = new DataColumn("LastName");
     lastNameColumn.DataType = System.Type.GetType("System.String");
     lastNameColumn.MaxLength = 30;
     lastNameColumn.Caption = "Last";
     studentTable.Columns.Add(lastNameColumn);

     DataColumn firstNameColumn =
          new DataColumn("FirstName", System.Type.GetType("System.String"));
     firstNameColumn.MaxLength = 20;
     firstNameColumn.Caption = "First";
     studentTable.Columns.Add(firstNameColumn);

     DataColumn birthdateColumn = new DataColumn("Birthdate");
     birthdateColumn.DataType = System.Type.GetType("System.DateTime");
     studentTable.Columns.Add(birthdateColumn);

     try                                         ┌─────────────────────┐
     {                                           │ Create object array to│
          object[ ] objArray = new Object[4];     │ hold column values  │
                                                 └─────────────────────┘
          objArray[1] = "Vbaby";                 ┌─────────────────────┐
          objArray[2] = "Ann";                   │  Define column      │
          objArray[3] = new DateTime(1952,1,1);  │  values             │
                                                 └─────────────────────┘
          studentTable.Rows.Add(objArray);        ┌─────────────────────┐
                                                 │  Add row to table's │
          DataRow newRow = studentTable.NewRow(); │  row collection     │
          newRow[1] = "Bergen";                  └─────────────────────┘
          newRow[2] = "Ormand";
          newRow[3] = new DateTime(1935,3,25);
          studentTable.Rows.Add(newRow);
     }
     catch (Exception ex)
     {
          msg.Text = "Exception: " + ex.Message;
     }

     int i;
     int rowCount;

     rowCount = studentTable.Rows.Count;
     msg.Text = msg.Text + "INITIAL TABLE" + "<br>" +
          "Row count: " + rowCount + "<br>" ;

     for(i = 0; i < rowCount; i++)
     {
          msg.Text = msg.Text +
          studentTable.Rows[i][0].ToString() + ", " +
          studentTable.Rows[i][1].ToString() + ", " +
          studentTable.Rows[i][2].ToString() + ", " +
          studentTable.Rows[i][3].ToString() + ", " + "<br>" ;
     }
```

FIGURE 8.10B
Page_Load method of DataTable application (DataTableBasics\BasicTable.aspx.cs).

```
          DataTable cloneTable = studentTable.Clone();  ──────  ┌─────────────┐
                                                                 │ Clone table │
                                                                 └─────────────┘
      msg.Text = msg.Text + "CLONE TABLE" + "<br>" +
                 "Row count: " + cloneTable.Rows.Count + "<br>" ;


          object[ ] valuesArray = new Object[4];       ⎫       ┌──────────────┐
          valuesArray[1] = "Denna";                    ⎬       │ Create object│
          valuesArray[2] = "Alenda";                   ⎪       │ array of column│
          valuesArray[3] = new DateTime(1985,7,7);     ⎭       │ values       │
                                                               └──────────────┘


          studentTable.BeginLoadData();  ──────  ┌────────────────────┐
                                                  │ Begin loading table│
                                                  └────────────────────┘
      DataRow loadedRow =
              studentTable.LoadDataRow(valuesArray, true);

      studentTable.EndLoadData();


      rowCount = studentTable.Rows.Count;
      msg.Text = msg.Text + "AFTER DATA LOAD" + "<br>" +
                 "Row count: " + rowCount + "<br>" ;

      for(i = 0; i < rowCount; i++)
      {
              msg.Text = msg.Text +
                      studentTable.Rows[i][0].ToString() + ", " +
                      studentTable.Rows[i][1].ToString() + ", " +
                      studentTable.Rows[i][2].ToString() + ", " +
                      studentTable.Rows[i][3].ToString() + ", " + "<br>" ;
      }

      DataRow[ ] selectRows;
      string filterExpression = "Birthdate > '1/1/1950'";

      string sort = "LastName ASC";

      selectRows = studentTable.Select(filterExpression, sort);

      rowCount = selectRows.Length;
      msg.Text = msg.Text + "SELECT TABLE" + "<br>" +
                 "Row count: " + rowCount + "<br>" ;

      for(i = 0; i < rowCount; i++)
      {
              msg.Text = msg.Text +
                      selectRows[i][0].ToString() + ", " +
                      selectRows[i][1].ToString() + ", " +
                      selectRows[i][2].ToString() + ", " +
                      selectRows[i][3].ToString() + ", " + "<br>" ;
      }

  }
```

FIGURE 8.10B (CONTINUED)
Page_Load method of DataTable application (DataTableBasics\BasicTable.aspx.cs).

Reporting software will caption a column with the Caption property value if it exists. If the Caption property value is not set, the software generally uses the ColumnName property. Though meaningful to an application developer, the column name will often prove offputting to a report reader. For example, the application developer will use the term "studentID" where the words "student" and "ID" are concatenated without space; however, the report reader would, in most cases, be satisfied with a simple "ID."

The Caption property is set with the statement

```
studentIDColumn.Caption = "ID";
```

The studentIDColumn column is added to the table's column collection with the following statement

```
studentTable.Columns.Add(studentIDColumn);
```

where:

- The Columns property of the DataTable object returns the DataColumnCollection object of the table.
- The Add method of the DataColumnCollection class adds the specified column to the collection. Although the object referenced by studentIDColumn is added to the collection, the object is referenced in the collection by:
  - Index value, in this case 0, because it is the first object added to the collection
  - ColumnName property value — in this case, "StudentID"

Additional columns are created, configured and added to the column collection to define the structure of the table fully, i.e., the table's schema. For example, the statements

```
DataColumn lastNameColumn = new DataColumn("LastName");
lastNameColumn.DataType = System.Type.GetType("System.String");
lastNameColumn.MaxLength = 30;
lastNameColumn.Caption = "Last";
studentTable.Columns.Add(lastNameColumn);
```

define a column with name "LastName," string data type, a maximum text length of 30 characters, and caption "Last." Note that this constuctor version initializes the new DataColumn object and assigns the string parameter to the ColumnName property.

Similarly, the statements

```
DataColumn firstNameColumn = new
DataColumn("FirstName",System.Type.GetType("System.String"));
firstNameColumn.MaxLength = 20;
firstNameColumn.Caption = "First";
studentTable.Columns.Add(firstNameColumn);
```

create and define a column with name "FirstName," string data type, a maximum text length of 20 characters, and caption "First." Note that this constuctor version initializes the new DataColumn object and assigns the first parameter, a string parameter, to the ColumnName property and the second parameter, also a string data type, to the DataType property.

A DataColumn object with ColumnName property "Birthdate" is created and defined with the following statements

```
DataColumn birthdateColumn = new DataColumn("Birthdate");
birthdateColumn.DataType =
System.Type.GetType("System.DateTime");
studentTable.Columns.Add(birthdateColumn);
```

Note!

The DataColumn objects added to the DataTable objects' DataCollectionObject define the table's schema.

The table's DataRowCollection containing DataRow objects holds the table's data. A DataRow object represents each row in a table. A DataTable's Rows property gets the table's DataRowCollection; for example, the DataRowCollection object of the studentTable is accessed with the expression:

```
studentTable.Rows
```

The Add method of the DataRowCollection adds a DataRow to the collection with column values specified by the elements of an object array parameter. For example, an object array named objArray, is created with the statement:

```
object[] objArray = new Object[4];
```

The elements of the array, which will become the values of the corresponding column values, are set with the following statements:

```
objArray[1] = "Vbaby";
objArray[2] = "Ann";
objArray[3] = new DateTime(1952,1,1);
```

The element at index position 0 is null. The element at index position 1 is a string data type object with the value Vbaby. The element at index position 2 is also a string data type object with value Ann. The element at index position 3 is a DataTime data type object representing the date February 1, 1952, created and initialized with the expression

```
new DateTime(1952,1,1)
```

The elements of the array correspond to the column values of a Student table row, which are Auto incrementing integral, string, string, and DateTime data type values. Note that the value of the element corresponding to the auto incrementing column named StudentID, automatically assigned by the database manage system, is not specified. On the other hand, values for the elements corresponding to the columns named LastName, FirstName and Birthdate are explicitly stated.

The Add method of the DataRowCollection creates a DataRow and adds it to the collection. The version illustrated below creates a DataRow with values specified by an object array of values corresponding to the row's column values and adds it to the collection.

```
studentTable.Rows.Add(objArray);
```

A DataRow object is returned by the DataTable NewRow method. For example, the statement

```
DataRow newRow = studentTable.NewRow();
```

creates a new DataRow object referenced by newRow. The column values of the DataRow object are accessed with the Index property. Consequently, the column value at index position 1, LastName, is set with the following statement

```
newRow[1] = "Bergen";
```

Similarly, the column values at index positions 2 and 3, FirstName and Birthdate, are set with the statements

```
newRow[2] = "Ormand";
newRow[3] = new DateTime(1935,3,25);
```

Another version of the DataRowCollection Add method adds a specified DataRow to the collection

```
studentTable.Rows.Add(newRow);
```

In this case, the DataRow object referenced by newRow is added to the collection.

The addition of the DataRow objects to the DataRowCollection is typically performed within a try statement enabling the processing of any exceptions in a catch statement. Of particular concern is the attempted addition of a row with values conflicting with constraints.

Integral variables to serve as a row iteration index, i, and store the number of records in the table, rowCount, are declared with the statements:

```
int i;
int rowCount;
```

The rows collection in a table is accessed with the DataTable's Rows property. The number of rows in the collection is accessed with DataRowCollection's Count property. As such, the number of rows in the studentTable is given by the expression

```
studentTable.Rows.Count;
```

and is assigned to the variable rowCount.

The row count of the table, as initially constructed and loaded, is concatenated to the text of the Label control msg with the statement

```
msg.Text = msg.Text + "INITIAL TABLE" + "<br>" +
"Row count: " + rowCount + "<br>" ;
```

Again, the rows collection in a table is accessed with the DataTable's Rows property. A specific member of the collection is accessed with the DataRowCollection's Index property. Thus, the expression

```
StudentTable.Rows[i]
```

accesses the ith DataRow in the collection. When i is 1, the first DataRow object in the collection is accessed. Similarly, when i is 2, the second DataRow object in the collection is accessed. Note that elements in the Row collection are accessed with a zero-based index. Thus, the expression

```
studentTable.Rows[i][j]
```

accesses the object representing the jth column's value in the ith table row. For example,

```
studentTable.Rows[0][0]
```

accesses the object representing the first column, i.e., the StudentID, in the first row of the table. Similarly,

```
studentTable.Rows[1][3]
```

accesses the object representing the fourth column, i.e., the Birthdate, in the second row of the table.

Similarly, the following statements iterate through the rows of the studentTable and concatenate the values of each column's value to the msg Label control's Text property. All the column values for a row are placed in the same line and separated by commas:

```
for(i = 0; i < rowCount; i++)
    {
msg.Text = msg.Text +
studentTable.Rows[i][0].ToString() + ," " +
studentTable.Rows[i][1].ToString() + ," " +
studentTable.Rows[i][2].ToString() + ," " +
studentTable.Rows[i][3].ToString() + ," " + "<br>" ;
    }
```

The "for" loop iterates through the rows in the DataRowCollection. The iteration starts at i = 0 and terminates when the iteration index i approaches the total number of rows in the collection given by the RowsCollection property Count assigned to the variable rowCount:

```
i < rowCount
```

Note that the ToString method of the object representing the column's value is invoked to convert the value to its string representation.

The DataTable's Clone method can be used to return a clone of the invoking table. The clone has the structure of the invoking table, i.e., schema, relationships and constraints, but does not have the data contained in the invoking table. For example, the statement returns a clone of the studentTable and assigns it to the reference cloneTable:

```
DataTable cloneTable = studentTable.Clone();
```

The absence of data in the cloned table is verified by a zero value for the table's row count. The row count of the cloned table is added to the Text property of the msg Label control with the statement

```
msg.Text = msg.Text + "CLONE TABLE" + "<br>" +
"Row count: " + cloneTable.Rows.Count + "<br>" ;
```

The DataTable's LoadDataRow method looks for a specific table row. The row is specified by an object array parameter containing the row's column values. The method seeks to match element values specified in the object array with corresponding columns of the primary key. If a match is found, the existing row is updated with the values specified in the object array parameter. If no matching row is found, a new row is created and loaded with the values corresponding to the object array parameter elements. For example, an object array, valuesArray, is created and loaded with objects representing the LastName, FirstName and Birthdate columns:

```
object[] valuesArray = new Object[4];
valuesArray[1] = "Denna";
valuesArray[2] = "Alenda";
valuesArray[3] = new DateTime(1985,7,7);
```

Note that the first element of the array, corresponding to the value of the StudentID column value that is the primary key, has a null value. The LoadDataRow method is used in conjunction with the BeginLoadData and the EndLoadData methods. The DataTable's BeginLoadData method initiates loading and turns off the notification, index maintenance and constraints during loading. The EndLoadData method terminates loading and resumes notification, index maintenance and constraint enforcement. The following statements either update or create and insert a row in the studentTable with values specified in the valuesArray.

Text detailing the number of rows in the table and the values of each row after the loading is completed is added to the Text property of the msg Label control with the following statements:

```
rowCount = studentTable.Rows.Count;
msg.Text = msg.Text + "AFTER DATA LOAD" + "<br>" +
"Row count: " + rowCount + "<br>" ;
for(i = 0; i < rowCount; i++)
    {
msg.Text = msg.Text +
```

```
studentTable.Rows[i][0].ToString() + ,"  " +
studentTable.Rows[i][1].ToString() + ,"  " +
studentTable.Rows[i][2].ToString() + ,"  " +
studentTable.Rows[i][3].ToString() + ,"  " + "<br>" ;
    }
```

The DataTable's Select method returns DataTable object with rows of the invoking table. The rows contained in the returned DataTable object can be filtered, sorted and limited to a specific DataViewRow state enumeration member value by various versions of the select method — for example, creation of a DataTable object derived from the studentTable in which the returned rows meet the following criteria:

- Only rows in which the Birthdate value is greater than January, 1, 1950, as specified by the string object, filterExpression, defined as follows:
  ```
  string filterExpression = "Birthdate > '1/1/1950'";
  ```
  Note also that complex filter criteria involving multiple columns can be specified.
- The rows are sorted in ascending LastName order, as specified by the string object, sort,
  ```
  string sort = "LastName ASC";
  ```
- The rows would be sorted in descending LastName order with the specification
  ```
  string sort = "LastName DESC";
  ```
  Note also that complex sort criteria involving multiple columns can be specified.

A DataTable reference is declared with the statement
```
DataRow[] selectRows;
```
The DataTable Select method is called and returns a DataTable object, with rows from the studentTable sorted in LastName order where Birthdate is greater than January 1, 1950. The returned DataTable object is assigned to the reference selectRows:
```
selectRows = studentTable.Select(filterExpression, sort);
```
Again, text detailing the number of rows in the table and the values of each row, after calling the Select method, is added to the Text property of the msg Label control with the following statements:
```
rowCount = selectRows.Length;
msg.Text = msg.Text + "SELECT TABLE" + "<br>" +
"Row count: " + rowCount + "<br>" ;
for(i = 0; i < rowCount; i++)
    {
msg.Text = msg.Text +
selectRows[i][0].ToString() + ,"  " +
selectRows[i][1].ToString() + ,"  " +
selectRows[i][2].ToString() + ,"  " +
selectRows[i][3].ToString() + ,"  " + "<br>" ;
    }
```

Rows in a table's row collection can be removed with the following DataRowCollection methods:

- **Remove** removes a specified DataRow object from the collection
- **RemoveAt** removes the row at the specified index

For example, the second row in the DataRowCollection is removed with the statement

```
studentTable.Rows.RemoveAt(1);
```

The table's row count and row details are attached to the msg Label control's Text property with the following statements:

```
rowCount = selectRows.Length;
msg.Text = msg.Text + "SECOND ROW REMOVED FROM STUDENTTABLE" +
"<br>" +
"Row count: " + rowCount + "<br>" ;
for(i = 0; i < rowCount; i++)
    {
msg.Text = msg.Text +
selectRows[i][0].ToString() + ," " +
selectRows[i][1].ToString() + ," " +
selectRows[i][2].ToString() + ," " +
selectRows[i][3].ToString() + ," " + "<br>" ;
    }
```

The individual columns of the table's column collection can be accessed with the Data-ColumnCollection's Item property. For example, the expression

```
studentTable.Columns
```

evaluates the table's DataRowCollection and the DataRowCollection's Item property accesses the DataColumn element at a specific index location. That is,

```
studentTable.Columns[i]
```

refers to the ith DataColumn element of the DataRowCollection. Subsequently, the ColumnName property of the ith DataColumn element in the DataRowCollection is accessed by the statement

```
studentTable.Columns[i].ColumnName
```

The table's column information is added to the msg Label's Text property with the following statements:

```
msg.Text = msg.Text + "COLUMNS INFORMATION" + "<br>" ;
for (i = 0; i < studentTable.Columns.Count; i++)
    {
msg.Text = msg.Text +
studentTable.Columns[i].ColumnName + ," " +
studentTable.Columns[i].DataType + ," " +
studentTable.Columns[i].Caption + ," " +
studentTable.Columns[i].AutoIncrement + "<br>";
    }
```

Note that the number of DataColumn elements in the DataColumnCollection is accessed with the expression

```
studentTable.Columns.Count
```

The Web page displayed at the requesting browser is shown in Figure 8.10C.

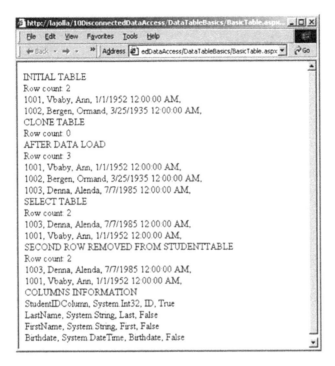

FIGURE 8.10C
Web page displayed at browser of DataTable application (DataTableBasics\BasicTable.aspx.cs).

9

Data Sets

DataSet Data Model

The **DataSet** object is a memory-resident database that provides a constant programming interface. The DataSet object model is shown in Figure 9.1.

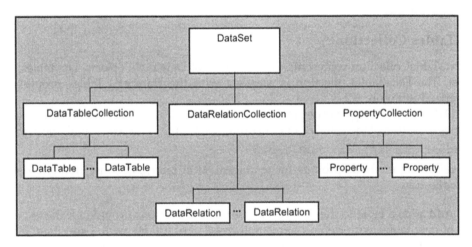

FIGURE 9.1
DataSet object model.

The primary components of the DataSet are the following:

- Data Table Collection: collection of DataTable objects representing the tables in the database
- Data Relations Collection: collection of DataRelation objects representing the relationship between the tables in the database
- Property Collection: collection of Property objects representing user information associated with the database

The DataSet models a relationship view of the data, including tables, their relationships and extended properties. New instances of a dataset are created with the constructor:

```
DataSet ContactDataSet = new DataSet("ContactDS");
```

where the argument is the dataset's name. An alternate constructor provides for creating a dataset without a name that can be assigned using the DataSet's **DataNameProperty**.

The DataSet is characterized by the properties of the DataSet class summarized below:

Property	Description
DataSetName	Gets or sets the name of the DataSet.
EnforceConstraints	Constraints are observed during update operations if set true and not observed if false. A ConstraintException is thrown when one or more constraints cannot be observed.
ExtendedProperties	Gets the ExtendedProperties, user information, associated with the dataset.
Relations	Gets the RelationshipCollection describing the relationship between the tables in the dataset.
Tables	Gets the TablesCollection.

Options for working with a DataSet include population of DataTables, DataRelations and Constraints programmatically, population with tables from an existing database using a DataAdapter, and population and persisting a database contents using XML.

Data Tables Collection

The DataTableCollection represents the collection of DataTable objects, i.e., tables, in the DataSet. The DataTableCollection is accessed with the DataSet's Tables property. It is summarized in Figure 9.2.

The DataSet's Tables property provides access to the DataTableCollection. For example, the tables collection of the DataSet studentAdministrationDS is accessed with the expression

```
studentAdministrationDS.Tables
```

The following methods provide for management of tables, i.e., insertion and deletion, in the collection:

- **Add** adds a table to the collection. Overloaded versions provide for the creation of new tables with default name and creation of a table with a specified Table-Name property, as well as the addition of a table with a specified reference.
- **Clear** removes all the tables in the collection.
- **Remove** removes a table from the collection. Overloaded versions provide for the removal of tables with a specified TableName property as well as for tables with a specified reference.
- **RemoveAt** removes a table at a specific position in the collection.

The existence of specific tables within the collection is facilitated with the following methods:

- **Contains** is used to determine if a DataTable object with a specified name or index exists in the collection.
- **Index** returns the relative position within the collection, i.e., the index, of a table with a specific name or reference.

These methods are used in conjunction with the Remove method.

Specific tables within the collection are accessed with the DataTableCollection Item property. For example, the first table in the data tables collection of the studentAdministrationDS DataSet is accessed with the expression

```
studentAdministrationDS.Tables[0]
```

public class **DataTableCollection** : InternalDataCollectionBase	
Hierarchy	
Object InternalDataCollectionBase DataTableCollection	
Public Instance Properties	
public DataTable **this**[int *index*] {get;}	Gets the DataTable object specified by the collection zero-based indexing value *index*.
public DataTable **this**[string *name*] {get;}	Gets the DataTable object with TableName property value *name*. The name search is not case-sensitive. A null is returned if the DataTable object is not found.
Public Instance Methods	
public virtual DataTable **Add**( );	Creates a new DataTable, with the default name Table*i* where *i* is a zero-based index reflecting relative order in the collection, and adds it to the collection. The created DataTable is returned by the method.
public virtual void **Add**(DataTable *table*);	Adds the DataTable object specified by the reference *table* to the collection.
public virtual DataTable **Add**(string *name*);	Creates a table with the TableName property value *name* and adds it to the collection. A default name is supplied if a null reference or an empty string argument is passed. The default name is Table*i* where *i* is a zero-based index reflecting relative order in the collection.
public virtual void **AddRange**(DataTable[ ] *table*);	Copies the DataTable objects in the DataTable array *tables* to the end of the collection.
public bool **CanRemove**(DataTable *table*);	Returns true if the DataTable object referenced by *name* table can be removed from the collection; false otherwise.
public void **Clear**( );	Clears the table collection of all DataTable members.
public bool **Contains**(string *name*);	Returns true if a DataTable with TableName property value *name* table exists in the collection; false otherwise.
Public Instance Methods	
public virtual int **IndexOf**(DataTable *table*);	Returns the index of the DataTable object referenced by *table* if it exists in the collection. The value −1 is returned if the specified object is not found.
public virtual int **IndexOf**(string *tableName*);	Returns the index of the DataTable object with the TableName property value *tableName* if it exists in the collection. The search comparison is not case sensitive. The value −1 is returned if the specified object is not found.
public void **Remove**(DataTable *table*);	Removes the DataTable object referenced by *table* if it exists in the collection.
public void **Remove**(string *tableName*);	Removes the DataTable object with the TableName property value *tableName* if it exists in the collection. The search comparison is not case sensitive. (*Not in Beta 2 documentation but verified.*) The value −1 is returned if the specified object is not found.
public void **RemoveAt**(int *index*);	Removes the DataTable object at the collection index position *index*.

FIGURE 9.2
DataTableCollection.

Similarly, the second table in the collection is accessed with the expression

```
studentAdministrationDS.Tables[1]
```

Note that the expression

```
studentAdministrationDS.Tables[n]
```

refers to a DataTable object and thus exposes all of the properties and methods of a DataTable object. For example, the TableName property of the first table in the student-AdministrationDS table collection is provided by the expression

```
studentAdministrationDS.Tables[0].TableName
```

Similarly, the expression

```
studentAdministrationDS.Tables[0].Columns
```

returns the columns collection and the expression

```
studentAdministrationDS.Tables[0].Rows
```

returns the rows collection of the first table in the studentAdministrationDS table collection. Note that the expression

```
studentAdministrationDS.Tables[0].Rows
```

references a DataRowCollection object and thus exposes its properties and methods, including the Item property. Thus, the expression

```
studentAdministrationDS.Tables[1].Rows[2]
```

references the third row in the second table in the DataTableCollection of the student-AdministrationDS DataSet. Note also that the expression represents a DataRow object and thus exposes its properties and methods.

Consequently, the expression

```
studentAdministrationDS.Tables[1].Rows[2][3]
```

refers to the object representing the value of the fourth column of the third row of the second table in the studentAdministrationDS DataSet. The expression exposes the properties and methods of the object. For example, if the object was of the DateTime type, then the expression

```
studentAdministrationDS.Tables[1].Rows[2][3].Year.ToString()
```

would reference the string equivalent of the year value.

Similarly, the expression

```
studentAdministrationDS.Tables[2].Columns
```

represents the DataColumnCollection of the third table in the studentAdministrationDS DataSet's DataTableCollection. Consequently, the expression

```
studentAdministrationDS.Tables[2].Columns.Count
```

evaluates to the number of columns in the table. In the same manner, the expression

```
studentAdministrationDS.Tables[2].Columns[0]
```

represents the first column of the third table in the studentAdministrationDS DataSet. As such, the expression references a DataColumn object and thus exposes its properties and methods. Accordingly,

```
studentAdministrationDS.Tables[2].Columns[0].ColumnName
```

represents the ColumnName property value of the column, and the expression

```
studentAdministrationDS.Tables[2].Columns[0].DataType
```

represents the column's DataType as a Type enumeration member.

public class **DataSet** : MarshalByValueComponent, IlistSource, IsupportInitialize, ISerializable	
Hierarchy	
Object	
MarshalByValueComponent	
DataSet	
Constructors	
public **DataSet**( );	Initializes a new instance of the DataSet class.
public **DataSet**(string *dataSetName*);	Initializes a new instance of the DataSet class and assigns *dataSetName* to the DataSetName property.
public **DataSet**(SerializationInfo *info*, StreamingContex contex);	Initializes a new instance of the DataSet class. Information to serialize or deserialize an object is specified by the SerializationInfo object *info*. The source and destination of the serialized stream is specified by the StreamingContex object *contex*.
Public Instance Properties	
public bool **CaseSensitive** {get; set;}	Gets or sets a value regarding string comparisons within the table. The value is true if the comparisons are case sensitive; false otherwise. The default value is false.
public string **DataSetName** {get; set;}	Gets or sets the name used as the name of the root element in an XML representation of the DataSet.
public DataViewManager **DefaultViewManager** {get;}	Gets the DataViewManager object enabling custom settings for each DataTable in the Dataset enabling filtering, searching and navigation.
public bool **EnforceConstraints** {get; set;}	Gets or sets a value determining enforcement of constraints in update operations. The value is true if the constraints are enforced; false otherwise. The default is true.
public PropertyCollection **ExtendedProperties** {get; set;}	Gets the collection of custom information.
public bool **HasErrors** {get;}	Gets a true value indicating the presence of errors in any of the rows in any of the tables in the DataSet; false otherwise.
public CultureInfo **Local** {get; set;}	Gets or sets a CultureInfo object that contains information about the user's machine locale that is used to compare strings during sorting. The default is a null reference.
public string **Namespace** {get; set;}	Gets or sets the namespace of the DataSet that is used when reading or writing an XML document.
public string **Prefix** {get; set;}	Gets or sets the XML prefix that aliases the DataSet's namespace.
public DataRelationCollection **Relations** {get;}	Gets the collection of relations linking tables in the DataSet. The value is null if no relations exist.
public override ISite **Site** {get; set;}	Gets or sets the ISite object for the DataSet that binds a component and container enabling communication between them and enabling management of the container's components.
public DataTableCollection **Tables** {get;}	Gets the collection of tables in the DataSet. The value is null if no tables exist.

FIGURE 9.3
DataSet.

Data Sets

DataSets are represented by the DataSet class, summarized in Figure 9.3. Properties and methods often used in data set management include the following:

Public Instance Methods	
public void **AcceptChanges** ( );	Commits all changes to the DataSet since loaded or the AcceptChanges method was called.
public void **BeginInit** ( );	Initiates initialization of DataSet.
public void **Clear** ( )	Removes all rows in all tables in the DataSet.
public DataSet **Clone** ( );	Returns a DataSet object with the structure of the invoking DataSet object including DataTable schemas, relations and constraints. Data is not included in the returned object.
public DataSet **Copy** ( );	Returns a copy of the invoking DataSet object including DataTable schemas, relations, constraints and data.
public void **EndInit** ( );	Terminates initialization started with the BeginInit method.
public DataSet **GetChanges** (DataRowState *rowStates*);	Returns a copy of the invoking DataSet object containing all changes since loaded or the AcceptChanges method was last called filtered by the DataRowState enumeration value *rowStates*.
public string **GetXml** ( );	Returns an XML representation of the data stored in the DataSet as a string.
public string **GetXmlSchema** ( );	Returns an XSD schema for the XML representation of the data stored in the DataSet as a string. (*Test of Beta 2 not successful.*)
public bool **HasChanges** ( );	Returns true if the DataSet has row changes including insertions, deletions and modifications; false otherwise.
public bool **HasChanges** ( ) DataRowState *rowState*);	Returns true if the DataSet has row changes including insertions, deletions and modifications filtered by the DataRowState enumeration value *rowState*; false otherwise.
public void **InferXmlSchema** (Stream *stream*, String[] *nsArray*);	Infers an XML schema into the DataSet where *stream* specifies the Stream object to read and *nsArray* specifies an array of namespace URI strings to be excluded from the schema inference.
public void **InferXmlSchema** (string *fileName*, String[ ] *nsArray*);	Infers an XML schema into the DataSet where *fileName* specifies the file to read and *nsArray* specifies an array of namespace URI strings to be excluded from the schema inference.
public void **InferXmlSchema** (TextReader *reader*, String[ ] *nsArray*);	Infers an XML schema into the DataSet where *reader* specifies the TextReader to read and *nsArray* specifies an array of namespace URI strings to be excluded from the schema inference.
public void **InferXmlSchema** (XmlReader *reader*, String[ ] *nsArray*);	Infers an XML schema into the DataSet where *reader* specifies the XmlReader to read and *nsArray* specifies an array of namespace URI strings to be excluded from the schema inference.
public virtual void **RejectChanges** ( );	Rolls back all changes to the DataSet since created or the AcceptChanges method of the DataSet was last called.

FIGURE 9.3 (CONTINUED)
DataSet.

CaseSensitive: The CaseSensitive property affects the sorting, searching and filtering operations performed in the table, DataTable objects, in the DataSet. The DataSet's CaseSensitive value is assigned by default to the CaseSensitive property of DataTable objects in the DataSet.

HasErrors: The HasErrors property has the value true if any of the rows in any of the tables in the DataSet have errors. If the DataSet has errors, the HasErrors property of the individual tables comprising the dataset is used to determine which tables have errors. The GetErrors method is then used to return an array of rows with errors.

Locale: The Locale property value of the Dataset is assigned by default to the Locale property of the DataTables in the DataSet.

Public Instance Methods	
public virtual void **Reset** ( );	Restores the DataSet to its original state.
public void **WriteXml** (Stream *stream*);	Writes the DataSet's schema and data to the Stream specified by *stream*.
public void **WriteXml** (string *fileName*);	Writes the DataSet's schema and data to the file specified by *fileName*.
public void **WriteXml** (TextWriter *writer*);	Writes the DataSet's schema and data using the TextWriter specified by *writer*.
public void **WriteXml** (XmlWriter *writer*);	Writes the DataSet's schema and data using the XmlWriter specified by *writer*.
public void **WriteXml** (Stream *stream* XmlWriteMode *mode*);	Writes the DataSet's schema and data to the Stream specified by *stream* with the XmlWriteMode enumeration value *mode*.
public void **WriteXml** (string *fileName* XmlWriteMode *mode*);	Writes the DataSet's schema and data to the file specified by *fileName* with the XmlWriteMode enumeration value *mode*.
public void **WriteXml** (TextWriter *writer* XmlWriteMode *mode*);	Writes the DataSet's schema and data using the TextWriter specified by *writer* with the XmlWriteMode enumeration value *mode*.
public void **WriteXml** (XmlWriter *writer* XmlWriteMode *mode*);	Writes the DataSet's schema and data using the XmlWriter specified by *writer* with the XmlWriteMode enumeration value *mode*.
public void **WriteXmlSchema**(Stream *stream*);	Writes the DataSet's schema as an XML schema to the Stream specified by *stream*.
public void **WriteXmlSchema**(string *fileName*);	Writes the DataSet's schema as an XML schema to the file specified by *fileName*.
public void **WriteXmlSchema**(TextWriter *writer*);	Writes the DataSet's schema as an XML schema using the TextWriter specified by *writer*.
public void **WriteXmlSchema**(XmlWriter *writer*);	Writes the DataSet's schema as an XML schema using the XmlWriter specified by *writer*.
Protected Instance Constructors	
public **DataSet**( );	Initializes a new instance of the DataSet class.
public **DataSet**(string *dataSetName*);	Initializes a new instance of the DataSet class and assigns *dataSetName* to the DataSetName property.
public **DataSet**(SerializationInfo *info*, StreamingContex context);	Initializes a new instance of the DataSet class. Information to serialize or deserialize an object is specified by the SerializationInfo object *info*. The source and destination of the serialized stream are specified by the StreamingContex object *contex*.

FIGURE 9.3 (CONTINUED)
DataSet.

Changes to the DataSet are committed with the AcceptChanges method. Furthermore, invoking the AcceptChanges method on the DataSet invokes the DataTable's AcceptChanges method on every table in the DataSet. Additionally, invoking the AcceptChanges method on each of the Dataset's tables invokes the AcceptChanges method of each row in the tables. Thus, invoking the AcceptChanges method on the DataSet invokes the AcceptChanges method on the components of the DataSet, i.e., tables and rows.

Programmatically Loading a DataSet

A DataSet's DataTables, DataRelations and Constraint can be populated programmatically. The application DataSetBasics provides an example of programmatic DataSet loading. Figure 9.4A illustrates the applications Web page BasicDataSet.aspx. The applications code-behind file is shown in Figure 9.4B.

```
<%@ Page language="c#" Codebehind="BasicDataSet.aspx.cs"
         AutoEventWireup="false" Inherits="DataSetBasics.BasicDataSet" %>
<HTML>
  <HEAD>
  </HEAD>
  <body MS_POSITIONING="GridLayout">

    <form id="BasicDataSet" method="post" runat="server">
          <asp:Label ID=msg Runat=server></asp:Label>
    </form>

  </body>
</HTML>
```

FIGURE 9.4A
DatasetBasics/BasicDataSet.aspx.

```
using System;
using System.Collections;
using System.ComponentModel;
using System.Data;
using System.Drawing;
using System.Web;
using System.Web.SessionState;
using System.Web.UI;
using System.Web.UI.WebControls;
using System.Web.UI.HtmlControls;

namespace DataSetBasics
{
    public class BasicDataSet : System.Web.UI.Page
    {
        protected System.Web.UI.WebControls.Label msg;

        DataSet studentAdministrationDS ;        ───── [ DataSet declaration ]

        public BasicDataSet()
        {
            Page.Init += new System.EventHandler(Page_Init);     [ Adding
        }                                                           tables to
                                                                    DataSet ]
        private void Page_Load(object sender, System.EventArgs e)
        {
            studentAdministrationDS = new DataSet("StudentAdministration");

            studentAdministrationDS.Tables.Add( CreateStudentTable() );
            studentAdministrationDS.Tables.Add( CreateContactTable() );

            DisplayTableRows("DATA - INITIAL LOAD");
            DisplayHasErrors("STATE AFTER INITIAL LOAD");      [ Committing
                                                                 DataSet
            studentAdministrationDS.AcceptChanges();            changes ]
            DisplayHasErrors("STATE AFTER AcceptChanges");

            ModifyStudentTableRow();
            DeleteStudentTableRow();          [ Adding, changing and deleting
            AddContactTableRows();              rows in DataSet's tables ]

            DisplayHasErrors("STATE AFTER CHANGES");
                                            [ DataSet declaration ]
            DataSet changesDS;

            changesDS =                 [ Extracting modified rows ]
                studentAdministrationDS.GetChanges(DataRowState.Modified);
            DisplayTableRows("MODIFIED DATA",changesDS);

            changesDS = studentAdministrationDS.GetChanges(DataRowState.Added);
            DisplayTableRows("ADDED DATA",changesDS);
            changesDS = studentAdministrationDS.GetChanges(DataRowState.Deleted);
            DisplayTableRows("DELETED DATA",changesDS);
                                              [ Write data and
            studentAdministrationDS.AcceptChanges();   schema to XML file ]
            DisplayHasErrors("STATE ");

            studentAdministrationDS.WriteXml("C://DB//StudentAdministrator.xml");
        }
```

FIGURE 9.4B
Code-behind file DataSetBasics/BasicDataSet.aspx.cs.

```
private void AddContactTableRows()
{
    object [] values = new object[4];

    values[1] = 1;
    values[2] = "Care, Joan";
    values[3] = "973 762 5465";
    studentAdministrationDS.Tables["Contact"].Rows.Add(values);
}

private DataTable CreateStudentTable()
{
    DataTable studentTable = new DataTable("Student");

    DataColumn dataColumn;
    dataColumn = new
        DataColumn("StudentID",System.Type.GetType("System.Int32"));
    dataColumn.AutoIncrement = true;
    dataColumn.Unique = true;
    studentTable.Columns.Add(dataColumn);
    dataColumn = new
        DataColumn("LastName",System.Type.GetType("System.String"));
    dataColumn.MaxLength = 30;
    studentTable.Columns.Add(dataColumn);
    dataColumn = new
        DataColumn("FirstName",System.Type.GetType("System.String"));
    dataColumn.MaxLength = 20;
    studentTable.Columns.Add(dataColumn);
    dataColumn = new
        DataColumn("Grade",System.Type.GetType("System.String"));
    dataColumn.MaxLength = 3;
    studentTable.Columns.Add(dataColumn);
    dataColumn = new
        DataColumn("Birthdate",System.Type.GetType("System.DateTime"));
    studentTable.Columns.Add(dataColumn);
    studentTable.PrimaryKey = new
        DataColumn[ ]{studentTable.Columns["StudentID"]};

    object [] values;
    values = new Object[5];
    values[1] = "Care";
    values[2] = "Helen";
    values[3] = "6";
    values[4] = new DateTime(1990,11,4);
    studentTable.Rows.Add(values);
    values = new Object[5];
    values[1] = "Dash";
    values[2] = "Thomas";
    values[3] = "6";
    values[4] = new DateTime(1990,9,4);
    studentTable.Rows.Add(values);

    return studentTable;
}
```

FIGURE 9.4B (CONTINUED)
Code-behind file DataSetBasics/BasicDataSet.aspx.cs.

A DataSet instance is created by invoking a DataSet constructor; for example,

```
DataSet studentAdministrationDS =
new DataSet("StudentAdministration");
```

In this case, the DataSet name is specified as "StudentAdministraton" by the optional argument. If the name is not specified, a default name, NewDataSet, is applied. Note that the name is required to ensure that any XML representation has a root element name. Another constructor option provides information needed to serialize or deserialize the DataSet.

Tables are added to the DataSet's table collection with the Add method. Assume that the CreateStudentTable method returns a DataTable object. The DataTable object returned by the CreateStudentTable method has the following characteristics:

```
    private DataTable CreateContactTable()
    {
        DataTable contactTable = new DataTable("Contact");

        DataColumn dataColumn;
        dataColumn = new
            DataColumn("ContactID",System.Type.GetType("System.Int32"));
        dataColumn.AutoIncrement = true;
        dataColumn.Unique = true;
        contactTable.Columns.Add(dataColumn);
        dataColumn = new
            DataColumn("StudentID",System.Type.GetType("System.Int32"));
        contactTable.Columns.Add(dataColumn);
        dataColumn = new
            DataColumn("Name",System.Type.GetType("System.String"));
        dataColumn.MaxLength = 50;
        contactTable.Columns.Add(dataColumn);
        dataColumn = new
            DataColumn("Telephone",System.Type.GetType("System.String"));
        dataColumn.MaxLength = 12;
        contactTable.Columns.Add(dataColumn);
        contactTable.PrimaryKey = new
            DataColumn[ ]{contactTable.Columns["ContactID"]};

        return contactTable;
    }

    private void DeleteStudentTableRow()
    {
        int studentTableIndex =
            studentAdministrationDS.Tables.IndexOf("Student");
        studentAdministrationDS.Tables[studentTableIndex].Rows[1].Delete();
    }

    private void DisplayHasErrors(string title )
    {
        msg.Text = msg.Text + title + "<br>";
        if (studentAdministrationDS.HasChanges(DataRowState.Added ))
            msg.Text = msg.Text + "State: Added" + "<br>";
        if (studentAdministrationDS.HasChanges(DataRowState.Deleted ))
            msg.Text = msg.Text + "State: Deleted" + "<br>";
        if (studentAdministrationDS.HasChanges(DataRowState.Detached ))
            msg.Text = msg.Text + "State: Detached" + "<br>";
        if (studentAdministrationDS.HasChanges(DataRowState.Modified ))
            msg.Text = msg.Text + "State: Modified" + "<br>";
        if (studentAdministrationDS.HasChanges(DataRowState.Unchanged ))
            msg.Text = msg.Text + "State: Unchanged" + "<br>";
    }
```

FIGURE 9.4B (CONTINUED)
Code-behind file DatasetBasics/BasicDataSet.aspx.cs.

- TableName property: Student
- Five columns:
  StudentID — AutoIncrement, Unique, Int32 data type
  LastName — String data type with MaxLength of 30 characters
  FirstName — String data type with MaxLength of 20 characters
  Grade — String data type with MaxLength of 3 characters
  Birthdate — DateTime data type
- Two data rows:
  1 Care   Helen   6   November 4, 1990
  2 Dash   Thomas   6   September 4, 1990

```
private void DisplayTableRows(string caption, DataSet dataSet)
{
    msg.Text = msg.Text + caption + "<br>";
    int noTables = dataSet.Tables.Count;
    for (int indexTable = 0; indexTable < noTables;indexTable++)
    {
        string tableName = dataSet.Tables[indexTable].TableName;
        int noCols = dataSet.Tables[indexTable].Columns.Count;
        int noRows = dataSet.Tables[indexTable].Rows.Count;
        msg.Text = msg.Text +
            "Table Name: " + tableName +
            " Columns: " + noCols +
            " Rows: " + noRows + "<br>";
        for (int indexRow = 0; indexRow < noRows; indexRow++)
        {
            if ( dataSet.Tables[indexTable].Rows[indexRow].RowState !=
                DataRowState.Deleted)
            {
                for (int columnIndex = 0; columnIndex < noCols; columnIndex++)
                {
                    msg.Text = msg.Text +
                        dataSet.Tables[indexTable].Rows[indexRow]
                            [columnIndex].ToString() + ", ";
                }
                msg.Text = msg.Text + "<br>";
            }
        }
    }
}

private void DisplayTableRows(string caption )
{
    msg.Text = msg.Text + caption + "<br>";
    int noTables = studentAdministrationDS.Tables.Count;
    for (int indexTable = 0; indexTable < noTables;indexTable++)
    {
        string tableNames =
            studentAdministrationDS.Tables[indexTable].TableName;
        int noCols =
            studentAdministrationDS.Tables[indexTable].Columns.Count;
        int noRows = studentAdministrationDS.Tables[indexTable].Rows.Count;
        msg.Text = msg.Text +
            "Table Names: " + tableNames +
            " Columns: " + noCols +
            " Rows: " + noRows + "<br>";
        for (int indexRow = 0; indexRow < noRows; indexRow++)
        {
            for (int columnIndex = 0; columnIndex < noCols; columnIndex++)
            {
                msg.Text = msg.Text +
                    studentAdministrationDS.Tables[indexTable].Rows[indexRow]
                        [columnIndex].ToString() + ", ";
            }
            msg.Text = msg.Text + "<br>";
        }
    }
}
```

FIGURE 9.4B (CONTINUED)
Code-behind file DatasetBasics/BasicDataSet.aspx.cs.

The table is added to DataSet's table collection with the statement

```
studentAdministrationDS.Tables.Add(CreateStudentTable());
```

where the expression

```
studentAdministrationDS.Tables
```

gets the DataSet's Tables property value that is the set's DataTableCollection object. The DataTableCollection's Add method is invoked with the reference of the table to be added as the parameter.

Similarly, assume that the method CreateContactTable returns a DataTable object representing the Contact table. The DataTable object returned by the CreateContactTable method has the following characteristics:

```
private void ModifyStudentTableRow()
{
    int studentTableIndex =
        studentAdministrationDS.Tables.IndexOf("Student");
    studentAdministrationDS.Tables[studentTableIndex].Rows[0][2] =
        "Linda";
}

private void Page_Init(object sender, EventArgs e)
{
    InitializeComponent();
}

#region Web Form Designer generated code
private void InitializeComponent()
{
    this.Load += new System.EventHandler(this.Page_Load);

}
#endregion

    }
}
```

FIGURE 9.4B (CONTINUED)
Code-behind file DatasetBasics/BasicDataSet.aspx.cs.

FIGURE 9.4C
Browser rendering of DatasetBasics/BasicDataSet.aspx.

- TableName: Contact
- Four columns:
  ContactID — AutoIncrement, Unique, Int32 data type
  StudentID — Int32 data type
  Name — String data type with MaxLength of 50 characters
  Telephone — String data type with MaxLength of 12 characters.

The Contact DataTable object returned does not have any data rows. The table is added to the studentAdministrationDS DataSet with the statement

```
studentAdministrationDS.Tables.Add(CreateContactTable());
```

After the tables are added, the DisplayTableRows method is called to display information regarding the tables comprising the DataSet. The information is displayed when the applications page is rendered in a browser (shown in Figure 9.4C). The method's single parameter serves as a caption line for the information displayed. The number of tables in the DataSet, represented by the integral variable noTables, is accessed with the DataTable-Collection's Count property in the statement

```
int noTables = studentAdministrationDS.Tables.Count;
```

A "for" loop is used to iterate through the tables in the DataSet's collection.

```
for (int indexTable = 0; indexTable < noTables;indexTable++)
{
}
```

The indexTable begins iterating at zero and increases by one in each iteration as long as it is less than noTables, i.e., the number of tables in the DataSet. Elements of the collection are accessed with a zero-based index.

A specific Table in the DataTableCollection is accessed with the collections Item property. As such, the statement

```
string tableNames =
studentAdministrationDS.Tables[indexTable].TableName;
```

accesses the TableName property of the Table in the collection with the index specified by indexTable.

Similarly, the DataColumnCollection of the Table in the collection with the index specified by indexTable is accessed with the statement

```
studentAdministrationDS.Tables[indexTable].Columns
```

The DataColumnCollection's Count property is accessed to ascertain the number of columns, noCols, in the table with the statement

```
int noCols =
studentAdministrationDS.Tables[indexTable].Columns.Count;
```

Similarly, the DataRowCollection's Count property is accessed to ascertain the number of rows in the table, noRows, with the statement

```
int noRows =
studentAdministrationDS.Tables[indexTable].Rows.Count;
```

These values are added to the text to be displayed with the following statements:

```
msg.Text = msg.Text +
"Table Names: " + tableNames +
" Columns: " + noCols +
" Rows: " + noRows + "<br>";
```

Within the loop iterating through the tables in the DataSet's table collection is the loop iterating through the rows of each table:

```
for (int indexRow = 0; indexRow < noRows; indexRow++)
{
}
```

In this loop, the table rows are indexed with the variable indexRow, which varies from 0, increasing by 1 in each iteration as long as the index is less than the number of rows in the table, noRows.

Within the loop iterating through the table rows is a loop that iterates through the columns in the row:

```
for (int columnIndex = 0; columnIndex < noCols; columnIndex++)
{
}
```

In this loop, the columns in each row are indexed with the variable columnIndex that varies from 0, increasing by 1 in each iteration as long as the index is less than the number of columns in the row, noCols. The value of each column is expressed with the expression

```
studentAdministrationDS.Tables[indexTable].Rows[indexRow][column
Index]
```

The expressions evaluation is broken down in Figure 9.5. The expression evaluates to the object representing the value in the column specified by columnIndex in the row specified by indexRow in the table specified by indexTable in the studentAdministrationDS DataSet. The object's ToString method converts the object's value to its string equivalent. Thus the statement

```
msg.Text = msg.Text +
studentAdministrationDS.Tables[indexTable].Rows[indexRow][column
Index].
ToString() + ," ";
```

appends each column's value to the information to be displayed as a comma-separated list.

The DataSet's HasChanges method returns true if the DataSet has new, modified or deleted rows since the DataSet was last loaded or the AcceptChanges method was last called; otherwise, the method returns false. Overloading provides for filtering the results by DataRowState enumeration values. For example,

```
studentAdministrationDS.HasChanges(DataRowState.Added)
```

returns true if the DataSet has added rows to its tables since last loaded or the AcceptChanges method was last called. The DisplayHasErrors method is called to list the type of changes to the DataSet with the following statements:

```
if (studentAdministrationDS.HasChanges(DataRowState.Added))
msg.Text = msg.Text + "State: Added" + "<br>";
if (studentAdministrationDS.HasChanges(DataRowState.Deleted))
msg.Text = msg.Text + "State: Deleted" + "<br>";
if (studentAdministrationDS.HasChanges(DataRowState.Detached))
msg.Text = msg.Text + "State: Detached" + "<br>";
if (studentAdministrationDS.HasChanges(DataRowState.Modified))
msg.Text = msg.Text + "State: Modified" + "<br>";
if (studentAdministrationDS.HasChanges(DataRowState.Unchanged))
msg.Text = msg.Text + "State: Unchanged" + "<br>";
```

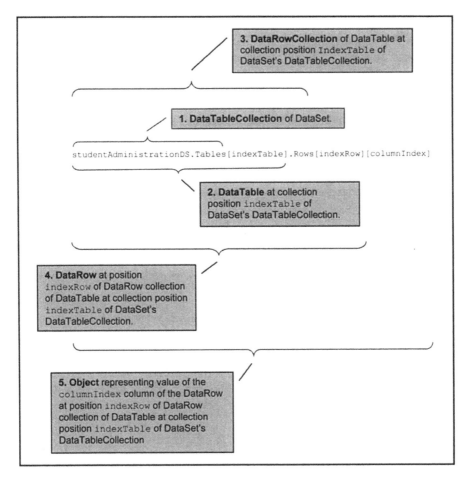

FIGURE 9.5
Evaluating an expression yielding the value of a specific column in a specific row in a specific table in a DataSet.

Whenever the HasChanges method returns true, the information to be displayed is appended with the type of change corresponding to the HasChanges parameter DataRowState enumeration value. The state after the initial load, consisting of the addition of the tables Student and Contact, corresponds to the DataRowState Added.

Changes to the DataSet, including the addition, modification and deletion of table rows, are managed with the following methods:

- **AcceptChanges** commits all changes since the DataSet was loaded or the last AcceptChanges was called. Invoking the AcceptChanges on the DataSet causes the AcceptChanges to be invoked on each table in the DataSet. In like fashion, the invocation of the AcceptChanges method on each DataTable causes the AcceptChanges to be invoked on each row in the DataTable. When the AcceptChanges method is called, rows in the Added or Modified state are changed to the Unchanged state and rows in the Deleted state are removed.

- **Clear** removes all rows in all tables.

- **HasChanges** returns a true value if the DataSet has new, modified or deleted rows.

- **RejectChanges** rolls back all changes to the DataSet since it was created or the last time the DataSet's AcceptChanges method was called.

The changes to the DataSet are committed by calling the AcceptChanges method

```
studentAdministrationDS.AcceptChanges();
```

After the AcceptChanges method is called, the state of the DataSet is Unchanged.

Tables in the DataSet can be manipulated bymodifying table schema (including the addition, modification and deletion of columns) and modifying table data (including the addition, modification and deletion of rows).

Consider the case in which the FirstName column value of the first row in the Student table is changed to the string Linda. First the index of the Student table in the DataSet's DataTableCollection is accessed with the following statement:

```
int studentTableIndex =

studentAdministrationDS.Tables.IndexOf("Student");
```

where the IndexOf method of theDataSet's DataTableCollection is used to access the position of the Student table in the collection. The index position is assigned to the variable studentTableIndex. The third column of the first row in the Student table is assigned the value Linda with the statement

```
studentAdministrationDS.Tables[studentTableIndex].Rows[0][2] =

"Linda";
```

Similarly, the second row of the Student table is deleted with the statement

```
studentAdministrationDS.Tables[studentTableIndex].Rows[1].Delete
();
```

An object array with values corresponding to row column values created and loaded with the following statements row is added to the Contact table with the following statements

```
object [] values = new object[4];
values[1] = 1;
values[2] = "Care, Joan";
values[3] = "973 762 5465";
```

The array element values corresponding to the table columns StudentID, Name and Telephone are assigned the values 1, Care, Joan and 973 762 5465, respectively. The Add method of the table in the DataRowCollection with the TableName property value Contact in the studentAdministrationDS DataSet's DataTableCollection is invoked with the statement

```
studentAdministrationDS.Tables["Contact"].Rows.Add(values);
```

where "values" is an object array with element values corresponding to the column values of the added row. A breakdown of the statement evaluation is shown in Figure 9.6.

After these changes, the HasChanges methods return true for the Added, Modified and Deleted DataRowState enumeration values.

The following methods provide for manipulation of the DataSet:

- **Clone**, which clones the structure of the DataSet including the schemas, relations and constraints
- **GetChanges**, which gets a copy of the DataSet since it was last loaded or the AcceptChanges method was last called. The method is overloaded and provides for filtering the changes by DataRowState.

A DataSet reference, changeDS, is declared with the statement

```
DataSet changesDS;
```

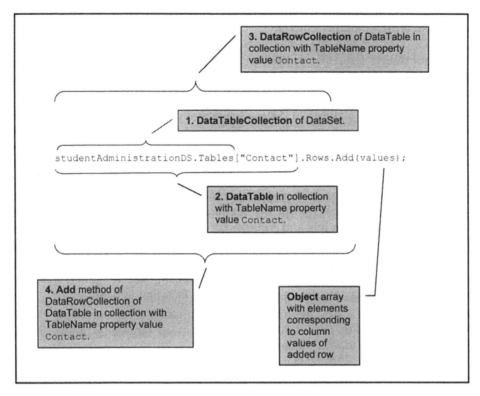

FIGURE 9.6
Adding a row to the Contact table in the studentAdministrationDS DataSet.

The DataSet's GetChanges method is called to return a copy of the DataSet containing only rows in the Modified state with the statement

```
changesDS =
studentAdministrationDS.GetChanges(DataRowState.Modified);
```

The returned copy is assigned to the reference changesDS. Information regarding the DataSet changesDS indicates the following:

- Student table — Rows: 1 Row Values: 0, Care, Linda, 6, 11/4/1990 12:00:00 AM
- Contact table — Rows: 0

The only row changed was the first row in the Student table. The DataSet returned by the GetChanges method contains the modified row values.

Similarly, the statement

```
changesDS =
studentAdministrationDS.GetChanges(DataRowState.Added);
```

returns a copy of the DataSet studentAdministrationDS containing only added rows, and the statement

```
changesDS =
studentAdministrationDS.GetChanges(DataRowState.Deleted);
```

returns a copy of the DataSet studentAdministrationDS containing only deleted rows. **Note, however, that rows marked Deleted cannot be accessed through the row.**

The DataSet has the following methods that facilitate coordination and use of industry-standard XML representations of data:

- **GetXml** returns the XML representation of the DataSet's data as a string.
- **GetXmlSchema** returns the XSD schema for the XML representation of the DataSet's data as a string.
- **ReadXml** reads the specified XML schema and data into the invoking DataSet. Overloaded versions provide for reading from various sources including streams, files, TextReaders and XmlReaders. Overloaded versions also provide for specifying how to read the XML data and schema with XmlReadMode enumeration members.
- **ReadXmlSchema** reads the specified XML schema into the invoking XSD DataSet. Overloaded versions provide for reading from various sources including streams, files, TextReaders and XmlReaders.
- **WriteXml** writes the XML schema and data from the invoking DataSet. Overloaded versions provide for writing to various targets including streams, files, TextReaders and XmlReaders. Overloaded versions also provide for specifying how to read the XML data and schema with XmlWriteMode enumeration members.
- **WriteXmlSchema** writes the XML schema and data from the invoking DataSet. Overloaded versions provide for writing to various targets including streams, files, TextReaders and XmlReaders.

The statement

```
studentAdministrationDS.WriteXml(
"C://DB//StudentAdministrator.xml");
```

writes an XML document representing the studentAdministrationDS DataSet's data and schema to the file named C://DB//StudentAdministrator.xml. The file's content is shown in Figure 9.7.

XML serialization provides for a format called DiffGram that includes the original and current data of an element as well as an identifier that associates the original and current versions. For example, an element that has been changed will appear twice in an XML document with DiffGram serialization. The first appearance represents the current data and is marked modified; a second represents the original data and is marked before.

The format used in reading and writing XML documents is specified by the XmlReadMode and XmlWriteMode enumerations, shown below. The XML document shown in

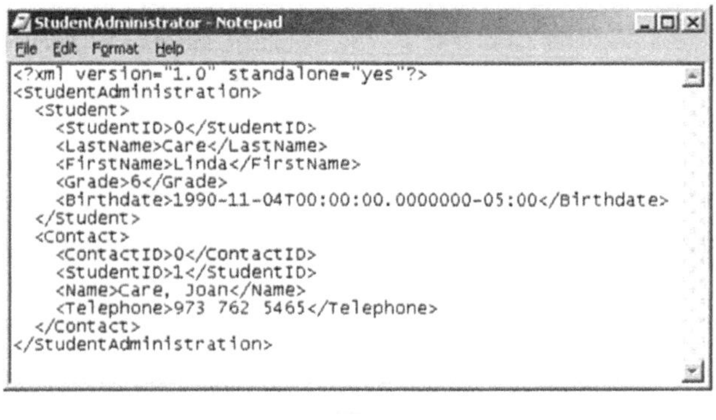


```
<?xml version="1.0" standalone="yes"?>
<StudentAdministration>
  <Student>
    <StudentID>0</StudentID>
    <LastName>Care</LastName>
    <FirstName>Linda</FirstName>
    <Grade>6</Grade>
    <Birthdate>1990-11-04T00:00:00.0000000-05:00</Birthdate>
  </Student>
  <Contact>
    <ContactID>0</ContactID>
    <StudentID>1</StudentID>
    <Name>Care, Joan</Name>
    <Telephone>973 762 5465</Telephone>
  </Contact>
</StudentAdministration>
```

FIGURE 9.7
Xml file written by application (DataSetBasics/BasicDataSet.aspx).

Figure 9.7 is written with the default WriteSchema mode in which the DataSet's contents are written as XML data and the relational structure as inline XSD schema. The XmlReadMode enumeration members specify how to read XML data and schema into a DataSet. Members of the enumeration are listed in Figure 9.8. The XmlWriteMode enumeration members specify how to write XML data and schema from a DataSet. Members of the enumeration are listed in Figure 9.9.

public enum XmlReadMode

Namespace: System.Data

Members

Name	Description
Auto	Performs one of the following as appropriate: Data is DiffGram The XmlReadMode is set to DiffGram DataSet has a schema or document has inline schema The XmlReadMode is set to ReadSchema DataSet does not have a schema and the document does not have an inline schema The XmlReadMode is set to InferSchema Auto is the Default XmlReadMode.
DiffGram	Read DiffGram applying changes from the DiffGram to the DataSet.
Fragment	Read XMl documents containing inline XDR schema fragments.
IgnoreSchema	Ignore any inline schema and read data into the existing DataSet schema. Data not matching the existing schema is discarded. If data is a DiffGram, the IgnoreSchema mode is the same functionally as the DiffGram mode.
InferSchema	Ignore any inline schema and infer schema from the data. If the DataSet has an existing schema, extend the existing schema by adding columns to existing tables and creating new tables where necessary to accommodate the data read.
ReadSchema	Read any inline schema and load data. Add new tables to the existing DataSet as required by the schema.

FIGURE 9.8
XmlReadMode enumeration.

public enum XmlWriteMode

Namespace: System.Data

Members

Name	Description
DiffGram	Writes the DataSet as a DiffGram including both the original and current values.
IgnoreSchema	Writes the current contents of the DataSet as XML data without an XSD schema. Nothing is written if the DataSet does not contain data.
InferSchema	Ignores any inline schema and infer schema from the data. If the DataSet has an existing schema, extend the existing schema by adding columns to existing tables and creating new tables where necessary to accommodate the data read.
WriteSchema	Writes the current contents of the dataset as XML data with the relational structure as an inline XSD schema. If the Dataset does not have any data only the inline schema is written. WriteSchema is the default mode.

FIGURE 9.9
XmlWriteMode enumeration.

After the initial load of the studentAdministrationDS DataSet and subsequent AcceptChanges method invocation, the following changes to the DataSet are made:

- The FirstName value in the first row of the Student table is changed to Linda.
- The second row, StudentID value of 1, is deleted from the Student table.
- A row is added to the Contact table.

Prior to invocation of the AcceptChanges method, the DataSet contains rows marked added, modified and deleted. The statement

```
studentAdministrationDS.WriteXml("C://DB//DataWithChanges.xml",
System.Data.XmlWriteMode.DiffGram);
```

writes the DataSet's data and schema to the file C://DB//DataWithChanges.xml in the DiffGram format. The file's content is shown in Figure 9.10.

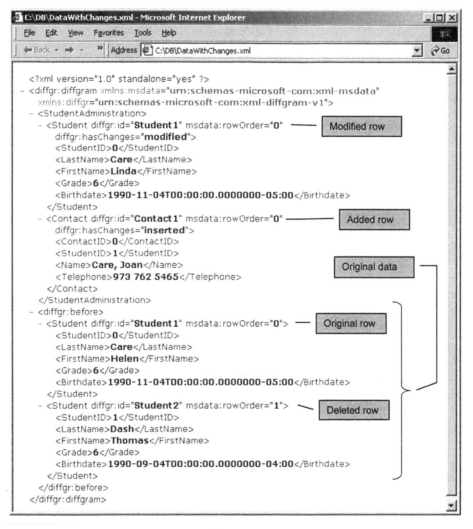

FIGURE 9.10
Xml file reflecting WriteXml with DiffGram XmlWriteMode.

Hands-On Exercise: Using the DataSet

1. Create and open an ASP.NET Web application named UsingDataSets in location http://LAJOLLA/11DisconnectedDataAccess.
2. In the Solution Explorer, delete WebForm1.aspx.
3. In Solution Explorer, add Web Form UseDataSet.aspx
4. Open the Toolbox; press the Ctrl+Alt+X key combination.
5. In the Toolbox, click the Data tab.
6. Drag a DataSet onto the UseDataSet.aspx page in the Designer window. The Add Dataset dialog box opens.
7. Check the Untyped dataset radio button.

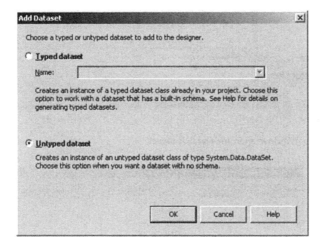

FIGURE HO9.1
Add DataSet dialog.

8. Click the OK button. The Add Dataset dialog box closes and the Designer gains focus. The DataSet control is displayed on the page.
9. Close the Toolbox.
10. Press F4 to open the Properties window.
11. Click the DataSet control in the Designer window.
12. Press F4 to open the Properties window.
13. Change the Name property value to AdministrationDS.
14. Click the ... at the right side of the Tables property to open the Tables Collection Editor.
15. Click the Add button.
16. A table is added to the collection. Change TableName property value to Student in the Properties pane of the Table Collection Editor. The (Name) entry in the Design section of the Properties pane is the name of the DataTable object declared by the Visual Studio.NET Designer and will appear in the code-behind file as

```
protected System.Data.DataTable dataTable1;
```

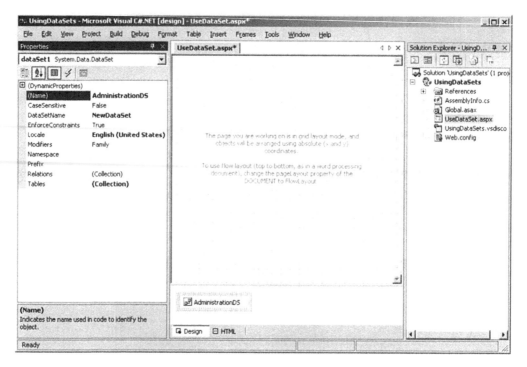

FIGURE HO9.2
Designer with Properties Window open for DataSet object.

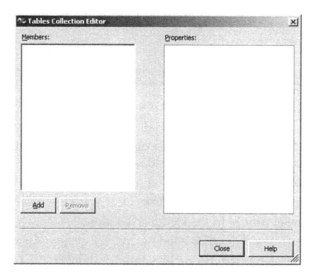

FIGURE HO9.3
Tables Collection Editor dialog.

Subsequent tables will be given the default name dataTable2, dataTable3 and so on. Good programming practice calls for assigning a meaningful name, for example, studentTable or studentTab. Enter studentTab in the (Name) box of the Design section of the Properties pane. The DataTable object will be declared with the name studentTab with the following statement:

```
protected System.Data.DataTable studentTab;
```

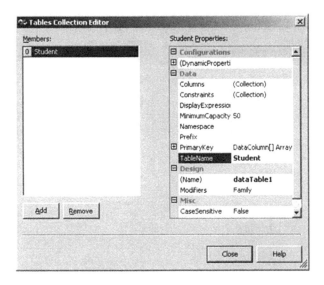

FIGURE HO9.4
Tables Collection Editor dialog with Student table added.

17. Click the ... at the right side of the Columns property in the Properties pane. The Column Collection Editor opens.

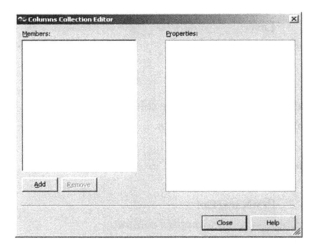

FIGURE HO9.5
Columns Collection Editor dialog.

18. Click the Add button to add a column to the table's column collection.

19. Assign the following property values:

AutoIncrement	**True**
Caption	**ID**
ColumnName	**StudentID** (replacing the default Column1)
DataType	**System.Int32** (replacing the default String)
Unique	**True**
(Name)	**studentIDCol**

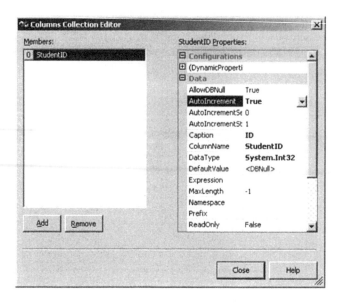

FIGURE HO9.6
Columns Collection Editor dialog with StudentID column added.

20. Click the Add button to add another column.
21. Assign the following property values:

Caption	**Last**
ColumnName	**LastName**
MaxLength	**30**
(Name)	**lastNameCol**

22. Click the Add button to add another column.
23. Assign the following property values:

Caption	**First**
ColumnName	**FirstName**
MaxLength	**20**
(Name)	**firstNameCol**

24. Click the Add button to add another column.
25. Assign the following property values:

Caption	**Grade**
ColumnName	**Grade**
MaxLength	**50**
(Name)	**gradeCol**

26. Click the Add button to add another column.
27. Assign the following property values:

Caption	**Birthdate**
ColumnName	**Birthdate**
DataType	**System.DateTime**
(Name)	**birthdateCol**

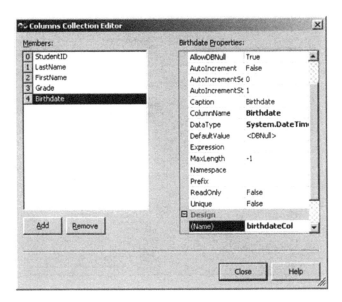

FIGURE HO9.7
Columns Collection Editor dialog with Student table's columns added.

28. Click the Close button. The Columns Collection Editor closes and the Tables Collection Editor regains the focus.

29. Click the down arrow at the right side of the PrimaryKey property to expose the Student table's columns.

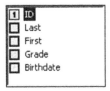

FIGURE HO9.8
Primary Key field selection list.

30. Click the ID column. The number 1 is entered, indicating that the ID is the first column of a multiple column key. In this case, the primary key is a single column: ID. Press the Enter key to close the list.

31. Click the + sign at the left side of the PrimaryKey property label to expand the PropertyKey value.

32. Click the Add button in the Tables Collection Editor to add another table to the collection. In the left pane, another table is added to the collection and the new table's properties are displayed in the right pane.

33. Change the table's TableName property value to Contact. Change the (Name) value in the Design section to contactTab.

34. Click the Enter key.

35. Click the ... at the right side of the Columns property box to open the Columns Collection Editor.

36. Click the Add button to add a column to the table's column collection.

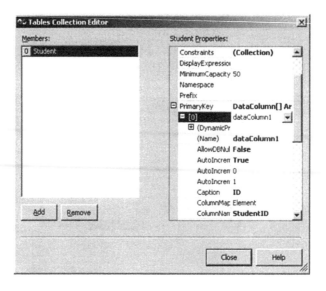

FIGURE HO9.9
Tables Collection Editor PrimaryKey property key values.

37. Assign the following property values:

    AutoIncrement   **True**
    Caption   **ID**
    ColumnName   **ContactID** (replacing the default Column1)
    DataType   **System.Int32** (replacing the default String)
    Unique   **True**
    (Name)   **contactIDCol**

38. Click the Add button to add another column.

39. Assign the following property values:

    Caption   **Student ID**
    ColumnName   **StudentID**
    DataType   **System.Int32** (Replacing the default String)
    (Name)   **studentIDCol**

40. Click the Add button to add another column.

41. Assign the following property values:

    Caption   **Name**
    ColumnName   **Name**
    MaxLength   **50**
    (Name)   **nameCol**

42. Click the Add button to add another column.

43. Assign the following property values:

    Caption   **Telephone**
    ColumnName   **Telephone**
    MaxLength   **12**
    (Name)   **telephoneCol**

44. Click the Close button. The Columns Collection Editor closes and the Tables Collection Editor regains the focus. If the Contact table in the left pane does not have focus, click the Contact table.

45. Click the down arrow at the right side of the PrimaryKey property to expose the Student table's columns.

46. Click the ID check box. Press the Enter key to accept the selection and close the list.

47. Click the Close button to close the Tables Collection Editor.

48. Close the Properties window.

49. In the View menu, select the Code option to open the code-behind file Use-DataSet.aspx.cs. Note the declaration of the DataSet, DataTable and DataColumn references and the code written by the Visual Studio.NET Designer in the InitializeComponent method.

50. Add the following statement to the Page_Load method:

    ```
    AdministrationDS.WriteXmlSchema("C://DB//AdministrationDS.xml");
    ```

51. Set the UseDataSet.aspx page as the application's start page.

52. Run the application.

53. Open the file C:\DB\AdministrationDS.xml. The file contains an Xml description of the DataSet's schema.

FIGURE HO9.10
XSD Schema.

10

Data Adapter and Disconnected Data Access

DataAdapter Bridge Model

The **DataAdapter** serves as a bridge between the data source and the DataSet. The bridge is conceptually shown in Figure 10.1.

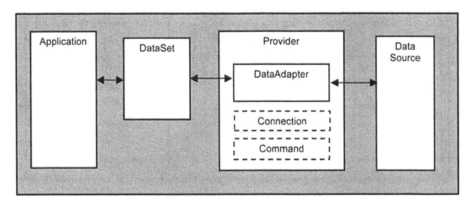

FIGURE 10.1
DataAdapter bridges the data source and DataSet.

The following DataAdapter methods provide the bridge foundation:

- **Fill** changes the data in the DataSet to match the data in the data source.
- **Update** changes the data in the data source to match the data in the DataSet.

The determination of which data in the data source correspond to which data in the data set is based on the DataAdapter's table mapping. The table mapping specifies which data source table's data, returned by the query against the data source in a Fill action, are used to insert or refresh rows in which dataset table. Similarly, the table mapping specifies which table's row additions, modifications and deletions in the data set are applied to which table in the data source in an Update action. In fact, a data table mapping is a master mapping used to define how data are transferred between tables in the data source and data set.
Properties of the table mapping include the following:

- **SourceTable**: name of the table in the data source
- **DatasetTable**: name of the table in the DataSet
- **ColumnMapping**: collection of DataColumnMapping objects describing the association of columns in the DataSet table with columns in the data source table

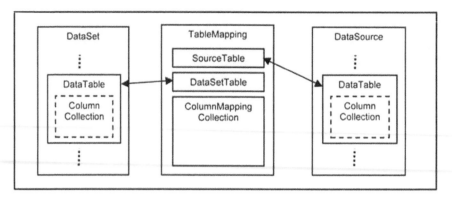

FIGURE 10.2
Table mapping model.

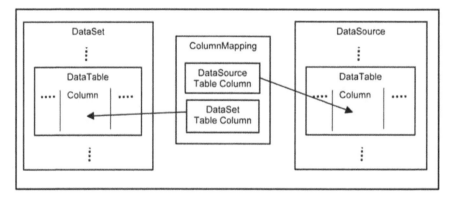

FIGURE 10.3
Column mapping model.

Each table mapping object maps a table in the data source to a table in the dataset. The model concept is shown in Figure 10.2. In the same fashion, each table mapping object contains a collection of column mapping objects that map the data source table's columns to the corresponding dataset table's columns. Figure 10.3 shows the column mapping model concept.

A column mapping is represented by the ColumnMapping object. The .NET Framework provides two DataAdapters:

- **OleDataAdapter** is used for connection to OLE DB-supported databases such as Access and Oracle. The OleDataAdapter is used in conjunction with OleDb-Connection and OleDbCommand.
- **SqlDataAdapter** is used for connection to the Microsoft SQL Server database in conjunction with SqlConnection and SqlCommand.

Characterizing Data Adapter Actions

The actions to be performed to change the schema of the DataSet when the schema of the DataSet does not match the schema of the incoming data are characterized by the members

public enum MissingSchemaActon	
Namespace: System.Data	
Members	
Name	**Description**
Add	Add necessary columns required to complete schema.
AddWithKey	Add necessary columns and primary key information required to complete schema.
Error	Raise a SystemException indicating a nonfatal recoverable error.
Ignore	Ignore extra columns.

FIGURE 10.4
MissingSchemaAction enumeration.

public enum MissingMappingActon	
Namespace: System.Data	
Members	
Name	**Description**
Error	Raise a SystemException indicating a nonfatal recoverable error.
Ignore	Ignore columns or tables that do not have a mapping.
Passthrough	Add the source column or table to the DataSet using its original name.

FIGURE 10.5
MissingMappingAction enumeration.

of the **MissingSchemaAction** enumeration, as shown in Figure 10.4. Similarly, the actions to be performed when a mapping is missing a source table or a source column are characterized by the members of the **MissingMappingAction** enumeration (Figure 10.5).

A **DataTableMapping** is a master mapping between the data returned from a data source query and a DataTable. The TableMapping name can be used in place of the DataTable name when the DataAdapter's fill method is called to populate a DataSet. Properties of the mapping provide the following:

- **SourceTable**: name of the table in the data source
- **DatasetTable**: name of the table in the DataSet
- **ColumnMapping**: collection of DataColumnMapping objects describing the association of columns in the DataSet table with columns in the data source table

---

Implementing Table Mappings

The data column mapping object enables the use of column names in the DataSet different from those in the data source. The DataColumnMapping class represents data column mapping; it is summarized in Figure 10.6.

Properties providing for mapping from a column in the data source to a column in the DataSet include:

- **SourceColumn**: name of the column in the data source to map from
- **DatasetColumn**: name of the column to which to map in the DataSet
- **ColumnMapping**: collection of DataColumnMapping objects describing the association of columns in the DataSet table with columns in the data source table

public sealed class **DataTableMapping** : MarshalByRefObject, ITableMapping, ICloneable	
Hierarchy	

Object
  MarshalByRefObject
    DataTableMapping	

Public Instance Constructors	
public **DataTableMapping** ( );	Initializes a new instance of the class setting all fields to default values.

public **DataTableMapping** (
  string *sourceTable*,
  string *dataSetTable*);
	Initializes a new instance of the class. The SourceTable property is assigned the value *sourceTable* and the DatasetTable is assigned the value *dataSetTable*. The SourceTable property value is case sensitive.

public **DataTableMapping** (
  string *sourceTable*,
  string *dataSetTable*
  DataColumnMapping[] *columnMappings*);
	Initializes a new instance of the class. The SourceTable property is assigned the value *sourceTable*, the DatasetTable is assigned the value *dataSetTable* and the ColumnsMappings property is assigned the array of ColumnMapping objects *columnMappings*. The SourceTable property value is case sensitive.

Public Instance Properties	
public DataColumnMappingCollection **ColumnMappings** {get;}	Gets the collection of DataColumnMapping objects.
public string **DataSetTable** {get; set;}	Gets or sets the DataSet table name.
public string **SourcetTable** {get; set;}	Gets or sets the data source table name. The SourceTable value is case sensitive.
Public Instance Methods	

public DataColumnMapping
  GetColumnMappingBySchemaAction (
  String *sourceColumn*,
  MissingMappingAction *mappingAction*);
	Returns a DataColumn with the name *sourceColumn* using the specified MissingMappingAction enumeration member value *mappingAction*.

public DataTable
  GetDataTableBySchemaAction (
  DataSet *dataSet*,
  MissingSchemaAction *schemaAction*);
	Returns the current DataTable for the DataSet *dataSet* using the specified MissingSchemaAction enumeration member value *schemaAction*.

FIGURE 10.6
DataTableMapping class summary.

The collection of DataColumnMapping objects describing the column mappings of a table is accessed as the TableMapping object's ColumnMapping property. The objects are represented by the DataColumnMapping class (Figure 10.7). The collection is represented by the DataColumnMappingCollection class shown in Figure 10.8.

The following methods enable management of the DataColumnMapping objects in the collection:

- **Add** adds a DataColumnMapping object to the collection.
- **Clear** removes all the DataColumnMapping objects in the collection.
- **IndexOf** returns the position of a specific DataColumnMapping object in the collection.
- **Remove** removes a specific DataColumnMapping object from the collection.
- **RemoveAt** returns the DataColumnMapping object at a specified position or with a specified data source column name from the collection.

A DataAdapter contains a collection of zero or more named TableMappings. It uses the DataTableMappingCollection when reconciling changes to associate column names in the data source with column names in the DataSet. How schema mappings are handled when

public sealed class **DataColumnMapping** : MarshalByRefObject, IColumnMapping, ICloneable	
Hierarchy	

Object
  MarshalByRefObject
    DataColumnMapping	

Public Instance Constructors	
public **DataColumnMapping** ( );	Initializes a new instance of the class setting all fields to default values.

public **DataColumnMapping** (
  string *sourceColumn*,
  string *dataSetColumn*);
	Initializes a new instance of the class. The SourceColumn property is assigned the value *sourceColumn* and the DatasetColumn is assigned the value *dataSetColumn*.

Public Instance Properties	
public string **DataSetColumn** {get; set;}	Gets or sets the name of the column in the DataSet to map to. The name is not case sensitive.
public string **SourceColumn** {get; set;}	Gets or sets the name of the column in the data source to map from. The name is case sensitive.
Public Instance Methods	

public DataColumn
  GetDataColumnBySchemaAction (
  DataTable *dataTable*,
  Type *dataType*,
  MissingSchemaAction *schemaAction*);
	Returns a DataColumn from the DataTable specified by *dataTable* of the Type specified by dataType using the action specified by the MissingSchemaAction enumeration member value *schemaAction*.

public override string **ToString** ( );	Returns the current SourceColumn name.

FIGURE 10.7
DataColumnMapping class summary.

a DataAdapter fills a DataSet — with the FillSchema method, for example — is specified by the members of the SchemaType ennumeration, Figure 10.9.

Implementing the Data Adapter

The OleDbDataAdapter class is summarized in Figure 10.10.
A data adapter is used to implement disconnected data access in application DataAdapterTableMapping. The application's Web page, UseTableMapping.aspx, is shown in Figure 10.11A; its code-behind file is shown in Figure 10.11B.

Functionality of the System.Data.OleDB namespace is exposed with the statement

```
using System.Data.OleDb;
```

The statement System.Data.Common exposes the mapping classes:

```
using System.Data.Common;
```

The data adapter associates with tables in a data set created with the statement

```
DataSet dataSet = new DataSet();
```

A data adapter object is created with the statement

```
OleDbDataAdapter dataAdapter =
new OleDbDataAdapter(cmdText, connection);
```

In this constructor version, the parameters specify the SQL statement text of the SelectCommand property and the connection string used to implement a connection to the data

public sealed class **DataColumnMappingCollection** : MarshalByRefObject, IColumnMappingCollection, IList, Icollection, IEnumerable

Hierarchy

Object
   MarshalByRefObject
      DataColumnMappingConnection

Public Static Methods

public static DataColumnMapping **getColumnMappingBySchemaAction** (DataColumnMappingCollection *collection*, string *sourceColumn*, MissingMappingAction *mappingAction*);	Returns the DataColumnMapping in the DataColumnMappingCollection specified by *collection* and data source column name *sourceColumn* and the action specified by the MissingMappingAction enumeration member value *mappingAction*.

Public Instance Constructor

public **DataColumnMappingCollection** ( );	Initializes a new instance of the class setting all fields to default values.

Public Instance Properties

public int **Count** {get;}	Gets the number of DataColumnMapping objects in the collection.
public DataColumnMapping **this** [int *index*] {get; set;}	Gets or sets the DataColumnMapping object at the collection position specified by *index*.
public DataColumnMapping **this** [string *sourceColumn*] {get; set;}	Gets or sets the DataColumnMapping object in the collection with the SourceColumn property value *sourceColumn*. The SourceColumn name is case sensitive.

Public Instance Methods

public int **Add** (object *value*);	Adds the object value to the collection and returns the index position of the added object.
public DataColumnMapping **Add** (string *sourceColumn* string *dataSetColumn*);	Adds a column mapping to the collection with the data source column name mapped from specified by *sourceColumn* and the DataSet column name mapped to specified by *dataSetColumn*. The method returns the DataColumnMapping added to the collection. Note that the *sourceColumn* is case sensitive and *dataSetColumn* is not case sensitive.
public void **AddRange** (DataColumnMapping [ ] *value*);	Adds the DataColumnMapping elements of the array *value* to the end of the collection.
public void **Clear** ( );	Removes all the DataColumnMapping objects in the collection.
public bool **Contains** (object *mappingObject*);	Returns true if the DataColumnMapping object *mappingObject* is in the collection; false otherwise.
public bool **Contains** (string *sourceColumn*);	Returns true if the DataColumnMapping object with the case-sensitive SourceColumn property value *sourceColumn* is in the collection; false otherwise.

FIGURE 10.8
DataColumnMappingCollection class summary.

source. Note that the SelectCommand, InsertCommand, DeleteCommand and Update-Command properties are OleDbCommand objects that include a connection property specifying a data source. These properties are used during data adapter operations involving the data source. If the connection is not opened, it is opened when the operation commences and closed when the operation is completed. If the connection is open before the data adapter operation begins, it must be explicitly closed with an explicit Close method call or an explicit Dispose method call, following completion of the data adapter operation.

Public Instance Methods	
public void **CopyTo** (Array *array*, int *index*);	Copies the elements of the collection to the Array object *array* starting at the array position *index*.
public DataColumnMapping **GetByDataSetColumn** (string *dataSetColumn*);	Returns the DataColumnMapping object with the DataSetColumn property value *dataSetColumn*.
public int **IndexOf** (object *mappingObject*);	Returns the index of the DataColumnMapping object *mappingObject* in the collection.
public int **IndexOf** (string *sourceColumn*);	Returns the index of the DataColumnMapping object with the case-sensitive SourceColumn value *sourceColumn*.
public int **IndexOfDataSetColumn** (string *dataSetColumn*);	Returns the index of the DataColumnMapping object with the DataSetColumn property value *dataSetColumn*. −1 is returned if the DataColumnMapping does not exist in the collection.
public void **Insert** (int *index*, object *mappingObject*);	Inserts the DataColumnMapping object *mappingObject* into the collection at the position specified by *index*.
public void **Remove** (object *mappingObject*);	Removes the DataColumnMapping object *mappingObject* from the collection.
public void **RemoveAt** (int *index*);	Removes the DataColumnMapping object at the index position *index* from the collection.
public void **RemoveAt** (string *sourceColumn*);	Removes the DataColumnMapping object with the case-sensitive SourceColumn property value *sourceColumn* from the collection.

FIGURE 10.8 (CONTINUED)
DataColumnMappingCollection class summary.

public enum SchemaType	
Namespace: System.Data	
Members	
Name	**Description**
Mapped	Apply existing table mappings to the incoming schema. Configure the DataSet with the transformed schema.
Source	Ignore any table mappings on the DataAdapter. Configure the DataSet using the incoming schema without applying any transformations.

FIGURE 10.9
SchemaType enumeration.

These properties are summarized below:

Property	Description

DeleteCommand	Gets or sets the OleDbCommand used during Update to delete rows in the data source corresponding to deleted rows in the DataSet. For example, the CommandText property of the OleDbCommand object is set to a statement of the fashion such as
	
	`dataAdapter.DeleteCommand.CommandText =`
	
	`"DELETE FROM Student WHERE StudentID = 21";`

InsertCommand	Gets or sets the OleDbCommand used during Update to insert rows in the data source corresponding to inserted rows in the DataSet. For example, the CommandText property of the OleDbCommand object is set to a statement of the fashion
	
	`dataAdapter.DeleteCommand.CommandText = "INSERT INTO Student`
	`('LastName',...`
	
	`'EnglishProficiencyCd')`
	
	`VALUES ('SomeLastName',... 2)";`

Property	Description
SelectCommand	Gets or sets the OleDbCommand used during Fill to return rows from the data source. For example, the CommandText property of the OleDbCommand object is set to a statement such as `dataAdapter.SelectCommand.CommandText = "SELECT * FROM Student";`

UpdateCommand	Gets or sets the OleDbCommand used during Update to update rows in the data source corresponding to modified rows in the DataSet. For example, the CommandText property of the OleDbCommand object is set to a statement such as
	
	`dataAdapter.UpdateCommand.CommandText =`
	
	`"UPDATE Student`
	
	`SET 'LastName' = 'SomeOtherLastName'`
	
	`WHERE StudentID = 21";`

During initialization, the following data adapter property values are assigned:

Property	Initial Value
MissingMappingAction	MissingMappingAction.Passthrough
MissingSchemaAction	MissingSchemaAction.Add
DeleteCommand	null
InsertCommand	null
SelectCommand	null if default constructor is used; otherwise, reflecting the command values passed as parameters in the constructor call
UpdateCommand	null

The data adapter's TableMapping property accesses a collection of DataTableMapping objects that are added to the collection with the collection's Add method:

```
DataTableMapping studentTM =
dataAdapter.TableMappings.Add("Student","StudentDS");
```

The Add method version shown has two parameters. The first is a string specifying the data source table, in this case Student. The second parameter is a string specifying the dataset table, in this case StudentDS. The Add method returns a reference to the DataTableMapping object added to the collection, which is assigned to studentTM. An alternate version of the Add method passes a DataTableMapping object parameter.

The table mappings are displayed as the Web page's msg control Text property by the DisplayTableMapping method. First, the number of mappings in the collection is determined with the expression

```
dataAdapter.TableMappings.Count
```

A loop starting with zero, corresponding to the first mapping in the collection and iterating as long as the iterator (in this case i) is less than the number of mappings in the collection, is represented by the statement

```
for(int i = 0;i < dataAdapter.TableMappings.Count;i++){}
```

The name of the mapping at the ith collection position is stated by

```
dataAdapter.TableMappings[i].ToString()
```

where the expression

```
dataAdapter.TableMappings[i]
```

evaluates to the TableMapping object at position i in the table mappings collection.

Each table mapping object contains a collection of column mapping objects accessed with the ColumnsMapping property of the DataTableMapping object. The number of column mapping objects in the collection is accessed with the collection's Count property:

public sealed class **OleDbDataAdapter** : DbDataAdapter, Icloneable, IdbDataAdapter	
Hierarchy	
Object	
MarshalByRefObject	
Component	
DataAdapter	
DbDataAdapter	
OleDbDataAdapter	
SqlDataAdapter	
Public Instance Constructors	
public **OleDbDataAdapter**( );	Initializes a new instance of the OleDbDataAdapter class.
public **OleDbDataAdapter**(OleDbCommand *selectCommand*);	Initializes a new instance and sets the SelectCommand property to the *selectCommand* object value.
public **OleDbDataAdapter**(string *selectCommandText* OleDbConnection *connection*);	Initializes a new instance and sets the SelectCommand property using the *selectCommandText* and uses the OleDBConnection *connection* object.
public **OleDbDataAdapter**(string *selectCommandText* string *connectionText*);	Initializes a new instance and sets the SelectCommand property using the *selectCommandText* and uses a OleDBConnection based on the *connectionText* string.
Public Instance Properties	
public bool **AcceptChangesDuringFill** {get; set;}	Gets or sets a value indicating whether the AcceptChanges method is called on a DataRow after it is added to a DataSet. The method is called if true. The default is true.
public OleDbCommand **DeleteCommand** {get; set;}	Gets or sets the OleDbCommand used during Update to delete rows in the data source corresponding to deleted rows in the DataSet.
public OleDbCommand **InsertCommand** {get; set;}	Gets or sets the OleDbCommand used during Update to insert rows in the data source corresponding to inserted rows in the DataSet.
public MissingMappingAction **MissingMappingAction** {get; set;}	Gets or sets the action performed when the incoming data does not have a matching table. The values are members of the MissingMatchingAction enumeration. The default value is Passthrough.
public MissingSchemaAction **MissingSchemaAction** {get; set;}	Gets or sets the action performed when the DataSet schema does not match the schema of the incoming data. The values are members of the MissingSchemaAction enumeration. The default value is Add.

FIGURE 10.10
OleDbDataAdapter class summary.

```
dataAdapter.TableMappings[i].ColumnMappings.Count
```

A loop starting with zero, corresponding to the first column mapping in the collection and iterating as long as the iterator (in this case j) is less than the number of column mappings in the column mapping collection, is represented by the statement.

```
for(int j = 0;
j < dataAdapter.TableMappings[i].ColumnMappings.Count;
j++) {}
```

The expression

```
dataAdapter.TableMappings[i].ColumnMappings[j]
```

evaluates to the jth column mapping object in the ith table mapping. The names of the source column and data set column associated by the column mapping object are expressed as

```
dataAdapter.TableMappings[i].ColumnMappings[j].SourceColumn
```

Public Instance Properties

public OleDbCommand **SelectCommand** {get; set;}	Gets or sets the OleDbCommand used during the Fill operation to select rows from the data source for insertion in the DataSet.
public DataTableMappingCollection **TableMappings** {get;}	Gets a collection containing the master mapping between data source and DataSet tables.
public OleDbCommand **UpdateCommand** {get; set;}	Gets or sets the OleDbCommand used during Update to update rows in the data source corresponding to modified rows in the DataSet.

Public Instance Methods

public override int **Fill**(DataSet *dataSet*);	Adds or refreshes rows in the DataSet specified by *dataSet*. The method returns the number of rows added or refreshed not including rows affected by statements that do not return rows.
public int **Fill**(DataTable *dataTable*);	Adds or refreshes rows in the designation DataTable specified by *dataTable*. The DataTable is created if it does not exist. The method returns the number of rows added or refreshed not including rows affected by statements that do not return rows.
public int **Fill**(DataTablet *dataTable*, string *sourceTable*);	Adds or refreshes rows and schema if necessary in the DataSet's DataTable specified by *dataTable*. The name of the table in the data source used for mapping is specified by *sourceTable*. The method returns the number of rows added or refreshed not including rows affected by statements that do not return rows.
protected virtual int **Fill**(DataTable *dataTable* IDbCommand *command*, CommandBehavior *behavior*);	Adds or refreshes rows and schema if necessary in the DataSet's DataTable specified by *dataTable*. The SQL SELECT statement is specified by the IdbCommand object *command* and the command behavior is specified by the CommandBehavior enumeration member value *behavior*. The method returns the number of rows added or refreshed not including rows affected by statements that do not return rows.
public int **Fill**(DataSet *dataSet* int *startRecord*, int *maxRecords*, string *sourceTable*);	Adds or refreshes rows and schema if necessary in the DataSet specified by *dataSet*. The range of rows in the DataSet is specified by the start row value *startRecord* and continues for the number of rows specified by the range value *maxRecords*. The data source table is specified by the table name *sourceTable*. The method returns the number of rows added or refreshed not including rows affected by statements that do not return rows.

FIGURE 10.10 (CONTINUED)
OleDbDataAdapter class summary.

and

```
dataAdapter.TableMappings[i].ColumnMappings[j].DataSetColumn
```

The values of the SourceColumn and DataSetColumn properties of each mapping are appended as a line to the Text property of the msg control. The browser rendering of the msg control's Text property is shown in Figure 10.11C. Note that the Student table mapping relates the columns as shown below:

Data Source Table Column	DataSet Table Column
LastName	Last
FirstName	First
StudentId	ID

public int **Fill**(DataSet *dataSet*
  int *startRecord*,
  int *maxRecords*,
  string *sourceTable*);
	Adds or refreshes rows and schema if
	necessary in the DataSet specified
	by *dataSet*. The range of rows in the DataSet is
	specified by the start row value *startRecord* and
	continues for the number of rows specified by the
	range value *maxRecords*. The data source table
	is specified by the table name *sourceTable*. The
	method returns the number of rows added or
	refreshed not including rows affected by
	statements that do not return rows.

protected int **Fill**(DataSet *dataSet* ,
  string *sourceTable*,
  IDataReader *dataReader*,
  int *startRecord*,
  int *maxRecords*);
	Adds or refreshes rows and schema if
	necessary in the DataSet specified by *dataSet*
	using the IDataReader object *dataReader*.
	The range of rows in the DataSet modified to
	match the data source are specified by the start
	row value *startRecord* and the range is specified
	by the *maxRecord* value. The data source table is
	specified by the table name *sourceTable*. The
	method returns the number of rows added or
	refreshed not including rows affected by
	statements that do not return rows.

protected int **Fill**(DataSet *dataSet* ,
  int *startRecord*,
  int *maxRecords*,
  string *sourceTable*,
  IDbCommand *command*;
  CommandBehavior *behavior*);
	Adds or refreshes rows and schema if
	necessary in the DataSet specified by *dataSet*.
	The range of rows in the DataSet modified to
	match the data source are specified by the start
	row value *startRecord* and the range is specified
	by the *maxRecord* value. The data source table is
	by *dataTable*. The SQL SELECT statement is
	specified by the IdbCommand object *command*
	and the command behavior is specified by the
	CommandBehavior enumeration member value
	behavior. The method returns the number of rows
	added or refreshed not including rows affected by
	statements that do not return rows.

public override DataTable[ ] **FillSchema** (
  DataSet *dataSet*
  SchemaType *schemaType*);
	Configures the DataSet, specified by *dataSet*,
	schema to match the data source schema based
	on the SchemaType enumeration member value
	schemaType. The method returns a collection of
	DataTable objects added to the DataSet.

public DataTable **FillSchema** (
  DataTable *dataTable*
  SchemaType *schemaType*);
	Adds a DataTable *dataTable* and configures the
	table's schema using the schema based on the
	SchemaType enumeration member value
	schemaType. The method returns a DataTable
	objects with the schema provided by the data
	source.

public override DataTable[ ] **FillSchema** (
  DataSet *dataSet*,
  SchemaType *schemaType*,
  String *sourceTable*);
	Configures the DataSet, specified by *dataSet*,
	schema to match the data source schema based
	on the SchemaType enumeration member value
	schemaType. The source table name is specified
	by *sourceTable*. The method returns a collection
	of DataTable objects added to the DataSet.

FIGURE 10.10 (CONTINUED)
OleDbDataAdapter class summary.

The columns of the DataSet's table corresponding to the data source's table LastName, FirstName and StudentID columns are referenced with the names Last, First and ID. Note that mappings for the other columns in the data source's Student table have not been defined.

The data adapter's MissingMappingAction property value, which is a member of the MissingMappingAction enumeration, specifies what action the adapter takes when incoming data do not have a matching mapping:

```
dataAdapter.MissingMappingAction =
MissingMappingAction.Passthrough;
```

In this case, the enumeration member Passthrough specifies that a missing table or column be created and, using its original name, added to the DataSet's representation of the

protected virtual DataTable[ ] **FillSchema** (DataTable *dataTable*, SchemaType *schemaType*, IDbCommand *command*, CommandBehavior *behavior*);	Adds the DataTable object *dataTable* and configures the table's schema to match the data source schema based on the SchemaType enumeration member value *schemaType*. The SQL SELECT statement is specified by the IDbCommand object *command* and the command behavior is specified by the CommandBehavior enumeration member value *behavior*. The method returns a collection of DataTable objects containing schema information from the data source.
public virtual DataTable[ ] **FillSchema** (DataSet *dataSet*, SchemaType *schemaType*, IDbCommand *command*, String *sourceTable*, CommandBehavior *behavior*)	Configures the DataSet, specified by *dataSet*, schema to match the data source schema based on the SchemaType enumeration member value *schemaType*. The source table name is specified by *sourceTable*. The SQL SELECT statement is specified by the IDbCommand object *command* and the command behavior is specified by the CommandBehavior enumeration member value *behavior*. The method returns a collection of DataTable objects containing schema information from the data source.
public override IdataParameter [ ] **GetFillParameters** ( );	Returns an array of IdataParameter objects representing parameters set by user when executing an SQL SELECT statement.
public int **Update** (DataRow [ ] *dataRows*);	Updates the data source by calling INSERT, UPDATE and DELETE statements for each inserted, updated or deleted row in the array of DataRow objects specified by *dataSet*. The method returns the number of rows affected.
public override int **Update** (DataSet *dataSet*);	Updates the data source by calling INSERT, UPDATE and DELETE statements for each inserted, updated or deleted row in the DataSet specified by *dataSet*. The method returns the number of rows affected.
public int **Update** (DataTable *dataTable*);	Updates the data source by calling INSERT, UPDATE and DELETE statements for each inserted, updated or deleted row in the DataTable specified by *dataTable*. The method returns the number of rows affected.
protected virtual int **Update** (DatRow[ ] *dataRow*, DataTableMapping *tableMapping*);	Updates the data source by calling INSERT, UPDATE and DELETE statements for each inserted, updated or deleted row in the array of DataRow objects specified by *dataRow* using the mapping specified by *tableMapping*. The method returns the number of rows affected.
public int **Update** (DataSet *dataSet*, string *sourceTable*);	Updates the data source by calling INSERT, UPDATE and DELETE statements for each inserted, updated or deleted row in the DataSet specified by *dataSet* using the source table with the name *sourceTable* for the mapping. The method returns the number of rows affected.

FIGURE 10.10 (CONTINUED)
OleDbDataAdapter class summary.

incoming data. Another enumeration member, Ignore, specifies that any incoming tables or columns without a mapping be ignored. The default enumeration value is Passthrough.

Similarly, the data adapter's MissingSchemaAction property value, which is a member of the MissingSchemaAction enumeration, specifies what action the adapter takes when the existing DataSet's schema does not match the schema of the incoming data. For example,

```
dataAdapter.MissingSchemaAction =
MissingSchemaAction.AddWithKey;
```

specifies that primary key information, including columns, be added to the DataSet's schema. The Add enumeration value specifies that columns required to complete the

```
<%@ Page language="c#" Codebehind="UseTableMapping.aspx.cs" AutoEventWireup="false"
            Inherits="DataAdapterTableMapping.UseTableMapping" %>
<HTML>
 <HEAD>
 </HEAD>
 <body MS_POSITIONING="GridLayout">

   <form id="UseTableMapping" method="post" runat="server">
       <asp:Label id=msg Runat=server></asp:Label>
   </form>

 </body>
</HTML>
```

FIGURE 10.11A
DataAdapterTableMapping/UseTableMapping.aspx.

schema be added. The Ignore enumeration value specifies that columns in the data source table not included in the DataSet's schema be ignored.

The Fill method retrieves rows from the data source using the SELECT statement specified by the SelectCommand property. A valid connection object is required. Note that, if the connection is not opened, it will be opened, the rows retrieved, and then closed. If the connection is open, it remains open. The Fill method adds the rows to the mapped table creating DataTable objects if they do not exist. In this Fill method version, the parameters are the DataSet into which the incoming data are to be loaded and the source data table name or, in this case, the table mapping name, to be used for the mapping. In this case, the data adapter's SelectCommand object effects a connection to the data source and return of all data in the Student table. The data are loaded in the DataSet object referenced by dataSet and the mapping studentTM is used to associate columns:

```
dataAdapter.Fill(dataSet, studentTM.ToString());
```

Other versions provide alternate means for specifying the target for the incoming data and applicable mapping.

The Fill method can be used multiple times on the same DataTable. The results depend on the existence of a primary key: if there is a primary key, data rows are merged with matching rows; if there is no primary key, data rows are appended to existing rows.

The contents of the StudentDS table in the DataSet are displayed by the PreviewData-SetTable method. The number of tables in the data set is evaluated with the statement

```
int noTables = dataSet.Tables.Count;
```

A for loop iterating over the tables in the DataSet is expressed with the following structure

```
for (int indexTable = 0; indexTable < noTables;indexTable++){}
```

The variable indexTable is used to index the DataTable object members of the DataSet's DataTableCollection property object values accessed with the DataSet's Tables property. As such, the name, number of columns and number of rows in a specific DataTable in the collection are evaluated with the statements

```
string tableName = dataSet.Tables[indexTable].TableName;
int noCols = dataSet.Tables[indexTable].Columns.Count;
int noRows = dataSet.Tables[indexTable].Rows.Count;
```

A loop providing for iterating over the rows of the specific table is effected with the structure

```
for (int indexRow = 0; indexRow < noRows; indexRow++) {}
```

```
using System;
using System.Collections;
using System.ComponentModel;
using System.Data;
using System.Drawing;
using System.Web;
using System.Web.SessionState;
using System.Web.UI;
using System.Web.UI.WebControls;            Exposes OleDb data
using System.Web.UI.HtmlControls;           access classes.

using System.Data.OleDb;
using System.Data.Common;                   Exposes DataTableMapping
                                            class.
namespace DataAdapterTableMapping
{
        public class UseTableMapping : System.Web.UI.Page
        {
                protected System.Web.UI.WebControls.Label msg;

                public UseTableMapping()
                {
                        Page.Init += new System.EventHandler(Page_Init);
                }

                private void Page_Load(object sender, System.EventArgs e)
                {
                        DataSet dataSet = new DataSet();    ——   Creates DataSet object.

                        string provider = "Provider=Microsoft.Jet.OLEDB.4.0";
                        string dataSource = "Data Source=C:\\DB\\StudentAdministratorDB.mdb";
                        string connectStg = provider + ";" + dataSource;
                        OleDbConnection connection = new OleDbConnection(connectStg);

                        string cmdText = "SELECT * FROM Student";  —  SQL SELECT statement.

 Creates
 OleDbDataAdapter
 specifying the         OleDbDataAdapter dataAdapter = new OleDbDataAdapter(cmdText, connection);
 SelectCommand
 property text and                                    Adds mapping relating
 connection.                                           source and DataSet tables.
                        DataTableMapping studentTM =
                                dataAdapter.TableMappings.Add("Student","StudentDS");

                        DataTableMapping contactTM =
                                dataAdapter.TableMappings.Add("Contact","ContactDS");

                        studentTM.ColumnMappings.Add("FirstName","First");  —   Column
                        studentTM.ColumnMappings.Add("LastName","Last");        mappings are
                        studentTM.ColumnMappings.Add("StudentID","ID");        added to table
                                                                               mapping.
                        DisplayTableMappings(dataAdapter);
```

FIGURE 10.11B
Code-behind file DataAdapterTableMapping/UseTableMapping.aspx.cs.

Note that data rows marked for deletion cannot be accessed. The expression

```
dataSet.Tables[indexTable].Rows[indexRow].RowState
```

evaluates to the RowState property value. When the value is DataRowState.Deleted, the row is marked for deletion and cannot be accessed. As such, the code block of the following statement

```
if (dataSet.Tables[indexTable].Rows[indexRow].RowState ! =
DataRowState.Deleted)
{
}
```

is only executed when the specified row is not marked for deletion.

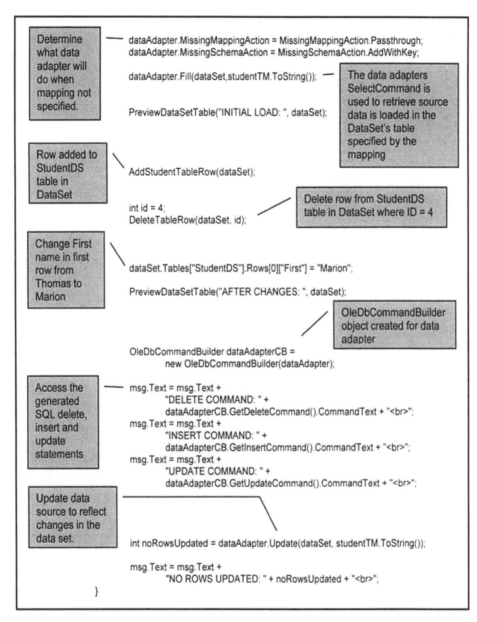

FIGURE 10.11B (CONTINUED)
Code-behind file DataAdapterTableMapping/UseTableMapping.aspx.cs.

A loop for iterating over the columns of a specific row is effected with the structure

```
for (int columnIndex = 0; columnIndex < noCols; columnIndex++)
{
}
```

The value of a specific column in a specific row in a specific table is expressed by

```
dataSet.Tables[indexTable].Rows[indexRow][columnIndex]
```

The string representation of the value is added to the msg control's Text property string with the statement

```
private void AddStudentTableRow(DataSet dataSet)
{
        object [] values = new object[14];

        values[1] = "Smith";
        values[2] = "Alexander";
        values[3] = "IV";
        values[4] = "6";
        values[5] = new DateTime(1989,10,11 );
        values[6] = "5642762973";
        values[7] = 1;
        values[8] = "5209 Arch Street";
        values[9] = "Spring Lake";
        values[10] = "Monmouth";
        values[11] = "NJ";
        values[12] = "07720";
        values[13] = 2;
        dataSet.Tables["StudentDS"].Rows.Add(values);
}

private void DeleteTableRow(DataSet dataSet, int id)
{
        // find index of row with ID value id
        for(int i=0;i < dataSet.Tables["StudentDS"].Rows.Count;i++)
        {
                if((int)dataSet.Tables["StudentDS"].Rows[i]["ID"] == id)
                        dataSet.Tables["StudentDS"].Rows[i].Delete();
        }
}

private void DisplayTableMappings(OleDbDataAdapter dataAdapter)
{
        msg.Text = "TABLE MAPPINGS" + "<br>";
        for(int i=0;i < dataAdapter.TableMappings.Count;i++)
        {
                msg.Text += i.ToString() + " "
                        + dataAdapter.TableMappings[i].ToString() + "<br>";

                for(int j=0; j < dataAdapter.TableMappings[i].ColumnMappings.Count;j++)
                {
                    msg.Text += j.ToString() + " " +
                        dataAdapter.TableMappings[i].ColumnMappings[j].SourceColumn
                        + "," +
                        dataAdapter.TableMappings[i].ColumnMappings[j].DataSetColumn
                        + "<br>";
                }
        }
}
```

FIGURE 10.11B (CONTINUED)
Code-behind file DataAdapterTableMapping/UseTableMapping.aspx.cs.

```
msg.Text = msg.Text +
dataSet.Tables[indexTable].Rows[indexRow][columnIndex].ToString()
+ ," ";
```

The contents of the DataSet are displayed with the caption "INITIAL LOAD" in the Web page's browser rendering.

The **FillSchema** method is similar to the Fill method. This method retrieves a schema from the data source using the SelectCommand property value; a valid connection object is required. As with the Fill method, if the connection is not open, it will be opened, the schema retrieved, and then closed; if the connection is open, it remains open. The FillSchema method adds DataTable objects to the DataSet. The DataColumnCollection of the DataTable objects is also configured with DataColumn objects. Additionally, the Data-Column objects are added, and selected properties including AllowDBNull, AutoIncrement and Unique are configured. Additionally, primary key and unique constraints are added to the ConstraintCollection.

```
                      private void PreviewDataSetTable(string caption, DataSet dataSet )
                      {
                            msg.Text = msg.Text + caption + "<br>";
                            int noTables = dataSet.Tables.Count;
                            for (int indexTable = 0; indexTable < noTables;indexTable++)
                            {
                                  string tableName = dataSet.Tables[indexTable].TableName;
                                  int noCols = dataSet.Tables[indexTable].Columns.Count;
                                  int noRows = dataSet.Tables[indexTable].Rows.Count;
                                  msg.Text = msg.Text +
                                        "Table Name: " + tableName +
                                        " Columns: " + noCols +
                                        " Rows: " + noRows + "<br>";
                                  for (int indexRow = 0; indexRow < noRows; indexRow++)
                                  {
                                        if ( dataSet.Tables[indexTable].Rows[indexRow].RowState !=
                                              DataRowState.Deleted)
                                        {
                                              for (int columnIndex = 0; columnIndex < noCols;
                                                    columnIndex++)
                                              {
                                                    msg.Text = msg.Text +
                                                    dataSet.Tables[indexTable].Rows[indexRow]
                                                          [columnIndex].ToString() + ", ";
                                              }
                                              msg.Text = msg.Text + "<br>";
                                        }
                                  }
                            }
                      }

                      private void Page_Init(object sender, EventArgs e)
                      {
                            //
                            // CODEGEN: This call is required by the ASP.NET Web Form Designer.
                            //
                            InitializeComponent();
                      }

                      #region Web Form Designer generated code
                      /// <summary>
                      /// Required method for Designer support - do not modify
                      /// the contents of this method with the code editor.
                      /// </summary>
                      private void InitializeComponent()
                      {
                            this.Load += new System.EventHandler(this.Page_Load);

                      }
                      #endregion
            }
}
```

FIGURE 10.11B (CONTINUED)
Code-behind file DataAdapterTableMapping/UseTableMapping.aspx.cs.

TheFillSchema method contrasts with the Fill method in that the FillSchema method does not return rows. A row is added to the StudentDS table by the method AddStudentTableRow. First, an object array is created with the statement

```
object [] values = new object[14];
```

Values are assigned to the array's elements corresponding to the column values of the row to be added, for example,

```
values[1] = "Smith";
```

and

```
values[5] = new DateTime(1989,10,11);
```

Finally, the row is added to the table with the statement

```
dataSet.Tables["StudentDS"].Rows.Add(values);
```

A row is deleted from the StudentDS table by the DeleteTableRow method. The ID value of the row to be deleted is passed as an argument, in this case 4:

```
int id = 4;
DeleteTableRow(dataSet, id);
```

The method iterates through the rows of the table with the structure

```
for(int i = 0;i < dataSet.Tables["StudentDS"].Rows.Count;i++)
{

}
```

Within the loop, the expression

```
(int)dataSet.Tables["StudentDS"].Rows[i]["ID"] =  = id
```

evaluates to true when the ID column value of the specific row is equal to the value passed as an argument. Note that the expression

```
dataSet.Tables["StudentDS"].Rows[i]["ID"]
```

is an object type and must be cast to type int. When the expression evaluates to true, the row is deleted with the statement

```
dataSet.Tables["StudentDS"].Rows[i].Delete();
```

The column named "First" in the first row, zero-based index value 0, in the table named "StudentDS" in DataSet dataSet is assigned a new value, "Marion," with the statement

```
dataSet.Tables["StudentDS"].Rows[0]["First"] = "Marion";
```

Contents of the revised table, StudentDS, are displayed with the caption "AFTER CHANGES" by the method PreviewDataSetTable:

```
PreviewDataSetTable("AFTER CHANGES: ," dataSet);
```

The OleDbCommandBuilder automatically generates the insert, delete and update commands for single-table updates by a data adapter. Figure 10.12 summarizes the OleDbCommandBuilder class. The OleDbCommandBuilder registers itself as a listener for the RowUpdating events raised by the OleDataAdapter specified in its DataAdapter property. The generated statements are based on the SQL SELECT statement encapsulated by the OleDbDataAdapter's SelectCommand property. The application should call the RefreshSchema method whenever the SELECT statement associated with the OleDb-CommandBuilder changes.

The OleDbCommandBuilder constructor version, used in this case, passes the OleDb-DataAdapter to be assigned to the DataAdapter property as a parameter:

```
OleDbCommandBuilder dataAdapterCB =
new OleDbCommandBuilder(dataAdapter);
```

The OleDbCommandBuilder's GetDeleteCommand, GetInsertCommand and GetUpdate-Command methods can be used to access the SQL statements generated. The methods return an OleDBCommand object whose CommandText property value is the statement. The statements are appended to the msg control's Text property value:

```
msg.Text = msg.Text + "DELETE COMMAND: " +
dataAdapterCB.GetDeleteCommand().CommandText + "<br>";
msg.Text = msg.Text + "INSERT COMMAND: " +
dataAdapterCB.GetInsertCommand().CommandText + "<br>";
```

```
msg.Text = msg.Text + "UPDATE COMMAND: " +
dataAdapterCB.GetUpdateCommand().CommandText + "<br>";
```

The generated SQL statements are displayed in Figure 10.11C. Note the use of question mark characters (?) as placeholders for parameters in the generated SQL statements.

Whenever a new OleDbCommandBuilder is created, any previously existing OleDb-CommandBuilder is released.

The data adapters Update method is called to update the data source to reflect changes in the data set. When the update method is called, the DataAdapter examines the RowState property of the rows in the DataSet's tables. The RowState property reflects the operations performed on the row since the AcceptChanges method was last called. For example, the RowState may indicate the row was Added, Deleted, Detached, Modified or Unchanged. Based on the RowState, the DataAdapter executes INSERT, UPDATE or DELETE statements required to bring the data source into synchronization with the DataSet.

In this case, the Update method is called with the following statement:

```
int noRowsUpdated =
dataAdapter.Update(dataSet, studentTM.ToString());
```

The delete, insert and update statements are called to update the data source to reflect the deleted, inserted and updated rows in the DataSet object, dataSet, using the table mapping specified by the TableMapping object studentTM. Note that the name of the table mapping can be used in place of the table name. Other versions of the Update method provide alternate options for specifying information required to update the data source. The Update method returns the number of rows in the data source successfully updated.

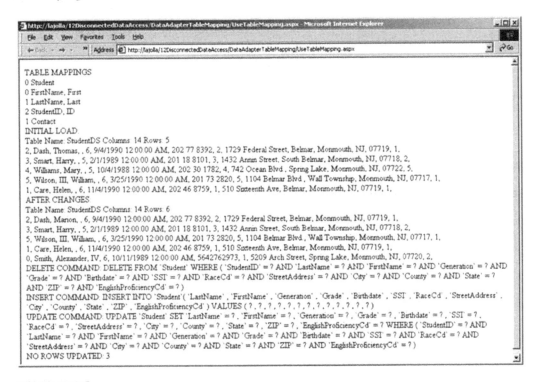

FIGURE 10.11C
DataAdapterTableMapping/UseTableMapping.aspx browser rendering.

public sealed class **OleDbCommandBuilder** : Component	
Hierarchy	

Object
  MarshalByRefObject
    Component
      OleDbCommandBuilder	

Public Instance Constructors	
public **OleDbCommandBuilder**( );	Initializes a new instance of the class.
public **OleDbCommandBuilde** (OleDbDataAdapter *adapter*);	Initializes a new instance and sets the DataAdapter property to the *adapter* object value.
Public Instance Properties	
public OleDbDataAdapter **DataAdapter** {get; set;}	Gets or sets a value specifying the DataAdapter for which statements enabling update operations are generated.
public string **QuotePrefix** {get; set;}	Gets or sets the beginning character or characters used for specifying database object names. The default value is the empty string.
public string **QuoteSuffix** {get; set;}	Gets or sets the ending character or characters used for specifying database object names. The default value is the empty string.
Public Instance Methods	
public OleDbCommand **GetDeleteCommand**();	Gets the automatically generated SQL statement used by the DataAdapter to effect row delete operations in the Update method call.
public OleDbCommand **GetInsertCommand**();	Gets the automatically generated SQL statement used by the DataAdapter to effect add row operations in the Update method call.
public OleDbCommand **GetUpdateCommand**();	Gets the automatically generated SQL statement used by the DataAdapter to effect row update operations in the Update method call.
public void **RefreshSchema**( );	Refreshes the database schema information used to generate the SQL delete, insert and update statements.

FIGURE 10.12
OleDbCommandBuilder.

Hands-On Exercise: Using the DataAdapter

Create and open an ASP.NET web application named UsingDataAdapters in location http://LAJOLLA/12DisconnectedDataAccess.

1. In Solution Explorer, delete WebForm1.aspx.
2. In Solution Explorer, add Web Form UseDataAdapter.aspx.
3. Open the Toolbox by pressing the Ctrl+Alt+X key combination.
4. In the Toolbox, click the Data tab.
5. Drag a DataAdapter onto the UseDataSet.aspx page in the Designer window. The Data Adapter Configuration Wizard opens.
6. Click the Next button.
7. Connect to the StudentAdministratorDB.mdb database.

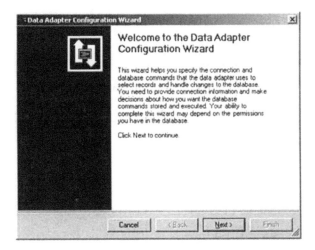

FIGURE HO10.1
Data Adapter Configuration Wizard.

8. Select from an existing connection or Click the new button to launch the Data Link Properties dialog box to create a new connection. (See the Hands-On Exercise in Chapter 7 for information regarding creating a connection.)

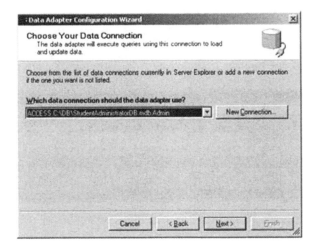

FIGURE HO10.2
Data Adapter Configuration Wizard Connection page.

9. Click the Next button. The Choose a Query Type window is displayed presenting options regarding the SQL statements or procedures that the data adapter will use to read and update the data source. The options are the following:

Option	Description
Use SQL statement	User-specified SELECT statement to read the data source. The Wizard will create the INSERT, DELETE and UPDATE statements that the data adapter will use to update the data source.
Create new stored procedures	User-specifed SELECT statement to read the data source. The Wizard creates the select, insert, delete and update procedures to read and update the data source.
Use existing stored procedures	Choose existing stored procedures for selecting, inserting, deleting, updating database operations.

10. Select the Use SQL statement option.

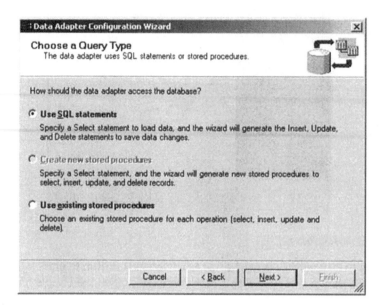

FIGURE HO10.3
Data Adapter Configuration Wizard Query Type page.

11. Click the Next button. A window for creating the SELECT statement opens.

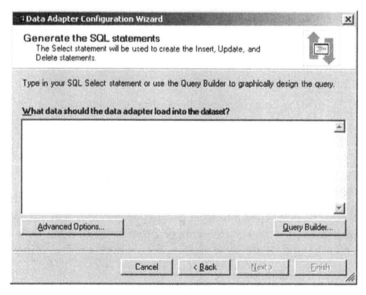

FIGURE HO10.4
Data Adapter Configuration Wizard SQL Statement page.

12. Click the Query Builder button to launch the Query Builder, which opens with the Add Table dialog box opened.

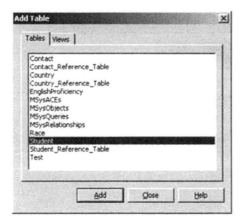

FIGURE HO10.5
Add Table dialog.

13. Select the Student table.
14. Click the Add button. The Student table is added to the Query Builder designer window.
15. Click the Close button to close the Add Table dialog box.

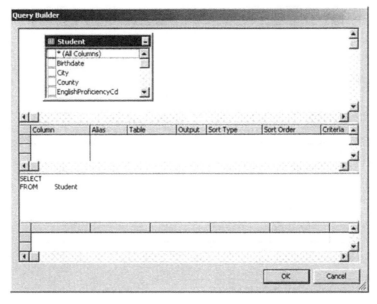

FIGURE HO10.6
Query Builder.

16. Click the All Columns options in the Student table in the Design window of the Query builder. The SELECT statement is changed to reflect the selection of "All Columns" representing a SELECT statement that returns values from all columns in the table:

```
SELECT Student.* FROM Student
```

17. Click the OK button to close the Query Builder.

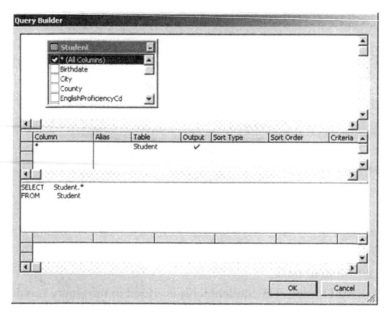

FIGURE HO10.7
Query Builder with all columns selected.

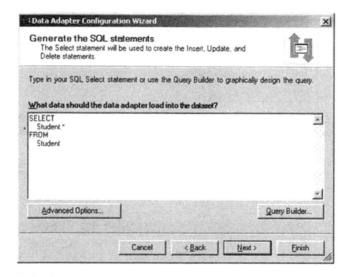

FIGURE HO10.8
Query Builder with generated SQL Statement.

18. Click the Next button. The Wizard configuration results are displayed.

    Note that the Wizard has created the following:

    Table Mappings

    Insert Statement

    Delete Statement

    Update Statement

19. Click the Finish button. The Wizard closes. Note that a connection object has been added to the Web page, UseDataAdapter.aspx, in the Designer window.

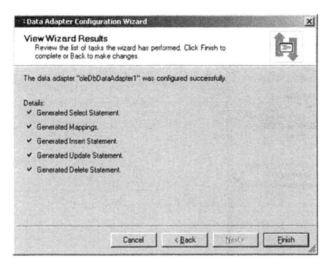

FIGURE HO10.9
Data Adapter Configuration Wizard Results.

FIGURE HO10.10
Designer showing DataAdapter and Connection controls.

20. Select the oleDbDataAdapter control in the Designer window.
21. Press F4 to open the Properties Window.
22. Change the Name property value to studentDA.
23. Click the ellipses at the right side of the TableMappings property to open the Table Mapping Window.

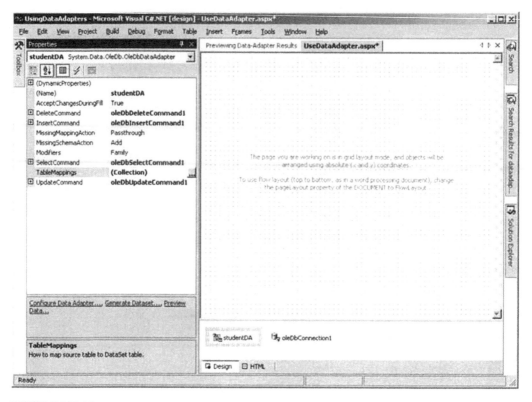

FIGURE HO10.11
DataAdapter Properties Window.

FIGURE HO10.12
Tables Mappings Window.

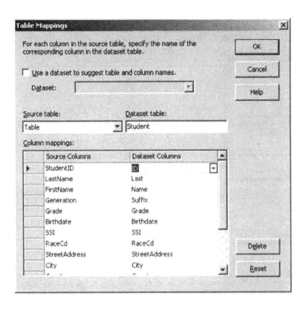

FIGURE HO10.13
Table Mappings Window with mappings entered.

24. Change the Dataset Column's names to the following, which presumably are easier to code:

Designer Generated	Easier to Code
StudentID	ID
LastName	Last
FirstName	First
Generation	Suffix

25. Click OK. The Table Mappings window closes.
26. Click the + sign to the left of the SelectCommand property to expose the properties of the SelectCommand object.
27. Place the cursor over the CommandText property box to expose the entire SQL statement.
28. Click the Preview Data... link located at the bottom of the Properties Window. The Data Adapter Preview Window opens.
29. Click the Fill Dataset button. The data loaded into the data set are displayed.
30. Click the Close button.
31. Expand the UpdateCommand property.
32. Place the cursor over the CommandText property to view the statement. Note the "?" placeholders for parameter values.
33. Click the ellipses at the right side of the UpdateCommand's Parameters property to open the OleDbParameter Collection Editor. The object members of the Parameter's collection are shown in the right pane. The properties of a selected parameter object are shown in the left pane.
34. Click OK to close the Editor.

Similarly, review the DeleteCommand and InsertCommand properties.

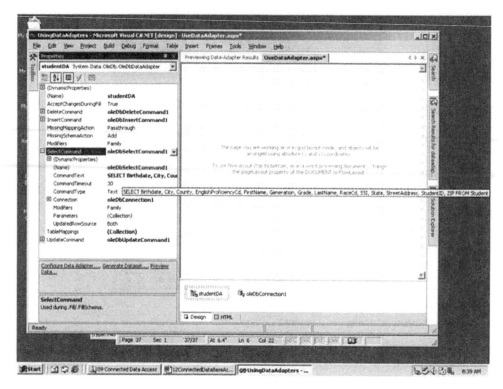

FIGURE HO10.14
DataAdapter with property values assigned.

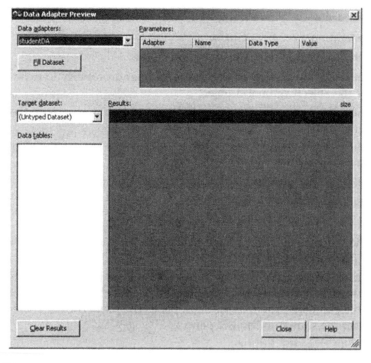

FIGURE HO10.15
DataAdapter Preview window.

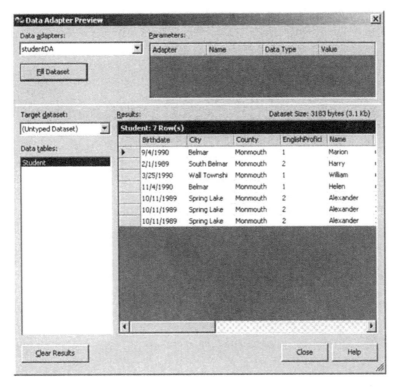

FIGURE HO10.16
DataAdapter Preview window with adapter selected.

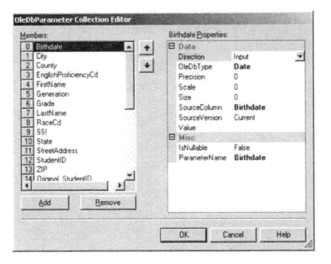

FIGURE HO10.17
OleDbParameter Collection Editor.

Part 4

Implementing Web Applications

11

Application Fundamentals

Panel Class

The Panel control is a container for other controls: it is useful as a container for controls created programmatically and for groups of controls that need to be managed programmatically. The **Panel** class, summarized in Figure 11.1, models the Panel Web Form control. The Web Form example in Figure 11.2 illustrates the use of the Panel control to contain other controls.

public class **Panel** : WebControl	
Heirarchy	
Object Control WebControl Panel	
Constructor	
public Panel( )	Initializes a new instance of the Panel class.

FIGURE 11.1
Panel class summarization.

```
<%@ Page language="c#" Codebehind="UsingPanel.aspx.cs
        AutoEventWireup="false" Inherits="PanelBackground.UsingPanel" %>
<!DOCTYPE HTML PUBLIC "-//W3C//DTD HTML 4.0 Transitional//EN" >
<HTML>
  <HEAD>
  </HEAD>                        Controls contained in the panel dataPanel
<body>

<form id=UsingPanel method=post runat="server">
      <asp:Panel ID="dataPanel" Runat=server BackColor=LightGray>
          <asp:Label id=labelID Runat="server">Name:</asp:Label>
          <asp:TextBox id=nameTextBox Runat="server"></asp:TextBox>
      </asp:Panel><br>
      <asp:Button ID="toggleButton" Runat=server Text="Toggle
                  Visibility"></asp:Button><br>
    <asp:Label ID="msgLabel" Runat=server></asp:Label>
</form>
</body>
</HTML>
```

FIGURE 11.2
Web Form illustrating Panel control as a container.

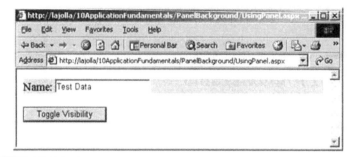

FIGURE 11.3
Panel containing a Label and Textbox controls.

The Panel control, identified as dataPanel, contains two other controls: first, a Label control identified as labelID and, second, a TextBox control identified as nameTextBox. The panel dataPanel is representative of many form fragments used to collect specific data. In this case, the datum Name is representative of many related data items. The Web Page is rendered in a browser as shown in Figure 11.3. Note that the panel's Backcolor attribute has been assigned the color Light Gray. The Label and TextBox controls are contained within the Light Gray panel. Note that the panel's width defaults to the width of the screen and its height defaults to a value sufficient to include the contained controls. Panel Height and Width attributes inherited from the WebControl class could be used to set the width and height of the panel.

The Panel can be used to control the visibility of a group of controls. This can be extremely useful when displaying or collecting data because the controls can be grouped in panels and only the panels with relevant controls are rendered visible. The example Web Page contains a button used to toggle the visibility attribute of the Panel control; when the button is clicked, the Web Page is sent to the server. Processing at the server is used to detect the current value of the visibility attribute, which is toggled.

Thus, when the panel is displayed, as in Figure 11.3, clicking the button results in a new Web Page with the panel rendered invisible, as shown in Figure 11.4. Note also that the contents of the TextBox are displayed below the button. Clicking the button will result in a Web Page displaying the panel and the controls contained within the panel. The code to toggle the visibility attribute and display the TextBox contents is contained in the code-behind file shown in Figure 11.5.

When the form is posted back to the server, the IsPostBack method parameter is true. In that case, the panel visibility attribute is tested:

```
if (dataPanel.Visible)
```

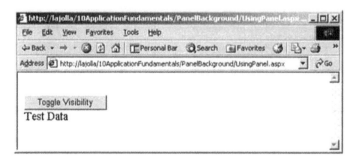

FIGURE 11.4
Panel containing a Label and Textbox controls rendered invisible.

```
using System;
using System.Web.UI.WebControls;

namespace PanelBackground
{
    public class UsingPanel : System.Web.UI.Page
    {
        protected System.Web.UI.WebControls.Label labelID;
        protected System.Web.UI.WebControls.TextBox nameTextBox;
        protected System.Web.UI.WebControls.Panel dataPanel;
        protected System.Web.UI.WebControls.Label msgLabel;
        protected System.Web.UI.WebControls.Button toggleButton;

        public UsingPanel()
        {
            Page.Init += new System.EventHandler(Page_Init);
        }

        private void Page_Load(object sender, System.EventArgs e)
        {
            if (IsPostBack)                          ── Test visibility
            {
                if (dataPanel.Visible)               ── Set invisible
                {
                    dataPanel.Visible = false;
                    msgLabel.Text = nameTextBox.Text;
                }
                else                                 ── Set visible
                {
                    dataPanel.Visible = true;
                    msgLabel.Text = nameTextBox.Text;
                }
            }                                        ── Display textbox content
        }

        public void Btn_Click(Object o, EventArgs ae)
        {
        }

        private void Page_Init(object sender, EventArgs e)
        {
            InitializeComponent();
        }

        #region Web Form Designer generated code
        private void InitializeComponent()
        {
            this.Load += new System.EventHandler(this.Page_Load);
        }
        #endregion
    }
}
```

FIGURE 11.5
Code-behind file with code to toggle visibility attribute and display text.

When the panel visibility attribute value is true, the panel is visible and the following statements are executed:

```
dataPanel.Visible = false;
msgLabel.Text = nameTextBox.Text;
```

First, the visibility attribute is set false; the panel will be rendered invisible. Next, the contents of the TextBox are assigned as the Text attribute value of the Label. Similarly, when the panel is not visible, the following statements are executed:

```
dataPanel.Visible = true;

msgLabel.Text = nameTextBox.Text;
```

In this case, the visibility attribute value is set to true and again the contents of the TextBox are displayed as the Text attribute of the Label.

User Controls

With a few modifications, a Web Forms page can be used as a control in another Web Forms page, thus enabling the development of custom **user controls**.

User Control Basics

A Web forms page used as a user control is of the System.Web.UI.**UserControl class**. Web Forms intended as user controls are contained in files with the **.ascx** extension. The UserControl class represents .ascx files intended for use in .aspx files. Note that the user controls cannot be called independently but can only be called from the Page that contains them. The UserControl class derives directly from the TemplateControl class, which enables the Page class and UserControl class with basic functionality. The TemplateControl class is summarized in Figure 11.6 and the UserControl class is summarized in Figure 11.7.

An example of a Web form intended as a user control is shown in Figure 11.8. The file is saved with an .ascx file extension. The form contains a label, textbox and literal control; the literal control is described next. The @ Control directive syntax is summarized in Figure 11.9. An example of an @ Control directive is shown in Figure 11.8.

```
<%@ Control Language = "c#" AutoEventWireup = "false"

    Codebehind = "DataPanel.ascx.cs" Inherits =
    "UserControls.DataPanel"%>
```

In this case, the compilation language is C#, auto event wiring is disabled, the code-behind class is DataPanel and the code behind is in the DataPanel.ascx.cs file.

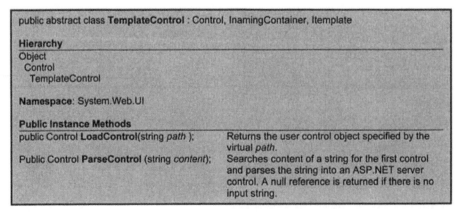

public abstract class **TemplateControl** : Control, InamingContainer, Itemplate

Hierarchy
Object
  Control
    TemplateControl

Namespace: System.Web.UI

Public Instance Methods

public Control **LoadControl**(string *path*);	Returns the user control object specified by the virtual *path*.
Public Control **ParseControl** (string *content*);	Searches content of a string for the first control and parses the string into an ASP.NET server control. A null reference is returned if there is no input string.

FIGURE 11.6
TemplateControl class summary.

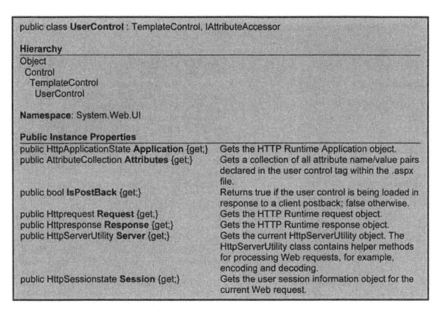

FIGURE 11.7
UserControl class summary.

```
<%@ Control Language="c#" AutoEventWireup="false"
       Codebehind="DataPanel.ascx.cs" Inherits="UserControls.DataPanel"%>

<asp:Label id=nameLabel runat=server text="Name:"></asp:Label>
<asp:Textbox id=nameTextbox runat=server></asp:Textbox>
<asp:Literal id=literal1 runat=server text="<br>"></asp:Literal>
<asp:Literal id="Literal2" runat=server text="<br>"></asp:Literal>
```

FIGURE 11.8
UserControl DataPanel.ascx.

An example of a Web Form using the DataPanel Web Form as a control is shown in Figure 11.10. First, the user control must be registered with the @ Register directive. The **@ Register** directive provides for the declarative addition of ASP.NET user control on a Web Page. The @ register syntax is presented in Figure 11.11.

In the example, the directive declares the tagprefix and tagname aliases NamePanel and NameData for the user control in the file DataPanel.ascx. The syntax for inserting an instance of a custom control is shown in Figure 11.12.

In the example, an instance of the custom control, declared in the @ Register directive, is inserted in the page with the statement

```
<NamePanel:NameData id = "nameData" runat = "server">
    </NamePanel:NameData>
```

The tagprefix and tagname aliases defined in the @ Register directive are used as a colon-separated pair, i.e., tagprefix:tagname. In the example, the colon-separated pair is NamePanel:NameData. An identification attribute, nameData, is declared enabling the control to be referenced programmatically. The mandatory runat = server attribute name/value pair is included in the control's opening tag. The version of the custom control syntax used in the example requires a closing tag that also includes the tagprefix:tagname colon-separated pair. When the Web Form is rendered, an instance of the DataPanel server control is included (see Figure 11.13).

`<%@ Control` attribute=*"value"* [attribute=*"value"*....]	
Attributes	
AutoEventWireup	true if the event auto wiring is enabled; otherwise false. Default is true.
ClassName	Class name of the page that is automatically compiled when the page is requested.
CompilerOptions	String indicating compiler options.
Debug	The page is compiled with debug symbols if true; false otherwise.
Description	Text description of the page.
EnableViewState	true if the user control's view state is maintained across page requests; false otherwise. The view state is the cumulative properties of the control.
Inherits	Specifies the code-behind class for the user control to inherit. The class specified must inherit from the UserControl class.
Language	Specifies the language to be used in compiling all inline rendering and server-side script blocks.
Src	Specifies the source file name of the code-behind class to be dynamically compiled when the user control is requested. When using Visual Studio.NET the Inherits attribute is used instead of the Src attribute.
WarningLevel	Specifies the level at which compilation is to be aborted. Valid values are 0 through 4.
Codebehind	Code-behind file's name.

FIGURE 11.9
@ Control directive summary.

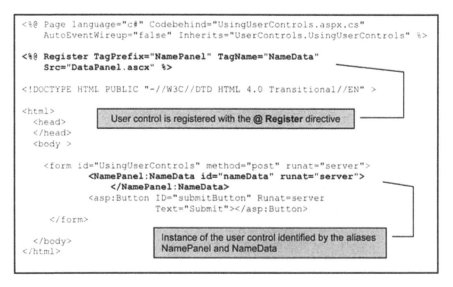

FIGURE 11.10
Web Form using the web Form DataPanel.ascx as a control.

Declaring User Control Properties

Properties can be declared for a user control and then manipulated declaratively when the control instance is inserted in the Web Form and programmatically at the server. The code in Figure 11.14 illustrates the declaration of properties for managing the BackColor and Text properties of the TextBox in the DataPanel control developed previously. A property called Background is defined that assigns the DataPanel's TextBox BackColor property:

```
<%@ Register tagprefix="tagprefix" Namespace="namespace" Assembly="assembly" %>
<%@ Register tagprefix="tagprefix" Tagname="tagname" Src="pathname" %>
```

Attributes

tagprefix	Alias that associates the control with a namespace.
Tagname	Alias that associates the control with a class.
Namespace	Namespace to be associated with the tagprefix.
Src	Location of the user control associated with the tagprefix and tagname. Either a relative or absolute location can be specified.
Assembly	Assembly in which the namespaces being associated with the tagprefix resides. Note that the *assembly* name does not include a file name extension.

FIGURE 11.11
@ Register directive syntax.

```
<tagprefix : tagname" id="ID" attributename="value" attributename-propertyname="value"
        eventname="eventhandlermethod" runat="server" />
Or
< tagprefix : tagname id="ID"  runat="server" >< /tagprefix : tagname>
```

Attributes

tagprefix	Alias that associates the control with a namespace declared with the @ Register directive.
tagname	Alias that associates the control with a class declared with the @ register directive.
id	Optional unique identifier that enables the control to be referenced.
attributename	Name of an attribute.
attributename-propertyname	Name of a property associated with a custom attribute. The *value* specifies the value assigned to the custom attribute-property.
eventname	Name of the event handler method defined in the code for the Web Forms page.
runat	The runat="server" name value pair is required in the opening tag of a server control.

FIGURE 11.12
User/Custom server control syntax.

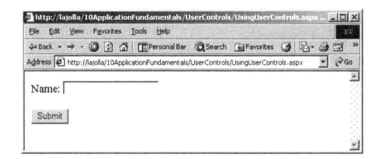

FIGURE 11.13
Rendering of Web Form including the custom server control DataPanel.

```
namespace UserControls
{
    using System;
    using System.Data;
    using System.Drawing;
    using System.Web;
    using System.Web.UI.WebControls;
    using System.Web.UI.HtmlControls;

    public abstract class DataPanel : System.Web.UI.UserControl
    {
        protected System.Web.UI.WebControls.Label nameLabel;
        protected System.Web.UI.WebControls.Literal literal1;
        protected System.Web.UI.WebControls.Literal Literal2;
        protected System.Web.UI.WebControls.TextBox nameTextbox;

        public Color Background
        {
            set
            {
                nameTextbox.BackColor = value;
            }
        }
        public string Content
        {
            set
            {
                nameTextbox.Text = value;
            }
            get
            {
                return nameTextbox.Text;
            }
        }

        public DataPanel()
        {
            this.Init += new System.EventHandler(Page_Init);
        }
        private void Page_Load(object sender, System.EventArgs e)
        {
        }
        private void Page_Init(object sender, EventArgs e)
        {
            InitializeComponent();
        }
        #region Web Form Designer generated code
        private void InitializeComponent()
        {
            this.Load += new System.EventHandler(this.Page_Load);
        }
        #endregion
    }
}
```

FIGURE 11.14
DataPanel with text and backcolor properties.

```
public Color Background
{
    set
    {
        nameTextbox.BackColor = value;
    }
}
```

A property called Content is defined that gets and sets the Text property of the TextBox control in the DataPanel:

```
public string Content
{
    set
    {
        nameTextbox.Text = value;
    }
    get
    {
        return nameTextbox.Text;
    }
}
```

```
<%@ Page language="c#" Codebehind="UsingUserControls.aspx.cs"
    AutoEventWireup="false" Inherits="UserControls.UsingUserControls" %>

<%@ Register TagPrefix="NamePanel" TagName="NameData"
    Src="DataPanel.ascx" %>

<!DOCTYPE HTML PUBLIC "-//W3C//DTD HTML 4.0 Transitional//EN" >

<html>
  <head>
  </head>
  <body >

    <form id="UsingUserControls" method="post" runat="server">
        <NamePanel:NameData id="nameData" runat="server"
                            Backcolor="Red">
        </NamePanel:NameData>
        <asp:Button ID="submitButton" Runat=server
                    Text="Submit"></asp:Button>
    </form>
                    ┌──────────────────────────────────────┐
  </body>           │ DataPanel property name/value pair declaration. │
</html>             └──────────────────────────────────────┘
```

FIGURE 11.15
DataPanel with Background property declared in instantiating element.

Declaratively Manipulating the Custom Control Properties

The custom control's properties are manipulated declaratively in the opening tag of the element inserting an instance of the control in the Web Form by declaring property name/value pairs. An example of a declarative property manipulation is shown in Figure 11.15. The Backcolor property is assigned the value "Red." The class DataPanel declaration contains code that assigns the value to the TextBox BackColor property. When the DataPanel is rendered in a browser, the textbox background color is "Red."

Programmatically Manipulating the Custom Control Properties

The custom control's properties are manipulated programmatically in methods of the control's class declaration. An example of programmatic manipulation of the DataPanel's

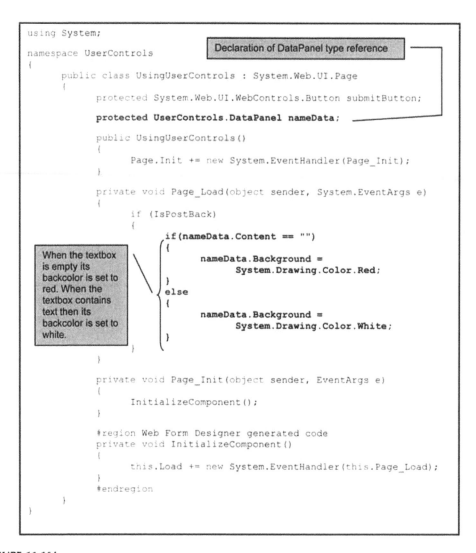

FIGURE 11.16A
Programmatically manipulating the DataPanel's properties.

properties is illustrated in Figure 11.16. Note the declaration of the DataPanel type reference of the custom control instantiated in the Web Form:

```
protected UserControls.DataPanel nameData;
```

In the example, the Content property of the DataPanel nameData is tested when the Web Form is posted back by the client. If the textbox's Content property is space, i.e., nothing has been entered in the textbox, the textbox's Background property is set to "Red." In practice, this would alert the client that a required entry is missing. On postback, if the textbox's Content property is not space, indicating that entries have been made in the textbox, the textbox's Background property is set to "White." Note that the DataPanel's Content property sets and gets the value of the TextBox contained in the DataPanel's Web Form. Similarly, the DataPanel's Background property sets the value of the Textbox contained in the DataPanel's Web Form.

The effect of the property manipulation is shown in Figure 11.16A; the initial rendering of the Web Form is shown in Figure 11.16B. In this case, the custom control's textbox

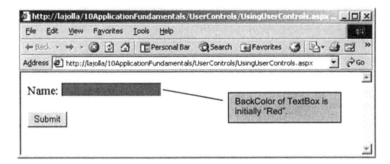

FIGURE 11.16B
Web Form containing DataPanel initial rendering.

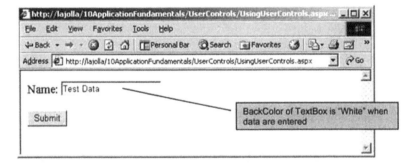

FIGURE 11.16C
Web Form containing DataPanel after postback with data entered in textbox.

BackColor property is "Red." This value is set declaratively. If data are entered in the textbox and the Web Form is posted back, the BackColor of the textbox is "White" (Figure 11.16C) and the data entry is "Test Data." If the textbox entry is removed and the Web Form posted back, the textbox will be rendered "Red."

User Control Events

User controls encapsulate their own events. That is, the event handlers are included in the code-behind file generating the user control. Information regarding events is sent through the page containing an instance of the user control. The DataPanel custom control is again defined and in this case includes a button (see Figure 11.17) captioned "Submit." Note also that the elements of the panel are contained within an ASP Panel control whose BackColor and BorderStyle properties are set to values "Light Gray" and "Solid," respectively. The intent is to provide a visual control definition at the user interface. The user control is declared in the file DataPanel.ascx. Note that the button OnClick attribute has the value "Submit_Click." The handler Submit_Click is defined in the code-behind file, i.e., the DataPanel class declaration, Figure 11.17B.

When a client clicks the button an event is raised. This event is passed to the DataPanel by the page containing the DataPanel user control. The Framework calls the DataPanel handler Submit_Click. The handler examines the content of the TextBox nameTextbox. If nameTextbox has no content, the BackColor property of the TextBox is set to the value

```
<%@ Control Language="c#" AutoEventWireup="false"
    Codebehind="DataPanel.ascx.cs"
    Inherits="UserControlEvents.DataPanel"
    Description="Client alerted when entry not made"%>

<asp:Panel id=panelID runat=server backcolor="LightGray"
         BorderStyle="Solid">
  <asp:Label id=nameLabel text="Name:" runat="server"></asp:Label>
  <asp:Textbox id=nameTextbox runat="server"></asp:Textbox>
  <asp:Literal id=Literal1 text="<br>" runat="server"></asp:Literal>
  <asp:Literal id=Literal2 text="<br>" runat="server"></asp:Literal>
  <asp:Button id=submitButton text="Submit" runat="server"
              onclick="Submit_Click"></asp:Button>
</asp:Panel>
```

Raises event

FIGURE 11.17A
DataPanel custom control with button.

```
namespace UserControlEvents
{
    using System;

    public abstract class DataPanel : System.Web.UI.UserControl
    {
        protected System.Web.UI.WebControls.Label nameLabel;
        protected System.Web.UI.WebControls.TextBox nameTextbox;
        protected System.Web.UI.WebControls.Literal Literal1;
        protected System.Web.UI.WebControls.Literal Literal2;
        protected System.Web.UI.WebControls.Panel panelID;
        protected System.Web.UI.WebControls.Button submitButton;

        public DataPanel()
        {
            this.Init += new System.EventHandler(Page_Init);
        }

        private void Page_Load(object sender, System.EventArgs e)
        {
            if(!IsPostBack)
                nameTextbox.BackColor = System.Drawing.Color.Red;
        }

        public void Submit_Click(object s, EventArgs ea)
        {
            if(nameTextbox.Text=="")
                nameTextbox.BackColor = System.Drawing.Color.Red;
            else
                nameTextbox.BackColor = System.Drawing.Color.White;
        }

        private void Page_Init(object sender, EventArgs e)
        {
            InitializeComponent();
        }

        #region Web Form Designer generated code
        private void InitializeComponent()
        {
            this.Load += new System.EventHandler(this.Page_Load);

        }
        #endregion
    }
}
```

FIGURE 11.17B
DataPanel custom control with button code-behind file.

"Red." On the other hand, if the TextBox contains any value, the BackColor property of the TextBox is set to the value "White." This process models in concept the data validation often done at the server.

On postback, the data presented are examined. When the data are invalid, the page is returned to the client with the TextBox BackColor property "Red" alerting the client that the entry has been determined to be invalid. In practice, when the posted data are valid, control is passed to another page containing information of interest to the client. Typically, the examination will involve accessing a database regarding the textbox's content. All of the processing can be encapsulated in the user control. The user control can be used in any Web Form, thereby promoting the reuse of tested code — a time- and cost-saving advantage.

Programmatically Creating User Controls

Controls can be added programmatically to a Web page. The value of this feature is that Web page content can be tailored to meet specific conditions uncovered at runtime. Enabling this dynamic insertion of controls are the @ Reference directive, PlaceHolder control and @ Control directive.

DataPanel User Control

Another version of the DataPanel user control Web page is shown in Figure 11.18A. In this example, the label, textbox and button are contained in a panel control. The panel's backcolor is set to LightGray. Note that the label control does not have a static caption and that the submitButton's OnClick handler, "Submit_Click," has been identified. The DataPanel's code-behind file is shown in Figure 11.18B.

```
<%@ Control Language="c#" AutoEventWireup="false"
    Codebehind="DataPanel.ascx.cs"
    Inherits="ProgramCreation.DataPanel"%>

<asp:Panel id="dataPanelControl" runat="server" backcolor="LightGray"
        borderstyle="solid">
    <asp:Label id=nameLabel runat="server"></asp:Label>
    <asp:TextBox id=nameTextBox runat="server"></asp:TextBox>
    <asp:Button id=submitButton onclick=Submit_Click runat="server"
            text="Submit"></asp:Button>
</asp:Panel>
```

FIGURE 11.18A
DataPanel user control Web page.

The control is loaded with the nameLabel's text set to "Enter Name:." Additionally, functionality for the OnClick handler, "Submit_Click," has been identified. In practice, the control's character would be exposed as properties allowing for user customization, depending on application circumstances. In this case, the textbox backcolor is set to "Red" whenever it is submitted without an entry, thereby alerting the client of the need to enter data for submission.

```
namespace ProgramCreation
{
    using System;

    public abstract class DataPanel : System.Web.UI.UserControl
    {
        protected System.Web.UI.WebControls.Button submitButton;
        protected System.Web.UI.WebControls.Label nameLabel;
        protected System.Web.UI.WebControls.TextBox nameTextBox;
        protected System.Web.UI.WebControls.Panel dataPanelControl;

        public DataPanel()
        {
            this.Init += new System.EventHandler(Page_Init);
        }

        public void Submit_Click(Object o, EventArgs ea)
        {
            if (nameTextBox.Text == "")
                nameTextBox.BackColor =
                    System.Drawing.Color.Red;
            else
                nameTextBox.BackColor =
                    System.Drawing.Color.White;
        }

        private void Page_Load(object sender, System.EventArgs e)
        {
            nameLabel.Text = "Enter Name:";
        }

        private void Page_Init(object sender, EventArgs e)
        {
            InitializeComponent();
        }

        #region Web Form Designer generated code
        private void InitializeComponent()
        {
            this.Load += new System.EventHandler(this.Page_Load);

        }
        #endregion
    }
}
```

FIGURE 11.18B
DataPanel user control code-behind file.

@ Reference Directive

The @ Reference (Figure 11.19) is declarative, indicating the user control Web Form source file that should be dynamically compiled and linked with the page in which the directive is declared. An @ Reference directive is included in a Web page that includes a user control. The directive specifies the user control's Web Form source file.

PlaceHolder Class

The **PlaceHolder** class represents a container to store dynamically added server controls on a Web page. The control does not have visible output. Controls are added, inserted and removed from the PlaceHolder control using the Control.Controls collection. The PlaceHolder class is summarized in Figure 11.20.

```
<%@  Reference page="pathoffile" %>
Or
<%@  Reference control="pathoffile" %>
```

Attributes	
page	Web Form that should be dynamically compiled and linked with the current page at runtime. *pathoffile* specifies the location of the Web Form source file.
control	User control that should be dynamically compiled and linked with the current page at runtime. *pathoffile* specifies the location of the Web Form source file.

FIGURE 11.19
@ Reference directive.

public class PlaceHolder : Control

Hierarchy

Object
   Control
      PlaceHolder

Control

`<asp:PlaceHolder id="PlaceHolderID" runat="server"/>`

Constructor

public PlaceHolder	Initializes a new instance of the PlaceHolder class.

Selected **Public Instance Property** *(Inherited from Control)*

public virtual ControlCollection Controls {get;}	Gets the ControlCollection object representing the server control's child controls. Controls can be added, inserted and removed from the ControlCollection.

FIGURE 11.20
PlaceHolder class summary.

An example of a Web page containing a PlaceHolder control is shown in Figure 11.21A. The PlaceHolder control is inserted with an identification attribute with value, dataPanel-PlaceHolder, that enables the control to be accessed programmatically and the required runat = server attribute/value pair. Note that the PlaceHolder control does not have any content and can also be specified as

```
<asp:PlaceHolder ID = "dataPanelPlaceHolder"
    Runat = "server"/>
```

that is, without the end tag.

The Web page's code-behind file is shown in Figure 11.21B. The DataPanel user control is added to the PlaceHolder control ControlCollection in the Page_Load method. First, the LoadControl method, inherited by the Page class from the TemplateControl class, is used to create a user control object from a file:

```
Control dataPanel = LoadControl("DataPanel.ascx");
```

In this case, a user control object corresponding to the control represented by the file DataPanel.ascx is created and returned by the method. The object is assigned the Control type reference dataPanel. The UserControl class is derived from the Control class, and thus the dataPanel is a Control type object.

The created control object is added to the dataPanelPlaceHolder's ControlCollection object with the ControlCollection's Add method:

```
dataPanelPlaceHolder.Controls.Add(dataPanel);
```

```
<%@ Page language="c#" Codebehind="CreateControl.aspx.cs"
         AutoEventWireup="false"
         Inherits="ProgramCreation.CreateControl" %>

<!DOCTYPE HTML PUBLIC "-//W3C//DTD HTML 4.0 Transitional//EN" >

<html>
  <head>
  </head>
  <body >

    <form id="CreateControl" method="post" runat="server">
        <asp:PlaceHolder ID="dataPanelPlaceHolder"
                         Runat="server">
        </asp:PlaceHolder>
    </form>

  </body>
</html>
```

PlaceHolder control

FIGURE 11.21A
Web page with placeholder for dynamically inserted control.

```
using System;
using System.Web.UI;

namespace ProgramCreation
{
    public class CreateControl : System.Web.UI.Page
    {
        protected System.Web.UI.WebControls.Label label1;
        protected System.Web.UI.WebControls.PlaceHolder
                                        dataPanelPlaceHolder;

        public CreateControl()
        {
            Page.Init += new System.EventHandler(Page_Init);
        }

        private void Page_Load(object sender, System.EventArgs e)
        {
            Control dataPanel = LoadControl("DataPanel.ascx");

            dataPanelPlaceHolder.Controls.Add(dataPanel);
        }

        private void Page_Init(object sender, EventArgs e)
        {
            InitializeComponent();
        }

        #region Web Form Designer generated code
        private void InitializeComponent()
        {
            this.Load += new System.EventHandler(this.Page_Load);

        }
        #endregion
    }
}
```

FIGURE 11.21B
Code-behind file of Web page with placeholder for dynamically inserted control.

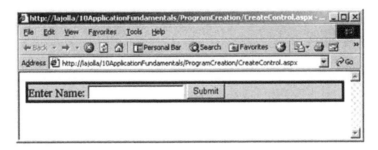

FIGURE 11.21C
Rendering of Web Page with user control DataPanel.

The Controls property of the dataPanelPlaceHolder control gets the dataPanelPlace-Holder's ControlCollection object. The control is added to the end of the ControlCollection's ordinal index array of child control objects.

The browser rendering of the Web page CreateControl is shown in Figure 11.21C. The user control DataPanel is inserted in the page and, when the submit button is clicked, the page is posted to the server. If the textbox holds content, the page is returned to the client with a "White" textbox backcolor. On the other hand, if the textbox does not hold content, the page is returned to the client with the textbox backcolor "Red."

12

Basic Navigation

Moving from page to page, referred to as Navigation, is a fundamental character of Web applications. The HyperLink control enables Navigation; the HttpResponse's redirect method enables server-side navigation. Data can be passed as name/value pairs attached to a URL, enabling pages to communicate with each other.

Hyperlink Class and Control

The **hyperlink** web server control creates a control that a user can click to move to another page. A hyperlink is typically rendered in a specified color, often blue, and underlined. The hyperlink control syntax is shown in Figure 12.1.

```
<asp:hyperlink
        id="hyperlinkid"
        NavigateUrl="url"
        Text="hyperlinkText"
        ImageUrl="url"
        Target="window"
        Runat="server">

   ContentText

</asp:hyperlink>
```

The <asp:hyperlink> element does not require content and thus the opening tag can be closed with a /> instead of > and a separate closing tag. Note that when both the text property and content are specified the content overrides the text property value.

FIGURE 12.1
Hyperlink server control syntax summary.

An example of a HyperLink control specification is as follows:

```
<asp:hyperlink
    id = sourceLinkID
    ImageUrl = "image.jpg"
    NavigateUrl = "TargetPage.aspx"
    Runat = "server"
    Text = "Link Control">
</asp:hyperlink>
```

public class HyperLink : WebControl	
Hierarchy	
Object	
Control	
WebControl	
HyperLink	
Constructor	
public HyperLink();	Initializes a new instance of the HyperLink class.
Public Instance Properties	
public virtual string **ImageUrl** {get; set;}	Gets or sets the path to the image displayed for the HyperLink control. When both the Text and ImageUrl are specified, the ImageUrl takes precedence.
public string **NavigateUrl** {get; set;}	Gets or sets the URL to link to when the HyperLink control is clicked by the user.

public string **Target** {get; set;}	Gets or sets the target window or frame to display the linked page when the HyperLink control is clicked by the user. When a value is not specified, the window with focus refreshes when the HyperLink control is clicked. Values must begin with a letter in the range a through z, that is, lower case. Additional valid values are the following:
	  _blank Content is rendered in a new window without frames.
	  _parent Content is rendered in the immediate frameset parent.
	  _self Content is rendered in the frame with focus.
	  _top Content is rendered in a full window without frames.

public virtual string **Text** {get; set;}	Gets or sets the text displayed for the control. When both the Text and ImageUrl are specified, the ImageUrl takes precedence. The text property also becomes the ToolTip in browsers supporting the functionality.

FIGURE 12.2
Hyperlink class summary.

In this example, the HyperLink control's NavigateUrl property specifies that the page TargetPage.aspx be rendered when the control is clicked. Additionally, the image, image.jpg, is displayed in place of the Text property value "Link Control" when the image is available. When the image is not available, the Text property value is displayed.

The **HyperLink class** represents a hyperlink control, i.e., a control that creates a link to another page. Figure 12.2 summarizes the HyperLink class.

Note!

Client-side navigation is affected with the HyperLink control.

Hands-On Exercise: Using the Create URL Dialog Box

Step 1: Create Application

1. Create a Web Form project: UsingHyperLinks.
2. Add the Web Form: SourcePage
3. Open the SourcePage in the HTML editor.
4. Add the HyperLink control:

Property	Value
id	sourceLinkID
Runat	server
Text	Link Control

5. In the <asp:HyperLink> element's opening tag, enter NavigateURL = .
6. The Pick URL ... prompt icon is displayed. Double-click the icon. The Create URL Dialog Box is displayed.

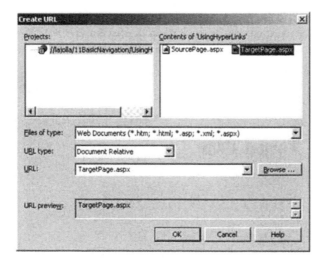

FIGURE HO12.1
Create URL dialog.

7. Select the TargetPage.aspx option in the Contents of UsingHyperLinks pane. The URL is previewed in the URP preview textbox:

   TargetPage.aspx

   Three forms of the URL can be created using URL-type drop-down list:

URL type	URL Created (as shown in the URL preview textbox)
Document Relative	TargetPage.aspx
Root Relative	/UsingHyperLinks/TargetPage.aspx
Absolute	http://lajolla/11BasicNavigation/UsingHyperLinks/TargetPage.aspx

8. Right-click SourcePage in the Solution Explorer and select the Set as the Start Page option.

9. Press Ctrl+F5 to start the application without debugging. Note that the Hyper-Link control is rendered with the Text property value Link Control.

FIGURE HO12.2
Page with hyperlink.

10. Click the Link Control. The Target Page is displayed.

FIGURE HO12.3
Target page.

Step 2: Create an Image File

1. Click Start. Move the cursor over the Programs option; the Program submenu is displayed. Move the cursor over the Accessories option and the Accessories submenu is displayed. Select the Imaging option in the accessories submenu and the Imaging window is opened.

2. Select the New option in the File menu. The New Blank Document dialog box is displayed. Select the JPG File option and click OK. A new JPG file is opened in the window.

3. Select the Straight Line annotation tool and draw a line.

4. Click the Annotation selection tool.

5. Place the cursor over the line and select the line by right-clicking. The selection of the line is indicated by the handles at each end of the line. A submenu is also displayed. Select the Properties option and a Straight Line Properties dialog box is displayed.

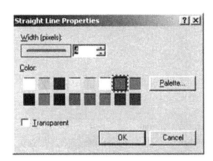

FIGURE HO12.4
Straight Line Properties dialog.

6. Increment the Width to 4 pixels. Select the Color Red. Click OK.
7. Select the Text Annotation tool and draw a textbox in the Window. Enter the word LINK in the text box.
8. Click the Annotation Selection tool.
9. Click the textbox in the Window. Selection is marked by the dashed line about the textbox and the sizing handles.
10. Drag the textbox and place it over the straight line.

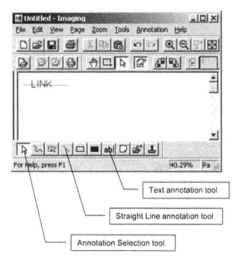

FIGURE HO12.5
Paint dialog.

11. Save the File. Select the Save As... option in the File menu. The Save As dialog box is opened. Navigate to the UsingHyperLinks folder and save the file with the name image.
12. Click Save.
13. Close the Imaging application.

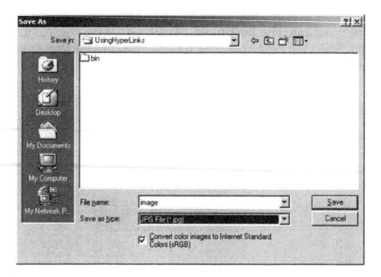

FIGURE HO12.6
Saving the image file.

Step 3: Display and Image HyperLink

1. Open the UsingHyperLink solution in Visual Studio.NET.
2. Click the Show All Files icon at the top of the Solution Explorer. Note that the image.jpg file is shown in the Solution Explorer.
3. Open SourcePage.aspx in the HTML editor.
4. Add the following attribute/value pair to the <asp:HyperLink> element:

   ImageUrl = "image.jpg"

5. Click Ctrl+F5 to Start Without Debugging.

FIGURE HO12.7
Browsing page with image link.

6. A link image is displayed. The ImageURL attribute when present takes precedence over the Text attribute.
7. Click the HyperLink to Link to a new page.

FIGURE HO12.8
Browsing linked page.

Accessing Client Information

HTTP-GET is a standard protocol that uses the HTTP (Hypertext transfer Protocol) verbs for the encoding and passing of parameters as name/value pairs as an appendage to the URI. The name/value pairs are preceded by a question mark (?) character and separated by an ampersand (&). The name and value comprising a pair are separated by an equal sign (=) and are referred to as a Query String. An example of name/value pair appended to a URI is shown in Figure 12.3.

A collection of names and values associated with an HTTP-GET query string is retrieved by the QueryString property of the HttpRequest object. The collection of names and values is represented as a **NameValueCollection** object, which represents a sorted collection of string keys and values that can be accessed by the hash code of the key or by index. The NameValueCollection class is summarized in Figure 12.4.

An example of a HyperLink control with an attached query string is shown in Figure 12.5. In this case the value of the HyperLink's NavigationUrl Property includes a query string with two name/value pairs. The first pair has name "Name1" and value "Value1" and the second has name "Name2" and value "Value2." The query string could contain many more name/value pairs. The target of the link is the page TargetPage.aspx. When the link is clicked, the application navigates to the page TargetPage.aspx. TargetPage.aspx is

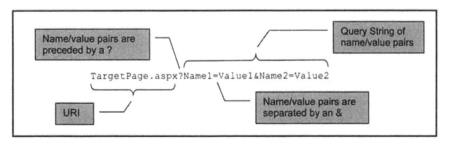

FIGURE 12.3
Example of a Query String, name–value pairs attached to a URI.

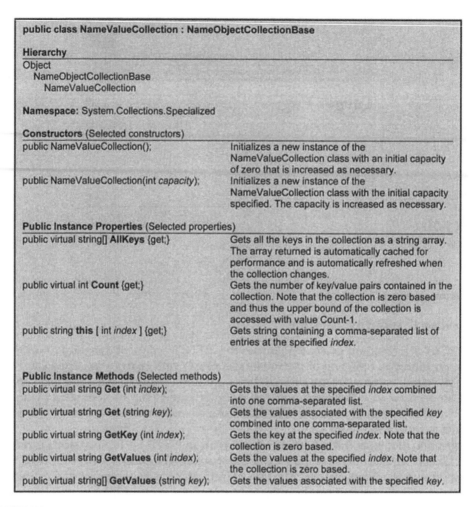

public class NameValueCollection : NameObjectCollectionBase	
Hierarchy	
Object	
NameObjectCollectionBase	
NameValueCollection	
Namespace: System.Collections.Specialized	
Constructors (Selected constructors)	
public NameValueCollection();	Initializes a new instance of the NameValueCollection class with an initial capacity of zero that is increased as necessary.
public NameValueCollection(int *capacity*);	Initializes a new instance of the NameValueCollection class with the initial capacity specified. The capacity is increased as necessary.
Public Instance Properties (Selected properties)	
public virtual string[] **AllKeys** {get;}	Gets all the keys in the collection as a string array. The array returned is automatically cached for performance and is automatically refreshed when the collection changes.
public virtual int **Count** {get;}	Gets the number of key/value pairs contained in the collection. Note that the collection is zero based and thus the upper bound of the collection is accessed with value Count-1.
public string **this** [int *index*] {get;}	Gets string containing a comma-separated list of entries at the specified *index*.
Public Instance Methods (Selected methods)	
public virtual string **Get** (int *index*);	Gets the values at the specified *index* combined into one comma-separated list.
public virtual string **Get** (string *key*);	Gets the values associated with the specified *key* combined into one comma-separated list.
public virtual string **GetKey** (int *index*);	Gets the key at the specified *index*. Note that the collection is zero based.
public virtual string **GetValues** (int *index*);	Gets the values at the specified *index*. Note that the collection is zero based.
public virtual string[] **GetValues** (string *key*);	Gets the values associated with the specified *key*.

FIGURE 12.4
Summary of the NameValueCollection class.

```
<%@ Page language="c#" Codebehind="SourcePage.aspx.cs"
    AutoEventWireup="false" Inherits="UsingHTTPRequest.SourcePage" %>
<!DOCTYPE HTML PUBLIC "-//W3C//DTD HTML 4.0 Transitional//EN" >
<HTML>
  <HEAD>
  </HEAD>
  <body >
    <form id="SourcePage" method="post" runat="server">
      <asp:HyperLink
          ID="sourceID"
          Runat="server"
          NavigateUrl="TargetPage.aspx?Name1=Value1&amp;Name2=Value2"
          Text="Link">
      </asp:HyperLink>
    </form>
  </body>
</HTML>
```

Query String

FIGURE 12.5
Web page with HyperLink control with attached query string (SourcePage.aspx).

```
<%@ Page language="c#" Codebehind="TargetPage.aspx.cs"
    AutoEventWireup="false" Inherits="UsingHTTPRequest.TargetPage" %>
<!DOCTYPE HTML PUBLIC "-//W3C//DTD HTML 4.0 Transitional//EN" >
<HTML>
  <HEAD>
  </HEAD>
  <body ">
    <form id="TargetPage" method="post" runat="server">
              <asp:Label ID="msgLabel" Runat="server"></asp:Label>
    </form>
  </body>
</HTML>
```

FIGURE 12.6A
TargetPage.aspx.

processed at the server and transmitted to the client for display. The listing for TargetPage.aspx is shown in Figure 12.6A.

The page contains a form element that contains a Label element, msgLabel. Processing associated with the page is contained in the code-behind file, i.e., TargetPage.aspx.cs, shown in Figure 12.6B. Note that the NameValueCollection class type in the System. Collections.Specialized namespace is exposed with the statement

```
using System.Collections.Specialized;
```

A string variable msg is declared and initialized with the statement

```
protected string msg = "";
```

The variable msg is used to record values to be displayed in the page's msgLabel control.

When the page is loaded at the server, information regarding the HttpRequest is retrieved by the Framework-provided Request object. First, the request method is ascertained by accessing the HttpMethod property.

```
Request.HttpMethod.ToString()
```

The property value returned is converted to a string and appended to the msg string variable. Note that a <br> element is also appended to the msg variable value. Next, the Params property of the Request object is used to obtain a collection of the name/value pairs associated with the Request object.

```
Request.Params
```

The value associated with the key value "Name1" is retrieved with the expression

```
Request.Params["Name1"]
```

and is appended to the msg string. The value of the second name/value pair is similarly ascertained and appended to the msg variable.

Care should be exercised because the collection returned by the Params property can contain name/value pairs other than those comprising the QueryString.

A reference to a NameValueCollection type object, coll, is declared with the statement

```
NameValueCollection coll;
```

The reference is assigned to the **NameValueCollection** returned by the request object's QueryString property. This collection contains the name/value pairs comprising the Request's Query String:

```
coll = Request.QueryString;
```

The number of name/value pairs in the collection is accessed as the collection's Count property:

```
int count = coll.Count;
```

```
using System;
using System.Collections.Specialized;  ———  Exposes
                                              NameValueCollection
namespace UsingHTTPRequest                    class
{
  public class TargetPage : System.Web.UI.Page
  {
    protected System.Web.UI.WebControls.Label msgLabel;
    protected string msg = "";

    public TargetPage()
    {
      Page.Init += new System.EventHandler(Page_Init);
    }

    private void Page_Load(object sender, System.EventArgs e)
    {
      msg = msg + "Method: " + Request.HttpMethod.ToString() + "<BR>";

      msg = msg + "Name1: " + Request.Params["Name1"] + "<BR>";
      msg = msg + "Name2: " + Request.Params["Name2"] + "<BR>";

      NameValueCollection coll;
      coll = Request.QueryString;
      int count = coll.Count;
      msg = msg + "Count: " + count.ToString() + "<BR>";

      for( int loop = 0; loop < count; loop++ )
      {
        msg = msg + coll.GetKey(loop) + "  " +
                coll.GetValues(loop)[0] + "<BR>";
      }

      msgLabel.Text = msg;
    }

    private void Page_Init(object sender, EventArgs e)
    {
      InitializeComponent();
    }

    #region Web Form Designer generated code
    private void InitializeComponent()
    {
      this.Load += new System.EventHandler(this.Page_Load);
    }
    #endregion
  }
}
```

FIGURE 12.6B
TargetPage.aspx code-behind file (TargetPage.aspx.cs).

The count of the number of name/value pairs in the collection is added to the msg variable with the statement

```
msg = msg + "Count: " + count.ToString() + "<BR>";
```

The collection's GetKey and GetValues methods are used to retrieve the name/value pairs by iterating through the collection with the following statements:

```
for(int loop = 0; loop < count; loop++)
{
    msg = msg + coll.GetKey(loop) + " " +
    coll.GetValues(loop)[0] + "<BR>";
}
```

The value pairs are added to the msg variable. Each name/value pair is added as a separate line. The <br> element is used to create the lines.

Finally, the msg value is assigned to the msgLabel control's Text property:

```
msgLabel.Text = msg;
```

When the application is executed, the SourcePage is first displayed, as shown in Figure 12.6C. When the Link control is clicked, the TargetPage.aspx is processed and displayed (Figure 12.6D).

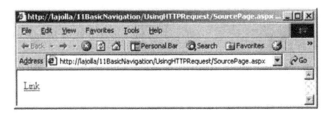

FIGURE 12.6C
Web Form page with HyperLink control (SourcePage.aspx).

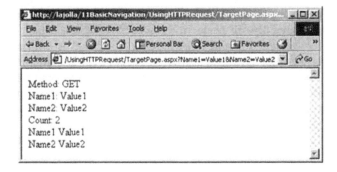

FIGURE 12.6D
Web Form page displaying HttpRequest values (TargetPage.aspx).

Server-Side Navigation

Server-side navigation is generally performed after submitted information has been examined and the appropriate link determined. The **HttpUtility** class provides utilities for URL encoding and decoding of text used in HTTP Web requests. Several selected members of the HttpUtility class are summarized in Figure 12.7.

Note that only ASCII-based characters can be transmitted using HTTP. Characters representing punctuation and blanks may not be properly interpreted and may result in improper encoding and decoding. The UrlEncode method properly encodes text for HTTP transmission. For example, the "<" character is encoded as &lt for HTTP transmission. The HttpUtility class's UrlEncode method reliability encodes strings and byte arrays for reliable HTTP transmission. The HttpUtility class also includes methods for reliability, decoding strings passed using HTTP.

public sealed class HttpUtility	
Class Hierarchy	
Object HttpUtility	
Namespace: System.Web	
Constructor	
public HttpUtility();	Initializes a new instance of the HttpUtility class.
Public Static Methods	
public static string **UrlEncode**(string url);	Encodes *str* for reliable HTTP transmission. The encoded string is returned by the method.
public static string **UrlEncode**(byte[] *urlByteArray*);	Encodes *urlByteArray* for reliable HTTP transmission. The encoded string is returned by the method.

FIGURE 12.7
HttpUtility class selected member summary.

A form that submits information to be used in a search provides an example of an application in which server-side redirection is appropriate. For example, the data submitted often require analysis and validation exceeding the capability of client-side validation. In this case, the search input data are submitted to the server for robust examination and validation. If the search input fulfills the examination and validation criteria, the application is redirected to a page able to perform the search using the input. If the examination and validation show the search input to be lacking, the client is informed accordingly.

Consider the page SourcePage.aspx, shown in Figure 12.8A, that contains a textbox for entry of a name to be used in a database search. Typically, additional controls will be used to enable the specification of added search criteria. The form also contains a button for posting the form to the server. A Label control is also provided for reporting server-side examination and validation results that require client-side attention.

When the form is posted, the submitted data are examined and validated in the Search_Click method declared in the code-behind file and wired to the page's searchButton

```
<%@ Page language="c#" Codebehind="SourcePage.aspx.cs"
    AutoEventWireup="false" Inherits="ServerSide.SourcePage" %>
<!DOCTYPE HTML PUBLIC "-//W3C//DTD HTML 4.0 Transitional//EN" >
<HTML>
  <HEAD>
  </HEAD>
  <body >
  <form id="SourcePage" method="post" runat="server">
    <asp:Label ID="Label1" Runat="server" Text="Enter Last
            Name:"></asp:Label>
    <asp:TextBox ID="searchName" Runat="server"></asp:TextBox>
    <asp:Literal id="Literal1" Runat="server"
            Text="<br>"></asp:Literal>
    <asp:Button ID="searchButton" Runat="server"
            OnClick="Search_Click" Text="Search"></asp:Button>
    <asp:Literal ID="Literal2" Runat="server" Text="<br>">
            </asp:Literal>
    <asp:Label ID="msgLabel" Runat="server"></asp:Label>
  </form>
  </body>
</HTML>
```

FIGURE 12.8A
Web Form SourcePage.aspx providing for input of search criteria.

```
using System;
using System.Web;

namespace ServerSide
{
  public class SourcePage : System.Web.UI.Page
  {
    protected System.Web.UI.WebControls.Literal literal1;
    protected System.Web.UI.WebControls.Literal Literal2;
    protected System.Web.UI.WebControls.Button searchButton;
    protected System.Web.UI.WebControls.Literal Literal1;
    protected System.Web.UI.WebControls.Label Label1;
    protected System.Web.UI.WebControls.TextBox searchName;
    protected System.Web.UI.WebControls.Label msgLabel;

    public void Search_Click(Object o, EventArgs e)
    {
      if (searchName.Text == "" )
        msgLabel.Text = "Name required to search";
      else
        Response.Redirect("TargetPage.aspx?searchName=" +
                          HttpUtility.UrlEncode(searchName.Text));
    }

    public SourcePage()
    {
      Page.Init += new System.EventHandler(Page_Init);
    }

    private void Page_Load(object sender, System.EventArgs e)
    {
    }

    private void Page_Init(object sender, EventArgs e)
    {
      InitializeComponent();
    }

    #region Web Form Designer generated code
    private void InitializeComponent()
    {
      this.Load += new System.EventHandler(this.Page_Load);
    }
    #endregion
  }
}
```

FIGURE 12.8B
Code-behind SourcePage.aspx.cs providing for input of search criteria.

control. The code-behind file is shown in Figure 12.8B. The content of the searchName textbox is examined:

```
if (searchName.Text =  = "")
```

If the box is blank, the form is returned to the client with the message

```
msgLabel.Text = "Name required to search";
```

If the box is not blank, the client's browser is redirected to the page TargetPage.aspx with the Response class Redirect method:

```
Response.Redirect("TargetPage.aspx?searchName = " +
    HttpUtility.UrlEncode(searchName.Text));
```

Additionally, a name/value pair is attached to the URL. The name part is "searchName" and the value part the encoded Text property of the form's searchName control. Encoding is performed with the HttpUtility class's URLEncode method.

```
<%@ Page language="c#" Codebehind="TargetPage.aspx.cs"
AutoEventWireup="false" Inherits="ServerSide.TargetPage" %>
<!DOCTYPE HTML PUBLIC "-//W3C//DTD HTML 4.0 Transitional//EN" >
<HTML>
  <HEAD>
  </HEAD>
  <body >
    <form id="TargetPage" method="post" runat="server">
      Search results for:
      <asp:Label ID="msgLabel" Runat="server"></asp:Label>
    </form>
  </body>
</HTML>
```

FIGURE 12.8C
Web Form TargetPage.aspx.

```
using System;

namespace ServerSide
{
      public class TargetPage : System.Web.UI.Page
      {
            protected System.Web.UI.WebControls.Label msgLabel;

            public TargetPage()
            {
                  Page.Init += new System.EventHandler(Page_Init);
            }

            private void Page_Load(object sender, System.EventArgs e)
            {
                  msgLabel.Text = Request.QueryString["searchName"];
            }

            private void Page_Init(object sender, EventArgs e)
            {
                  InitializeComponent();
            }

            #region Web Form Designer generated code
            private void InitializeComponent()
            {
                  this.Load += new System.EventHandler(this.Page_Load);

            }
            #endregion
      }
}
```

FIGURE 12.8D
Web Form TargetPage.aspx code-behind file (TargetPage.aspx.cs).

Redirection at the browser is to the page TargetPage.aspx shown in Figure 12.8C. The page contains static text and a Label control for displaying search results. Results of the search are performed in the Page_Load method defined in the code-behind file, Figure 12.8D. In this case, the search results are simply the value of the searchName passed in the posting as a name/value pair attached to the URL.

The SourcePage.aspx appears as shown in Figure 12.8E, in which a name with punctuation has been entered. When the Search button is clicked, the form is posted to the server. The searchName textbox is not empty and the client is redirected to the page targetPage with the search name attached to the URL as a name/value pair. TargetPage.aspx is displayed at the browser in Figure 12.8F.

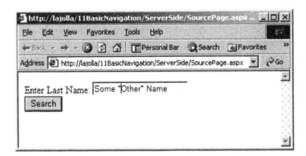

FIGURE 12.8E
Web Form SourcePage.aspx with punctuated name entered.

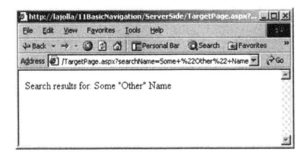

FIGURE 12.8F
Web Form TargetPage.aspx with passed name.

Tip!

The HttpResponse's redirect method redirects a client to a new URL.

13

Value Selection

Lists

List Web server controls provide for user selection of items in the list. The list Web server controls are ListBox, DropdownList, CheckBoxList and RadioButtonList. The List Web controls are containers for items displayed in the list. Figure 13.1 illustrates a list control that contains three items.

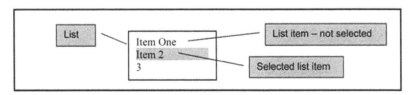

FIGURE 13.1
List control architecture.

The list items are user selectable; in the example, the second item in the list is selected. Values associated with a list item are accessible programmatically. In the example, only one item in the list is selected. Some lists provide for selection of more than one item. The **ListSelectionMode** enumeration summarized in Figure 13.2 represents list selection mode options.

public enum ListSelectionMode	
Namespace: System.Web.UI.WebControl	
Member Name	**Description**
Multiple	Multiple item selection.
Single	Single item selection.

FIGURE 13.2
ListSelectionMode enumeration summary.

Properties common to list-type controls are defined in the **ListControl** class summarized in Figure 13.3.

The AutoPostBack property is useful in that, when set true, the page is automatically posted back to the server whenever a user changes the list selection. This property is often used to reconfigure the user interface based on a list selection. For example, in a health user interface, the selection options and default values might change based on the user's sex. The default value is false, and changing the selection does not result in an automatic postback.

public abstract class ListControl : WebControl	
Hierarchy	
Object 　Control 　　WebControl 　　　ListControl	
Namespace: System.Web.UI.WebControls	
Constructor	
public ListControl()	Initializes a new instance of the ListControl class.
Public Instance Properties	
public virtual bool **AutoPostBack** {get; set;}	Gets or sets the value indicating that a postback automatically occurs whenever a user changes the list selection. If set true, postback occurs automatically whenever the list selection changes; false otherwise. The default value is false.
public virtual string **DataMember** {get; set;}	Gets or sets the value indicating the DataSource table to bind to the control. The property value is a string specifying the table in the DataSource.
public virtual object **DataSource** {get; set;}	Gets or sets the data source used to populate the list's items. The property value is a data source object.
public virtual string **DataTextField** {get; set;}	Gets or sets the value indicating that a postback automatically occurs whenever a user changes changes; false otherwise. The default value is false.
public virtual string 　**DataTextFormatString** {get; set;}	Gets or sets the formatting string that specifies how the control is displayed.
public virtual string **DataValueField** {get; set;}	Gets or sets the field that provides the value of the list item.
public virtual ListItemCollection **Items** {get;}	Gets the collection of items in the list. The property value is a ListItemCollection object representing the items in the list. The default is an empty list.
public virtual int **SelectedIndex** {get; set;}	Gets and sets the lowest ordinal index of the selected items. The default is −1 indicating no items are selected.
public virtual ListItem **SelectedItem** {get;}	Gets the ListItem object representing the selected item with the lowest index. The default is a null reference indicating nothing is selected.

FIGURE 13.3
ListControl class summary.

ListItem Control

A **ListItem** control represents an individual item in a list control; it is summarized in Figure 13.4.

The Text and Value properties provide for separation of the item's caption and the value associated with the item. For example, an item can be displayed with the caption "Fee" and be associated with the value 5.75 if the Text property is assigned the value Fee and the Value property is assigned the value 5.75. The ListItem controls in the example are declared with the following statements:

```
public sealed class ListItem : IstateManager, IparserAccessor, IattributeAccessor

Hierarchy
Object
   ListItem

Namespace: System.Web.UI.WebControls

Control Syntax
<asp:ListItem Value=value, Text=text, Selected=selectValue>InnerHTMLContnent</asp:ListItem>

Public Instance Constructors
public ListItem()                          Initializes a new instance of the ListItem class with
                                           all fields set to their default values.
public ListItem(string text)               Initializes a new instance of the ListItem class with
                                           the specified text.
public ListItem(string text, string value)) Initializes a new instance of the ListItem class with
                                           the specified text and value.

Public Static Method
Public static ListItem FromString(string s); Creates a ListItem from the string s.

Public Instance Properties (Selected)
public bool Selected {get; set;}           Gets and sets the selected value of the item. The
                                           item is selected if true and not selected if false. The
                                           default is false.
public string Text {get; set;}             Gets and sets the item's text displayed. When not
                                           specified, the Value content is displayed if it exists.
                                           The default is the String.Empty, an empty string.
public string Value {get; set;}            Gets and sets the item's Value content. When not
                                           specified, the Text content is used if it exists.
```

FIGURE 13.4
ListItem summary.

```
<asp:ListItem Selected = False Text = "item 1" Value = "1">Item One
    </asp:ListItem>
<asp:ListItem Selected = true Text = "Item 2" Value = "2">
    </asp:ListItem>
<asp:ListItem Selected = false Value = "3">
    </asp:ListItem>
```

User-selected items are rendered highlighted. The Selected property of selected ListItem controls is set true and false otherwise. Some controls, such as the ListBox control, provide for multiple item selection. The text displayed and value exposed depend on the item's Text, Value and Inner HTML Content, as specified in Figure 13.5.

Text Property	Value Property	Inner HTML Content	Text Displayed	Value Exposed
Set	Set	Set	Inner HTML Content	Value Property
Set	Set	Not Set	Text Property	Value Property
Set	Not Set	Set	Inner HTML Content	Inner HTML Content
Set	Not Set	Not Set	TextProperty	Text Property
Not Set	Set	Set	Inner HTML Content	Value Property
Not Set	Set	Not Set	Value Property	Value Property
Not Set	Not Set	Set	Inner HTML Content	Inner HTML Content
Not Set	Not Set	Not Set	Not Set	Not Set

FIGURE 13.5
ListItem text displayed.

Correspondingly, the first item specifies an Inner HTML Content, "Item One," and, even though the Text property is specified, the Inner HTML Content is displayed. The second item does not have an Inner HTML Content, but has a Text property value, which is displayed. In the third item, neither an Inner HTML Content nor Text property value is specified; consequently, the value of the Value property is displayed. Because the Text and Value properties provide for empty string default values, a list can have empty list items.

ListBox Control

The ListBox control serves as a container for ListItem controls and represents the ListBox control. Figure 13.6 summarizes the **ListBox** class. A ListBox is useful when a long list of selection options must be presented to the user for selection.

public class ListBox : ListControl, IPostBackDataHandler	
Hierarchy	

Object
  Control
    WebControl
      ListControl
        ListBox	

Namespace: System.Web.UI.WebControls	
Constructor	
public ListBox()	Initializes a new instance of the ListBox class
Public Instance Properties	
public override Color **BorderColor** {get; set;}	Not applicable. Gets or sets the BorderColor.
public override BorderStyle **BorderStyle** {get; set;}	Not applicable. Gets or sets the BorderStyle.
public override Unit **BorderWidth** {get; set;}	Not applicable. Gets or sets the BorderWidth.
public virtual int **Rows** {get; set;}	Gets or sets the number of rows displayed in the ListBox. The number or rows displayed must be in the range 1 to 2000. The default value is 4.
public virtual **ListSelectionMode** {get; set;}	Gets or sets the selection mode. Only a single item in the ListBox can be selected when set to ListSelectionMode.Single. Multiple items can be selected when set to ListSelectionMode.Multiple. Default is Single.
public override string **ToolTip** {get; set;}	Not applicable. Gets or sets the ToolTip displayed when the pointer cursor rests over the ListBox.

FIGURE 13.6
ListBox class summary.

Note that the BorderColor, BorderStyle, BorderWidth and ToolTip properties inherited from the WebControl class are overridden and are applicable to the ListBox class.

Typically, the user selects one of the options from the list. By default, the user can only select one of the list items; the selected item is highlighted. Clicking another item deselects the previously selected item and selects the clicked item. Multiple items can be selected if the ListSelectionMode property is set to "Multiple."

Normally, only four rows of a list are displayed in the list box. The number of rows displayed can be specified with the Rows property. A scroll bar is automatically provided

```
<%@ Page language="c#" Codebehind="ValueSelection.aspx.cs" AutoEventWireup="false"
Inherits="UsingListBoxes.ValueSelection" %>
<HTML>
 <HEAD>
 </HEAD>
 <body MS_POSITIONING="GridLayout">

   <form id="ValueSelection" method="post" runat="server">
     <asp:Label ID="Label1" Runat="server" Text="Birthdate Verification:"></asp:Label><br>
     <asp:ListBox ID=verificationList Runat=server Rows=7>
       <asp:ListItem Text="Baptism or church certification" Value="01"></asp:ListItem>
       <asp:ListItem Text="Birth certificate" Value="02"></asp:ListItem>
       <asp:ListItem Text="Entry in Family Bible" Value="03"></asp:ListItem>
       <asp:ListItem Text="Hospital certificate" Value="04"></asp:ListItem>
       <asp:ListItem Text="Parent's affidavit" Value="05"></asp:ListItem>
       <asp:ListItem Text="Passport" Value="06"></asp:ListItem>
       <asp:ListItem Text="Physican's certificate" Value="07"></asp:ListItem>
       <asp:ListItem Text="Previously verified school records" Value="08"></asp:ListItem>
       <asp:ListItem Text="State-issued ID" Value="09"></asp:ListItem>
       <asp:ListItem Text="Driver's license" Value="10"></asp:ListItem>
       <asp:ListItem Text="Immigration document" Value="11"></asp:ListItem>
       <asp:ListItem Text="None" Value="98"></asp:ListItem>
       <asp:ListItem Text="Other" Value="99"></asp:ListItem>
     </asp:ListBox>
     <br>
     <br>
     <asp:Label ID=msgLabel Runat=server></asp:Label>
     <br>
     <asp:Button ID=enterButton Runat=server Text=Enter
                 OnClick=Enter_Click></asp:Button>
   </form>

 </body>
</HTML>
```

FIGURE 13.7A
Web page with birthdate verification list box (UsingListBoxes.ValueSelectin.aspx).

when the number of items in the list is greater than the number of items displayed. The page shown in Figure 13.7A illustrates the use of a list box enabling indication of the method used to verify a birthdate.

The page contains a ListBox named verificationList. The number of rows displayed is explicitly set to seven with the Rows property. The list box contains 13 list items; each is represented by a ListItem control and specifies the text displayed and the item's value. The page also contains a label for displaying messages named msgLabel and a button for initiating the postback to the server named enterButton. When displayed, the page appears as shown in Figure 13.7B.

Note that seven of the thirteen list items are displayed and that a scroll bar is provided to enable viewing and selection of the other items. Note also that the list is initially displayed with none of the items selected and that an item could have been selected by setting the Selected property of one of the list items to true.

Clicking the Enter button posts the page back to the server and invokes the method Enter_Click. The code-behind file is shown in Figure 13.7C.

The ListBox's SelectedIndex property is tested to ascertain if an item has been selected:

```
if(verificationList.SelectedIndex =  = -1)
```

If the SelectedIndex property value is –1, no item has been selected, and the BackColor of the list box is set to LightPink to alert the user to the problem area; a bright red message to the user is displayed in the msgLabel:

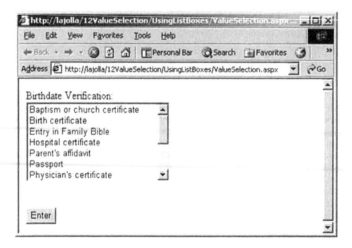

FIGURE 13.7B
Page UsingListBoxes/ValueSelection.aspx displayed in browser.

```
verificationList.BackColor = System.Drawing.Color.LightPink;
msgLabel.ForeColor = System.Drawing.Color.Red;
msgLabel.Text = "Select Birthdate Verification method!";
```

The page displayed is shown in Figure 13.7D. If an item has been selected, the list box backcolor is set to White and the Value and Test properties of the selected list item are displayed:

```
verificationList.BackColor = System.Drawing.Color.White;
msgLabel.ForeColor = System.Drawing.Color.Black;
msgLabel.Text = "Birthdate Verification Selection " + "<br>" +
    "Value: " + verificationList.SelectedItem.Value + "<br>" +
    "Text: " + verificationList.SelectedItem.Text;
```

Figure 13.7E shows the page returned to the user when "Baptism or church certificate" is selected and the Enter button clicked.

Dynamically Loaded List

Often the list items are not static but dependent upon information available to the application. In these cases, the items are added to the list programmatically. An example of an application in which the list items are added dynamically is the application Dynamically-LoadedList. Consider the page shown in Figure 13.8A.

The page contains an empty ListBox control. The list items are added during execution of the Page_Load method defined in the code-behind file. Although in this case the items are added as "hard code" they typically are the result of a data query based on user data input. The "hard code" in this case builds the table itemList (Figure 13.8B).

The code-behind file is shown in Figure 13.8C. The statement

```
using System.Data;
```

is required to expose members of the namespace System.Data.

```
using System;

namespace UsingListBoxes
{
  public class ValueSelection : System.Web.UI.Page
  {
    protected System.Web.UI.WebControls.Label Label1;
    protected System.Web.UI.WebControls.Label msgLabel;
    protected System.Web.UI.WebControls.Button enterButton;
    protected System.Web.UI.WebControls.ListBox verificationList;

    public void Enter_Click(Object o, EventArgs ea) {
      if(verificationList.SelectedIndex == -1) {
         verificationList.BackColor=System.Drawing.Color.LightPink;
         msgLabel.ForeColor = System.Drawing.Color.Red;
         msgLabel.Text="Select Birthdate Verification method!";
      }
      else {
         verificationList.BackColor=System.Drawing.Color.White;
         msgLabel.ForeColor = System.Drawing.Color.Black;
         msgLabel.Text = "Birthdate Verification Selection " + "<br>" +
            "Value: " + verificationList.SelectedItem.Value + "<br>" +
            "Text: " + verificationList.SelectedItem.Text;
      }
    }

    public ValueSelection() {
      Page.Init += new System.EventHandler(Page_Init);
    }

    private void Page_Load(object sender, System.EventArgs e) {
      // Put user code to initialize the page here
    }

    private void Page_Init(object sender, EventArgs e) {
      InitializeComponent();
    }

    #region Web Form Designer generated code
    private void InitializeComponent() {
      this.Load += new System.EventHandler(this.Page_Load);
    }
    #endregion
  }
}
```

FIGURE 13.7C
Code-behind file.

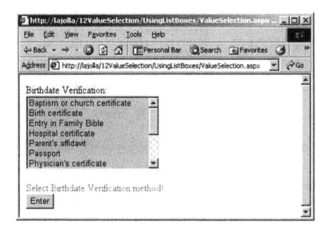

FIGURE 13.7D
Page returned to user when an item has not been selected.

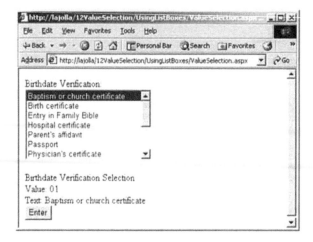

FIGURE 13.7E
Page returned to user when an item has been selected.

```
<%@ Page language="c#" Codebehind="DataEntry.aspx.cs" AutoEventWireup="false"
Inherits="DynamicallyLoadedList.DataEntry" %>
<HTML>
  <HEAD>
  </HEAD>
  <body MS_POSITIONING="GridLayout">
    <form id="DataEntry" method="post" runat="server">
      <asp:Label ID=verificationLabel Runat=server text="Birthdate
                 Verication"></asp:Label>
      <br>
      <asp:ListBox ID=verificationList Runat=server></asp:ListBox>
      <br>
      <br>
      <asp:Label ID=msgLabel Runat=server></asp:Label>
      <br>
      <asp:Button ID=enterButton Runat=server Text=Enter ></asp:Button>
    </form>
  </body>
</HTML>
```

FIGURE 13.8A
Page with an empty list box (DynamicallyLoadedList/DataEntry.aspx).

Code	Description
01	Baptism or church certificate
02	Birth certificate
03	Entry in Family Bible
04	Hospital certificate
05	Parent's affidavit
98	None

FIGURE 13.8B
Table itemList.

The DataTable itemList is created; the table's columns are created and added to the table itemList:

```
DataTable itemList = new DataTable();
```

The table's columns are created, initialized and added to the table:

```
itemList.Columns.Add(new DataColumn("code",typeof(string)));
itemList.Columns.Add(new
    DataColumn("description",typeof(string)));
```

```
using System;
using System.Data;

namespace DynamicallyLoadedList {
  public class DataEntry : System.Web.UI.Page {
    protected System.Web.UI.WebControls.ListBox verificationList;
    protected System.Web.UI.WebControls.Label msgLabel;
    protected System.Web.UI.WebControls.Button enterButton;

    public DataEntry() {
      Page.Init += new System.EventHandler(Page_Init);
    }

    private void Page_Load(object sender, System.EventArgs e) {
      if(!IsPostBack){
```
                              [Table created and columns defined]
```
        DataTable itemList = new DataTable();
        itemList.Columns.Add(new DataColumn("code",typeof(string)));
        itemList.Columns.Add(new
                      DataColumn("description",typeof(string)));

        DataRow listItem;
        listItem = itemList.NewRow();
        listItem[0] = "01";
        listItem[1] = "Baptism or church certificate";
        itemList.Rows.Add(listItem);

        listItem = itemList.NewRow();
        listItem[0] = "02";
        listItem[1] = "Birth certificate";
        itemList.Rows.Add(listItem);

        listItem = itemList.NewRow();
        listItem[0] = "03";
        listItem[1] = "Entry in family Bible";          [ Table rows
        itemList.Rows.Add(listItem);                       created and
                                                           initialized ]
        listItem = itemList.NewRow();
        listItem[0] = "04";
        listItem[1] = "Hospital certificate";
        itemList.Rows.Add(listItem);

        listItem = itemList.NewRow();
        listItem[0] = "05";
        listItem[1] = "Parent's affidavit";
        itemList.Rows.Add(listItem);

        listItem = itemList.NewRow();
        listItem[0] = "98";
        listItem[1] = "None";
        itemList.Rows.Add(listItem);
```

FIGURE 13.8C
Code-behind file with "hard-coded" list box items (DynamicallyLoadedList/DataEntry.aspx.cs).

The first column is initialized with name "code" and data type string. The second column is initialized with name "description" and data type string. A DataRow object reference, listItem, is declared:

```
DataRow listItem;
```

A new itemList table row is created and returned by the table's NewRow method and assigned to the reference listItem:

```
listItem = itemList.NewRow();
```

The columns of the row are initialized:

```
listItem[0] = "01";

listItem[1] = "Baptism or church certificate";
```

```
        verificationList.DataSource = itemList;
        verificationList.DataValueField ="code";
        verificationList.DataTextField ="description";
        verificationList.DataBind();
    }
}

public void Enter_Click(Object o, EventArgs ea){
    if(verificationList.SelectedIndex == -1)
    {
        verificationList.BackColor=System.Drawing.Color.LightPink;
        msgLabel.ForeColor = System.Drawing.Color.Red;
        msgLabel.Text="Select Birthdate Verification method!";
    }
    else
    {
        verificationList.BackColor=System.Drawing.Color.White;
        msgLabel.ForeColor = System.Drawing.Color.Black;
        msgLabel.Text = "Birthdate Verification Selection " + "<br>" +
                        "Value: " +
                        verificationList.SelectedItem.Value + "<br>" +
                        "Text: " + verificationList.SelectedItem.Text;
    }
}

private void Page_Init(object sender, EventArgs e)
{
    InitializeComponent();
}

#region Web Form Designer generated code
private void InitializeComponent()
{
    this.Load += new System.EventHandler(this.Page_Load);
}
#endregion
    }
}
```

FIGURE 13.8C (CONTINUED)
Code-behind file with "hard-coded" list box items (DynamicallyLoadedList/DataEntry.aspx.cs).

The first column is initialized to value "01" and the second column to value "Baptism or church certificate." Finally, the row, listItem, is added to the table's Rows collection property with the collection's Add method.

```
itemList.Rows.Add(listItem);
```

Additional rows, comprising the table, are similarly created, initialized and added to the table.

The table's items are then identified as the verificationList's list items with the ListBox using the DataSource property:

```
verificationList.DataSource = itemList;
```

The table's "code" column is specified as the list's value property with the statement

```
verificationList.DataValueField = "code";
```

Similarly, the table's "description" column is specified as the list's text property with the statement

```
verificationList.DataTextField = "description";
```

Note the interchange of field and column.

Finally, the ListBox control, verificationList, is data-bound to the DataSouce specified by its DataSource property:

```
verificationList.DataBind();
```

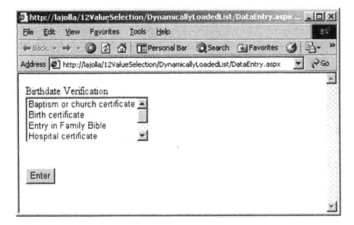

FIGURE 13.8D
DynamicallyLoadedList/DataEntry.aspx as first displayed at a client browser.

The code to dynamically load the list items is contained in the Page_Load method invoked every time the page is loaded. However, the code is enclosed in a selection block that is only executed when the IsPostBack page property is not true, i.e., the first time the page is loaded. Figure 13.8D illustrates the page as first displayed at a client browser.

Finally, the list can be modified dynamically by the addition of new rows and modification and deletion of existing rows.

Tip!

Use dynamically loaded lists to tailor the list to user characteristics thereby creating a user-friendly and efficient interface.

DropDownList Control

The **DropDownList** Web server control enables users to select a single item from a predefined list; the list can be defined statically or dynamically. The DropDownList displays only the selected item and a drop-down button. When the drop-down button is clicked, the hidden items are displayed, enabling the user to make a selection. Upon selection, the list disappears and only the selected item is displayed. Regarding appearance, the following conditions should be observed:

- Some browsers do not support the width and height property values.
- The browser determines the number of items displayed when the drop-down button is clicked.

The DropDownList Web control (Figure 13.9) is a container for ListItems objects that represent the list's items. One item is always selected. The list's items can be added statically or dynamically.

```
public class DropDownList : ListControl, IpostBackHandler

Hierarchy

Object
   Control
      WebControl
         ListControl
            DropDownList

Namespace: System.web.UI.WebControls

Constructor
public DropDownList()                        Initializes a new instance of the DropDownList
                                             class.

Public Instance Properties
public override Color BorderColor {get; set;}   Not applicable. Gets or sets the BorderColor.
public override BorderStyle BorderStyle {get; set;}  Not applicable. Gets or sets the BorderStyle.
public override Unit BorderWidth {get; set;}    Not applicable. Gets or sets the BorderWidth.
public override int SelectedIndex {get; set;}   Gets or sets the index of the selected item.
                                                The default value is zero.
public override string ToolTip {get; set;}      Not applicable. Gets or sets the ToolTip
                                                displayed when the pointer cursor rests over
                                                the DropDownList.
```

FIGURE 13.9
DropDownList class summary.

```
<%@ Page language="c#" Codebehind=" DataEntry.aspx.cs" AutoEventWireup="false"
         Inherits="UsingDropDownLists.DataEntry" %>
  <HEAD>
  </HEAD>
  <body MS_POSITIONING="GridLayout">
    <form id="DataEntry" method="post" runat="server">
      <asp:Label ID=verificationLabel Runat=server text="Birthdate
                 Verication"></asp:Label>
      <br>
      <asp:DropDownList ID=verificationList Runat=server></asp:DropDownList>
      <br>
      <br>
      <asp:Label ID=msgLabel Runat=server></asp:Label>
      <br>
      <asp:Button ID=enterButton Runat=server Text=Enter ></asp:Button>
    </form>
  </body>
</HTML>
```

FIGURE 13.10A
Page with an empty drop-down list (UsingDropDownLists/DataEntry.aspx).

The application UsingDropDownLists provides an example of an application using the DropDownList Web control with dynamically loaded list items. The Web page is shown in Figure 13.10A.

The page contains an empty DropDownList control. The list items are added during execution of the Page_Load method defined in the code-behind file. The list items "hard-code," in this case, builds the table itemList.

The code-behind file is shown in Figure 13.10B. Items are added to the DropDownList, verificationList, in the Page_Load method. The code is similar to that used to create, initialize and load the list items in the ListBox control in DynamicallyLoadedList/DataEntry.aspx.cs.

The initially selected item is specified by assigning a value to the SelectedIndex property with the statement

```
verificationList.SelectedIndex = 1;
```

```
using System;
using System.Data;

namespace UsingDropDownLists
{
    public class DataEntry : System.Web.UI.Page
    {
        protected System.Web.UI.WebControls.Label verificationLabel;
        protected System.Web.UI.WebControls.DropDownList verificationList;
        protected System.Web.UI.WebControls.Label msgLabel;
        protected System.Web.UI.WebControls.Button enterButton;

        public DataEntry()
        {
            Page.Init += new System.EventHandler(Page_Init);
        }

        private void Page_Load(object sender, System.EventArgs e)
        {
            if(!IsPostBack)
            {
```
| | DataTable itemList created and its columns defined |
```
                DataTable itemList = new DataTable();
                itemList.Columns.Add(new DataColumn("code",typeof(string)));
                itemList.Columns.Add(new
                            DataColumn("description",typeof(string)));

                DataRow listItem;
                listItem = itemList.NewRow();
                listItem[0] = "01";
                listItem[1] = "Baptism or church certificate";
                itemList.Rows.Add(listItem);

                listItem = itemList.NewRow();
                listItem[0] = "02";
                listItem[1] = "Birth certificate";
                itemList.Rows.Add(listItem);

                listItem = itemList.NewRow();
                listItem[0] = "03";
                listItem[1] = "Entry in family Bible";
                itemList.Rows.Add(listItem);
```
| | Rows created, initialized and added to table itemList |
```
                listItem = itemList.NewRow();
                listItem[0] = "04";
                listItem[1] = "Hospital certificate";
                itemList.Rows.Add(listItem);

                listItem = itemList.NewRow();
                listItem[0] = "05";
                listItem[1] = "Parent's affidavit";
                itemList.Rows.Add(listItem);

                listItem = itemList.NewRow();
                listItem[0] = "98";
                listItem[1] = "None";
                itemList.Rows.Add(listItem);
```

FIGURE 13.10B
Code-behind dynamically loads the list's items (UsingDropDownLists/DataEntry.aspx.cs).

Note that the items are identified ordinal with a zero-based index. Thus, the second item in the list is selected when the value 1 is assigned to the SelectedIndex property. The default value of the SelectedIndex property is zero, and thus the first item in the list is the default selection when the SelectedIndex property is not set.

The drop-down list is initially displayed with the second list item selected (Figure 13.10C).

Tip!

The DropDownList Web control can be used to allow user selection of a single item in a list displayed when the user clicks the list's drop-down button. Minimal user interface page space is required to implement a drop-down list.

```
        verificationList.DataSource = itemList;
        verificationList.DataValueField ="code";          }  ── Data
        verificationList.DataTextField ="description";     }     binding
        verificationList.DataBind();

        verificationList.SelectedIndex = 1;    ──    Selecting second item
    }                                                    using zero-based index
}

public void Enter_Click(Object o, EventArgs ea)
{
    if(verificationList.SelectedIndex == -1)
    {
        verificationList.BackColor=System.Drawing.Color.LightPink;
        msgLabel.ForeColor = System.Drawing.Color.Red;
        msgLabel.Text="Select Birthdate Verification method!";
    }
    else
    {
        verificationList.BackColor=System.Drawing.Color.White;
        msgLabel.ForeColor = System.Drawing.Color.Black;
        msgLabel.Text = "Birthdate Verification Selection " + "<br>" +
            "Value: " + verificationList.SelectedItem.Value + "<br>" +
            "Text: " + verificationList.SelectedItem.Text;
    }
}


private void Page_Init(object sender, EventArgs e)
{
    InitializeComponent();
}

#region Web Form Designer generated code
private void InitializeComponent()
{
    this.Load += new System.EventHandler(this.Page_Load);

}
#endregion
    }
}
```

FIGURE 13.10B (CONTINUED)
Code-behind dynamically loads the list's items (UsingDropDownLists/DataEntry.aspx.cs).

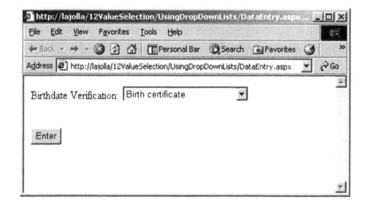

FIGURE 13.10C
Page UsingDropDownLists/DataEntry.aspx displayed in a browser illustrating DropdownList.

CheckBoxes and Radio Buttons

Check boxes are used to enable multiple selections within a group. Radio buttons are used to restrict selection to one and only one item in a group.

Text associated with the control can be situated to the left or to the right of the control. The **TextAlign** enumeration represents the text alignment options for the checkbox and radio button controls. The TextAlign enumeration is listed in Figure 13.11.

public enum TextAlign	
Namespace: System.Web.UI.Web.Controls	
Member Name	**Description**
Left	Text appears to the left of the control.
Right	Text appears to the right of the control.

FIGURE 13.11
TextAlign enumeration listing.

Checkbox Control

The **Checkbox** control creates a checkbox on the Web Forms page. Clicking the control toggles the control between the checked and unchecked state. The checkbox control enables the user to respond with a "yes" by clicking the checkbox or "no" by unchecking the checkbox.

Tag	Property	Description
<asp:CheckBox		Opening tag.
	id	Unique identification. Required if the control is to be accessed programmatically.
	AutoPostBack	Default is false.
	Text	String specifying the caption appearing to the left or right of the control.
	TextAlign	TextAlign enumeration member specifying the alignment of the control's Text property value. The default value is Right.
	Checked	Specifies if the control appears checked. Default is false.
	OnCheckedChanged	Handler for the CheckedChanged event. The CheckedChanged event is raised when the Checked property is changed.
	Runat	Required property with value "server."
/>		The element does not have content and thus can be closed with the /> tag instead of a separate closing tag.

FIGURE 13.12
Textbox control syntax.

The CheckBox control syntax is shown in Figure 13.12.

The following example shows the declaration of a CheckBox control. The control has a caption (Enrolled) specified by the Text attribute. The TextAlign attribute assumes the default value and thus the caption appears to the right of the control. The checkbox appears unchecked initially because the Checked attribute is not set true; the default value is false.

The AutoPostBack attribute is set true and thus the form is posted to the server whenever the checkbox is clicked.

```
<asp:CheckBox ID = enrolled Runat = server
    AutoPostBack = True
    Text = Enrolled>
</asp:CheckBox>
```

The declaration could also be expressed as

```
<asp:CheckBox ID = enrolled Runat = server
    AutoPostBack = True
    Text = Enrolled>
/>
```

The control does not have content and can be closed with the /> instead of a separate closing tag as above. The control is rendered as shown in Figure 13.13.

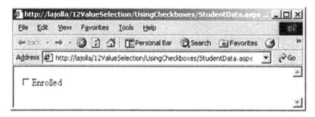

FIGURE 13.13
Example of a CheckBox control.

The CheckBox control is represented by the CheckBox class summarized in Figure 13.14.

Figure 13.15A illustrates a Web Form page with a CheckBox control. The control's caption, specified with the Text attribute, appears at the right side of the control, the TextAlign attribute default position. Note that the page will be posted to the server whenever the control is clicked because the AutoPostBack attribute has been set true. Note also that a handler, Enrolled_Checked, has been declared for the CheckedChanged event that is raised at the server whenever the control is clicked, i.e., the Checked property has been changed. The page appears as shown in Figure 13.15B.

The check box is initially shown with the default Checked setting, false. When the unchecked box is clicked, the control toggles to the checked state. The Web Form page is immediately posted to the server. The page's code-behind file is shown in Figure 13.15C. When the page is loaded, the pageLoadMsg control's Text property is assigned the value of the enrolled Checkbox control's Checked property.

```
pageLoadMsg.Text = "Page-Load Message: " +
    enrolled.Checked.ToString();
```

When the CheckedChanged event is raised, the checkedChangedMsg control's Text property is also assigned the value of the enrolled Checkbox control's Checked property. This is performed in the CheckedChanged event handler, Enrolled_Checked.

The returned page appears as shown in Figure 13.15D. Note that the state of the control has been toggled to the checked state. Note also that the messages clearly indicate that the current state of the control has been ascertained in the Page_Load method and the Enrolled_Checked method.

Typically, more extensive processing is performed. In the "real world" StudentData page, enrollment change procedures are initiated whenever the student's enrollment status changes.

public class CheckBox : WebControl, IPostBackDataHandler	
Hierarchy	
Object	
Control	
WebControl	
CheckBox	
Public Instance Constructor	
Public CheckBox();	Initializes a new instance of the CheckBox class.
Public Instance Properties	
public virtual bool **AutoPostBack** {get; set;}	The web form is automatically posted back to the server every time the CheckBox is clicked if set true; false otherwise. The default is false.
public virtual bool **Checked** {get; set;}	The CheckBox appears checked if set true; false otherwise. The default is false.
public virtual string **Text** {get; set;}	Caption appearing next to the control.
public virtual bool **Checked** {get; set;}	The CheckBox appears checked if set true; false otherwise. The default is false.
public virtual TextAlign **TextAlign** {get; set;}	Specifies where the caption appears. The default is Right.
Public Instance Event	
public event EventHandler **CheckedChanged**;	The CheckedChanged event occurs when the Checked property is changed.
Public Instance Method	
protected virtual void OnCheckedChanged(EventArgs *e*);	Handler for the CheckedChanged event. The parameter *e* contains information regarding the event.

FIGURE 13.14
CheckBox class summary.

```
<%@ Page language="c#" Codebehind="StudentData.aspx.cs"
         AutoEventWireup="false" Inherits="UsingCheckboxes.StudentData" %>
<HTML>
  <HEAD>
  </HEAD>
  <body MS_POSITIONING="GridLayout">
    <form id=StudentData method=post runat="server">
      <asp:checkbox id=enrolled Text="Enrolled"
                    AutoPostBack="True"
                    Runat="server"
                    OnCheckedChanged="Enrolled_Checked">
        </asp:checkbox><br>



    <asp:label id=checkedChangedMsg Runat="server"></asp:label><br>
    <asp:Label ID=pageLoadMsg Runat=server></asp:Label></FORM>
  </body>
</HTML>
```

Web Form is automatically posted to server when check box is clicked

Handler for CheckedChanged event raised at server

FIGURE 13.15A
Web Form illustrating a CheckBox control (UsingCheckBoxes.StudentData.aspx).

Tip!
Checkboxes are useful in collecting and displaying data characterized with two values such as yes/no, true/false or 1 and 2.

FIGURE 13.15B
Web Form page (UsingCheckBoxes.StudentData.aspx).

```
using System;

namespace UsingCheckboxes
{
  public class StudentData : System.Web.UI.Page
  {
    protected System.Web.UI.WebControls.Label checkedChangedMsg;
    protected System.Web.UI.WebControls.Label pageLoadMsg;
    protected System.Web.UI.WebControls.CheckBox enrolled;

    public void Enrolled_Checked(Object o, EventArgs e)
    {
      checkedChangedMsg.Text = "Enrolled_Checked: " +
                                 enrolled.Checked.ToString();
    }

    public StudentData()
    {
      Page.Init += new System.EventHandler(Page_Init);
    }

    private void Page_Load(object sender, System.EventArgs e)
    {
      if(IsPostBack)
      {
        pageLoadMsg.Text = "Page-Load Message: " + enrolled.Checked.ToString();
      }
    }

    private void Page_Init(object sender, EventArgs e)
    {
      InitializeComponent();
    }

    #region Web Form Designer generated code
    private void InitializeComponent()
    {
      this.Load += new System.EventHandler(this.Page_Load);

    }
    #endregion
  }
}
```

FIGURE 13.15C
Code-behind file (UsingCheckBoxes.StudentData.aspx.cs).

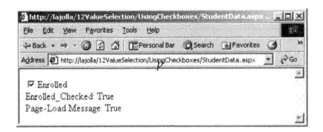

FIGURE 13.15D
Web Form page (UsingCheckBoxes.StudentData.aspx) after roundtrip initiated by clicking CheckBox.

RadioButton Control

The **RadioButton** control creates a radio button on the Web Forms page, which appears as a circle. The control has two states: checked and unchecked. The checked state is indicated by the appearance of a solid circle within the radio button. Clicking the control toggles the control between the checked and unchecked state. The RadioButton control enables the user to respond with a "yes" by checking the radio button or "no" by unchecking the radio button. Checked and unchecked radio buttons are illustrated in Figure 13.16.

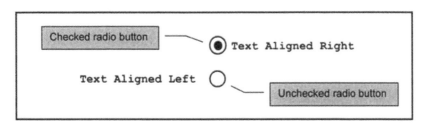

FIGURE 13.16
Illustrating RadioButton checked state, unchecked state and text alignment.

The text associated with a radio button can be aligned to the left or the right. Additionally, radio buttons can be grouped together to allow a single selection within the group. The RadioButton control syntax is shown in Figure 13.17.

RadioButton controls grouped to enable sex identification are illustrated in Figure 13.18A. The buttons are assigned to the group Sex with the GroupName property. The first button has the Text property value Female and ID property female. The second button has the Text property value Male and ID property male. In both cases, the text is aligned in the default position: right. Additionally, the Checked property is not set, and thus both buttons have the default value: false.

Tag	Property	Description
<asp:RadioButton		Opening tag.
	id	Unique identification. Required if the control is to be accessed programmatically.
	AutoPostBack	Default is false.
	Checked	Specifies if the control appears checked. Default is false.
	GroupName	String specifying the name of the group to which the radio button belongs.
	Text	String specifying the caption appearing to the left or right of the control.
	TextAlign	TextAlign enumeration member specifying the alignment of the control's Text property value. The default value is Right.
	OnCheckedChanged	Handler for the CheckedChanged event. The CheckedChanged event is raised when the Checked property is changed.
	Runat	Required property with value "server."
/>		The element does not have content and thus can be closed with the /> tag instead of a separate closing tag.

FIGURE 13.17
RadioButton control syntax.

```
<%@ Page language="c#" Codebehind="DataEntry.aspx.cs" AutoEventWireup="false"
         Inherits="UsingRadioButtonGroups.DataEntry" %>
<HTML>
  <HEAD>
  </HEAD>
  <body >
    <form id="DataEntry" method="post" runat="server">
      <asp:Label ID=sexLabel Runat=server text="Sex: "></asp:Label>
      <asp:RadioButton ID=female Runat=server Text=Female
                       GroupName=Sex></asp:RadioButton>
      <asp:RadioButton ID=male Runat=server Text=Male
                       GroupName=Sex></asp:RadioButton>
      <br>
      <br>
      <asp:Button ID=enterButton Runat=server Text=Enter
                  OnClick=Enter_Click></asp:Button>
      <br>
      <asp:Label ID=msgLabel Runat=server></asp:Label>
    </form>
  </body>
</HTML>
```

FIGURE 13.18A
RadioButton controls grouped to enable sex identification (UsingRadioButtongroups.DataEntry.aspx).

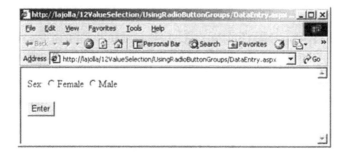

FIGURE 13.18B
Initial display of UsingRadioButtongroups.DataEntry.aspx.

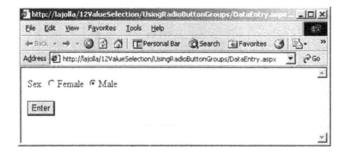

FIGURE 13.18C
UsingRadioButtongroups.DataEntry.aspx with Male radio button checked.

The initial display of the page is shown in Figure 13.18B. Note that the radio buttons are unchecked. If more than one button in a group is assigned the checked value, only the last button in the group with the Checked property set true will appear checked.

The female and male radio buttons belong to the group named Sex. As such, only one can be checked at a time. Checking one button in the group unchecks the other button in the group. Figure 13.18C shows the page with the Male radio button checked.

Although the AutoPostBack property can be set true, resulting in automatic posting of the form whenever the radio button Checked property is changed. At the server, the CheckChanged event is raised if the Checked property of a radio button has been changed. Note that the event is raised by each control individually; the radio button group does not raise the event. Identification of the checked control and subsequent processing can be performed in a handler for the CheckedChanged event.

Posting is usually initiated by clicking a button, such as the Entry button on the form shown. The code-behind file in Figure 13.18D illustrates the identification of the checked radio button.

The identification of the checked button is performed in the Enter_Click method. The Checked state of each radio button is ascertained in turn. The female radio button's Checked state is tested with the statement

```
if(female.Checked)
```

If the Checked property value is true, the message text value is set with the statement

```
msgLabel.Text = "Female selected";
```

Similarly, the `male` radio button's Checked state is tested with the statement

```
if(male.Checked)
```

Again, if the Checked property value is true, the message text value is set with the statement

```
msgLabel.Text = "Male selected";
```

If neither button's Checked property is true, the initial value of the message is displayed:

```
msgLabel.Text = "Select Sex";
msgLabel.ForeColor = System.Drawing.Color.Red;
```

alerting the user that a Sex selection is required.

Figure 13.18E shows that, when the male radio button is selected, the page is returned to the user.

The **RadioButton class** represents the RadioButton control and is summarized in Figure 13.18F. Note that the RadioButton class is derived from the CheckBox class and thus inherits its characteristics and functionality.

CheckBox and RadioButton Lists

The **CheckBoxList** control enables a group of CheckBox controls to be treated collectively, like items in a list. Similarly, the **RadioButtonList** control enables a group of RadioButton controls to be treated collectively.

The CheckBox and RadioButton controls comprising the list can be arranged in a tabular layout or simply one after the other. Members of the **RepeatLayout enumeration** represent the layout options (Figure 13.19).

The direction in which the members of a list control can be arranged is specified by the members of the **RepeatDirection enumeration,** as illustrated in Figure 13.20.

The list controls are declared with the ListItem control. The ListItem controls are rendered as check boxes when included in a CheckBoxList control. Similarly, ListItem controls are rendered as radio buttons when included in a RadioButtonList control.

A typical tabular layout is shown in Figure 13.21. The value of the CellPadding property is added to the height and width of the highest and widest control to determine the cell dimensions applied to all the cells in the list. The value of the CellSpacing property determines the spacing between the cells. The CellPadding and CellSpacing properties

```
using System;

namespace UsingRadioButtonGroups
{
        public class DataEntry : System.Web.UI.Page
        {
                protected System.Web.UI.WebControls.RadioButton female;
                protected System.Web.UI.WebControls.RadioButton male;
                protected System.Web.UI.WebControls.Button enterButton;
                protected System.Web.UI.WebControls.Label msgLabel;
                protected System.Web.UI.WebControls.Label sexLabel;

                public void Enter_Click(Object o, EventArgs e)
                {
                        msgLabel.Text = "Select Sex";
                        msgLabel.ForeColor = System.Drawing.Color.Red;

                        if(female.Checked)
                        {
                                msgLabel.Text = "Female selected";
                                msgLabel.ForeColor = System.Drawing.Color.Black;
                        }
                        if(male.Checked)
                        {
                                msgLabel.Text = "Male selected";
                                msgLabel.ForeColor = System.Drawing.Color.Black;
                        }
                }

                public DataEntry()
                {
                        Page.Init += new System.EventHandler(Page_Init);
                }

                private void Page_Load(object sender, System.EventArgs e)
                {
                }

                private void Page_Init(object sender, EventArgs e)
                {
                        InitializeComponent();
                }

                #region Web Form Designer generated code
                private void InitializeComponent()
                {
                        this.Load += new System.EventHandler(this.Page_Load);

                }
                #endregion
        }
}
```

FIGURE 13.18D
UsingRadioButtongroups.DataEntry.aspx.cs.

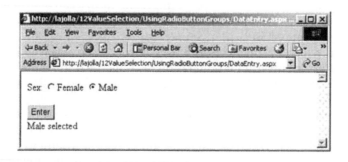

FIGURE 13.18E
UsingRadioButtongroups.DataEntry.aspx page returned to user when Male radio button was checked.

public class RadioButton : CheckBox	
Hierarchy	
Object	
Control	
WebControl	
CheckBox	
RadioButton	
Namespace: System.Web.UI.WebControls	
Public Instance Constructor	
public RadioButton();	Initializes a new instance of the RadioButton class.
Public Instance Properties	
public virtual string **GroupName** {get; set;}	The value specifies the name of the group that the radio button belongs to. Note only one button in the group can be selected at a time. Radio buttons on a form are logically grouped with the GroupName property. The default value is String.Empty.

FIGURE 13.18F
RadioButton class summary.

public enum RepeatLayout	
Namespace: System.Web.UI.Web.Controls	
Member Name	**Description**
Flow	Items displayed without tabular structure.
Table	Items displayed in tabular structure.

FIGURE 13.19
RepeatLayout enumeration.

public enum RepeatDirection	
Namespace: System.Web.UI.Web.Controls	
Member Name	**Description**
Horizontal	Items are arranged in left to right rows. The number of columns in each row is specified by the control's RepeatColumns property.
Vertical	Items are arranged from top to bottom in columns. The number of columns is specified by the control's RepeatColumns property.

FIGURE 13.20
RepeatDirection enumeration.

are specified in pixels. The default value for these properties is –1, signifying that the property value is not set.

The number of columns is determined by the RepeatColumns property. The default value for the RepeatColumn property is 0, indicating that the property value is not set.

Both the ListBoxList and the RadioButtonList classes inherit the SelectedIndexChanged event from the ListControl class. This event is raised at the server whenever a selection in the list occurs. If the list control's AutoPostBack property is set true, the form is automatically posted back to the server when the user selects any check box in the list. A handler for the event can be defined to process the selection. Typically, the selection processing is accomplished in a method associated with a button click.

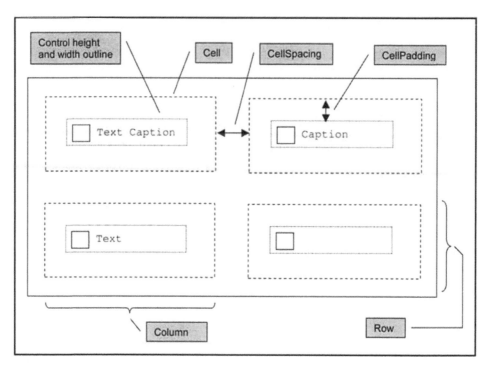

FIGURE 13.21
List layout illustrating CellPadding and CellSpacing properties.

RadioButtonList Control and Class

The RadioButtonList control syntax is shown in Figure 13.22. The **RadioButtonList** class represents the RadioButtonList control. Figure 13.23 summarizes the RadioButtonList class.

An example of a RadioButtonList control is shown in Figure 13.24A. The element describes a two-column list named englishProficiencyList:

```
<asp:RadioButtonList ID = englishProficiencyList Runat = server
    RepeatColumns = 2>

</asp:RadioButtonList>
```

The list contains five list items describing the various levels of English proficiency. The page's rendering is shown in Figure 13.24B.

Note that the list items are rendered as radio buttons in a two-column table and that an initial selection has not been made.

Server-side processing is defined in the code-behind file, shown in Figure 13.24C. Processing related to the list is handled in the Enter_Click method. The SelectedItem property, inherited from the ListControl class, gets the selected item with the lowest index in the list. The default value is a null reference. When none of the list items (radio buttons in this case) is selected, the SelectedItem property returns the default null.

First the value obtained by the SelectedItem property is tested for null:

```
if(englishProficiencyList.SelectedItem =  = null)
{
    msgLabel.Text = "Select English Proficiency";
```

Tag	Property	Description
<asp:RadioButtonList		Opening tag.
	id	Unique identification. Required if the control is to be accessed programmatically.
	AutoPostBack	The form is automatically posted to the server when the user selects a radio button in the list if true. Default is false.
	CellPadding	The padding in pixels between the border of the cell containing the widest and highest radio button in the list to determine the cell size to apply to all cells in the control. The default is –1 which indicates the property is not set.
	DataSource	String specifying the source used to initialize the list items text and value field values.
	DataTextField	String specifying the data source field used to initialize list item Text properties.
	DataValueField	String specifying the data source field used to initialize list item Value properties.
	RepeatColumns	Specifies the number of columns in which the list items are displayed. Default is 0 indicating property not set.
	RepeatDirection	RepeatDirection enumeration. Default is Vertical.
	RepeatLayout	RepeatLayout enumeration specifying the layout arrangement of the list items. Default is Table.
	TextAlign	TextAlign enumeration member specifying the alignment of the control's Text property value. The default value is Right.
	OnSelectedIndexChanged	Handler for the CheckedChanged event. The CheckedChanged event is raised when an item in the list's Checked property is changed.
	Runat	Required property with value "server".
>		Opening tag closing character.
</asp: RadioButtonList >		Closing tag.

FIGURE 13.22
RadioButtonList control syntax.

```
msgLabel.ForeColor = System.Drawing.Color.Red;
}
```

If null, indicating none of the list items is selected, a message is returned to the user. If not null, the ListItem class' object representing the selected object is returned by the property get operation. The selected ListItem's Text and Value property values are returned to the user in a message. Typically, they would be used in a database access:

```
else
{
    msgLabel.Text = "Selected Item: " +
        englishProficiencyList.SelectedItem.Value +
        " " + englishProficiencyList.SelectedItem.Text;
        msgLabel.ForeColor = System.Drawing.Color.Black;
}
```

The page returned to the user after processing, where the user selected the "Fluent Speaker" radio button, is shown in Figure 13.24D.

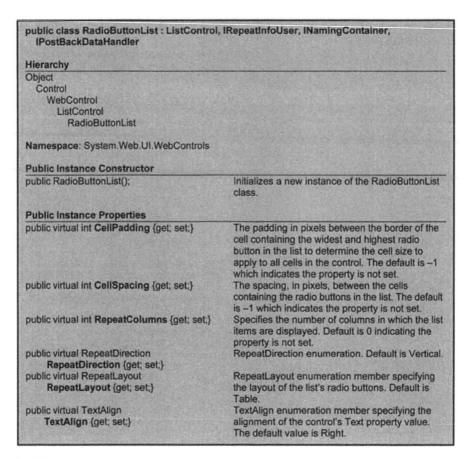

FIGURE 13.23
RadioButtonList class summary.

```
<%@ Page language="c#" Codebehind="DataEntry.aspx.cs" AutoEventWireup="false"
Inherits="UsingRadioButtonLists.DataEntry" %>
<!DOCTYPE HTML PUBLIC "-//W3C//DTD HTML 4.0 Transitional//EN" >
<HTML>
  <HEAD>
  </HEAD>
  <body MS_POSITIONING="GridLayout">
    <form id="DataEntry" method="post" runat="server">
      <asp:Label ID=label1 Runat=server Text="English Proficiency"></asp:Label>
      <br>
      <asp:RadioButtonList ID=englishProficiencyList Runat=server RepeatColumns=2>
        <asp:ListItem Text="Native Speaker" Value="01"/>
        <asp:ListItem Text="Fluent Speaker" Value="02"/>
        <asp:ListItem Text="Limited Proficiency" Value="03"/>
        <asp:ListItem Text="Non_English Speaking" Value="04"/>
        <asp:ListItem Text="Status Unknown" Value="99"/>
      </asp:RadioButtonList>
      <br>
      <asp:Button ID=enterButton Runat=server OnClick=Enter_Click
                  Text="Enter"></asp:Button>
      <br>
      <asp:Label ID=msgLabel Runat="server"></asp:Label>
      <br>
      <br>
    </FORM>
  </body>
</HTML>
```

FIGURE 13.24A
RadioButtonList example (UsingRadioButtons.DataEntry.aspx).

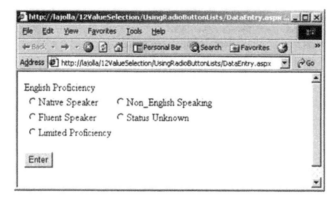

FIGURE 13.24B
RadioButtonList (UsingRadioButtons.DataEntry.aspx).

```
using System;

namespace UsingRadioButtonLists
{
    public class DataEntry : System.Web.UI.Page
    {
        protected System.Web.UI.WebControls.Label label1;
        protected System.Web.UI.WebControls.Button enterButton;
        protected System.Web.UI.WebControls.Label msgLabel;
        protected System.Web.UI.WebControls.RadioButtonList
                                    englishProficiencyList;

        public DataEntry()
        {
            Page.Init += new System.EventHandler(Page_Init);
        }

        public void Enter_Click(Object o, EventArgs ea)
        {
            if(englishProficiencyList.SelectedItem == null)
            {
                msgLabel.Text = "Select English Proficiency";
                msgLabel.ForeColor = System.Drawing.Color.Red;
            }
            else
            {
                msgLabel.Text = "Selectd Item: " +
                                englishProficiencyList.SelectedItem.Value +
                                    " " + englishProficiencyList.SelectedItem.Text;
                msgLabel.ForeColor = System.Drawing.Color.Black;
            }
        }

        private void Page_Load(object sender, System.EventArgs e)
        {
        }

        private void Page_Init(object sender, EventArgs e)
        {
            InitializeComponent();
        }

        #region Web Form Designer generated code
        private void InitializeComponent()
        {
            this.Load += new System.EventHandler(this.Page_Load);

        }
        #endregion
    }
}
```

FIGURE 13.24C
RadioButtonList example code-behind file (UsingRadioButtons.DataEntry.aspx.cs).

FIGURE 13.24D
RadioButtonList page returned after processing (UsingRadioButtons.DataEntry.aspx).

Tip!

Both the RadioButton and RadioButtonList controls provide for the selection of one, and only one, item from a list of predefined items. The RadioButtonList provides for the representation of the items as ListItem objects, and thus the selected item has a Value as well as a Text property. The RadioButton can be logically assigned to a group containing other radio buttons scattered over the form, thereby affording maximum flexibility in interface design. Properties of the selected RadioButton used for processing include the identification and Text.

CheckBoxList Control and Class

The CheckBoxList control provides for the selection of multiple list options; syntax of the CheckBoxList control is shown in Figure 13.25.

An example of the CheckBoxList control is shown in Figure 13.26A. The control is named assistanceList and is intended to enable a user to specify all of the various forms of assistance to which a student is entitled. Often a student is entitled to more than one; thus, a list providing for selection of more than one item is required. In the example, the list contains four items, defined with the ListItem element. Note that the list has a Horizontal RepeatDirection layout. The page's rendering is shown in Figure 13.26B.

Note that the list items are rendered as CheckBoxes in a Horizontal layout and that initial selection has not been made.

The **CheckBoxList** class represents the CheckBoxList control. The CheckBoxList class is summarized in Figure 13.27.

Server-side processing is defined in the code-behind file shown in Figure 13.26C. Processing related to the list is handled in the Enter_Click method. A ListItemCollection object reference, listItems, is declared and assigned to the collection of list items returned by the assistanceList Items property get:

```
ListItemCollection listItems = assistanceList.Items;
```

The Items property is inherited from the ListControl class.

The using directive

```
using System.Web.UI.WebControls;
```

enables the unqualified reference to the ListItemCollection class.

Tag	Property	Description
<asp:CheckBoxList		Opening tag.
	id	Unique identification. Required if the control is to be accessed programmatically.
	AutoPostBack	The form is automatically posted to the server when the user selects a check box in the list if true. Default is false.
	CellPadding	The padding in pixels between the border of the cell containing the widest and highest check box in the list to determine the cell size to apply to all cells in the control. The default is –1 which indicates the property is not set.
	DataSource	String specifying the source used to initialize the list items text and value field values.
	DataTextField	String specifying the data source field used to initialize list item Text properties.
	DataValueField	String specifying the data source field used to initialize list item Value properties.
	RepeatColumns	Specifies the number of columns in which the list items are displayed.
	RepeatDirection	RepeatDirection enumeration. Default is Vertical.
	RepeatLayout	RepeatLayout enumeration specifying the layout arrangement of the list items. Default is Table.
	TextAlign	TextAlign enumeration member specifying the alignment of the control's Text property value. The default value is Right.
	OnSelectedIndexChanged	Handler for the CheckedChanged event. The CheckedChanged event is raised when the Checked property is changed.
	Runat	Required property with value "server".
>		Opening tag closing character.
</asp:CheckBoxList>		Closing tag.

FIGURE 13.25
CheckBoxList control syntax.

The collection contains items in the list control. The number of items in the collection is returned by the collection's Count property:

```
int count = listItems.Count;
```

The items in the list can be referenced with an ordinal zero-based index value and the properties of the item ascertained:

```
for(int i = 0; i < count; i++)
{
    if(listItems[i].Selected)
        msgLabel.Text = msgLabel.Text + listItems[i].Value + " " +
            listItems[i].Text + "<br>";
}
```

In the above code, the Selected property is tested:

```
listItems[i].Selected
```

If the property value is true, the Value and Text properties are added to the Text property string of the msgLabel control. Note the expressions

```
listItems[i].Value
```

and

```
listItems[i].Text
```

The page returned to the user after processing, where the user selected the "State Tuition Voucher" and "Federal Impact Program" check boxes, is selected, as shown in Figure 13.26D.

```
<%@ Page language="c#" Codebehind="DataEntry.aspx.cs" AutoEventWireup="false"
         Inherits="UsingCheckBoxLists.DataEntry" %>
<HTML>
  <HEAD>
  </HEAD>
  <body MS_POSITIONING="GridLayout">
    <form id="DataEntry" method="post" runat="server">
      <asp:Label ID=label1 Runat=server text="Assistance"></asp:Label><br>
      <asp:CheckBoxList ID=assistanceList Runat=server
                        RepeatDirection=Horizontal>
      <asp:ListItem text="City: Breakfast" Value="05"></asp:ListItem>
      <asp:ListItem Text="State: Tuition Voucher" Value="42"></asp:ListItem>
      <asp:ListItem Text="Federal: Impact Program" Value="71"></asp:ListItem>
      <asp:ListItem Text="Federal: Title 21" Value="74"></asp:ListItem>
      </asp:CheckBoxList>
      <br>
      <br>
      <asp:Button ID=enterButton Runat=server OnClick="Enter_Click"
                  Text=Enter></asp:Button>
      <br>
      <asp:Label ID=msgLabel Runat=server></asp:Label>
    </form>
  </body>
</HTML>
```

FIGURE 13.26A
CheckBoxList example (UsingCheckbox.DataEntry.aspx).

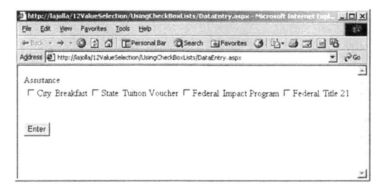

FIGURE 13.26B
CheckBoxList example (UsingCheckbBoxLists.DataEntry.aspx).

Tip!

Both the CheckBox and CheckBoxList controls provide for the selection of multiple items from a list of predefined items. The CheckBoxList provides for the representation of the items as ListItem objects, and thus the selected item has a Value as well as a Text property. The CheckBox controls can be scattered over the form, thereby affording the maximum flexibility in interface design. Properties of the selected CheckBox used for processing include ID, Selected and Text.

```
using System;
using System.Web.UI.WebControls;

namespace UsingCheckBoxLists
{
    public class DataEntry : System.Web.UI.Page
    {
        protected System.Web.UI.WebControls.Label label1;
        protected System.Web.UI.WebControls.CheckBoxList assistanceList;
        protected System.Web.UI.WebControls.Button enterButton;
        protected System.Web.UI.WebControls.Label msgLabel;

        public void Enter_Click(Object o, EventArgs ea)
        {
            msgLabel.Text = "";

            ListItemCollection listItems = assistanceList.Items;

            int count = listItems.Count;
            for(int i = 0; i < count; i++)
            {
                if(listItems[i].Selected)
                    msgLabel.Text = msgLabel.Text + listItems[i].Value + " " +
                                    listItems[i].Text + "<br>";
            }
        }

        public DataEntry()
        {
            Page.Init += new System.EventHandler(Page_Init);
        }

        private void Page_Load(object sender, System.EventArgs e)
        {
        }

        private void Page_Init(object sender, EventArgs e)
        {
            InitializeComponent();
        }

        #region Web Form Designer generated code
        private void InitializeComponent()
        {
            this.Load += new System.EventHandler(this.Page_Load);

        }
        #endregion
    }
}
```

FIGURE 13.26C
CheckBoxList example code-behind file (UsingRadioButtons.DataEntry.aspx.cs).

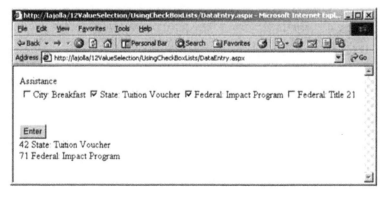

FIGURE 13.26D
CheckBoxList page returned after processing (UsingCheckBoxLists/DataEntry.aspx).

public class CheckBoxList : ListControl, IRepeatInfoUser, INamingContainer, **IPostBackDataHandler**	
Hierarchy	

Object
  Control
    WebControl
      ListControl
        CheckBoxList	

Namespace: System.Web.UI.WebControls	
Public Instance Constructor	
public CheckBoxList();	Initializes a new instance of the CheckBoxList class.
Public Instance Properties	
public virtual int **CellPadding** {get; set;}	The padding in pixels between the border of the cell containing the widest and highest radio button in the list to determine the cell size to apply to all cells in the control. The default is −1 which indicates the property is not set.
public virtual int **CellSpacing** {get; set;}	The spacing, in pixels, between the cells containing the radio buttons in the list. The default is −1 which indicates the property is not set.
public virtual int **RepeatColumns** {get; set;}	Specifies the number of columns in which the list items are displayed. Default is 0 indicating the property is not set.
public virtual RepeatDirection **RepeatDirection** {get; set;}.	RepeatDirection enumeration member specifying layout direction of the check boxes. Default is Vertical.
public virtual RepeatLayout **RepeatLayout** {get; set;}	RepeatLayout enumeration member specifying the layout of the list's check boxes. Default is Table.
public virtual TextAlign **TextAlign** {get; set;}	TextAlign enumeration member specifying the alignment of the control's Text property value. The default value is Right.

FIGURE 13.27
CheckBoxList class summary.

14

Data Presentation

Data Binding

ASP.NET supports binding of a data source to any property on an ASP.NET Web page, including properties of server controls. The formal data binding syntax is shown in Figure 14.1.

Data binding in the opening tag of a server control
<tagprefix : tagname property="<%# databinding expression %> runat=server />

Data binding anywhere on the page
literal text <%# databinding expression %>

FIGURE 14.1
Data binding syntax.

When binding the data source to a server control, the binding expression is placed on the value side of an attribute/value pair in the control's opening tag. The databinding expression must evaluate to the type expected by the property. The binding occurs when a control's DataBind method is called. When called, the method results in the resolution of the control's data binding and the data bindings of all of its child controls.

The application DataBindingBasics illustrates binding (1) a program variable to a page property and (2) a control property to another control property. The application's page, BindData.aspx, is shown in Figure 14.2A. The application contains a textbox name; the value of the Text property of the name textbox control is bound to the Text property of the nameLabel server control with the element declaration

```
<asp:Label ID = nameLabel Runat = server text = <%# name.Text%>/>
```

where the databinding expression is

```
name.Text
```

In a similar manner, the syntax

```
<%# dateTime%>
```

binds the dateTime variable to the page property declared by the <%# and%> tags.

The code-behind file is shown in Figure 14.2B. The dateTime variable is declared with the statement

```
protected System.String dateTime;
```

Every time the page is loaded, the variable is initialized in the Page_Load method with the statement

```
dateTime = DateTime.Now.ToShortTimeString();
```

```
<%@ Page language="c#" Codebehind="BindData.aspx.cs"
        AutoEventWireup="false" Inherits="DataBindingBasics.BindData" %>
<HTML>
  <HEAD>
  </HEAD>
  <body MS_POSITIONING="GridLayout">
    <form id="BindData" method="post" runat="server">
      Name: <asp:TextBox ID=name Runat=server></asp:TextBox>
      <p></p>
      <asp:Button ID=submit Runat=server OnClick=Submit_Click Text="Submit" />
      <p></p>
      Submitted Name: <asp:Label ID=nameLabel Runat=server text=<%# name.Text%> />
      <p></p>
      Time Submitted: <%# dateTime %>
    </form>
  </body>
</HTML>
```

Binding control (name) property to another control (nameLabel) property

Binding variable dateTime to page property

FIGURE 14.2A
Web page DataBindingBasics/BindData.aspx.

The current date and time are accessed with the static Now method of the DataTime class. The current date and time are formatted to a short-time version that displays only the hour, minutes and AM or PM. Other dateTime formats provide for displaying both the data and time in many versions. The initial rendering of the Web page BindData is shown in Figure 14.2C with the user-entered Name "Somename."

Clicking the Submit button posts the page and invokes the Submit_Click method, which calls the DataBind method of the Page with the statement

```
Page.DataBind();
```

Bindings of the Page and all child controls are affected: the user-entered value in the name textbox control, i.e., the Text property value, is bound to the Text property value of the label control nameLabel. Similarly, the dateTime variable declared in the code-behind file and initialized in the Page_Load file is bound to a page property. The returned page's rendering is shown in Figure 14.2D.

Data Grids Model

Data grids effectively display tabular data. The data grid shown in Figure 14.3 illustrates the use of a data grid displaying data returned by an SQL query against a Student table. Each row of the data source is displayed as a row in the data grid; the rows of the data grid are list items. Each item consists of cells that correspond to the data source's row columns. Grid lines can be used to separate the row, columns or cells.

Grid-formatting properties also provide for distinctly displaying specific categories of items:

- Selected item: an item selected for distinct display
- Alternate items: every other data item
- Header items: item at the top of the grid generally used to list the column headings
- Footer items: item positioned at the bottom of the grid

```
using System;
using System.Collections;
using System.ComponentModel;
using System.Data;
using System.Drawing;
using System.Web;
using System.Web.SessionState;
using System.Web.UI;
using System.Web.UI.WebControls;
using System.Web.UI.HtmlControls;

namespace DataBindingBasics
{
        public class BindData : System.Web.UI.Page
        {
                protected System.Web.UI.WebControls.TextBox name;
                protected System.Web.UI.WebControls.Button submit;
                protected System.Web.UI.WebControls.Label nameLabel;

                protected System.String dateTime;      ———      Program variable dateTime

                public BindData()
                {
                        Page.Init += new System.EventHandler(Page_Init);
                }

                private void Page_Load(object sender, System.EventArgs e)
                {
                        dateTime = DateTime.Now.ToShortTimeString();   ——   Variable
                }                                                           initialized

                public void Submit_Click(object o, System.EventArgs e)
                {
                        Page.DataBind();            ———          DataBind
                }                                                 method called
                                                                  for Page and all
                private void Page_Init(object sender, EventArgs e)   child controls
                {
                        InitializeComponent();
                }

                #region Web Form Designer generated code
                private void InitializeComponent()
                {
                        this.Load += new System.EventHandler(this.Page_Load);

                }
                #endregion
        }
}
```

FIGURE 14.2B
Code-behind file DataBindingBasics/BindData.aspx.cs.

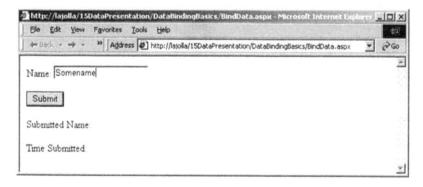

FIGURE 14.2C
Initial browser rendering of Web page DataBindingBasics/BindData.aspx with name entered.

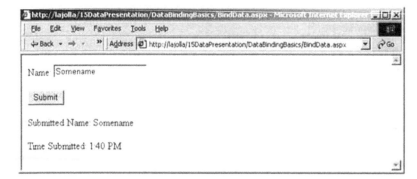

FIGURE 14.2D
Browser rendering of Web page DataBindingBasics/BindData.aspx after Submit button is clicked.

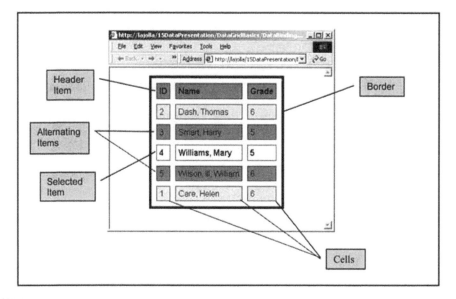

FIGURE 14.3
Browser rendering of data grid displaying SQL query results.

public enum GridLines

Namespace: System.Web.UI.WebControls

Member	Description
Both	Both horizontal and vertical grid lines rendered.
Horizontal	Only horizontal grid lines rendered.
None	No grid lines rendered.
Vertical	Only vertical grid lines rendered.

FIGURE 14.4
GridLine enumeration.

Members of the **GridLines** enumeration (Figure 14.4) characterize the grid lines rendered. The horizontal alignment of items within a container is characterized by the **HorizontalAlign** enumeration shown in Figure 14.5.

The **BaseDataList** class is an abstract class that serves as the base class for the DataList and DataGrid controls. The class is summarized in Figure 14.6. Of particular importance

public enum HorizontalAlign	
Namespace: System.Web.UI.WebControls	
Member	**Description**
Center	Contents are centered.
Justify	Contents are spread to align both left and right margins.
Left	Contents are left justified.
NotSet	Horizontal alignment is not set.
Right	Contents are right justified.

FIGURE 14.5
Horizontal alignment enumeration.

is the DataBind method that results in binding the control and all child controls to specified data sources.

The DataSource property specifies the data source to which the control is bound, i.e., members of the data source are used to populate the grid or list. Note that lists derived from the ICollection interface — the Array class, for example — can be used as a DataSource. The ICollection interface defines the size, enumerators and synchronization methods for collections.

Additionally, the IsBindableType method returns true if the specified data type is not bindable to the control. Data types that are bindable to controls derived from the BaseDataList are the following: System.Boolean, System.Byte, System.SByte, System.Int16, System.UInt16, System.Int32, System.UInt32, System.Int64, System.UInt64, System.Char, System.Double, System.Single, System.DateTime, System.Decimal and string.

The BaseDataList class also contains properties that enable formatting the grid and its contents:

- CellPadding determines the space between the cell's contents and its border; the space is the same on all sides. Note that individual cell sizes cannot be specified.
- CellSpacing determines the space between cells. The space is the same on all sides.
- GridLines sets grid lines rendered. Options include horizontal and vertical, vertical only, horizontal only and no lines. A member of the GridLines enumeration specifies the value.
- HorizontalAlign sets the horizontal alignment of the contents. A member of the HorizontalAlign enumeration specifies the value.

Cell spacing and cell padding are illustrated in Figure 14.7. Note that column width is determined by its widest content. The cell padding is added on all sides to determine the cell's border. The cell spacing is the distance between the cells on all sides. The use of horizontal and vertical grid lines is illustrated in Figure 14.8.

Instances of the BaseDataList class are not created directly. The constructor is called during construction of derived classes to initialize properties defined in the BaseDataList class.

Data Grid Items

Like other list type controls such as the DataList and Repeater, the DataGrid has sections (Figure 14.9). The header section typically captions the columns. The header is shown by

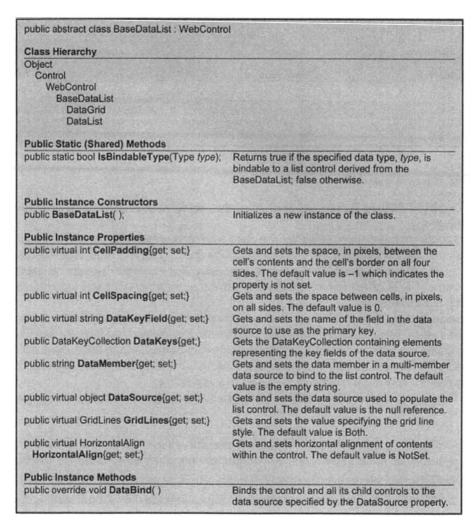

```
public abstract class BaseDataList : WebControl
```

Class Hierarchy

Object
  Control
    WebControl
      BaseDataList
        DataGrid
        DataList

Public Static (Shared) Methods

public static bool **IsBindableType**(Type *type*);	Returns true if the specified data type, *type*, is bindable to a list control derived from the BaseDataList; false otherwise.

Public Instance Constructors

public **BaseDataList**( );	Initializes a new instance of the class.

Public Instance Properties

public virtual int **CellPadding**{get; set;}	Gets and sets the space, in pixels, between the cell's contents and the cell's border on all four sides. The default value is −1 which indicates the property is not set.
public virtual int **CellSpacing**{get; set;}	Gets and sets the space between cells, in pixels, on all sides. The default value is 0.
public virtual string **DataKeyField**{get; set;}	Gets and sets the name of the field in the data source to use as the primary key.
public DataKeyCollection **DataKeys**{get;}	Gets the DataKeyCollection containing elements representing the key fields of the data source.
public string **DataMember**{get; set;}	Gets and sets the data member in a multi-member data source to bind to the list control. The default value is the empty string.
public virtual object **DataSource**{get; set;}	Gets and sets the data source used to populate the list control. The default value is the null reference.
public virtual GridLines **GridLines**{get; set;}	Gets and sets the value specifying the grid line style. The default value is Both.
public virtual HorizontalAlign **HorizontalAlign**{get; set;}	Gets and sets horizontal alignment of contents within the control. The default value is NotSet.

Public Instance Methods

public override void **DataBind**( )	Binds the control and all its child controls to the data source specified by the DataSource property.

FIGURE 14.6
BaseDataList class summary.

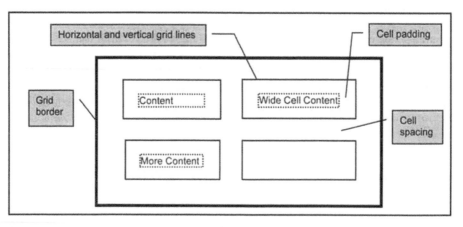

FIGURE 14.7
Illustrating cell spacing and cell padding.

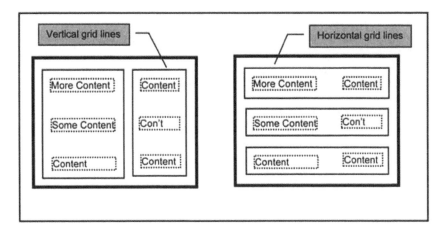

FIGURE 14.8
Horizontal and vertical grid lines.

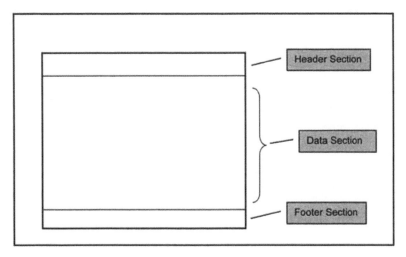

FIGURE 14.9
Data grid sections.

default and uses the data source field names as default values. The Footer section provides an additional option for captioning. Data from the data source are displayed as items, i.e., rows, in the data section.

The type of the items is characterized by the **ListItemType** enumeration, which is summarized in Figure 14.10. An item (row) in the DataGrid is represented by the **DataGridItem** class, summarized in Figure 14.11.

DataItem and DataSetIndex Properties

The DataGridItem class inherits the Cells property from the TableRow class. The Cells property gets the collection of TableCell objects that represent the collection of cells, or in this case columns, of the DataGridItem. The DataGrid's items are contained in the Data-Grid's **DataGridItemCollection** object. The collection is accessed by the DataGrid's Items property. The DataGridItemCollection class is summarized in Figure 14.12.

public enum ListItemType

Namespace: System.Web.UI.WebControls

Member	Databound	Description
AlternatingItem	Yes	Item in alternating cells.
EditItem	Yes	Item in the edit mode.
Footer	No	Footer section item.
Header	No	Header section item.
Item	Yes	Item in data section.
Pager	No	Control for navigating pages associated with the DataGrid.
SelectedItem	Yes	Selected item.
Separator	No	Separator between items in the list.

FIGURE 14.10
ListItemType enumeration.

public class DataGridItem : TableRow, INamingContainer

Class Hierarchy

Object
   Control
      WebControl
         TableRow
            DataGridItem

Public Instance Constructors

public **DataGridItem**(int *itemIndex* int *dataSourceIndex* ListItemType *itemType*);	Initializes a new instance of the class. The position of the item in the DataGrid's items collection is specified by *itemIndex*. The position of the item in the bound data source is specified by *dataSourceIndex*. The type of item is specified by the ListItemType enumeration member *itemType*.

Public Instance Properties

public virtual object **DataItem**{get; set;}	Gets and sets the properties of the data item represented by the DataGridObject.
public virtual int **DataSetIndex**{get;}	Gets the index number of the DataGridItem object from the bound data source.
public virtual int **ItemIndex**{get;}	Gets the index specifying the position of the DataGridItem object in the Items collection of the DataGrid.
public virtual ListItemType **ItemType**{get;}	Gets the type of the object represented by the DataGridItem object.

FIGURE 14.11
DataGridItem class summary.

Data Grid

The DataGrid class is derived from BaseDataList and represents a data grid; it is summarized in Figure 14.13. The application DataGridBasics illustrates implementation of the DataGrid. The application's Web page is shown in Figure 14.14A.

The DataGrid is included in an .aspx file with the element

```
<asp:DataGrid ID = studentGrid Runat = server></asp:DataGrid>
```

```
public class DataGridItemCollection : ICollection, IEnumerable

Class Hierarchy
Object
    DataGridItemCollection

Public Instance Constructors
```

public **DataGridItemCollection**(ArrayList *items*);	Initializes a new instance of the class. The items used to initialize the list are specified by the array *items*.

Public Instance Properties

public int **Count**{get;}	Gets the number of dataGridItem objects in the collection.
public bool **IsReadOnly**{get;}	Always returns the value false indicating the DataGridItem objects in the collection can be modified.
public bool **IsSynchronized**{get;}	Always returns the value false indicating access to the DataGridItemCollection is not synchronized.
public DataGridItem **this** [int *index*]{get;}	Gets the DataGridItem object at the collection position specified by zero-based *index*.
public object **SyncRoot**{get;}	Gets the object that can be used to synchronize access to the collection.

FIGURE 14.12
DataGridItemCollection class summary.

```
public class DataGrid : BaseDataList, INamingContainer

Class Hierarchy
Object
    Control
        WebControl
            BaseDataList
                DataGrid

Public Instance Constructors
```

public **DataGid**( );	Initializes a new instance of the class.

Public Instance Properties

public virtual bool **AllowCustomPaging**{get; set;}	Gets and sets the value true if custom paging is enabled; false otherwise. The default value is false.
public virtual bool **AllowPaging**{get; set;}	Gets and sets the value true if paging is enabled; false otherwise. The default value is false.
public virtual bool **AllowSorting**{get; set;}	Gets and sets the value true if sorting is enabled; false otherwise. The default is false.
public virtual TableItemStyle **AlternatingItemStyle**{get;}	Gets the TableItemStyle object specifying the style properties for alternating items in the DataGrid.
public virtual bool **AutoGenerateColumns**{get; set;}	Gets and sets the value true if the bound column elements are automatically created and displayed; false otherwise. The default value is true.
public virtual string **BackImageUrl**{get; set;}	Gets and sets the URL of an image to display in the DataGrid's background. The default value is the empty string.
public virtual DataGridColumnCollection **Columns**{get;}	Gets the DataGrid's collection of explicitly declared columns.
public virtual int **EditItemIndex**{get; set;}	Gets and sets the zero-based index of the item to edit. The default −1 indicates no item is selected for edit.
public virtual TableItemStyle **EditItemStyle**{get;}	Gets the TableItemStyle object specifying the style properties for the DataGrid item selected for edit. The default is the empty TableItemStyle object.
public virtual TableItemStyle **FooterStyle**{get;}	Gets the TableItemStyle object specifying the style properties for the DataGrid's footer section. The default is the empty TableItemStyle object.
public virtual TableItemStyle **HeaderStyle**{get;}	Gets the TableItemStyle object specifying the style properties for the DataGrid's header section. The default is the empty TableItemStyle object.
public virtual DataGridItemCollection **Items**{get;}	Gets the DataGrid's item collection.
public virtual TableItemStyle **ItemStyle**{get;}	Gets the TableItemStyle object specifying item style. The default is the empty TableItemStyle object.

FIGURE 14.13
DataGrid class summary.

Public Instance Properties (Cont.)	
public int **PageCount**{get;}	Gets the number of pages required to display the items in the DataGrid.
public virtual DataGridPagerStyle **PagerStyle**{get;}	Gets the DataGridPagerStyle object specifying the style properties of the DataGrid's paging section. The default is the empty DataGridPagerStyle object.
public virtual int **PageSize**{get; set;}	Gets and sets the number of items to display on a page. The default is 10.
public virtual int **SelectedIndex**{get; set;}	Gets and sets the index of the selected item. The default value −1 indicates no item is selected.
public virtual DataGridItem **SelectedItem**{get;}	Gets the DataGridItem object representing the selected dataGrid item.
public virtual TableItemStyle **SelectedItemStyle**{get;}	Gets the TableItemStyle object specifying the style properties for selected item in the DataGrid. The default is the empty TableItemStyle object.
public virtual bool **ShowFooter**{get; set;}	Gets and sets the value true if the footer is displayed; false otherwise. The default is false.
public virtual bool **ShowHeader**{get; set;}	Gets and sets the value true if the header is displayed; false otherwise. The default is true.
public virtual int **VirtualItemCount**{get; set;}	Gets and sets the virtual number of items in the DataGrid when custom paging is used.

FIGURE 14.13 (CONTINUED)
DataGrid class summary.

```
<%@ Page language="c#" Codebehind="DataBinding.aspx.cs" AutoEventWireup="false"
         Inherits="DataGridBasics.DataBinding" %>
<HTML>
  <HEAD>
  </HEAD>
  <body MS_POSITIONING="GridLayout">

    <form id="DataBinding" method="post" runat="server">
          <asp:DataGrid ID=studentGrid Runat=server></asp:DataGrid>
    </form>

  </body>
</HTML>
```

FIGURE 14.14A
Web page DataGridBasics/DataBinding.aspx.

The page's browser rendering is shown in Figure 14.3 and the application's code-behind page is shown in Figure 14.14B.

The DataGrid class is exposed with the statement

```
using System.Web.UI.WebControls;
```

The DataGrid, studentGrid, is declared with the statement

```
protected System.Web.UI.WebControls.DataGrid studentGrid;
```

The DataGrid displays data in a data set's StudentName table. The table's data are returned with the SQL statement

```
string cmdText = "SELECT StudentID AS ID, " +
    "LastName + ', '' + FirstName AS Name, Grade " +
    "FROM Student";
```

The statement returns three items from each row in the database's Student table:

- StudentID field with the alias ID
- A field concatenating the LastName field, literally consisting of a comma and space, and FirstName field with the alias Name
- Student Grade field

```
using System;
using System.Collections;
using System.ComponentModel;
using System.Data;
using System.Drawing;
using System.Web;
using System.Web.SessionState;
using System.Web.UI;
using System.Web.UI.WebControls;          ┌──────────────────┐
using System.Web.UI.HtmlControls;  ───────┤ Exposes DataGrid │
                                          │ functionality    │
using System.Data.OleDb;                  └──────────────────┘

namespace DataGridBasics                        ┌──────────────┐
{                                               │ DataGrid     ┐
        public class DataBinding : System.Web.UI.Page  declaration │
        {                                       └──────────────┘
                protected System.Web.UI.WebControls.DataGrid studentGrid;

                public DataBinding()
                {
                        Page.Init += new System.EventHandler(Page_Init);
                }

                private void Page_Load(object sender, System.EventArgs e)
                {
                        string cmdText = "SELECT StudentID AS ID, " +
    ┌──────────┐              "LastName + ', ' + FirstName AS Name, Grade " +
    │ SQL      ├────          "FROM Student";
    │ statement│
    └──────────┘        string provider = "Provider=Microsoft.Jet.OLEDB.4.0";
                        string dataSource =
                                "Data Source=C:\\DB\\StudentAdministratorDB.mdb";

                        string connectStg = provider + ";" + dataSource;

                        OleDbConnection connection = new OleDbConnection(connectStg);

    ┌──────────┐        OleDbCommand command = new OleDbCommand(cmdText, connection);
    │ The      │
    │ DataGrid's├──      DataSet studentDataSet = new DataSet();
    │ data source│
    └──────────┘        OleDbDataAdapter studentDataAdapter =
                                new OleDbDataAdapter(command);
    ┌──────────┐
    │ Data adapter│
    │ loading data│
    │ set with SQL│
    │ query results├──  studentDataAdapter.Fill(studentDataSet,"StudentName");
    └──────────┘
                                                          ┌──────────┐
                        studentGrid.GridLines= GridLines.Both;  ┐ Grid lines│
                                                          │ and cell │
                        studentGrid.CellSpacing = 10;     │ formatting│
    ┌──────────┐        studentGrid.CellPadding = 5;      └──────────┘
    │ Grid     │
    │ alignment in│
    │ its container├──  studentGrid.HorizontalAlign = HorizontalAlign.Center;
    └──────────┘
```

FIGURE 14.14B
Code-behind Web page DataGridBasics/DataBinding.aspx.

The returned data are loaded into the studentDataSet table studentName.
Horizontal and vertical grid lines are specified with the statement

```
studentGrid.GridLines = GridLines.Both;
```

Cell spacing and padding are specified with the following statements:

```
studentGrid.CellSpacing = 10;
studentGrid.CellPadding = 5;
```

Horizontal alignment of the data grid in its container, in this case the browser window, is specified with HorizontalAlign property in the statement

```
studentGrid.HorizontalAlign = HorizontalAlign.Center;
```

that locates the grid in the center of the container. Other alignment options are left and right.

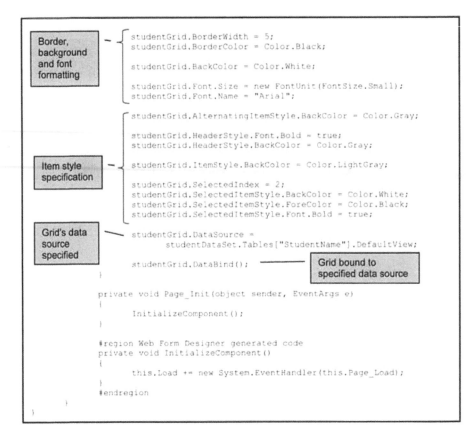

FIGURE 14.14B (CONTINUED)
Code-behind Web page DataGridBasics/DataBinding.aspx.

The data grid's basic format characteristics are assigned to properties inherited from the WebControl class with the statements

```
studentGrid.BorderWidth = 5;
studentGrid.BorderColor = Color.Black;
studentGrid.BackColor = Color.White;
studentGrid.Font.Size = new FontUnit(FontSize.Small);
studentGrid.Font.Name = "Arial";
```

Style properties are assigned to the different list item types; corresponding to selected list item types, these style properties provide for specifying the presentation of the data grid:

Property Name	DataGrid Items Affected
AlternatingItemStyle	Alternating items
EditItemStyle	Items selected for editing
ItemStyle	All items
SelectedItemStyle	Selected items

The back color of alternating items, i.e., lines in the grid, is set to the color Gray with the statement

```
studentGrid.AlternatingItemStyle.BackColor = Color.Gray;
```

The presentation of alternating lines in a contrasting color is very helpful in reading long lists with small font size. The header item can be set with the HeaderStyle property as in the statements

```
studentGrid.HeaderStyle.Font.Bold = true;
studentGrid.HeaderStyle.BackColor = Color.Gray;
```

which specify a bold font on a Gray background.

The basic item's style is specified with the ItemStyle property. For example, the statement

```
studentGrid.ItemStyle.BackColor = Color.LightGray;
```

specifies a light-gray background.

The selected item is specified with the SelectedItem property. For example,

```
studentGrid.SelectedIndex = 2;
```

specifies that the third item is marked "selected." Note that the items are addressed with a zero-based index.

The style of the selected item is specified with the SelectedItemStyle property as in the statements

```
studentGrid.SelectedItemStyle.BackColor = Color.White;
studentGrid.SelectedItemStyle.ForeColor = Color.Black;
studentGrid.SelectedItemStyle.Font.Bold = true;
```

The style properties are applied with precedence, as shown in Figure 14.15. For example, the style for presentation of alternating items is superseded by the SelectedItemStyle when an alternating item is selected.

Precedence	Style Property
1	EditItemStyle
2	SelectedItemStyle
3	AlternatingItemStyle
4	ItemStyle
5	ControlStyle

FIGURE 14.15
Precedence of style properties.

The footer's appearance is specified with the FooterStyle property. The data grid's data source is assigned with the DataSource property. The following statement assigns the studentDataSet's StudentName table as the data grid's data source:

```
studentGrid.DataSource =
    studentDataSet.Tables["StudentName"].DefaultView;
```

The data grid is bound to the data source with the DataBind method

```
studentGrid.DataBind();
```

During binding, a bound column object is automatically created and displayed for each field in the data source if the AutoGenerateColumns property is set true, which is the default value. Auto-generated columns are not added to the column's collection. Auto-generated columns are rendered after explicitly declared columns.

Properties contributing to the control's functionality include:

Paging — If AllowPaging is set true and the PageSize property is not set, the DataGrid control will display 10 items on a page.

Sorting — When sorting is enabled, a LinkButton control is rendered in the heading section of each column where a SortExpression property is set. The LinkButton enables sorting the dataGrid by the selected column; the SortCommand event is raised when the LinkButton is clicked. Typically, the handler sorts the data and rebinds the sorted data to the dataGrid. When a TemplateColumn column type is used with the HeaderTemplate property set, a Button control must be provided.

BackImageUrl — The BackImageUrl specifies the image to display in the data grid's background. The image is tiled if it is smaller than the data grid. The statement

```
studentGrid.BackImageUrl = "Image.jpg";
```

specifies the relative path name of a .jpg image.

EditItemIndex — The EditItemIndex specifies the zero-based index of the item to edit. The default value, –1, indicates that no item is selected for edit. Editing control is rendered in the item corresponding to the index in an EditCommandColumn. The index must be explicitly set to –1 to cancel editing.

Paging — The PageCount properties specify the number of pages required to display the items in the DataGrid. This property is only applicable when the AllowPaging property is set to true. Likewise, the Page Sizer property is only applicable when the AllowPaging property is set to true.

Accessing Items

The Items property accesses the DataGrid's item collection. Only items containing fields bound to the data source are contained in the collection; the header, footer and separator sections are not included. An application, DataItemBasics, illustrates DataGrid item access. The application's Web page is shown in Figure 14.16A.

```
<%@ Page language="c#" Codebehind="AccessItemCells.aspx.cs"
         AutoEventWireup="false" Inherits="DataItemBasics.AccessItemCells" %>
<HTML>
  <HEAD>
  </HEAD>
  <body MS_POSITIONING="GridLayout">

    <form id="AccessItemCells" method="post" runat="server">
      <asp:DataGrid ID=studentGrid Runat=server ></asp:DataGrid>
      <p></p>
      <asp:Label ID=itemList Runat=server></asp:Label>
      <p></p>
      <asp:Button ID=accessItems Runat=server OnClick=SelectItem_Click
                  Text="Select Item 3 Cells"></asp:Button>
      <p></p>
      <asp:Label ID=selectedItem Runat=server></asp:Label>
    </form>
  </body>
</HTML>
```

FIGURE 14.16A
Web page DataGridBasics/DataBinding.aspx.

The DataGrid is included in the .aspx file with the element

```
<asp:DataGrid ID = studentGrid Runat = server></asp:DataGrid>
```

```
using System;

using System.Data.OleDb;

namespace DataItemBasics
{
        public class AccessItemCells : System.Web.UI.Page
        {
                protected System.Web.UI.WebControls.DataGrid studentGrid;
                protected System.Web.UI.WebControls.Button accessItems;
                protected System.Web.UI.WebControls.Label itemList;
                protected System.Web.UI.WebControls.Label msg;

                public AccessItemCells()
                {
                        Page.Init += new System.EventHandler(Page_Init);
                }
```

`Load data set with student names`

```
                private void Page_Load(object sender, System.EventArgs e)
                {
                        System.Data.DataSet studentDataSet = LoadDataSet();
```

`Bind data grid to data set`

```
                        studentGrid.DataSource =
                                studentDataSet.Tables["StudentName"].DefaultView;
                        studentGrid.DataBind();

                        ListNames();
```

`List names in data grid`

```
                }

                public System.Data.DataSet LoadDataSet( )
                {
                        string cmdText = "SELECT StudentID AS ID, " +
                                "LastName + ', ' + FirstName AS Name, Grade " +
                                "FROM Student";

                        string provider = "Provider=Microsoft.Jet.OLEDB.4.0";
                        string dataSource =
                                "Data Source=C:\\DB\\StudentAdministratorDB.mdb";

                        string connectStg = provider + ";" + dataSource;

                        OleDbConnection connection = new OleDbConnection(connectStg);

                        OleDbCommand command = new OleDbCommand(cmdText, connection);

                        System.Data.DataSet studentDataSet = new
                                System.Data.DataSet();

                        OleDbDataAdapter studentDataAdapter = new
                                OleDbDataAdapter(command);

                        studentDataAdapter.Fill(studentDataSet,"StudentName");

                        return studentDataSet;
                }
```

FIGURE 14.16B
Code-behind Web page DataItemBasics/AccessItemCells.aspx.

The label control itemList will be used to list the grid's Name column and the label control selectedItem will be used to display the Name column and collection position of the three items in the grid's item collection. The application's code-behind page is shown in Figure 14.16B.

The StudentName table in the studentDataset is loaded with the StudentID, Name and Grade data from rows in the Student table in the StudentAdministrator database. The StudentName table in the studentDataSet is set as the data grid's DataSource property value:

```
studentGrid.DataSource =

    studentDataSet.Tables["StudentName"].DefaultView;
```

```
                    public void SelectItem_Click(object o, System.EventArgs e)
                    {
┌─────────┐           studentGrid.SelectedIndex = 3;              ┌────────────────────┐
│ Select  │────────                                         ──── │ Accessing second   │
│grid item│                                                /     │ column in selected │
└─────────┘                                               /      │ item               │
                   msg.Text += "You selected " +         /       └────────────────────┘
                         studentGrid.SelectedItem.Cells[1].Text +
                         " with index number " +
                         studentGrid.SelectedIndex.ToString() + ".";
                    }

                    public void ListNames()
                    {
                        itemList.Text =
                            "Number of items: " + studentGrid.Items.Count + "<br>";

                        for(int i=0; i < studentGrid.Items.Count; i++)
                        {
                            itemList.Text +=
                                studentGrid.Items[i].Cells[1].Text + "<br>";
                        }
                    }

                    private void Page_Init(object sender, EventArgs e)
                    {
                        InitializeComponent();
                    }

                    #region Web Form Designer generated code
                    private void InitializeComponent()
                    {
                        this.Load += new System.EventHandler(this.Page_Load);
                    }
                    #endregion
                }
```

FIGURE 14.16B (CONTINUED)
Code-behind Web page DataItemBasics/AccessItemCells.aspx.

The DataBind method is called to bind the data grid to the data source:

```
studentGrid.DataBind();
```

The ListNames method is called to iterate through the items of the data grid and list the name contained in each item:

```
ListNames();
```

The collection of items in the data grid is accessed with the data grid's Items property. For example, the expression

```
studentGrid.Items
```

evaluates to the DataGridItemCollection object representing the studentGrid's collection of DataGridItems. The number of items in the studentGrid's items collection is given by the expression

```
studentGrid.Items.Count
```

A loop iterating over the items in the data grid's item collection is effected by the following structure

```
for(int i = 0; i < studentGrid.Items.Count; i++)
{
}
```

The iterator i begins with value zero and increases by one in each iteration. The iteration continues as long as the iterator value is less than the number of items in the collection.

A specific item in the collection is accessed with the collection index property. That is, the item associated with the index position i in the collection is represented by the expression

```
studentGrid.Items[i]
```

The collection of objects representing an item's cells or columns is accessed with the DataGridItem Cells property. For example, the expression

```
studentGrid.Items[i].Cells
```

accesses the TableCellCollection representing the cells of the item in the studentGrid item collection with index position i. A particular object in the collection, i.e., the object representing a specific column value, is accessed with the TableCellCollection index property. For example, the item's second column is accessed with the expression

```
studentGrid.Items[i].Cells[1]
```

The Text property is used to get and set the text content of the TableCell, as in the expression

```
studentGrid.Items[i].Cells[1].Text
```

that gets the text content of the second column. Remember that position in the collection is zero based. The second column contains the student names that are added to the itemList's Text property.

The application Web page's browser is shown in Figure 14.16C. The contents of the data grid's Name column are displayed in the itemList Label control.

The page is returned to the server when the "Select Item 3 Cells" is pressed and the method SelectItem_Click is invoked. The studentGrid's SelectedIndex property is used to set the zero-based index value of the selected item:

```
studentGrid.SelectedIndex = 3;
```

The index is zero based; thus, the value 3 refers to the fourth item in the grid's item collection.

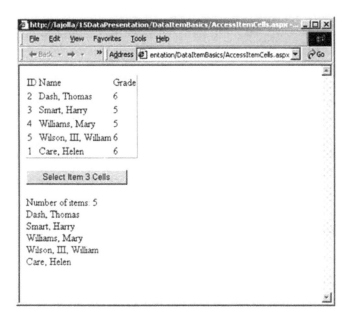

FIGURE 14.16C
Initial browser rendering of the Web page DataItemBasics/AccessItemCells.aspx.

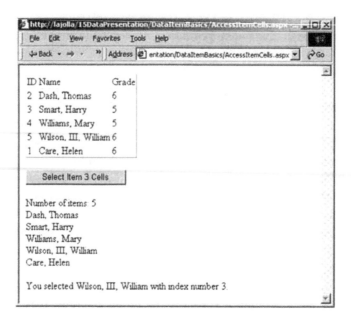

FIGURE 14.16D
Browser rendering of the Web page DataItemBasics/AccessItemCells.aspx after Select button is clicked.

The data grid's SelectItem property gets the DataGridItem that represents the selected item. Thus, the expression evaluates to the DataGridItem representing the selected item:

```
studentGrid.SelectedItem
```

The cells' collection of the DataGridItem representing the selected item is accessed with the Cell property:

```
studentGrid.SelectedItem.Cells
```

The cells' collection is represented by a TableCellCollection object. The TableCell objects comprising the collection are accessed with the collection's index. For example,

```
studentGrid.SelectedItem.Cells[1]
```

evaluates to the TableCell object representing the second TableCell object in the collection — the object representing the Name column. The text content of the TableCell is accessed with the Text property, for example,

```
studentGrid.SelectedItem.Cells[1].Text
```

The text content of the Name column and index of the selected item are assigned to the msg control's Text property. Figure 14.16D shows the browser of the returned page displaying the name and index of the selected item.

Paging

The DataGrid has the ability to display the contents of the data source in segments, called pages. An example of a data source displayed in a paged mode is shown in Figure 14.17. The number of items displayed in the DataGrid is referred to as the page size; the items in the data source are grouped into pages based on this page size. The specific page

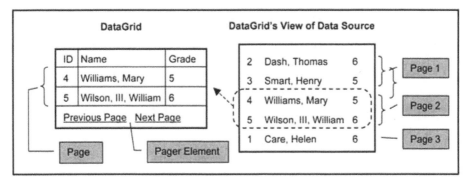

FIGURE 14.17
Paging model.

public enum PagerMode	
Namespace: System.Web.UI.WebControls	
Member	**Description**
NextPrev	Previous and Next buttons to access the next and previous pages are displayed.
NumericPages	Numbered buttons to directly access a page are displayed.

FIGURE 14.18
PagerMode enumeration.

displayed in the DataGrid is called the current page. In the example, the second page is the current page. A pager element is appended to the DataGrid to effect navigation between the pages: The links at the bottom of the DataGrid can be used to display the previous page or the next page. The type of link buttons displayed are characterized by the PagerMode enumeration, shown in Figure 14.18.

In the example, the NextPrev PagerMode is effected and the text of the Previous and Next buttons are Previous Page and Next Page, respectively. The DataGrid is instantiated with the statement

```
<asp:DataGrid
ID = nameGrid
Runat = server
OnPageIndexChanged = ChangePage>
</asp:DataGrid>
```

The ChangePage method is wired to the PageIndexChanged event. The **PageIndex-Changed** event is raised when a link button in a DataGrid's pager element is clicked.

```
public event DataGridPageChangedEventHandler PageIndexChanged

EventHandler Delegate
public delegate void DataGridPageChangedEventHandler(
        Object source,
        DataGridPageChangedEventArgs e
);
```

FIGURE 14.19
PageIndexChanged event.

```
public sealed class DataGridPageChangedEventArgs : EventArgs

Class Hierarchy
Object
    EventArgs
        DataGridPageChangedEventArgs

Namespace: System.Web.UI.WebControls

Public Instance Constructors
public DataGridPageChangedEventArgs (     Initializes a new instance of the class. The
                                          CommandSource property is initialized to the
                                          value
    object commandSource,                 commandSource and the NewPageIndex property
    int newPageIndex );                   is set to the value newPageIndex.

Public Instance Properties
public object CommandSource{get;}         Gets the object representing page selection
                                          element that is the source of the command.
public int NewPageIndex{get;}             Gets the index of the page selected in the page
                                          selection element.
```

FIGURE 14.20
DataGridPageChangedEventArgs class summary.

The event handler receives an argument of the type **DataGridPageChangedEventArgs** (Figure 14.20). The arguments provide information regarding the PageIndexChanged event raised whenever a button in the Pager section of the DataGrid is clicked.

The Pager can be located at the top edge, the bottom edge or the top and the bottom edges of the DataGrid. In the example, the Pager is located at the bottom of the DataGrid. The members of the **PagerPosition** enumeration (Figure 14.21) characterize the location of the Pager. The Pager's style is represented by the **DataGridPagerStyle** class, summarized in Figure 14.22.

```
public enum PagerPosition

Namespace: System.Web.UI.WebControls

Member              Description
Bottom              Pager positioned at the bottom of the DataGrid.
Top                 Pager positioned at the top of the DataGrid.
TopAndBottom        Pager positioned at the top and bottom of the DataGrid.
```

FIGURE 14.21
PagerPosition enumeration.

The Web application, DataGridPaging, illustrates paging. The DataGrid is implemented in the application's page, PagedNames.aspx (Figure 14.23A).

The code-behind page is shown in Figure 14.23B. The DataGrid, nameGrid, properties allowing paging and specifying the number of items shown on a page are set with the statements

```
nameGrid.AllowPaging = true;
nameGrid.PageSize = 2;
```

The nameGrid's PagerStyle property is used to access the DataGridPagerStyle object representing the pager element's style. The pager elements BackColor, NextPageText and PrevPageText style property values are set with the following statement:

```
nameGrid.PagerStyle.BackColor = Color.Gray;
nameGrid.PagerStyle.NextPageText = "Next Page";
nameGrid.PagerStyle.PrevPageText = "Previous Page";
```

```
public sealed class DataGridPagerStyle : TableItemStyle
```

Class Hierarchy

Object
  MarshalByRefObject
    Component
      Style
        TableItemStyle
          DataGridPagerStyle

Namespace: System.Web.UI.WebControls

Public Instance Properties

public PagerMode **Mode**{get; set;}	Gets and sets the PagerMode enumeration member that specifies the buttons enabling navigation from page to page. The default value is NextPrev.
public string **NextPageText**{get; set;}	Gets and sets the text displayed in the Next page button. The default value is ">" which is rendered as the greater than character ">".
public int **PageButtonCount**{get; set;}	Gets and sets the number of numbered buttons to display concurrently on the page. The default value is 10.
public PagerPosition **Position**{get; set;}	Gets and sets the PagerPosition enumeration member specifying the position of the pager element. The default value is Bottom.
public string **PreviousPageText**{get; set;}	Gets and sets the text displayed in the Previous page button. The default value is "<" which is rendered as the less than character "<".
public bool **Visible**{get; set;}	Gets and sets the value true if the pager is to be displayed; false otherwise. The default value is true.

Public Instance Methods

public override void **Reset**( )	Restores the DataGridPagerStyle object to its default values.

FIGURE 14.22
DataGridPagerStyle class summary.

```
<%@ Page language="c#" Codebehind="PagedNames.aspx.cs" AutoEventWireup="false"
                Inherits="DataGridPaging.PagedNames" %>
<HTML>
  <HEAD>
  </HEAD>
  <body MS_POSITIONING="GridLayout">
    <form id="PagedNames" method="post" runat="server">
      <asp:DataGrid ID=nameGrid Runat=server
                OnPageIndexChanged=ChangePage></asp:DataGrid>
      <p></p>
      <asp:Button ID=resetButton Runat=server OnClick=SetDefaultStyle
              Text="Set Default Style"></asp:Button>
      <p></p>
      <asp:Button ID=setRutton Runat=server OnClick=SetCustomStyle
              Text="Set Custom Style"></asp:Button>
      <p></p>
      <asp:Button ID=goLast Runat=server OnClick=GoLast
              Text="Go Last"></asp:Button>
      <p></p>
      Current Page Index: <asp:Label ID=msg Runat=server></asp:Label>
    </form>
  </body>
</HTML>
```

FIGURE 14.23A
Web page DataGridPaging\PagedNames.aspx.

```
using System;
using System.Drawing;
using System.Web.UI.WebControls;

using System.Data.OleDb;

namespace DataGridPaging
{
        public class PagedNames : System.Web.UI.Page
        {
                protected System.Web.UI.WebControls.Label msg;
                protected System.Web.UI.WebControls.DataGrid nameGrid;

                protected System.Boolean IsDefaultProperties;
                protected System.Web.UI.WebControls.Button resetButton;
                protected System.Web.UI.WebControls.Button setButton;
                protected System.Web.UI.WebControls.Button goLast;
                protected System.Data.DataSet studentDataSet;

                public PagedNames()
                {
                        Page.Init += new System.EventHandler(Page_Init);
                }

                private void Page_Load(object sender, System.EventArgs e)
                {
                        if(!IsPostBack)
                        {
                                nameGrid.AllowPaging = true;       ┌─────────────────────┐
                                nameGrid.PageSize = 2;         ╱   │ Enable paging and   │
                                                                   │ set page size.      │
                                nameGrid.BorderWidth = 2;          └─────────────────────┘
                                nameGrid.BorderColor = Color.Black;
                                nameGrid.Width = 200;
          ┌──────────────┐
          │ Set initial  │
          │ PagerStyle   │ ╲        nameGrid.PagerStyle.BackColor = Color.Gray;
          │ properties   │          nameGrid.PagerStyle.NextPageText = "Next Page";
          └──────────────┘          nameGrid.PagerStyle.PrevPageText = "Previous Page";

                                BindData();
                        }
                }

                public void BindData()
                {
                        nameGrid.DataSource = LoadDataSet();
                        nameGrid.DataBind();
                        DisplayProperties();
                }

                public void ChangePage(Object o, DataGridPageChangedEventArgs e )
                {
                        nameGrid.CurrentPageIndex = e.NewPageIndex;

                        BindData();
                }
```

FIGURE 14.23B
Code-behind file DataGridPaging\PagedNames.aspx.cs.

The NextPageText and PrevPageText property values only have effect when the PagerMode property is set to the NextPrev value, which is the default PagerMode property value.

The initial rendering of the Web page is shown in Figure 14.23C. The DataGrid's page contains two items corresponding to the data items constituting the page with index value zero when the data source is viewed as consisting of two item pages. The index of the page is displayed in the text box labeled "Current Page Index." The index of the current page is accessed with the DataGrid's CurrentPageIndex property. The value is assigned to the text box in the DisplayProperties method with the statement

```
msg.Text = nameGrid.CurrentPageIndex.ToString();
```

```
        public void GoLast(Object o, EventArgs e)
        {
                nameGrid.CurrentPageIndex = nameGrid.PageCount -1 ;
                BindData();
        }                          [ Set CurrentPageIndex to index of last page ]

        public System.Data.DataSet LoadDataSet( )
        {
                string cmdText = "SELECT StudentID AS ID, " +
                        "LastName + ', ' + FirstName AS Name, Grade " +
                        "FROM Student";
                string provider = "Provider=Microsoft.Jet.OLEDB.4.0";
                string dataSource =
                        "Data Source=C:\\DB\\StudentAdministratorDB.mdb";
                string connectStg = provider + ";" + dataSource;
                OleDbConnection connection = new OleDbConnection(connectStg);
                OleDbCommand command = new OleDbCommand(cmdText, connection);
                System.Data.DataSet studentDataSet =
                        new System.Data.DataSet();
                OleDbDataAdapter studentDataAdapter =
                        new OleDbDataAdapter(command);
                studentDataAdapter.Fill(studentDataSet,"StudentName");
                return studentDataSet;
        }
                                            [ Access the index of the
                                              currently displayed page ]
        public void DisplayProperties()
        {
                msg.Text = nameGrid.CurrentPageIndex.ToString();
        }

        public void SetDefaultStyle(Object o, EventArgs e)
        {
                nameGrid.PagerStyle.Reset();
                nameGrid.PagerStyle.Mode = PagerMode.NextPrev;
        }

        public void SetCustomStyle(Object o, EventArgs e)
        {
                nameGrid.PagerStyle.BackColor = Color.LightGray;
                nameGrid.PagerStyle.Position = PagerPosition.Top;
                nameGrid.PagerStyle.Mode = PagerMode.NumericPages;
        }

        private void Page_Init(object sender, EventArgs e)
        {
                InitializeComponent();
        }

        #region Web Form Designer generated code
        private void InitializeComponent()
        {
                this.Load += new System.EventHandler(this.Page_Load);

        }
        #endregion
}
```

[Reset pager style to default]

[Specify custom pager style properties]

FIGURE 14.23B (CONTINUED)
Code-behind file DataGridPaging\PagedNames.aspx.cs.

Note that the Pager section is located in the default position located at the bottom edge of the DataGrid. The Pager section displays the Gray backcolor and the page navigation buttons contain the captions "Previous Page" and "Next Page." When the "Next Page" button in the Pager section is clicked, the page is posted back to the server. The Selected-IndexChanged event is raised and handled by the ChangePage method. The arguments passed in the method are represented by the DataGridPageChangedEventArgs class. The NextPageIndex property of this class represents the index of the page selected in the Pager element. The NextPageIndex value is assigned to the DataGrid's CurrentPageIndex with the expression

```
nameGrid.CurrentPageIndex = e.NewPageIndex;
```

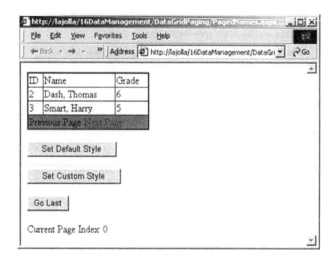

FIGURE 14.23C
Initial rendering of Web page DataGridPaging\PagedNames.aspx.cs.

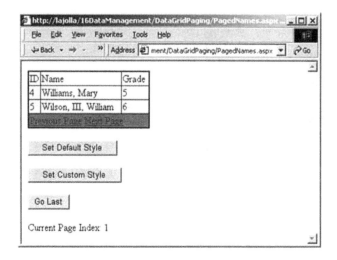

FIGURE 14.23D
Rendering of Web page DataGridPaging\PagedNames.aspx after the Next Page button is clicked.

The returned page's rendering is shown in Figure 14.23D, in which the items constituting the second page are displayed. Note that the CurrentPageIndex value is one.

Paging can also be programmatically affected. For example, clicking the Go Last button results in the display of the last page. When the Go Last button is clicked, the page is posted to the server and the GoLast method is invoked. The number of pages reflecting segmenting the data source according to the DataGrid's PageSize property is accessed with the PageCount property. The page index is zero based; thus, the index of the last page is evaluated by the expression

```
nameGrid.PageCount -1
```

The value of the last page is assigned to the CurrentPageIndex with the expression

```
nameGrid.CurrentPageIndex = nameGrid.PageCount -1 ;
```

The DataGrid is bound to the data source and the page is returned for rendering (Figure 14.23E). Note that the value of the first page is zero.

When the Set Custom Style is clicked, the page is posted and the method SetCustomStyle is invoked. The pager's style properties are set to custom values. The back color is changed to light gray with the statement

```
nameGrid.PagerStyle.BackColor = Color.LightGray;
```

Similarly, the pager's position is changed to the top edge of the DataGrid with the statement

```
nameGrid.PagerStyle.Position = PagerPosition.Top;
```

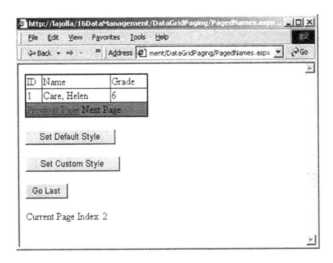

FIGURE 14.23E
Rendering of Web page DataGridPaging\PagedNames.aspx after the Go Last button is clicked.

Finally, the PagerMode property is set with the statement

```
nameGrid.PagerStyle.Mode = PagerMode.NumericPages;
```

When in the NumericPages mode, number buttons are displayed in the Pager element. The page corresponding to the button's number is displayed when the page is rendered. The number of button displayed is specified by the PageButtonCount property. When the number of pages exceeds the number of buttons that can be concurrently displayed, ellipsis buttons (...) are displayed in place of the buttons that cannot be displayed. When the ellipsis button is clicked, the next or previous set of numbered buttons is displayed. This property only has an effect when the PagerMode property is set to the NumericPages value. Figure 14.23F shows the page rendering after the Set Custom Style button is clicked. Clicking the Set Default Style results in invocation of the method SetDefaultStyle. The DataGridPagerStyle's Reset method is invoked with the statement

```
nameGrid.PagerStyle.Reset();
```

The Reset method restores the DataGridPagerStyle object's properties to their default values. For example, the NextPageText property is set to ">," the PrevPageText property is set to "<," and the Position property is set to Bottom.

In the Beta 2 version, the statement

```
nameGrid.PagerStyle.Mode = PagerMode.NextPrev;
```

is required to set the PagerMode to its default value after the Reset method is called. The page rendering after the Set Default Style button is clicked is shown in Figure 14.23G.

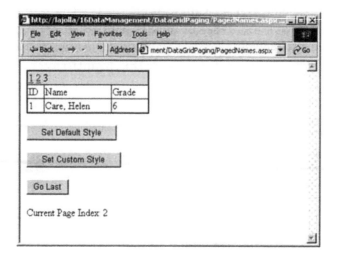

FIGURE 14.23F
Rendering of Web page DataGridPaging\PagedNames.aspx after the Set Custom Style button is clicked.

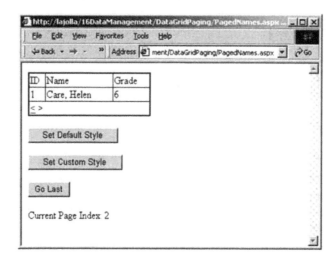

FIGURE 14.23G
Rendering of Web page DataGridPaging\PagedNames.aspx after the Set Default Style button is clicked.

15

Parameterized Data Operations

The Command class CommandText property represents an SQL statement. Placeholders can be used to represent fields in an SQL statement that will be replaced with values at runtime. The type of placeholder depends on the type of data adapter:

- With OleDbDataAdapter, question marks, "?," are used to identify the parameters because the OLE DB.NET Provider does not support named parameters. The parameters must be provided in an order corresponding to the position of its placeholder
- With SqlDataAdapter, named placeholders are required. The name must be preceded with an "@" sign, for example, "@StudentID."

The Command class Parameters property contains a list of Parameter type objects representing the replacement values. These objects are used at runtime to pass values to the SQL statement or stored procedure. Basically, each parameter object relates a name, data type and data value. When the SQL statement, or stored procedure, is executed, the placeholders are replaced by corresponding values from the parameters collection. Figure 15.1 illustrates the relationship between placeholders in the CommandText property

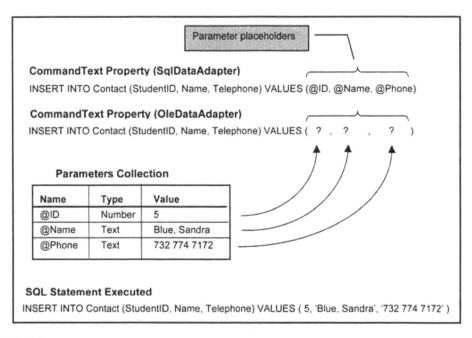

FIGURE 15.1
Command class CommandText and Parameters properties.

SQL statement and the Parameters property collection of Parameter objects. The OLE DB.NET Provider does not support named parameters; consequently, the members of the collection must correspond to the position of the placeholders in the SQL statement.

Data adapters can be configured with four command objects: SelectCommand, Insert-Command, DeleteCommand and UpdateCommand. Each command object contains an SQL statement or stored procedure, as well as a collection of parameter objects. This chapter describes the implementation of parameters for the OLE DB environment.

Note:

The SqlCommand class has comparable parameter and parameter collection classes:

SqlParameterCollection
SqlParameter

Type characterization is provided by the SqlDbType enumeration.

Data Type, Direction and Version

DbType enumeration members (Figure 15.2) characterize the parameter's data type. The enumeration member names are not case sensitive. The **ParameterDirection** enumeration (Figure 15.3) characterizes the direction of the data relative to a target, *not the data source*. The ParameterDirection values are applicable to OleDbParameters and SqlParameters. If the ParameterDirection is Output, the execution of the command does not return a value. The InputOutput, Output and ReturnValue are updated after the last row of the result set is read. The **DataRowVersion in** Figure 15.4 describes the version state of the data row's values.

The version of the data row's values depends on the operation last performed on the data row; Figure 15.5 shows the relation between version and operations. When the row's BeginEdit method is called and a row value changed, the row's Current and Proposed values are available. If the row's CancelEdit method is called, the Proposed value is discarded. When the EndEdit is called, the Proposed value becomes the Current value. When the RejectChanges method is called, the Proposed value is discarded and the version becomes Current. When the row's AcceptChanges method is called, the Proposed value becomes the Current value. When the Table's AcceptChanges method is called, the Current value becomes the row's new original value. Note that the Table's AcceptChanges method invokes the row's AcceptChanges, thus the Proposed values made Current in turn become the row's new original value.

The DataRowVersion values are used by the data adapter's UpdateCommand and Update operations to determine whether the parameter is set to the Current or Original value. The data adapter's InsertCommand and DeleteCommand ignore the DataRow-Version values.

Parameters and Parameter Collections

The **OleDbParameter** class illustrated in Figure 15.6 represents parameters. The OLE DB parameters are contained in a collection relative to their position in the command and

DbType	OleDbType	Description
public enum DbType	public enum OleDbType	
Namespace: System.Data.OleDb		
Member Name		
DbType	**OleDbType**	**Description**
AnsiString		A variable-length stream of 1 to 8,000 non-Unicode characters.
Binary	Array of type Byte LongVarBinary	A variable-length stream of 1 to 8,000 bytes.
Boolean	Boolean	Boolean value: true or false values.
Byte		8-bit unsigned integer.
Currency		A currency value ranging from -922,337,203, 685,477.5808 to +922,337,203, 685,477.5808.
DateTime	DBDate DBTimeStamp FileTime	Date and time value.
Decimal	Currency Numeric	Real number ranging from 1.0×10^{-28} to approximately 7.9×10^{28} with 28 to 29 significant digits.
Double		Floating-point ranging from approximately 5.0×10^{-324} to 1.7×10^{308} with a precision of 15 to 16 digits.
Guid		Globally unique identifier.
Int16	SmallInt	16-bit signed integer ranging from –32768 to 32767.
Int32	Integer	32-bit signed integer ranging from –2147483648 to 2147483647.
Int64	BigInt	32-bit signed integer ranging from -9223372036854775808 to 9223372036854775807.
Object	PropVariant IUnknown	General representation of any reference or value type.
SByte	TinyInt	8-bit integer ranging from –128 to 127.
Single	Single	Floating-point ranging from approximately 1.5×10^{-45} to 3.4×10^{38} with a precision of 7 digits.
String	BSTR Char LongVarChar	Unicode character string.
Time		Date and time ranging from January 1, 1753 to December 31, 9999 with an accuracy of 3.33 milliseconds.
UInt16	UnsignedSmallInt	16-bit unsigned integer ranging from 0 to 65535.
UInt32	UnsignedInt	32-bit unsigned integer ranging from 0 to 4294967295.
UInt64	UnsignedBigInt	64-bit unsigned integer ranging from 0 to 18446744073709551615.
VarNumeric		Variable-length numeric value. Not supported by SQL Server .NET Provider.
	Empty	No value.
	Error	Maps to Exception.

FIGURE 15.2
DbType enumeration.

Member Name	Description
public enum ParameterDirection	
Namespace: System.Data	
Member Name	**Description**
Input	Input-only parameter.
InputOutput	Input and output parameter.
Output	Output parameter only.
ReturnValue	A return value from an operation such as stored procedure, built-in function, or user-defined function.

FIGURE 15.3
ParameterDirection enumeration.

public enum DataRowVersion	
Namespace: System.Data	
Member Name	**Description**
Current	Current values.
Default	Default values.
Original	Original values.
Proposed	Proposed values.

FIGURE 15.4
DataRowVersion enumeration.

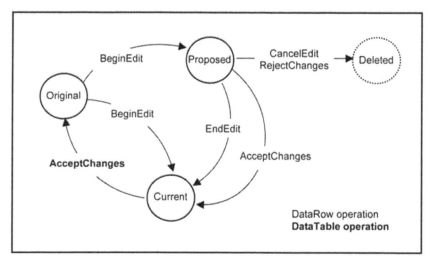

FIGURE 15.5
DataRow values version transition diagram.

associated DataSet mapping. The number of parameters in the command must equal the number of placeholders or the provider may raise an error. The **OleDBParameterCollection** class shown in Figure 15.7 represents the collection of parameters.

Application Using Parameters

The application ParameterizedSelect illustrates use of a parameterized SQL statement. The application's Web page GetContact.aspx is shown in Figure 15.8A and the browser rendering is shown in Figure 15.8B. The user has entered the value 5 in the textbox, indicating to the application that the contacts for the student with ID value 5 are desired.

The page's code-behind file is shown in Figure 15.8C. Note that the contactGrid's EnableViewState property value is set to false in the Page_Load method with the statement

```
contactGrid.EnableViewState = false;
```

Because the data grid is to be populated with results specific to the request, maintaining the data grid's state from request to request has no benefit. The EnableViewState property value is set to false, so the state information is not stored, thereby improving performance. Conversely, if the data grid is always populated with the same information,

public sealed class OleDbParameter : MarshallByrefObject, IDataParameter, ICloneable	
Hierarchy	
Object	
MarshalByRefObject	
OleDbParameter	
Namespace: System.Data.OleDb	
Public Instance Constructors	
public OleDbParameter( );	Initializes a new instance of the class.
public OleDbParameter(string *name*, object *value*);	Initializes a new instance of the class and sets the ParameterName property value to *name* and the Value property to the object *value*.
public OleDbParameter(string *name*, OleDbType *dataType*);	Initializes a new instance of the class and sets the ParameterName property value to *name* and the OleDbType property to the value *dataType*. The Size and Precision properties are inferred when possible.
public OleDbParameter(string *name*, OleDbType *dataType*, int *size*);	Initializes a new instance of the class and sets the ParameterName property value to *name*, the OleDbType property to the value *dataType* and the Size property to the integral value *int*.
public OleDbParameter(string *name*, OleDbType *dataType*, int *size* , string *sourceColumn*);	Initializes a new instance of the class and sets the ParameterName property value to *name*, the OleDbType property to the value *dataType*, the Size property to the integral value *size*, and the SourceColumn name to *sourceColumn*.
public OleDbParameter(string *name*, OleDbType *dataType*, int *size* , ParameterDirection *direction*, bool *isNullable*, byte *precision*, byte *scale*, string *sourceColumn*, DataRowVersion *version*, object *value*);	Initializes a new instance of the class and sets the ParameterName property value to *name*, the OleDbType property to the value *dataType*, the Size property to the integral value *size*, the Direction property to the value *direction*, the InNullable property to the value *isNullable*, the Precision property to the value *precision*, the Scale property to the value *scale*, the SourceColumn property to the name *sourceColumn*, and the Value property to the object *value*.
Public Instance Properties	
public DbType **DbType** {get; set;}	Gets and sets the DbType of the parameter. The default is type Object.
public ParameterDirection **Direction** {get; set;}	Gets and sets the value indicating the parameters direction. The default is Input.
public bool **IsNullable** {get; set;}	Gets and sets the value true if null values are accepted; false otherwise. The default is false.
public OleDbType **OleDbType** {get; set;}	Gets and sets the OleDbType of the parameter.
public string **ParameterName** {get; set;}	Gets and sets the parameter's name. The default is the empty string.

FIGURE 15.6
OleDbParameter class.

the EnabledViewState property should be set to true, in which case the data grid will store the state information that also results in improved performance under the circumstances.

When the button is clicked, the page is posted and the method GetContacts is invoked at the server.

A parameterized SQL select statement is created with the statement

```
String selectCmd = "SELECT * FROM Contact WHERE StudentID = ?";
```

which represents the value of the data adapter's select command object text property. The question mark is a placeholder; the statement presumes that, when it is executed, a paramater in the adapter's parameter collection will provide the value to substitute for

Public Instance Properties (Cont.)	
public byte **Precision** {get; set;}	Gets and sets the value representing the maximum number of digits used to represent the parameter's value. The default is 0. The Precision property is only applicable to decimal and numeric input parameters.
public byte **Scale** {get; set;}	Gets and sets the value representing the number of decimal places to which the parameter's value is resolved. The default is 0. The Precision property is only applicable to decimal and numeric input parameters.
public int **Size** {get; set;}	Gets and sets the maximum number of bytes of binary and string type parameter values. The default is inferred from the parameter's value.
public string **SourceColumn** {get; set;}	Gets and sets the name of the source column. The default is the empty string.
public DataRowVersion **SourceVersionColumn** {get; set;}	Gets and sets the DataRowVersion applicable during loading. The default is Current.
public object **Value** {get; set;}	Gets and sets the parameter's value. The default is null.
Public Instance Methods	
public override string ToString( );	Returns the ParameterName property value.

FIGURE 15.6 (CONTINUED)
OleDbParameter class.

the placeholder. The adapter's select command object parameter's collection is accessed with the expression

```
dataAdapter.SelectCommand.Parameters
```

The collection's Add method is used to add a parameter to the collection. For example,

```
dataAdapter.SelectCommand.Parameters.Add("@StudentID",DbType.Int32);
```

adds a parameter with name @StudentID and type DbType.Int32 to the collection. The Value property's value is set to the user-entered value in the studentID textbox with the statement

```
dataAdapter.SelectCommand.Parameters["@StudentID"].Value =
    studentID.Text;
```

When the data adapter's Fill method is invoked,

```
dataAdapter.Fill(dataSet, "Student Contacts");
```

the following actions occur:

- The connection with the data source is automatically opened.
- The parameter's value, in this case the user-entered student identification value, is substituted for the placeholder.
- The resolved SQL statement is used to retrieve the applicable rows.
- The data set is populated with the returned rows.
- The Web page's data grid is bound to the data set.
- The connection is automatically closed.
- The Web page is returned to the user's browser.

The returned page's rendering is shown in Figure 15.8D. In the example, the user entered student ID value 5 prior to clicking the Get Contacts button.

public sealed class OleDbParameterCollection : MarshallByRefObject, IDataParameterCollection, IList, ICollection, IEnumerable	
Hierarchy	

Object
  MarshallByrefObject
    OleDbParameterCollection	

Namespace: System.Data.OleDb	
Public Instance Properties	
public int **Count** {get;}	Gets the number of OleDbParameter objects in the collection.
public OleDbParameter **this** [string *parameterName*] {get; set;};	Gets and sets the OleDbParameter object in the collection with the ParameterName property value *parameterName*.
public OleDbParameter **this** [int *index*] {get; set;};	Gets and sets the OleDbParameter object in the collection with zero-based position value *index*.
Public Instance Methods	
public OleDbParameter **Add** (OleDbParameter *parameter*);	Adds the OleDbParameter *parameter* to the collection. The method returns a reference to the OleDbParameter object.

public OleDbParameter **Add** (
  string *name*
  object *value*);
	Adds the OleDbParameter object to the collection with ParameterName property *name* and Value property *value*.

public OleDbParameter **Add** (
  string *name*
  OleDbType *type*);
	Adds the OleDbParameter object to the collection with ParameterName property *name* and OleDbType property *type*.

public OleDbParameter **Add** (
  string *name*
  OleDbType *type*
  int size);
	Adds the OleDbParameter object to the collection with ParameterName property *name*, OleDbType property *type* and Size property *size*.

public OleDbParameter **Add** (
  string *name*
  OleDbType *type*
  int size
  string *sourceColumn*);
	Adds the OleDbParameter object to the collection with ParameterName property *name*, OleDbType property *type*, Size property *size*, and SourceColumn property *sourceColumn*.

public void **Clear**( );	Removes all the parameter objects from collection.
public bool **Contains** (OleDbParameter *parameter*	Returns true if OleDbParameter object *parameter* is in the collection; false otherwise.
public bool **Contains** (string *name*);	Returns true if OleDbParameter object with ParameterName property value *name* is in the collection; false otherwise.

public void **CopyTo**(
  Array *array*,
  int *index*);
	Copies the OleDbParameter objects in the collection into the Array object *array* starting with the array index value *index*.

Public Instance Methods	
public int **IndexOf** (OleDbParameter *parameter*);	Returns the zero-based index of the OleDbParameter object *parameter* in the collection.
public int **IndexOf** (string *name*);	Returns the zero-based index of the OleDbParameter with ParameterName property value *name* in the collection.

public void **Insert** (
  int *index*,
  object *parameter*);.
	Inserts an OleDbParameter object *parameter* to the collection at the zero-based index position *index*.

public void **Remove** (object *parameter*);	Removes the OleDbParameter object *parameter* from the collection.
public void **RemoveAt** (int *index*);	Removes the OleDbParameter object at the zero-based index *index* from the collection.
public void **RemoveAt** (string *name*);	Removes the OleDbParameter object with the ParameterName property value *name* from the collection.

FIGURE 15.7
OleDbParameterCollection class.

```
<%@ Page language="c#" Codebehind="GetContacts.aspx.cs" AutoEventWireup="false"
         Inherits="ParameterizedSelect.GetContacts" %>
<HTML>
  <HEAD>
  </HEAD>
  <body MS_POSITIONING="GridLayout" style="FONT-SIZE: 10pt; FONT-FAMILY: Arial">
    <form id="GetContacts" method="post" runat="server">
      Enter valid student ID: <asp:TextBox ID=studentID Runat=server>
                                </asp:TextBox>
      <p></p>
      <asp:Button ID=getContactsButton Runat=server Text="Get Contacts"
                  OnClick="GetContacts_Click"></asp:Button>
      <p></p>
      <asp:DataGrid id=contactGrid Runat=server></asp:DataGrid>
      <p></p>
      <asp:Label ID=msg Runat=server></asp:Label>
    </form>
  </body>
</HTML>
```

FIGURE 15.8A
Web page ParameterizedSelect/GetContacts.aspx.

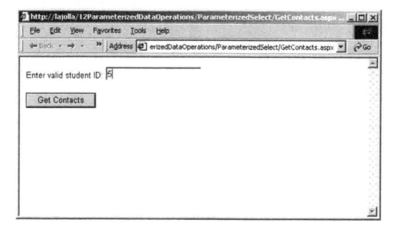

FIGURE 15.8B
Browser rendering of Web page ParameterizedSelect/GetContacts.aspx.

Hands-On Exercise: Using the Parameters Collection Editor

Step 1: Create Project: UsingParametersCollectionEditor

1. Create the application.
2. Delete the Web page WebForm1.aspx.

Step 2: Create Web Form page StudentSearch.aspx

1. Add Web Form StudentSearch.aspx.
2. Drag an HTML Label element onto the page. Change the content to read:
   First:.

```
using System;
using System.Data;
using System.Drawing;

using System.Data.OleDb;

namespace ParameterizedSelect
{
        public class GetContacts : System.Web.UI.Page
        {
                protected System.Web.UI.WebControls.TextBox studentID;
                protected System.Web.UI.WebControls.Button getContactsButton;
                protected System.Web.UI.WebControls.Label msg;
                protected System.Web.UI.WebControls.DataGrid contactGrid;

                public GetContacts()
                {
                        Page.Init += new System.EventHandler(Page_Init);
                }

                private void Page_Load(object sender, System.EventArgs e)
                {
                        contactGrid.EnableViewState = false;
                }

                public void GetContacts_Click(object o, EventArgs e)
                {
```

> **Parameterized SQL statement**

```
                        String selectCmd =
                                "SELECT * FROM Contact WHERE StudentID = ?";

                        string provider = "Provider=Microsoft.Jet.OLEDB.4.0";
                        string dataSource =
                          "Data Source=C:\\DB\\StudentAdministratorDB.mdb";
                        string connectStg = provider + ";" + dataSource;

                        OleDbConnection connection = new OleDbConnection(connectStg);

                        OleDbCommand command =
                                new OleDbCommand(selectCmd, connection);

                        OleDbDataAdapter dataAdapter = new OleDbDataAdapter(command);
```

> **Parameter object added to collection and its value set to user-entered datum**

```
                        dataAdapter.SelectCommand.Parameters.Add("@StudentID",DbType.Int32);
                        dataAdapter.SelectCommand.Parameters["@StudentID"].Value =
                          studentID.Text;

                        DataSet dataSet = new DataSet();

                        dataAdapter.Fill(dataSet, "Student Contacts");

                        msg.Text =
                                "Select Command Text: "
                                + dataAdapter.SelectCommand.CommandText;

                private void Page_Init(object sender, EventArgs e)
                {
                        InitializeComponent();
                }

                #region Web Form Designer generated code
                private void InitializeComponent()
                {
                        this.Load += new System.EventHandler(this.Page_Load);

                }
                #endregion
        }
}
```

FIGURE 15.8C
Code-behind file ParameterizedSelect/GetContacts.aspx.cs.

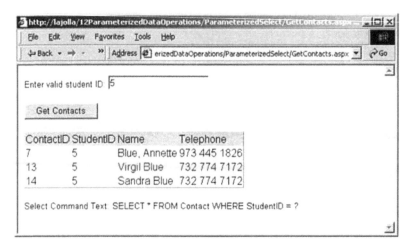

FIGURE 15.8D
Browser rendering of ParameterizedSelect/GetContacts.aspx.cs.

3. Drag a Web Forms textbox control onto the page. Assign the following property values:

   (ID): lastName

   Text: %

4. Drag a Web Forms button control onto the page. Assign the following property values:

   (ID): search

   Text: search

   Click: searchClick

5. Drag a Web Forms datagrid control onto the page. Assign the following property values:

   (ID): nameGrid

Step 3: Create and Configure Data Adapter

1. In the Toolbox window, click the Data tab.
2. Drag an OleDbDataAdapter onto Web. The Data Adapter Configuration Wizard opens.
3. Click the Next button.

   Page 1: Data Connection

   • Select the StudentAdministration database.

   • Click Next.

   Page 2: Query Type

   • Accept the Use SQL Statement selection.

   • Click Next; the Select SQL statement window opens.

   Page 3: Generate SQL Statements

   • Click Query Builder button.

   Page 4: Query Builder

   The Add Table window opens.

- Select Student Table.
- Click Add.
- Click Close button.
- Enter the following:

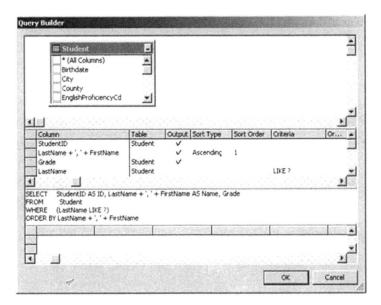

FIGURE HO15.1
Query Builder.

- Click the OK button.

Page 3: Reopens

- Click the Advance Options....

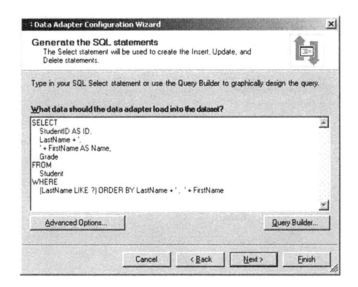

FIGURE HO15.2
Data Adapter Configuration Wizard SQL statements page.

Page 5: Advanced SQL Generation Options

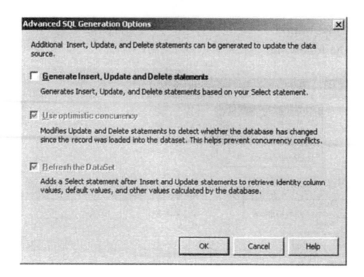

FIGURE HO15.3
Advanced SQL Generation Options dialog.

- Uncheck the Generate Insert, Update and Delete Statements.
- Click OK.

Page 3: Reopens

- Click Next.

Page 6: View Wizard Results

The Wizard's results are displayed.

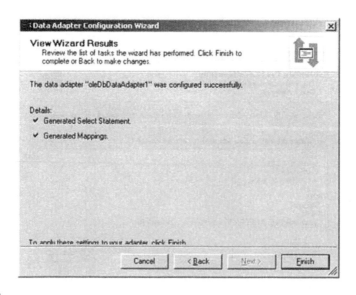

FIGURE HO15.4
Configuration Wizard results page.

4. Click Finish.

Step 4: Manually Configure Data Adapter Properties.

1. In the Web page Designer Window, open the Properties Window.
2. Assign the following property values:
   (Name)   **nameAdapter**

Step 5: Edit the Parameters Collection

1. Expand the Select Command node by clicking the + sign. Note: the parameters are automatically configured by the DataAdapter Configuration Wizard.
2. Click the ellipses in the InsertCommand Parameter property. The OleDbParameter-Collection Editor opens.

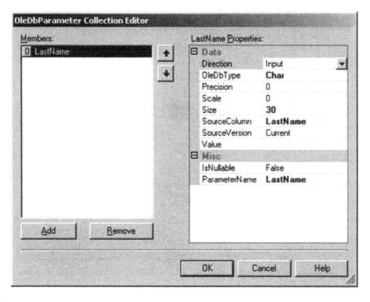

FIGURE HO15.5
OleDbParameter Collection Editor.

3. Click OK to close the editor. The editor is divided into two panes. The left pane is used to add and remove parameters:

   The Add button creates a new parameter in the collection with default name Parameter*n* where *n* is a sequential number.

   The Remove button removes the selected parameter from the collection.

4. The right pane is used to set the properties of the parameter selected in the left pane:

   Direction: Select from a drop-down list of ParameterDirection enumeration members.

   OleDbType: Select from a drop-down list of OleDbTypes.

   Precision: Enter the parameter's precision.

   Scale: Enter the parameter's scale.

   Size: Enter the parameter's size.

SourceColumn: Enter the parameter's data source column.

SourceVersion: Select from a drop down list of DataRowVersion enumeration members.

Value: **explicit literal** passed as the parameter; this property overrides the SourceColumn property.

IsNullable: Enter true if null values are accepted; false otherwise.

ParameterName: Enter name used for programmatic reference. Note: preface SqlParameter names with @.

Step 6: Create DataSet

1. Drag a DataSet onto page. The Data Adapter Configuration Wizard opens.

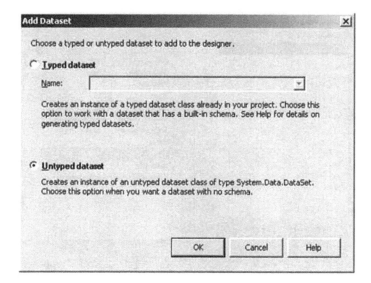

FIGURE HO15.6
Add Dataset dialog.

2. Select the Untyped dataset option.
3. Click the OK button.
4. Assign the following property values:
   (Name) **nameSet**
5. Assign DataGrid's Data Source
6. Select the DataGrid.
7. Assign the following property values:
   DataSource **nameSet**

Step 7: Code the Searchclick Method

1. Enter the following boldface code in the skeletal SearchClick method in the code-behind file StudentSearch.aspx.cs:

```
private void SearchClick(object sender, System.EventArgs e)
{
nameAdapter.SelectCommand.Parameters["LastName"].Value =
   lastName.Text;
nameAdapter.Fill(nameSet, "Student Names");
nameGrid.DataSource = nameSet.Tables["Student Names"];
nameGrid.DataBind();
}
```

Step 8: Set Start Page

1. In Solution Explorer, set StudentSearch as the Start Page.

Step 9: Execute the Application

1. Enter W% in the textbox. (% is the wildcard character.) Click the Search button.

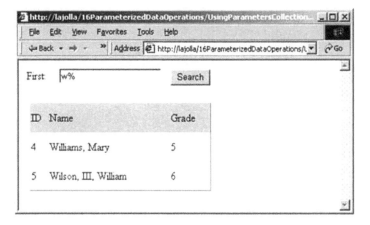

FIGURE HO15.7
Browser rendering of returned results.

2. The students with last names beginning with "W" are listed.
3. Close the application.

16

Data Management

Column Types

Explicitly declared columns can be programmatically added to the DataGrid's columns collection. The bottom column shown in Figure 16.1 is an explicitly declared column. These columns provide greater formatting flexibility than automatically generated columns. The collection is accessed with the DataGrid's Columns collection. These explicitly declared columns are displayed (1) in an order corresponding to their order in the collection and (2) before auto-generated columns. Note that the auto-generated columns are not added to the columns collection. The types of columns are described in Figure 16.2.

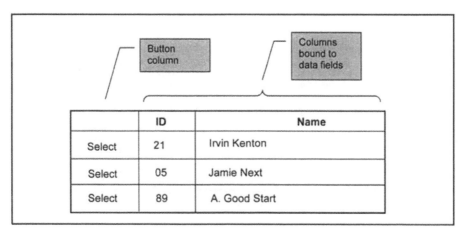

FIGURE16.1
Declared columns.

Type	Description
BoundColumn	Displays a column bound to a field in the data source. BoundColumn is the default column type.
ButtonColumn	Displays a column with a command button for each item.
EditCommandColumn	Displays a column containing editing commands for each item.
HyperLinkColumn	Displays a column in which the contents are represented as a hyperlink. The column contents can be bound to a field in the data source or static text.
TemplateColumn	Displays a column in which the item's content is based on a specified template.

FIGURE 16.2
Types of explicitly declared columns.

```
public abstract class DataGridColumn : IStateManager

Class Hierarchy
Object
   DataGridColumn
      BoundColumn
      ButtonColumn
      EditCommandColumn
      HyperLinkColumn
      TemplateColumn

Namespace: System.Web.UI.WebControls

Public Instance Constructors
public DataGidColumn( );                         Initializes a new instance of the class.

Public Instance Properties
public virtual TableItemStyle                    Gets the TableItemStype object specifying the
   FooterStyle{get; }                            the column's footer style. The default is the empty
                                                 TableItemStyle object.
public virtual string FooterText{get; set;}      Gets and sets the text displayed in the column's
                                                 footer section. The default value is the empty
                                                 string.
public virtual string HeaderImageUrl{get; set;}  Gets and sets the location of the image to display
                                                 in the header section of the column. The default
                                                 value is the empty string.
public virtual TableItemStyle                    Gets the TableItemStype object specifying the
   HeaderStyle{get; }                            the column's header style. The default is the empty
                                                 TableItemStyle object.
public virtual string HeaderText{get; set;}      Gets and sets the text displayed in the column's
                                                 header section. The default value is the empty
                                                 string.
public virtual TableItemStyle ItemStyle{get; }   Gets the TableItemStype object specifying the
                                                 the column's item style. The default is the empty
                                                 TableItemStyle object.
public virtual string SortExpression{get; set;}  Gets and sets the field name to pass to the
                                                 OnSortCommand method. The default value is the
                                                 empty string.
public bool Visible{get; set;}                   Gets and sets the value true to display the column
                                                 in the DataGrid control; false otherwise. The
                                                 default value is true.

Protected Instance Properties
protected bool DesignMode{get;}                  Gets the value true if the column is in design mode;
                                                 false otherwise.
protected DataGrid Owner{get;}                   Gets the DataGrid object of which the column is a
                                                 member.
```

FIGURE 16.3
DataGridColumn class.

A class derived from the DataGridColumn class represents each of these column types. Selected members of the DataGridColumn class are presented in Figure 16.3.

Button Column

The ButtonColumn class represents a column that contains a command button for each row in the column. The button's caption, such as "SELECT," can be specified with a Text property, in which case all buttons contain the same caption. Another option is to bind

```
public enum ButtonColumnType

Namespace: System.Web.UI.WebControls

Member                          Description
LinkButton                      Hyperlink style buttons.
PushBotton                      Push button style.
```

FIGURE 16.4
ButtonColumnType enumeration.

```
public event DataGridCommandEventHandler ItemCommand

EventHandler Delegate
public delegate void DataGridCommandEventHandler(
        Object source,
        DataGridCommandEventArgs e
);
```

FIGURE 16.5
ItemCommand event.

```
public sealed class DataGridCommandEventArgs : CommandEventArgs

Class Hierarchy
Object
    EventArgs
        CommandEventArgs
            DataGridCommandEventArgs

Namespace: System.Web.UI.WebControls

Public Instance Constructors
public DataGridCommandEventArgs (         Initializes a new instance of the class. The
    DataGridItem item,                    DataGridItem object item represents the DataGrid
    object commandSource,                 item or row. The CommandSource property is
    CommandEventArgs originalArgs );      initialized to the value commandSource. The
                                          CommandEventArgs object originalArgs
                                          represents the command argument and name.

Public Instance Properties
public object CommandSource{get;}         Gets the object representing the source of the
                                          command.
public DataGridItem Item{get;}            Gets the DataGridItem object representing the
                                          selected item.
```

FIGURE 16.6
DataGridCommandEventArgs class summary.

the column to a field in the data source with the DataTextField property so the button's caption will reflect the bound fields value. Additionally, a formatting string can be included in the DataTextField property to format the data displayed.

Members of the **ButtonColumnType** enumeration, shown in Figure 16.4, characterize the type of button displayed in a button column. Clicking a button in the ButtonColumn raises the **ItemCommand** event (Figure 16.5). The event handler receives an argument of the type **DataGridCommandEventArgs** (Figure 16.6). The arguments provide information regarding the ItemCommand event raised whenever a button in the DataGrid is clicked. The ButtonColumn class, summarized in Figure 16.7, represents the button column.

public class ButtonColumn : DataGridColumn	
Class Hierarchy	
Object	
DataGridColumn	
ButtonColumn	
Namespace: System.Web.UI.WebControls	
Public Instance Constructors	
public **ButtonColumn** ( );	Initializes a new instance of the class.
Public Instance Properties	
public virtual ButtonColumnType **ButtonType** {get; set;}	Gets or sets the ButtonColumnType enumeration value specifying the button type. The default type is LinkButton.
public virtual string **CommandName**{get; set;}	Gets or sets the string representing the command to be performed when the button is clicked. The default value is the empty string.
public virtual string **DataTextField** {get; set;}	Gets or sets the data source field name to bind to the ButtonColumn. The default value is the empty string.
public virtual string **DataTextFormatString** {get; set;}	Gets or sets the string specifying the display format applied to data displayed as the button caption. The default value is the empty string.
public virtual string **Text** {get; set;}	Gets or sets the caption displayed in the buttons. The default value is the empty string.
Public Instance Methods	
public override void **Initialize** ( );	Restores the ButtonColumn to its initial state.
public override void **InitializeCell** (TableCell *cell*, int *columnIndex*, ListItemType *itemType*);	Resets the TableCell object *cell* to its initial state where *columnIndex* is the column index of the column containing the cell and *itemType* is a ListItemType member.
Protected Instance Methods	
protected virtual string **FormatDataTextValue** (object *dataValue*);	Formats the assigned value to the format specified by the DataTextFormatString property.

FIGURE 16.7
ButtonColumn class summary.

The application ButtonColumnBasics illustrates the following:

- Creation and initialization of a ColumnButton object
- Adding a ColumnButton to a data grid
- Handling the ItemCommand event raised when a ColumnButton is clicked

The application's SelectStudent page is shown in Figure 16.8A.

The page contains a data grid nameGrid. The handler for the ItemCommand event is declared with the attribute–value pair expression

```
OnItemCommand = ItemSelected
```

in the opening tag of the data grid element. The code-behind file is shown in Figure 16.8B. A ButtonColumn object is created and initialized with the statements

```
ButtonColumn selectButtonColumn = new ButtonColumn();
```

The caption on the button, displayed in each row, is set with the statement

```
selectButtonColumn.Text = "Select";
```

The same caption appears on every button. The button type is specified with the statement

```
selectButtonColumn.ButtonType = ButtonColumnType.PushButton;
```

```
<%@ Page language="c#" Codebehind="SelectStudent.aspx.cs" AutoEventWireup="false"
        Inherits="ButtonColumnBasics.SelectStudent" %>
<HTML>
  <HEAD>
  </HEAD>
  <body MS_POSITIONING="GridLayout">

    <form id="SelectStudent" method="post" runat="server">
      <asp:DataGrid ID=nameGrid Runat=server OnItemCommand=ItemSelected>
      </asp:DataGrid>
      <p></p>
      <asp:Label ID=msgLabel Runat=server></asp:Label>
    </form>
  </body>
</HTML>
```

Handler for ItemCommand event

FIGURE 16.8A
Web page ButtonColumnBasics/SelectStudent.aspx.

```
using System;
using System.Web.UI.WebControls;
using System.Data.OleDb;

namespace ButtonColumnBasics
{
      public class SelectStudent : System.Web.UI.Page
      {
            protected System.Web.UI.WebControls.DataGrid nameGrid;
            protected System.Web.UI.WebControls.Label msgLabel;

            public SelectStudent()
            {
                  Page.Init += new System.EventHandler(Page_Init);
            }

            private void Page_Load(object sender, System.EventArgs e)
            {
                        ButtonColumn selectButtonColumn =
                              new ButtonColumn();

                        selectButtonColumn.Text = "Select";
                        selectButtonColumn.ButtonType =
                              ButtonColumnType.PushButton;
                        selectButtonColumn.HeaderText = "Select Student";
                        selectButtonColumn.ItemStyle.HorizontalAlign =
                              HorizontalAlign.Center;

                        nameGrid.Columns.Add(selectButtonColumn);

                        nameGrid.DataSource = LoadDataSet();
                        nameGrid.DataBind();
            }

            public System.Data.DataSet LoadDataSet( )
            {
                        string cmdText = "SELECT StudentID AS ID, " +
                              "LastName + ', ' + FirstName AS Name, Grade " +
                              "FROM Student";
                        string provider = "Provider=Microsoft.Jet.OLEDB.4.0";
                        string dataSource =
                              "Data Source=C:\\DB\\StudentAdministratorDB.mdb";
                        string connectStg = provider + ";" + dataSource;
                        OleDbConnection connection =
                              new OleDbConnection(connectStg);
                        OleDbCommand command =
                              new OleDbCommand(cmdText, connection);
                        System.Data.DataSet studentDataSet =
                              new System.Data.DataSet();

                        OleDbDataAdapter studentDataAdapter =
                              new OleDbDataAdapter(command);
                        studentDataAdapter.Fill(studentDataSet,"StudentName");
                        return studentDataSet;
            }
```

Button column creation

Button column style, like caption, type and alignment defined

Column added to grid

FIGURE 16.8B
Code-behind file ButtonColumnBasics/SelectStudent.aspx.cs.

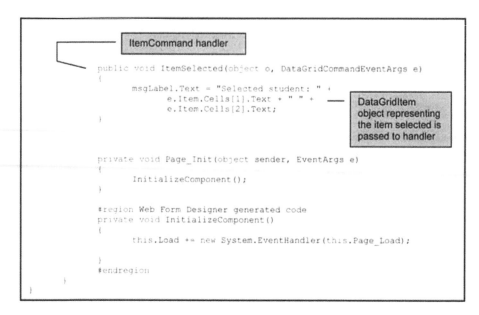

FIGURE 16.8B (CONTINUED)
Code-behind file ButtonColumnBasics/SelectStudent.aspx.cs.

Alternatively, a hyperlink type button can be specified. The column's header caption is specified with the statement

```
selectButtonColumn.HeaderText = "Select Student";
```

A TableItemStyle object that is accessed with the ButtonColumn's ItemStyle property represents the button's style. Properties represented by the TableItemStyle class include HorizontalAlign, which specifies the horizontal alignment of the item, in this case a button, within its container. The following statement specifies that the button be centrally located within its cell:

```
selectButtonColumn.ItemStyle.HorizontalAlign =
HorizontalAlign.Center;
```

Alignment options include Left and Right.

The Add method is used to add the ButtonColumn object, `selectButtonColumn`, to the data grids column collection.

```
nameGrid.Columns.Add(selectButtonColumn);
```

The DataGrid is bound to a data set containing student identification, name and grade data. The initial browser rendering of the page is shown in Figure 16.8C. The members of the data grids column collection, in this case the single button column, are positioned in front of the auto-generated columns reflecting the fields of the bound data source.

When a button is clicked, the page is posted back and the ItemCommand is raised. The handler SelectItem is invoked. This handler is passed a DataGridCommandEventArgs object that includes a DataGridItem representing the item associated with the button clicked. For example, the DataGridItem object member of the passed DataGridCommandEventArgs object e is accessed with the expression

```
e.Item.Cells
```

Figure 16.8D shows the page returned to the browser when the button of the third item in the list is clicked.

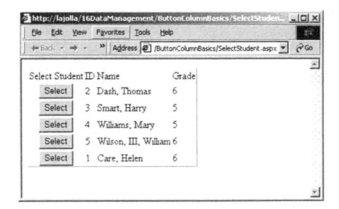

FIGURE 16.8C
Initial rendering of Web page ButtonColumnBasics/SelectStudent.aspx.

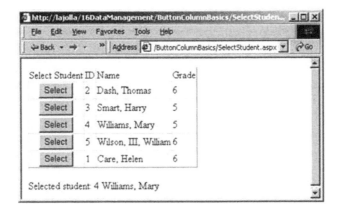

FIGURE 16.8D
Returned Web page ButtonColumnBasics/SelectStudent.aspx.cs.

The DataTextField enables the binding of a field name from the data source to the button. In this case, the value displayed in the button is the value of the field in the item in which the button appears. The DataTextFormatString property provides for specifying a string that effects formatting of the value displayed. The format string syntax is shown in Figure 16.9.

Bound Column

A **BoundColumn** class (Figure 16.10) represents a column that is bound to a field in the data source. Updates to the data source field bound to the column are reflected in the column. The application BoundColumnBasics illustrates use of the BoundColumn to display selected fields in a data source. For example, consider a data set with a table consisting of student ID, name and grade fields that is used to populate a data grid with name and grade columns.

Syntax	
{ *cellIndex* : *formatCharacter x...x* }	
cellIndex	Index of the cell to be formatted. **Always zero as the column only contains one cell.**
formatCharacter	Character specifying the format.
x...x	Precision specifier determines the number of decimal places, for example xx indicates two decimal places.

Format Character	Description
C or c	Currency
D or d	Decimal
E or e	Scientific or exponential
F or f	Fixed
G or g	General
N or n	Number
X	Hexadecimal in upper case
x	Hexadecimal in lower case

FIGURE 16.9
Format string syntax.

public class BoundColumn : DataGridColumn	
Class Hierarchy	
Object	
DataGridColumn	
BoundColumn	
Public Instance Constructors	
public **BoundColumn**( );	Initializes a new instance of the class.
Public Instance Properties	
public virtual string **DataField**{get; set;}	Gets and sets the name of the data source field bound to the column. The default value is the empty string.
public virtual string **DataFormattingString**{get; set; }	Gets and sets the string specifying the format for items displayed in the column. The default is the empty string.
public virtual bool **ReadOnly**{get; set;}	Gets and sets the value true if the items in the BoundColumn can be edited; false otherwise. The default value is false.
Public Instance Methods	
public override void **Initialize**( )	Resets the BoundColumn value to its initial state.
public override void **InitializeCell**( )	Resets the specified TableCell object, *cell*, in the BoundColumn represented by the index *columnIndex* and item type specified by the ListItemType enumeration member *itemType*.
Protected Instance Properties	
protected virtual string **FormatDataValue**(object *dataValue*);	Converts the specified object, dataValue, to the format specified by the DataFormatString property. The formatted value is returned.

FIGURE 16.10
BoundColumn class.

The applications start page is shown in Figure 16.11A. The Web page contains the DataGrid server control nameGrid. The code-behind file is shown in Figure 16.11B. A BoundColumn object, nameColumn, intended to display the name field, is created with the statement

```
BoundColumn nameColumn = new BoundColumn();
```

```
<%@ Page language="c#" Codebehind="DataInBoundColumns.aspx.cs"
        AutoEventWireup="false"
        Inherits="BoundColumnBasics.DataInBoundColumns" %>
<HTML>
  <HEAD>
  </HEAD>
  <body MS_POSITIONING="GridLayout">
    <form id="DataInBoundColumns" method="post" runat="server">
      <asp:DataGrid ID=nameGrid Runat=server></asp:DataGrid>
    </form>
  </body>
</HTML>
```

FIGURE 16.11A
Web page BoundColumnBasics/DataInBoundColumns.aspx.

```
using System;
using System.Drawing;
using System.Web.UI.WebControls;
using System.Data.OleDb;

namespace BoundColumnBasics
{
    public class DataInBoundColumns : System.Web.UI.Page
    {
        protected System.Web.UI.WebControls.DataGrid nameGrid;

        public DataInBoundColumns()
        {
            Page.Init += new System.EventHandler(Page_Init);
        }

        private void Page_Load(object sender, System.EventArgs e)
        {
            BoundColumn nameColumn = new BoundColumn();
            nameColumn.HeaderText = "Student Name";
            nameColumn.DataField = "Name";               // Column bound to Name field
            nameColumn.HeaderStyle.BackColor = Color.LightGray;
            nameGrid.Columns.Add(nameColumn);

            BoundColumn gradeColumn = new BoundColumn();
            gradeColumn.HeaderText = "Grade";
            gradeColumn.DataField = "Grade";             // Column bound to Grade field
            gradeColumn.HeaderStyle.BackColor = Color.LightGray;
            nameGrid.Columns.Add(gradeColumn);

            nameGrid.AutoGenerateColumns = false;        // Columns in data set not
            nameGrid.DataSource = LoadDataSet();         // automatically generated
            nameGrid.DataBind();
        }

        public System.Data.DataSet LoadDataSet( )
        {
            string cmdText = "SELECT StudentID AS ID, " +
                "LastName + ', ' + FirstName AS Name, Grade " +
                "FROM Student";
            string provider = "Provider=Microsoft.Jet.OLEDB.4.0";
            string dataSource =
                "Data Source=C:\\DB\\StudentAdministratorDB.mdb";
            string connectStg = provider + ";" + dataSource;
            OleDbConnection connection =
                new OleDbConnection(connectStg);
            OleDbCommand command =
                new OleDbCommand(cmdText, connection);
            System.Data.DataSet studentDataSet =
                new System.Data.DataSet();
            OleDbDataAdapter studentDataAdapter =
                new OleDbDataAdapter(command);
            studentDataAdapter.Fill(studentDataSet,"StudentName");
            return studentDataSet;
        }
```

FIGURE 16.11B
Code-behind file BoundColumnBasics/DataInBoundColumns.aspx.cs.

```
        private void Page_Init(object sender, EventArgs e)
        {
                InitializeComponent();
        }

        #region Web Form Designer generated code
        private void InitializeComponent()
        {
                this.Load += new System.EventHandler(this.Page_Load);

        }
        #endregion
    }
}
```

FIGURE 16.11B (CONTINUED)
Code-behind file BoundColumnBasics/DataInBoundColumns.aspx.cs.

The column's properties are set. For example, the statements

```
nameColumn.HeaderText = "Student Name";

nameColumn.DataField = "Name";
```

assign the HeaderText caption and the name of the data source's field that the column will display. The TableItemStyle object representing the grid's header style is accessed with the expression

```
nameColumn.HeaderStyle
```

The TableItemStyle's Backcolor property is assigned a light gray color with the statement

```
nameColumn.HeaderStyle.BackColor = Color.LightGray;
```

The BoundColumn object nameColumn is added to the nameGrid's collection with the Add method:

```
nameGrid.Columns.Add(nameColumn);
```

A second bound column, intended to display the Grade field, is created, configured and added to the grid's collection with the statement

```
BoundColumn gradeColumn = new BoundColumn();

gradeColumn.HeaderText = "Grade";

gradeColumn.DataField = "Grade";

gradeColumn.HeaderStyle.BackColor = Color.LightGray;

nameGrid.Columns.Add(gradeColumn);
```

The grid's AutoGenerateColumns property is set to false to prevent the automatic generation of columns to display source data:

```
nameGrid.AutoGenerateColumns = false;
```

The grid's DataSource property is set to the DataSet returned by the LoadDataSet method and the data bound with the statements

```
nameGrid.DataSource = LoadDataSet();

nameGrid.DataBind();
```

The application's browser rendering is shown in Figure 16.11C. Only the name and grade fields of the data set are displayed in the grid. This is in contrast to the display of all fields in the data set, StudentID, Name and Grade, that would result if the grid's AutoGenerateColumns property were set true.

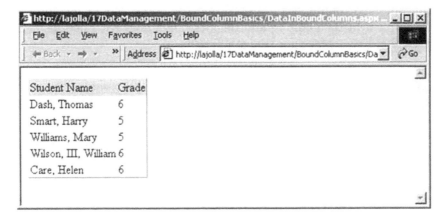

FIGURE 16.11C
Browser rendering of Web page BoundColumnBasics/DataInBoundColumns.aspx.

Edit Command Column

The Edit Command column displays an Edit command button in each row. Clicking the button selects the row for editing and raises the EditCommand event. When a row is selected for editing, the Edit button is replaced by Update and Cancel command buttons; clicking these buttons raises the UpdateCommand and CancelCommand events, respectively. The handler for the UpdateCommand updates the data set, rebinds the data and deselects the row. Similarly, the CancelCommand handler deselects the row and rebinds the data. The Edit Command column is represented by the **EditCommandColumn** class, shown in Figure 16.12.

public class EditCommandColumn : DataGridColumn	
Hierarchy	

Object
   DataGridColumn
      EditCommandColumn	

Public Instance Constructor	
public **EditCommandColumn( );**	Initializes a new instance of the class.
Public Instance Properties	
public virtual ButtonColumnType **ButtonType** {get; set;}	Gets and sets a ButtonColumnType enumeration member specifying the button type. The default is LinkButton.
public virtual string **CancelText** {get; set;}	Gets and sets the caption displayed in the Cancel command button.
public virtual string **EditText** {get; set;}	Gets and sets the caption displayed in the Edit command button.
public virtual string **UpdateText** {get; set;}	Gets and sets the caption displayed in the Update command button.

FIGURE 16.12
EditCommandColumn.

The EditCommandColumnBasics application illustrates use of the EditCommand-Column to implement data editing and database updating. For example, consider the Contact table that lists contacts for students (Figure 16.13).

ContactID	StudentID	Name	Telephone
1	1	Care, Joan	973 762 5465
2	2	Dash, Thomas, Jr.	973 330 9101
3	2	Dash, Evelyn	973 330 9101
4	3	Smart, Wilma	973 239 4751
5	4	Williams, Neville	414 539 6249
6	4	Williams, Ronda	973 775 4802
7	5	Blue, Annette	973 445 1826
13	5	Virgil Blue	732 774 7172
14	5	Sandra Blue	732 774 7172

FIGURE 16.13
Contact table.

In this case, the student identified by StudentID value 2 has two contacts: Thomas Dash Jr. and Evelyn Dash. Loading the data into a data grid with an EditCommandColumn affects editing of these data. The initial browser rendering of the application start page is shown in Figure 16.14A.

The grid's first column is an EditCommandColumn with a button in each row, in this case captioned "Edit." The Contact table data are loaded into BoundColumns. The ContactID that uniquely identifies rows in the Contact table is loaded into a column with the Visible property set to value false.

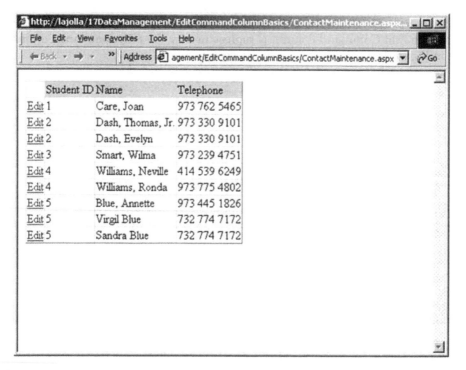

FIGURE 16.14A
Initial browser rendering of EditCommandColumnBasics/ContactMaintenance.aspx.

Clicking the Edit button posts the page and raises the EditCommand event. The page is returned to the browser in the edit mode. Figure 16.14B shows the page returned in response to user clicking of the Edit button containing the contact name Virgil Blue for the student with identification code 5. Note that the selected row is returned in the Edit mode:

- The EditCommandColumn contains Update and Cancel buttons.
- Editable fields are presented in textboxes.

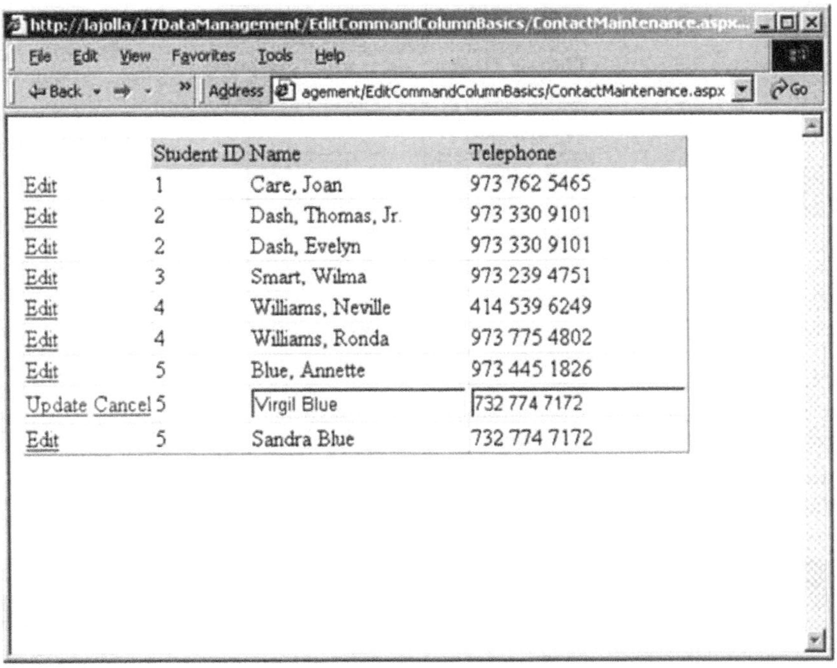

FIGURE 16.14B
Browser rendering of EditCommandColumnBasics/ContactMaintenance.aspx page in Edit mode.

The framework changes the buttons displayed in the EditCommandColumn automatically. The captions displayed are explicitly stated; if the captions of the Edit, Update and Cancel buttons are not explicitly stated, the column will not be displayed.

The Name and Telephone fields are loaded into columns that are visible and not read-only and are rendered in textboxes. Data in the Name and Telephone fields can be user modified. The StudentID field is loaded into a column with the ReadOnly property value set to true. Figure 16.14C illustrates user modification of the telephone number.

Clicking the Update button posts the page and raises the UpdateCommand event. The following programmatic steps are explicitly performed in the UpdateCommand event handler:

- A parameterized update command is created

  UPDATE Contact SET Name = ?, Telephone = ? WHERE ContactID = ?

- The columns containing Name, Telephone and ContactID number are accessed and assigned to OleDbParameter objects.
- An ExecuteNonQuery command is executed.
- The selected item is deselected.
- The updated table's data are loaded into the grid.

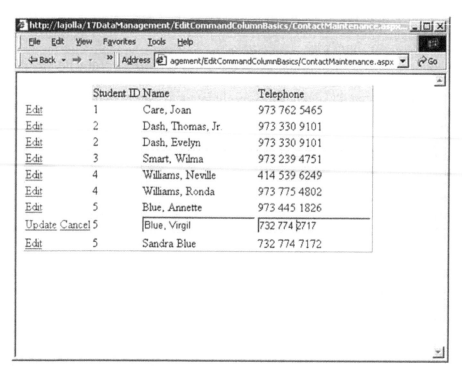

FIGURE 16.14C
User modification of the Name and Telephone fields.

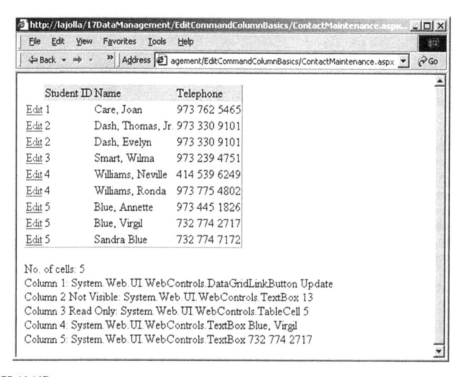

FIGURE 16.14D
Browser rendering of page after update of database.

```
<%@ Page language="c#" Codebehind="ContactMaintenance.aspx.cs"
        AutoEventWireup="false"
        Inherits="EditCommandColumnBasics.ContactMaintenance" %>
<!DOCTYPE HTML PUBLIC "-//W3C//DTD HTML 4.0 Transitional//EN" >
<HTML>
  <HEAD>
  </HEAD>
  <body MS_POSITIONING="GridLayout">
    <form id="ContactMaintenance" method="post" runat="server">
      <asp:DataGrid ID=contactGrid Runat=server
                   OnEditCommand=EditContact
                   OnCancelCommand=CancelEdit
                   OnUpdateCommand=UpdateContact>
      </asp:DataGrid>
      <p></p>
      <asp:Label ID=msg Runat=server></asp:Label>
    </form>
  </body>
</HTML>
```

Methods raising
Edit, Cancel and
Update events
when the Edit,
Cancel and Update
buttons are clicked

FIGURE 16.14E
Web page EditCommandBasics/ContactMaintenance.aspx.

The rendering of the page returned to the browser is shown in Figure 16.14D. Note that the Name and Telephone fields reflect the modifications.

For this example, the message field normally used to display error messages is used to display characteristics of the selected items columns when handled by the UpdateCommand handler. Note that the second column, though not visible, contains a textbox control with the value of the ContactID 13. Note also that the third column, in read-only status, contains a table cell control that displays the StudentID value 5. The fourth and fifth columns contain textbox controls displaying the Name and Telephone values. The text box controls in the Name and Telephone columns provide for user data entry. The text box control in the ContactID is not visible and precludes user modification of the value.

Both the Name and Telephone fields require nonzero-length values and thus result in failure of the update operation if either is an empty string. A message field is generally included on the page to present any error messages to the user. The application's page, EditCommandBasics/ContactMaintenance.aspx, is shown in Figure 16.14E.

Assignment of methods to handle the data grid's Edit, Update and Cancel events is made with the following value–attribute pairs:

```
OnEditCommand = EditContact

OnCancelCommand = CancelEdit

OnUpdateCommand = UpdateContact>
```

The page's code behind file is shown in Figure 16.14F. During the Page_Load method execution, the EditCommandColumn is created:

```
EditCommandColumn editColumn = new EditCommandColumn();
```

The edit, update and cancel button captions are set with the statements

```
editColumn.EditText = "Edit";

editColumn.CancelText = "Cancel";

editColumn.UpdateText = "Update";
```

If these values are not explicitly specified, the column will not display. The column is added to the grid's Columns collection with the statement

```
contactGrid.Columns.Add(editColumn);
```

```
using System;
using System.Drawing;
using System.Web.UI.WebControls;
using System.Data.OleDb;

namespace EditCommandColumnBasics
{
      public class ContactMaintenance : System.Web.UI.Page
      {
            protected System.Web.UI.WebControls.DataGrid contactGrid;
            protected System.Web.UI.WebControls.Label msg;

            protected System.Data.OleDb.OleDbConnection connection;

            public ContactMaintenance()
            {
                  Page.Init += new System.EventHandler(Page_Init);
            }

            private void Page_Load(object sender, System.EventArgs e)
            {
                  connection = CreateConnection();
```

```
                  EditCommandColumn editColumn = new EditCommandColumn();
                  editColumn.EditText = "Edit";
                  editColumn.CancelText = "Cancel";
                  editColumn.UpdateText = "Update";
                  contactGrid.Columns.Add(editColumn);
```
Column for edit and update buttons

```
                  BoundColumn contactColumn = new BoundColumn();
                  contactColumn.HeaderText = "Contact ID";
                  contactColumn.DataField = "ContactID";
                  contactColumn.HeaderStyle.BackColor = Color.LightGray;
                  contactColumn.Visible = false;
                  contactGrid.Columns.Add(contactColumn);
```
Nonvisible column for ContactID

```
                  BoundColumn studentColumn = new BoundColumn();
                  studentColumn.HeaderText = "Student ID";
                  studentColumn.DataField = "StudentID";
                  studentColumn.HeaderStyle.BackColor = Color.LightGray;
                  studentColumn.ReadOnly = true;
                  contactGrid.Columns.Add(studentColumn);
```
Read-only column for StudentID

```
                  BoundColumn nameColumn = new BoundColumn();
                  nameColumn.HeaderText = "Name";
                  nameColumn.DataField = "Name";
                  nameColumn.HeaderStyle.BackColor = Color.LightGray;
                  contactGrid.Columns.Add(nameColumn);
```
Editable Column for Name

```
                  BoundColumn telephoneColumn = new BoundColumn();
                  telephoneColumn.HeaderText = "Telephone";
                  telephoneColumn.DataField = "Telephone";
                  telephoneColumn.HeaderStyle.BackColor = Color.LightGray;
                  contactGrid.Columns.Add(telephoneColumn);
```
Editable column for Telephone

```
                  contactGrid.AutoGenerateColumns = false;
                  contactGrid.DataSource = LoadDataSet();
                  contactGrid.DataBind();
            }
```
Columns not created automatically

FIGURE 16.14F
Code-behind file EditCommandBasics/ContactMaintenance.aspx.cs.

A BoundColumn to represent the ContactID field is created, configured and added to the grid's Columns collection with the statements

```
BoundColumn contactColumn = new BoundColumn();
contactColumn.HeaderText = "Contact ID;"
contactColumn.DataField = "ContactID;"
contactColumn.HeaderStyle.BackColor = Color.LightGray;
contactColumn.Visible = false;
contactGrid.Columns.Add(contactColumn);
```

Note that the column's Visible property value is set false, thus the column will be rendered invisible.

```
public System.Data.DataSet LoadDataSet( )
{
    string selectText = "SELECT ContactID, StudentID, Name, "
        + "Telephone  FROM Contact";
    OleDbCommand command =
        new OleDbCommand(selectText, connection);
    System.Data.DataSet contactDataSet =
        new System.Data.DataSet();
    OleDbDataAdapter contactDataAdapter =
        new OleDbDataAdapter(command);
    contactDataAdapter.Fill(contactDataSet,"Contact");
    return contactDataSet;
}

public void CancelEdit(Object o, DataGridCommandEventArgs e)
{
    contactGrid.EditItemIndex = -1;
    BindData();
}

public void EditContact(Object o, DataGridCommandEventArgs e)
{
    contactGrid.EditItemIndex = e.Item.ItemIndex;
    BindData();
}

public void UpdateContact(Object o, DataGridCommandEventArgs e)
{
    DisplayItemCells(e);

    string updateText = "UPDATE Contact SET Name=?, "
        + " Telephone=? WHERE ContactID = ? ";

    OleDbCommand updateCommand =
        new OleDbCommand(updateText, connection);

    updateCommand.Parameters.Add(new OleDbParameter("name",
        OleDbType.Char));
    updateCommand.Parameters.Add(new OleDbParameter("telephone",
        OleDbType.Char));
    updateCommand.Parameters.Add(new OleDbParameter("id",
        OleDbType.Integer));

    updateCommand.Parameters["id"].Value =
        ((TextBox)e.Item.Cells[1].Controls[0]).Text;
    updateCommand.Parameters["name"].Value =
        ((TextBox)e.Item.Cells[3].Controls[0]).Text;
    updateCommand.Parameters["telephone"].Value =
        ((TextBox)e.Item.Cells[4].Controls[0]).Text;

    updateCommand.Connection.Open();
```

Callouts: *Row deselected and grid rebound* · *Selected row set for editing* · *Accessing the selected item's columns* · *Parameterized update statement* · *Update command* · *Create parameter objects* · *Assign values to parameters*

FIGURE 16.14F (CONTINUED)
Code-behind file EditCommandBasics/ContactMaintenance.aspx.cs.

Similarly, a BoundColumn to represent the StudentID field is added to the grid's Columns collection with the statements

```
BoundColumn studentColumn = new BoundColumn();
studentColumn.HeaderText = "Student ID;"
studentColumn.DataField = "StudentID;"
studentColumn.HeaderStyle.BackColor = Color.LightGray;
studentColumn.ReadOnly = true;
contactGrid.Columns.Add(studentColumn);
```

The StudentID field should not change; consequently, the column's ReadOnly property value is set true. When in the edit mode, the cell will be represented as a TableCell control.

BoundColumn columns are also added to the grid's Columns collection to represent the Name and Telephone fields. The default values for the Visible and ReadOnly property are

```
                        try
                        {
  ┌──────────┐                   updateCommand.ExecuteNonQuery();
  │ Update   │          }
  │ database │          catch (OleDbException oleDbEx)
  └──────────┘          {
                                msg.Text += "Exception: " + oleDbEx.Message + "<br>";
                        }

                        updateCommand.Connection.Close();

                        contactGrid.EditItemIndex = -1;  ──────  ┌──────────────────┐
                        BindData();                              │ Deselect item and │
                }                                                │ rebind grid       │
                                                                 └──────────────────┘
                public void BindData()
                {
                        contactGrid.DataSource = LoadDataSet();
                        contactGrid.DataBind();
                }

                public OleDbConnection CreateConnection()
                {
                        string provider = "Provider=Microsoft.Jet.OLEDB.4.0";
                        string dataSource =
                                "Data Source=C:\\DB\\StudentAdministratorDB.mdb";
  ┌──────────┐          string connectStg = provider + ";" + dataSource;
  │ Create   │          OleDbConnection connection =
  │ parameter│                  new OleDbConnection(connectStg);
  │ objects  │          connection = new OleDbConnection(connectStg);
  └──────────┘          return connection;
                }

                public void DisplayItemCells(DataGridCommandEventArgs e)
                {
                        msg.Text += "No. of cells: " + e.Item.Cells.Count + "<br>";
                        msg.Text += "Column 1: "
                                + e.Item.Cells[0].Controls[0].ToString() + " "
                                + ((LinkButton)e.Item.Cells[0].Controls[0]).Text
                                + "<br>";
  ┌──────────┐          msg.Text += "Column 2 Not Visible: "
  │ Access   │                  + e.Item.Cells[1].Controls[0].ToString() + " "
  │ TextBox  │                  + ((TextBox)e.Item.Cells[1].Controls[0]).Text
  └──────────┘                  + "<br>";
  ┌──────────┐          msg.Text += "Column 3 Read Only: "
  │ Access   │                  + e.Item.Cells[2].ToString() + " "
  │ TableCell│                  + e.Item.Cells[2].Text + "<br>";
  └──────────┘          msg.Text += "Column 4: "
                                + e.Item.Cells[3].Controls[0].ToString() + " "
                                + ((TextBox)e.Item.Cells[3].Controls[0]).Text
                                +"<br>";
                        msg.Text += "Column 5: "
                                + e.Item.Cells[4].Controls[0].ToString() + " "
                                + ((TextBox)e.Item.Cells[4].Controls[0]).Text
                                + "<br>";
                }

                private void Page_Init(object sender, EventArgs e)
                {
                        InitializeComponent();
                }

                #region Web Form Designer generated code
                private void InitializeComponent()
                {
                        this.Load += new System.EventHandler(this.Page_Load);
                }
                #endregion
        }
}
```

FIGURE 16.14F (CONTINUED)
Code-behind file EditCommandBasics/ContactMaintenance.aspx.cs.

accepted. Consequently, these cells of the selected item are represented by TextBox controls when in the edit mode. The content of these controls can be user modified:

```
BoundColumn nameColumn = new BoundColumn();
nameColumn.HeaderText = "Name";
nameColumn.DataField = "Name";
nameColumn.HeaderStyle.BackColor = Color.LightGray;
contactGrid.Columns.Add(nameColumn);
BoundColumn telephoneColumn = new BoundColumn();
telephoneColumn.HeaderText = "Telephone;"
telephoneColumn.DataField = "Telephone;"
telephoneColumn.HeaderStyle.BackColor = Color.LightGray;
contactGrid.Columns.Add(telephoneColumn);
```

Data filling the grid are bound to columns added to the Columns collection. Consequently, the grid's AutoGenerateColumns property value is set false.

```
contactGrid.AutoGenerateColumns = false;
```

Finally, the DataSource property is set to a DataSet object filled with Contact table data. The grid is bound to the data set

```
contactGrid.DataSource = LoadDataSet(); contactGrid.DataBind();
```

The result is the page rendering shown in Figure 16.14A.

When the Edit button is clicked, the page is posted and the EditCommand is raised. During server processing, the EditCommand event handler EditContact is invoked. The Framework passes a DataGridCommandEventArgs object representing the event, as shown in Figure 16.6. The selected item is represented by the argument's Item property, a DataGridItem object. The item's position in the Items collection of the data grid is represented by the value of the DataGridItem's ItemIndex property. Consequently, the index of the selected item is provided by the expression

```
e.Item.ItemIndex
```

The index of the data grid item set for editing is represented as the value of the data grid's EditItemIndex. Thus, the statement

```
contactGrid.EditItemIndex = e.Item.ItemIndex;
```

sets the selected item to edit mode. Finally, the grid is bound to a freshly filled data set

```
BindData();
```

The page is returned with the selected item in the edit mode (Figure 16.14B).

If the user clicks the Cancel button, the page is posted and the CancelCommand raised. During processing the CancelEdit method is invoked. The grid's EditItemIndex is set to the value –1, indicating that no item in the grid is selected for editing:

```
contactGrid.EditItemIndex = -1;
```

Again, the grid is bound to a freshly filled data set

```
BindData();
```

The page is returned with no items in the edit mode (Figure 16.14A).

On the other hand, if the user clicks the Update button, the page is posted and the UpdateCommand raised. During processing the UpdateContact method is invoked and passed a DataGridCommandEventArgs argument. The argument's Item property represents the selected grid item.

The method DisplayItems is called to illustrate access of the selected item's cells. The number of cells in the selected item is evaluated with the following expression:

```
e.Item.Cells.Count
```

Specifically, the Cells property accesses the TableCellCollection of TableCell objects representing the grid's columns. The number of TableCell objects, i.e., the number of columns represented, is accessed with the collection's Count property.

The item's first cell, corresponding to the grid's first column, is accessed with the expression

```
e.Item.Cells[0]
```

that indexes the collection of TableCell. The Controls property accesses the collection of Controls comprising the cell. There is only one control, which is accessed with the expression

```
e.Item.Cells[0].Controls[0]
```

A string representation of the type of control is expressed as

```
e.Item.Cells[0].Controls[0].ToString()
```

The first column is a LinkButton type of control. The type of control and value represented are summarized below:

Column	Field Represented	Type of Web Control	Value
1	EditCommandColumn	LinkButton	Update
2	ContactId	TextBox	13
3	StudentID	TableCell	5
4	Name	TextBox	Blue, Virgil
5	Telephone	textBox	732 774 2717

The Control object is cast to the appropriate control type; for example, the first column control is cast to a LinkButton type with the expression

```
(LinkButton)e.Item.Cells[0].Controls[0]
```

and the button's Text property is expressed with

```
((LinkButton)e.Item.Cells[0].Controls[0]).Text
```

Similarly, the column values in columns represented by text boxes are accessed with expressions such as the following:

```
((TextBox)e.Item.Cells[1].Controls[0]).Text
```

On the other hand, the Read-Only column is represented by a TableCell and the type of control is expressed with the statement

```
e.Item.Cells[2].ToString()
```

and the value represented is accessed with the expression

```
e.Item.Cells[2].Text + "<br>";
```

A parameterized update type of SQL statement is created:

```
string updateText = "UPDATE Contact SET Name = ?, Telephone = ? "
+ "WHERE ContactID = ? ";
```

The "?" placeholders are replaced at runtime by parameters. The order of the parameters in the collection must parallel the order of the placeholders in the SQL statement:

Parameter Position	Field	Purpose
1	Name	Updated value
2	Telephone	Updated value
3	ContactID	Identifier of table row to be updated

The update command object is created with the statement

```
OleDbCommand updateCommand =
    new OleDbCommand(updateText, connection);
```

Next, the Parameter objects are created and added to the command's parameter collection

```
updateCommand.Parameters.Add(new OleDbParameter("name",
    OleDbType.Char));
updateCommand.Parameters.Add(new OleDbParameter("telephone",
    OleDbType.Char));
updateCommand.Parameters.Add(new OleDbParameter("id",
    OleDbType.Integer));
```

Note that the type of the parameters representing the Name and Telephone field values is OleDbType.Char. On the other hand, the type of the parameter representing the ContactID value is OleDbType.Integer.

The parameter object value is assigned with the following statements that access the selected item's column values:

```
updateCommand.Parameters["id"].Value =
    ((TextBox)e.Item.Cells[1].Controls[0]).Text;
updateCommand.Parameters["name"].Value =
    ((TextBox)e.Item.Cells[3].Controls[0]).Text;
updateCommand.Parameters["telephone"].Value =
    ((TextBox)e.Item.Cells[4].Controls[0]).Text;
```

Next, the connection with the data source is opened:

```
updateCommand.Connection.Open();
```

The update command is executed in a try block:

```
try
{
    updateCommand.ExecuteNonQuery();
}
catch (OleDbException oleDbEx)
{
    msg.Text + = "Exception: " + oleDbEx.Message + "<br>";
}
```

Exceptions raised are reported in the catch block. For example, the Name and telephone fields require nonempty strings; if the Name field value is an empty string, an error will be raised and the message displayed:

Field 'Contact.Name' cannot be a zero-length string.

Finally, the connection is closed, the data set is filled with the current, i.e., updated, data source values, and the grid is bound to the data set:

```
updateCommand.Connection.Close();
contactGrid.EditItemIndex = -1;
BindData();
```

The page returned to the browser is shown in Figure 16.14D.

Hands-On Exercise: Insert and Delete Database Operations

Step 1: Create Application Contact Maintenance

1. Create Project ContactMaintenance.
2. Delete the Web page WebForm1.aspx.

Step 2: Create Web page AddDeleteContact.aspx

1. Add web form AddDeleteContact.aspx.

Step 3: Create and Configure Data Adapter

1. Drag an OleDbDataAdapter onto the Web page. Assign the following property values: (Use the Wizard where applicable.)

   Data Connection   StudentAdministration

   Table   Contact

   Select Command   **SELECT * FROM Contact ORDER BY Name**

   Do not generate insert, delete and update commands.

   (Name)   **contactAdapter**

Step 4: Create and Configure DataSet

1. In the data adapter's Properties window, click the Generate Dataset... link.
2. Select the DataSet and assign the following property value:

   (Name)   **contactSet**
3. In the data adapter's Properties window, click the Preview Data... link. The Data Adapter Preview window opens.
4. Click the Fill data set button. The data are displayed in the results area.
5. Click the Close button.

Step 5: Create and Configure DataGrid

1. Drag a Web forms datagrid onto the page. Assign the following property value:

   DataSource   **ContactSet**

   DataMember   **Contact**

   (ID)   **contactGrid**

Step 6: Fill the Data Set and Bind the DataGrid to the DataSet

1. In the code-behind file Page_Load method, call the data adapter's Fill method to load the data set's Contact table and the data grid's DataBind method to bind the grid to the data source when the page is initially loaded.

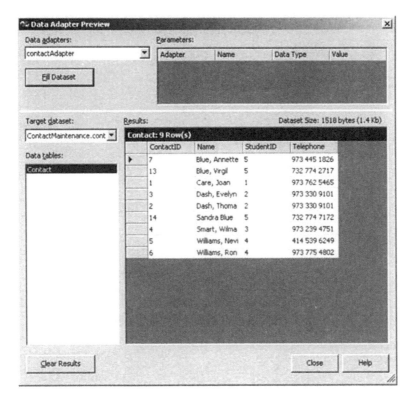

FIGURE HO16.1
Data Adapter Preview.

```
if (!IsPostBack)
{
    contactAdapter.Fill(contactSet, "Contact");
    contactGrid.DataBind();
}
```

Step 7: Execute Application

Step 8: Complete Data Grid Configuration

1. In the DataGrid's properties window, click the ellipses at the left end of the Columns property. The contactGrid properties dialog window with the Columns tab is selected. Click the General tab.
2. Review the settings.
3. Click the Columns tab.
4. In the Available columns list, expand the Button Column entry.
5. Add the Delete column to the Selected columns list.
6. Select the **PushButton** option in the ButtonType drop-down list when the Delete Contact column is selected in the Selected columns list.
7. Enter Delete Contact in the Text textbox.

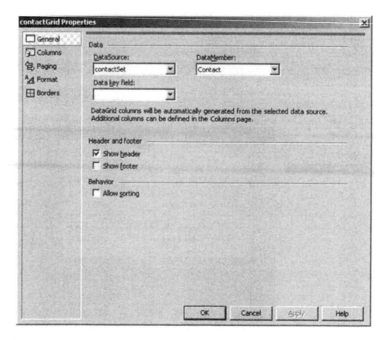

FIGURE HO16.2
ContactGrid Properties.

8. Check the Create columns automatically at runtime.

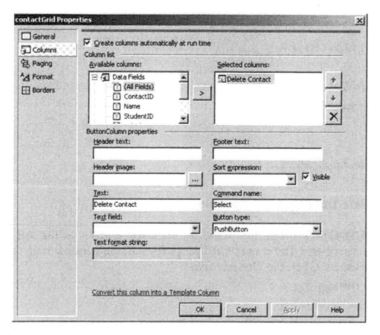

FIGURE HO16.3
ContactGrid Properties.

9. Click the Apply button.
10. Click the OK button.

Step 9: Create a Label Control for Messages

1. Drag a Web Forms Label control onto the Web page to the left of and below the DataGrid. Assign the following property values:

   (ID)   messageLabel

   Text

   ForeColor   **Red**

   Note that the Text property is the empty string.

Step 10: Create Handler for Delete Contact Button Click

1. In the DataGrid's Properties, click the Events tab button. (The Events are listed when the *Lightning Bolt* is clicked.) Enter the following handler name:

   ItemCommand   **contactGridItemCommand**

2. Double-click the ItemCommand caption in the Properties window and the Code Editor opens with the cursor at the ContactGridItemCommand method. Add the bold-face code to the method:

```
private void ContactGridItemCommand(object source,
    System.Web.UI.WebControls.DataGridCommandEventArgs e)
{
    int selectedContactID =
        Convert.ToInt32(e.Item.Cells[1].Text);

    string deleteText =
        "DELETE FROM Contact WHERE ContactID = ? ";

    string provider = "Provider=Microsoft.Jet.OLEDB.4.0";
    string dataSource =
        "Data Source=C:\\DB\\StudentAdministratorDB.mdb";
    string connectStg = provider + ";" + dataSource;
    OleDbConnection connection =
        new OleDbConnection(connectStg);
    connection = new OleDbConnection(connectStg);

    OleDbCommand deleteCommand =
        new OleDbCommand(deleteText, connection);
    deleteCommand.Parameters.Add(new OleDbParameter(
        "contactID", OleDbType.Integer));

    deleteCommand.Parameters["contactID"].Value =
        Convert.ToInt32(e.Item.Cells[1].Text);

    deleteCommand.Connection.Open();
    try
    {
        deleteCommand.ExecuteNonQuery();
    }
    catch (OleDbException oleDbEx)
    {
        messageLabel.Text +=
            "Exception: " + oleDbEx.Message + "<br>";
    }
```

```
        deleteCommand.Connection.Close();

        contactAdapter.Fill(contactSet, "Contact");
        contactGrid.DataBind();
}
```

Step 11: Execute the Application

Step 12: Configure Web Page Insert Controls

1. Drag a Web forms Label onto the page. Assign the following property value:
   Text   **Student ID:**

2 Drag a Web forms Textbox onto the page. Assign the following property value:
   (ID)   **studentID**

3. Drag a Web forms Label onto the page. Assign the following property value:
   Text   **Name:**

4. Drag a Web forms Textbox onto the page. Assign the following property value:
   (ID3)   **name**

5. Drag a Web forms Label onto the page. Assign the following property value:
   Text   **Telephone:**

6. Drag a Web forms Textbox onto the page. Assign the following property value:
   (ID)   **telephone**

7. Drag a Web forms Button onto the page. Assign the following property values:
   (ID)   **insertButton**
   Text   **Insert Contact**
   Click   **InsertContact**

Step 13: Code Insert Procedure

1. Double-click the Insert Contact button on the Web Page Designer. The Code
   Editor opens with the cursor at the InsertContact method:

```
private void InsertContact(object sender, System.EventArgs e)
{
        messageLabel.Text = "";

        if (studentID.Text == "" || name.Text == "" ||
            telephone.Text == "")
        {
            messageLabel.Text = "Error: Student ID, Name "
                + " and Telephone values are required!";
            contactAdapter.Fill(contactSet, "Contact");
            contactGrid.DataBind();
            return;
        }
```

```
try
{
    Int32.Parse( studentID.Text );
}
catch (FormatException fe)
{
    messageLabel.Text = fe.Message;
    contactAdapter.Fill(contactSet, "Contact");
    contactGrid.DataBind();
    return;
}

string insertText = "INSERT INTO Contact (StudentID," +
    " Name, Telephone) + VALUES (?, ?, ?)";

string provider = "Provider=Microsoft.Jet.OLEDB.4.0";
string dataSource =
    "Data Source=C:\\DB\\StudentAdministratorDB.mdb";
string connectStg = provider + ";" + dataSource;
OleDbConnection connection =
    new OleDbConnection(connectStg);
connection = new OleDbConnection(connectStg);

OleDbCommand insertCommand =
    new OleDbCommand(insertText, connection);

insertCommand.Parameters.Add(
    new OleDbParameter("studentID", OleDbType.Integer));
insertCommand.Parameters.Add(new OleDbParameter("name",
    OleDbType.Char));
insertCommand.Parameters.Add(
    new OleDbParameter("telephone", OleDbType.Char));

insertCommand.Parameters["studentID"].Value =
    Convert.ToInt32(studentID.Text);
insertCommand.Parameters["name"].Value = name.Text;
insertCommand.Parameters["telephone"].Value =
    telephone.Text;

insertCommand.Connection.Open();
try
{
    insertCommand.ExecuteNonQuery();
}
catch (OleDbException oleDbEx)
{
    messageLabel.Text += "Exception: " +
        oleDbEx.Message + "<br>";
}
insertCommand.Connection.Close();

contactAdapter.Fill(contactSet, "Contact");
contactGrid.DataBind();
}
```

Step 14: Execute Application

FIGURE HO16.4
Page rendering.

17

Data Lists and Templates

Template Overview

A **template** is a group of HTML elements, literal text, data binding expressions, and ASP.NET server controls declarative syntax that are treated as a unit within another control. For example, the template shown in Figure 17.1 illustrates a combination of Label Checkbox and Image controls; it provides for utilization of diverse controls and developer-specified format. Typically, the template would be used to present the items in a list. Editing or entry of the information is affected with the template shown in Figure 17.2.

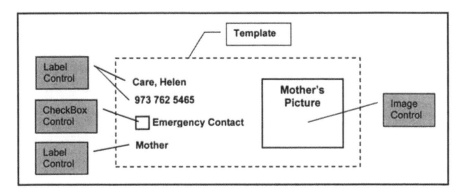

FIGURE 17.1
Typical template control for data presentation.

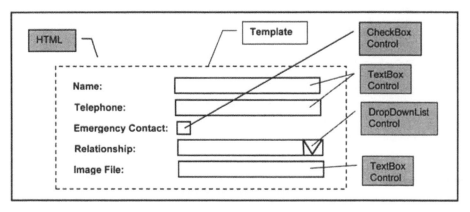

FIGURE 17.2
Template for data editing or entry.

In this case, the template provides TextBox controls for entry of the contact name and telephone. Also provided are a TextBox control for entry of the location of the image file containing the contact's picture and a CheckBox control for checking emergency contacts. A DropDownList control is provided to enable selection of the contact's relationship to the student from a predefined list — for example, Mother, Father, Brother, Sister, Aunt, Uncle, Grandparent and Not Known. Finally, the controls are captioned with HTML.

Note that templates differ from style in that style speaks to the appearance of a control or element, i.e., features such as background color, font face and size. Note also that style can be used to define the appearance of the controls comprising a template. Each template supports its own style object, which enables styling the template at both design and runtime.

Different templates can be used to customize a control. Templates are useful for customizing the layout of data in list-type structures. Framework-defined templates are summarized in Figure 17.3. Figure 17.4 lists the types off templates applicable to the Repeater, DataGrid and DataList controls.

Type	Description
ItemTemplate	Customizes HTML elements and controls displayed once for each row in the data source.
AlternatingItemTemplate	Customizes HTML elements and controls, like the ItemTemplate, but rendered for every other row. Typically, the AlternatingItemTemplate is like the ItemTemplate but with a different background color.
SelectedItemTemplate	Customizes HTML elements and controls for a selected item in the data list or grid. The selected item can be simply rendered with a different background color or be expanded to include HTML and controls displaying other data source fields.
EditItemTemplate	Layout of HTML and controls when the item is in the edit mode. TextBoxes are typically rendered for data input.
HeaderTemplate	HTML and controls rendered at the top, header section, of the list or grid.
FooterTemplate	HTML are controls rendered at the bottom, footer section, of the list or grid.
SeparatorTemplate	Layout rendered between the items. For example, a line represented by the <hr> element.
Pager	Section rendered on paged grids

FIGURE 17.3
Types of templates.

Type	Repeater	DataList	DataGrid
AlternatingItemTemplate	X	X	
EditItemTemplate		X	(Column)
FooterTemplate	X	X	X
HeaderTemplate	X	X	X
ItemTemplate	X	X	(Column)
Pager			X
SelectedItemTemplate		X	
SeparatorTemplate	X	X	

FIGURE 17.4
Web server controls supporting templates.

Characterizing Lists

List items can be displayed in columns; the number of columns is specified with the **RepeatColumns** property. The default value is zero. If the RepeatColumn property is not

public enum RepeatLayout	
Namespace: System.web.UI.WebControls	
Member	**Description**
Flow	Items displayed one after another without tabular structure.
Table	Items displayed in tabular structure.

FIGURE 17.5
RepeatLayout enumeration.

set, the list items will be displayed in a single column. The RepeatColumn property enables spreading the list over the width of the page.

The items can be arranged is a tabular fashion. The list items can also be arranged one after another in a flow fashion. The arrangement of the items is characterized by the **RepeatLayout** property with RepeatLayout enumeration member values (Figure 17.5).

When the RepeatLayout property is set to RepeatLayout.Table, the items are displayed in an HTML tabular structure. When the tabular layout is used, the **GridLines** property can be used to specify the display of grid lines. The options characterized by the GridLines enumeration members are none, vertical lines, or horizontal lines, as well as both horizontal and vertical lines. The items can be loaded from top to bottom or left to right. The direction of loading is specified by the **RepeatDirection** property using RepeatDirection enumeration member values, as shown in Figure 17.6.

public enum RepeatDirection	
Namespace: System.web.UI.WebControls	
Member	**Description**
Horizontal	Items displayed horizontally left to right. When the numbers of columns in a row are filled, the next row is filled in the same manner. The process continues until all items are displayed.
Vertical	Items displayed vertically from top to bottom. Items are displayed in all columns. The columns are filled from left to right.

FIGURE 17.6
RepeatDirection enumeration.

DataList Control

The **DataList** is a bound control that provides for the customized display of data-source row content using templates. The DataList control is summarized in Figure 17.7.

Declaring the <asp:DataList> control element in the .aspx file creates a DataList control. Declaring the **<template> element** within theDataList's opening and closing tags creates the templates. The syntax is summarized in Figure 17.8. HTML text and controls comprise the template's content. Each of the embedded control's property and data-binding values defines the control's appearance and data content. The template element's type is defined by the type name, for example, ItemTemplate or SeparatorTemplate.

```
public class DataList : BaseDataList, InamingContainer, IRepeatInfoUser
```

Class Hierarchy

```
Object
   Control
      WebContol
         BaseDataList
            DataList
```

Public Static (Shared) Fields

public const string **CancelCommandName**	Name of the Cancel command.
public const string **DeleteCommandName**	Name of the Delete command.
public const string **EditCommandName**	Name of the Edit command.
public const string **SelectCommandName**	Name of the Select command.
public const string **UpdateCommandName**	Name of the Update command.

Public Instance Constructor

public DataList( )	Initializes a new instance of the class.

Public Instance Properties

public virtual TableItemStyle **AlternatingItemStyle** {get;}	Gets the TableItemStyle object representing the style properties of alternating items. The default is the empty TableItemStyle object.
public virtual ITemplate **AlternatingItemTemplate** {get; set;}	Gets or sets the template representing alternating items. The default is a null reference.
public virtual int **EditItemIndex** {get; set;}	Gets or sets the zero-based index of the selected for editing. The default is –1 indicating no item is selected.
public virtual TableItemStyle **EditItemStyle** {get;}	Gets the TableItemStyle object representing the style properties of the item selected for editing. The default is the empty TableItemStyle object.
public virtual ITemplate **EditItemTemplate** {get; set;}	Gets or sets the template representing the item selected for editing. The default is a null reference.
public virtual bool **ExtractTemplateRows** {get; set;}	Gets or sets the value true if the rows of a Table control defined in each template are extracted and displayed; false otherwise. The default is false.
public virtual TableItemStyle **FooterStyle** {get;}	Gets the TableItemStyle object representing the style properties of the footer section. The default is the empty TableItemStyle object.
public virtual ITemplate **FooterTemplate** {get; set;}	Gets or sets the template representing the footer section. The default is a null reference.
public override GridLines **GridLines** {get; set;}	Gets or sets the GridLines enumeration value representing the grid line style. The default is None.

FIGURE 17.7
DataList control.

The application DataListBasics illustrates use of the DataList control and templates. The DataList is bound to a DataSet, contactSet, filled with data extracted from the Student and ContactMaster tables with the SQL statement

```
SELECT Student.LastName + ', ' + Student.FirstName AS StudentName,
    ContactMaster.Name, ContactMaster.Telephone,
    ContactMaster.Emergency
FROM ContactMaster
INNER JOIN Student
ON ContactMaster.StudentID = Student.StudentID
ORDER BY Student.LastName + ', ' + Student.FirstName
```

Public Instance Properties (Cont.)	
public virtual TableItemStyle **HeaderStyle** {get;}	Gets the TableItemStyle object representing the style properties of header section. The default is the empty TableItemStyle object.
public virtual ITemplate **HeaderTemplate** {get; set;}	Gets or sets the template representing the header section. The default is a null reference.
public virtual DataListItemCollection **Items** {get;}	Gets the DataListItemCollection object representing the collection of DataListItems.
public virtual TableItemStyle **ItemStyle** {get;}	Gets the TableItemStyle object representing the item style properties. The default is the empty TableItemStyle object.
public virtual ITemplate **ItemTemplate** {get; set;}	Gets or sets the template representing the item. The default is a null reference.
public virtual int **RepeatColumns** {get; set;}	Gets or sets the number of list columns displayed. The default is zero.
public virtual RepeatDirection **RepeatDirection** {get; set;}	Gets or sets the RepeatDirection enumeration member value specifying the display direction. The default is Vertical.
public virtual RepeatLayout **RepeatLayout** {get; set;}	Gets or sets the RepeatLayout enumeration member value specifying the layout mode. The default is Table.
public virtual int **SelectedIndex** {get; set;}	Gets or sets the zero-based index of the selected item. The default is –1 indicating no item is selected.
public virtual DataListItem **SelectedItem** {get;}	Gets the DataListItem object representing the selected item.
public virtual TableItemStyle **SelectedItemStyle** {get;}	Gets the TableItemStyle object representing the style properties of the selected item. The default is the empty TableItemStyle object.
public virtual ITemplate **SelectedItemTemplate** {get; set;}	Gets or sets the template representing the selected item. The default is a null reference.
public virtual TableItemStyle **SeparatorStyle** {get;}	Gets the TableItemStyle object representing the separator. The default is the empty TableItemStyle object.
public virtual ITemplate **SeparatorTemplate** {get; set;}	Gets or sets the template representing the separator. The default is a null reference.
public virtual bool **ShowFooter** {get; set;}	Gets or sets the value true if the footer section is displayed; false otherwise. The default is true.
public virtual bool **ShowHeader** {get; set;}	Gets or sets the value true if the header section is displayed; false otherwise. The default is true.

FIGURE 17.7 (CONTINUED)
DataList control.

Typical data returned are the following:

StudentName	Name	Telephone	Emergency
Care, Helen	Care, Joan	973 762 5465	true
Dash, Thomas	Dash, Thomas, Jr.	973 330 9101	false
Dash, Thomas	Dash, Evelyn	973 330 9101	true
Smart, Harry	Smart, Wilma	973 239 4751	true
Williams, Mary	Williams, Neville	414 539 6249	true
Williams, Mary	Williams, Ronda	973 775 4802	false
Wilson, III, William	Blue, Annette	973 445 1826	true
Wilson, III, William	Virgil Blue	973 774 7172	false
Wilson, III, William	Sandra Blue	973 774 7172	true

Selected fields — StudentName, Name and Emergency — are displayed in a DataList control, contactList, bound to the DataSet, contactSet (Figure 17.9A). The list contains an item for each row of the returned data. The embedded controls comprising the item layout include the following:

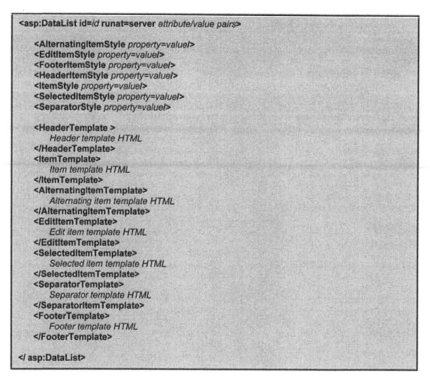

FIGURE 17.8
DataList control syntax.

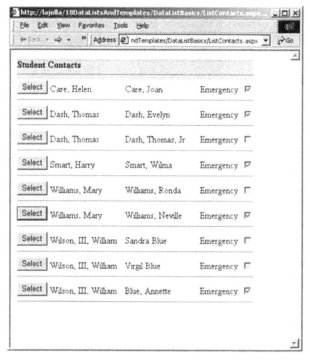

FIGURE 17.9A
Initial rendering of Web page DataListBasics/ListContacts.aspx.

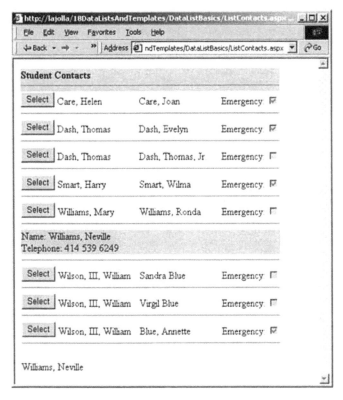

FIGURE 17.9B
Rendering of Web page DataListBasics/ListContacts.aspx when Mary Williams' emergency contact is clicked.

- Button control with the caption "Select"
- Label control containing the StudentName field composed of the Student table's FirstName and LastName fields
- Label control containing the Name field from the ContactMaster table
- HTML text "Emergency"
- CheckBox control containing a representation of the value of the Emergency field extracted from the ContactMaster table

Note that several students — Thomas Dash, Mary Williams and William Wilson III — have more than one contact. Every student has a contact checked as an emergency contact. Background color, LightGray, and bold font set off the header section of the list. In the "real world," the header section would also include column captions. A line separates the list items.

When the user clicks the Select button, the item layout is replaced with a layout that displays the contact name and telephone number of the selected contact. In the "real world," additional information would also be displayed, such as alternate telephone numbers and image of the contact. For example, if the user clicks the emergency contact for Mary Williams, the telephone number for Neville Williams is displayed (Figure 17.9B).

The application's web page DataListBasics/ListContacts.aspx is shown in Figure 17.9C. The DataList control, contactList, is created with the opening tag

```
<%@ Page language="c#" Codebehind="ListContacts.aspx.cs" AutoEventWireup="false"
         Inherits="DataListBasics.ListContacts" %>
<!DOCTYPE HTML PUBLIC "-//W3C//DTD HTML 4.0 Transitional//EN" >
<HTML>
  <HEAD>
    <meta name="GENERATOR" Content="Microsoft Visual Studio 7.0">
    <meta name="CODE_LANGUAGE" Content="C#">
    <meta name=vs_defaultClientScript content="JavaScript (ECMAScript)">
    <meta name=vs_targetSchema
          content="http://schemas.microsoft.com/intellisense/ie5">
  </HEAD>
  <body MS_POSITIONING="GridLayout">
    <form id="ListContacts" method="post" runat="server">
      <asp:DataList ID=contactList Runat=server
                    DataSource="<%# contactSet %>"
                    OnItemCommand=ContactCommand>

        <HeaderStyle BackColor=LightGrey />
        <SelectedItemStyle BackColor=LightGrey/>

        <HeaderTemplate>
          <B>Student Contacts <br><hr></B>
        </HeaderTemplate>
        <FooterTemplate>
          <hr>
        </FooterTemplate>

        <ItemTemplate>
          <asp:Button ID=selectButton Runat=server Text=Select
              CommandName=ContactSelected></asp:Button>
          <asp:Label ID=studentNameLabel Runat=server
              Text='<%# DataBinder.Eval(Container, "DataItem.StudentName")%>'
              Width=128></asp:Label>
          <asp:Label ID=nameLabel Runat=server
              Text='<%# DataBinder.Eval(Container, "DataItem.Name")%>'
              Width=128></asp:Label>
          Emergency:
          <asp:CheckBox ID=emergencyCheckBox Runat=server
              Checked='<%# DataBinder.Eval(Container, "DataItem.Emergency") %>'
              Enabled="false" />
        </ItemTemplate>

        <SeparatorTemplate>
          <hr>
        </SeparatorTemplate>

        <SelectedItemTemplate>
          Name: <%# DataBinder.Eval(Container, "DataItem.Name")%>
          <br>
          Telephone:
          <asp:Label ID="telephoneLabel" Runat=server
              Text='<%# DataBinder.Eval(Container, "DataItem.Telephone") %>'
              width=128></asp:Label>
        </SelectedItemTemplate>

      </asp:DataList>
      <p></p>
      <asp:Label ID=messageLabel Runat=server></asp:Label>
    </form>
```

Callout annotations:
- Handler name for events raised by List buttons
- Header and selected style settingsStyle
- Header and Footer templates and embedded HTML
- Embedded controls and HTML comprising ItemTemplate
- Separator template
- Embedded controls and HTML comprising the SelectedItemTemplate

FIGURE 17.9C
Web page DataListBasics/ListContacts.aspx.

```
<asp:DataList ID = contactList Runat = server
    DataSource = "<%# contactSet%>"
    OnItemCommand = ContactCommand>
</asp:DataList>
```

The DataSet contactSet is defined as the data source. When data binding, the binding is specified for the data list as a whole. Controls embedded within the data list control, such as Labels, TextBoxes, DropDownLists and CheckBoxes, are in turn bound to the container, which is the data list. The data list can be bound to any data source represented by a class that supports the IEnumerable interface.

Binding is brought about when the page is first loaded by the following code in the Page_Load method of the code-behind file ListContacts.aspx.cs:

```
if(!IsPostBack)

{

    contactAdapter.Fill(contactSet);

    contactList.DataBind();

}
```

The handler ContactCommand is specified to handle the Item event that is raised whenever any button in the data list is clicked.

Template and template style elements are declared within the DataList's opening and closing tags. For example, the style of the header section is defined with the

```
<HeaderStyle BackColor = LightGrey/>
```

that specifies a light-gray color background. Similarly, the selected item is also rendered with a light-gray color background:

```
<SelectedItemStyle BackColor = LightGrey/>
```

The template element tags

```
<HeaderTemplate>

</HeaderTemplate>
```

define the header template. Inside the template, HTML

```
<B>Student Contacts <br><hr></B>
```

defines the header content. Similarly, the footer template is defined with the tags and HTML content

```
<FooterTemplate>

    <hr>

</FooterTemplate>
```

In this case, the footer is simply a line across the bottom of the list.

The template for list items is declared with the ItemTemplate element tags:

```
<ItemTemplate>

</ItemTemplate>
```

HTML and Web controls defining the template's content are defined with the statements

```
<asp:Button ID = selectButton Runat = server Text = Select
    CommandName = ContactSelected></asp:Button>
<asp:Label ID = studentNameLabel Runat = server
    Text = '<%# DataBinder.Eval(Container,
        "DataItem.StudentName")%>'
    Width = 128></asp:Label>
<asp:Label ID = nameLabel Runat = server
    Text = '<%# DataBinder.Eval(Container, "DataItem.Name")%>'
    Width = 128></asp:Label>
Emergency:
<asp:CheckBox ID = emergencyCheckBox Runat = server
```

```
Checked = '<%# DataBinder.Eval(Container,
    "DataItem.Emergency")%>'
Enabled = "false"/>
```

The Web controls include a Button, several Labels and a Checkbox; HTML is included to describe the significance of the CheckBox control. A CommandName, ContactSelected, is declared for the Button control. The Label control's Text property is bound to the container's, in this case, the datalist, data source StudentName and Name fields. The CheckBox's Checked property is bound to the container's data source Emergency field.

A separator, a line rendered between the list items, is specified with the Separator-Template element tags and content:

```
<SeparatorTemplate>

    <hr>

</SeparatorTemplate>
```

The template specifying the layout of the selected item is created with the Selected-ItemTemplate element tags. The template's contents are specified within the element's opening and closing tags:

```
<SelectedItemTemplate>

    Name: <%# DataBinder.Eval(Container, "DataItem.Name")%>

    <br>

    Telephone:

    <asp:Label ID = "telephoneLabel" Runat = server

    Text = '<%# DataBinder.Eval(Container,
        "DataItem.Telephone")%>'

    width = 128></asp:Label>

</SelectedItemTemplate>
```

Embedded HTML and a data binding rendered as HTML are used to display the contact name and caption. The contact telephone is captioned with HTML and represented as the Text property of a Label control.

Note!

Templates provide flexibility in the layout of data presented in lists.

DataList Events

The DataList control supports events, including events typically raised by button clicks: Edit, Cancel, Update and Delete. The commands are summarized in Figure 17.10.

The exact event raised is specified by the button's CommandName property. For example, if the CommandName property value is "cancel," the CancelCommand event is raised when the button is clicked. In addition, the DataList supports the ItemCommand event raised whenever a button in the datalist is clicked. The ItemCommand facilitates the implementation of specialized functionality such as item selection or detail presentation.

```
public event DataListCommandEventHandler CancelCommand;
public event DataListCommandEventHandler DeleteCommand;
public event DataListCommandEventHandler EditCommand;
public event DataListCommandEventHandler UpdateCommand;
public event DataListCommandEventHandler ItemCommand;
```

EventHandlerDelegate	Argument Description
public delegate void DataListCommandEventHandler(object *source*, DataListCommandEventArgs *e*);	*source* represents the event source. *e* is the DataListCommandArgs object passed by the Framework describing the event.

FIGURE 17.10
Cancel, Delete, Edit and Update commands.

public sealed class DataListCommandEventArgs : CommandEventArgs

Hierarchy	
Object EventArgs Commandeventargs DataListcommandEventArgs	

Namespace: System.Web.UI.WebControls

Public Instance Constructors	
public **DataListCommandArgs**(DataListItem *item*, object *commandSource*, CommandEventArgs *originalArgs*);	Initializes a new instance of the class. The DataGridItem object *item* represents the DataList item or row. The CommandSource property is initialized to the value commandSource. The CommandEventArgs object *originalArgs* represents the command argument and name.

Public Instance Properties	
public object **CommandSource** {get;}	Gets the object representing the source of the command.
public DataListItme **Item** {get;}	Gets the DataListItem representing the selected item.

FIGURE 17.11
DataListCommandEventArgs class.

```
public void ContactCommand(object o, DataListCommandEventArgs e)
{
     contactList.SelectedIndex = e.Item.ItemIndex;

     messageLabel.Text =
          ((Label)e.Item.FindControl("nameLabel")).Text
          +  "<br>";

     contactAdapter.Fill(contactSet);
     contactList.DataBind();
}
```

FIGURE 17.12
Handler for the ItemCommand event raised when the Select button is clicked.

The event handler receives an argument of the type DataListCommandEventArgs summarized in Figure 17.11. The argument provides information regarding the command event raised. Figure 17.12A shows the handler for the ItemCommand event raised when the Select button in the ItemTemplate is clicked. The handler is coded in the code-behind file.

The Framework calls the handler and passes the arguments. An object representing the selected item is passed as an argument member. The index of the selected item is accessed with the expression

```
e.Item.ItemIndex
```

The data list's SelectedIndex property is set with the statement

```
contactList.SelectedIndex = e.Item.ItemIndex;
```

Additionally, the item template embedded control named "nameLabel" is accessed, cast to a Label control type and its Text property assigned to the Text property for the mesageLabel control with the statement

```
messageLabel.Text =
    ((Label)e.Item.FindControl("nameLabel")).Text + "<br>";
```

Note!

The SelectedIndexChanged event inherited from BaseDataList is raised when a list item is selected and can be used to implement selected item functionality.

A Templates Editor facilitates creation of templates in .aspx files. See the following Hands-On Exercise.

Hands-On Exercise: Creating Templates in the Web Forms Designer

Step 1: Create Application Using Template Editor

1. Create Project UsingTemplateEditor.
2. Delete the Web page WebForm1.aspx.

Step 2: Create Web Page Contacts.aspx

1. Add web form **Contacts.aspx**.

Step 3: Create and Configure Data Adapter

1. Drag an OleDbDataAdapter onto the Web page. Assign the following property values (use the Wizard where applicable):

   Data Connection   `StudentAdministration`

2. Select Query.

   Do not generate insert, delete and update commands.

   (Name)   **contactAdapter**

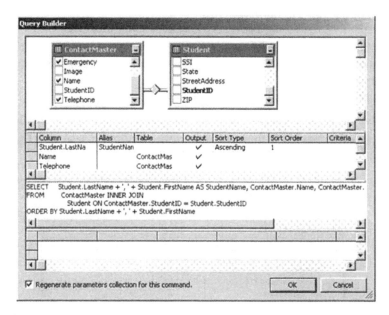

FIGURE HO17.1
Query Builder

Step 4: Create and Configure DataSet

1. In the data adapter's Properties window, click the Generate Dataset... link.
2. Select the DataSet and assign the following property value:
   (Name) **contactSet**
3. In the data adapter's Properties window, click the Preview data... link. The Data Adapter Preview window opens.
4. Click the Fill dataset button. The data are displayed in the results area.

Step 5: Create and Configure DataList

1. Drag a Web forms data list onto the page. Assign the following property value:
   DataSource   **ContactSet**
   DataMember   **ContactMaster**
   (ID)   **contactList**
   ItemCommand   **ContactCommand**
2. Fill the Data Set and Bind the DataList to the DataSet.
3. In the code-behind file Page_Load method, call the data adapter's Fill method to load the data set's Contact table and the data list's DataBind method to bind the grid to the data source when the page is initially loaded:

```
if (!IsPostBack)
{
    contactAdapter.Fill(contactSet, "ContactMaster");
    contactList.DataBind();
}
```

Step 6: Edit Header and Footer Templates

1. Right-click the data list control. Select the Edit Template option. Click the Header and Footer Templates in the submenu. The data list is displayed in the template-editing mode.
2. Enter HTML text in the HeaderTemplate **Student Contacts**.
3. Drag the HTML line element onto the HeaderTemplate and FooterTemplate.
4. Right-click the data list in the template-editing mode and select the End Template Editing option.

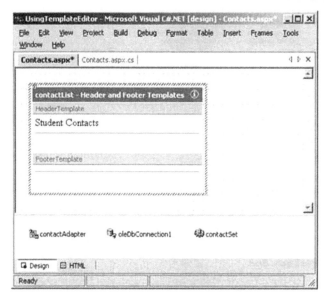

FIGURE HO17.2
Template Header and Footer Editor selector.

Step 7: Edit Item Template

1. Right-click the data list control. Select the Edit Template option. Click the Item Templates option in the submenu. The data list is displayed in the template-editing mode.
2. Drag a button control onto the ItemTemplate.
3. Select the button and set the following properties in the Properties window:

   (ID)   **selectButton**
   CommandName   **ContactSelected**
   Text   **Select**

4. Drag a Label control onto the ItemTemplate.
5. Select the label and set the following properties in the Properties window:

   (ID)   **studentNameLabel**
   Width   128

6. Click the ellipsis at the left side of the DataBindings property. The DataBinding dialog opens. Select the Text property in the Bindable Properties pane. Select the Simple binding radio button. Expand the Container selection in the Simple binding pane. Expand the DataItem selection. Select the StudentName entry.

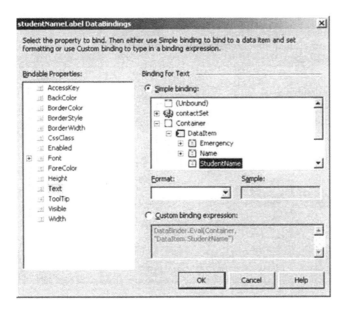

FIGURE HO17.3
Binding dialog.

7. Click the OK button.

8. Drag a Label control onto the ItemTemplate.

9. Select the label and set the following properties in the Properties window:

(ID)   **NameLabel**

Width   128

10. Click the ellipsis at the left side of the DataBindings property. The DataBinding dialog opens. Select the Text property in the Bindable Properties pane. Select the Simple binding radio button. Expand the Container selection in the Simple binding pane. Expand the DataItem selection. Select the Name entry. Click the OK button.

11. Enter the HTML text: **Emergency:**.

12. Drag a CheckBox control onto the ItemTemplate.

13. Select the checkbox and set the following properties in the Properties window:

(ID)   **emergencyCheckBox**

Enabled   **false**

14. Click the ellipsis at the left side of the DataBindings property. The DataBinding dialog opens. Select the Checked property in the Bindable Properties pane. Select the Simple binding radio button. Expand the Container selection in the Simple binding pane. Expand the DataItem selection. Select the Emergency entry. Click the OK button.

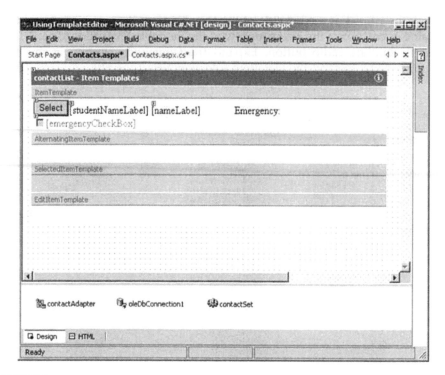

FIGURE HO17.4
Item Template editor.

15. Right-click the data list in template-editing mode and select the End Template Editing option.

Step 8: Selected Item Template

1. Right-click the data list control. Select the Edit Template option. Click the Item Templates option in the submenu. The data list is displayed in the item template-editing mode.
2. Enter in SelectedItemTemplate the HTML text: **Name:**.
3. Drag a Label control onto the ItemTemplate.
4. Select the label and set the following properties in the Properties window:

    (ID)   **selectedNameLabel**

    Width   128
5. Click the ellipsis at the left side of the DataBindings property. The DataBinding dialog opens. Select the Text property in the Bindable Properties pane. Select the Simple binding radio button. Expand the Container selection in the Simple binding pane. Expand the DataItem selection. Select the Name entry. Click the OK button.
6. Position the blinking cursor at the end of the selectedNameLabel control. Press the Enter key to start a new line.
7. Enter, at the new line, the HTML text: **Telephone:**.
8. Drag a Label control onto the SelectedItemTemplate.

9. Select the label control and set the following properties in the Properties window:

(ID)   **telephoneLabel**

Width   128

10. Click the ellipsis at the left side of the DataBindings property. The DataBinding dialog opens. Select the Text property in the Bindable Properties pane. Select the Simple binding radio button. Expand the Container selection in the Simple binding pane. Expand the DataItem selection. Select the Telephone entry. Click the OK button.

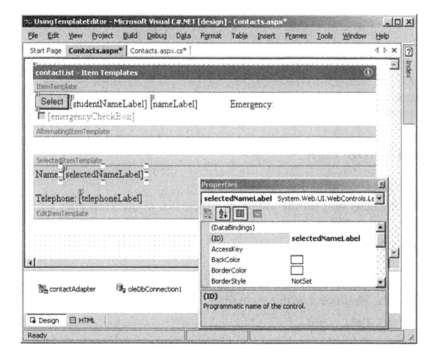

FIGURE HO17.5
Item Template editor.

11. Right-click the data list in template-editing mode and select the End Template Editing option.

Step 9: Style HeaderTemplate and SelectedItemTemplate

1. Select the data list control. Press F4 to display the Properties window. Double-click the Properties window's title Bar to float the window. Size the window.
2. Expand the HeaderStyle property.
3. Enter, or select, the BackColor property value: **LightGray.**
4. Expand the HeaderStyle's Font property.
5. Enter, or select, the Bold property value: **True.**
6. Expand the SelectedItemStyle property.
7. Enter, or select, the BackColor property value: **LightGray.**
8. Close the Properties window.

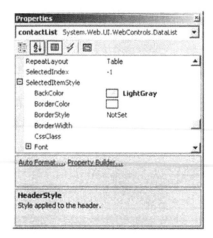

FIGURE HO17.6
DataList Properties window.

Step 10: Add Message Label

1. Drag a Label control onto the Web page.
2. Select the label and set the following properties in the Properties window.

   (ID)   **messageLabel**

   Width   **256**

   Text

3. In the code-behind file's ContactCommand method, add the following line of code at the beginning of the method:

   ```
   messageLabel.Text =
   ((Label)e.Item.FindControl("nameLabel")).Text + "<br>";
   ```

Step 11: Execute the Application

The application's browser renderings are shown in Figures 17.9A and 17.9B.

18

Web Applications

The StudentInformation application represents a typical Web application. The application provides the functionality required by a school to compile and maintain student information. Basic information regarding a student is presented in the primary information form illustrated in Figure 18.1.

A text box in the upper left corner of the form provides for entry of a search string. For example, if the letter "w" is entered only the students with a last name beginning with the letter "w" will be listed when the Search button is clicked. Names of the selected students are listed in the drop down list at the top right corner of the form; details of the selected student are displayed in the form. Details regarding student Harry V. Smart are displayed in the example. The data are divided into sections relevant to student administration: biographical, enrollment and address. Buttons at the bottom of the form provide for the updating or deletion of a selected student's data or the addition of a new student: Update, Add and Delete buttons.

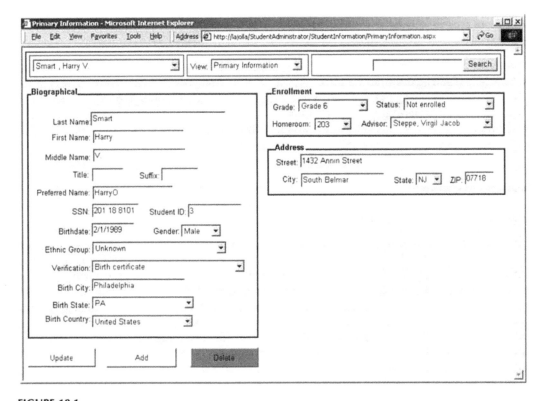

FIGURE 18.1
Primary information form (PrimaryInformation.aspx).

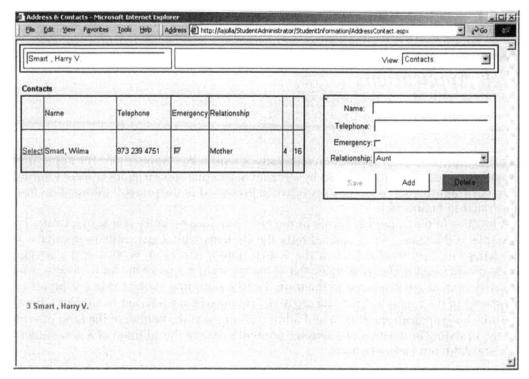

FIGURE 18.2.
Contacts form (AddressContact.aspx).

A drop-down list in the top center of the form provides for the selection of different views of the selected student's information. In the "real world," views are available for characterizing the selected student, for example, Contacts, Parents/Guardians, Medical, Transportation, Attendance and Guidance views. In the example, only the Primary Information and Contact views are available. The Contact view is shown in Figure 18.2.

Application Architecture

The application's architecture is summarized in Figure 18.3. **Clients** of the application interact through Web browsers. Web forms facilitate client interaction and are an integral part of the Web application. For example, in the application Student Information, the Primary Information form is requested by entering its Web address at the browser, for example, http://www.buildingwebapplications.com. The forms are returned to the application with user input. The Web application also contains business rules used to process the user input contained in the returned form. Communications between the application and client use HTTP transport protocol and HTML markup and, as such, are able to go through firewalls.

In the Student Information application architecture, a Web Service, UtilityService.asmx.cs, provides access to the database. Communication with the Web service is provided by HTTP-POST, HTTP-GET and SOAP protocols. These are in text form and thus able to cross firewalls. The Web service receiving an HTTP/SOAP request invokes a method on

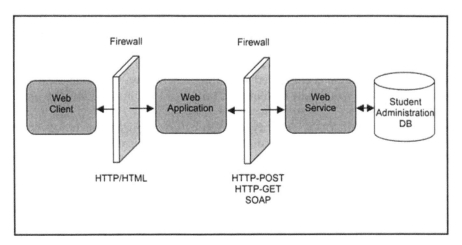

FIGURE 18.3
Application architecture.

Method Name	Returned Tables	Description
UtilityDataSet	BirthdateVerification	Basis used to verify student's birthdate.
	Country	Country code used to identify student's country of birth.
	EnrollmentStatus	Student's current enrollment status.
	EthnicGroup	Codes used to characterize student's ethnicity.
	Grade	Code used to specify student's current grade including early childhood and ungraded.
	Room	Code used to specify student's homeroom.
	State	State codes used to identify student's state of birth and state of residence.
	Teacher	Names of teachers used to specify student's homeroom teacher.
	Relationship	Codes used to characterize the student's contact relationship.
SelectStudent	Student	Data pertaining to a specific student identified by the student's identification code.
SelectStudents	Names	Names of students whose last name is like a specified search string.
SelectContacts	Contact	Contact data pertaining to a specific student identified by the student's identification code. Note, a student can have multiple contacts.
InsertContact		Inserts new Contact table record.
DeleteContact		Deletes a Contact record identified by the ContactID.
UpdateContact		Updates a Contact record identified by the ContactID.
InsertStudent		Inserts a new Student table record.
DeleteStudent		Deletes a Student table record identified by the StudentID.
UpdateStudent		Updates a Student record identified by the StudentID.

FIGURE 18.4
Web service UtilityService.asmx.cs.

the appropriate object that returns a dataset containing the requested data. Methods exposed in the Web service UtilityService are summarized in Figure 18.4. These methods provide the access to the StudentAdministrationDB.

The value of the Web service is its ability to be located anywhere on the Internet. Moreover, its functionality is universally accessible and described in the XML format of the Web Service Description Language (WSDL). In the example, only a single Web service is employed; in practice, multiple Web services are used.

The preceding application is an example of multiple-tier architecture. The Web browser is the traditional client tier. The Web application is the traditional server tier combining the presentation and business logic. In the two-tier architecture, data access is also performed in the server tier. In this case, the Web service is the data tier. Note that, although the business logic is combined with the presentation in the classical server tier, a sophisticated design would encapsulate the business logic in its own Web service that would be another tier.

Firewalls are essential to the security of Web-based applications; however, they are unable to understand binary data formats and thus complicate distributed application technologies that employ binary data formats. However, Web service utilization is not hindered by firewalls because the data are communicated in a textual format.

Asp.Net Application

An **ASP.NET application**, simply called an **application**, is the collection of all files, pages, handlers, modules and executable code that can be invoked in the scope of a virtual directory and its subdirectories on a Web application server. Every ASP.NET application is executed within a unique .NET Framework application domain. The **application domain** is created by the runtime host and provides isolation between applications. That is, the application domain prevents code in one domain from accessing code running in another domain.

An application is created when an application resource is accessed. For example, simply accessing a .aspx page in the application's virtual directory triggers the application's creation. The creation is signaled by the Application_Start event. When the application is created, ASP.NET also creates a pool of instances of the HttpApplication class. An HttpApplication instance is assigned to every incoming request. The HttpApplication object is responsible for managing the request over its lifetime and is returned to the pool when the request has been completed. When the last instance exits, the Application_End event is raised.

Note!

The Application_Start and Application_End events mark the lifetime of an ASP.NET application.

Every request is assigned to an HttpApplication instance. An application will typically consist of multiple requests; as such, the HttpApplication's Init and Dispose methods are raised several times during the lifetime of the application.

Global.asax File

The **Global.asax** file, also known as the Application file, contains code handlers for application-level events. The file is located in the root directory of the application's virtual directory and users cannot access it. The Global.aspx file is optional. When changes are saved to the Global.asax file, all current requests are completed, an Application_OnEnd event is broadcast to all listeners, and the application is restarted. In effect, the application is stopped and rebooted. All state information is lost. Note that the first request results in the reparsing and compilation of the Global.aspx file and firing of the Application_OnStart event.

The Global.asax file is parsed and compiled into a .NET Framework class derived from the HttpApplication class.

Application- and Session-Level Events

The Global.asax file provides for handling application-level events in Web applications. These events, referred to as **application-level** and **session-level events**, are not invoked in response to individual page request but are invoked by higher-level conditions such as:

- **Application_Start**, which is raised the first time an application resource is accessed, e.g., a page is requested
- **Application_End**, which is raised when the application ends
- **Session_Start**, which is raised when a session begins; typically, multiple requests are made during a session
- **Session_End**, which is raised when a session ends

Handlers for these events are implemented in the application's Global.asax.cs file. The Global.asax.cs file of the StudentInformation Web application is shown in Figure 18.5.

In this case, the Application_Start event is used to load relatively static tables. In the real world, data used to build relatively static lists such as state codes are maintained in a special file. For example, the state code changes infrequently and thus can be maintained over the lifetime of the application. Other data of a similar nature include birthdate verification methods, terms used to characterize a student–contact relationship and room numbers in a building. These data are used in drop-down list controls. Because they do not change, it would be a waste of resources to retrieve them every time the page is created.

The tables are contained in a dataset returned by the Web service method `Service-Utility.UtilityDataSet`. A reference to the Web service object is created in the Application_Start method with the expression

```
localhost.UtilityService us
```

The reference is assigned to a proxy for the Web service object created with the expression

```
new localhost.UtilityService()
```

A UtilityService class method in the Application_Start method is automatically invoked on the remote object; thus, the expression

```
us.UtilityDataSet();
```

returns a data set containing data retrieved from the StudentAdministratorDB database.

The UtilityService class is defined in the file UtilityService.asmx.cs file. Note the Global.asax file also contains request level events:

- Application_BeginRequest
- Application_EndRequest

These methods are called at the beginning and end of each request.

```
using System;
using System.Collections;
using System.ComponentModel;
using System.Web;
using System.Web.SessionState;

using System.Data;

namespace StudentInformation
{
    public class Global : System.Web.HttpApplication
    {
        protected void Application_Start(Object sender, EventArgs e)
        {
            localhost.UtilityService us = new
                localhost.UtilityService();
            DataSet ds = us.UtilityDataSet();

            Application["UtilityDataSet"] = ds;
        }

        protected void Session_Start(Object sender, EventArgs e)
        {
        }

        protected void Application_BeginRequest(Object sender,
            EventArgs e)
        {
        }

        protected void Application_EndRequest(Object sender,
            EventArgs e)
        {
        }

        protected void Session_End(Object sender, EventArgs e)
        {
        }

        protected void Application_End(Object sender, EventArgs e)
        {
        }
    }
}
```

FIGURE 18.5
Global.asax.cs.

Application and Session State

HTTP is a stateless protocol in that it does not provide for indicating if a sequence of requests is from the same client or if a specific browser is viewing a specific page. ASP.NET provides for storing application scope data throughout the lifetime of the application and storing session scope data across multiple requests.

The HttpApplicationState class exposes a **Contents** collection that enables sharing global information across multiple sessions and requests within an ASP.NET application. For example, the Dataset ds, returned by the Web service, is stored as a collection element with the statement

```
Application["UtilityDataSet"] = ds;
```

As such, the data in the tables are available to all requests over the lifetime of the application. For example, the PrimaryInformation form's code-behind file, Primary-Information.aspx.cs, defines the LoadBirthdateVerificationDDL method that is invoked when the form is first loaded. The method code is shown in Figure 18.6.

```
private void LoadBirthdateVerificationDDL()
{
      DataSet uds = (DataSet) Application["UtilityDataSet"];

      ListItem li;

      foreach(DataRow row in uds.Tables["BirthdateVerification"].Rows)
      {
            li = new ListItem();
            li.Value = row[0].ToString();
            li.Text = (string)row[1];

            birthdateVerificationDDL.Items.Add(li);
      }
}
```

Content collection object named "UtilityDataSet"

Tables collection element named "BirthdateVerification"

FIGURE 18.6
LoadBirthdateVerificationDDL method in PrimaryInformation.aspx.cs.

The Dataset in the application's Content collection named `"UtilityDataSet"` is retrieved with the expression

```
Application["UtilityDataSet"]
```

The object expressed is cast to a Dataset type and assigned to Dataset type reference `uds`. Each of the rows in the BirthdateVerification table in the data set are sequentially accessed with the `foreach` statement

```
foreach(DataRow row in
    uds.Tables["BirthdateVerification"].Rows)
{


}
```

The rows' column values are used to create a list item that is added to the birthdateVerificationDDL control in the PrimaryInformation form. These list items are summarized in Figure 18.7.

Value	Text
1	Baptismal or church certificate
2	Birth certificate
3	Entry in family Bible
4	Hospital certificate
5	Parent's affidavit
6	Passport
7	Physician's certificate
8	Previously verified school records
9	State-issued ID
10	Driver's license
11	Immigration document
98	None
99	Other

FIGURE 18.7
List items loaded in the PrimaryInformation form's birthdateVerificationDDL control.

This control provides for user interaction regarding the birthdate verification. The data set also contains tables providing information required to initialize the other list controls: Ethnic Group, Birth State, Birth Country, Grade, Enrollment Status, Home Room, Advisor and State of Residence.

Note!

Relatively static data, of the type used to load interface controls, can be loaded **once** and stored in the Application Content collection and thus made available over the lifetime of the application.

Session-level data are maintained by the .NET Framework in a Session object collection. These data are available stored at the end of every request and made available at the beginning of the next request. As such, they are available across multiple client visits. For example, the user is able to transfer between a student's PrimaryInformation form and Contacts form by selecting the corresponding item in the View drop-down list at the top of the forms. The selected form needs to know the identification of the student currently displayed.

Everything starts with the PrimaryInformation form. Assume a student has been selected. When a new view is selected, the SelectedIndexChanged event, associated with the View drop-down list, is fired. This event is wired to the ViewSelected methods in the form's code-behind file, as shown in Figure 18.8. If an item is selected, the value of the selected item is assigned to the Session collection object named "studentID" with the statement

```
Session["studentID"] = nameDDL.SelectedItem.Value;
```

Similarly, the text of the selected item is assigned to the Session collection object named "name" with the statement

```
Session["name"] = nameDDL.SelectedItem.Text;
```

These values are available throughout the life of the Session and thus available to subsequent requests.

After the selected name and student identification are stored, the page corresponding to the selected item is returned to the user:

```
if(viewDDL.SelectedIndex == 1)
        Response.Redirect("AddressContact.aspx");
```

In this case, the page represented by the file AddressContact.aspx is returned to the user. The form's `Page_Load` method is shown in Figure 18.9.

```
private void ViewSelected(object sender, System.EventArgs e)
{
        if (nameDDL.SelectedIndex > -1)
        {
                Session["studentID"] = nameDDL.SelectedItem.Value;
                Session["name"] = nameDDL.SelectedItem.Text;

                if(viewDDL.SelectedIndex == 1)
                        Response.Redirect("AddressContact.aspx");
        }
        .
        .
        .
}
```

"studentID" and "name" objects are added to the Session collect

FIGURE 18.8
ViewSelected method in the PrimaryInformation form's code-behind file (PrimaryInformation.aspx.cs).

```
private void Page_Load(object sender, System.EventArgs e)
{
    nameTB.Text = (string)Session["name"];

    LoadContact(Convert.ToInt32(Session["studentID"]));

    Session["ContactAddMode"] = false;

    saveB.Enabled = false;

    if(!IsPostBack)
    {
        LoadViewDDL();

        LoadRelationship();
    }
}
```

nameTB text set to value of
Session collection object "name."

Session collection object
"studentID" passed as parameter
in the LoadContact method.

FIGURE 18.9
Page_Load method in the AddressContact form's code-behind file (AddressContact.aspx.cs).

The nameTB textbox in the upper-left corner of the form is loaded with the student name stored in the Session collection with the statement

```
nameTB.Text = (string)Session["name"];
```

The student's contact information is retrieved form the database and loaded in the form's data grid by the LoadContact method. The method's parameter is the student identification code of the student whose contacts are to be retrieved. The student's identification code is obtained by converting the Session collection object named "studentID" to an integer with the expression

```
Convert.ToInt32(Session["studentID"])
```

Note that the mode of the forms is also retained as a Session collection object. For example, when the Add button is clicked, the Add method is called (see Figure 18.10).

The Session collection object named "ContactAddMode" is set to the value true with the statement

```
Session["ContactAddMode"] = true;
```

Subsequent requests can ascertain the mode by accessing the Session collection object named "ContactAddMode."

```
private void Add(object sender, System.EventArgs e)
{
    Session["ContactAddMode"] = true;
    deleteB.Visible = false;
    addB.Visible = false;

    addNameTB.Text = "";
    addTelephoneTB.Text = "";
    addEmergencyCB.Checked = false;
    addRelationshipDDL.SelectedIndex = -1;
}
```

When the Add button is clicked
the Session collection object
named "ContactAddMode" is set
true.

FIGURE 18.10
Add method in the AddressContact form's code-behind file (AddressContact.aspx.cs).

Note!

The Session collection can be used to maintain Session-level state values over the life of the Session.

Appendices

Appendix A.1

Class Data Type

The concept of class underlies the practice of object-oriented analysis and design. The object model of an account, used in all types of commercial endeavors, is shown in Figure A1.1.

Account
acctNo : Integer
acctBalance : Money
setAcctNo(acctNo : Integer)
getAcctNo( ) : acctNo
setAcctBalance(acctBalance : Money)
getAcctBalance ( ) : AcctBalance

FIGURE A1.1
Object defined in an object-oriented design.

The C# **class data type** models the class concept of object-oriented analysis and design. At the most basic level, classes consist of attributes characterizing a modeled object and functions to manipulate the attributes. A C# class modeling the basic business account shown in Figure A1.1 is illustrated in Figure A1.2.

The class definition provides for characterizing an account by account number and account balance attributes. An integer-type number identified by the name acctNo characterizes the attribute account number. Similarly, the account balance is characterized by a money-type number — a special type of number suitable for representing financial numbers — identified by the name acctBalance. The characterization of class attributes is addressed in Appendix A.2.

The class definition also provides methods for managing the class attributes. For example, the function

```
setAcctNo(int an)
```

assigns an integral value identified by the name an to the variable acctNo. Similarly, the function

```
setAcctBalance(decimal ab)
```

assigns a money-type value identified by the name ab to the variable acctBalance. Additionally, the functions getAcctNo() and getAcctBalance() give the value of the attributes acctNo and acctBalance. The characterization of the methods for managing class attributes is addressed in Appendix B.3.

Note!

The C# class data type represents the attributes and functions of objects underlying the concepts of object-oriented design and analysis.

A class is declared using the keyword class, which is preceded by modifiers that determine how the class can be accessed or used. The keyword class is followed by an identifier

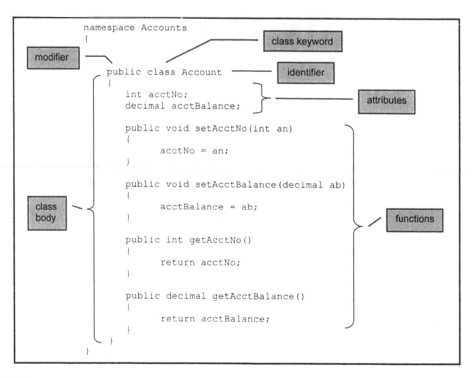

FIGURE A1.2
C# class representing a basic business account (Accounts\Account.cs).

naming the class. The class name is followed by the class body, the class attributes and methods definitions enclosed in braces. These elements of the class declaration are called out in Figure A1.2 and summarized as

```
modifiers class identifier { class body }
```

Additional elements provide for incorporating the attributes and functions of existing classes in the class being declared. Additionally, elements provide for definition of attributes that can be used in the class declaration.

The class data type can be used in programs to model objects represented by the class. Consider the process of creating a new account illustrated by a flow in Figure A1.3. The process is typically initiated by the business need to record an activity such as a new customer. Data regarding the account such as identification number and initial balance are input at the terminal of the account representative. The input data are used to update the programmatic model of the account. The details of the account are recorded.

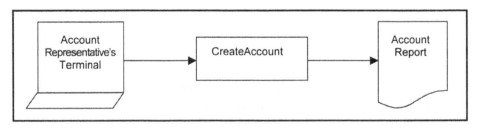

FIGURE A1.3
Creation of a new account.

```
namespace Accounts
{
    using System;

    public class CreateAccount                    [Main method]
    {
        public static void Main( )
        {                                          [Create new
                                                    account]
            Account acct = new Account();

            acct.setAcctNo(10);                    [Set the account
            acct.setAcctBalance(100.01m);           attribute values]


            Console.WriteLine("Account No.     " +  [Report
                        acct.getAcctNo() );          details
            Console.WriteLine("Account Balance " +   of the
                        acct.getAcctBalance() );     new
                                                     account]

        }
    }
}
```

FIGURE A1.4
Creating and using an Account object (Accounts\CreateAccount.cs).

Although simplistic, this process underlies many business applications. For example, in most "real world" applications, the account number is supplied by the system and the account information is recorded in a database. Information in the database is used for analysis and reporting and is typically accessible for display. However, the input of initial data, updating of a programmatic account model and recording of account detail are ever-present in some form or another.

A program to create a new account is shown in Figure A1.4. The class CreateAccount models the account creation process. The class has a function, **Main,** where program control starts and ends. Within the Main function, objects representing elements of the process modeled are created and manipulated. For example, an object representing an account is created with the statement

```
Account acct = new Account();
```

In this statement, an object of the class Account is created; this object is referenced by the name acct. The function Account(), which is a special type of function, called a constructor, is called upon to create the object. The constructor is invoked by the keyword **new** and results in allocating memory to store values of the objects attributes, i.e., the account number and balance.

Functions of the Account class object, referenced by acct, are invoked to set the attribute values:

```
acct.setAcctNo(10);
```

```
acct.setAcctBalance(100.01m);
```

Note that the invocation begins with the object's reference, followed by a period called the member selection operator, followed by the name of the function. In the example, the setAcctNo function is invoked to set the acctNo attribute to the value 10. Similarly, the setAcctBalance function is invoked to set the money type variable acctBalance attribute to the value 100.01. In the example, the values of the account number and balance, 10 and

100.01 respectively, are simply assumed. In the "real world," their determination is generally more complex.

A **namespace** is used to organize C# components and declare scope. A namespace is declared with the namespace keyword followed by the name of the namespace and the components of the namespace enclosed in braces. A namespace name can be any legal name and can include periods. One or more classes can be declared within a namespace; Account class and CreateAccount class are declared in the Accounts namespace.

The .NET Framework contains many namespaces, each containing classes useful in application development. For example, the namespace System contains predefined classes supplied as part of the .NET framework. The classes defined in the System namespace are made accessible to the class CreateAccount with the keyword "using" followed by the name of the namespace:

```
using System;
```

Included in the namespace System is the Console class that provides access to the standard input, output and error streams. Typically, the output stream is the display and the input stream is the keyboard. Included in the Console class is the function WriteLine ( ) that writes a line to the console display. This method is invoked to output the values of the account number and balance:

```
Console.WriteLine("Account No." + acct.getAcctNo() );
```

The account number is accessed with the expression

```
acct.getAcctNo()
```

which invokes the getAcctNo() function for the object referenced by acct. The expression returns the account number value of the object referenced by acct as an integer. The value of the account number is appended to the string "Account No." and output at the Console. Similarly, the account balance is displayed at the Console with the statement

```
Console.WriteLine("Account Balance" + acct.getAcctBalance());
```

When executed, the application including the classes Account and CreateAccount produces the output shown in Figure A1.5.

```
Account No.      10
Account Balance  100.01
```

FIGURE A1.5
Output of application containing Account and CreateAccount classes.

The defining and use of the class data type are fundamental to object-oriented programming and are the subject of this appendix. Preliminary elements basic to using the C# language are the following:

- Identifiers for naming program components
- Keyword, i.e., words that have a special meaning in the language
- Literals for the specification of values in the program
- Lexical considerations, factors involved in the translation of program source code to a machine-executable object

These preliminary elements are described next.

Identifiers

Identifiers are the names used to identify the various components of C# programs, including classes, attributes and functions.

For the most part, identifiers follow the Unicode 3.0 standard, Technical Report 15, Annex 7 guidelines, available on-line at http://www.unicode.org/unicode/reports/tr15/.

Valid identifiers are formed with the following rules:

- Identifiers must start with a letter character (a through z and A through Z), underscore or "@" symbol.
- Identifiers cannot be keywords.
- Characters after the starting character can be a letter character, decimal digit (0 through 9), or connecting characters such as underscore (_).

Figures A1.6 and A1.7 show examples of valid identifiers and invalid identifiers, respectively.

Programming tips:

Guidelines for effective naming:

Use concatenated nouns and adjectives that describe the attribute or class represented, for example, account and generalAccount, account911.

Avoid identifiers similar to the keywords, for example, For.

Use concatenated verbs and adverbs that describe the purpose of a function, for example, setCustomerName and getAccountBalance.

Use a consistent capitalization style. A popular style is to start names of attributes with small letters and classes with capital letters. The first letters of subsequent words of an attribute or class name are capitalized.

Use consistent terms throughout namespaces, libraries and applications.

Identifier	Explanation
TypicalIdentifier1	Valid starting letter and continuing characters
_valid_identfier	_ is a valid starting and connecting character
@break	@ prefix enables keywords to be used as identifiers
Break	Break is not a keyword, break is a keyword – C# is case sensitive

FIGURE A1.6
Valid C# identifiers.

Identifier	Explanation
1InvalidIdentifier	Invalid starting letter
break	Identifiers cannot be keywords
invalid-connector	Hyphen is not a valid connector
$amount	Invalid starting connector

FIGURE A1.7
Invalid C# identifiers.

Keywords

Keywords are reserved words that have special meaning to the compiler, can only be used as intended and cannot be used as identifiers unless prefixed with @. Note that identifiers are names used to identify components, attributes and functions included in a C# program. For example, @this is a valid identifier, whereas this is not. The C# keywords are listed in Figure A1.8.

abstract	enum	long	stackalloc
as	event	namespace	static
base	explicit	new	string
bool	extern	null	struct
break	false	object	switch
byte	finally	opertor	this
case	fixed	out	throw
catch	float	override	true
char	for	params	try
checked	foreach	private	typeof
class	goto	protected	unit
const	if	public	ulong
continue	implicit	readonly	unchecked
decimal	in	ref	unsafe
default	int	return	ushort
delegate	interface	sbyte	using
do	internal	sealed	virtual
double	is	short	void
else	lock	sizeof	while

FIGURE A1.8
C# keywords.

C# is a case-sensitive language, i.e., lower-case and upper-case letters are different. Thus, short and SHORT are different; in fact, short is a keyword and SHORT is not a keyword. Keywords used in the program to define the Account class include the following: class, decimal, int, public, return, static, using and void.

Literals

Literals (summarized in Figure A1.9) are representations of values in the source code. The character literals include the escape sequences representing Unicode character encodings. These sequences are summarized in Figure A1.10.

Type	Representation	Example
boolean	Boolean values true and false.	true and false
integer	Integral number.	711 \
real	Real number.	3.1415
character	Single character, enclosed in single quotes.	'C'
string	Zero or more characters enclosed in double quotes.	"C# Now and Forever!"
null	A reference that does not refer to any object.	null

FIGURE A1.9
Literal types: descriptions and examples.

Sequence	Character Name	Unicode Encoding
\'	Single quote	0x0027
\"	Double quote	0x0022
\\	Backslash	0x005C
\0	Null	0x0000
\a	Alert	0x0007
\b	Backspace	0x0008
\f	Form feed	0x000C
\n	New line	0x000A
\r	Carriage return	0x000D
\t	Horizontal tab	0x0009
\v	Vertical tab	0x000B

FIGURE A1.10
Escape sequences.

A string literal consists of zero or more characters enclosed in double quotes. Note that the simple escape sequences can be included. For example,

```
"\x0007first part\nsecond part\a"
```

is a valid string literal including the alarm and new line escape sequences. The alarm escape sequence is coded as a Unicode escape sequence, \u0007; hexadecimal, \x0007; and simple escape sequence \a. For the most part, the escape sequences are processed, when included in a string literal.

A second form of string literal, the verbatim string literal, consists of an @character followed by a zero or more characters enclosed in double quotes. For example,

```
@"\x0007first part\nsecond part\a"
```

For the most part, the characters between the double quotes are interpreted verbatim. Moreover, a verbatim string literal can span several lines, as in

```
"\x0007first part\nsecond part\a

multiple line span"
```

The program shown in Figure A1.11A illustrates handling of regular and verbatim strings. The output of the program is shown in Figure A1.11B. Note that the first string output is a regular string that contains the alarm and new line escape sequences. The escape sequences are processed, the alarm is sounded and the "second part" of the string is placed on a new line. On the other hand, the verbatim string is processed verbatim. The characters forming the escape sequences are displayed just as the other characters in the string are. Note that the spacing between the characters and the multiple line span of the verbatim string literal are preserved.

```
namespace CharacterLiteralsandStrings
{
    using System;

    public class CharacterLiteralsandStrings          ┌──────────────┐
    {                                                  │   regular    │
        public static int Main(string[] args)          │ string literal│
        {                                              └──────────────┘

            string s = "\x0007first part\u0007\nsecond part\a";
            string vs = @"\x0007first part\u0007\nsecond part\a


        multiple line span";

        Console.WriteLine( s );
        Console.WriteLine( vs );                       ┌──────────────┐
                                                       │   verbatim   │
        return 0;                                      │ string literal│
    }                                                  └──────────────┘
  }
}
```

FIGURE A1.11A
Regular and verbatim string literals.

```
first part
second part
\x0007first part\u0007\nsecond part\a

              multiple line span
```

FIGURE A1.11B
Regular and verbatim strings.

Lexical Considerations

The text comprising a program, including editorial comments, white space and line terminators, is treated as a continuous stream at the start of the transition to an executable object. C# provides two forms of comments. The **regular comment** begins with the characters /* and ends with the characters */. A regular comment can be a single line, multiple lines or portions of a line. A **one-line comment** begins with the characters // and extends to the end of the line. Comments help to explain the CreateAccount program shown in Figure A1.12.

Tip!

Comments are essential to good programming practice; they help to make a program written by someone else understandable. In fact, comments will help to make a program that you wrote years, months or even days ago understandable. *Any programmer who has had to revise a previously written program will attest to this point!*

```
/*   This program creates an instance of the Account class
 *   Programmer: Dudley Gill
 *   Date:        October 15, 2001
 */
using System;
public class CreateAccount
{
    public static void Main( )
    {
        // Create instance of the Account class
        Account acct = new Account();

        /* In the "real world" initial values of the
         * account, that is account number and balance, are
         * retreived from the account creator, which could
         * be an account representative at a terminal or another
         * program.
         */
        acct.setAcctNo(10);              // Initial values assigned
        acct.setAcctBalance(100.01m);

        /* In the "real world" the account information would
         * be stored in a database at this point as well as
         * reported.
         */
        Console.WriteLine("Account No.     " + acct.getAcctNo() );
        Console.WriteLine("Account Balance " +
                                acct.getAcctBalance() );
    } /* Program End */
}
```

FIGURE A1.12
Commenting the CreateAccount program.

Typically, the characters expressing a program stream are posed as lines of characters. A line termination character signals the end of a line. It is these characters that enable text editors and browsers to know when to start a new line. The characters interpreted as line terminators are summarized in Figure A1.13. During the transition from source code to machine executable object, characters that appear as spaces in the source code are often ignored and are referred to as **white space**. The white-space characters are summarized in Figure A1.14.

Line terminating character	Escape Sequence	Unicode Encoding
Carriage return	\r	u000D
Line feed	\n	u000A
Carriage return line feed	\r\n	
Line separator		u2028
Paragraph separator		u2029

FIGURE A1.13
Line terminators.

Description	Escape Sequence	Unicode Encoding
New line	\n	u000A
Tab	\t	u0009
Vertical tab	\v	u000B
Form feed		u000C
Control-Z or Substitute		u001A

FIGURE A1.14
White-space characters.

Appendix A.2

Data Types

Class type is just one of the types available for representing data. C# data representations can be divided into two categories: value and reference. Value types store their data; reference types store a reference to their data referred to as objects. Class is a reference data type.

Value Types

Value types called simple types are identified by reserve words and always have a value of that type. Consequently, value types cannot have the value null. One of the value types is the byte type used to represent unsigned integers in the range 0 to 255. A byte type value is represented in memory using eight binary values called bits and shown conceptually in Figure A2.1. The byte type value represented is the number 129.

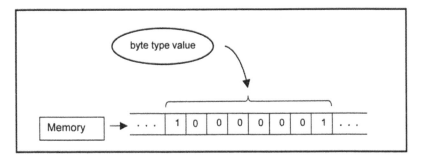

FIGURE A2.1
Memory representation of the byte value type.

Other value types are similarly represented. Other value types are type bool representing Boolean values and numeric types representing integral-type data, floating-point-type data and decimal-type data. A strut type and enumeration type are also value types. The **integral types** are summarized in Figure A2.2.

The char values correspond to the Unicode character set. Although it is classified as an integral type, there are no implied conversions from the other integral types to type char. char type constants are expressed as character literals, for example,

```
'A'
'3'
'\x000D'
```

Reserved Word	Size	Range of Values
sbyte	signed 8-bit integers	-128 to 127
byte	unsigned 8-bit integers	0 to 255
short	signed 16-bit integers	-32768 to 32767
ushort	unsigned 16-bit integers	0 to 65535
int	signed 32-bit integers	-2147483648 to 2147483647
uint	unsigned 32-bit integers	0 to 4294967295
long	signed 64-bit integers	-9223372036854775808 to 9223372036854775807
ulong	unsigned 64-bit integers	0 to 18446744073709551615
char	unsigned 16-bit integers	0 to 65535

FIGURE A2.2
Integral types.

Reserved Word	Size	Approximate Range of Values	Precision
float	32-bit single-precision	1.5×10^{-45} to 3.4×10^{38}	7 digits
double	64-bit double-precision	5.0×10^{-324} to 1.7×10^{308}	15 - 16 digits

FIGURE A2.3
Floating-point types.

Value	Description
-0 and +0	Although displayed as zero, both positive zero and negative zero values are used in certain operations. When the result of a floating-point operation is too small to be represented the result becomes either positive or negative zero.
Infinity and –Infinity	Positive Infinity and negative Infinity are produced by operations such as dividing a non-zero number by zero. When the result of a floating-point operation becomes too large to be represented the result becomes either positive or negative zero.
NaN	Not-a-Number values represent values that are not a number which are produced by invalid operations such as dividing a non-zero number by zero. If either operand in a floating-point operation is NaN the result is NaN.

FIGURE A2.4
Special floating-point values.

The **floating-point** types are float and double. The types are represented as 32-bit and 64-bit numbers according to specifications of the IEEE 745 format. The floating-point types are summarized in Figure A2.3. Special values used to characterize unique floating-point values are summarized in Figure A2.4.

The program in Figure A2.5A illustrates infinity, negative infinity and NaN values. The program's output is shown in Figure A2.5B.

The **decimal** type is suitable for representing numbers used in business, financial or monetary computations. Whereas the float and double types represent numbers subject to rounding errors, the decimal types represent numbers exactly. The decimal type can represent numbers as small as 1.0×10^{-28} to numbers in the range of 7.9×10^{28} with 28 to 29 significant digits. The number of decimal places is limited to 28 digits.

When decimal operations produce a result too small to be represented as a decimal, the result becomes zero. On the other hand, when the result of an operation becomes too large to be represented as a decimal, an exception is raised. The **bool** type represents the Boolean logical values true and false. The other types cannot be converted to type bool. The default values of the value types are summarized in Figure A2.6.

```
namespace Values
{
    using System;

    public class Values
    {
        public static int Main(string[] args)
        {
            System.Console.WriteLine( "1.0 / 0.0 = " + (1.0 / 0.0) );
            System.Console.WriteLine( "1.0 / -0.0 = " + (1.0 / -0.0) );
            System.Console.WriteLine( "0.0 / 0.0 = " + (0.0 / 0.0) );
            System.Console.WriteLine( "0.0 / -0.0 = " + (0.0 / -0.0) );
            return 0;
        }
    }
}
```

FIGURE A2.5A
Program illustrating computations resulting in special values (SpecialFloatingPointValues\SpecialValues.cs).

```
1.0 / 0.0 = Infinity
1.0 / -0.0 = -Infinity
0.0 / 0.0 = NaN
0.0 / -0.0 = NaN
```

FIGURE A2.5B
Output of program illustrating computations resulting in special values (SpecialFloatingPointValues\Special-Values.cs).

C and C++ Programmers' Tip

Unlike C and C++, a non-zero value cannot be converted to true and a zero value cannot be converted to false.

Type	Default Value
sbyte, byte, short, ushort, int, uint, long, ulong	0
char	'\x0000'
float	0.0f
double	0.0d
decimal	0.0m
bool	false

FIGURE A2.6
Value type default values.

An **enumeration** type is a set of named constants called an enumeration list. The elements of an enumeration are called **enumerators**. The keyword **enum** identifies the declaration of an enumeration type. The enum declaration syntax is shown in Figure A2.7. Declaration of an enum type named Region, underlying type long with members EAST, MIDATLANTIC, CENTRAL, SOUTH, and WEST, is shown in Figure A2.8.

The enum type body declares the elements, which are the named members. Each enumerator, i.e., member of the list, has an associated constant integral value. Each enum

[attributes] [modifiers] **enum** identifier [: underlying-type] { members }	
attributes	Declarative tags used to specify additional information. Attributes are optional.
modifiers	Valid modifiers are new, public, private, protected and internal. Modification is optional.
identifer	enum name.
underlying-type	Optional enumerator type specification. Storage allocated for each enumerator is based on the type specification.The default is int.
members	Comma-separated list of enumerator identifiers with optional value assignment.

FIGURE A2.7
Enum type syntax.

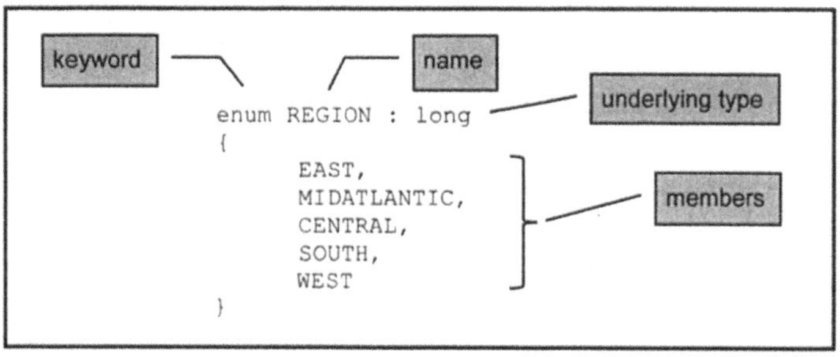

FIGURE A2.8
Enum type syntax.

type has a corresponding integral type called the **underlying type** of the enum type. The enumerator values must be within the range of the underlying type of the enum.

Specification of an underlying type is optional. If not specified, the default type is int. The valid types are byte, sbyte, short, ushort, int, uint, long or ulong. Note that char is not a valid enumeration underlying type.

The **enumerators** or **members** of the enumeration are enclosed in braces; the members are sequentially associated with a value starting with zero. In this case, the first enumerator, EAST, is associated with the value 0, the enumerator MIDATLANTIC 1, the enumerator CENTRAL 2 and so on. A value may be explicitly assigned to an enumerator. For example,

```
enum REGION : long
{
EAST,
MIDATLANTIC,
CENTRAL = 9,
SOUTH,
     WEST
}
```

In this case, the enumerators EAST and MIDATLANTIC are associated with values zero and one. The enumerator CENTRAL is explicitly assigned the value nine. When the value of an enumerator is explicitly assigned, the following enumerators are sequentially numbered starting with the next integral value. Thus SOUTH is assigned the value 10 and WEST is assigned the value 11. The values must be within the range of the enum's underlying type.

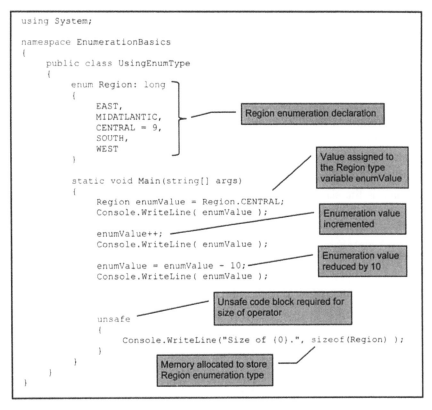

FIGURE A2.9A
Program illustrating use of the enum data type.

A program illustrating use of the enum data type is shown in Figure A2.9A. A Region type variable enumValue is declared and initialized to the value of the CENTRAL member with the statement

```
Region enumValue = Region.CENTRAL;
```

The value of the CENTRAL enumerator, defined in the enumeration's declaration, is the long 9. The following operators are valid with enum types:

Comparison operators — ==, !=, <, >, <=, >= simply compare the underlying integral values of the operators.

Arithmetic operators — Addition is evaluated as the sum of the underlying integral values of the operators. Subtraction is evaluated as the difference of the underlying integral values of the operators or the difference between an underlying operator value and an integral value within the underlying types' range.

Enumeration logical operators — ^, &, | simply perform the logical operation on the underlying enum operators.

Bitwise complement operator — ~ simply performs the bitwise complementation of the underlying value and the result is cast to the enum type.

Postfix increment and decrement — ++ and -- are evaluated by incrementing or decrementing the decrement operators associated value of the enum operator and casting the result to the enum type.

Sizeof operator — Returns the size of the underlying type.

The value of the enumerator is incremented with the statement

```
enumValue++;
```

The resulting value is 10, corresponding to the enumerator SOUTH.

The literal integral value 10 is subtracted from the enumerator with the statement

```
enumValue = enumValue - 10;
```

resulting in a value of 1 that corresponds to the enumerator EAST.

The sizeof operator is used to evaluate the memory allocated to store a Region type with the expression

```
sizeof(Region)
```

The size of the underlying integral type is returned and displayed. Note that value 8 is returned, which is the size of the underlying type: long. The sizeof operator requires an unsafe context, declared with the **unsafe** keyword. The program's output is shown in Figure A2.9B.

Note!

The Project's Build "Allow unsafe code block" property must be set to true.

```
CENTRAL
SOUTH
EAST
Size of 8.
```

FIGURE A2.9B
Output of the program illustrating use of the enum data type.

Every enum type automatically derives from the **System.Enum** class and thus inherits its properties and methods as well as the properties and methods inherited by the System.Enum class from the object and ValueType classes. The Enum class is summarized in Figure A2.10 and a program illustrating the enum class is shown in Figure A2.11A.

Invoking the GetType method, which is inherited from the Object class, provides the type of the enumeration:.

```
Type enumType = Region.EAST.GetType();
```

The Enum class GetName method returns the name constant associated with the value in the enumeration.

```
Console.WriteLine("Name: " + Enum.GetName(enumType, 11));
```

The string WEST, which is the current value of the region type enumValue, is displayed at the console. The program's output is shown in Figure A2.11B.

It is the responsibility of the programmer to ensure that the appropriate values are assigned to enumeration type variables.

The **struct** type is a value type and can be used to represent "lightweight" data elements that do not require the robust capability of a class. Note that a class type is a reference type. The struct type syntax is shown in Figure A2.12; an example of a structure is shown in Figure A2.13A.

public abstract class **Enum** : IComparable, Iformattable, IConvertible	
Hierarchy	
Object ValueType Enum	
Public Static Methods	

public static string **Format**(
  Type *enumType*,
  Object *value*,
  String *format*);
	Returns a string representation of the enumerator, *value* of the enumeration type *enumType* formatted as *format*. Valid format values are "G" or "g" for enumerted constant or decimal, "X" or "x" for hexadecimal and "D" or "d" for decimal.

public static string **GetName**(
  Type *enumType*,
  Object *value*);
	Returns a string name representation of enumerator *value* of the enumeration type *enumType*.

public static string[ ] **GetNames**(Type *enumType*);	Returns an array of string representations of the enumerator names of the enumeration type *enumType*.
public static Type **GetUnderlyingType**(Type *enumType*);	Returns the underlying type of the enumeration type *enumType*.
public static Array **GetValues**(Type *enumType*);	Returns an array of constants of the enumeration type *enumType* enumerators.

public static bool **IsDefined**(
  Type *enumType*,
  Object *value*);
	Returns true if an enumerator has the value *value* in the enumeration *enumType*.

public static object **Parse**(
  Type *enumType*,
  string *value*);
	Returns the enumerator object corresponding to the enumerator name value in the enumeration *enumType*.

public static object **Parse**(
  Type *enumType*,
  string *value*
  bool *noCase*);
	Returns the enumerator object corresponding to the enumerator name value in the enumeration *enumType*. The operation is case sensitive if *noCase* is true.

public static object **ToObject**(
  Type *enumType*,
  byte *value*);
	Returns an instance of the enumeration type *enumTyp* with *value* of byte type.
	Note: overloaded versions return the value to short, int, long, object, sbyte, ushort, uint and ulong type.

Public Instance Methods	
public int **CompareTo**(object *target*);	Compares the current instance with the object *target*. The value returned is as follows: | Integral Value	Description
Negative	this instance less than *target*
Zero	this instance equal to *target*
Positive	this instance greater than *target*	
public override bool **Equals**(object *target*);	Compares the current instance with the object *target*. The value true is returned if equal and same type; false if unequal.
public override int **GetHashCode**( );	Returns hash code for this instance.
public TypeCode **GetTypeCode**( );	Returns TypeCode enumeration member representing the underlying type.
public override string **ToString**( );	Converts the enumerator value to its string representation. Overloaded versions provide for formatting the string.
Protected Instance Constructor	
protected **Enum**( );	Initializes a new instance of the class. This constructor is called by derived class constructors.

FIGURE A2.10
Enum class summary.

```
using System;

namespace EnumClassBasics
{
      class UsingEnumClass
      {
            enum Region : long
            {
                  EAST,
                  MIDATLANTIC,
                  CENTRAL = 9,
                  SOUTH,
                  WEST
            }

            static void Main(string[] args)
            {
                  Type enumType = Region.EAST.GetType();
                  Console.WriteLine("Type: " + enumType.ToString() );

                  Console.WriteLine("Name: " + Enum.GetName(enumType, 11));
            }
      }
}
```

FIGURE A2.11A
Program illustrating the enum class.

```
Type: EnumClassBasics.UsingEnumClass+Region
Name: WEST
```

FIGURE A2.11B
Output of program illustrating the enum class.

[attributes] [modifiers] **struct** identifier [: interfaces] { body } [;]	
attributes	Declarative tags used to specify additional information. Attributes are optional.
modifiers	Valid modifiers are new, public, private, protected and internal. Modification is optional.
identifer	Struct name.
interfaces	Optional comma-separated list of implemented interfaces.
body	Member declarations.

FIGURE A2.12
Struct type syntax.

A struct LanguageStruct is declared. In this case the structure represents a student or parent's language proficiency. Inheritance of structs is characterized as follows:

- A struct cannot inherit from other structs or any class except the Object class.
- A struct can implement interfaces.
- A struct cannot be the base of a class.

The struct declares four members: an instance variable, a constructor, a property and a method.

A string, englishProficiency, represents English proficiency. In "real life," the string would be replaced with a ProficiencyLevel enumeration with the members NATIVE,

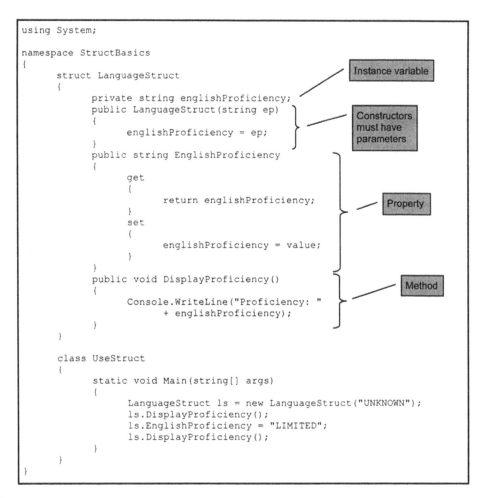

```
using System;

namespace StructBasics
{
    struct LanguageStruct                                    [ Instance variable ]
    {
        private string englishProficiency;
        public LanguageStruct(string ep)                     [ Constructors
        {                                                      must have
            englishProficiency = ep;                           parameters ]
        }
        public string EnglishProficiency
        {
            get
            {
                return englishProficiency;                   [ Property ]
            }
            set
            {
                englishProficiency = value;
            }
        }
        public void DisplayProficiency()                     [ Method ]
        {
            Console.WriteLine("Proficiency: "
                    + englishProficiency);
        }
    }

    class UseStruct
    {
        static void Main(string[] args)
        {
            LanguageStruct ls = new LanguageStruct("UNKNOWN");
            ls.DisplayProficiency();
            ls.EnglishProficiency = "LIMITED";
            ls.DisplayProficiency();
        }
    }
}
```

FIGURE A2.13A
Program illustrating struct type.

FLUENT, LIMITED, NONE and UNKNOWN. A more ambitious struct would include fields to represent speaking, writing and reading proficiency. The struct would also include additional fields — native language, for instance.

A constructor is declared and takes a single parameter that initializes the variable englishProficiency. *Struct constructors must have parameters.* A default constructor is always provided and initializes the struct members with default values. Declared constructors must take parameters and initialize all of the instance variables within the constructor body. A property EnglishProficiency is declared that accesses the variable englishProficiency. The method DisplayProficiency that displays the instance variable englishProficiency at the Console is also declared.

An instance of the struct is declared with the statement

```
LanguageStruct ls = new LanguageStruct("UNKNOWN");
```

Structs can also be created without the new operator. When this is done, the variables must be initialized before use. Memory for structs is allocated on the stack and can result in improved performance. Note that memory allocated for a class is on the heap. The program's output is shown in Figure A2.13B.

```
Proficiency: UNKNOWN
Proficiency: LIMITED
```

FIGURE A2.13B
Output of program illustrating struct type.

Reference Types

A **reference** type value is a reference to an instance of the type referred to as an **object**. A value type's value is actually a value of the type, but the reference type's value refers to an object of the type. Instances of the type are created with object creation expressions. Reference types are summarized in Figure A2.14.

Type	Description
class	A data structure that contains data members and function members.
object	The base class from which all other classes are derived.
string	The class represents Unicode character strings.
interface	A type that defines a contract that specifies the members that must be supplied by classes or interfaces implementing the interface.
array	A data structure composed of elements, all of the same type, that can be accessed using indices.
delegate	A data structure that refers to a static method, methods that are the same for all instances of the class, or to an object instance and a method of that instance.

FIGURE A2.14
Reference types.

Variables

Variables represent stored values, i.e., a storage location. The data type of the variable determines the type of data stored. For example, a variable that is an unsigned short data type holds a number between 0 and 65535. Sixteen bits, i.e., two bytes, are set aside in memory to hold the value of the variable. For organizations that need to uniquely identify less than 65,000 accounts, an unsigned short data type enables a unique number to be assigned to each account. Similarly, a decimal-type variable holds a decimal-type datum. The range of values of the decimal data type is sufficient to represent the balance of countries and nations as well as the typical individual or company.

Local variables are variables that are defined within a method, property or indexer. A variable declaration includes a type, identifier and optional assignment:

```
string englishProficiency = "LIMITED";
```

In this case, the type is string, the identifier is englishProficiency and the initial value is "LIMITED." The declaration without initialization is

```
string englishProficiency;
```

Multiple variables can be declared in a single declaration, for example,

```
string nativeLanguage, englishProficiency = "LIMITED";
```

A **field** is a variable declared in a class or struct. If the field is modified with the static modifier, it is said to be a **static** variable. A field that is not a static variable is said to be an **instance** variable.

Appendix A.3

Defining Methods

A **method** is a class member that can implement a computation that can be performed by an object of the class or the class.

Method Declaration

The functionality of a method is defined in the method's declaration. The basic syntax of a method declaration is shown in Figure A3.1.

attributes method-modifiers return-type method-name (parameter-list) { method-body }	
attributes	Optional programmer-specified declaratives pertaining to the method.
method-modifiers	The method-modifiers modify the method declaration. Valid modifiers are the following: new, public, protected, internal, private, static, virtual, override, abstract and extern.
return-type	The return-type of the value computed by the method. The value computed is said to be the value "returned" by the method. If the method does not return a value the return-type is void.
method-name	Name of the method, that is, the identifier used to programatically refer to the method.
parameter-list	An optional list of parameters passed to the method. The parameter list is a comma-separated list of parameter declarations enclosed in parentheses.
method-body	Typically, the method consist of a block containing the statements defining the computation performed by the method. Special types of methods have bodies that consist of a semicolon following the method-name.

FIGURE A3.1
Method declaration syntax.

An example of a method named TravelTime is shown in Figure A3.2. The method is declared public by its method modifier and returns a type double value. The method has a parameter list containing the declaration of two parameters of type double, the value distance and the value rate. These values are used in the method's body to compute the travel time. The computed value is returned by the method.

The parameter list consists of a comma-separated list of parameter declarations. Figure A3.3 shows the parameter declaration syntax. Each parameter identifies the type and name of values passed to the method.

The syntax elements of the parameter list for the method TravelTime are shown in Figure A3.4. Each parameter has a type and name. The first parameter is type double and named distance. The second is also type double but is named rate. Note also that the

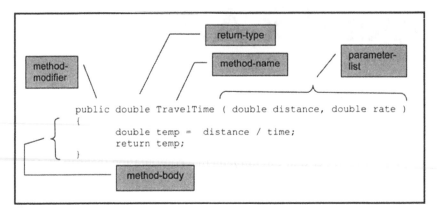

FIGURE A3.2
Example of a method declaration.

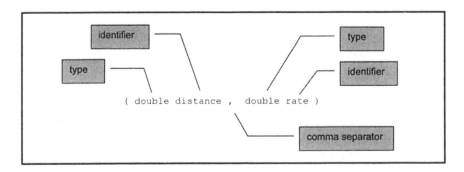

FIGURE A3.3
Parameter list declaration.

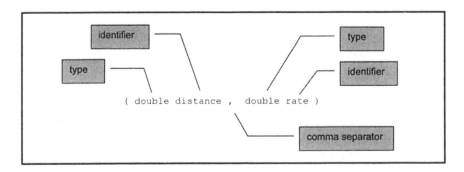

FIGURE A3.4
Syntax elements of the TravelTime method parameter list.

parameter list is enclosed in parentheses. If the enclosing parentheses do not contain a declaration, the parameter list is said to be empty.

The method name and parameter list are referred to as the method's **signature**. The parameter names must be unique. The ref and out modifiers are part of the method's signature, but the params modifier is not considered to be part of it. The following guidelines should be followed in naming method parameters:

- Choose names that describe or are easily associated with the meaning of the parameter. Note that, in the example, the parameters are named distance and rate, names that completely describe their meaning.

- Do not use Hungarian notation, i.e., do not prefix each name with a type identifier such as dDistance for a double parameter representing distance.

- Capitalize the first letter of words comprising the parameter name except for the first letter of the first word, e.g., firstDaysDistance and secondDaysDistance.

- Check all parameters for validity. This check can be performed as part of the method or can be accomplished before the method is called. Inclusion of validity checking as part of the method makes for reusable code because it helps to avoid misuse of the method and accompanying unpredictable results. For example, what is the meaning of a negative rate in the previous example? Is a negative rate a valid parameter value?

The computation performed by the method is defined in the method body, which can be a block (a set of braces) or a semicolon. The block contains the statements executed when the method is invoked. Names are introduced in the method's body by local variable declarations or by the parameter list. The names in the body must be unique. As such, a local variable cannot have the same name as another local variable or parameter.

When the return type of the method is void, return statements are not permitted. When the return type is not void, the method must terminate with a return statement or a throw statement, i.e., raise an exceptional condition. The value returned must be the type specified by the method's declared return type. Note that a method can have many return statements.

Method Invocation

A method's computational capability is brought into play by "invoking" or "calling" the method. Most methods use information passed during the method call in their computation. These information values are the parameters defined in the method declaration; they are referred to as arguments in the method's call or invocation. A method argument is the actual value or variable reference passed as a method's parameter. The argument declaration syntax is shown in Figure A3.5.

expression	
expression	A sequence of operators and operands that specifies a computation. For example, x + y where x is added to y to yield a value. Another example is the literal value 5. A string type argument could be "AnyString".
modifier variable-reference	
modifier	A keyword. Valid values are the following
	ref The argument is passed as a reference parameter. If a variable, it must be initialized.
	out The argument is passed as an output parameter. Initialization is not required.
variable-reference	A variable reference.

FIGURE A3.5
Argument declaration syntax.

type . *identifier* (*argument-list*)		
type	An instance reference of a type or the type name. Valid combination of type and static method characterization are as follows:	
	type name	if the method is a static method, that is, declared with the static modifier.
	instance reference	if the method is an instance method, that is, non-static.
identifier	A member of the type specified by *type*.	
argument-list	A comma-separated list of arguments representing the values or variable references for the method's parameters. The argument list is enclosed in parentheses and is optional.	

FIGURE A3.6
Method invocation syntax.

An argument can take two forms. One form is an expression whose evaluated result is the value of the argument. The other form of an argument is a variable reference that can refer to a predefined value type or to an instance of a reference type. Variable reference arguments can be modified with the ref and out modifiers. The statements comprising the body of the method are executed through a method invocation expression, the syntax of which is shown in Figure A3.6.

Using a Method

A program illustrating the declaration and invocation of the method TravelTime is shown in Figure A3.7.

The method TravelTime is declared and defined as a member of the Travel class. In the real world, the class Travel would also define other travel-related methods such as AverageSpeed, CostPerMile and ExpectedFuelConsumption; travel-related fields such as travelDistance, travelSpeed, fuelConsumptionRate and fuelCost; and constructors to initialize new Travel objects.

The method TravelTime takes two parameters: distance and rate, and computes the time required to travel the specified distance at the specified rate. The computed time is stored in a temporary type double variable temp. The value stored in the variable temp is the value returned by the method. The method is invoked by an instance of the class TravelTime. Figure A3.8 describes the elements of the method's invocation.

In Figure A3.7, double type variables d, r and tt, representing distance to be traveled, rate of travel and travel time, respectively, are declared. The variables d and r are initialized to the values 120 and 65, respectively. An instance, travelObject, of the class Travel is also created.

The method TravelTime of the class Travel is invoked for the instance travelObject with the variables d and r as arguments. The argument d corresponds to the method's parameter distance and the argument r corresponds to its parameter rate. The method performs the computation defined in the body of the declaration and returns the computed result, i.e., the distance divided by the rate. The returned value is assigned to the variable tt. The value of the variable tt is displayed at the console.

The program shown in Figure A3.7 produces the following console display:

```
Travel time: 1.8461538461538463
```

Note that some methods do not return a value, or the value returned is void. For example, the method WriteLine, which displays to the console, does not return a value.

```
namespace TravelTime
{
    using System;

    public class Travel
    {
        public double TravelTime (double distance, double rate )
        {
            double temp;
            temp = distance / rate;
            return temp;
        }
    }

    public class UsingTravel
    {
        public static int Main(string[] args)
        {
            double d;    // travel distance
            double r;    // travel rate or speed
            double tt;   // travel time

            d = 120;     // Assume 120 mile travel distance
            r = 65;      // Assume 65 mile per hour speed

            Travel travelObject = new Travel();

            tt = travelObject.TravelTime( d, r );

            Console.WriteLine("Travel time: " + tt);

            return 0;
        }
    }
}
```

Declaration of method TravelTime in the class Travel

Invocation of method TravelTime by Travel class object travelObject

FIGURE A3.7
Program illustrating the method TravelTime.

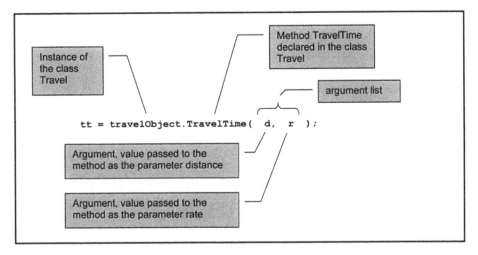

Method TravelTime declared in the class Travel

Instance of the class Travel

argument list

```
tt = travelObject.TravelTime( d, r );
```

Argument, value passed to the method as the parameter distance

Argument, value passed to the method as the parameter rate

FIGURE A3.8
Elements of the method TravelTime's invocation.

```
namespace MethodInvocation
{
    using System;

    public class Methods
    {
        public static void StaticMethod( )
        {
            Console.WriteLine("Static Method");
        }

        public void InstanceMethod( )
        {
            Console.WriteLine("Instance Method");
        }
    }
```

FIGURE A3.9A
Program illustrating accessing of class and instance methods.

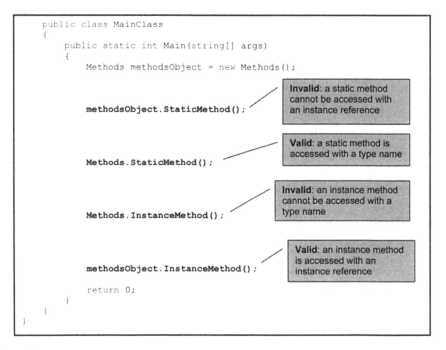

FIGURE A3.9B
Program illustrating accessing of class and instance methods.

Instance and Static Methods

Methods of a class are either static methods or instance methods. Generally, static methods provide computational results common to all instances of the class, while instance methods provide computational results specific to a particular instance of the class. When the method declaration includes the static modifier, the method is a static method and is often referred to as a **class method**. When the method is declared without the static modifier, it is an **instance method**. A Methods class that contains static and instance methods is declared in Figures A3.9A and A3.9B.

The class Methods is declared and includes the declaration of two methods: StaticMethod and InstanceMethod. The method StaticMethod's declaration includes the modifier static; therefore, StaticMethod is a class or a static method. On the other hand, the method InstanceMethod is not declared with the static modifier and thus is an instance method.

MethodsObject, an instance of the class Methods, is declared in the method main. A static method is invoked with an expression that contains the class name. For example, StaticMethod is a static method and is invoked with the statement

```
Methods.StaticMethod( );
```

Trying to invoke a static method with an instance of the class is not valid. Similarly, an instance method is invoked with an expression that contains an instance reference or a predefined type. For example, InstanceMethod is an instance method and is invoked with the statement

```
methodsObject.InstanceMethod( );
```

where methodsObject is an instance of the Methods class. Trying to invoke an instance method with a class type name is not valid.

Ref and Out Modifiers

When a value-type variable is passed as a parameter, a copy of the parameter is created. Along with the method's local variables, this copy is used in the computations defined in the method's body. Changes to the parameters inside the method's body have no effect on the data stored in the variable passed as a parameter. The parameters are said to be passed **by-value**.

The **ref** method parameter modifier causes the method's computation to refer to the variable passed to the method. That is, changes made to the parameter in the method's computation are reflected in the variable referenced in the method's argument list. Note that a variable passed as a ref parameter must first be initialized. Use of an uninitialized variable as a ref argument will raise a compilation error.

A program illustrating use of the ref method parameter modifier is shown in Figure A3.10. A class UsingRef is declared that declares two methods: PassingRefValue and PassingValue. The PassingRefValue has a single integer parameter, i, that is modifier with the ref modifier. The method's computation consists of a statement that increments the value of the passed value. The method displays the value of the parameter when the computation is completed.

A method PassingValue is also declared. PassingValue also has a single integer parameter. However, the parameter is not modified. The computation, as with PassingRefValue, consists of a statement that increments the value of the passed value. The method displays the value of the parameter when the computation is completed.

The methods PassingRefValue and PassingValue are invoked in the Main method. First, the integer variable i is declared and assigned the value 1 and the value is displayed at the console. The method PassingRefValue is invoked with the variable i as a ref-modified argument. The statements comprising the body of the method are executed. The value of the parameter i is incremented and displayed at the console. The value displayed is 2. Control returns to the method Main and the statement following the method invocation is executed. The value of the variable i is displayed at the console. The value is 2. The parameter manipulated in the method **referred** to the variable passed as the argument.

Next, the method PassingValue is invoked and the variable i is passed as an argument. Within the method, the value of the parameter is incremented and its value within the

```
namespace RefAndOutParameters
{
    using System;

    public class UsingRef
    {
        public static void PassingRefValue( ref int i )
        {
            i++;
            Console.WriteLine("i inside PassingRefValue method: "
                + i );
        }

        public static void PassingValue( int i )
        {
            i++;
        }

        public static int Main(string[] args)
        {
            int i = 1;
            Console.WriteLine("i: " + i);

                                                    ┌─────────────────┐
                                                    │ i passed as a   │
                                                    │ ref argument    │
            PassingRefValue(ref i);                 └─────────────────┘
            Console.WriteLine("i: " + i);

            PassingValue(i);
            Console.WriteLine("i: " + i);

            return 0;
        }
    }
}
```

FIGURE A3.10
Program illustrating ref modifier.

method is displayed at the console. The value displayed is 3. Control returns to the Main method and the value of the variable i is displayed. The displayed value is 2. Note that the value of the variable i did not increase. The value passed as an argument was not passed as a reference variable, and thus the methods manipulations did not refer to the actual variable.

The program's output is the following console display:

```
i passed to method: 1
i inside PassingRefValue method: 2
i after PassingRefValue completed: 2
i inside PassingValue method: 3
i after PassingValue completed: 2
```

Note!

To use a ref parameter, the argument must be passed as a ref argument. A variable passed as a ref argument must first be initialized.

The **out** method parameter modifier causes the method's computation to refer to the variable passed to the method. That is, changes made to the parameter in the method's

```
namespace OutParameters
{
    using System;

    public class UsingOut
    {
        public static void
            PassingOutValues( int i, out int i2, out int i3 )
        {
            i2 = i * i;
            i3 = i * i * i;
        }

        public static int Main(string[] args)
        {
            int i = 2;
            int iSquared;
            int iCubed = 21;

            PassingOutValues( i, out iSquared, out iCubed );

            Console.WriteLine("i:        " + i);
            Console.WriteLine("iSquared: " + iSquared);
            Console.WriteLine("iCubed:   " + iCubed);

            return 0;
        }
    }
}
```

FIGURE A3.11
Program illustrating out modifier.

computation are reflected in the variable referenced in the method's argument list. In this sense, an out parameter is similar to a ref parameter. However, a variable passed as an out parameter need not be initialized. Moreover, a value must be assigned to an out parameter before the method returns. Failure to assign a value will raise a compilation error. Use of an out parameter before a value is assigned within the method will also result in a compilation error.

A program illustrating use of the out method parameter modifier is shown in Figure A3.11. A class UsingOut is declared. The class contains a method PassingOutValues that has three integer parameters: i, i2 and i3. The parameters i2 and i3 are modified with out. Because i2 and i3 are out parameters, the actual variables passed as arguments in the method's call are referenced by the corresponding parameters in the methods body. Thus the squared value of i is assigned to the variable passed as the argument corresponding to the parameter i2. Similarly, the squared value of i is assigned to the variable passed as the argument corresponding to the parameter i3.

An integer variable i is declared and initialized to the value 2 in the method Main. Integer variables iSquared and iCubed are also declared. iSquared is not initialized but iCubed is initialized to the value 21.

The method PassingOutValues is invoked. The value i is passed as an argument corresponding to the parameter i. The values iSquared and iCubed are passed as out arguments corresponding to the out parameters i2 and i3. During execution of the method, values are assigned to the variable referenced by i2, i.e., iSquared, and the variable referenced by i3, i.e., iCubed. When the method returns, the values of i, iSquared and iCubed are displayed at the console:

```
I:        2
ISquared: 4
ICubed:   8
```

Note that any value initializing value assigned to a variable passed as an out argument is overwritten during the methods invocation.

When a reference-type variable is passed as a parameter, the reference does not contain the data; it "points" to the data. As such, changes inside the method's body are made to the variable referenced by the parameter. Note that the reference cannot be changed in the method. That is, the reference cannot be assigned to a newly created object of the type, inside the method, that will persist outside the method. In order to change the reference inside the method, the reference-type variable must be passed with the ref or out keywords. Variables passed as parameters in a manner that enables the actual values to be changed within the method's body are said to be passed **by-reference**.

Constructors and Destructors

Constructors and **destructors** have the same name as the enclosing class declaration. All other methods must have names that differ from the enclosing class.

An **instance constructor** is a class member that initializes an instance of a class. The syntax for instance constructor declaration is shown in Figure A3.12. The declaration begins with optional defined attributes followed by optional access modification.

The constructor body is a code block that contains statements executed to initialize a new class. Note that the constructor does not contain a return statement. The constructor name must be the same as the name of the class in which the constructor is declared. The constructor name is followed by an optional parameter list enclosed in parentheses. The types of the parameters in the parameter list must be as accessible as the constructor. This will be important when class types are used as variable, class member, parameters and arguments.

When no constructor is declared, a default constructor is automatically provided; it can be viewed as a parameterless constructor. Constructors are invoked by the object creation expressions and through constructor initializers. The syntax of the object creation expression is shown in Figure A3.13.

attributes constructor-modifiers identifier (parameter-list) {constructor-body}	
attributes	Optional programmer-specified declaratives pertaining to the constructor.
constructor-modifiers	Optional access modifiers. Valid modifiers are the following: public Access is not limited. protected Access is limited, including derived types. Internal Access is limited to this program. private Access is limited. With the exception of the protected internal combination, only one modifier can be specified at a time.
identifier	Name of the class in which the constructor is declared.
parameter-list	An optional list of parameters passed to the method. The parameter list is a comma-separated list of parameter declarations enclosed in parentheses.
constructor-body	Statements constituting the constructor's action are specified in the constructor body.

FIGURE A3.12
Syntax for instance constructor declaration.

new *type* (*argument-list*)	
type	A class type or a value type. The type cannot be an abstract type. (The concept of an abstract type class is explained in Appendix A.9.) The object creation expression evaluates to a *type* reference.
argument-list	An optional list of arguments passed to the constructor.

FIGURE A3.13
Object creation expression syntax.

```
namespace Constructors
{
    using System;

    public class ClassType
    {
        private string sField;
        private int iField;



        public ClassType(string sParm, int iParm)
        {
            sField = sParm;
            iField = iParm;
            this.dField = 1.1;
        }


        public void DisplayFields()
        {
            Console.WriteLine("sField: " + sField);
            Console.WriteLine("iField: " + iField);
            Console.WriteLine("dField: " + dField);
        }
    }

    public class MainClass
    {
        public static int Main(string[] args)
        {
            string sVar = "anInstance";
            int iVar = 21;



            ClassType ct = new ClassType( sVar, iVar );

            ct.DisplayFields();

            return 0;
        }
    }
}
```

type name

argument list

constructor

object creation expression

FIGURE A3.14
Program illustrating constructor declaration and object creation.

The expression begins with the **new** keyword, followed with the name of the type and then by an optional argument list enclosed in parentheses. The expression evaluates to a reference to a new object of the specified type. An example of a constructor declaration and its use in an object creation expression is shown in Figure A3.14. The program declares

Run-time object creation steps	
Step	**Description**
1	A new instance of the class is created and memory space is allocated. An outOfMemoryException is raised if there is not enough memory for the allocation. (Exceptions are described in Appendix A.9.)
2	Fields, declared in the new class, are initialized to their default values.
3	The class's constructor is invoked. Note that a reference to the new instance is passed to the constructor and can be accessed with the this keyword.
4	The invocation expression evaluates a reference to the newly created instance.

FIGURE A3.15
Runtime object creation steps.

a class ClassType. The class declares a constructor ClassType with two parameters: a string type sParm and an int type iParm. The constructor assigns the passed values to the fields sField and iField. Note that the constructor has the same name as the class in which it is declared and also that the other members in the class, in this case the method Display-Values, have a name that is not the same as the name of the class.

An instance of the class is created in the Main method of the program's ClassMain. An instance of the ClassType is created with an object creation expression. Steps in the creation of objects at runtime are summarized in Figure A3.15.

The class's constructor is invoked. The constructor, ClassType, initializes sField and iField fields in the newly created instance, with values passed as the constructor's argument list. The constructor is passed a reference to the newly created instance. This self-reference is accessed with the keyword this and is used to initialize the dField of the newly created instance.

The expression returns a reference to the newly created ClassType object. The returned reference is assigned to the ClassType object reference ct. The instance's DisplayFields method is invoked to display the instance's field values. The console display is shown below:

```
sField: anInstance
iField: 21
dField: 1.1
```

A **static constructor** is a class member which implements actions that initialize a class as opposed to members, i.e., instance constructors that initialize an instance of the class. The syntax for static constructor declaration is shown in Figure A3.16.

attributes static identifier ( ) {constructor-body}	
attributes	Optional programmer-specified declaratives pertaining to the constructor.
identifier	Name of the class in which the constructor is declared.
constructor-body	Statements constituting the constructor's action are specified in the constructor body.

FIGURE A3.16
Syntax for static constructor declaration.

Attributes are optional in a static constructor declaration. Note that a static constructor cannot be modified with access modifiers. A static constructor declaration includes the keyword static preceding the identifier, which must be the class name and is followed by

Static constructor invocation

- Static constructors are invoked automatically and cannot be invoked explicitly.
- The static constructor is invoked before any instance of the class is created.
- A static constructor for a class never executes more than one time.
- A static constructor is executed before any static member of the class is referenced.

FIGURE A3.17
Static constructor invocation.

```
namespace StaticConstructor
{
    using System;

    public class ClassType
    {
        static ClassType()
        {
            Console.WriteLine("ClassType static constructor invoked");
        }

        public ClassType()
        {
            Console.WriteLine("ClassType instance constructor invoked");
        }
    }

    public class MainClass
    {
        public static int Main(string[] args)
        {
            new ClassType();
            new ClassType();
            return 0;
        }
    }
}
```

static constructor declaration

FIGURE A3.18
Program illustrating declaration and invocation of static constructors.

parentheses. The static constructor does not have a parameter list. The constructor's body defines the actions taken when the constructor is invoked.

Invocation of static constructors is described in Figure A3.17. The program in Figure A3.18 illustrates static constructor declaration and invocation.

A class ClassType is declared. A constructor ClassType is declared and defines an action that writes a message to the console. Two instances of the class are created; the program produces the following console display:

```
ClassType static constructor invoked

ClassType instance constructor invoked

ClassType instance constructor invoked
```

Note that the static constructor is only invoked once.

Tip!

Static constructors are used to effect class initialization, for example, opening a communication link that will be used by all instances of the class.

attributes ~ identifier ( ) {destructor-body}	
attributes	Optional programmer-specified declaratives pertaining to the destructor.
identifier	Name of the class in which the destructor is declared.
destructor-body	Statements constituting the destructor's action are specified in the destructor body.

FIGURE A3.19
Syntax for destructor declaration.

A destructor is a class member that implements actions required to destruct an instance of the class. The syntax for destructor declaration is shown in Figure A3.19.

Attributes are optional. Note that the destructor declaration does not permit access modification. A destructor declaration includes the tilde "~" character preceding the identifier, which must be the class name. The class name is followed by parentheses. Note that the destructor does not provide for parameters; action undertaken when the destructor is invoked is specified in the destructor's body. Destructor invocation is described in Figure A3.20. A program illustrating declaration of a destructor is shown in Figure A3.21.

Destructor invocation

- Destructors are invoked **automatically** and cannot be invoked explicitly.
- A destructor is invoked any time after an instance of the class becomes eligible for destruction, that is, program code cannot use the instance.

FIGURE A3.20
Destructor invocation.

```
namespace Destructors
{
    using System;

    public class ClassType
    {
        ~ClassType()
        {
            // instance destruction actions
        }
    }

    public class MainClass
    {
        public static int Main(string[] args)
        {
            {
                new ClassType();
            }

            return 0;
        }
    }
}
```

Destructor declaration Note: "~"

Destructor invoked any time after program reaches this point. The instance of ClassType is no longer visible.

FIGURE A3.21
Program illustration destructor declaration and invocation.

The destructor is called automatically at some point after the instance is no longer available to the program code. In the example, the instance of ClassType is created within a block of code. The instance is not accessible outside the block, and thus the instance destructor is called *automatically* sometime after the program reaches the code block's closing brace.

Tip!

Destructors are used to effect destruction of an instance of a class, for example, releasing system-related resources consumed by the instance.

Overloading

Methods and constructors have signatures. A method's or constructor's **signature** consists of the name and the type of each parameter, including ref or out modifiers. Note that a method's signature does not include the method's return type. Several methods or constructors can have the same name providing their signatures are unique. Methods with the same name but different signatures are said to be **overloaded**.

Note!

Overloading facilitates code reuse in that methods with the same functionality and differing in parameters can use the same name, thereby reducing the programmer familiarization curve. The use of the same name to represent similar functionalities is known as **polymorphism**.

The program example in Figure A3.22 illustrates method overloading. Five methods with the same name, Overload, are declared. In each case, the parameters are different and thus the signatures of the methods are unique. Note that the ref and out parameter modifiers are part of the signature and thus Overload (int i) and Overload (ref int i) are unique signatures.

The program's output is the following:

```
Overload(int i);
Overload(double d);
Overload(string s);
Overload(ref int r);
Overload( );
```

The .NET Framework has elaborate procedures for distinguishing between methods with different signatures and ensuring that the appropriate version is invoked.

```
namespace Overloading
{
    using System;

    public class OverloadingMethods
    {
            public static void Overload( int i)
            {
                    Console.WriteLine("Overload(int i)");
            }
            public static void Overload( double d)
            {
                    Console.WriteLine("Overload(double d)");
            }
            public static void Overload( string s)
            {
                    Console.WriteLine("Overload(string s)");
            }
            public static void Overload( ref int r)
            {
                    Console.WriteLine("Overload(ref int r)");
            }
            public static void Overload( )
            {
                    Console.WriteLine("Overload( )");
            }


        public static int Main(string[] args)
        {
                    Overload( 1 );
                    Overload( 1.0 );
                    Overload( "s" );
                    int r = 1;
                    Overload ( ref r );
                    Overload ( );

                    return 0;
        }
    }
}
```

FIGURE A3.22
Program illustrating method overloading.

Appendix A.4

Properties

A **property** is a member of a class that provides access to an attribute of an object or class. A property is like a field in that it is named; it differs from a field in that properties have **accessors** that specify the assignment and retrieval of the property's value.

Property Declaration

The property declaration syntax is shown in Figure A4.1.

[attributes] [modifiers] type identifier {accessor declaration}	
attributes	Declarative tags used to specify additional information. Attributes are optional.
modifiers	Modifiers are optional. Valid modifiers are new, static, virtual, abstract, override and an access modifier: public, protected, internal and private. Note, the virtual, abstract and overrride are not valid modifiers on an accessor of a static property.
type	Property type.
identifier	Property name.
accessor declaration	Declaration of the accessors used to read and write the property.

FIGURE A4.1
Property declaration syntax.

The example in Figure A4.2 illustrates the declaration of a property named Rate of type double with public access. A property declaration includes an optional attribute, optional modifier, type, property name and accessor declarations. The accessor declarations specify how the reading and writing of the property value follow the property identifier and are enclosed in braces.

Accessor Declaration

The accessors of a property contain the statements that specify how a property value is read, written or computed. Accessor declaration syntax is shown in Figure A4.3.

The **set** accessor assigns a value to the property. The **get** accessor retrieves the value of the property. The accessor declaration consists of **get** or **set** words followed by the accessor body, which is a block. The block contains the statements defining the value returned or assigned when the accessor is invoked in a program. In the example in Figure A4.1, the

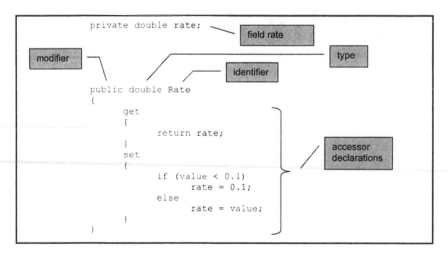

FIGURE A4.2
Example of a property Rate declaration.

```
set { accessor-body }
get { accessor-body }

accessor-body              Block containing the statements that are executed when the
                           accessor is invoked.
```

FIGURE A4.3
Accessor declaration syntax.

value returned by the get accessor for the property Rate is the value of the field rate defined as:

```
get
{
    return rate;
}
```

Note that the get accessor can also compute the value returned; for example,

```
get
{
    return 0.9 * rate;
}
```

returns a value that is nine tenths of the value of rate. The get accessor must terminate with a return statement or a throw statement.

The value assigned to the Rate property is defined by the set accessor:

```
set
{
    if (value < 0.1)
        rate = 0.1;
    else
        rate = value;
}
```

Note that the variable **value** represents the implied value of the property. In the example, if the implied value of the property Rate is less than 0.1, then the value 0.1 is assigned to the variable rate. However, when the implied value is greater than or equal to 0.1, then the value of the property is assigned to the variable rate.

The accessor declaration can contain a set accessor, a get accessor or both a set and get accessor. A property with an accessor declaration that contains only a set accessor is called a **read-only** property. Similarly, a property with an accessor declaration that contains only a get accessor is called a **write-only** property. A property with an accessor declaration that contains both a get and set accessor is called a **read-write** property.

Accessing Properties

A property is referenced just like a field member. The program in Figure A4.4 illustrates the declaration and accessing of properties. The program declares the class Account with private data members rate and fee. Properties Rate and Fee are also declared. A main method illustrating accessing the properties Rate and Fee is also shown.

```
namespace UsingProperties
{
    using System;

    public class Account
    {
            private double rate;
            public double Rate
            {
                get
                {
                    return rate;
                }
                set
                {
                    if (value < 0.1)
                        rate = 0.1;
                    else
                        rate = value;
                }
            }
    }
```

FIGURE A4.4
Program illustrating declaring and accessing properties.

First, an Account object, named act, is instantiated. Accession of the property Rate is shown in Figure A4.5. Properties are accessed like fields. In this case the set accessor

```
set
{
    if (value < 0.1)
        rate = 0.1;
    else
        rate = value;
}
```

```
                static double fee;
                static double Fee
                {
                        get
                        {
                                if (fee < 0.15)
                                        return fee;
                                else
                                        return 0.15;
                        }
                        set
                        {
                                fee = value;
                        }
                }

        public static int Main(string[] args)
        {
                Account act = new Account();

                act.Rate = 0.05;
                Console.WriteLine("Rate: " + act.Rate);

                act.Rate = 0.2;
                Console.WriteLine("Rate: " + act.Rate);

                Account.Fee = 0.05;
                Console.WriteLine("Fee: " + Account.Fee);

                Account.Fee = 0.25;
                Console.WriteLine("Fee: " + Account.Fee);

                return 0;
        }
    }
}
```

FIGURE A4.4 (CONTINUED)
Program illustrating declaring and accessing properties.

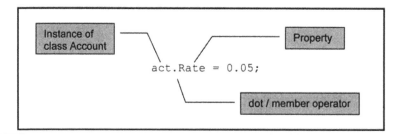

FIGURE A4.5
Accessing the property Rate.

is invoked with an *implied* value of 0.05. The statements comprising the accessor are executed, resulting in the assignment of 0.1 to the member rate. Note that the value is 0.05, which is less than 0.1.

Retrieving a property is similar, except the statements comprising the get accessor are executed. The statement

```
Console.WriteLine("Rate: " + act.Rate);
```

in particular, the expression

```
act.Rate
```

invokes the get accessor

```
get
{
    return rate;
}
```

The current value of the data member rate is returned, resulting in a console display

```
Rate: 0.1
```

 The program also illustrates accessing the property Fee. The program's output is

```
Rate: 0.1
Rate: 0.2
Fee: 0.05
Fee: 0.15
```

Note that, when the Rate is assigned a value 0.05, rate is assigned the value 0.1, but when Rate is assigned the value 0.5, rate is assigned the value 0.5. The value returned by the property Fee depends on the value of the member fee. When fee is less than 0.15, the value of fee is returned; otherwise, the value 0.15 is returned.

Static Properties

Properties declared using the **static** modifier are said to be static. Static properties are like other static members in that the property is associated with all instances of the class rather than with a particular instance. The program in Figure A4.6 illustrates the declaration and accessing of a static property.
 Static properties are declared with the static keyword:

```
static double GeneralFee
```

The property Fee is accessed as a class member, as shown in Figure A4.7.
The program's output is:

```
GeneralFee: 0.05
```

Hiding and Accessing Inherited Properties

The **new** modifier explicitly hides a property inherited from a base class. An example of using the new modifier to hide an inherited member is shown in Figure A4.8.
A BaseAccount class, declaring a property OtherFee, is defined. A class DerivedAccount, inheriting the members of BaseAccount, is also defined. The member OtherFee is also defined and is modified with new and thus explicitly hides the base class member OtherFee.
 A DerivedAccount class object, da, is created with the statement

```
DerivedAccount da = new DerivedAccount();
```

The property OtherFee of the DerivedAccount instance da is set with the statement

```
da.OtherFee = 1.1;
```

```
namespace StaticProperty
{
    using System;

    public class Account
    {

        static double generalFee;
        static double GeneralFee
        {
            get
            {
                return generalFee;
            }
            set
            {
                generalFee = value;
            }
        }

        public static int Main(string[] args)
        {
            Account act = new Account();

            Account.GeneralFee = 0.05;
            Console.WriteLine("GeneralFee: " + Account.GeneralFee);

            return 0;
        }
    }
}
```

FIGURE A4.6
Declaring and accessing a static property.

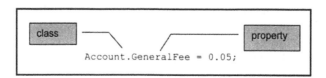

FIGURE A4.7
Accessing a static property.

The value of the property OtherFee is retrieved by invoking the get accessor with the statement

```
Console.WriteLine("Derived Class Fee: " + da.OtherFee);
```

and displays the following at the console

```
Derived Class Fee: 1.1
```

The expression

```
(BaseAccount) da
```

casts the DerivedAccount type to BaseAccount type. As such, the base class set accessor is invoked by the statement

```
((BaseAccount)da).OtherFee = 0.7;
```

and the otherFee data member is set to 0.7.

Similarly, the statement

```
Console.WriteLine("Derived Class Fee: " +
((BaseAccount)da).OtherFee);
```

```
namespace InheritedProperties
{
    using System;

    public class BaseAccount
    {
            private double otherFee;
            public double OtherFee
            {
                    get
                    {
                            return otherFee + 1.0;
                    }
                    set
                    {
                            otherFee = value;
                    }
            }
    }

    public class DerivedAccount : BaseAccount
    {
            private double otherFee;
            public new double OtherFee
            {
                    get
                    {
                            return otherFee;
                    }
                    set
                    {
                            otherFee = value;
                    }
            }
    }

    public class MainClass
    {
            public static int Main(string[] args)
            {

                    DerivedAccount da = new DerivedAccount();

                    da.OtherFee = 1.1;
                    Console.WriteLine("Derived Class Fee: " +
                            da.OtherFee);

                    ((BaseAccount)da).OtherFee = 0.7;
                    Console.WriteLine("Derived Class Fee: " +
                            ((BaseAccount)da).OtherFee);

                    return 0;
            }
    }
}
```

FIGURE A4.8
Program illustrating hiding an inherited member with the new modifier.

invokes the base class get accessor and

```
Base Class Fee: 1.7
```

as the base class get accessor returns the value of otherFee plus 1.0.

Tip!

The program will compile and run if the new keyword is omitted, but the development environment editor will issue a warning indicating that an override or a new keyword is required.

Interface Properties

Properties can be declared in interfaces. The interface property declaration syntax is shown in Figure A4.9. A program illustrating the use of interface properties is shown in Figure A4.10. An interface IAccount is defined. The interface IAccount has a read-write property, OtherFee.

The class Account implements the interface IAccount. The inherited property OtherFee is implemented in the class Account. The inherited property OtherFee *must* be implemented as declared in the interface, i.e., it must have the same type and same accessors.

The property is accessed in the method Main of the class MainClass with the statements

```
a.OtherFee = .11m;

Console.WriteLine("Other Fee: " + a.OtherFee);
```

where a is an instance of the Account class.

The program output is:

```
Other Fee: 0.11
```

Summary

The following points characterize properties:

- Properties are characterized as read-write, read or write, based on the declaration of their accessors.

Property Characterization	get accessor	set accessor
Read-write	X	X
Read	X	
Write		X

- Properties differ from fields in that they do not represent storage locations.
- Properties are accessed just like fields.

Properties provide for the implementation of procedures similar to methods.

[*attributes*] [*new*] *type identifier* {*interface-accessors*}	
attributes	Declarative tags used to specify additional information. Attributes are optional.
new	new modifier. The new modifier is optional.
type	Property type.
identifier	Property name.
interface-accessors	Property get and set accessors. The accessor body consists of a terminating semicolon only. The accessors serve as placeholders indicating whether a property is read-only, write-only or read-write.

FIGURE A4.9
Interface property declaration syntax.

```
namespace InterfaceProperties
{
    using System;

    public interface IAccount
    {
        decimal OtherFee
            {
                get;
                set;
            }
    }

    public class Account : IAccount
    {
        private decimal otherFee;

        public decimal OtherFee
            {
                get
                {
                    return otherFee;
                }
                set
                {
                    otherFee = value;
                }
            }
    }

    public class MainClass
    {
        public static int Main(string[] args)
    {
        Account a = new Account();

        a.OtherFee = .11m;
        Console.WriteLine("Other Fee: " + a.OtherFee);

        return 0;
    }
    }
}
```

FIGURE A4.10
Program illustrating interface properties, their inheritance and use.

Appendix A.5

Access Modifiers

Access Modifiers

Classes and class member access are determined by **access modifiers**. The intuitive meaning of the access modifiers is summarized in Figure A5.1.

Modifier	Access Description
public	Not limited.
protected	Limited to containing class or types derived from the class.
private	Limited to containing type.
internal	Limited to this program.
protected internal	Limited to this program or types derived from the containing class.
*Note: Derived classes are dealt with in Appendix A.9.	

FIGURE A5.1
Intuitive meaning of the access modifiers.

The validity of these modifiers depends on the context in which they are used. For example,

- Namespace elements cannot be declared private or protected; they can only be declared public or internal. Note that internal is the default.
- Class members can have any of the access modifiers. The default accessibility is private.
- Struct members can have public, internal or private access modification. The default accessibility is private.
- Interface members are implicitly declared public. Access modification declaration of interface members is prohibited.
- Enumeration members are implicitly declared public. Access modification declaration of enumeration members is prohibited.

A major strength of object-oriented languages is the ability to create new classes, called derived classes, based on existing classes. The existing class is called the base class. The use of access modifiers in base class influences its own member access as well as the member access of the derived class. These effects are presented in Appendix A.9: Inheriting Classes.

Class Modifiers

Class modifiers include:

new — Specifies that the same method in a class used as the basis for the current class is hidden: Appendix A.9.

access modifiers — Public, protected, internal and private.

abstract — Specifies a class that can only be used as basis for other classes: Appendix A.9.

sealed — Specifies that a class cannot be used as the basis for another class: Appendix A.9.

Note that some of the modifiers are used to declare access of derived classes. The program ClassModifiers illustrates class access modification.

```
using System;

namespace AccessModifiers
{                                          Namespace elements are either public
                                           or internal: internal by default.
    class Account
    {
        private class PrivateAccount       ———  Contained type
        {                                        declared private.

        }

        public class PublicAccount         ———  Contained type
        {                                        declared public.
            public string publicAccountDesc =
                "PublicAccount Description";
        }
    }

    class ClassModifiers
    {
        static void Main(string[] args)         PublicAccount
        {                                        is accessible.

  Syntax error:
  PrivateAccount  ————
  is inaccessible.
            Account.PrivateAccount pa =
                new Account.PrivateAccount();

            Account.PublicAccount pa = new Account.PublicAccount();
            string outString = pa.publicAccountDesc;
            Console.WriteLine(outString);
        }
    }
}
```

FIGURE A5.2A
Program illustrating class access modification (AccessModifiers\ClassModifiers.cs).

Class declarations in a namespace, for example,

```
class Account
{


}
```

have the default internal access. As such, the class is accessible to other elements within the namespace. For example, the statement

```
Account a = new Account();
```

in the Main method of the ClassModifiers class accesses the Account class.

The access modifiers can be used with classes declared within a class. For example, the class PrivateAccount is declared private in the class Account.

```
private class PrivateAccount
{

}
```

If the class is accessed in another class, for example, with the statement

```
Account.PrivateAccount pa =
new Account.PrivateAccount();
```

in the class ClassModifiers, a compile error is raised:

```
`Account.PrivateAccount' is inaccessible
    due to its protection level
```

Note that the default for class types is private; thus the declaration

```
class PrivateAccount
{

}
```

gives rise to the same error. On the other hand, the class PublicAccount declared in the class Account

```
public class PublicAccount
{
    public string publicAccountDesc = "PublicAccount Description";
}
```

is accessible in the class ClassModifier, as with the statement

```
Account.PublicAccount pa = new Account.PublicAccount();
```

When the erroneous reference to a private member is removed, the program can be built and executed. The program's output is shown in Figure A5.2B.

```
PublicAccount Description
Press and key to continue_
```

FIGURE A5.2B
Output of program illustrating class access modification (AccessModifiers\ClassModifiers.cs).

Note!

The protected and private access modifiers are only allowed on nested classes.

Member Access Modifiers

Access to members of a class is also declared with access modifiers. The program, Access-Modifiers\ClassModifiers.cs, illustrates member access modification. A class Account is declared. The class has a field member name with private access by default, a member accountNo with declared internal access and a member balance with declared private access.

The class MemberModifiers, Figure A5.3A, defines the method `Main`. An instance of the class Account is declared with the statement

```
Account a = new Account();
```

The expression

```
a.name
```

accesses the Account class instance field member name. The member has private access by default and thus is not accessible outside the class in which it is declared. Note that the statement is "commented out." Similarly, the expression

```
a.balance
```

accesses the Account class instance field member balance, which is declared private and thus is not accessible outside the class in which it is declared. On the other hand, the expression

```
a.accountNo
```

accesses the `Account` class instance field member accountNo, which is declared internal and thus is accessible within the program in which it is declared.

```
namespace MemberAccess
{
    class Account
    {
        string name = "Account Name";
        internal int accountNo = 21;
        private decimal balance = 10.01m;

        public decimal getBalance()          ┌─ private class
        {                                     │  members are
            return balance;                   └─ accessible
        }
    }

    public class MemberModifiers
    {
        static void Main(string[] args)       ┌─ name access
        {                                     │  is private by
            Account a = new Account();        └─ default

            // Console.WriteLine(a.name);      ┌─ accountNo
                                              │  declared
            Console.WriteLine("No.: " + a.accountNo);  └─ public

                                              ┌─ balance declared
            // Console.WriteLine(a.balance);   └─ private

            Console.WriteLine("Balance: " + a.getBalance());
        }
    }                ┌─ getBalance declared public
}
```

FIGURE A5.3A
Program illustrating class member access modification (MemberAccess\MemberModifiers.cs).

Members of the class Account can access balance; thus it can be referenced in the Account method getBalance. The method getBalance returns the value of the private member field balance:

```
public decimal getBalance()
{
    return balance;
}
```

The method getBalance has public access and thus is accessible outside its class.

As a private member, balance is not accessible outside the class but is accessible inside the class; hence it is available to the method getBalance, as in the expression:

```
a.getBalance()
```

Program output is shown in Figure A5.3B.

```
PublicAccount Description
Press and key to continue_
```

FIGURE A5.3B
Output of program illustrating class member access modification (MemberAccess\MemberModifiers.cs).

Note!

Members modified public are accessible outside the class of declaration, but members modified private are only accessible within the class of declaration.

Static Modifier

The **static** modifier declares a member as belonging to a type rather than an instance of the type. Static modification is applicable with fields, methods, properties, operators and constructors. Constant and type declarations are implicitly static. Static modification cannot be used with indexers, destructors or types. For example, a general fee applied to all accounts should be considered as belonging to the account class rather than a particular account. The general fee should be declared a static member of the class.

Only one copy of a static field is shared by all instances of the type, whereas each instance of the class has a copy of the type's instance fields. The program in Figure A5.4A illustrates the static modifier.

A member is declared static with the static keyword

```
public static decimal generalFee;
```

Static members are referenced through the type. For example,

```
Account.generalFee = 10.01m;
```

assigns the value 10.01m to the static field member generalFee of the class Account.

Note that an instance reference, such as

```
a10.generalFee
```

where a10 is an instance of the class Account, is **invalid**.

The program's output is shown in Figure A5.4B.

```
using System;

namespace StaticModifierBasics
{
    public class Account
    {
        public Account(int an)
        {
            accountNo = an;
        }

        public int accountNo;
        public static decimal generalFee;

        public decimal getGeneralFee()
        {
            return generalFee;
        }
    }

    public class AccessStaticMember
    {
        public static void Main()
        {
            Account a10 = new Account(10);
            Account a20 = new Account(20);

            Account.generalFee = 10.01m;

            Console.WriteLine("a10 Account No:   " + a10.accountNo);
            Console.WriteLine("a10 General Fee: "
                + a10.getGeneralFee());

            Console.WriteLine("a20 Account No:   " + a20.accountNo);
            Console.WriteLine("a20 General Fee: "
                + a20.getGeneralFee());
        }
    }
}
```

FIGURE A5.4A
Program illustrating static member modification (StaticModifierBasics\AccessStaticMember.cs).

```
a10 Account No:   10
a10 General Fee: 10.01
a20 Account No:   20
a20 General Fee: 10.01
Press any key to continue_
```

FIGURE A5.4B
Output of program illustrating static member modification (StaticModifierBasics\AccessStaticMember.cs).

Encapsulation

The program MemberModifiers illustrates the elements of the object-oriented notion of encapsulation. The notion of **encapsulation** speaks to the concept of completeness and controlled access; the class Account illustrates this concept. First, the Account class completely models an account. It includes provision for a unique identifier, name and balance. In "real life," the account class would include many more fields, including address and telephone numbers. Second, access to these fields is through defined methods. For example, an instance of the account class is created with the statement

```
Account a = new Account( );
```

The following expression **does not** provide access to the field balance

```
a.balance
```

because balance is declared private and thus is only accessible to a member of the class Account.

The method getBalance is a member of the class Account and thus has access to balance. If access to a member is permitted, it is said to be **accessible**. Because getBalance is declared public, it is accessible. The method getBalance returns the value of the field member balance. As such, access to the private field member balance is controlled in that it is accessed through the member method getBalance. Access to the private field member balance is illustrated in Figure A5.5. First, the getBalance method is invoked by the Account class instance a. Second, the method getBalance, a member of Account access the private field member balance. Third, the value of the field balance is returned. Fourth, the value of the private field member balance is made available in the calling object.

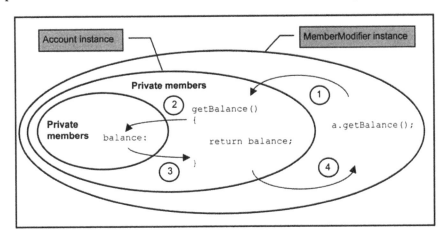

FIGURE A5.5
Access to the private field member balance.

Note that the concept of encapsulation suggests that all field members should be private with access provided though public methods. As such, the Account fields name and accountNo should be declared private. In this manner, methods setName, setAccountNo, setBalance, getName and getAccountNo should be defined public.

Note!
The private modifier is the default access modifier for all members.

Object Class

The Object class is the base for all classes of the .NET Framework and defines basic functionality. It is summarized in Figure A5.6. A program illustrating use of the Object class is shown in Figure A5.7A. The program's output is shown in Figure A5.7B.

public class **Object**	
Namespace: System	
Public Static Methods	
static bool **Equals** (object *objX*, object *objY*);	Returns true if objX and objY are the same instance or both are null references; false otherwise.
Public Instance Constructors	
Object ( );	Initializes a new instance of the class.
Public Instance Methods	
virtual bool **Equals** (object *obj*);	Returns the value true if the specified object *obj* is equal to the current object; false otherwise.
virtual int **GetHashCode** ( );	Returns a hash code for the current Object.
Type **GetType** ( );	Returns the Type object representing the runtime type of the current instance.
virtual string **ToString** ( );	Returns a String object representing the current object.
Protected Instance Methods	
~**Object** ( );	Enables freeing of resources before the Object is reclaimed by garbage collection and is called automatically after an object becomes inaccessible. This method is also known as the Finalize method and uses destructor syntax.
Object **MemberwiseClone** ( )	Creates a shallow copy of the current Object. Note a shallow copy simply creates a copy of the object. If the object contains references to other objects it does not create copies of the referenced objects. The clone points to the original referenced objects. On the other hand, a deep copy creates a copy of the object and every object referenced by the object, directly or indirectly.

FIGURE A5.6
Object class.

```
using System;

namespace ObjectClassBasics
{
    public class Account { }

    public class UsingObject
    {
        public static void Main()
        {
            Object o = new Object();
            Object x = new Object();
            Object y = o;

            Console.WriteLine("o = x: " + o.Equals(x));

            Console.WriteLine("o = y: " + o.Equals(y));

            Console.WriteLine("o = y: " + Object.Equals(o,x));

            Console.WriteLine("Hash: "
                + o.GetHashCode().ToString());

            Console.WriteLine("String representation: "
                + o.ToString().ToString());
        }
    }
}
```

FIGURE A5.7A
Program illustrating use of the Object class (ObjectClassBasics\UsingObjects.cs).

```
o = x: False
o = y: True
o = y: False
Hash: 3
String representation: System.Object
Press any key to continue_
```

FIGURE A5.7B
Output of program illustrating use of the Object class (ObjectClassBasics\UsingObjects.cs).

Appendix A.6

Expressions

Identifiers reference data in memory. Manipulations of these data are expressed in statements in which **operators** relate the data identifiers, called **operands** or arguments, to each other. For example, the statement

```
z = x + y;
```

instructs the computer to add the data represented by the identifiers x and y and assign the sum to the memory location associated with the identifier z. In the statement, x, y and z are operands or arguments and the symbols + and = are operators.

Operators can operate on one, two or three operands. Those that operate on two arguments are called **binary operators**, while an operator that operates on one argument is called a **unary operator**. An operator with three arguments is called a **ternary operator**. The manner in which the operations in an expression are performed is determined by the operator's **precedence** and **associativity**.

An **expression** is a sequence of operators and operands. Thus the statement z = x + y; contains the expression x + y, which is evaluated to a value that is the sum of the values of the variable represented by the identifiers x and y. This value is assigned to the variable z. Note that the assignment of the sum to the variable z also forms an expression. C# has well-defined rules for evaluating expressions; some operations are always performed before others are. This precedence of some operators over others is implied. For example, multiplication is always performed before addition. Consider the expression: a + b * c. The product of b * c is evaluated first and the result then added to a.

Parentheses are used to specify the order of evaluation. Consider, for example, the expression (a + b) * c; the expression inside the parentheses is evaluated first. Care must be taken to ensure that the intended evaluation of an expression is identical to the way that C# evaluates the expression because the results can differ widely for different evaluation orders. Selected operators can be overloaded, providing for user-defined operations.

Operators

C# operators are summarized in Figure A6.1.

Simple Assignment Operator

The **simple assignment** operator, =, changes the value of the operand to the left of the operator to the value of the operand to the right. In the example below, the variable A is assigned the value 711:

Category	Operator	Name	Associativity
Primary	(x)	Parenthesized expression	
	x . y	Member access	
	f(x)	Method invocation	
	a[x]	Element access	
	x++	Postfix increment	
	x—	Postfix increment	
	new	new	
	typeof	typeof	
	sizeof	sizeof	
	checked	checked expression	
	unchecked	unchecked expression	
Unary	+	Unary olus	
	-	Unary minus	
	!	Logical negation	
	~	Bitwise complement	
	++x	Prefix increment	
	--x	Prefix decrement	
	(T)x	Cast expression	
Multiplicative	*	Multiplication	Left-associative
	/	Division	
	%	Remainder	
Additive	+	Addition	Left-associative
	-	Subtraction	
Shift	<<	Shift left	Left-associative
	>>	Shift right	
Relational	<	Less than	Left-associative
	>	Greater than	
	<=	Less than or equal to	
	>=	Greater than or equal to	
	is	is	
Equality	==	Equal to	Left-associative
	!=	Not equal to	
Logical AND	&		Left-associative
Logical XOR	^		Left-associative
Logical OR	|		Left-associative
Conditional AND	&&		Left-associative
Conditional OR	||		Left-associative
Conditional	? :		Right-associative
Assignment	=		Right-associative
	*=		
	/+		
	%=		
	+=		
	-=		
	<<=		
	>>=		
	&=		
	^=		
	|=		

FIGURE A6.1
Operators listed in order of precedence.

```
A = 711
```

If the type of the right-hand operand is not implicitly convertible to the type of the left-hand one, a compile-time error results. Note that the result is the same type as the left operand and is a value.

Assignment is right associative, i.e., groups from right to left. For example,

```
A = B = C
```

means

```
A = (B = C)
```

In this case, the expression B = C is evaluated and the value of C is assigned to B. The value of the expression is then assigned to A.

The simple assignment operator sets the value of the variable on the left equal to the value of the expression on the right. Thus the statement

```
result = 5 + 3 * 2;
```

assigns the value 11 to the variable result. Note that the multiplication 3 * 2 is performed first and the result added to 5. Finally, the value of the expression on the right, 11, is assigned to the memory location referenced by the identifier result. Assignment has the lowest precedence of the operators and is performed after all other operations.

Note that the assignment operator in C# is not the equality operator in algebra. In C#, the expression on the right side of the assignment operator is completely evaluated and then the result is assigned to the variable on the left side.

Primary Operators

A primary expression can be a **literal**, i.e., a value represented by source code. For example, the expression

```
7
```

is a source code representation of the integral value seven.

A primary expression can also be a simple name, i.e., a **single identifier**. Remember that an identifier represents a variable. For example, the statement

```
int i = 11;
```

defines an identifier i that is assigned the value 11. Thus, the expression

```
i
```

is an example of a single identifier expression.

A **parenthesized expression** is an expression enclosed within parentheses. The value of this expression is the value of the expression contained within. For example, the value of the parenthesized expression

```
( 7 + 11 + 21 )
```

is 39. Note: 7, 11 and 21 are literals.

A member access expression can consist of a namespace or data structure followed by a period "." followed by an identifier. The period is often referred to as the **member access operator**. As an example, consider a namespace, HumanResource, containing a member data structure Person that contains a data member identifier, name. The value of name is given with the following expression

```
HumanResource.Person.name
```

The **method invocation** operator identifies a method, i.e., a computation described elsewhere, to be called or invoked. For example, the expression

```
getBalance( 12 )
```

specifies that a method named getBalance should be performed. Note that method also identifies further information, called parameters, such as the particular account to be referenced, which in this case is the account 12.

C# provides for grouping elements into collections. The **element access** operator provides for accessing a specific element of the collection. For example,

```
Msg[ 3 ]
```

refers to the third message in the collection of messages called Msg.

The **postfix increment** operator, **++**, results in adding 1 to the value of the operand *after* the operand has been evaluated. Similarly, the **postfix decrement** operator, **--**, results in subtracting 1 from the value of the operand *after* the operand has been evaluated. The postfix increment and decrement operators are defined for the following data types: sbyte, byte, short, ushort, int, uint, long, ulong, char, float, double and decimal. Note that the postfix increment and decrement operators are also defined for any enum type.

The **new** operator creates an instance of a type and is used to create objects, i.e., instances of class types. Additionally, the new operator is used to create instances of array types and delegate types. The **typeof** expression is used to obtain the System.Type object for a type. Note that the predefined types have an object type representation referenced in the Type class in the System namespace. For example, the program

```
namespace PrimaryExpressions
{
    using System;

    public class Class1
    {
        public static int Main(string[] args)
        {
            Console.WriteLine( typeof(int) );
            Console.WriteLine( typeof(System.Double) );
            Console.WriteLine( typeof(string) );

            return 0;
        }
    }
}
```

produces the output

```
Int32
Double
System.String
```

The **sizeof** operator returns the size of a value type in bytes. For example, the sizeof an int type is expressed as

```
sizeof( int )
```

The program

```
namespace PrimaryExpressions
{
    using System;
```

```
public class Class1
{
    public static int Main(string[] args)
    {
    unsafe
    {
        Console.WriteLine( sizeof(int) );
        Console.WriteLine( sizeof(System.Double) );
    }

    return 0;
    }
}
}
```

produces the following output:

```
4
8
```

where 4 and 8 are the sizes of the int and System.Double types, respectively, in bytes. Note that the sizeof operator is used in the unsafe context that enables the use of pointers.

The **checked** and **unchecked** operators control overflow checking for integral-type arithmetic operations. The checked operator evaluates the contained expression and throws an overflow exception if an overflow occurs. For example, at runtime the value of i exceeds the range for type int after incrementing and results in a runtime error:

```
int i = 2,147,483,647
checked {
i++;
};
```

Similarly, the definition

```
int i = 2,147,483,648
```

results in a compile time error because the value assigned is outside the valid int range.

An expression evaluated in the unchecked mode will be truncated to fit the designated type. For example, the program

```
namespace PrimaryExpressions
{
    using System;

    public class Class1
    {
        public static int Main(string[] args)
        {
        int i = 2147483647;
        unchecked
        {
            Console.WriteLine( i++ ) ;
        }
```

```
        return 0;
        }
    }
}
```

produces the output

```
2147483647
```

where the value of I, which is incremented to the value 2147483648, is truncated to the maximum value in the type int range.

Unary Operators

The **unary plus** operator, **+**, simply returns the value of the operand. The **unary minus** operator, **-**, result is obtained by subtracting the operand from zero. For example, given

```
i = 342;
```

the unary operation

```
-i
```

results in the variable i value of −342. The unary minus operator is defined for integer, floating-point and decimal negation.

The **logical negation** operator, expressed as !, results in the value true if the operand is false and false if the operand is true. For example, assume that the Boolean variable b has value true. The expression

```
!b
```

results in a value of false.

The **bitwise complement** operation, **~**, results in the bitwise complementation of the operand. For example, the statement

```
i = 5;
```

results in the memory of allocation of four bytes of memory associated with the identifier i that have the following bit values:

```
10100000000000000000000000000000
```

After the variable i is bitwise complemented,

```
~i
```

the allocated memory contains the following values:

```
01011111111111111111111111111111
```

The **prefix increment** operator, **++**, results in adding 1 to the value of the operand *before* the operand has been evaluated. Similarly, the **prefix decrement** operator, **--**, results in subtracting 1 from the value of the operand *before* the operand has been evaluated. The prefix increment and decrement operators are defined for the following data types: sbyte, byte, short, ushort, int, uint, long, ulong, char, float, double and decimal. Note that the prefix increment and decrement operators are also defined for any enum type.

The **cast** operation, **(type)**, results in an explicit conversion of the expression cast to the type specified. The default of a real number literal on the right-hand side of an assignment is double. Thus, the statement

```
float f = 7.11; // Build Error: Cannot implicitly convert
                // type 'double' to 'float'
```

results in a compile time error because a double type cannot be stored as a float type. The double can be explicitly cast to type float with a cast operation:

```
float f = (float) 7.11;
```

Similarly, because there is no implicit conversion from double to long, the following statement results in a compile time error:

```
long l = 7.11; // Compile error, no implicit conversion
```

A cast is required to prevent a compile time error:

```
long l = (long) 7.11;
```

The program shown in Figure A6.2A demonstrates unary operations including unary minus, logical negation, bitwise complement and cast. The program's output is shown in Figure A6.2B.

```
namespace UnaryOperators
{
    using System;
    using System.Collections;

    public class Class1
    {
        public static int Main(string[] args)
        {
            int i = 432;
                System.Console.WriteLine( -i );

                bool b = true;
                System.Console.WriteLine( !b );

                int bc = 5;
                System.Console.Write( "Bits Before Complement: " );
                int [ ] ia = ( bc );
                BitArray ba = new BitArray( ia );
                for (int index=0 ; index < 32; index++)
                {
                        if (ba[index]== true)
                            System.Console.Write( "1" );
                        else
                            System.Console.Write( "0" );
                }
                System.Console.WriteLine( " " );
                System.Console.Write( "Bits After Complement:  " );
                int [ ] cia = ( ~bc );
                BitArray cba = new BitArray( cia );
                for (int index=0 ; index < 32; index++)
                {
                        if (cba[index]== true)
                            System.Console.Write( "1" );
                        else
                            System.Console.Write( "0" );
                }
                System.Console.WriteLine( " " );

                // float f =   5.5; Results in compile error

                float f = (
        float) 5.5; // cast converts double to float

                return 0;
        }
    }
}
```

FIGURE A6.2A
Illustrating unary operations (UnaryOperators\Class1.cs).

```
-432
False
Bits Before Complement: 10100000000000000000000000000000
Bits After Complement:  01011111111111111111111111111111
```

FIGURE A6.2B
Output of program illustrating unary operations (UnaryOperators\Class1.cs).

Arithmetic Operators

The arithmetic operators are similar to those in other languages. The operations are defined for selected operand types: integer, floating and decimal. The two arguments need not be of the same type because conversion is performed, where possible, according to predefined conversion rules, to a type for which the operation is defined.

The **multiplication operator**, *, performs multiplication producing the product of the operands. For example, where A represents 5 and B represents 6, the expression

    A * B

evaluates to 30.

The **division operator**, /, performs division producing the quotient of the operands. The left-hand operator is the dividend and the right-hand one is the divisor. Note that the result of integer division is rounded toward zero. The absolute value of the result of the operation is the largest possible integer that is less than the absolute value of the quotient. For example, the expression

    –   22 / 8

evaluates to –2. Consider now the case

    –   22 / 8.00

The division operation dividend is converted to a floating point –22.00 and a floating-point division is performed, resulting in the value –2.75. The result is positive or zero when the two operands have the same sign and negative or zero when the operands have different signs. Note also that a runtime exception is thrown when the divisor is zero.

The **remainder** operator, %, yields the remainder of a divide operation. This operator, sometimes called the **modulus** operator, computes the remainder of the division of the operands. For example, the statement

    remainder = 22 % 8 ;

assigns the value 6 to remainder, because 22 divided by 8 is 2 with 6 left over or remaining. For integers, the expression x % y is the same as the expression x – (x / y) * y. For decimals, the expression x % y is evaluated as x – n * y, where n is the largest possible integer that is equal to or less than x / y. For example, the expression

    –22 % 8

evaluates to –6.

The **addition operator**, +, computes the sum of the operands. For example, when A represents the integer 5 and B represents the integer 6, the expression

    A + B

evaluates to 11. When the sum is outside the range that can be represented, an exception condition is raised. *Note that the + operator is also used to represent string concatenation.*

```
namespace ArithmeticOperations
{
    using System;

    public class ArithmeticOperations
    {
        public static int Main(string[] args)
        {
                int A = -22;
                int B = 8;
                double C = 8.00;
                int D = 3;
                double F = 3.33;

                System.Console.WriteLine( "(-22/8) = " + A/B);

                System.Console.WriteLine( "(-22/8.00) = " + A/C);

                System.Console.WriteLine( "-22/8 + 3 = " + (A/B + D));
                System.Console.WriteLine( "-22/8.00
                    + 3 = " + (A/C + D));

                System.Console.WriteLine( "-22/8
                    + 3.33 = " + (A/B + F));

                System.Console.WriteLine( "-22%8 = " + (A % B));
                System.Console.WriteLine( "-22%8.00 = " + (A % C));

                System.Console.WriteLine( "B + '' is eight'' = "
                    + (B + " is eight") );

                return 0;
        }
    }
}
```

FIGURE A6.3A
Program illustrating arithmetic operations (ArithmeticOperations\Class1.cs).

The **subtraction operator, -,** computes the difference of the operands. For example, when A represents the integer 5 and B represents the integer 6, the expression

    A - B

evaluates to −1. When the difference is outside the range that can be represented, an exception condition is raised.

The **multiplicative** operators, ***, /** and **%,** have the same precedence and are left associative. The **additive** operators, **+** and **−,** have the same precedence and are left associative. The program shown in Figure A6.3A illustrates the use of the arithmetic operators. The program illustrates implicit conversions as well as string concatenation.

If one, or both, of the operands of the addition operator is a string, the operator performs string concatenation. For example:

    int A;

    A = 10;

    A + " is Ten"

results in the string expression

    "10 is Ten"

The operand that is not a string is converted to a string at runtime. The two string operands are concatenated; the characters in the left-hand operand string precede the characters in the right-hand string in the resultant string. The program also illustrates the remainder operator. Figure A6.3B shows the output of the program.

```
(-22/8) = -2
(-22/8.00) = -2.75
-22/8 + 3 = 1
-22/8.00 + 3 = 0.25
-22/8 + 3.33 = 1.33
-22%8 = -6
-22%8.00 = -6
B + '' is eight'' = 8 is eight
```

FIGURE A6.3B
Program illustrating arithmetic operations (ArithmeticOperations\Class1.cs)

Shift Operators

The **shift operators**, also known as the **bitwise shift operators**, move the bits in the left operand to the left or right of the number of bits specified in the right operand. The **left shift operator** is shown as **<<** and the **right shift operator** is shown as **>>**. An example of the left shift operator is shown in Figure A6.4.

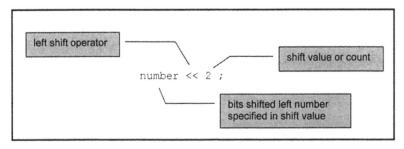

FIGURE A6.4
Shift operator.

The left and right shift operators are defined for int, uint, long and ulong right operands. The shift value or count is int. The shift value is the low-order 5 bits of the shift value if the left operand is int or uint. The shift value is the low-order 6 bits of the shift value if the left operand is long or ulong.

When the bits are shifted left, the rightmost bits are padded with 0. An example illustrating the left bitwise shift operation is shown below. Given the value 8, the contents of the memory location of the operand number are shown in Figure A6.5. The low-order bit is shown on the left.

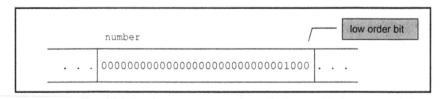

FIGURE A6.5
Bit values associated with the number 8 stored as an int type.

The value of the expression

```
number = number << 2
```

reflects the bits being shifted two positions to the left and the result assigned to the variable number. The high-order bits are discarded and the low-order empty positions are filled with zeros. The memory location associated with the datum after the shift is shown in Figure A6.6, in which the bits have been shifted two places to the left and the low-order bits have been set to zero. Note that after the shift the memory location holds the number 32, which is 8 * (2 * 2). Left-shifting is a fast and efficient way of multiplying numbers by two or powers of two.

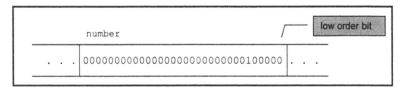

FIGURE A6.6
Bit values associated with the number 8 stored as an int type.

The right shift operator is similar except the bits are shifted right. If the left operand is int or long, the low-order bits are discarded, the remaining bits are shifted right and the high-order empty bits are set to zero if the operand is non-negative and to one if the operand is negative. If the left operand is uint or ulong, the low-order bits are discarded, the remaining bits are shifted right and the high-order empty bits are set to zero. Note that right-shifting provides a quick method of dividing by two or powers of two in what is described as "truncating" integer division. A program illustrating left-shifting is shown in Figure A6.7A.

The program's output is shown in Figure A6.7B. Note that the orientation of the bits is reversed and the low-order bit is shown to the left. However, the left shift results in shifting the bits to increase the value of the number represented.

Relational and Equality Operators

The **equal to, ==; not equal to, !=; less than, <; greater than, >; less than or equal to, <=;** and **greater than or equal to, >=,** operators are referred to as the **comparison operators**. The result returned by the comparison operators is shown in Figure A6.8. The return type is always type bool. The comparison operators are defined for the integral types int, uint, long and ulong.

The comparison operators are also defined for the floating-point types float and double. If either operand is NaN, the result is false for the ==, <, >, <= and >= operators and true for the != operator. When neither operand is NaN, comparison results reflect the following:

- Negative and positive zero are considered equal.
- Negative infinity is considered smaller or less than all other values but equal to another negative infinity.
- Positive infinity is considered larger or greater than all other values but equal to another positive infinity.

The comparison operators are defined for the decimal type.

```
namespace ShiftOperators
{
    using System;
    using System.Collections;

    public class ShiftOperators
    {
        public static int Main(string[] args)
        {
                int x = 8;
                System.Console.WriteLine("x before shift: " + x);

                int [ ] ia = { x };
                BitArray ba = new BitArray( ia );
                for (int index=0 ; index < 32; index++)
                {
                        if (ba[index]== true)
                            System.Console.Write( "1" );
                        else
                            System.Console.Write( "0" );
                }
                System.Console.WriteLine( " " );

                x = x<<2;
                System.Console.WriteLine("x after 2 bit left shift: "
                    + x);

                ia[0] = x ;
                ba = new BitArray( ia );
                for (int index=0 ; index < 32; index++)
                {
                        if (ba[index]== true)
                            System.Console.Write( "1" );
                        else
                            System.Console.Write( "0" );
                }
                System.Console.WriteLine( " " );

                return 0;
        }
    }
}
```

FIGURE A6.7A
Program illustrating the left shift operation (ShiftOperators\Class1.cs).

```
x before shift: 8
00010000000000000000000000000000
x after 2 bit left shift: 32
00000100000000000000000000000000
```

FIGURE A6.7B
Output of program illustrating the left shift operation (ShiftOperators\Class1.cs).

Operation	Results
X == y	true if x is equal to y, false otherwise
X != y	true if x is not equal to y, false otherwise
X < y	true if x is less than y, false otherwise
x > y	true if x is greater than y, false otherwise
x <= y	true if x is less than or equal to y, false otherwise
x >= y	true if x is greater than or equal to y, false otherwise

FIGURE A6.8
Results of comparison operations.

The == and != operators are referred to as the **equality operators**. The == and !=, i.e., equal and not equal operators, are defined for the Boolean type and are referred to as the **Boolean equality** operators. The == operation result is true if both operands are true or both are false, and false otherwise. The != operation result is false if both operands are true or both are false, and true otherwise. These results are summarized in Figure A6.9.

x	y	x == y	X != y
true	True	true	false
true	False	false	true
false	True	false	true
false	False	true	false

FIGURE A6.9
Results of Boolean equality operations.

The equality operators are also defined for reference types and delegate types and are developed with object-oriented programming. The comparison operators are defined for enumeration types and are developed with the enumeration types. The == and != operators are defined for the string types and are referred to as the **string equality** operators. The == and != operators compare the values of the strings. Two strings are considered equal if one of the following is true:

- Both strings have value null.
- Both strings are not null, are of equal length and have identical characters in each character position.

The **is** operator is used to check if the runtime type of an object is compatible with a specified type. This operator is described in the development of object-oriented programming.

Logical Operators

The logical **AND, &,** logical **exclusive OR, ^,** and the **inclusive OR, |,** are referred to as **logical operators**. The logical operations defined for int, uint, long and ulong integral types are referred to as **integer logical operators**. The & operator computes the bitwise logical AND of the operands. The | operator computes the bitwise logical OR of the operands. The ^ operator computes the logical exclusive OR of the two operands.

x	y	&	|	^
0	0	0	0	0
0	1	0	1	1
1	0	0	1	1
1	1	1	1	0

FIGURE A6.10
Integer bitwise logical operations.

The bit patterns associated with the results of the integer logical operators are illustrated in the Figure A6.11A program. The program's output, i.e., resultant bit patterns, is shown in Figure A6.11B.

```
namespace LogicalOperators
{
    using System;
    using System.Collections;

    public class LogicalOperators
    {

        public static int Main(string[] args)
        {
                int x = 11;

                int y = 5;

                int [ ] ia = { 0 };
                BitArray ba;

                System.Console.Write( "x bit pattern:    " );
                ia[0] = x;
                ba = new BitArray( ia );
                for (int index=0 ; index < 32; index++)
                {
                        if (ba[index]== true)
                            System.Console.Write( "1" );
                        else
                            System.Console.Write( "0" );
                }
                System.Console.WriteLine( " " );

                System.Console.Write( "y bit pattern:    " );
                ia[0] = y;
                ba = new BitArray( ia );
                for (int index=0 ; index < 32; index++)
                {
                        if (ba[index]== true)
                            System.Console.Write( "1" );
                        else
                            System.Console.Write( "0" );
                }
                System.Console.WriteLine( " " );

                System.Console.Write( "x&y bit pattern: " );
                ia[0] = x&y;
                ba = new BitArray( ia );
                for (int index=0 ; index < 32; index++)
                {
                        if (ba[index]== true)
                            System.Console.Write( "1" );
                        else
                            System.Console.Write( "0" );
                }
                System.Console.WriteLine( " " );
```

FIGURE A6.11A
Integer bitwise logical operations (LogicalOperators\Class1.cs).

The logical operators are defined for Boolean types and are referred to as **Boolean logical** operators. The results of Boolean logical operations are summarized in Figure A6.12.

The logical operators are evaluated from left to right; therefore, the expression x is evaluated before expression y in the statement

```
x & y;
```

An example of a logical operation is the following:

```
boolean x, y, z;
x = 10;
```

```
                        System.Console.Write( "x^y bit pattern: " );
                        ia[0] = x^y;
                        ba = new BitArray( ia );
                        for (int index=0 ; index < 32; index++)
                        {
                                if (ba[index]== true)
                                        System.Console.Write( "1" );
                                else
                                        System.Console.Write( "0" );
                        }
                        System.Console.WriteLine( " " );

                        System.Console.Write( "x|y bit pattern: " );
                        ia[0] = y|x;
                        ba = new BitArray( ia );
                        for (int index=0 ; index < 32; index++)
                        {
                                if (ba[index]== true)
                                        System.Console.Write( "1" );
                                else
                                        System.Console.Write( "0" );
                        }
                        System.Console.WriteLine( " " );

                        return 0;
                }
        }
}
```

FIGURE A6.11A (CONTINUED)
Integer bitwise logical operations (LogicalOperators\Class1.cs).

```
x bit pattern:   11010000000000000000000000000000
y bit pattern:   10100000000000000000000000000000
x&y bit pattern: 10000000000000000000000000000000
x^y bit pattern: 01110000000000000000000000000000
x|y bit pattern: 11110000000000000000000000000000
```

FIGURE A6.11B
Output of program illustrating integer bitwise logical operations (LogicalOperators\Class1.cs).

x	y	x & y	x ^ y	x | y
true	true	true	False	true
true	false	false	True	true
false	true	false	true	true
false	false	false	false	false

FIGURE A6.12
Summary of Boolean logical operations.

```
y = 9;

(x != 11) & (y < 10)
```

The fact that x is not equal to 11 results in a true value for the first parenthetical expression; y is less than 10, which results in a true value for the second parenthetical expression. The result of a logical AND is true when both of the operands are true; thus, the value of the overall expression is false.

Note that the precedence of the bitwise and logical operators must be observed when they are being evaluated. The logical operators are also defined for enumeration types.

Conditional Logical Operators

The **AND**, **&&**, and **OR**, **| |**, are called the **conditional logical operators**. These operators are defined for Boolean types and are referred to as **Boolean conditional logical operators**. The results of Boolean conditional logical operations are summarized in Figure A6.13. A program illustrating Boolean logical operators is shown in Figure A6.14A. The output of the program in Figure A6.14A illustrating Boolean logical operators is in Figure A6.14B.

x	y	x && y	x | | y
true	true	true	true
true	false	false	true
false	true	false	true
false	false	false	false

FIGURE A6.13
Summary of Boolean conditional logical operations.

```
namespace ConditionalLogicalOperators
{
    using System;

    public class Class1
    {
        public static int Main(string[] args)
        {
            System.Console.WriteLine( "true && true:   " + (true && true) );
            System.Console.WriteLine( "true && false:  " + (true && false) );
            System.Console.WriteLine( "false && true:  " + (false && true) );
            System.Console.WriteLine( "false && false: " + (false && false) );

            System.Console.WriteLine( "true || true:   " + (true || true)  );
            System.Console.WriteLine( "true || false:  " + (true || false) );
            System.Console.WriteLine( "false || true:  " + (false || true) );
            System.Console.WriteLine( "false || false: " + (false || false) );

            return 0;
        }
    }
}
```

FIGURE A6.14A
Program illustrating Boolean conditional operators (ConditionalLogicalOperators\Class1.cs).

```
true && true:   True
true && false:  False
false && true:  False
false && false: False
true || true:   True
true || false:  True
false || true:  True
false || false: False
```

FIGURE A6.14B
Output of program illustrating Boolean conditional operators (ConditionalLogicalOperators\Class1.cs).

Conditional Operator

The **conditional** operator (? :) is made up of three operands: the first is an expression, the second is a value assigned to the result if the expression is true, and a third operand's value is assigned to the result if the expression is false. For example, when the statement

```
result = ( w < x ) ? y : z;
```

is evaluated, the result is set to y if w is less than x. If w is greater than x, the result is set to z. The first operand expression of the conditional operator must be type Boolean.

Note!

The conditional operator (? :) is similar to the if–else construct:

```
if ( w < x )
  result = y;
else
  result = z;
```

Compound Assignment Operators

Compound assignment operators provide for the performance of a binary operation and the assignment of the result to the left-hand operand. These operators are shown in Figure A6.15.

Operator	Use	Meaning
*=	a *= b	a = a * b
/=	a */ b	a = a / b
%=	a %= b	a = a % b
+=	a += b	a = a + b
-=	a -= b	a = a - b
<<=	a <<= b	a = a << b
>>=	a >>= b	a = a >> b
&=	a &= b	a = a & b
^=	a ^= b	a = a ^ b
|=	a |= b	a = a | b

FIGURE A6.15
Compound assignment operators.

Note that:

- The equal sign always follows the other sign in a compound assignment operator.
- The compound assignment operators are right associative.
- The left-hand operand must be a variable.

The expression is evaluated in four steps:

1. The left-hand operand is evaluated to obtain a variable.
2. The value of the left-hand operand is saved to a temporary memory location and the right-hand operand is evaluated.
3. The saved value of the left-hand operand and the value of the right-hand operand are evaluated according to the first operator of the compound operator.
4. The result is assigned to the left-hand operand, which is a variable.

Consider the expression

```
amt = amt * commission;
```

This statement can also be expressed as

```
amt *= commission;
```

using the *= compound assignment operator.

Note!

C# does not have the following operators:

```
exponentiation
comma
```

Appendix A.7

Program Flow

C# provides a robust assortment of statements enabling procedures required to effect application rules and procedures. Traditionally these procedures are known as algorithms. An **algorithm** is a sequence of steps that, if followed, will produce a determined outcome. C# provides the sequence, selection and iteration statements required to implement algorithms effectively.

Statement Fundamentals

A **statement list** consists of one or more statements in sequence. When control is transferred to the start point of the statement list, control is passed to the first statement in the list. At the end of the statement, control is passed to the next statement in the list. Eventually, control reaches the end of the last statement in the list and is transferred to the end point of the statement list.

Statement lists occur in blocks. A **block** consists of an optional statement list enclosed in braces. When the statement list is omitted, the block is said to be an **empty block**. A block and statement list are shown in Figure A7.1.

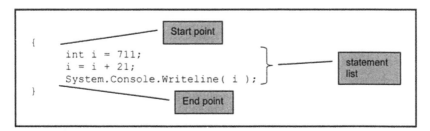

FIGURE A7.1
Block as enclosed statement list.

When control is passed to a block, it is passed to the start point of the block and transferred to the statement list, i.e., the first statement in the list. At the end point of the list, control is transferred to the end point of the block. If the block is empty, control is transferred to the end point of the block.

At times, nothing is to be done in a programming context that provides for an operation. In such cases an **empty statement** is used. Typically, the empty statement is simply a terminating semicolon, for example,

```
; // example of an empty statement
```

Control is simply passed to the end of the empty statement.

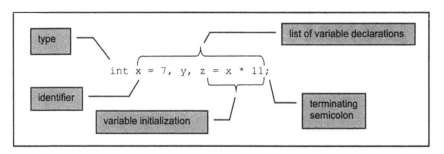

FIGURE A7.2
Local variable declaration.

Declaration statements declare a local variable or constant. A typical variable declaration is shown in Figure A7.2.

A variable declaration begins with specification of the variables type. The type is followed by a comma-separated list of the variables declared. Each variable in the list consists of an identifier and optional initial value. The initial value is specified by an "=" operator and the initial value. For example, the declaration in Figure A7.2 declared three type int variables identified as x, y and z. The variable x is initialized to integer value 7; the value z is initialized to the value of x multiplied by 11.

The declaration and initialization of multiple variables in a single statement is equivalent to the declaration of a single variable in a statement followed by a simple assignment to initialize the variable. An equivalent declaration of the variables x, y and z is shown in Figure A7.3.

```
int x;
x = 7;
int y;
int z;
z = x * 11;
```

FIGURE A7.3
Single declarations followed by simple assignment.

A **constant declaration** begins with the **const** keyword, followed by the type of the constant. The type is followed by a comma-separated list of the constants declared. Each constant in the list consists of an identifier and optional initial value. The initial value is specified by an "=" operator followed by the initial value. For example, the declaration in Figure A7.4 declared three type int constants identified as X, Y and Z. The constant X is initialized to integer value 7 and the value Z is initialized to the value of X multiplied by 11. A typical constant declaration is shown in Figure A7.4.

The **scope** of a local variable or constant begins with the declaration and ends at the end of the block in which it was declared. Formally, the scope of a name is the region of the program within which it is possible to refer to the entity declared by the name without qualification of the name. Within its scope, another variable or constant with the same name cannot be declared.

A statement can be labeled. A **labeled** statement is prefixed by a label. This statement is declared by stating an identifier, the label, followed by a colon, which in turn is followed by the referenced statement. Control can be transferred to labeled statements, as in the switch statement and iteration statements. An example of a labeled statement is shown in Figure A7.5.

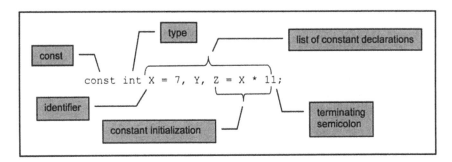

FIGURE A7.4
Local constant declaration.

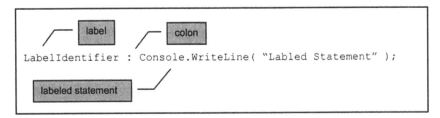

FIGURE A7.5
Example of a labeled statement.

Selection Statements

Selection statements, also known as decision statements, select one of a number of possible statements to perform based on the outcome of an evaluation expression. C# provides two types of selection statements: the if statement and the switch statement.

The **if statement** selects a statement for execution based on the evaluated value of a Boolean expression; it begins with the if keyword, followed by a Boolean expression enclosed in parentheses. The Boolean expression is followed by a single statement or a block, i.e., embedded statements. The Boolean expression in the if statement shown in Figure A7.6 is followed by a block consisting of a single statement. A typical if statement is shown in Figure A7.6.

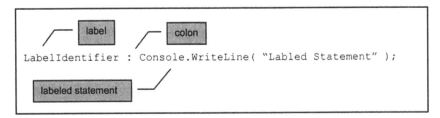

```
if ( bEOF )
{
        System. Console.WriteLine ("End Processing") ;
}
```

FIGURE A7.6
If statement.

When the Boolean expression evaluates to the value true, the statement following the expression is executed. After the statement is executed, control passes to the following statement. If the Boolean expression evaluates to false, the statement is not executed and control passes immediately to the statement following the if statement. The statement is often referred to as the **if statement body**. This body can be an empty statement, a single statement or a block of statements. If the body is empty or consists of a single statement, the if statement must end with a semicolon. For example,

```
if ( bEOF );
```

is an example of an empty if statement. Note that the if statement is terminated with a semicolon. If the body consists of several statements, i.e., embedded statements, they must be enclosed in braces as a block of code:

```
if ( bEOF ) {
    System.Console.WriteLine("Statement 1");
    System. Console.WriteLine ("Statement 2");
}
```

A semicolon is not placed after the closing brace. However, statements within the braces must be terminated with a semicolon. The flow chart in Figure A7.7 illustrates the flow of control in an if statement.

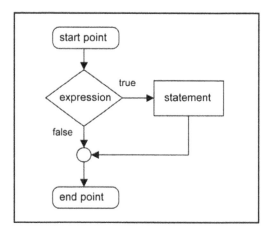

FIGURE A7.7
Flow chart illustrating flow of control.

The if statement is often referred to as the "if–then" statement. For example, if the expression is true, then perform the statement. Some languages include the word *then* as part of the if statement, but it is not included in the C# if statement.

Tip for Visual Basic Programmers!
The C# if statement does not contain then as an element.

An **else** part is used with the if statement and provides for programming either–or situations, i.e., execute one set of actions if the expression is true, but a different set of actions if the expression is false. A flowchart depicting the if–else statement flow of control is shown in Figure A7.8.

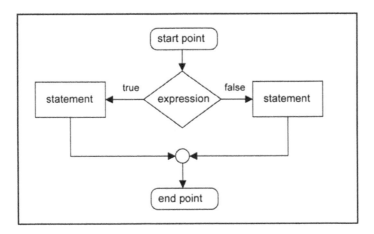

FIGURE A7.8
Flow chart illustrating if–else flow of control.

If the Boolean expression is true, the statement in the left box is performed; however, if the expression is false, the statement in the right box is performed. Note that the paths lead to the same end point. The if–else structure is said to have a single entrance, the start point, and single exit, the end point. The if–else statement is often referred to as the "if–then–else" statement.

Consider the program statements required to calculate pay based on hours worked and pay rate. For hours worked less than or equal to 40, the pay is simply the pay rate times the hours worked. However, if the hours worked exceeds 40, pay is calculated as pay rate times hours plus a premium for hours exceeding 40, often one half the regular rate. This programming circumstance is implemented with the if–else statement as illustrated with the code fragment shown in Figure A7.9.

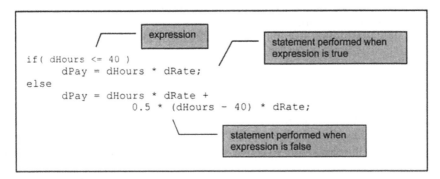

FIGURE A7.9
Pay calculation.

Note that, in the example, statements following the if and else keywords are simple and thus need not be enclosed in braces. If, however, several statements are to be performed in either case, the multiple statements must be enclosed in braces. Remember that statements following if and else keywords can be a null statement terminated with a semicolon, a simple statement terminated with a semicolon or multiple statements, each of which is terminated with a semicolon and all of the statements are enclosed in braces.

If statements and if–else statements can be nested. In nested if statements, each else statement is associated with the closest preceding if statement that has not already been

```
01  int x, y, z;
02  // value assigned to x
03  // value assigned to y
04  // value assigned to z
05  if(x > y)
06      if(x > z)
07          System.Console.WriteLine ( "x is largest!" );
08      else
09          System.Console.WriteLine ( "z is largest!" );
10  else
11      if(y > z)
12          System. Console.WriteLine ( "y is largest!" );
13      else
14          System. Console.WriteLine ( "z is largest!" );
```

FIGURE A7.10
Matching the nearest else in nested if–else statements.

associated with an else. Indentation, used to improve readability, is ignored by the compiler but is helpful in matching ifs and elses.

Consider the code fragment shown in Figure A7.10. In this example, three integer values — x, y and z — are compared. The variable representing the values is declared at line 01. Values are assigned to the variables at lines 2 through 4; x and y are compared at line 5. The values represented by the variables x and y are compared at line 5. If x is greater than y, then expression x > y is true and the following statement is performed. In this case, the statement is another if:

```
if(x > z)
```

If x is also greater than 3, the if expression evaluates to true. The statement following this if is then performed and

```
x is largest!
```

is displayed at the console. Control passes to the statement following the statement on line 14.

Consider now the case in which z > x > y. As before, the condition x > y is true and control passes to the if statement at line 6. In this case, however, the condition x > z is false, so the statement following the else is performed. That is, the statement at line 9 is executed and

```
z is largest!
```

is displayed at the console. Again, control passes to the statement following statement 14.

Now consider the case y > x > z. In this case, the condition x > y is false and control passes to the else at line 10. Remember that an else is associated with the nearest preceding if not associated with an else. Hence, the else at line 8 is associated with the if at line 6. The statement following the else at line 10 is performed. This statement contains an if expression

```
if(y > z)
```

which evaluates to true. Consequently,

```
y is largest!
```

is displayed. Again, control passes to the statement following statement 14.

Finally, when z > y > x, the condition x > y is false and control passes to else at line 10. In this case, however, the condition y > z is false, so the statement

```
z is largest!
```

is displayed at the console and control again passes to the statement following statement 14.

If and else statements can be nested to test for multiple conditions. For example, the code shown in Figure A7.11 can be used to execute different actions, depending on the value of a message code.

```
char msgCd;
// value assigned to msgCd
if (msgCd == '1')
      System.Console.WriteLine("Message 1");
else if (msgCd == '2')
      System.Console.WriteLine("Message 2");
else if (msgCd == '3')
      System.Console.WriteLine("Message 3");
System.Console.WriteLine("Next Statement");
```

FIGURE A7.11
Nested if statements testing for multiple conditions.

If msgCd is assigned the value 1, the message

```
Message 1
```

```
Next Statement
```

is displayed at the console. On the other hand, if msgCd is assigned the value 3, the message

```
Message 3
```

```
Next Statement
```

is displayed at the console.

This style of indenting saves space and is used by most programmers. The flowchart in Figure A7.12 illustrates the flow of control.

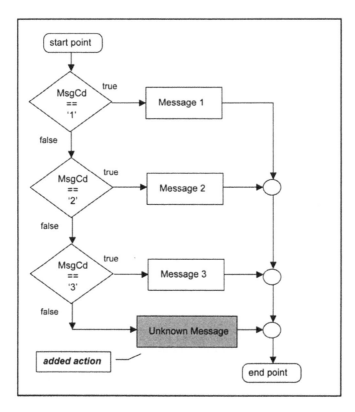

FIGURE A7.12
Nested if statements testing for multiple conditions.

Note the addition of the additional else to display

```
Unknown Message
Next Statement
```

when the value assigned to msgCd is other than 1, 2 or 3.

Programming Tip!

Handling of the unexpected is a professional programming requirement.

Braces can be used to tie an else to an if that is separated from the else by another if, as shown in Figure A7.13.

```
        string transCd;
        bool creditApproved;
        // value assigned to transCd and creditApproved
        if (transCd == "Buy")
            {
    block       if ( creditApproved )
    if              System.Console.WriteLine("Complete Sale");
            }
        else
                System.Console.WriteLine("Continue Shopping");
```

FIGURE A7.13
Using blocks to define if–else association.

This code will display

```
Complete Sale
```

when the variable transCd has the value "Buy" for completing the sale and the variable creditApproved has the value true, indicating a credit-worthy customer. When transCd code has the value "Buy" and creditApproved is false, nothing is displayed. Whenever the transaction code is not "Buy," such as when the transaction code variable has the value "Cont" for continue, the statement

```
Continue Shopping
```

is displayed, regardless of the credit worthiness of the customer.

Programming Tip!

Use of indentation and parentheses in the coding of complicated if–else logic is a good programming practice and a welcome tool in debugging.

The **switch** statement provides for programming decisions with multiple outcomes. The outcome is dependent upon the value of a controlling expression. Figure A7.14 shows a flowchart illustrating the switch's logical structure. The switch is entered with an expression value; the expression is evaluated and converted to the governing type and control is transferred to the switch block. The switch block consists of multiple sections, each associated with a specified constant value and statements to be executed when the value

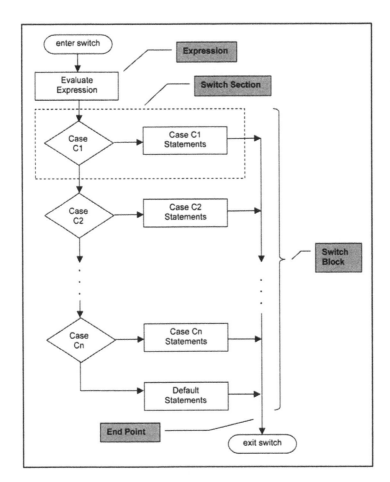

FIGURE A7.14
Illustrating switch concept and flow of control.

of the governing expression is equal to the value of the specified constant. Control is passed from switch section to the next switch section until the switch section's constant value is equal to the value of the governing expression, in which case control is passed to the switch section's statement list.

Statements in the list are executed. If the end point of the statement list is reached, control is passed to the end point of the switch. Alternately, control can be passed to another switch section. If none of the switch section constant values is equal to the value of the governing expression, an optional statement list in a default switch section is executed. The constant value of each switch section is labeled with the word *Case*. Thus, if the controlling expression evaluates to the value C2, the statement list in the block labeled "Case C2 Statements" is executed. Following execution of the statements, control is passed to the end point of the switch. Upon reaching the end point of the switch statement, control is transferred to the statement immediately following the switch statement.

C+ and C++ Programmers' Tip

Unlike C and C++, the switch does not have a "fall through" to subsequent switch sections after the switch section's statements have been executed.

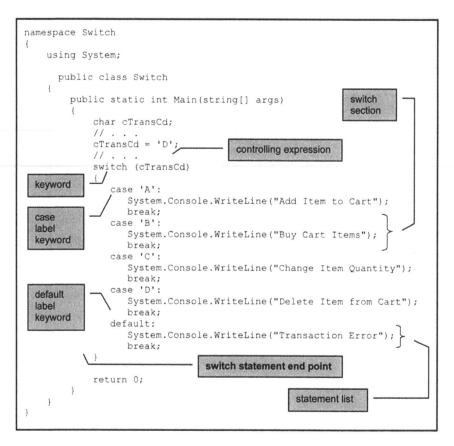

FIGURE A7.15
Switch representation of online shopper input processing.

Consider the classical problem of responding to an application user's selection. Typically, this datum is referred to as a transaction. Consider an online user's reaction signaling regarding disposition of items in a shopping cart.

The transaction code 'A' signals the intent to add a new item, 'B' implies the items in the cart are to be bought, 'C' implies the quantity of an item in the cart is to be changed and 'D' implies that an item in the cart is to be deleted. The decision process has multiple outcomes — four to be exact. The switch statement efficiently models this decision process. The code shown in Figure A7.15 effectively models the process.

The switch statement begins with the **switch** keyword, which is followed by an expression, enclosed in parentheses, called the **switch expression** or **controlling expression**. A **switch block** enclosed in braces follows the parenthesized controlling expression. The switch block consists of zero or more switch sections. A **switch section** consists of one or more switch labels followed by a statement list. The **switch labels** are **case** and **default**.

The type of the switch expression determines the type of the switch statement. In the example shown in Figure A7.15, the expression evaluates to the type of the variable cTransCd, which is a char type. The valid types for switch expressions are the following: sbyte, byte, short, ushort, int, uint, long, ulong and char. The string and enum types, discussed later, are also valid switch expression types.

The switch section begins with one or more switch labels. The switch label consists of the case keyword followed by a constant expression and terminated with a colon. For example,

```
case 'C' :
```

The constant expression type must match the type of the switch expression. Additionally, the same constant value cannot be specified in more than one case label. In Figure A7.1, the constant expressions are of type char, which is the type of the switch expression. The switch block can have at most one default switch label, which consists of the **default** keyword followed by a colon. For example,

```
default :
```

Evaluation of the switch statement is as follows. First the switch expression is evaluated. If one of the constants in the case label is equal to the value of the switch expression, control is passed to the statement list following the case label. If none of the constants in the case label is equal to the value of the switch expression, control is passed to the statement list following the default label. Additionally, if none of the constants in the case label is equal to the value of the switch expression and there is no default label, control is passed to the end point of the switch statement.

In the example shown in Figure A7.1, the switch expression value is 'D,' resulting in execution of the statement list of the switch section labeled case 'D' : which is

```
System.Console.WriteLine("Delete Item from Cart");

break;
```

The output displayed at the System console is the following:

```
Delete Item from Cart
```

Programming Tip!

Generally the default case is put at the bottom of the switch and the other case alternatives are arranged in numerical or alphabetical order for program readability.

Note that each switch section in the example, Figure A7.15, ends with a break statement, which causes control to be transferred immediately to the end point of the switch section. If the execution of a switch section is to be followed by the execution of another switch section, an explicit goto case or goto default statement must be used. Execution of the goto statement results in the immediate transfer of control to the statement immediately following the label. Figure A7.16 illustrates the use of goto case statements and the use of multiple case labels in a switch section.

When the cTransCd expression evaluates to either 'P' or 'B,' the statement list

```
System.Console.WriteLine("Buy Cart Items");

break;
```

is executed and control is transferred to the end point of the switch statement.

Note that many of the statement lists end with the statement

```
Goto case 'R';
```

When this statement is executed, control is transferred to the switch section with case label

```
case 'R';
```

Note!

The switch statements provide for programming decision procedures with multiple outcomes. In fact, a switch statement can have as many case alternatives as needed.

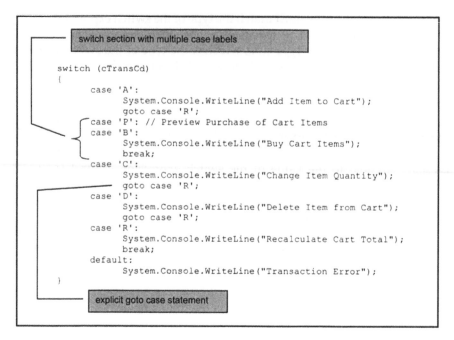

FIGURE A7.16
Illustrating multiple switch section labels and explicit goto statements.

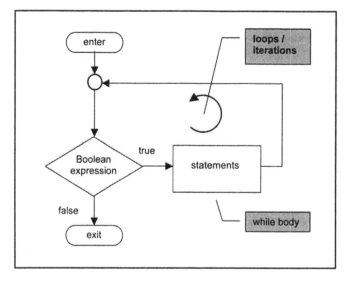

FIGURE A7.17
Logical structure of the while statement.

Iteration Statements

The **while** statement executes statements as long as a Boolean expression is true. The logical structure of the while statement is shown in Figure A7.17.

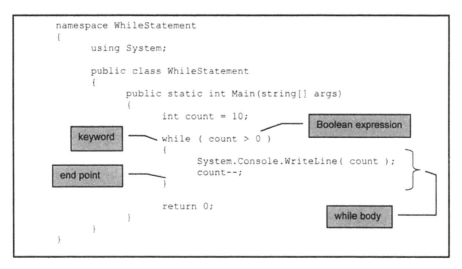

```
namespace WhileStatement
{
        using System;

        public class WhileStatement
        {
                public static int Main(string[] args)
                {
                        int count = 10;

                        while ( count > 0 )
                        {
                                System.Console.WriteLine( count );
                                count--;
                        }

                        return 0;
                }
        }
}
```

FIGURE A7.18
The while statement in a count-down loop.

Note that a controlling Boolean expression is evaluated first. If the expression is true, control is transferred to statements comprising what is known as the **while body**. After completion of the body statements, the expression is reevaluated. Again, if the statement evaluates false, control is transferred to the while body statements followed by reevaluation of the expression. This sequence of events, called **looping** or **iterating**, continues until the expression evaluates to the value false, in which case control is transferred to the statement immediately following the while statement.

The while statement begins with the **while** keyword, which is followed with a Boolean expression enclosed in parentheses. The parenthesized expression is followed by statements referred to as the while body. Figure A7.18 contains a program illustrating the while loop. The Boolean expression compares the value of the integral variable count with a constant value, 10. When the expression evaluates to true, i.e., the value of count is greater than zero, statements comprising the while body are executed. When the expression evaluates to false, i.e., count is equal to less that zero, control transfers to the end point of the while statement and subsequently to the statement immediately following the while statement. Note that the value of count is output at every iteration or loop, as well as decremented at every loop. The program's output, displayed at the System console, is:

10

9

8

7

6

5

4

3

2

1

Within the while body a **break** statement can be used to transfer control to the end point of the while statement, i.e., looping ends. When a **continue** statement is executed in the

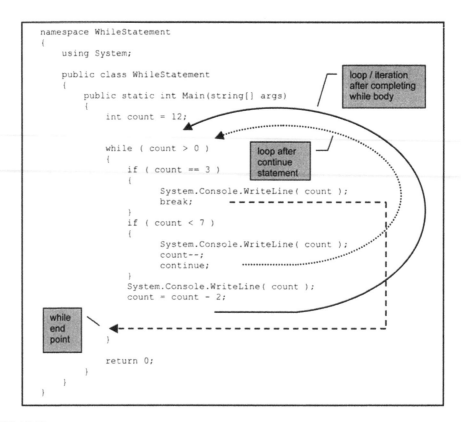

FIGURE A7.19
Illustrating effects of break and continue statements in while body.

while body, control is transferred to the beginning of the while statement, i.e., a new loop is begun. A program illustrating the effects of the continue and break statements in a while body is shown in Figure A7.19.

The while statement is entered with the Boolean expression evaluating to true, 12 is greater than zero, resulting in execution of the statements comprising the while body. The if statements are not executed, and count is not equal to 3 and is greater than 7. Statements displaying count and decrementing count by two are executed and control returns to the beginning of the while statement. This loop is continued until count is decremented to value 6, at which point the if statement comparing count and the constant 7 evaluates true. The block of statements

```
System.Console.WriteLine( count );

count--;

continue;
```

is executed. The value of count is displayed at the console, count is decremented by one and the continue statement is executed. When the continue statement is executed within a while statement, control is transferred to the beginning of the while statement. This process is continued in subsequent loops until count is decremented to the value 3. At that point, the if statement comparing count and the constant 3 evaluates true and the block of statements associated with the if is executed:

```
System.Console.WriteLine( count );

break;
```

In this case, the value of count is displayed at the console and the break statement is executed. When a break statement is executed within a while statement, control is transferred to the end point of the while statement and subsequently to the statement following the while statement. The program produces the following output:

```
12
10
8
6
5
4
3
```

Note!

The statements comprising the while body are only executed if the Boolean expression is true. In other words, if the expression is false when execution of the while statement commences, the statements comprising the while body are not executed.

The **do** statement conditionally executes statements one or more times. The logical structure of the do statement is illustrated in Figure A7.20.

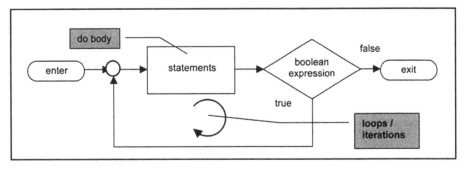

FIGURE A7.20
Logical structure of the do statement.

The do statement is entered and the statements comprising the do body are immediately executed. After all of the statements comprising the do body are executed, a controlling expression is evaluated. If the expression evaluates to true, control is transferred to the beginning of the do statement, i.e., control is looped to the beginning. This process is continued until the expression evaluates false and control passes to the statement following the do statement.

Figure A7.21 illustrates the do statement, which begins with the do keyword followed by parenthesized statements comprising the do body. The parenthesized statements, i.e., the do body, are followed by the keyword **while** which in turn is followed by a parenthesized Boolean expression. The do statement is often referred to as the **do while** statement. Note that the do statement is terminated with a semicolon.

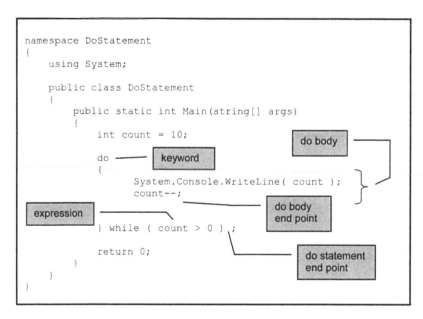

FIGURE A7.21
Illustrating the do statement.

In Figure A7.21, the variable count is assigned the value 10. When the do statement is executed, the do body statements are executed:

```
System.Console.WriteLine( count );
count--;
```

The value of the variable count is displayed at the console and decremented to 9. The program reaches the do body end point and the controlling expression is evaluated. The value of the variable count is 9, the expression evaluates true and control is transferred to the start of the do statement. This looping process is continued until the expression evaluates false.

The program's console display is as follows:

```
10
9
8
7
6
5
4
3
2
1
```

Within the do body, a **break** statement can be used to transfer control to the end point of the do statement, i.e., looping ends. When a **continue** statement is executed in the do body, control is transferred to the beginning of the do statement, i.e., a new loop is begun. A program illustrating the effects of the continue and break statements in a do body is shown in Figure A7.22.

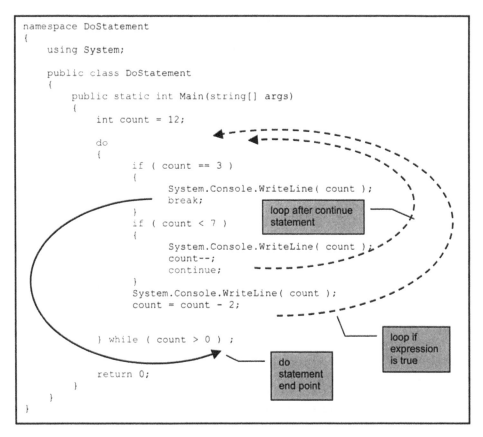

FIGURE A7.22
Illustrating effects of break and continue statements in the do body.

The program's console display is as follows:

12

10

8

6

5

4

3

The do statement is entered with a count value of 12, and the statements comprising the do body are executed. The if statements are not executed when count is not 3 and is less than 7. The statements displaying count at the console and decrementing count by 2 are executed. The Boolean expression is evaluated and evaluates to true and the count value 10 is greater than zero, resulting in control returning to the start of the do statement. This loop is continued until count is decremented to value 6, at which point the if statement comparing count and the constant 7 evaluates true. The block of statements

```
System.Console.WriteLine( count );
count--;
continue;
```

is executed. The value of count is displayed at the console, count is decremented by one and the continue statement is executed. When the continue statement is executed within a do statement, control is transferred to the beginning of the do statement. This process is continued in subsequent loops until count is decremented to the value 3. At that point, the if statement comparing count and the constant 3 evaluates true and the block of statements associated with the if is executed:

```
System.Console.WriteLine( count );
break;
```

In this case, the value of count is displayed at the console and the break statement is executed. When a break statement is executed within a do statement, control is transferred to the end point of the do statement and subsequently to the statement following the do statement.

Note!

The statements comprising the do body are executed prior to evaluation of the Boolean expression. The statements comprising the do body are executed again and again, only if the Boolean expression evaluates to true.

The **for** statement evaluates a list of initializing expressions, evaluates a Boolean expression and repeatedly executes statements comprising a for body as long as the Boolean expression evaluates true. A flow chart illustrating the for statement's logical structure is shown in Figure A7.23. The for statement begins with the for keyword, which is followed

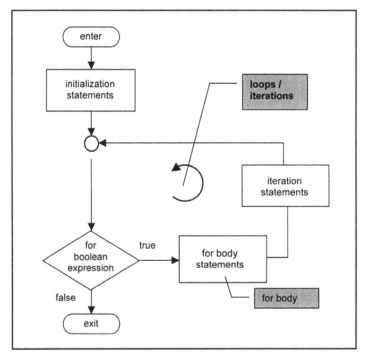

FIGURE A7.23
Logical structure of the for statement.

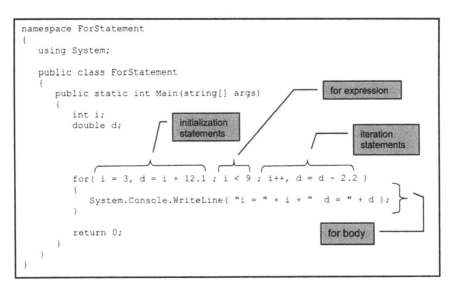

FIGURE A7.24
Illustrating the for statement.

by a parenthesized semicolon list consisting of initialization statements; a controlling Boolean expression, referred to as the for expression; and iteration statements. The parenthesized initialization statements, controlling for expression and iteration statements, are followed by statements comprising the for body. When the for statement is executed, the initialization statements are evaluated. The Boolean for expression is evaluated. If the expression is true, the statements comprising the for body are executed and then the iteration statements are executed.

The expression evaluation, execution of the for body statements and execution of the iteration statements are repeatedly performed as long as the Boolean for expression evaluates to true. An example of a for statement is shown in Figure A7.24. In the listing, the initialization statements consist of a list of comma-separated statements

```
i = 3, d = i + 12.1
```

The variable i is initialized to the value 3 and the variable d to the value 15.1, i.e., the current value of i plus the 12.1. Note that the initialization statements can consist of a local declaration statement. The scope of variables declared in the initialization extends to the end of the for body statements, which are in a comma-separated list.

The for expression is optional but, if present, must be a Boolean expression. In the example, the Boolean expression compares the value of the variable i with the constant 9.

```
i < 9
```

When the expression is true, the body of the for statement is executed, the iteration statements are executed and control returns to the top of the for statement. The for body, in this case, consists of the statement

```
System.Console.WriteLine( "i = " + i + "  d = " + d );
```

which displays the values of the variables i and d at the console.

The iteration statements are then executed:

```
i++, d = d - 2.2
```

Note that the iteration statements are optional and, if present, are a comma-separated list of statements. In the example, the statements decrement the value of i and subtract 2.2 from the value of d.

Control is transferred to the start of the for statement. The process of evaluating the control expression, executing the for body and executing the iteration statement is repeated until the control for expression evaluates to the value false.

The program output is

```
i = 3   d = 15.1
i = 4   d = 12.899999999999999
i = 5   d = 10.7
i = 6   d = 8.5
i = 7   d = 6.3
```

Note!

The initialization statements are only executed once — at the beginning of the for statement.

Note that the break statement can be used to transfer control to the end point of the "for" statement and thus to the statement immediately following the for statement. Additionally, the continue statement can be used to transfer control to the end point of the for body and thus another execution of the for loop if the expression evaluates to the value true. An example of a for statement using a break statement to stop looping is shown in Figure A7.25.

```
namespace ForStatementAdvanced
{
    using System;

    public class ForStatementAdvanced
    {
        public static int Main(string[] args)
        {
            int i = 4;

            for ( string s = " Loop" ;  ; i-- )
            {
                System.Console.WriteLine( i + s );
                s = s + " Loop";
                if ( i < 2 ) break;
            }

            return 0;
        }
    }
}
```

when break statement
is executed

FIGURE A7.25
Using the break statement to break out of an endless loop.

When the break statement is executed, control is passed to the end point of the for statement, ending looping or iteration. The program's output is the following:

```
4 Loop
3 Loop Loop
2 Loop Loop Loop
1 Loop Loop Loop
```

Without execution of the break statement, the for statement would loop forever.

Jump Statements

The **jump** statements transfer control. The program point to which the control is to be transferred is referred to as the **target** of the jump statement. The **break** statement transfers control to the end point, and thus exits, an enclosing switch, while, do, for or foreach statement. The **continue** statement starts a new iteration or loop of the enclosing while, do, for or foreach statement. When the looping statements are nested, the continue applies only to the innermost, often referred to as the nearest, looping statement. The **goto** statement transfers control to a labeled statement. This statement begins with the keyword goto, followed by the label of a labeled statement. An example of the goto statement is shown in Figure A7.26. When the expression i == 3 evaluates to the value true, the goto statement is executed and control is transferred to the statement labeled exitPoint.

```
namespace GoToStatement
{
    using System;

    public class GoToStatement
    {
        public static int Main(string[] args)
        {

                                          Endless loop
            for (int i =0;     ;i++)
            {
                Console.WriteLine( i );
                if ( i == 3 )
                    goto exitPoint;                Unconditional
            }                                      transfer of
                                                   control
            exitPoint:
                Console.WriteLine( "Exit Point" );

            return 0;
        }
    }
}
```

FIGURE A7.26
Using the goto statement to exit a loop.

The program output is

0

1

2

3

```
Exit Point
```

The goto keyword can also be used to transfer control to switch sections in a switch statement body.

Other jump type statements include the following:

- The **return** statement is used to effect an exit, transfer control, from the current function and return a value.

- The **throw** statement throws an exception when an exceptional condition arises and enables exception handling.

Appendix A.8

Exceptions

Traditionally, when an abnormal condition was encountered, control was passed to the system. Unable to handle problems for all applications, the system stopped the program abruptly, a condition referred to as **abnormal termination**. Generally, the system issued a cryptic message intended to describe the problem and listed selected memory locations intended to provide the developer with information required for debugging.

C# provides an alternative approach to handling abnormal conditions. When a problem is encountered, an exception is thrown. Control is passed to a block of code, called a **handler**, intended to handle the exception, not the system. The handler assumes control and the program block throwing the exception expires. Handlers are designed to correct the abnormal condition or provide for "graceful" program termination. In an abnormal termination, communication links are not closed and volatile data are not saved, but in a "graceful" program, termination data are saved and communication links are properly closed.

Exception Class

Exceptions fall generally into two categories: system exceptions thrown by the runtime when an abnormal condition arises during program execution and application exceptions thrown by a user program. The base class for representing all exceptions is the Exception class summarized in Figure A8.1. The Exception class derives directly from the Object class and is extended by the SystemException class to represent system exceptions. The .NET Framework contains built-in exception classes derived from the SystemException class, including the classes listed in Figure A8.2.

Exception Handling Overview

When an exception (referred to as **thrown**) occurs, the system searches for the nearest catch clause. This clause begins with the **catch** keyword. The search begins at the try statement that encloses the method giving rise to the exception. A **try** statement begins with the try keyword. The search continues until a catch clause is located that can handle the exception. A catch clause can specify the type of exception handled; if it does not specify a type of exception, it can handle any exception. When an appropriate catch clause is found, program control passes to the first statement in the catch clause.

public class **Exception** : ISerializable	
Hierarchy	
Object Exception	
Public Instance Constructors	
public **Exception**( );	Initializes a new instance of the class.
public **Exception**(string *message*);	Initializes a new instance of the class with the Message property value *message*.
public **Exception**(string *message*, Exception *innerException*);	Initializes a new instance of the class with the Message property value *message* and InnerException value *innerException*.
Public Instance Properties	
public virtual string **HelpLink** {get; set;}	A uniform resource name (URN) or uniform resource locator (URL) representing a link to help file associated with the exception.
public Exception **InnerException** {get;}	An exception object representing the root or causative exception, referred to as the inner exception. Default is the null reference. A null reference indicates the exception was not caused by another exception.
public virtual string **Message** {get;}	A text string describing the exception. Default is the empty string.
public virtual string **Source** {get; set;}	A string representing the name of the application or object causing the error. The default is the name of the assembly where the exception was created.
public virtual string **StackTrace** {get;}	A string representing the name of the application or object causing the error. The default is the name of the assembly where the exception was created.
public MethodBase **Target** {get;}	A MethodBase object that provides information about the method or constructor that creates the exception.
Public Instance Methods	
public virtual Exception **GetBaseException** ( )	Returns an exception object representing the original, that is, the innermost, exception.
public virtual void **GetObjectData** (SerializationInfo *info*, StreamingContext context);	Sets a SerializationInfo object, *info*, with information about the exception where the StreamingContext object, *context*, contains information about the source or destination of the serialized stream. Note that a SerializationInfo object contains information needed to serialize or deserialize an object.
public override string **ToString** ( )	Returns a string representing the fully qualified name of the exception and possibly the error message.
Protected Instance Constructor	
protected **Exception** (SerializationInfo *info*, StreamingContext context);	Initializes a new instance of the class with SerializationInfo object, *info*, information and StreamingContext object, *context*, information about the source or destination of the serialized stream.
Protected Instance Properties	
protected int **HResult** {get; set;}	Numerical code assigned to the exception.

FIGURE A8.1
Exception class summary.

A "finally" clause can be used to specify code executed regardless of how the try clause is exited. This clause begins with the **finally** keyword. Finally clause statements are executed after the try block is exited or the catch block is executed. The finally block is typically used to release resources. A program illustrating exception handling is shown in Figure A8.3A. The statement

```
r = d / q
```

results in a divide-by-zero condition because q has been assigned the value 0.

Name	Exceptional Condition Description
OutOfMemoryException	Memory allocation failure.
StackOverflowException	Execution stack exhaustion.
NullReferenceException	Required reference is null.
TypeInitializationException	No catch clause for exception thrown in a static constructor.
InvalidCastException	Explicit conversion failure.
ArrayTypeMismatchException	Element type and array type mismatch.
IndexOutOfRangeException	Index value less than zero or greater than the array's upper bound.
MulticastNotSupportedException	Delegate combining operation fails.
ArithmeticException	Arithmetic operation failure.
DivideByZeroException	Division of integral value by zero.
OverflowException	Arithmetic operation overflow.

FIGURE A8.2
Exceptions represented by classes in namespace System.

```
using System;

namespace ExceptionBasics
{
      class HandleException
      {
            static void Main(string[] args)
            {
                  int d = 1, q=0, r;

                  try
                  {
                        r = d/q;
                  }
                  catch(ArithmeticException e)
                  {
                        Console.WriteLine("Message:     " + e.Message);
                        Console.WriteLine("Source:      " + e.Source);
                        Console.WriteLine("StackTrace:  " + e.StackTrace);
                        Console.WriteLine("TargetSite:  " + e.TargetSite);
                  }
                  finally
                  {
                        Console.WriteLine("Finally Clause");
                  }
            }
      }
}
```

FIGURE A8.3A
Program illustrating exception handling (ExceptionBasics\HandleExceptions.cs).

When the exception is thrown, the search for the nearest appropriate catch clause is initiated. The clause

```
catch(DivideByZeroException e)
{
      Console.WriteLine("Message:     " + e.Message);
      Console.WriteLine("Source:      " + e.Source);
      Console.WriteLine("StackTrace:  " + e.StackTrace);
      Console.WriteLine("TargetSite:  " + e.TargetSite);
}
```

will handle a divide-by-zero exception. Note that the DividebyZeroException class is derived from the ArithmeticException class. As such, the clause

```
catch(ArithmeticException e)
{
    Console.WriteLine("Message:      " + e.Message);
    Console.WriteLine("Source:       " + e.Source);
    Console.WriteLine("StackTrace: " + e.StackTrace);
    Console.WriteLine("TargetSite: " + e.TargetSite);
}
```

would also catch the DivideByZeroException.

Control is passed to the first statement in the catch clause. In this case, the properties of the exception are written to the console. After the catch clause is executed control is passed to a finally clause if it exists. If an exceptional condition is not encountered in the try clause, control is also passed to a finally clause. The program's output is shown in Figure A8.3B.

```
Message:        Attempted to divide by zero.
Source:         ExceptionBasics
StackTrace:        at ExceptionBasics.HandleException.Main(String[] args)
TargetSite:     Void Main(System.String[])
Finally Clause
```

FIGURE A8.3B
Output of program illustrating exception handling (ExceptionBasics\HandleExceptions.cs).

Note!

Try–catch–finally statements enable exceptional conditions to be handled within the application, thus enabling "graceful" recovery.

Exception Handling Statements

The try, catch and finally clauses enable the robust handling of exceptional conditions within the application. There are three combinations:

- Try clause followed by a catch clause consisting of one or more catch blocks
- Try clause followed by a finally clause
- Try clause followed by a catch clause consisting of one or more catch blocks followed by a finally clause

---

Try–Catch Statement

The **try–catch** statement provides for exception handling within an application The syntax of this statement is shown in Figure A8.4.

```
try { try-body }
catch ( exception-declaration-1 ) { catch-body-1 }
catch ( exception-declaration-2 ) { catch-body-2 }

...
or
try try-body catch { catch-body }
```

try-body	Code block containing statements with potential for creating abnormal or exceptional conditions.
exception_declaration	Declaration of the exception object associated with the catch clause.
catch-body	Code block containing statements defining the exception handler.

FIGURE A8.4
Try–catch statement syntax.

The try block contains code with the potential for creating exceptional conditions. If the try block completes without an exception, control passes to the next statement. If, on the other hand, an exception occurs, control passes to the closest catch statement declared to handle the exception. Each catch clause contains an optional exception declaration and a code block. The catch clause can have an argument, i.e., an exception-declaration, that specifies the exception handled. The catch clause can also be declared without an exception-declaration, in which case any type of exception is handled.

When multiple catch clauses are declared, the order of catch statements is important. The catch block intended to catch a specific exception should be placed before a catch block intended to catch a more general exception. For example, the catch block to catch a divide-by-zero exception should be placed before the catch block intended to catch an arithmetic error. Note that the divide-by-zero exception is a represented by a class inheriting the class representing the more general arithmetic exception. Catch block selection is performed by matching the type of exception with the type of exception declared in the catch statement.

Try–Finally Statement

The try–finally statement provides a program flow structure in which control is passed to the finally block of the try–finally statement, regardless of how the try block is exited. Statements in the finally block are always executed. The try–finally statement syntax is shown in Figure A8.5.

```
try { try-body } finally { finally-body }
```

try-body	Code block containing statements with potential for creating abnormal or exceptional conditions.
finally-body	Code block containing statements executed regardless of the try block exit.

FIGURE A8.5
Try–finally statement syntax.

Try–Catch–Finally Statement

The catch and finally clauses can be used together with the try clause to handle exceptional conditions in the catch clauses and handle procedures that should always be performed in the finally clause. The program HandleExceptions.cs, illustrated in Figure A8.3A, illustrates use of try, catch and finally.

User-Defined Exceptions

The Exception class is extended by the ApplicationException class (Figure A8.6) to represent application exceptions. Classes developed to represent new application exceptions should be derived from the ApplicationException class.

public class **ApplicationException** : Exception	
Hierarchy	
Object Exception ApplicationException	
Public Instance Constructors	
public **ApplicationException**( );	Initializes a new instance of the class.
public **ApplicationException**(string *message*);	Initializes a new instance of the class with the Message property value *message*.
public **ApplicationException**(string *message*.; Exception *innerException*);	Initializes a new instance of the class with the Message property value *message* and InnerException value *innerException*.
Protected Instance Constructor	
protected **ApplicationException** (SerializationInfo *info*, StreamingContext *context*);	Initializes a new instance of the class with SerializationInfo object, *info*, information and StreamingContext object, *context*, information about the source or destination of the serialized stream.

FIGURE A8.6
ApplicationException class.

A user-defined custom exception is declared in a class derived from the ApplicationException class. Consider an application that has to open a special connection. Failure to open the connection could result in application failure and should be signaled by an exception. A user-defined exception, ConnectionException, is defined in Figure A8.7. The definition includes a constructor that calls the base class constructor with parameter used to set the Message property.

Tip!

End the name of the exception's class with the word "Exception" as in "Connection-Exception."

```
using System;

namespace UserExceptionBasics
{
    public class ConnectionException : ApplicationException
    {
        public ConnectionException(string msg)
            : base (msg)
        {
        }
    }
}
```

FIGURE A8.7
Definition of a user-defined exception (UserExceptionBasics\ConnectionException.cs).

Throw Statement

The **throw** statement is used to signal an abnormal condition during program execution. The syntax of the throw statement is given in Figure A8.8.

throw [*exception-expression*]	
exception-expression	Optional expression declaring the exception object. When omitted the current exception object in a catch clause is thrown.

FIGURE A8.8
Throw statement syntax.

The thrown exception is an instance of a class derived from the System.Exception class. When an exception is thrown, control is transferred to the nearest catch clause that can handle the exception. The transfer of control is unconditional. If no suitable catch clause is identified, an implementation termination is effected. An example of the use of a user-defined exception is shown in Figure A8.9.

The application calls the OpenConnection method with the statement

```
ua.OpenConnection();
```

within a try statement.

The OpenConnection method consists of a single statement

```
throw new ConnectionException("Connection failure");
```

that throws a new instance of the ConnectionException class in which the Message property is initialized to the value "Connection failure."

The search for the catch statement begins and continues to the Main method, where a suitable handler is identified. Control passes to the catch block, resulting in execution of statement writing a message to the Console. The message includes the value of the expression

```
e.Message
```

where e is the thrown ConnectionException object. Note that the exception's Message property was initialized to the value "Connection failure."

```
using System;

namespace UserExceptionBasics
{
      class UserApplication
      {
            static void Main(string[] args)
            {
                  try
                  {
                        UserApplication ua = new UserApplication();
                        ua.OpenConnection();
                  }
                  catch (ConnectionException e)        Handler for
                  {                                    ConnectionException
                        Console.WriteLine("Message: " + e.Message);
                  }
            }

            public void OpenConnection()              ConnectionException
            {                                          thrown
                  throw new ConnectionException("Connection failure");
            }
      }
}
```

FIGURE A8.9
Program illustrating use of a user-defined exception (UserExceptionBasics\UserApplication.cs).

Appendix A.9

Inheriting Classes

Inheritance is the ability of a class, called the derived class, to extend the functionality of a base class. A class hierarchy diagram represents the relationship between a derived class and its base class. Figure A9.1 shows several forms of a class hierarchy diagram.

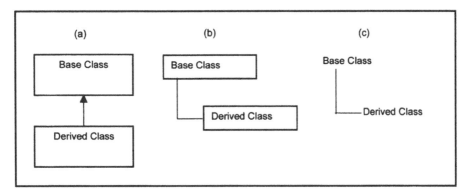

FIGURE A9.1
Class hierarchy diagram.

The derived class inherits all of the members of the base class except for instance constructors, static constructors and destructors of its base class. The class declaration syntax illustrated in Figure A9.2 provides for inheritance. The Account class, shown in Figure A9.3A, represents a basic account. The account provides for representation of account identification and balance; the class also provides for management of these data. A class representing a checking account is shown in Figure A9.3B.

[attributes] [modifiers] class *identifier* [: *base-list*] { *body* } [;]	
attributes	Provide additional information about the class.
modifiers	Modify the declaration. Valid values are new, abstract, sealed and the access modifiers. The access modifiers are private, protected, internal and public. The protected and private modifiers are only allowed on contained, often referred to as nested, classes.
identifier	Class name.
base-list	Comma-separated list containing at most one base class and the implemented interfaces. (Interfaces are described in Appendix A.10.)
body	Class member declaration. Allowed members include the following: Constructors, Destructors, Constants, Fields, Methods, Properties, Indexers and Operators.

FIGURE A9.2
Class declaration syntax.

```
using System;

namespace InheritanceBasics
{
      public class Account
      {
            int acctNo;
            decimal acctBalance;

            public void setAcctNo(int an)
            {
                  acctNo = an;
            }
            public void setAcctBalance(decimal ab)
            {
                  acctBalance = ab;
            }
            public int getAcctNo()
            {
                  return acctNo;
            }
            public decimal getAcctBalance()
            {
                  return acctBalance;
            }
      }
}
```

FIGURE A9.3A
Account class (InheritanceBasics\Account.cs).

```
using System;

namespace InheritanceBasics                    ┌──────────────────────────┐
{                                              │ Fields and methods of    │
      public class CheckingAccount : Account   │ Account class inherited by│
      {                                        │ CheckingAccount class     │
            public static decimal interestRate;└──────────────────────────┘

            public decimal interestEarned( )
            {
                  return interestRate * getAcctBalance();
            }
      }
}
```

FIGURE A9.3B
CheckingAccount class (InheritanceBasics\CheckingAccount.cs).

The class declaration provides for the inheritance of the fields and methods of the Account class.

```
public class CheckingAccount : Account { . . . }
```

The class declares a new field, interestRate, common to all checking accounts. The class also declares a method, interestEarned, that computes the product of the field interestRate and the inherited field acctBalance. Note that acctBalance is declared with private access and thus is only accessible by members of the Account class. Thus the expression

```
return interestRate * acctBalance;
```

is *invalid*. The getAcctBalance method that returns the value of the field acctBalance is public and thus is accessible, therefore the statement

```
return interestRate * getAcctBalance();
```

is *valid*.

The class UsingInheritance (Figure A9.3C) illustrates use of the class CheckingAcount. The statement

```
CheckingAccount.interestRate = 0.030m;
```

assigns the interest rate value common to all instances of the CheckingAccount class. An instance of the CheckingAccount class is created and initialized with the statement

```
CheckingAccount ca = new CheckingAccount( );
```

```
using System;

namespace InheritanceBasics
{
    class UsingInheritance
    {
        static void Main(string[] args)
        {
            CheckingAccount.interestRate = 0.030m;

            CheckingAccount ca = new CheckingAccount( );

            ca.setAcctBalance(1000.00m);

            Console.WriteLine("Interest Earned: "
                + ca.interestEarned() );
        }
    }
}
```

FIGURE A9.3C
UsingInheritance class (InheritanceBasics\UsingInheritance.cs).

The account balance is set by calling the inherited method setAcctBalance

```
ca.setAcctBalance(1000.00m);
```

The interest earned by the account represented by the object ca is given by the statement

```
Console.WriteLine("Interest Earned: " + ca.interestEarned() );
```

The output is shown in Figure A9.3D.

```
Interest Earned: 30
Press any key to continue_
```

FIGURE A9.3D
Output of UsingInheritance class (InheritanceBasics\UsingInheritance.cs).

Protected Access Modifier

A member declared **protected** is accessible from within the class in which it is declared and from any class derived from the class in which it is declared. Struct members cannot have protected access modification because the struct type cannot be inherited. For example, the acctBalance field in the Account class can be declared protected as shown in Figure A9.4A.

As a protected member, acctBalance is accessible in classes derived from Account. For example, the CheckingAccount class derived from the Account class accesses the inherited member as if it were declared public (Figure A9.4B).

```
using System;

namespace ProtectedAccess
{
        public class Account                    ┌─ Protected access member
        {
                int acctNo;
                protected decimal acctBalance;

                public void setAcctNo(int an)
                {
                        acctNo = an;
                }
                public void setAcctBalance(decimal ab)
                {
                        acctBalance = ab;
                }
                public int getAcctNo()
                {
                        return acctNo;
                }
                public decimal getAcctBalance()
                {
                        return acctBalance;
                }
        }
}
```

FIGURE A9.4A
Account class with protected members (ProtectedAccess\Account.cs).

```
using System;

namespace ProtectedAccess
{                                                    ┌─ acctBalance is
        public class CheckingAccount : Account          declared protected
        {                                                in the Account
                public static decimal interestRate;      class and thus is
                                                         accessible in
                public decimal interestEarned( )         derived classes
                {
                        return interestRate * acctBalance;
                }
        }
}
```

FIGURE A9.4B
CheckingAccount class accessing inherited protected member (ProtectedAccess\CheckingAccount.cs).

In this case, because CheckingAccount is derived from Account, acctBalance is accessible:

```
return interestRate * acctBalance;
```

The class UsingProtectedAccess illustrates use of the CheckingAccount class, as shown in Figure A9.4C.

Although acctBalance is protected, it is accessible within the class CheckingAccount. However, it is not accessible in the class UsingProtectedAccess which is not derived from the class Account. Thus, the statement

```
a.acctBalance = 1000.00m;
```

is **invalid**. The output is shown in Figure A9.4D.

```
using System;

namespace ProtectedAccess
{
    class UsingProtectedAccess
    {
        static void Main(string[] args)
        {
            CheckingAccount.interestRate = 0.030m;

            Account a = new Account();
            // Protected access
            // a.acctBalance = 1000.00m;

            CheckingAccount ca = new CheckingAccount();
            ca.setAcctBalance(1000.00m);

            Console.WriteLine("Interest Earned: "
                + ca.interestEarned());
        }
    }
}
```

FIGURE A9.4C
UsingProtectedAccess class (ProtectedAccess\UsingProtectedAccess.cs).

```
Interest Earned: 30
Press any key to continue_
```

FIGURE A9.4D
Output of UsingInheritance class (ProtectedAccess\Using ProtectedAccess.cs).

Sealed Access Modification

A **sealed** class cannot be inherited; the sealed class modifier is used to prevent unintended derivation. Selected classes in the .NET Framework are sealed classes, for example,

Class	Description
HttpRequest	Enables access to HTTP values sent in a Web request
HttpResponse	Encapsulates HTTP response information

Consider a special account class representing unique conditions not present in any other type of account. This account should be declared sealed to prevent unintentional derivation. For example, the class is declared with the statements

```
public sealed class SpecialAccount { }
```

Derivation from this class, as in

```
public class InvalidDerivation : SpecialAccount
```

is **invalid** and will give rise to a compile time error. A struct is implicitly sealed because it cannot be inherited.

Hiding, Overriding and Virtual Keywords

Hiding of a member occurs when a member with the same name is declared in a derived class:

Methods — A method declared in a class hides all base class non-method members with the same name and all base class methods with the same signature.

Constants, Fields, Properties — These members, declared in the derived class or struct, hide all.

Events and Types — These base class members have the same name.

Indexers — An indexer declared in the derived class or struct hides all base class indexers with the same signature.

For example, consider the classes defined in Figure A9.5A. The method interestEarned is defined in the class Account and also in the class CheckingAccount derived from the class Account.

```
public class Account
{
        public decimal interestEarned()
        {
                return 0.10m;
        }
}

public class CheckingAccount : Account
{
        public decimal interestEarned()
        {
                return 0.20m + base.interestEarned();
        }
}
```

Warning issued at compilation indicating InterestEarned in Account class is hidden

FIGURE A9.5A
Hidden method.

At compilation, a warning is issued:

```
warning CS0108: The keyword new is required on warning CS0108: The
keyword new is required on
'HidingBasics.CheckingAccount.interestEarned()' because it hides
inherited member 'HidingBasics.Account.interestEarned()'
```

The warning is eliminated with the **new** modifier, which indicates that the declared method is a "new implementation" of the inherited member (Figure A9.5B).

Note!

The new modifier explicitly hides an inherited base class member.

The **base** keyword is used to access members of the base class from within a derived class. Use of the base keyword is permitted within the derived class in order to:

- Call a base class overridden method, as in Figures A9.5A and A9.5B
- Call a base class constructor in the creation of derived class instances

```
public class Account
{
        public decimal interestEarned()
        {
                return 0.10m;
        }
}

public class CheckingAccount : Account
{
        public new decimal interestEarned()
        {
                return 0.20m + base.interestEarned();
        }
}
```

FIGURE A9.5B
New modifiers indicate intentional hiding.

For example, the interestEarned method of the base class Account is called within the derived class CheckingAccount method interestEarned with the expression

```
base.interestEarned()
```

A member modified by the keyword **virtual** is referred to as a virtual member. An overriding member in a derived class can change the implementation of a virtual member. At runtime, the type of the invoking object is determined and the overriding member of the closest derived class is called. The virtual modifier can be used to modify method declarations because methods are non-virtual by default. The virtual modifier cannot be used with the static, abstract and override modifiers. The virtual modifier can also be used to modify property declarations, but cannot be used on a static property declaration.

The **override** modifier declares a new implementation of a member inherited from a base class. Override method modification is restricted:

- A non-virtual or static member cannot be overridden.
- The accessibility of the overridden method cannot be changed.
- The new, static, virtual and abstract modifiers cannot be used in an override method declaration.

Override property declarations must specify the same access modifier, type and name as the inherited property and must override a virtual, abstract or inherited property. An example of a class declared with virtual modification is shown in Figure A9.6A. The method interestEarned is declared with virtual modification.

```
using System;

namespace HidingBasics
{
        public class Account
        {
                public virtual decimal interestEarned()
                {
                        return 0.10m;
                }
        }
}
```

FIGURE A9.6A
Account class (HidingBasics/Account.cs).

```
using System;

namespace HidingBasics
{
     public class CheckingAccount : Account
     {
          public override decimal interestEarned()
          {
               return 0.20m + base.interestEarned();
          }
     }
}
```

FIGURE A9.6B
CheckingAccount class (HidingBasics/CheckingAccount.cs).

The class CheckingAccount in Figure A9.6B inherits the Account class and overrides the base class method interestEarned.

If the override modifier was not used, a compilation warning would be raised:

```
warning CS0114: 'HidingBasics.CheckingAccount.interestEarned()'
hides inherited member 'HidingBasics.Account.interestEarned()'.
To make the current member override that implementation, add the
override keyword. Otherwise add the new keyword.
```

A class SpecialCheckingAccount (Figure A9.6C) inherits the CheckingAccount class. A class ComputeInterest illustrates use of the classes Account, CheckingAccount and SpecialCheckingAccount, as shown in Figure A9.6D. Figure A9.6E shows the output.

```
using System;

namespace HidingBasics
{
     public class SpecialCheckingAccount : CheckingAccount
     {
     }
}
```

FIGURE A9.6C
SpecialCheckingAccount class (HidingBasics/SpecialCheckingAccount.cs).

```
using System;

namespace HidingBasics
{
     class ComputeInterest
     {
          static void Main(string[] args)
          {
               Account a = new Account();
               Console.WriteLine("Account:                "
                    + a.interestEarned());

               CheckingAccount ca = new CheckingAccount();
               Console.WriteLine("CheckingAccount:        "
                    + ca.interestEarned());

               SpecialCheckingAccount sca =
                    new SpecialCheckingAccount();
               Console.WriteLine("SpecialCheckingAccount: "
                    + sca.interestEarned());
          }
     }
}
```

FIGURE A9.6D
ComputeInterest class (HidingBasics/ComputeInterest.cs).

```
Account:                   0.1
CheckingAccount:           0.3
SpecialCheckingAccount: 0.3
Press any key to continue
```

FIGURE A9.6E
Output of ComputeInterest class (HidingBasics/ComputeInterest.cs).

Note that the inherited method of the CheckingAccount class is invoked by the instance of the SpecialCheckingAccount.

Constructors and Destructors

Base class constructor invocation is permitted in a derived class constructor and is effected with the **base** keyword. The base class constructor is invoked immediately before the body of the declared constructor. Consider the class BaseClass in Figure A9.7A. The class defines two constructors:

BaseClass( )   A default constructor

BaseClass(string)   A constructor representative of constructors with arguments

```
using System;

namespace ConstructorBasics
{
     public class BaseClass
     {
          public BaseClass()
          {
               Console.WriteLine("BaseClass( )");
          }

          public BaseClass(string s)
          {
               Console.WriteLine("BaseClass(" + s + ")");
          }
     }
}
```

FIGURE A9.7A
BaseClass class (ConstructorBasics/BaseClass.cs).

The class DerivedClass of Figure A9.7B is derived from the class BaseClass. The derived class defines four constructors and illustrates invocation of selected base class constructors. The base class constructor is declared with the constructor initialized expression

```
base : (parameter-list)
```

The parameter-list is used to select the base class constructor to invoke. All of the base class constructors are included in the selection process. For example, in the constructor

```
public DerivedClass() : base( )
{
    Console.WriteLine("DerivedClass()");
}
```

```
using System;

namespace ConstructorBasics
{
      public class DerivedClass : BaseClass
      {
            public DerivedClass() : base(  )
            {
                  Console.WriteLine("DerivedClass()");
            }
            public DerivedClass(string s) : base(s)
            {
                  Console.WriteLine("DerivedClass("   + s + ")");
            }
            public DerivedClass(string s, string ss) : base()
            {
                  Console.WriteLine("DerivedClass("   + s + ", "
                        + ss +  ")");
            }
            public DerivedClass(string s, string ss, string sss)
            {
                  Console.WriteLine("DerivedClass("   + s + ", "
                        + ss + ", " + sss + ")");
            }
      }
}
```

FIGURE A9.7B
DerivedClass class (ConstructorBasics/DerivedClass.cs).

the expression base( ) matches the base class constructor

```
public BaseClass()
{
    Console.WriteLine("BaseClass( )");
}
```

that is invoked prior to execution of the derived class constructor's body statements.
   The parameters specified in the parameter-list have access to the parameters specified in the constructor declaration. In the same fashion, in the constructor

```
public DerivedClass(string s)  : base(s)
{
    Console.WriteLine("DerivedClass(" + s + ")");
}
```

the expression base(s) matches the base class constructor

```
public BaseClass(string s)
{
    Console.WriteLine("BaseClass(" + s + ")");
}
```

that is invoked prior to execution of the derived class constructor's body statements. The parameters specified in the constructor initializer's parameter-list have access to the parameters specified in the derived class's constructor declaration. In this case, the Base-Class constructor argument is the DerivedClass parameter "s."
   The number of parameters of the base class constructor referenced as an initializer is not related to the number of parameters in the derived class constructor. For example, the derived class constructor

```
public DerivedClass(string s, string ss) : base()
{
    Console.WriteLine("DerivedClass(" + s + ", " + ss + ")");
}
```

has two parameters, "s" and "ss," whereas the referenced base class constructor has zero parameters.

Moreover, when no initializer is explicitly specified, the default initializer is implied. For example, the derived class constructor

```
public DerivedClass(string s, string ss, string sss)
{
    Console.WriteLine("DerivedClass(" + s + ",
    " + ss + ", " + sss + ")");
}
```

does not explicitly specify an initializer constructor. However, when an instance of the class is created and initialized with the derived class constructor, the base class default constructor is invoked. A class with Main method illustrating constructor initialization is shown in Figure A9.7C. The output is shown in Figure A9.7D.

```
using System;

namespace ConstructorBasics
{
    class UsingConstructors
    {
        static void Main(string[] args)
        {
            DerivedClass dc = new DerivedClass();

            DerivedClass dcs =
                new DerivedClass("dcs Argument");

            DerivedClass dcss =
                new DerivedClass("dcss Argument",
                    "Second Argument");

            DerivedClass dcsss =
                new DerivedClass("dcsss Argument",
                    "Second Argument","Third Argument");
        }
    }
}
```

FIGURE A9.7C
UsingConstructors class (ConstructorBasics/UsingConstructors.cs).

```
BaseClass( )
DerivedClass()
BaseClass(dcs Argument)
DerivedClass(dcs Argument)
BaseClass( )
DerivedClass(dcss Argument, Second Argument)
BaseClass( )
DerivedClass(dcssss Argument, Second Argument, Third Argument)
Press any key to continue_
```

FIGURE A9.7D
Output of UsingConstructors class (ConstructorBasics/UsingConstructors.cs).

Destructors cannot be inherited; thus, the only destructor available to a class instance is the declared destructor.

Abstract Modifier

An **abstract** class is a class intended to be used as a base class only; it is declared with the **abstract** modifier. Abstract classes have the following restrictions:

- They cannot be instantiated. Abstract classes are intended to be used as base classes.
- They can contain abstract methods and accessors. Abstract methods and accessors do not have implementation, i.e., defining, bodies.
- They cannot be declared with the sealed modifier, which indicates that the class is not to be inherited.
- A non-abstract class derived from an abstract class must include implementations of the abstract methods and accessors.

An abstract class declaration is shown in Figure A9.8A.

```
using System;

namespace AbstractClassBasics
{
      public abstract class Account
      {
            public abstract decimal Fee();
      }
}
```

FIGURE A9.8A
Account class (HidingBasics/Account.cs).

The **abstract** modifier is used to indicate that a method is not implemented. In the Account class, the method Fee is declared abstract and is not implemented. Abstract method declarations are characterized as:

- Implicitly virtual in that they are intended for implementation in derived classes
- Only permitted in abstract classes
- Not having a body and terminated with a semicolon following the signature, for example, public abstract decimal interestEarned();
- Implemented in derived classes by an overriding method
- Prohibiting static, virtual and override modifiers

An example of an implementation of an abstract method is provided in Figure A9.8B. The derived class SavingsAccount is derived from the base class Account; the method Fee is modified override and implemented. Use of the derived class SavingsAccount is illustrated in Figure A9.9C.

```
using System;

namespace AbstractClassBasics
{
        public class SavingsAccount : Account
        {
                public override decimal Fee()
                {
                        return 5.50m;
                }
        }
}
```

FIGURE A9.8B
SavingsAccount class (HidingBasics/SavingsAccount.cs).

```
using System;

namespace AbstractClassBasics
{
        class UseAbsactClass
        {
                static void Main(string[] args)
                {
                        // Account a = new Account();

                        SavingsAccount ca = new SavingsAccount();
                        Console.WriteLine("Fee: " + ca.Fee());
                }
        }
}
```

Instantiation of an abstract class is an error

FIGURE A9.8C
UseAbstractClass class (HidingBasics/UseAbstactClass.cs).

```
Fee: 5.5
Press any key to continue
```

FIGURE A9.8D
Output of UseAbstractClass class (HidingBasics/UseAbstactClass.cs).

Note that the instantiation of the abstract class is commented out or an error would result: an abstract class cannot be instantiated. The output, when the Main method of UseAbstractClass is called, is shown in Figure A9.9D.

Appendix A.10

Interfaces

The **interface** keyword declares a reference type with abstract members. A class or struct inheriting the interface must implement these members. As such, an interface is said to define a contract because implementing classes or structs must provide implementation of the interface members. For example, consider development of a name class. Typically, different name classes will be developed to meet specific requirements. For example, a DirectoryName class would represent names expressed as

Doe, John

whereas a MailingName class would represent names expressed as

John Doe

Creation of an interface defining properties first and last would ensure that all classes inheriting the interface would implement these properties and thus provide minimum representation of a name. Additionally, inheritance of the interface IComparable would ensure the implementation of a comparison method for the specific name type. In other words, classes inheriting the interface would contract to implement properties and methods required to represent names.

Declaring Interfaces

The syntax for declaring an interface is summarized in Figure A10.1. An example of an interface declaration, defining properties first and last and inheriting the IComparable interface, is shown in Figure A10.2A. Interfaces can be members of a namespace, in this case, UsingInterfaces. Interfaces can also be members of a class.

{attributes} [modifiers] **interface** identifier [:base-list] { body }	
attributes	Declarative tags used to specify additional information. Attributes are optional.
modifiers	Valid modifers are new, public, private, protected and internal.
identifer	Interface name.
base-list	Comma-separated list of explicit base interfaces.
body	Member declarations. Valid members are nonimplemented methods, properties and indexers. Fields and constructors are not permitted.

FIGURE A10.1
Interface declaration syntax.

```
using System;

namespace UsingInterfaces
{
      interface IName : IComparable
      {
            string first
            {
                  get;
                  set;
            }
            string last
            {
                  get;
                  set;
            }

      }
}
```

FIGURE A10.2A
Interface declaration (UsingInterfaces/Iname.cs).

An interface can inherit from one or more interfaces. In the example, the interface IName inherits from the interface IComparable, which is a member of the System namespace provided by .NET and contains the abstract method CompareTo. When implemented, the CompareTo method will provide a comparison of name types useful in sorting operations essential to list building and searching.

Interfaces can declare the following abstract members:

- Methods: only the return type and signature are declared.
- Properties: only the signature is declared; the get and set blocks are not defined.
- Indexers: the accessor block is not defined.

The interface IName declares two properties: first and last. Note that only the signature of the properties is specified.

Using Interfaces

Classes (Figure A10.2B) can implement interfaces, for example. In the base list, i.e., the class and interfaces inherited, the class is listed first followed by the list of interfaces. In the example, the class DirectoryName inherits the interface IName. The class that inherits an interface also inherits the interface's bases. In the example, the class DirectoryName also inherits the interface IComparable even though it is not explicitly stated in the class declaration. Typically, the class would contain additional fields, properties and methods. In this case, the class declares two fields that represent a name: firstName and lastName.

A constructor is defined:

```
public DirectoryName(string f, string l)
{
      firstName = f;
      lastName = l;
}
```

```
using System;

namespace UsingInterfaces
{
      public class DirectoryName : IName
      {
            string firstName, lastName;

            public DirectoryName(string f, string l)    ── Constructor
            {
                  firstName = f;
                  lastName = l;
            }

            public string first
            {
                  get
                  {
                        return firstName;
                  }
                  set
                  {
                        firstName = value;
                  }
            }                                            ── Property
            public string last                              implementations
            {
                  get
                  {
                        return lastName;
                  }
                  set
                  {
                        lastName = value;         ── Method
                  }                                   implementation
            }

            public int CompareTo(Object o)
            {
                  string stringThis = this.lastName + ", "
                        + this.firstName;
                  string stringObj = ((DirectoryName)o).last + ", "
                        + ((DirectoryName)o).first;

                  return String.Compare (stringThis, stringObj);
            }
      }
}
```

FIGURE A10.2B
Interface Implementation (UsingInterfaces/DirectoryName.cs).

The constructor provides for initialization of the fields firstName and lastName.

In a more robust Name class, fields representing title, suffix and sex would be included. Though not included in the example, the class would probably contain a field returning the name as a formatted string:

```
public string formattedName( )
{
    return this.last + ", " + this.first;
}
```

The class DirectoryName contains the interface's property and method implementations.

In this example, the inherited IName properties first and last are implemented:

```
public string first
{
    get
    {
        return firstName;
    }
    set
    {
        firstName = value;
    }
}
public string last
{
    get
    {
        return lastName;
    }
    set
    {
        lastName = value;
    }
}
```

The properties provide access to the class's private members, firstName and lastName. The inherited IComparable interface's method CompareTo is also implemented.

```
public int CompareTo(Object o)
{
    string stringThis = this.lastName + ", "
        + this.firstName;
    string stringObj = ((DirectoryName)o).last + ", "
        + ((DirectoryName)o).first;
    return String.Compare (stringThis, stringObj);
}
```

The implementation of the CompareTo method is intended to provide a comparison of the current DirectoryName instance with another DirectoryName object.

First a string, stringThis, is created representing the directory-formatted name of the current object. Then a string, stringObj, is created representing the directory-formatted name of the object to be compared. Although in use the CompareTo method will be passed a DirectoryName argument, the CompareTo method is defined with an Object-type parameter. The argument is cast to a DirectoryName type with the expression

```
(DirectoryName)o
```

```
using System;

namespace UsingInterfaces
{
        class CompareNames
        {
                static void Main(string[] args)
                {
                        DirectoryName n1 =
                                new DirectoryName("Jack", "BNimble");

                        DirectoryName n2 =
                                new DirectoryName("Jack", "BQuick" );

                        Console.WriteLine("BNimble, Jack < BQuick, Jack: "
                                + n1.CompareTo(n2));

                        n2.last = "BFast";

                        Console.WriteLine("BNimble, Jack > BFast, Jack:  "
                                + n1.CompareTo(n2));
                }
        }
}
```

[Implemented first property] — pointing to `n2.last = "BFast";`

[Implemented CompareTo method] — pointing to `+ n1.CompareTo(n2));`

FIGURE A10.2C
Illustrating using interfaces (UsingInterfaces/CompareNames.cs).

Finally, the two strings are compared using the String class's Compare method. This method returns a value consistent with the return value defined for the IComparable interface CompareTo method. A class illustrating use of the DirectoryName class is shown in Figure A10.2C.

Two instances, n1 and n2, of the DirectoryName class are created and initialized. The instance n2 is compared with the n1 instance with the expression

```
n1.CompareTo(n2)
```

and the result written to the console. The string "BNimble, Jack" is less than the string "BQuick, Jack" and thus a negative value is returned by Compare and, subsequently, CompareTo methods.

The lastName value of the n2 instance is assigned a value with the statement

```
n2.last = "BFast";
```

The revised instance n2 is compared with the n1 instance and the result written to the console. In this case, the string "BNimble, Jack" is greater than the string "BFast, Jack" and thus a positive value is returned

```
BNimble, Jack < BQuick, Jack: -1
BNimble, Jack > BFast, Jack:  1
Press any key to continue_
```

FIGURE A10.2D
Output of programming illustrating using interfaces (UsingInterfaces/CompareNames.cs).

Note!

Structs can also implement interfaces.

Appendix A.11

Delegates

The **delegate** type represents an object that refers to a static method or an instance object and a method of the instance. The **Delegate** class is the base class of all delegates; this class is derived directly from the Object class.

Declaring a Delegate

The syntax for declaring a delegate is shown in Figure A11.1. A delegate declaration defines a type that encapsulates methods, returning a specific type and taking a specific parameter list. For example, a delegate, named FeeDelegate, encapsulating methods returning a double and taking a single char type parameter is declared as shown in Figure A11.2.

```
[attributes] [modifiers] delegate result-type identifier
       ([formal-parameters]);

attributes                  New, developer-defined kinds of declarative information
                            that are defined through the declaration of attribute
                            classes derived from the abstract class
                            System.Attribute.
modifiers                   Valid modifiers are the following: new, public, protected,
                            internal and private.
result-type                 Return type of the methods encapsulated by the
                            delegate.
identifier                  Name of the delegate.
formal-parameters           Parameter list of methods encapsulated by the delegate.
```

FIGURE A11.1
Delegate declaration syntax.

A delegate type, FeeDelegate, has been declared. Note that the return type of the delegate has been specified as double and that a formal parameter list has also been specified — in this case, a single char. The declared delegate type, FeeDelegate, is only valid for the specified return type and argument.

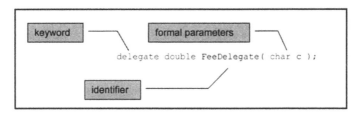

FIGURE A11.2
Declaration of a delegate.

Instantiating a Delegate

A delegate object is created with a new expression where the method encapsulated passes as a method call without its arguments. For example, consider a method Fee defined in a class Customer

```
public class Customer
{
    .  .  .
public double Fee( char c )
    {
        if (c == 'G')
            return baseFeeGold + accountFeeGold;
        else
            return baseFee + accountFee;
    }
    .  .  .
}
```

Gold-rated customers, identified by a field with value "G," receive a special fee. A delegate object encapsulating this method is created with a new expression, as shown in Figure A11.3.

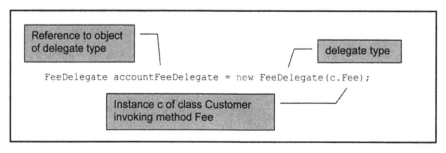

FIGURE A11.3
Instantiating a FeeDelegate object.

The delegate type encapsulates a method returning the same type and the same arguments as specified in its declaration. Note that the declaration of the delegate FeeDelegate specifies a return type of double and a parameter list consisting of a single char parameter.

In the instantiation of a delegate object, a reference of the delegate's type is assigned to a newly created object of the delegate's type. The delegate is passed a call of the method it is to represent, in this case, Fee. Note that Fee returns a double and has a single char parameter.

Assume the class Customer also contains a method Fee defined as follows:

```
public double Fee()
{
    return baseFee + accountFee + unclassedFee;
}
```

The delegate does not reference this method, even though it has the same name and return type, because the method's parameters are different. In this case, the parameter list is empty.

Delegates are similar to method pointers in C++. Note that delegates are objects.

Using a Delegate

The delegate

```
accountFeeDelegate('G')
```

is a reference to the method

```
Fee( char c )
```

invoked by an object of the Customer type with a single char argument. If the argument is 'G,' the method returns the value as

```
baseFeeGold + accountFeeGold;
```

A program illustrating the use declaration and use of delegates is shown in Figure A11.4A. A delegate, FeeDelegate, is declared with the statement

```
delegate double FeeDelegate( char c );
```

```csharp
namespace UsingDelegates
{
  using System;

  delegate double FeeDelegate( char c );

  public class Customer
  {
    static double baseFee = 0.25;
    static double baseFeeGold = 0.2;
    private double accountFee = 0.2;
    private double accountFeeGold = 0.11;
    private double unclassedFee = 0.05;

    public double Fee( char c )
    {
      if (c == 'G')
            return baseFeeGold + accountFeeGold;
      else
            return baseFee + accountFee;
    }

    public double Fee()
    {
       return baseFee + accountFee + unclassedFee;
    }

    static double BaseFee( char c )
    {
      if (c == 'G')
         return baseFeeGold;
      else
         return baseFee;
    }
```

FIGURE A11.4A
Using delegates (UsingDelegates/Customer.cs).

```
public static int Main(string[] args)
{
  Customer c = new Customer();

  FeeDelegate baseFeeDelegate =
    new FeeDelegate(Customer.BaseFee);

  System.Console.WriteLine( "Base Fee Gold Customer:       " +
    baseFeeDelegate('G'));
  System.Console.WriteLine( "Base Fee Regular Customer:    " +
    baseFeeDelegate('R'));

  FeeDelegate accountFeeDelegate =
    new FeeDelegate(c.Fee);

  System.Console.WriteLine( "Account Fee Gold Customer:    " +
    accountFeeDelegate('G'));
  System.Console.WriteLine( "Account Fee Regular Customer: " +
    accountFeeDelegate('R'));
  System.Console.WriteLine( "Account Fee Unclassed Customer: " +
    c.Fee());

  return 0;
  }
 }
}
```

FIGURE A11.4A (CONTINUED)
Using delegates (UsingDelegates/Customer.cs).

The following statement declares a reference to a FeeDelegate type, called baseFee-Delegate, that encapsulates the method BaseFee:

```
FeeDelegate baseFeeDelegate = new FeeDelegate(Customer.BaseFee);
```

Note that BaseFee is a static method and is referenced by the class name Customer.

The statements

```
System.Console.WriteLine( "Base Fee Gold Customer:
" + baseFeeDelegate('G'));
```

```
System.Console.WriteLine( "Base Fee Regular Customer:
" + baseFeeDelegate('R'));
```

result in invocation of the method

```
static double BaseFee( char c )
{
    if (c == 'G')
        return baseFeeGold;
    else
        return baseFee;
}
```

first with parameter 'G' and then 'R.' The resultant browser renderings are:

```
Base Fee Gold Customer:     0.2
```

```
Base Fee Regular Customer:  0.25
```

The following statement declares a reference to a FeeDelegate type, called account-FeeDelegate, that encapsulates the method Fee:

```
FeeDelegate accountFeeDelegate = new FeeDelegate(c.Fee);
```

Note that Fee is an instance method and must be invoked by an instance of the class Customer.

The statements

```
System.Console.WriteLine( "Account Fee Gold Customer:
" + accountFeeDelegate('G'));
System.Console.WriteLine( "Account Fee Regular Customer:
" + accountFeeDelegate('R'));
```

result in invocation of the method

```
public double Fee( char c )
{
    if (c == 'G')
        return baseFeeGold + accountFeeGold;
    else
        return baseFee + accountFee;
}
```

first with parameter 'G' and then 'R.' The resultant browser renderings are:

```
Account Fee Gold Customer:        0.31
Account Fee Regular Customer:     0.45
```

The method Fee(char c) is called and not the method Fee() because the delegate accountFeeDelegate associates with methods returning a double and having a single char parameter.

Consider now the statement

```
System.Console.WriteLine( "Account Fee Unclassed Customer: " +
    c.Fee());
```

In this case, the method

```
public double Fee()
{
    return baseFee + accountFee + unclassedFee;
}
```

is invoked by an instance of the Customer class. The resultant browser renderings are:

```
Account Fee Unclassed Customer: 05
```

The program's output is shown in Figure A11.4B. Note the use of the delegate objects; delegates are immutable, i.e., once a delegate object is created, the method associated with the object never changes.

```
Base Fee Gold Customer:          0.2
Base Fee Regular Customer:       0.25
Account Fee Gold Customer:       0.31
Account Fee Regular Customer:    0.45
Account Fee Unclassed Customer:  0.5
```

FIGURE A11.4B
Output of program using delegates (UsingDelegates/Customer.cs).

Delegates are immutable. Delegates can reference both static and instance methods. C++ function pointers can only reference static methods.

Composing Delegates

A delegate instance of two or more delegate instances can be composed with the plus (+) operator. Delegates comprising the composition must be of the same type and encapsulate static methods with return type void. When the composed delegate is called, the comprising delegates are called in order. A program illustrating the composition of delegates is shown in Figure A11.5A.

The delegate display encapsulation methods with void return type and a single string type parameter are declared with the statement

```
delegate void display(string s);
```

```
namespace ComposingDelegates
{
    using System;

      delegate void display(string s);

      public class Customer
    {
            public static void TypeCustomer(string s)
            {
                    if (s == "G" )
                            Console.Write("Gold ");
                    else
                            Console.Write("Regular ");
            }

            public static void AnnualVolume(string s)
            {
                    if (s == "G" )
                            Console.WriteLine("More than $1,000,000");
                    else
                            Console.WriteLine("Less than $1,000,000");
            }

    public static int Main(string[] args)
    {
      Customer customer = new Customer();

      display typeDelegate = new display(TypeCustomer);

      display volumeDelegate = new display(Customer.AnualVolume);

      typeDelegate("G");
      volumeDelegate("G");

      display composedDelegate = typeDelegate + volumeDelegate;

      composedDelegate("G");

      display decomposedDelegate = composedDelegate - typeDelegate;

      decomposedDelegate("R");

      return 0;
    }
    }
}
```

FIGURE A11.5A
Program illustrating composed delegates (ComposingDelegates\Class.cs).

Two methods, TypeCustomer and AnnualVolume, with void return type and single string parameter, are also declared in a class Customer:

```
public static void TypeCustomer(string s)
{
    if (s == "G" )
        Console.Write("Gold ");
    else
        Console.Write("Regular ");
}
public static void AnnualVolume(string s)
{
    if (s == "G" )
        Console.WriteLine("More than $1,000,000");
    else
        Console.WriteLine("Less than $1,000,000");
}
```

Delegate object references associated with the methods TypeCustomer and AnnualVolume are created with the statements

```
display typeDelegate = new display(TypeCustomer);
display volumeDelegate = new display(Customer.AnnualVolume);
```

Methods referenced by the delegates are called with the statements

```
typeDelegate("G");
volumeDelegate("G");
```

and the following output is rendered:

```
Gold More than $1,000,000
```

The typeDelegate and volumeDelegate are composed with the statement

```
display composedDelegate = typeDelegate + volumeDelegate;
```

The composed delegates are assigned to a displayDelegate reference composedDelegate. The methods referenced by all of the delegates comprising the composed delegate are called in order with the statement

```
composedDelegate("G");
```

First, the typeDelegate and then the volumeDelegate are called and the following output is rendered:

```
Gold More than $1,000,000
```

The minus (–) operator can be used to remove a delegate from a composed delegate, for example, when the following code results in the removal of the typeDelegate from the composedDelegate:

```
display decomposedDelegate = composedDelegate - typeDelegate;
```

The statement

```
decomposedDelegate("R");
```

calls the methods delegated by the delegates comprising the decomposedDelegate. The resultant console display is:

```
Less than $1,000,000
```

The output of a program is shown in Figure A11.5B.

```
Gold More than $1,000,000
Gold More than $1,000,000
Less than $1,000,000
```

FIGURE A11.5B
Output of program illustrating composed delegates (ComposingDelegates\Class.cs).

Anonymous Invocation

The delegate is not class-sensitive; the method's return type and argument types are the important factors. In other words, the delegate is not sensitive to the object that it references, only the object's method return type and argument types. Thus, the actual method that will be called when a delegate object is passed to code need not be known at compile time, i.e., delegates are suitable for **anonymous invocation**. The program shown in Figure A11.6 illustrates anonymous invocation.

Two classes are defined: AFee and BFee. Both define a static method with return type void and no arguments: aFeeMethod and bFeeMethod. A delegate is declared with the following statement

```
delegate void abFeeDelegate();
```

that encapsulates methods with return type void and no arguments.

At runtime, a delegate, abFee, of the type abFeeDelegate is declared with the statement

```
abFeeDelegate abFee;
```

A delegate object is created at runtime and assigned to the reference with the statements

```
if (inputBuffer == 'A')
    abFee = new abFeeDelegate(AFee.aFeeMethod);
else
    abFee = new abFeeDelegate(BFee.bFeeMethod);
```

The aFeeMethod of class AFee is passed as the argument if the user inputs the character 'A,' whereas the bFeeMethod of class BFee is passed as the argument if the user inputs a character other than 'A.' It is not known at compile time which method will be passed in the delegate object creation at runtime. Thus, the actual method called when the statement

```
abFee();
```

is executed depends on what the user has entered at the console at runtime. For example, if the user enters the character 'A' at the console, the program displays the following at the console:

```
aFeeMethod called
```

On the other hand, when a character other than 'A' is entered, the program displays the following at the console:

```
bFeeMethod called
```

Delegates are similar to C++ method/function pointers, but are object oriented and type safe.

```
namespace AnonymousInvocation
{
    using System;

    delegate void abFeeDelegate();

    public class AFee
    {
        static public void aFeeMethod()
        {
            System.Console.WriteLine("aFeeMethod called");
        }
    }

    public class BFee
    {
        static public void bFeeMethod()
        {
            System.Console.WriteLine("bFeeMethod called");
        }
    }

    public class MainClass
    {
      public static int Main(string[] args)
      {
          abFeeDelegate abFee;

          System.Console.Write("Enter fee class code 'A' or 'B':");
          char inputBuffer = (char) System.Console.Read();

          if (inputBuffer == 'A')
                abFee = new abFeeDelegate(AFee.aFeeMethod);
          else
                abFee = new abFeeDelegate(BFee.bFeeMethod);

          abFee();

          return 0;
      }
    }
}
```

FIGURE A11.6
Illustrating anonymous invocation with delegates (AnonymousInvocation\Class1.cs).

Appendix B.1

HTML Basics

HyperText Markup Language (HTML) is a markup language intended for Internet documents. A **markup language** provides, in the form of symbols, for marking, i.e., describing, parts of a document. For example, a part of the document might be identified as a title. Another part might be identified as a heading and still another as a list. These parts of the document can be said to comprise the structure of the document. The markup can also provide for presentation of the document; for example, how the document should be displayed. HTML differs from the proprietary markups used in word processors in that it is intended to be used across a worldwide network employing disparate hardware and software.

HyperText Markup Language (HTML 4.01)

HyperText Markup Language (HTML) is the markup language for Internet publication. Tim Berners-Lee originally developed HTML while at CERN. The development of browsers, starting with Mosaic, has popularized the medium and led to its rapid growth and utilization. The early work of the Internet Engineering Task Force (IETF) and the recent efforts of the World Wide Web Consortium, a nonprofit standards-setting body, have resulted in the current HTML specification. HTML provides authors with the ability to create documents with the following features:

1. Structure: identification of the parts of documents, for example, title, headings and lists
2. Presentation: definition of how browsers should display the markedup text, for example color, font size, and location including features such as Cascading Style (CSS) and absolute positioning of text and graphics on the page.
3. Links to other resources enabling users to navigate from document to document by clicking highlighted text, which results in retrieval of a resource for display
4. Forms for the collection of user input, which can be used as the basis for transaction processing
5. Inclusion of multimedia resources such as video and sound

Information regarding the HyperText Markup Language (HTML) is available at http:// www.w3.org/TR/html401/

HTML also differs from most markup languages in that it supports **hypertext** — a method of organizing information so that the reader can select a path through the material. This approach contrasts with the traditional passage effected by moving from one page to the next sequentially. With hypertext, the reader selects the next unit of information by clicking highlighted text, called a **hyperlink** or **link** for short. In effect, a hyperlink specifies the address of an Internet resource. Clicking the hyperlink retrieves the resource.

Basic HTML Document

A basic HTML document is shown in Figure B1.1A. Figure B1.1B illustrates how HTML documents are displayed in browsers. Note that the title is displayed in the browser's title bar and the document's content is displayed in the browser's window.

```
<!DOCTYPE HTML PUBLIC "-//W3C//DTD HTML 4.01 Frameset//EN"
      http://www.w3.org/TR/html4/frameset.dtd>
<HTML>
  <HEAd>
    <TITLE>Basic HTML Document</TITLE>        Title appears in
  </HEAD>                                      browser Title Bar
  <BODY  >

    Basic HTML Document Content        Document content
                                       appears in browser
                                       window

  </BODY>
</HTML>
```

FIGURE B1.1A
Basic HTML document.

    The HTML documents includes special words enclosed in "<" and ">" symbols. These words and enclosing symbols are called tags and specify the document's structure and how the document should be displayed. For example, text between the <HEAD> tags describes the document and the text between the <TITLE> tags is displayed in the browser's title bar. On the other hand, text between the <BODY> tags is displayed in the browser's window. The tags are said to **markup** the document; HTML is a markup language.

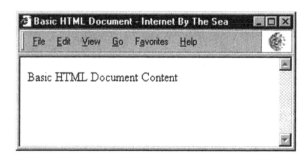

FIGURE B1.1B
Basic HTML document rendered in browser.

Defining HTML

Standard Generalized Markup Language (SGML) is a language for defining markup languages; a language defined using SGML is called an SGML **application**. HTML is an SGML application. Elements, attributes, character references and comments are the SGML constructs used to define HTML. These constructs provide for the markup of documents so as to specify structure and presentation.

An **Element type**, simply referred to as an **element**, specifies document structure. Typical elements represent tables, lists and paragraphs. Element declarations generally describe three parts: a start tag, content and end tag. The element's name appears in the start tag and the end tag. The **start tag** is written as <element-name> and the **end tag** is written as </element-name>. If the slash is omitted in the end tag, the structure and behavior intended by the element will not be realized. For example, the start and end tags of the BODY element define the beginning and end of the document part containing content:

```
<BODY>
     Basic HTML Document Content
</BODY>
```

Element names are case-insensitive.

The end tag of selected element types can be omitted: The P element that describes a paragraph is an example of an element with optional end tag:

```
<P>First paragraph content<P>Second paragraph content
```

Note the division of the content into paragraphs when the document is displayed.

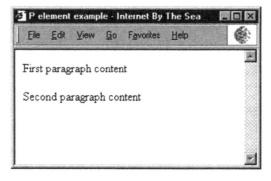

FIGURE B1.2
The P element defines paragraphs.

Use of the optional end tag yields the same structure:

```
<P>First paragraph content</P><P>Second paragraph content</P>
```

On the other hand, the content

```
First paragraph content
Second paragraph content
```

is displayed as a single line.

The element's content appears between the start tag and the end tag. For example,

```
<H1>Document Heading</H1>
```

the phrase "Document Heading" is the content part of the H1 element illustrated. The H1 element specifies the font size the browser should use to display the content. Some elements do not have content; these elements are said to be **empty** elements. For example, the line break element, BR, has no content.

Note!

Elements prescribe structure and behavior.

Elements have properties called **attributes**. Properties are specified with a space-separated list of attribute–value pairs that appear before the final ">" of the start tag. For example,

```
<H1 id="documentheading">Document Heading</H1>
```

the id attribute is set to the value "documentheading," enabling the identification of the specific element programmatically. The following rules guide the specification of attribute values:

- Values should be defined using either double quotation marks or single quotation marks. Note that single quotation marks can be included within a value delimited by double quotation marks.

- Values may be defined without quotation marks if the value is composed of the following: letters (A to Z and a to z), digits (0 to 9), hyphens, periods, underscores and colons.

- Attribute names are case insensitive and, for the most part, attribute values are case insensitive. The language reference specifies when attribute values are case sensitive.

Note!

Elements have properties called attributes.

Character references are symbolic names for characters that can be included in HTML documents. These references are used to specify characters or symbols that cannot be entered with authoring tools, such as a typical computer keyboard. For example, some authoring tools might not be able to enter the letter "a" with an accent sign above it.

Character references begin with the ampersand "&" sign and end with the semi-colon ";". Examples of several character references are shown below.

Symbolic Name	Numeric Name	Character Name	Character Appearance
<	<	less-than sign	<
"	"	double quotation mark	"

The numeric name can also be expressed as a hexadecimal number. The hexadecimal number is preceded by a lower-case x. Thus the double quotation mark is also represented by the character reference "

Comments provide a means for documenting HTML; they are ignored by the browser. Comments begin with the symbols <!– and end with the symbols -->. Any text placed between the beginning and ending symbols is comments. It is common practice to place the name of the author creating the HTML file and the date of installation at the top of the document as comments. For example:

```
<!–Dudley Gill    June, 26, 2001-->
```

Comments can span several lines and the above comment could also be written as:

```
<!–Dudley Gill
    June, 26, 2001-->
```

HTML Document Structure

An HTML document is composed of three parts. The first part provides version information and is called a document type declaration. The second, delimited by a HEAD element and known as the **head**, includes the title and other information. The third part, delimited by a BODY element and known as the **body**, contains the document's contents, in this case, the simple statement "Basic HTML Document Content". Note that the head and body parts of the document are delimited by an HTML element. White space (i.e., spaces, new lines, tabs and comments) before or after each part is ignored.

Version Information

The **version information** is specified in a **document type declaration,** which specifies the document type definition (DTD) used for authoring the document. The syntax of the HTML markup constructs is defined in a **document type definition** (DTD). HTML 4.01 currently specifies three DTDs:

- Strict DTD, a specification that includes all elements that have not been deprecated or do not appear in frameset documents (special documents in which the browser's window is divided into many frames, each of which can display an HTML document)
- Transitional DTD that includes everything in the Strict DTD plus deprecated elements and attributes
- Frameset DTD that includes everything in the Transitional DTD plus elements and attributes for framesets

A URI is included in the declaration that enables user agents to download the DTD. Most HTML editors will provide for incorporation of the version information.

HTML Element

The **HTML element** is the document's root element. After the version information in the document type declaration, the rest of the document is contained within the HTML element. Although the start and ending tags are optional, it is general practice to include

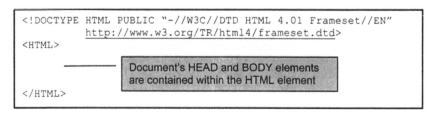

```
<!DOCTYPE HTML PUBLIC "-//W3C//DTD HTML 4.01 Frameset//EN"
           http://www.w3.org/TR/html4/frameset.dtd>
<HTML>

                ————————  Document's HEAD and BODY elements
                          are contained within the HTML element
</HTML>
```

FIGURE B1.3
Fundamental HTML document.

them. The HTML element contains the HEAD and BODY elements. An example of the fundamental HTML document structure is shown in Figure B1.3.

Tip!

Good authoring practice calls for insertion of the optional HTML start and end tags.

HEAD Element

The **HEAD element** contains data about the document that are not content. An example is the document title, which is not rendered as content in the browser's window but is displayed by most browsers in the window's title bar. Similarly, meta-information used by search engines to index the document's content is included in the HEAD element.

The HEAD element start and end tags are optional. The following example illustrates a HEAD element with TITLE and META element contents.

```
<HEAD>
    <TITLE>About Us</TITLE>
    <META http-equiv="Content-Type" content="text/html;
        charset=iso-8859-1">
</HEAD>
```

The **TITLE element** is used to identify the document. The title is not displayed as content but should be made available to the user; it is displayed by many browsers in the Title Bar. The TITLE element start and end tags are required. The title can contain character entities, for example, special characters. Titles cannot contain other markup elements or comments. The title should be descriptive of the content. For example, the title used above describes the page

```
<HEAD>
    <TITLE>Basic HTML Document</TITLE>
</HEAD>
```

and is displayed in the browser's title bar in Figure B1.1B.

The **META element** enables authors to provide information about a document, for example, the document author's name. The META element's information is described with "name/content" pairs. The name component describes the information in the content component. The content component contains information associated with the name component. For example, the following META element describes information regarding the author. The name component describes the type of information, i.e., "Author," and the content component assigns the value "Dudley Gill" to it.

```
<META name="Author" content="Dudley Gill">
```

The META element start tag is required and the end tag is forbidden. This is commonly used to provide information to search engines indexing documents. For example,

```
<META name="keywords" lang="en-us" content="HTML, syntax, basic">
```

Note that the keywords are specified as a comma–space-separated list. In this case, the keywords are "HTML," "syntax" and "basic." The lang attribute is used to specify the language, enabling search engines to filter search results based on language preferences.

BODY Element

The document's contents are contained within the BODY element; its end and start tags are optional. The body must contain at least one instance of the block elements or script.

HTML Documentation

Element documentation is available at http://www.w3.org/html4/index/elements.htm

Attribute documentation is available at http://www.w3.org/html4/index/attribute.htm

---

Content Model

HTML documents have two types of content markup elements:

- **Block elements** reflect major and large structural aspects of the document. Tables are an example of a block element. Block elements contain other block elements as well as inline elements.
- **Inline elements** reflect document content and text markup. Typically, inline elements only contain other inline elements.

The inline and block elements are formatted differently by rendering agents, i.e., browsers. For example, block level elements generally begin with a new line, whereas inline elements do not. The table element, used to organize data in a tabular format, is presented in Appendix B.2. All the HTML elements are summarized in Appendix B.4.

Block and inline elements markup the document to specify its structural and textural rendering, respectively.

Attributes

The following attributes are generic in nature and apply to most elements:

class — Assign one or more class names to an element. Classes are defined in the style element. The element is said to belong to the class. For example,

```
<HEAD>
  <STYLE>
    P.bold {font: 24pt Arial bold;}
    P.indent   {text-indent: 24pt;}
  </STYLE>
<HEAD>
<BODY>
  <P class="bold">Bold heading text</H2>
  <P class="indent">Indented content!
</BODY>
```

specifies that the first paragraph belongs to the class "bold" and the second to the class "indent."

dir — Specifies the base direction of text and tables. Valid values are "ltr" and "rtl." For example,

THIS READS <BDO **DIR="rtl"**>ltr sdaer sihT</BDO> LEFT TO RIGHT

specifies that the directionality of the enclosed text is right to left.

id — Assigns a document-wide unique id to the element. For example, the paragraph marked up in the following element has a unique identification:

<P **id="uniqueparagraph"**>This paragraph has id!</P>

Throughout the document, the paragraph can be referenced by its unique id "uniqueparagraph".

lang — Specifies the language used to interpret the document content. For example,

<HTML **lang="fr"**>

denotes document content interpreted as French.

style — Specifies style at the element level. For example, the style of a P element is specified as follows:

Regular text<P **style="font: 24pt Arial bold; color: blue; text-indent: 1in;"**>Styled text paragraph</P>Regular text continued

In this case, the paragraph is rendered in 24-point Arial bold font, indented 1 inch and in the color blue. The style is specified with property/value pairs as follows:

- Property and value are separated with a colon.
- Each property/value pair is terminated with a semicolon.
- Space-separated list of property/value pairs are enclosed in double quotation marks.

Style is presented in Appendix B.3.

title — Provides advisory information about the element, often displayed as a popup or "tool tip" when the cursor is over the element.

<H1 **title="Heading title popup"**>Heading element with title
  </H1>

href — Specifies the URL of a Web resource. For example,

```
<A href=http://www.w3.org/html4/index/attribute.htm>Attribute
   Documentation </A>
```

specifies the location of the HTML Attribute documentation.

src — Specifies the URL of a resource such as an image or file. For example,

```
<IMG width=450 height=150 src="mapImage.gif">
```

height — Specifies the intended height. For example,

```
<IMG width=450 height=150 src="mapImage.gif">
```

specifies an image height of 150 pixels.

width — Specifies the intended width of a table or image. The value can be specified in several ways:

- **Fixed**: fixed width. For example,
  ```
  <IMG width=450 height=150 src="mapImage.gif">
  ```
  specifies a fixed width of 450 pixels.

- **Percentage**: the width is a percentage of the horizontal space available. For example,
  ```
  <IMG width="50%" height="20%" src="mapImage.gif">
  ```
  specifies a width of 50% of the available space.

- **Proportional**: for example, the specification
  ```
  width="4*"
  ```
  refers to a portion of the space.

Appendix B.2

HTML Tables

Tables are composed of rows and columns of cells and provide a useful structure for organizing and presenting information. The cells can contain text as well as other objects, including images, links, forms, form fields and other tables.

Basic Structure

A typical table rendering illustrating the basic structure of a table is shown in Figure B2.1A. Note that the table is aligned to the right of the window and occupies 50% of the available window width. This table has a caption and is composed of cells arranged in four columns and three rows. Note that the first two rows have three cells, whereas the fourth row has four. The table is specified by the HTML statements shown in Figure B2.1B.

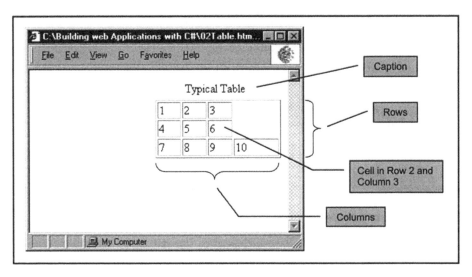

FIGURE B2.1A
Typical table rendering in a browser.

HTML tables are declared with the **TABLE** element. TABLE element start and end tags are required. This element contains other elements that specify the table's caption, rows and content (Figure B2.2). The TR elements specify the table's rows; the cells in a row are specified by the TD elements. Note that the number of table columns is automatically configured. In this case, four columns are required. The TABLE element has generic attributes as well as the attributes shown in Figure B2.3.

```
<TABLE border="1" align="right" width="50%">
  <CAPTION>Typical Table
  <TR>
    <TD>1
    <TD>2
    <TD>3
  </TR>
  <TR>
    <TD>4
    <TD>5
    <TD>6
  </TR>
  <TR>
    <TD>7
    <TD>8
    <TD>9
    <TD>10
  </TR>
</TABLE>
```

FIGURE B2.1B
Typical table definition.

Element	Description
CAPTION	Describes the character of the table. No or at most one caption element can be included in the table specification.
COL or COLGROUP	Specifies the table's columns or groups of columns. The specification can contain zero or more COL or COLGROUP elements.
TBODY	Groups rows into a table body.
TD	Specifies a cell.
TFOOT	Groups rows into a table foot. A table can contain none or at most one TFOOT element.
TH	Specifies a header column. Header columns are centered within a cell and bold.
THEAD	Groups rows into a table head. A table can contain no or at most one THEAD element.
TR	Specifies a table row.

FIGURE B2.2
TABLE element contents.

Caption Element

The **CAPTION** element, when declared, describes the nature of the table. This element must follow the TABLE element start tag immediately. Each TABLE element can contain, at most, one CAPTION element. The CAPTION element start and end tags are required.

The CAPTION element has the generic attributes as well as an align attribute, which is deprecated. Valid values of the align attribute are the following:

top   Caption located at the top of the table. Top is the default value.

bottom Caption located at the bottom of the table.

left   Caption located at the left side of the table.

right   Caption located at the right side of the table.

Note that the align attribute is deprecated.

Attribute	Description
summary	Text that describes the table's purpose and structure for user agents rendering non-visual media.
align	Specifies the table's alignment relevant to the document. Valid values are the following:
	left Table placed at left side of document.
	center Table placed at right center of document.
	right Table placed at right side of document.
width	Number describing the table's width. The number can be expressed as number of pixels or as a percentage of the available horizontal space. When not specified, the width is determined by the browser.
border	Number setting the width of the border surrounding the table in terms of pixels. For example, border="1" specifies a border 1 pixel wide.
frame	Value specifying which sides of the frame surrounding the table will be visible. Valid values are the following:
	void No sides, the default value.
	above Top side only.
	void No sides, the default value.
	hsides Top and bottom sides only.
	vsides Left-hand and right-hand sides only.
	lhs Left-hand side only.
	rhs Right-hand side only.
	box All four sides.
	border All four sides.
rules	Value specifying which rules will appear between the table's cells. Valid values are the following:
	none No rules, the default value.
	groups Rows will be rendered only between row groups (specified by the THEAD, TFOOT and TBODY elements) and the column groups (specified by the COL and COLGROUP elements).
	rows Rules will be rendered between rows only.
	cols Rules will be rendered between columns only.
	all Rules will be rendered between columns and rows.
cellspacing	Number that specifies the space between the left side of the table and the left-most cells, the space between the top of the table and the top of the upper-most cell and so forth for the right side and bottom of the table. The number also specifies the space between the cells. Cell spacing can be expressed as a number of pixels or as a percentage of available space.
cellpadding	Number specifying the space between the edge of the cell and the cell's contents. The number can be expressed as the number of pixels or as the percentage of available space.

FIGURE B2.3
Selected TABLE element attributes.

TR Element

The **TR** element specifies a table row and acts as a container for table cells. The start tag is required and the end tag is optional. The TR element contains the TH and TD elements.

Attribute	Description
align	Value specifying the horizontal alignment of data and justification of text in a table cell. Valid values are the following:
	left — Left-flush data/Left-justify text. Default value for table data.
	center — Center data/Center-justify text. Default value for table headers.
	right — Right-flush data/Right-justify text.
	justify — Justify text left and right.
	char — Align text about a specific character, for example, a decimal point. Results are unpredictable for browsers that do not support the feature.
valign	Value specifying the vertical position of data in a table cell. Valid values are the following:
	top — Data flush with cell top
	center — Data centered vertically in cell. Default value.
	bottom — Data flush with bottom of cell
	baseline — Justify text left and right.
	char — Align text about a specific character, for example, a decimal point. Results are unpredictable for browsers that do not support the feature.
char	Character that specifies a single character that is used for alignment within a cell. The default value is the decimal point. Browsers are not required to support this feature. Note that the default depends on the value assigned to the lang attribute.
charoff	Number, when present, specifying the offset to the first occurrence of the alignment character on each line. When the line does not include an alignment character, the text should be shifted horizontally to the number specified. Browsers are not required to support this feature.

FIGURE B2.4
Selected TR element attributes.

The TH element specifies a header cell; the TD element specifies a data cell and can also serve as a header cell. The TR element has generic attributes as well as attributes shown in Figure B2.4.

The following script illustrates a table containing three rows:

```
<TABLE>
  <CAPTION>Illustrating Table Rows</CAPTION>
  <TR>
  <TR></TR>
  <TR>
</TABLE>
```

Note that the TR end tag is optional.

TH and TD Elements

The **TH** element specifies a table header cell and the **TD** element specifies a table data cell. The start tags are required but the end tags are optional. The TH and TD element

Attribute	Description
headers	List, space separated, of ids of header cells that provide information for the current data cell. Useful for non-visual user agents.
scope	Value specifying the set of data cells for which the current header cell provides header information. Valid values are the following:
	row Header information pertains to the rest of the row
	col Header information pertains to the rest of the column
	rowgroup Header information pertains to the rest of the row group
	colgroup Header information pertains to the rest of the column group
abbr	Text that is substituted as an abbreviated form for the cell's content.
axis	List, comma separated, of categories to which the cell belongs.
rowspan	Number specifying the number of rows spanned by the cell. The default value is one. The value zero means the cell spans all rows from the current row to the last row of the table section, that is, header, body or foot, in which the cell is defined.
colspan	Number specifying the number of columns spanned by the cell. The default value is one. The value zero means the cell spans all columns from the current column to the last column of the column group in which the cell is defined.
nowrap	When true the automatic wrapping is disabled; false otherwise. *Deprecated* attribute.
width	Length, either number of pixels or percentage of available horizontal space, specifying a recommended cell width. *Deprecated* attribute.
height	Length, either number of pixels or percentage of available vertical space, specifying a recommended cell height. *Deprecated* attribute.

FIGURE B2.5
TH and TD attributes for structuring and styling the table.

contents include block elements, inline elements and text. They also include the generic attributes and the cell alignment attributes, as well as additional attributes for structuring and styling the table. TH and TD attributes are summarized in Figure B2.5.

The table in Figure B2.6A illustrates use of TH and TD elements to specify table headers and data. Note that the TH and TD element end tags are optional. The browser rendering is shown in Figure B2.6B.

Note that the cells defined with the TH element are rendered differently than the cells defined with the TD element. Cells 1 through 4 and 5 are defined with the TH element, which can also be used to define a header cell, as in Cell 11. However, a header cell defined with a TD element is not rendered any differently than other TD-defined cells.

The number of rows in a table is set by the number of TR elements in the table's definition. In the absence of grouping, the number of columns in a table is set by the number of cells in the row with the most cells. In the preceding example, row 2 has the most cells (five). Consequently, the table is structured with five columns. In those rows where the number of cells defined is less than five, the row is padded as required. For example, Row 1 and Row 3 are padded with spaces that correspond to what would be cell 5 and cell 15.

When rendering the header cells, the browser can render either the content of the TH element or the element's abbr attribute value. Cells can span several rows. For example, a table with a cell spanning two columns is shown in Figure B2.7A and is shown rendered in Figure B2.7B.

```
<TABLE border="1">
  <CAPTION>Illustrating TH and TD Elements</CAPTION>
  <TR>
    <TH>Col 1</TH>
    <TH>Col 2
    <TH>Col 3</TH>
    <TH>Col 4</TH>
  <TR>
    <TH>Row 2</TH>
    <TD>Cell 7
    <TD>Cell 8</TD>
    <TD>Cell 9</TD>
    <TD>Cell 10</TD>
  </TR>
    <TD>Row 3</TD>
    <TD>Cell 12
    <TD>Cell 13</TD>
    <TD>Cell 14</TD>
  <TR>
</TABLE>
```

FIGURE B2.6A
Table illustrating TH and TD elements.

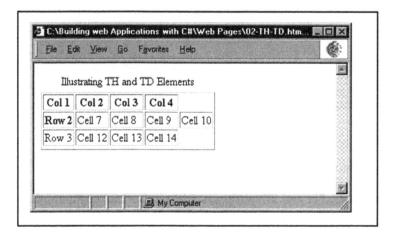

FIGURE B2.6B
Browser rendering of TH and TD elements.

Cell 4 spans two columns because the cell's colspan attribute is set to 2. Note also that the second cell defined in the second row corresponds to the cell that occupies the third column. Similarly, cells can be defined to span multiple rows with the rowspan attribute (Figure B2.8A). The table is rendered as shown in Figure B2.8B.

Note that Cell 2 spans the first and second rows. This fact is taken into account in the rendering and the second TD element in the second row defines the cell that appears in the table's third column.

Note!

Defining overlapping cells is an error, i.e., if Cell 5 above is defined by Cell 4 spanning two columns and Cell 2 spanning two rows.

```
<TABLE border="1">
  <CAPTION>Illustrating Cell Spanning 2 Columns</CAPTION>
  <TR>
    <TD>Cell 1
    <TD>Cell 2
    <TD>Cell 3
  <TR>
    <TD colspan="2" >Cell 4
    <TD>Cell 6
  <TR>
    <TD>Cell 7
    <TD>Cell 8
    <TD>Cell 9
</TABLE>
```

Spans two columns

Second element defines cell in third column

FIGURE B2.7A
Table with cell spanning two columns.

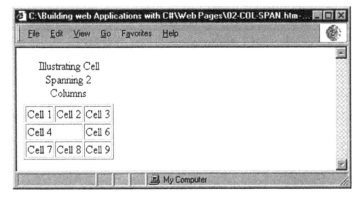

FIGURE B2.7B
Rendering of table with cell spanning two columns.

```
<TABLE border="1">
  <CAPTION>Illustrating Cell Spanning 2 Rows</CAPTION>
  <TR>
    <TD>Cell 1
    <TD rowspan="2">Cell 2
    <TD>Cell 3
  <TR>
    <TD>Cell 4
    <TD>Cell 6
  <TR>
    <TD>Cell 7
    <TD>Cell 8
    <TD>Cell 9
</TABLE>
```

Cell spanning two rows

FIGURE B2.8A
Table with cell spanning two rows.

The frame, rules and border attributes provide for styling the table's external frame and internal rules, e.g., the table shown in Figure B2.9A defines a table with external top and bottom frame lines 4 pixels wide and horizontal rules between the rows.

Horizontal and vertical alignment of the cell contents are set with the **align** and **valign** attributes. For example, the table shown in Figure B2.10A illustrates horizontal alignment

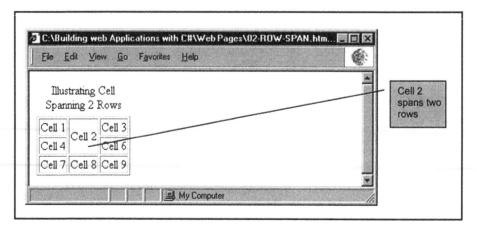

FIGURE B2.8B
Rendering of table with cell spanning two rows.

```
<TABLE border="4" rules=rows frame="hsides">
  <CAPTION>Illustrating Borders and Rules</CAPTION>
  <TR>
    <TD>Cell 1
    <TD>Cell 2
    <TD>Cell 3
  <TR>
    <TD>Cell 4
    <TD>Cell 5
    <TD>Cell 6
  <TR>
    <TD>Cell 7
    <TD>Cell 8
    <TD>Cell 9
</TABLE>
```

FIGURE B2.9A
Table with rules and borders.

of the contents of a cell. In this case, the contents of the cell in the first row are justified left. Similarly, the contents of the second and third rows are aligned to the center and to the right, respectively. The table is shown rendered in Figure B2.10B.

Cell contents are aligned vertically with the valign attribute. For example, Figure B2.11A illustrates aligning cell contents at the top, middle and bottom of the cell. The table is rendered as shown in Figure B2.11B.

The first cell in the first row is located in the upper left-hand corner of the table. The orientation of table cells is shown in Figure B2.12. Alternate direction provides for the first cell to be located in the upper right-hand corner of the table with subsequent cells to its left.

Cell margins are specified by the cellspacing and the cellpadding attributes. As shown in Figure B2.13A, the table specifies that the cell spacing and the cell padding will be 25 and 15 pixels, respectively.

The table rendering is shown in Figure B2.13B. Note that the distance from the table frame to the cells is 20 pixels. Note also that the spacing between the cells is 20 pixels. These values, the space between the cells and the frame as well as the space between cells, are specified by the value of the cellspacing attribute. The space of 10 pixels between the cell's border and the cell's contents is specified by the cellpadding attribute.

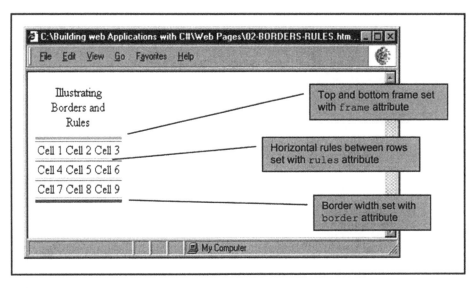

FIGURE B2.9B
Rendering of table with rules and borders.

```
<TABLE border="1">
  <CAPTION>Illustrating Alignment of Cell Contents</CAPTION>
  <TR><TD align="left" width = "200">Align Left
  <TR><TD align="center">Align Center
  <TR><TD align="right">Align Right
</TABLE>
```

FIGURE B2.10A
Table with cell alignment.

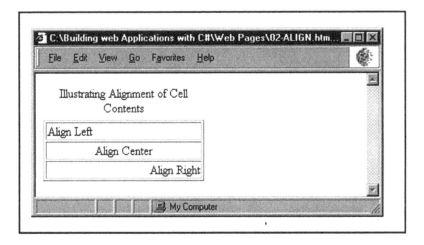

FIGURE B2.10B
Rendering of table with cell alignment.

```
<TABLE border="1">
  <CAPTION>Illustrating Vertical Alignment of Cell
Contents</CAPTION>
  <TR><TD valign="top" height="50">Align Top
  <TR><TD valign="middle" height="50">Align Middle
  <TR><TD valign="bottom" height="50">Align Bottom
</TABLE>
```

FIGURE B2.11A
Vertical alignment.

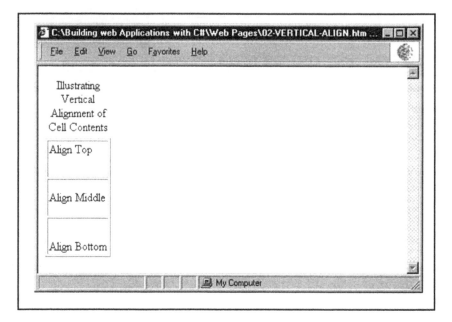

FIGURE B2.11B
Rendering of table with vertical alignment.

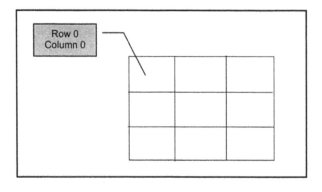

FIGURE B2.12
Table cell orientation.

```
<TABLE border="5" cellspacing="20" cellpadding="10">
  <CAPTION>Illustrating Cell Spacing</CAPTION>
  <TR>
    <TD >20 pixel space
    <TD >Cell padding, the distance from
         the cell contents to the cell border,
         is 10 pixels.
  <TR>
    <TD>Other data
</TABLE>
```

FIGURE B2.13A
Table illustrating cell spacing.

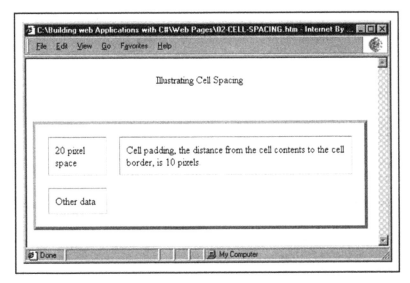

FIGURE B2.13B
Rendering of table illustrating cell spacing.

COL Element

The **COL** element provides for attributing columns spanned by the element. This element does not group columns structurally; it requires a start tag, has no content and the end tag is forbidden. The element has the generic attributes and horizontal and vertical alignment attributes, as well as the span and width attributes (Figure B2.14).

The table in Figure B2.15A illustrates the COL element. The first COL element is associated with the first column and defines a column with default attributes. The second is associated with the next three columns because the span attribute is set to value 3. The width and text justifications of these columns are set to 60 pixels and right justification. Although the table has five columns, the COL elements are associated with only the first four. Consequently, the column not associated with a COL element assumes the default attribute values. The table is rendered as shown in Figure B2.15B.

Attribute	Description
span	Number, N, specifying the number of columns spanned by the element, that is, the current column and the next N-1 columns. The number must be greater than zero. The default value is "1". All of the spanned columns share the attributes specified.
width	Length specifying the width of the columns spanned. The length can be specified as the number of pixels or as a percentage of the available space.

FIGURE B2.14
COL element span and width attributes.

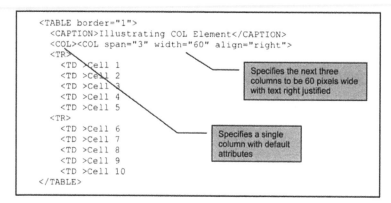

FIGURE B2.15A
Table illustrating COL element.

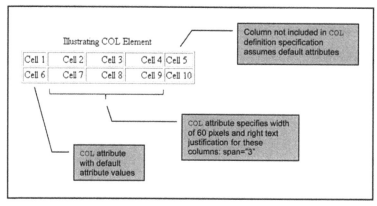

FIGURE B2.15B
Rendering of table illustrating COL element.

COLGROUP Element

Columns are grouped structurally with the **COLGROUP** element. The start tag is required and the end tag is optional. The element's content consists of zero or more COL elements. The element has the generic attributes and the cell alignment attributes, as well as the span and width attributes (Figure B2.16). A table illustrating the COLGROUP element is shown in Figure B2.17A.

Attribute	Description
span	Number N, where N is greater than zero, specifying the number of columns spanned by the element, that is, the current column and the next N-1 columns. The number must be greater than zero. The default value is "1". All of the spanned columns share the attributes specified. Note that the span attribute is ignored if the COLGROUP element contains one or more COL elements.
width	Length specifying the width of the columns spanned. The length can be specified as the number of pixels or as a percentage of the available space. A special value "0*", referred to as zero asterisk, specifies that the width of each column in the group should be the minimum width necessary to contain the column's content. Note that this requires the contents of every row in the column be known prior to rendering and thereby precluding incremental rendering of the table. The width attribute is overridden by any column in the spanned group whose width is specified with a COL element width attribute.

FIGURE B2.16
COLGROUP element span and width attributes.

```
<TABLE border="1">
  <CAPTION>Illustrating COLGROUP Element</CAPTION>
  <COLGROUP span = 3 width="80" align="center">
  <COLGROUP span="2" width="60" align="right">
  <TR>
    <TD >Cell 1
    <TD >Cell 2
    <TD >Cell 3
    <TD >Cell 4
    <TD >Cell 5
  <TR>
    <TD >Cell 6
    <TD >Cell 7
    <TD >Cell 8
    <TD >Cell 9
    <TD >Cell 10
</TABLE>
```

FIGURE B2.17A
Table illustrating COLGROUP element.

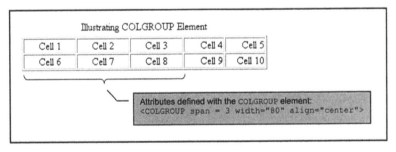

FIGURE B2.17B
Rendering of table component illustrating COLGROUP element.

The table uses the COLGROUP element to define the width and text alignment of the first three columns to be 80 pixels wide and center justified. A second COLGROUP element defines the width and text alignment of the next two columns to be 60 pixels wide and right justified. The table is rendered as shown in Figure B2.17B.

Note that when the COLGROUP contains a COL element the span attribute of COLGROUP element is ignored. Consider the case where a column must be assigned an id. (This will prove useful later when the format of elements is set programmatically.) For example, assume the third column of the above table must be assigned an id, as shown in Figure B2.17C.

```
<TABLE border="1">
  <CAPTION>Illustrating COLGROUP Element</CAPTION>
  <COLGROUP width="80" align="center"> ──────
    <COL span=2>                               span attribute
    <COL id="format-dynamically">             not used when
  <COLGROUP span="2" width="60" align="right"> COL elements
  <TR>                                          are declared
    <TD >Cell 1
    <TD >Cell 2
    <TD >Cell 3
    <TD >Cell 4
    <TD >Cell 5
  <TR>
    <TD >Cell 6
    <TD >Cell 7
    <TD >Cell 8
    <TD >Cell 9
    <TD >Cell 10
</TABLE>
```

FIGURE B2.17C
Assignment of id to third column.

Row Groups

The **THEAD**, **TFOOT** and **TBODY** elements divide a table into head, foot and body sections, respectively. The header and footer sections describe the table's content. The body section contains the table's data. The head and foot sections can be repeated on every page of a table that spans multiple pages. The THEAD and TFOOT elements require a start tag, whereas the end tag is optional. Both the start and end tags of the TBODY element are optional. The THEAD, TFOOT and TBODY elements are subject to the following:

- When included in the table's definition, the THEAD, TFOOT and TBODY must define at least one row.
- The THEAD, TFOOT and TBODY sections of the table must have the same number of columns.
- The TFOOT section must be defined prior to the TBODY section.
- The THEAD, TFOOT and TBODY elements have the generic attributes and the cell alignment attributes.

A sample table illustrating the use of THEAD, TFOOT and TBODY elements is shown in Figure B2.18A.

The table is defined with two body sections. Note the first TBODY element prior to Row 1 of the table and the second TBODY element between Rows 3 and 4. The table is rendered as shown in Figure B2.18B. The section defined by the TFOOT element appears at the bottom of the table even though it is declared prior to the body section of the table defined by the TBODY element.

Note!

The THEAD, TFOOT and TBODY elements divide a table into head, foot and body sections.

```
<TABLE  rules="groups">
  <CAPTION>Illustrating Table Sections</CAPTION>
  <THEAD>
    <TR>
      <TH>Header Cell
  <TFOOT>
    <TR>
      <TH>Footer Cell
  <TBODY>
    <TR><TD >Data Cell Row 1
    <TR><TD >Data Cell Row 2
    <TR><TD >Data Cell Row 3
  <TBODY>
    <TR><TD >Data Cell Row 4
    <TR><TD >Data Cell Row 5
    <TR><TD >Data Cell Row 6
    <TR><TD >Data Cell Row 7
    <TR><TD >Data Cell Row 8
    <TR><TD >Data Cell Row 9
    <TR><TD >Data Cell Row 10
</TABLE>
```

> TFOOT must be declared prior to TBODY

FIGURE B2.18A
Illustration of THEAD, TFOOT and TBODY elements.

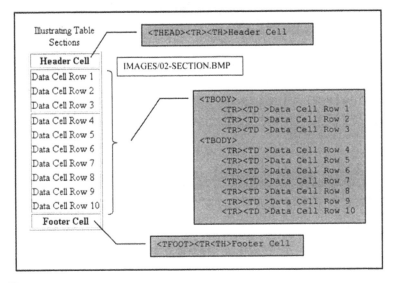

FIGURE B2.18B
Rendering of table illustrating THEAD, TFOOT and TBODY elements.

Nesting Tables

Tables can be nested. Because these elements require a start and an end tag, it is very easy for a user agent to discern when a table begins and ends. This ability to nest tables provides the ability to create complex structures. The table in Figure B2.19A illustrates the nesting of a table within the first cell of a table. The table's rendering is shown in Figure B2.19B; note that the nested table, including the caption, is included as the content of the first cell.

Note!

Tables can be nested.

```
<TABLE border="1">
  <CAPTION>Illustrating Nesting Tables</CAPTION>
  <TR>
    <TD>Table 1 Row 1 Col1
      <TABLE border="1">
        <CAPTION>Nested Table</CAPTION>
        <TR>
          <TD>Table 2 Row 1 Col 1
          <TD>Table 2 Row 1 Col 2
        <TR>
          <TD>Table 2 Row 2 Col 1
          <TD>Table 2 Row 2 Col 2
      </TABLE>
    <TD>Table 1 Row 1 Col 2
  <TR>
    <TD>Table 1 Row 2 Col 1
    <TD>Table 1 Row 2 Col 2
</TABLE>
```

Nested
Table

FIGURE B2.19A
Nested tables.

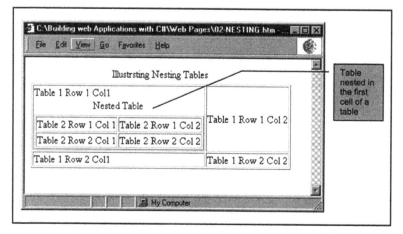

FIGURE B2.19B
Rendering of nested tables.

Appendix B.3

Cascading Style Sheet Basics

Cascading style sheets (CSS) allows authors to attach style, for example, color, fonts and spacing, for a structural document. In other words, the CSS is a template specifying style over a Web page or site. Three options exist for attaching the style sheets to a document:

- CSS style attributes can be attached to the existing HTML tags.
- A style block can be incorporated in the document.
- The document can be linked to a separate style document.

The separation of style and content facilitates development and efficient maintenance. The latest versions of the widely used browsers support CSS.

> W3C has endorsed cascading style sheets as part of the HTML 4 standard. The full W3C cascading style sheet recommendation is available at http://www/w3.org/TR/REC-CSS2.

Property–Value Pairs

A style is declared with a property and associated value. A **property–value** pair is called a declaration. A property–value pair specifying a font weight of 14 points is shown in Figure B3.1.

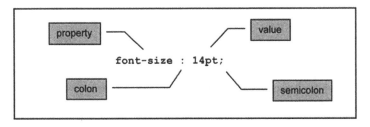

FIGURE B3.1
Property–value pair specifying a 14-point font weight.

CSS defines the properties, for example, font-size. Other properties associated with a font include font-family and font-style. The values that can be associated with a property depend on the property. For example, font size can be expressed as an absolute value such as xx-small or xx-large, a relative value such as larger or smaller, or as a measurement such as pt or em, or as a percentage in relation to overall font size, later to be recognized as the font size of the parent element. A colon separates the property and value and a semicolon follows the property–value pair.

CSS style declarations can be used as the value in the style attribute of most HTML elements. Examples are shown in Figure B3.2A. The first line is shown in 14-point font weight and the second in a bold red forecolor. The third line is shown normally.

```
<!-- File Name: SingleItem.html -->

<P style="font-size: 14pt">AN00031-00</P>
<P style="color: red; font-weight: bold">Garden Park Bench</P>
<P>$189.95</P>
```

FIGURE B3.2A
Incorporating CSS declarations in HTML style attributes.

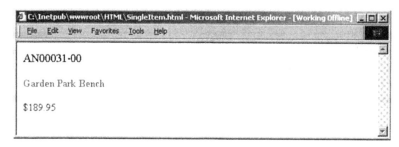

FIGURE B3.2B
Page incorporating CSS declarations in HTML style attributes.

DIV and SPAN Tags

The **DIV** tag is used to divide a document into logical divisions. Typically each division will have its own style. For example, the DIV could be used to divide a document into a header section with banner size type, a content section with normal type and a footer section with very small type. The DIV tag is called a block-level tag because it can enclose block-level elements such as headers, paragraphs and tables. The SPAN tag, on the other hand, is used to block together or group together a few words or characters. Typically, the DIV tag is used to apply style to a single element and the SPAN tag is used to apply style to multiple elements. An example of the use of the DIV and SPAN tags is presented in Figure B3.3A.

The page is displayed as shown in Figure 3.3B. The content "Inventory Report" is contained within a SPAN element with style attributes of color red and font-weight of extra large. Note that the following line is displayed normally. A DIV element is used to set off the report content. All of the paragraphs within the division are displayed with the same style, i.e., with a font weight of 16 points. Finally, another DIV element is used to

```
<HTML>
   <HEAD>
      <TITLE> DIV and SPAN Tags</TITLE>
   </HEAD>
   <BODY>
         <SPAN STYLE="color:red; font:x-large">
            Inventory Report
         </SPAN>
         <P>Selected item summary:</P>
      <DIV STYLE="font:16pt">
         <P>AN00031-00</P>
         <P>Garden Park Bench</P>
         <P>$189.95</P>
      </DIV>
      <DIV STYLE="color:blue; font:x-small">
         <P>Date: September 28, 2001</P>
         <P>Time: 1:29 PM</P>
      </DIV>
   </BODY>
</HTML>
```

FIGURE B3.3A
Page illustrating use of the DIV and SPAN tags.

FIGURE B3.3B
Browser rendering of page illustrating DIV and SPAN tags.

set off the report's date and time. Note again that all of the paragraphs within the DIV element are displayed with the same style.

The style values specified in a DIV element can be augmented with style values in the elements contained within the DIV element. For example, in Figure B3.4A, the values of the first DIV element are overridden in the P element containing the item number. In this case, the style is augmented to display the item number in a bold font weight.

Similarly, the style values specified in the DIV element can be overridden. The paragraph containing the price of the item is displayed in 12-point type, which overrides the 16-point value specified in the DIV element containing the paragraph. The browser rendering is shown in Figure B3.4B.

```
<HTML>
    <HEAD>
        <TITLE> DIV and SPAN Tags</TITLE>
    </HEAD>
    <BODY>
        <SPAN STYLE="color:red; font:x-large">
          Inventory Report
        </SPAN>
        <P>Selected item summary:</P>
      <DIV STYLE="font:16pt Helvetica">
        <P STYLE="font-weight:bold">AN00031-00</P>
        <P>Garden Park Bench</P>
        <P STYLE="font:12pt">$189.95</P>
      </DIV>
        <DIV STYLE="color:blue; font:x-small">
          <P>Date: September 28, 2001</P>
          <P>Time: 1:29 PM</P>
        </DIV>
    </BODY>
</HTML>
```

> Augmenting the DIV style values to display element contents **bold**

> DIV 16pt value overridden with 12pt value

FIGURE B3.4A
Page illustrating use of overriding the DIV tag style values.

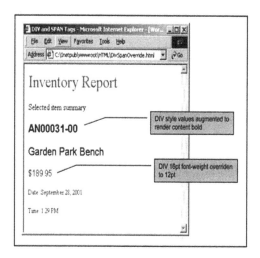

FIGURE B3.4B
Browser rendering of page illustrating augmenting and overriding DIV style values.

Inheritance

Elements within a container inherit the characteristics of the container. Thus, all of the paragraph elements in a division inherit all of the characteristics of the division. For example, the DIV element shown below defines a DIV element with font style characteristics of 16-point Helvetica:

```
<DIV STYLE="font:16pt Helvetica">
  <P STYLE="font-weight:bold">AN00031-00</P>
  <P>Garden Park Bench</P>
  <P STYLE="font:12pt">$189.95</P>
</DIV>
```

The first paragraph inherits these characteristics and augments them to include font-weight. Consequently, the font style characteristics are 16 point, Helvetica and bold. The second paragraph simply displays the item name with the inherited characteristics. The third paragraph, however, overrides its inherited value to render the price of the item in 12-point font size.

Inheritance enables the defining of style characteristics at the highest level.

Note!

Style values "trickle down"; consequently, formatting should be defined at the highest possible level.

Statement Syntax

When included in a style attribute of an HTML tag, the CSS statements are specified as a list. For example, the elements contained within the division shown in Figure B3.5 are rendered with 16-point Helvetica font in color red.

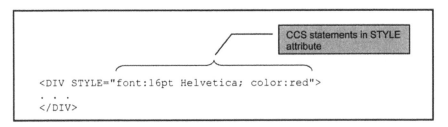

```
                                              CCS statements in STYLE
                                              attribute

<DIV STYLE="font:16pt Helvetica; color:red">
. . .
</DIV>
```

FIGURE B3.5
List of CSS statements in STYLE attribute.

The CSS statement syntax, when not included in the style attribute of an HTML tag, consists of a selector followed by CSS statements in a block enclosed in braces sometimes referred to as "curly braces." One form of the selector is an HTML tag. In Figure B3.6, the selector is the BODY tag. Consequently, all of the elements contained in the body of the documents will be rendered with the characteristics specified within the block following the selector. In this case, the font characteristics are specified as 12 point, sans-serif and bold.

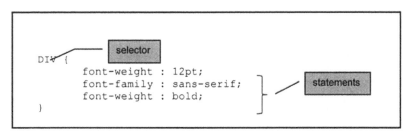

```
                      selector
DIV {
         font-weight : 12pt;
         font-family : sans-serif;       statements
         font-weight : bold;
   }
```

FIGURE B3.6
Illustrating CSS statement syntax.

Similarly, the style characteristics for all P elements are specified by the following:

```
P {
    font-weight : normal
}
```

All P elements of the document will be rendered with normal font weight.

These two specifications can be combined as:

```
DIV {
    font-weight : 12pt;
    font-family : sans-serif;
    font-weight : bold;
}
P {
    font-weight : normal
}
```

An HTML page illustrating the association of CSS statements with HTML tags is shown in Figure B3.7A.

```
<HTML>
    <HEAD>
        <TITLE>Statements Syntax</TITLE>
    </HEAD>
    <BODY>
        <STYLE type="text/css">
            BODY {
                font-weight : 16pt;
                font-family : sans-serif;
                font-weight : bold;
            }
            P {
                font-weight : normal;
            }
        </STYLE>
        Inventory Report
        <P>Selected item summary:</P>
        <P>AN00031-00</P>
        <P>Garden Park Bench</P>
        <P>$189.95</P>
        <P>Date: September 28, 2001</P>
        <P>Time: 1:29 PM</P>
    </BODY>
</HTML>
```

CCS statement
in an HTML
STYLE element

FIGURE B3.7A
CSS statements selecting BODY and P HTML tags.

The browser rendering results in the first line of the document's content being rendered in the style statement associated with the BODY tag. That is, the content is rendered with the style characteristics specified for the BODY tag: 16 point, sans-serif and normal weight. The following lines, all tagged with P, are rendered with the inherited weight and typeface but with an overridden font weight. The browser rendering of the page defined in Figure B3.7A is shown in Figure B3.7B. In this case, the first line is rendered according to the style statements associated with the BODY tag. The following lines are rendered with

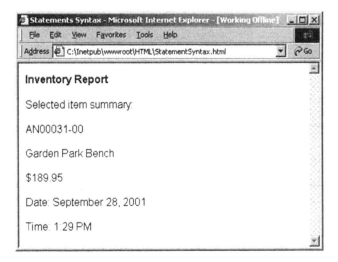

FIGURE B3.7B
Rendering of page with CSS statement with HTML selectors.

the inherited BODY style statements and the overriding P element style statement. That is, the first line is rendered in a bold font weight, whereas the following lines are rendered in a normal font weight.

Class and id Attributes

The **class** and **id** attributes are element identifiers. Almost all elements have these attributes, which are summarized in Figure B3.8.

Attribute	Used in	Value Type	Description
class	All elements except the following: BASE, BASEFONT, HEAD, HTML, META, PARAM, SCRIPT, STYLE, TITLE	CDATA	Space-separated list of class names
id	All elements except the following: BASE, BASEFONT, HEAD, HTML, META, PARAM, SCRIPT, STYLE, TITLE	string	Document-wide unique identifier

FIGURE B3.8
Class and id attributes summary.

The id attribute assigns a unique identifier to an element. The identifier must be unique within the document. For example, the following paragraphs are distinct in that their id values are unique:

```
<P id="itemno">AN00031-00</P>
<P id="name">Garden Park Bench</P>
<P id="unitprice">$189.95</P>
```

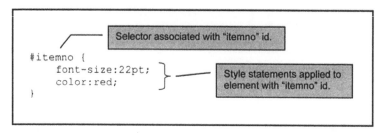

FIGURE B3.9
Style statements associated with "itemno" id.

```
<HTML>
    <HEAD>
        <TITLE>id Attribute Selector</TITLE>
        <STYLE TYPE="text/css">
            #itemno {font-size:22pt; color:red;}
            #name {font-size:16pt; font-weight:bold; color:black;}
            #uniteprice {font-size:16pt; color:black;}
        </STYLE>
    </HEAD>
    <BODY>
        <P id="itemno">AN00031-00</P>
        <P id="name">Garden Park Bench</P>
        <P id="unitprice">$189.95</P>
    </BODY>
</HTML>
```

FIGURE B3.10A
Assigning style with the id attribute.

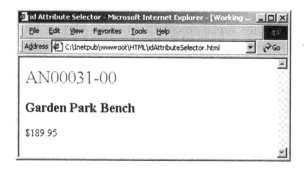

FIGURE B3.10B
Rendering of page assigning style with the id attribute.

The id attribute can be used as a style selector. The CSS id selector is formed with the "#" immediately followed by the id value. For example, the selector associated with the id "itemno" is "#itemno" (Figure B3.9). A page illustrating assigning style with the id attribute is shown in Figure B3.10A. The page is rendered as shown in Figure B3.10B. The class attribute assigns an element to a class. More than one element instance can belong to a class:

```
<P><SPAN id="msg01" class="warning">Warning Message 1</SPAN></P>
<P><SPAN id="msg02" class="warning">Warning Message 2</SPAN></P>
<P><SPAN id="msg11" class="error">Error Message 1</SPAN></P>
<P><SPAN id="msg12" class="error">Error Message 2</SPAN></P>
```

```
<HTML>
   <HEAD>
      <TITLE>id Attribute Selector</TITLE>
      <STYLE TYPE="text/css">
            P.warning {font-size:16pt; color:yellow;}
            P.error {font-size:22pt; font-weight:bold; color:red;}
      </STYLE>
   </HEAD>
   <BODY>
      <P class="warning">Item not found</P>
      <P id="msg1" class="error">System Failure</P>
      <P id="msg2" class="error">Notify Administrator</P>
   </BODY>
</HTML>
```

FIGURE B3.11A
Assigning style with the class attribute.

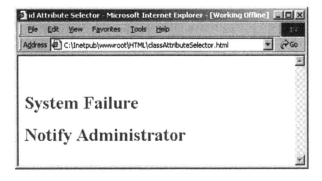

FIGURE B3.11B
Rendering of page assigning style with the class attribute.

Both of the warning messages belong to the same class; they are distinct in that they have unique id. Similarly, both error messages belong to the same class and are unique in that they have unique id. The class attribute can also be used as a style selector. An example of assigning style using the class attribute is illustrated in Figure B3.11A.

Paragraphs in class "warning" are rendered in 16-point yellow type. Paragraphs in class "error" are rendered in 22-point bold red type. The browser rendering is shown in Figure B3.11B.

Grouping Selectors

Selectors sharing the same style declaration can be grouped in a comma-separated list. For example,

```
P.note {font-size:16pt; color:yellow;}
P.warning {font-size:16pt; color:yellow;}
P.error {font-size:22pt; font-weight:bold; color:red;}
```

can be expressed as

```
P.note, P.warning {font-size:16pt; color:yellow;}
P.error {font-size:22pt; font-weight:bold; color:red;}
```

Pseudo-Selectors

The pseudo-selectors provide for formatting based on abstractions or concepts not represented in the document tree. For example, the pseudo-selector :anchor results in a rendering in which the color of an element that has focus changes, i.e., the background color of all anchor elements will change to red when the element is given focus:

```
A:focus { background-color : red }
```

Pseudo-selectors are case-insensitive. Not all browsers support pseudo-selectors.

HTML STYLE Element

The HTML **STYLE** element provides for specifying style for more than one element. Both the start and end tags are required. Attributes of the element are specified in Figure B3.12.

Attribute	Value Type	Required	Description
lang	Language Code		Base language of the element's attributes and text content (case insensitive).
dir	LTR or RTL		Base directionality (case insensitive).
type	Content Type	X	Content type of the style language.
media	Media Descriptions		Intended for use with media.
title	Text		Advisory title.

FIGURE B3.12
Attributes of the STYLE element.

The **type** attribute specifies the style sheet language. For example,

```
<STYLE type="text/css">
```

specifies a style type value of type text and subtype "CSS." This is the value of the type attribute used with Cascading Style Sheets. Other examples of content type include "text/ html", "image/gif", "audio/basic" and "video/mpeg." Note that the content types are case insensitive. This attribute is required, i.e., authors must specify a value, because there is no default value.

The **media** attribute specicfies the destination media for the style; typical media types include projection and print. Media attribute values can be expressed as a comma-separated list. The default value is "screen." A list of media descriptors is presented in Figure B3.13.

Color and Unit Values

CSS provides a multitude of ways to specify units of measurement and color. Units of measurement include **px** for pixels, **pt** for points, **in** for inches, **cm** for centimeters and **em** for em-spaces. Additionally, size can be specified as a percentage, for example, font-size=150%, and with mnemonics, for example, **x-small** and **x-large**.

Attribute Value	Intended Device or Terminal
screen	Non-paged computer screens.
tty	Teletype type terminals.
tv	Television type devices.
projection	Projectors.
handheld	Handheld devices.
print	Paged and opaque material and material viewed in "print preview" mode.
braille	Braille tactile feedback devices.
aural	Speech synthesizers.
all	All devices.

FIGURE B3.13
Media attributes values.

Color can be specified in terms of the color names, for example, **red, blue** or **green**; as a HTML color specification, for example **#0000FF**; or in terms of the rgb components of the color, for example, **rbg(255,0,0)**. An HTML page illustrating the variety of ways for specifying unit of measurement and color is shown in Figure B3.14A. A browser rendering of Figure B3.14A is shown in Figure B3.14B.

```
<HTML>
   <HEAD>
      <TITLE>Color and Units</TITLE>
      <STYLE TYPE="text/css">
        H1 {
            color : #0000FF;
            font-size : 2cm;
        }
         H3 {
            color : green;
            font-size : 12px;
        }
        P {
            color : rgb(255,0,0);
            font-size : x-large;
        }
      </STYLE>
   </HEAD>
   <BODY  >
      <H1>Header</H1>
      <P>Paragraph</P>
      <H3>Footer</H3>
   </BODY>
</HTML>
```

FIGURE B3.14A
Using various units of measurement and color values.

Typeface Specifications

The typeface can be specified as the typeface name or the typeface family. CSS defines five typeface families, **font-family**, summarized in Figure B3.15.

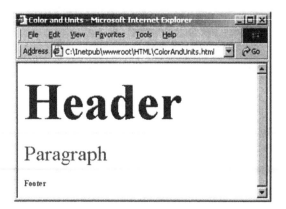

FIGURE B3.14B
Rendering of page using various units of measurement and color.

Family name	Description
cursive	Appears as handwriting.
fantasy	Graphical symbols. An example is Dingbat.
monospace	Uniform character spacing. An example is Courier.
sans-serif	Typeface without feet. An example is Arial.
serif	Typeface with feet. An example is Times.

FIGURE B3.15
Font-family property values.

For example,

```
P { font-family : Courier, monospace }
```

The specification calls for rendering of text with a Courier typeface and, if it is not available, the monospace typeface is implemented.

The weight of the text rendering is specified with the **font-weight** property. Font-weight can be expressed as multiples of 100 between the range of 100 through 900, where 100 is the lightest and 900 the boldest, or as a weight value as defined in Figure B3.16. For example, rendering in a light text face is specified as

```
P { font-weight : light }
```

Family name	Description
light	Light weight text.
normal	Normal text
bold	Bold text.
bolder	Boldest text.

FIGURE B3.16
Font-weight property values.

The **font-size** property provides for specifying the text size. A variety of values are available for specifying font size in terms of points, inches, centimeters, millimeters and em-spaces. There are 72 points in an inch and an em-space is equivalent to the width of the largest letter in proportional font (typically, the letter "m"). A set of mnemonic values are also provided for specification of point size: xx-small, x-small, small, medium, large,

Style name	Description
normal	Normal text.
italic	Slanted text with designer typeface.
oblique	Slanted text.

FIGURE B3.17
Font-style property values.

x-large and xx-large. Additionally, font size can be specified proportionally with the mnemonic values smaller and larger, as well as with a percentage value, such as 125%.

The **font-style** property provides for specifying italicized text. Valid values for expressing text style are listed in Figure B3.17. For the most part, italic and oblique property values produce similar renderings with current browsers.

The **font-variant** property provides for rendering text as small capitals. Valid values for expressing font variant are listed in Figure B3.18. The font: tag enables all of the font-related properties to be listed in a space-separated list. Note that values of a property specified as a comma-separated list must still include the comma.

Variant name	Description
normal	Normal text.
small-caps	All letters are rendered as capitals with a height slightly larger than the lowercase letters.

FIGURE B3.18
Font-style property values.

Text Specifications

The text properties define the visual presentation of characters, spaces, words, lines and paragraphs; they apply to visual media.

The **text-indent** property specifies the indentation of the first line in a block. The indentation is on the left when the base direction of text is left to right and on the right when the base direction is right to left. The property's value can be specified as a fixed length or as a percentage of the containing block width. The fixed-length values can be expressed in a variety of units of measure, as illustrated in Figure B3.19.

Unit of Measure	Description
em	Relative measure typically based on the widest character, for example, the letter "m."
ex	The x-height of the relevant font.
px	Pixel width.
in	Inch.
cm	Centimeter.
mm	Millimeter.
pt	Points (72 points are equal to 1 inch).
pc	Picas (1 pica is equal to 12 points).

FIGURE B3.19
Units for specifying text-indent values.

Value	Alignment Description
left	Left.
right	Right.
center	Center without interword spacing.
justify	Interword spacing used to render text flush left and right.

FIGURE B3.20
Text-align values.

```
<HTML>
   <HEAD>
     <TITLE>Text Indent and Align</TITLE>
     <STYLE TYPE="text/css">
     P {
           text-indent : 16pt;
               text-align : justify;
     }
     </STYLE>
   </HEAD>
   <BODY  >
     <P>The first line of a paragraph is indented 16 points.
        Note that subsequent lines in the same paragraph are
        rendered flush left. Note also that the text is justified
        both right and left.</P>
     <P>All paragraphs are similarly indented. Again, subsequent
        lines in a paragraph are rendered flush left without
        indentation.</P>
   </BODY>
</HTML>
```

FIGURE B3.21A
Illustrating text-indent and text-align properties.

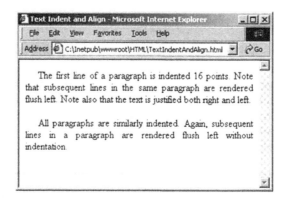

FIGURE B3.21B
Illustrating indentation and justify alignment.

The **text-align** property defines text alignment. Valid values are listed in Figure B3.20. Note that the actual justification algorithm is dependent upon the browser or, more generally, the user agent. For example, Figure B3.21A specifies indentation of the first line of each paragraph and flush left and right text alignment.

Figure B3.21A is rendered as shown in Figure B3.21B. Note the 16-point indentation of all paragraphs and that the interword spacing has been adjusted to enable the text to be flush left and flush right.

Value	Decoration Description
none	No decoration.
underline	Each line of text is underlined.
overline	Each line of text is overlined.
line-through	Each line is rendered with a strike through, that is, a line through the center of the line.
blink	Lines of text alternate between being visible and invisible.

FIGURE B3.22
Decoration values.

```
<HTML>
   <HEAD>
      <TITLE>Decoration</TITLE>
      <STYLE TYPE="text/css">
      H1 {
                  text-decoration : overline;

         }
         P   {
                  text-decoration : blink;
                  text-decoration : line-through;
         }
      H4 {
                  text-decoration : underline;

         }
      </STYLE>
   </HEAD>
   <BODY  >
      <H1>Overline</H1>
      <P>Blinking text with line-through</P>
      <H4>Underline</H4>
   </BODY>
</HTML>
```

FIGURE B3.23A
Illustrating the text-decoration property.

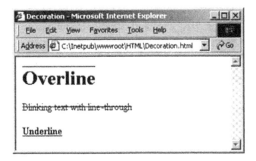

FIGURE B3.23B
Illustrating the overline, underline and line-through text-decoration property values.

The **text-decoration** property defines the decorations that are added to the text. Valid decoration values and their meaning are presented in Figure B3.22. The use of the decoration properties underlining, overlining and striking through text are shown in Figure B3.23A. The blink decoration property value is not implemented in all browsers. Figure B3.23B shows a browser rendering of Figure B3.23A.

Value	Letter Spacing Description
normal	Normal character spacing for the font adjusted when necessary to justify text.
Length Values	Space added to the default intercharacter space.

FIGURE B3.24
Letter-spacing values.

Value	Letter Spacing Description
normal	Normal word spacing.
Length Values	Space added to the default interword space.

FIGURE B3.25
Word-spacing values.

The **letter-spacing** property specifies character spacing. The spacing depends on the algorithm implemented and the text alignment property value. For example, the justify text-align property value calls for character spacing that may differ from the value specified with letter spacing. Valid letter-spacing values are listed in Figure B3.24. Similarly, the **word-spacing** property specifies the space between words. Valid word-spacing values and their meaning are listed in Figure B3.25.

The letter and word spacing algorithms are user agent dependent and thus may vary from browser to browser. The word-spacing and letter-spacing properties are illustrated in Figure B3.26A. The between-letter spacing in paragraphs falling in the letter class is increased by 0.5 em. The interword spacing in paragraphs falling in the word class is increased by 5 em. Figure B3.26B shows a rendering of Figure B3.26A. Note that the letter spacing property is implemented but the word-spacing property is not in the particular browser rendering the listing.

```
<HTML>
    <HEAD>
        <TITLE>Spacing</TITLE>
        <STYLE TYPE="text/css">
        P.normal {
             font-size : 16pt;
        }
        P.letter {
             font-size : 16pt;
             letter-spacing : 0.5em;
        }
        P.word {
             font-size : 16pt;
             word-spacing : 5em;
        }
        </STYLE>
    </HEAD>
    <BODY  >
        <P class="normal">Normal Letter and Word Spacing</P>
        <P class="letter">0.5em Letter and Default Word Spacing</P>
        <P class="word">Default Letter and 5em Word Spacing</P>
    </BODY>
</HTML>
```

FIGURE B3.26A
Illustrating word-spacing and letter-spacing.

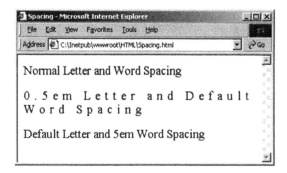

FIGURE B3.26B
Rendering an implementation of the letter- and word-spacing properties.

Value	Text-Transform Value Description
capitalize	First letter of each word is rendered uppercase.
uppercase	All letters of each word are rendered uppercase.
lowercase	All letters of each word are rendered lowercase.
none	Capitalization effects are not applied.

FIGURE B3.27
Text-transform values.

```
<HTML>
   <HEAD>
      <TITLE>Capitalization Effects</TITLE>
      <STYLE TYPE="text/css">
      P.none {
           font-size : 16pt;
      }
      P.capitalize {
           font-size : 16pt;
           text-transform : capitalize;
      }
      P.uppercase {
           font-size : 16pt;
           text-transform : uppercase;
       }
      P.lowercase {
           font-size : 16pt;
           text-transform : lowercase;
       }
   </STYLE>
   </HEAD>
   <BODY  >
      <P class="none">Capitalization effect: none</P>
      <P class="capitalize">Capitalization effect: capitalize</P>
      <P class="uppercase">Capitalization effect: uppercase</P>
      <P class="lowercase">Capitalization effect: lowercase</P>
   </BODY>
</HTML>
```

FIGURE B3.28A
Illustrating capitalization effects of various text-transform property values.

The **text-transform** property specifies capitalization effects. Valid text-transform properties are listed in Figure B3.27, while Figure B3.28A illustrates capitalization effects of the text-transform property. The text in paragraph class capitalize illustrates the capitalize property value in which the first letter of each word is rendered in uppercase. The text in

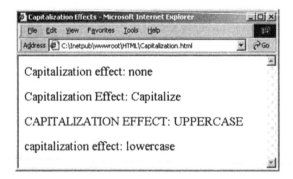

FIGURE B3.28B
Rendering illustrating capitalization effects of various text-transform property values.

Value	White Space Value Description
normal	White space is collapsed and lines are broken as necessary to fill the display area, that is, wrapped.
pre	White space is not collapsed. Lines are not wrapped.
nowrap	White space is collapsed and lines are not broken to fill the display area, that is, text is not wrapped.

FIGURE B3.29
White-space values.

paragraph uppercase and lowercase is rendered in uppercase and lowercase letters, respectively. The browser rendering of Figure B3.28A is shown in Figure B3.28B.

White space can be formatted, as seen in Figure B3.29. An example of white-space formatting is shown in Figure B3.30A. Figure B3.30A illustrates the white-space text formatting property and the HTML PRE element.

Figure B3.30B shows a browser rendering of Figure B3.30A. Note that the normal property value results in collapsed white space and line wrapping. Note also that white space is not collapsed and the lines are not wrapped when the white-space property value is set to nowrap.

The HTML element **PRE** is deprecated. The PRE element's enclosed text is assumed to be preformatted. Suggested guidelines for handling preformatting include:

- Leave white space intact, i.e., do not collapse the white space.
- Default the font to fixed-pitch. Note that the default is overridden in Figure B3.30A.
- Disable word wrap.

The white-space **pre** property specifies that the referenced text is preformatted and text is rendered as with the HTML PRE element's enclosed text. Implementation of the white-space pre property value is uncertain.

Tables

Tables can be viewed as a grid of cells. For example, consider the cells in Figure B3.31, in which the table has cells arranged in three rows and four columns. Note that not all elements of the grid contain cells.

```
<HTML>
    <HEAD>
        <TITLE>Whitespace</TITLE>
        <STYLE TYPE="text/css">
        P.normal {
               font-size : 16pt;
               white-space : normal;
        }
        P.nowrap {
               font-size : 16pt;
               white-space : nowrap;
            }
        PRE {
                   font-family : serif;
               font-size : 16pt;
        }
        </STYLE>
    </HEAD>
    <BODY  >
        <H2>normal white-space Property Value</H2>
        <P class="normal">White space is normally
collapsed and

lines are broken as necessary to fill the display area!
A new line is not necessarily a new line. <BR> However, an HTML
break

element will create a new line!</P>
        <H2>nowrap white-space Property Value</H2>
        <P class="nowrap">White space is normally
collapsed and

lines are not wrapped!
A new line is not necessarily a new line. <BR> However, an HTML
break

element will create a new line!</P>
        <H2>PRE HTML Element</H2>
        <PRE class="nocollapse">White space is not
collapsed and

lines are not wrapped!
A new line is a new line. <BR>Additionally, an HTML break element
will

create a new line!</PRE>
    </BODY>
</HTML>
```

FIGURE B3.30A
Illustrating the white-space property and the HTML PRE element.

Typically, the topmost row and the leftmost column of a table contain information describing the row and column and are called **header cells**. These cells are also referred to as the stub row and column. The other cells contain the table's data. HTML provides for arranging cells in a grid arrangement and specifying the cells as header cells or data cells. Figure B3.32A illustrates the specifying of a table containing cells in the arrangement shown in Figure B3.31.

The table's browser rendering is shown in Figure B3.32B. The table has three rows defined by a TR element. The header cells are defined with a TH element and the data cells are defined with a TD element. Note that the header cells are rendered in a bold font weight.

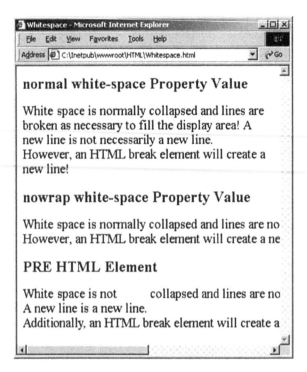

FIGURE B3.30B
Rendering illustrating white-space text formatting property and the PRE element.

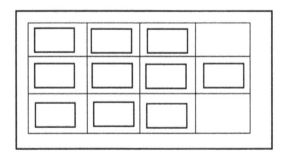

FIGURE B3.31
Cells arranged in a grid.

Additionally, note that the number of columns is based on the number of cells. For example, the second row has four cells, one header and three data, and thus the table has four columns. By default, the table's caption is centered on top of the table.

CSS provides for styling tables; Figure B3.33A illustrates typical CSS table style specifications. The styled table's rendering is shown in Figure B3.33B.

```
<HTML>
   <HEAD>
      <TITLE>Table Basics</TITLE>
   </HEAD>
   <BODY  >
      <TABLE>
         <CAPTION>Basic Table Caption</CAPTION>
         <TR>
            <TH>Header Cell
            <TH> Header Cell
            <TH> Header Cell
         <TR>
            <TH>Header Cell
            <TD> Data Cell
            <TD> Data Cell
            <TD> Data Cell
         <TR>
            <TH>Header Cell
            <TD> Data Cell
            <TD> Data Cell
      </TABLE>
   </BODY>
</HTML>
```

FIGURE B3.32A
Basic table specification.

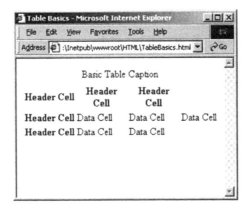

FIGURE B3.32B
Rendering of a basic table.

```
<HTML>
   <HEAD>
      <TITLE>Table With Style</TITLE>
      <STYLE>
        TABLE {
                border : 5px solid black;
        }
        CAPTION {
                text-align : left;
        }
        TD {
           text-align : center;
           vertical-align : middle;
                border : 2px solid red;
        }
        TH {
           text-align : center;
           vertical-align : middle;
                border : 2px dashed blue;
        }
      </STYLE>
   </HEAD>
   <BODY  >
      <TABLE>
         <CAPTION>Basic Table Caption</CAPTION>
         <TR>
            <TH>Header Cell
            <TH> Header Cell
            <TH> Header Cell
         <TR>
            <TH>Header Cell
            <TD> Data Cell
            <TD> Data Cell
            <TD> Data Cell
         <TR>
            <TH>Header Cell
            <TD> Data Cell
            <TD> Data Cell
      </TABLE>
   </BODY>
```

FIGURE B3.33A
Basic table with CSS style specifications.

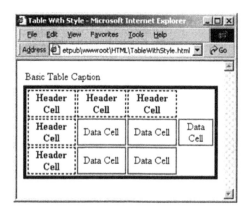

FIGURE B3.33B
Rendering of basic table with CSS specifications.

Appendix B.4

HTML Elements

This appendix provides a summary of selected elements defined in the HTML 4.01 Specifications. Depreciated elements are not included. An example of the element is provided; full documentation is available at **www.w3.org/TR/html401/index/elements.html.** Selected attributes are illustrated; full documentation regarding the attributes is available at **www.w3.org/TR/html401/index/attribute.htm.**

A   Indicates the target or destination of a hyperlink.

The A element is an inline element and requires an opening and closing tag. The href or name attribute is required:

  href Destination URL or anchor point. The href must be enclosed in parentheses.

Example: Link to a server.

```
<A HREF="http://www.buildingwebapplications.com">
   Building Web Applications home page.
</A>
```

Example: Define an anchor.

```
<A NAME="anchor">
   Anchor.
</A>
```

Example: Link to an anchor.

```
<A HREF="#anchor">Link to an anchor.</A>
```

ABBR   Indicates an abbreviated form.

The ABBR element is an inline element and requires an opening and closing tag. The title attribute is the full or expanded form of the abbreviation used in the text.

Example:

```
<ABBR TITLE=" Building Web Applications">BWA</ABBR>
```

ACRONYM Indicates an acronym.

The ACRONYM element is an inline element and requires an opening and closing tag. The title attribute is the full or expanded form of the acronym used in the text.

Example:

```
<ACRONYM TITLE=" Building Web Applications">BWA
   </ACRONYM>
```

ADDRESS   Provides author information.

The ADDRESS element is an inline element and requires opening and closing tags. The href attribute specifies the destination url.

Example:

```
<ADDRESS>Author: Dudley Gill Address:
   <A HREF="mailto:mail@buildingwebapplications.com">
   mail@buildingwebapplications.com
   </A>.
</ADDRESS>
```

AREA   Defines a client-side image map area including shape, coordinates and image.

The AREA element is an inline element that requires an opening; the closing tag is forbidden. The AREA element is nested within a MAP element. AREA element attributes include the following:

> **shape**   Shape of the object. Valid values are "circ," "circle," "poly," "polygon," "rect" and "rectangle."
>
> **coords** Coordinates of the object
>
> **href**   Destination URL
>
> **alt**   Alternate text or graphic

Example:

```
<P>Click on element to see example rendering.
<P><IMG width=300 height=80 src="mapImage.gif""
USEMAP"= "#aMap"" border="2">
<MAP NAME="aMap">
   <AREA    SHAPE="rect"  COORDS="10,10,50,40"
      href="b.html" alt="bold"  >
   <AREA    SHAPE="rect"  COORDS="60,10,110,40"
      href="i.html" alt="bold"  >
   <AREA    SHAPE="rect"  COORDS="120,10,200,40"
      href="em.html" alt="bold"  >
</MAP>
```

B   Indicates the text should be rendered bold.

The B element is an inline element and requires opening and closing tags.

Example:

```
<B>Text rendered bold</B>
```

BASE   Specifies the document's base URI.

The BASE element is nested within the head element and requires an opening tag; the closing tag is forbidden.

Example:

```
<BASE HREF="http://buildingwebapplications/
   htmlelements/" />
```

BDO   Overrides the bidirectional algorithm for selected text fragments.

The bdo element is an inline element and requires opening and closing tags.

Example:

```
THIS READS <BDO DIR="rtl">ltr sdaer sihT</BDO> LEFT
    TO RIGHT
```

BIG   Indicates the text should be rendered in a font larger than the current font.

The BIG element is an inline element and requires opening and closing tags.

Example:

```
<BIG>Text rendered larger</BIG>
```

BLOCKQUOTE   Indents and sets apart a quotation.

The BLOCKQUOTE element is a block element and requires opening and closing tags.

Example:

```
Regular text<BLOCKQUOTE>A very long quotation that
spans many lines and should be set apart from the
regular text</BLOCKQUOTE>Regular text continued
```

BODY   Defines the document's body.

The BODY element is a block element. Opening and closing tags are optional.

Example:

```
<BODY>
    Document content
</BODY>
```

BR   Forces a line break.

The BR element is an inline element. An opening tag is required and a closing tag is forbidden.

Example:

```
A break in the text<BR>is inserted.
```

BUTTON   Forces a line break.

The BUTTON element is an inline element. Opening and closing tags are required.

> **type**   Specifies the type of button. Valid types are submit, button and reset.

Example:

```
<BUTTON type="submit">Press to Login</BUTTON>
```

CAPTION   Specifies a table's caption.

The CAPTION element is an inline element. Opening and closing tags are required.

The align attribute specifies the location of the caption relative to the table's contents. Valid values are "bottom" for center-bottom, "center," "left," "right" and "top" for top-center.

Example:

```
<TABLE BORDER="solid">
    <CAPTION ALIGN="bottom" >
      Table Caption
    </CAPTION>
    <TBODY>
      <TR>
      <TD>
          Table Content
      </TD>
      </TR>
    </TBODY>
</TABLE>
```

CITE   Renders content in italics as used for citations.

The CITE element is a block element. Opening and closing tags are required.

Example:

```
Book
<CITE>
    Building Web Applications
</CITE>
```

CODE   Renders content in font used to represent computer code.

The CODE element is an inline element. Opening and closing tags are required.

Example:

```
Regular Text
<CODE>
    Computer Code
</CODE>
```

COL   Specifies a table column's default properties.

The COL element is a block element. An opening tag is required and a closing tag is forbidden. The element's attributes specify the table column's properties:

    span   Specifies the number of columns covered by the specification.

    style   Specifies the properties of the covered columns.

Example:

```
<TABLE BORDER="solid">
    <CAPTION ALIGN="right" >
      Table Caption
    </CAPTION>
```

```
<TBODY>
   <COL SPAN="2", STYLE="color:red">    .
   <TR>
      <TD>
         Cell 1
      </TD>
      <TD>
         Cell 2
      </TD>
      <TD>
         Cell 3
      </TD>
   </TR>
</TBODY>
</TABLE>
```

Note that only two columns are covered by the COL element declaration.

COLGROUP   Groups columns in a table.

The COLGROUP element is a block element. An opening tag is required and a closing tag is optional. The element's attributes specify the table column's properties. The COLGROUP element properties are overridden by the COL element properties.

span   Specifies the number of columns covered by the specification.

style   Specifies the properties of the covered columns.

Example:

```
<TABLE BORDER="solid" RULES="groups">
   <CAPTION ALIGN="right" >
      Table Caption
   </CAPTION>
   <TBODY>
      <COLGROUP SPAN="2", STYLE="color:red">
      <COLGROUP STYLE="color:blue">
      <TR>
         <TD>
            Cell 1
         </TD>
         <TD>
            Cell 2
         </TD>
         <TD>
            Cell 3
         </TD>
      </TR>
   </TBODY>
</TABLE>
```

	Note: When the Table element's rules attribute is set to "group," lines are placed between the column groups.
DD	Defines a definition in a definition list.
	The DD element is a block element. An opening tag is required and a closing tag is optional.
	Example:

```
<DL>
    <DT>Native
       <DD>English is the native language.
    <DT>Fluent
       <DD>English is a second language but mastered.
</DL>
```

DEL	Marks deleted text.
	The DEL element is an inline element and requires opening and closing tags.
	Example:

```
The <DEL>deleted</DEL> text is marked.
```

DFN	Indicates a definition.
	The DFN element is an inline element and requires opening and closing tags.
	Example:

```
The book BWA <DFN>Building Web Applications</DFN> is
a complete reference.
```

DIV	Indicates a container.
	The DIV element is a block element and requires opening and closing tags.
	Example:

```
<DIV ALIGN="left">
    A division
</DIV>
<DIV ALIGN="right">
    Another division
</DIV>
```

DL	Defines a definition list.
	The DL element is a block element. An opening tag is required and a closing tag is optional.
	Example:

```
<DL>
    <DT>Native
       <DD>English is the native language.
    <DT>Fluent
       <DD>English is a second language but mastered.
</DL>
```

DT   Defines a definition term in a definition list.

The DT element is a block element. An opening tag is required and a closing tag is optional.

Example:

```
<DL>
   <DT>Native
      <DD>English is the native language.
   <DT>Fluent
      <DD>English is a second language but mastered.
</DL>
```

EM   Emphasizes text.

The EM element is an inline element and requires opening and closing tags.

Example:

```
Emphasized text <EM>is usually an italic</EM> rendering.
```

FIELDSET   Defines a container for related controls enabling client-side users to submit data.

The FIELDSET element is a block element and requires opening and closing tags.

Example:

```
Text <FIELDSET>within the FIELDSET element</FIELDSET>
is boxed.
```

FORM   Defines a container for controls enabling client-side users to submit data.

The FORM element is a block element and requires opening and closing tags.

Example:

```
<HTML>
   <FORM ACTION="http://application.com/login.asp"
      METHOD="POST">
      Enter name: <INPUT TYPE="text" NAME="name"><BR>
      Enter password: <INPUT TYPE="password"
      NAME="pw"><BR>
      <INPUT TYPE="SUBMIT" VALUE="Login">
   </FORM>
</HTML>
```

FRAME   Defines a frame within a frameset.

The FRAME element is a block element. An opening tag is required. A closing tag is forbidden.

Example:

```
<FRAME SRC="DFN.html">
```

FRAMESET   Defines a window composed of multiple frames.

The FRAMESET element is an inline element and requires opening and closing tags.

Example:

```
<FRAMESET COLS="33%, *">
    <FRAME SRC="DFN.html">
    <FRAME SRC="B.html">
</FRAMESET>
```

H1 through H6   Renders text as a heading.

The H1 through H6 elements are block elements and require opening and closing tags.

Example:

```
<H2>Heading Rendering</H2>
```

Note: H1 is the most prominent and H6 is the least prominent.

HEAD   Defines a part of the document containing information about the document.

The opening and the closing tags are optional.

Example:

```
<HEAD>
    <TITLE>A Simple Document</TITLE>
</HEAD>
```

HR   Inserts a horizontal rule.

The HR element is a block element. An opening tag is required. A closing tag is forbidden.

Example:

```
Insertion of<HR>horizontal line
```

HTML   Defines a document containing HTML elements.

The opening and the closing tags are optional.

Example:

```
<HTML>
    <BODY>
        An HTML Document
    </BODY>
</HTML>
```

I   Indicates the text should be rendered in italics.

The I element is an inline element and requires opening and closing tags.

Example:

```
<I>Italicized text</I>
```

IFRAME   Creates an inline subwindow.

The IFRAME element is a block element and requires opening and closing tags.

The attributes characterize the inline window:

     width   specifies the width of the subwindow.

     height   Specifies the height of the subwindow.

     src   Specifies the page displayed in the window.

Example:

```
<IFRAME width=300 height=100 src="b.html"></IFRAME>
```

IMG   Creates an embedded image.

The IMG element is an inline element. An opening tag is required and a closing tag is forbidden. The src is required and specifies the url of the image to be inserted. The width and height attributes define the image boundary.

Example:

```
<IMG width=450 height=150 src="mapImage.gif ">
```

INPUT   Creates form input controls.

The INPUT element is an inline element. An opening tag is required and a closing tag is forbidden. The type attribute is required and specifies the type of control. Valid values are button, checkbox, file, hidden, image, password, radio, reset, submit and text.

Example:

```
<HTML>
    <FORM ACTION="http://application.com/login.asp"
       METHOD="POST">
       Enter name: <INPUT TYPE="text" NAME="name"><BR>
       Enter password: <INPUT TYPE="password"
       NAME="pw"><BR>
       <INPUT TYPE="SUBMIT" VALUE="Login">
    </FORM>
</HTML>
```

INS   Marks text inserted in the document.

The INS element is an inline element. Opening and closing tags are required.

Example:

```
Inserted <INS>text</INS> is marked.
```

KBD   Marks text to be entered by user, usually as monospaced font.

The KBD element is an inline element. Opening and closing tags are required.

Example:

```
Enter the following: <KBD>Text to be entered!</KBD>
```

LABEL   Form field.

The LABEL element is an inline element. Opening and closing tags are required.

Example:

```
<LABEL>Name: </LABEL>
<INPUT type="text">
```

LEGEND   Inserts caption in box drawn by FIELDSET control.

The LEGEND element is a block element. Opening and closing tags are required.

Example:

```
<FIELDSET>
    <LEGEND>Login Controls</LEGEND>
        ID: <INPUT type="text" id="ID">
        Password: <INPUT type="text" id="PW">
</FIELDSET>
```

LI   Defines a list item.

The LI element is a block element. An opening is required and the closing tag is optional.

Example:

```
<DIR>
    <LI>1 Native
    <LI>2 Fluent</LI>
    <LI>3 Limited
    <LI>4 None
</DIR>
```

LINK   Defines a link to a document.

The LINK element is only used in the head element. The LINK element has no content. An opening is required and the closing tag is forbidden. Attributes include:

    rel   Specifies a forward type link. Valid types are "rev," "rel" and "index."

    href   URI of the linked resource

Example:

```
<LINK rel="Index" HREF="b.html">
```

Typically the linked document is the next page, previous page or index of content.

MAP   Defines a client-side image map.

The element is not rendered. Opening and closing tags are required. The name attribute assigns a name to the image map defined by the map element.

Example:

```
<P>Click on element to see example rendering.
<P><IMG width=300 height=80 src="mapImage.gif"
USEMAP="#aMap" border="2">
<MAP NAME="aMap">
    <AREA SHAPE="rect" COORDS="10,10,50,40"
        href="b.html" alt="bold" >
    <AREA SHAPE="rect" COORDS="60,10,110,40"
        href="i.html" alt="bold" >
    <AREA SHAPE="rect" COORDS="120,10,200,40"
        href="em.html" alt="bold" >
</MAP>
```

META   Provides information about the document.

The element is not rendered. An opening tag is required and the closing tag is forbidden. The META element is only used in the HEAD element.

Example:

```
<HTML>
    <HEAD>
        <META name="CODE_LANGUAGE" Content="C#">
    </HEAD>
    <BODY>
    </BODY>
</HTML>
```

NOFRAMES   Alternate content container for non-frame-based renderings.

The NOFRAMES element is an inline element. Opening and closing tags are required.

Example:

```
<FRAMESET>
    <NOFRAMES>
        Alternate content for browsers not supporting
            frames.
    </NOFRAMES>
</FRAMESET>
```

Note: Frames are supported in Internet Explorer version 3.0 or later.

NOSCRIPT   Alternate content container for non-script-based renderings.

The NOSCRIPT element is an inline element. Opening and closing tags are required.

Example:

```
<NOSCRIPT>
    Alternate content for browsers not script-based
        renderings.
</NOSCRIPT>
```

OBJECT   Inserts a generic object into the HTML page.

The OBJECT element is an inline element. Opening and closing tags are required.

Example:

```
<OBJECT CLASSID="someObject.obj"></OBJECT>
```

OL   Defines an order list.

The OL element is a block element. Opening and closing tags are required.

Example:

```
<OL START="10">
    <LI>Native
    <LI>Fluent
    <LI>Limited
    <LI>None
</OL>
```

OPTGROUP   Groups items in a selection list.

The OPTGROUP element is a block element. Opening and closing tags are required. This element is used within a select element.

The label attribute captions the items in the group.

Example:

```
<SELECT>
    <OPTGROUP LABEL="English">
        <OPTION>USA</OPTION>
        <OPTION>Other</OPTION>
    </OPTGROUP>
    <OPTGROUP LABEL="Other than English">
        <OPTION>French</OPTION>
        <OPTION>German</OPTION>
        <OPTION>Spanish</OPTION>
        <OPTION>Other</OPTION>
    </OPTGROUP>
</SELECT>
```

OPTION   Choice in a selection list.

The OPTION element is a block element. An opening tag is required. A closing tag is optional. The OPTION element is used within a select element.

Example:

```
<SELECT>
    <OPTGROUP LABEL="English">
        <OPTION>USA</OPTION>
        <OPTION>Other</OPTION>
    </OPTGROUP>
    <OPTGROUP LABEL="Other than English">
        <OPTION>French</OPTION>
        <OPTION>German</OPTION>
        <OPTION>Spanish</OPTION>
        <OPTION>Other</OPTION>
    </OPTGROUP>
</SELECT>
```

P   Defines a paragraph.

The P element is a block element. An opening tag is required. A closing tag is optional.

Example:

```
A paragraph<P>Another paragraph
```

PARAM   Named property value of an OBJECT.

The PARAM element is empty. An opening tag is required. A closing tag is forbidden. The param element is valid within an object element.

Attributes include:

   name   Name of the param element

   value   Value of an input parameter for the param element

Example:

```
<OBJECT CLASSID="someObject.obj">
    <PARM NAME="size" VALUE="large">
</OBJECT>
```

PRE

Renders text as previously formatted.

The PRE element is a block element. Opening and closing tags are required.

Example:

```
<PRE>
Text
   is
      rendered
   exactly
      as formatted
</PRE>
```

Note: Spaces and line breaks are preserved.

Q

Marks text as a quotation.

The Q element is an inline element. Opening and closing tags are required.

Example:

```
The short inline quotation <Q>"A quote"</Q> is set apart.
```

SAMP

Renders text as program output, code or script.

The SAMP element is an inline element. Opening and closing tags are required.

Example:

```
<SAMP>Code is rendered in fixed-width font</SAMP>
```

SCRIPT

Specifies script statements.

The SCRIPT element is not rendered. Opening and closing tags are required.

Example:

```
<SCRIPT type="C#">
<!-- Script should be hidden within comments to
prevent rendering by down-level browsers -->
</SCRIPT>
```

SELECT

Defines an option selector.

The SELECT element is an inline element. Opening and closing tags are required.

The size attribute sets the number of rows in the list box. A multiple attribute provides for multiple option selection.

Example:

```
<SELECT SIZE="3">
    <OPTION VALUE="1" SELECTED>Native
    <OPTION VALUE="2">Fluent
    <OPTION VALUE="3">Limited
    <OPTION VALUE="4">None
    <OPTION VALUE="99">Unknown
</SELECT>
```

SMALL　　　Indicates the text should be rendered in a font smaller than the current font.

The SMALL element is an inline element and requires opening and closing tags.

Example:

```
Regular text <SMALL>Small text</SMALL>
```

SPAN　　　Specifies an inline container.

The SPAN element is an inline element and requires opening and closing tags.

Example:

```
Regular text <SPAN STYLE="font-size:24;color:red;">
Text in SPAN element</SPAN>
```

The span element shown uses the style color and font-size properties to change the enclosed text to color red and font size 24.

STRONG　　　Renders text with emphasis.

The STRONG element is an inline element and requires opening and closing tags.

Example:

```
Regular text <STRONG>Text rendered with emphasis
</STRONG>
```

STYLE　　　Specifies style.

The STYLE element is declared in the head section. This element is not rendered and requires opening and closing tags.

Example:

```
<HEAD>
    <STYLE>
        BODY {background-color: gray; color: black;}
        H2 {font: 24pt Arial bold;}
        P   {text-indent: 24pt;}
    </STYLE>
<HEAD>
<BODY>
    <H2>Heading text</H2>
    <P>Body content!
</BODY>
```

SUB   Renders enclosed text as subscript.

The SUB element is an inline element and requires opening and closing tags.

Example:

```
Illustrating a subscript<SUB>The subscript</SUB> and
superscript<SUP>The superscript</SUP>
```

SUP   Renders enclosed text as superscript.

The SUP element is an inline element and requires opening and closing tags.

Example:

```
Illustrating a subscript<SUB>The subscript</SUB> and
superscript<SUP>The superscript</SUP>
```

TABLE   Defines a table.

The TABLE element is a block element. Opening and closing tags are required.

Example:

```
<TABLE BORDER="solid">
   <CAPTION ALIGN="left" >
      Table Caption
   </CAPTION>
   <TBODY>
      <TR>
         <TH>
            Row 1
         </TH>
         <TD>
            Cell 2
         </TD>
         <TD>
            Cell 3
         </TD>
      </TR>
      <TR>
         <TH>
            Row 2
         </TH>
         <TD>
            Cell 5
         </TD>
         <TD>
            Cell 6
         </TD>
      </TR>
   </TBODY>
</TABLE>
```

TBODY
Defines a table's body rows.

The TBODY element is not rendered. Opening and closing tags are optional.

Example:

```
<TABLE BORDER="solid">
   <CAPTION ALIGN="left" >
      Hours Worked
   </CAPTION>
   <THEAD>
      <TR>
         <TH>Employee
         <TH>M
         <TH>T
         <TH>W
         <TH>T
         <TH>F
   </THEAD>
   <TFOOT>
      <TR>
         <TH>Total
         <TD>16
         <TD>8
         <TD>16
         <TD>8
         <TD>8
   </TFOOT>
   <TBODY>
      <TR>
         <TD>Tony
         <TD>8
         <TD>0
         <TD>8
         <TD>0
         <TD>0
      <TR>
         <TD>Rosa
         <TD>8
         <TD>8
         <TD>8
         <TD>8
         <TD>8
   </TBODY>
</TABLE>
```

TD Defines a table's data cell.

The TD element is a block element. An opening tag is required. A closing tag is optional.

Example:

```
<TABLE BORDER="solid">
    <CAPTION ALIGN="left" >
        Hours Worked
    </CAPTION>
    <THEAD>
        <TR>
            <TH>Employee
            <TH>M
            <TH>T
            <TH>W
            <TH>T
            <TH>F
    </THEAD>
    <TFOOT>
        <TR>
            <TH>Total
            <TD>16
            <TD>8
            <TD>16
            <TD>8
            <TD>8
    </TFOOT>
    <TBODY>
        <TR>
            <TD>Tony
            <TD>8
            <TD>0
            <TD>8
            <TD>0
            <TD>0
        <TR>
            <TD>Rosa
            <TD>8
            <TD>8
            <TD>8
            <TD>8
            <TD>8
    </TBODY>
</TABLE>
```

TEXTAREA   Specifies a multiline text field.

The TEXTAREA element is an inline element and requires opening and closing tags. The COLS attribute sets the character width of the text area.

Example:

```
<TEXTAREA COLS=16>
A text area is a multiline text input control.
</TEXTAREA>
```

TFOOT   Defines a table's foot rows.

The TFOOT element is not rendered. An opening tag is required. A closing tag is optional.

Example:

```
<TABLE BORDER="solid">
  <CAPTION ALIGN="left" >
    Hours Worked
  </CAPTION>
  <THEAD>
    <TR>
      <TH>Employee
      <TH>M
      <TH>T
      <TH>W
      <TH>T
      <TH>F
  </THEAD>
  <TFOOT>
    <TR>
      <TH>Total
      <TD>16
      <TD>8
      <TD>16
      <TD>8
      <TD>8
  </TFOOT>
  <TBODY>
    <TR>
      <TD>Tony
      <TD>8
      <TD>0
      <TD>8
      <TD>0
      <TD>0
```

```
            <TR>
               <TD>Rosa
               <TD>8
               <TD>8
               <TD>8
               <TD>8
               <TD>8
         </TBODY>
   </TABLE>
```

TH Specifies a table's header cell.

The TH element is a block element. An opening tag is required.
A closing tag is optional.

Example:

```
<TABLE BORDER="solid">
   <CAPTION ALIGN="left" >
      Hours Worked
   </CAPTION>
   <THEAD>
      <TR>
         <TH>Employee
         <TH>M
         <TH>T
         <TH>W
         <TH>T
         <TH>F
   </THEAD>
   <TFOOT>
      <TR>
         <TH>Total
         <TD>16
         <TD>8
         <TD>16
         <TD>8
         <TD>8
   </TFOOT>
   <TBODY>
      <TR>
         <TD>Tony
         <TD>8
         <TD>0
         <TD>8
         <TD>0
         <TD>0
```

```
        <TR>
            <TD>Rosa
            <TD>8
            <TD>8
            <TD>8
            <TD>8
            <TD>8
    </TBODY>
</TABLE>
```

THEAD

Defines a table's header rows.

The THEAD element is not rendered. An opening tag is required. A closing tag is optional.

Example:

```
<TABLE BORDER="solid">
    <CAPTION ALIGN="left" >
        Hours Worked
    </CAPTION>
    <THEAD>
        <TR>
            <TH>Employee
            <TH>M
            <TH>T
            <TH>W
            <TH>T
            <TH>F
    </THEAD>
    <TFOOT>
        <TR>
            <TH>Total
            <TD>16
            <TD>8
            <TD>16
            <TD>8
            <TD>8
    </TFOOT>
    <TBODY>
        <TR>
            <TD>Tony
            <TD>8
            <TD>0
            <TD>8
            <TD>0
            <TD>0
```

```
                    <TR>
                        <TD>Rosa
                        <TD>8
                        <TD>8
                        <TD>8
                        <TD>8
                        <TD>8
                </TBODY>
            </TABLE>
```

TITLE   Contains the document title.

The TITLE element is typically displayed in the browser's title bar and is a block element. Opening and closing tags are required. The TITLE element is only used in the head element.

Example:

```
<HTML>
    <HEAD>
        <TITLE>Document Title</TITLE>
    <BODY>
        Document Content
    </BODY>
</HTML>
```

TR   Defines a table row.

The TR element is a block element. An opening tag is required. A closing tag is optional.

Example:

```
<TABLE BORDER="solid">
    <CAPTION ALIGN="left" >
        Hours Worked
    </CAPTION>
    <THEAD>
        <TR>
            <TH>Employee
            <TH>M
            <TH>T
            <TH>W
            <TH>T
            <TH>F
    </THEAD>
    <TFOOT>
        <TR>
            <TH>Total
            <TD>16
            <TD>8
            <TD>16
            <TD>8
            <TD>8
    </TFOOT>
```

```
         <TBODY>
           <TR>
             <TD>Tony
             <TD>8
             <TD>0
             <TD>8
             <TD>0
             <TD>0
           <TR>
             <TD>Rosa
             <TD>8
             <TD>8
             <TD>8
             <TD>8
             <TD>8
         </TBODY>
       </TABLE>
```

TT   Specifies fixed-width rendering of enclosed text.

The TT element is an inline element and requires opening and closing tags.

Example:

```
Regular text <TT>Fixed-width text</TT>
```

UL   Specifies an unordered list.

The UL element is a block element and requires opening and closing tags.

Example:

```
<UL>
<LI>First item
<LI>Second item
<LI>Third item
</UL>
```

VAR   Marks text as an instance of a variable.

The VAR element is an inline element and requires opening and closing tags.

Example:

```
Enter the variable <VAR>value</VAR> in the Name field.
```

Appendix C.1

Introduction to XML

Just as HTML provides a universal method for viewing data, XML provides a universal method for describing data.

An inventory file is typical of a file containing data. For example, the inventory of a company selling exotic wood porch, balcony and patio furniture is shown in Figure C1.1. Notice the structure of the data. First, each inventory item is represented by a single line. Second, each inventory item has the same characteristics: Item No., Description, Color, Quantity and Unit Price. In some cases, the entry is blank; however, provisions exist for its use.

Item No.	Description	Color	Quantity	Unit Price
AN00031-00	Garden Park Bench		529	189.95
ANF00032-00	Trellis Trough		447	229.95
AN04332-00	Square Planter 15"		48	109.95
AN04332-01	Square Planter 19"		581	149.95
ANF00012-01	Table 36"		199	229.95
ANF00012-00	Chair		896	74.95
ANF00012-02	Chair Cushion	White	754	54.95
ANF00012-02	Chair Cushion	Green	547	54.95

FIGURE C1.1
Example of data describing the inventory of a store selling exotic wood furniture.

The table, which can be viewed as a document, is referred to as the Inventory. Note that the Inventory consists of rows describing the inventory objects. Each of these rows is referred to as an Item. Each Item consists of five components, referred to as Item No., Description, Color, Quantity and Unit Price.

Describing Data With XML

Extensible Markup Language (**XML**) is a markup language that can be used to describe most documents. The inventory shown in Figure C1.1 is a document and thus can be described using XML. Names used to describe the document's contents are called elements;

they are not standard, but custom designed. Consequently, it is possible to create any element needed to describe a document. Along with this flexibility, however, is the need to adhere to a very rigid syntax that makes it possible for users or readers of the document to understand exactly what is being presented.

XML elements are named using capital letters. An element describing the inventory is named INVENTORY. An element describing the inventory items is named ITEM. Each inventory item consists of five components specifying the item's number, description, color, quantity and unit price, which are described by ITEMNO, DESCRIPTION, COLOR, QUANTITY and UNITPRICE elements, respectively. In general, element names should be descriptive of their representation, but contractions are the general practice. The following table illustrates the preferred element name as well as names that might be used by authors and developers.

Preferred	Expected Variations
INVENTORY	INV
ITEM	ITEM, PROD
ITEMNO	IN, NO, NUM
DESCRIPTION	DESC
COLOR	COL
QUANTITY	QTY
UNITPRICE	UP, PRICE

An XML document describing part of the inventory is shown in Figure C1.2.

```
<INVENTORY>
  <ITEM>
    <ITEMNO>AN00031-00</ITEMNO>
    <DESCRIPTION>Garden Park Bench</DESCRIPTION>
    <COLOR></COLOR>
    <QUANTITY>529</QUANTITY>
    <UNITPRICE>$189.95</UNITPRICE>
  </ITEM>
  <ITEM>
    <ITEMNO>AN00032-00</ITEMNO>
    <DESCRIPTION>Trellis Trough</DESCRIPTION>
    <COLOR></COLOR>
    <QUANTITY>447</QUANTITY>
    <UNITPRICE>$229.95</UNITPRICE>
  </ITEM>
  <ITEM>
    <ITEMNO>AN04332-00</ITEMNO>
    <DESCRIPTION>Square Planter 15"</DESCRIPTION>
    <COLOR></COLOR>
    <QUANTITY>48</QUANTITY>
    <UNITPRICE>$109.95</UNITPRICE>
  </ITEM>
</INVENTORY>
```

FIGURE C1.2
Inventory.xml.

Note!

.NET Framework provides for the automatic creation of XML documents.

Interpreting an XML Document

Only the data are important to the user. Thus, opening the file Inventory.xml as a text file, in Notepad for example, presents the user with the task of extracting the data (Figure C1.3).

```
Inventory.xml - Notepad                           _ □ ×
File  Edit  Search  Help
<INVENTORY>
   <ITEM>
      <ITEMNO>AN00031-00</ITEMNO>
      <DESCRIPTION>Garden Park Bench</DESCRIPTION>
      <COLOR></COLOR>
      <QUANTITY>529</QUANTITY>
      <UNITPRICE>189.95</UNITPRICE>
   </ITEM>
   <ITEM>
      <ITEMNO>AN00032-00</ITEMNO>
      <DESCRIPTION>Trellis Trough</DESCRIPTION>
      <COLOR></COLOR>
      <QUANTITY>447</QUANTITY>
      <UNITPRICE>229.95</UNITPRICE>
   </ITEM>
   <ITEM>
      <ITEMNO>AN04332-00</ITEMNO>
      <DESCRIPTION>Square Planter 15"</DESCRIPTION>
      <COLOR></COLOR>
      <QUANTITY>48</QUANTITY>
      <UNITPRICE>109.95</UNITPRICE>
   </ITEM>
</INVENTORY>
```

FIGURE C1.3
Inventory.xml opened in browser.

The XML rendering is readable; XML documents are intuitive. The quantity of the Garden Park Benches available is clearly 529. However, reading an XML document is cumbersome because the makeup is interspersed with the data. However, the XML document provides information that would not be available in the common Comma-Separated Values rendering of the Inventory file:

```
"AN0031.00","Garden Park Bench",529,$189.95

"AN0032-00","Trellis Trough",447,$229.95

"AN04332-00","Square Planter 15",48,$109.95
```

In this type of file, the meaning of the data is not indicated in the file. Its interpretation is dependent upon knowledge of a template specifying what each position in the list means. Every Computer Science major has written a program that, given the Comma Separated Values file above, would produce the printed listing that follows:

```
AN0031-00

Garden Park Bench

529

$189.95

AN0032-00

Trellis Trough
```

```
447
$229.95
AN04332-00
Square Planter 15
48
$109.95
```

The XML framework provides a more robust manner for describing and interpreting data.

Specifying How an XML File Is Displayed

The contents of an XML file can be displayed according to rules specified in a style sheet, as illustrated in Figure C1.4. Information from the Inventory.xml file is input to the browser, as well as information from a style sheet file. The style sheet contains information that the browser uses to display information contained in the XML file.

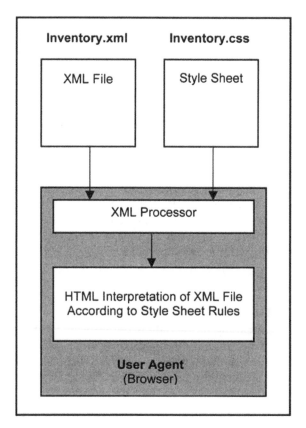

FIGURE C1.4
Interpreting and displaying an XML file.

A **Cascading Style Sheet (CSS)** is a file specifying the rules for displaying an XML file. An example of a CSS file that specifies how elements of the Inventory.xml file are to be displayed is shown in Figure C1.5.

```
/* file: Inventory.css   */

ITEM
  {display:block;
   margin-top:10;
   font-size:12pt}

ITEMNO
  {display:block;
   font-weight:bold;
   color:red}

DESCRIPTION
  {display:block}

COLOR
  {display:block}

QUANTITY
  {display:block}

UNITPRICE
  {display:block}
```

FIGURE C1.5
Style sheet describing the display of Inventory.css file data (Inventory.css).

Specifically, the style sheet specifies how each of the XML elements is to be displayed. In this case, the style sheet specifies the following rules for displaying the Inventory.xml file's elements:

Element	Display Rules
ITEM	Insert a line break above and below.
	Insert a 10-point space above.
	Size font at 12 point.
ITEMNO	Insert a line break above and below.
	Color red.
	Weight font bold.
DESCRIPTION	Insert a line break above and below.
COLOR	Insert a line break above and below.
QUANTITY	Insert a line break above and below.
UNITPRICE	Insert a line break above and below.

The XML file must contain a reference to the style sheet file containing the rules for displaying the XML file's content. An inventory file with a reference to an appropriate style sheet file is shown in Figure C1.6.

When the XML file is opened in a browser, such as Internet Explorer 5, the document is displayed according to the rules specified in the style sheet to which the document is linked. In the example, the XML file contains a reference to the style sheet file Inventory.css. The XML file is displayed according to the rules specified in file Inventory.css. Note the following:

- The item numbers are shown in bold red type.
- Each item is displayed with a 12-point space above.
- Each element is displayed on a separate line.

Cascading style sheets are just one of the many ways of specifying how an XML file is displayed.

```
<?xml-stylesheet type="text/css" href="Inventory.css"?>

<INVENTORY>
  <ITEM>
    <ITEMNO>AN00031-00</ITEMNO>                   Reference
    <DESCRIPTION>Garden Park Bench</DESCRIPTION>  to style
    <COLOR></COLOR>                               sheet file
    <QUANTITY>529</QUANTITY>
    <UNITPRICE>$189.95</UNITPRICE>
  </ITEM>
  <ITEM>
    <ITEMNO>AN00032-00</ITEMNO>
    <DESCRIPTION>Trellis Trough</DESCRIPTION>
    <COLOR></COLOR>
    <QUANTITY>447</QUANTITY>
    <UNITPRICE>$229.95</UNITPRICE>
  </ITEM>
  <ITEM>
    <ITEMNO>AN04332-00</ITEMNO>
    <DESCRIPTION>Square Planter 15"</DESCRIPTION>
    <COLOR></COLOR>
    <QUANTITY>48</QUANTITY>
    <UNITPRICE>$109.95</UNITPRICE>
  </ITEM>
</INVENTORY>
```

FIGURE C1.6
Inventory.xml file with reference to style sheet (InventoryWithStyleSheetRef.xml).

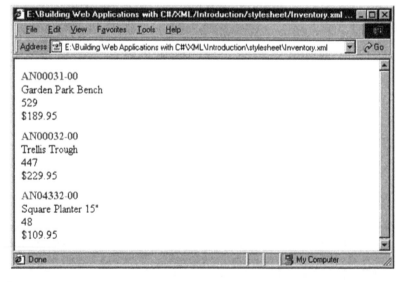

FIGURE C1.7
Inventory.xml with reference to style sheet Inventory.css opened in browser.

What Is XML?

XML has emerged as the common language of program data interchange. Developed under the auspices of the World Wide Consortium, XML thus has the status of standard.

XML was developed by the XML Working Group under the auspices of the World Wide Consortium (W3C). In its published specification for *XML: Extensible Markup Language (XML) 1.0 (Second Edition)*, the design goals are stated as:

1. XML shall be straightforwardly usable over the Internet.
2. XML shall support a wide variety of applications.
3. XML shall be compatible with SGML.
4. It shall be easy to write programs that process XML documents.
5. The number of optional features in XML is to be kept to the absolute minimum.
6. XML documents should be human legible and reasonably clear.
7. The XML design should be prepared quickly.
8. The design of XML shall be formal and concise.
9. XML documents shall be easy to create.
10. Terseness in XML markup is of minimal importance.

XML fulfills these design goals. The full specification is available at the Web address http://www.w3.org/TR/REC-xml.

The character of XML is summarized as follows:

Internet Usability, Easy Processing and Readability

The previous example illustrates that XML is well suited to use over the Internet. Many browsers incorporate the ability to process XML documents. The previous example illustrates the human readability of an XML document. Consider, for example, the XML file representing an inventory. The price of the Trellis Trough is clearly $229.95. Similarly, the quantity of Garden Park Benches on hand is clearly 529. Though cumbersome, the organization is straightforward and, for the most part, self-explanatory, resulting in an extremely readable document.

Compatible with SGML

XML is a subset of the Standard Generalized Markup Language (SGML). Like SGML, XML is independent of platforms and vendors. The XML standard was developed in a relatively short timeframe. XML processors have been developed by many vendors; they are available in browsers, which speaks to the ease of implementation.

The XML standard is formal and concise. In complexity, it is comparable to a language such as COBOL — a procedural programming language used to develop most applications between the years 1960 and 2000. COBOL can be described as a language, with approximately a dozen verbs and nouns defined by the application developer.

Application Variety and Terseness in XML

Documents expressed in XML are not terse, but this is of minimal importance. On the other hand, XML is intended to be a robust language that supports a variety of applications, and it can. For example, consider the use of XML to mark up a sentence to reflect its elements as their respective parts. In this case, the sentence

```
Ship the square planter.
```

would be expressed as

```
<DECLARATION>
  <VERB>Ship</VERB>
  <OBJECT>
    <ARTICLE>the</ARTICLE>
    <NOUNMODIFIER>
      <ADJECTIVE>square</ADJECTIVE>
      <NOUN>planter</NOUN>
    </NOUNMODIFIER>
  </OBJECT>
</DECLARATION>
```

Note that the XML document is much longer than the non-XML. Note also that XML is able to effectively mark up a sentence in a manner that should satisfy the most demanding language teacher. Thus, this example illustrates the ability to use XML in applications other than those involved in transferring data from program to program. It also illustrates that XML documents need not be terse; the original sentence required 23 characters, whereas the XML rendering required more than 150 characters — a possibly heavy price to pay if bandwidth is limited.

Hands-On Exercise: Introducing XML

Step 1: Create XML File

1. Open new text file in a text editor, for example, Notepad.
2. Type in the XML document shown in Figure C1.2.

```
<INVENTORY>
  <ITEM>
    <ITEMNO>AN00031-00</ITEMNO>
    <DESCRIPTION>Garden Park Bench</DESCRIPTION>
    <COLOR></COLOR>
    <QUANTITY>529</QUANTITY>
    <UNITPRICE>189.95</UNITPRICE>
  </ITEM>
  <ITEM>
    <ITEMNO>AN00032-00</ITEMNO>
    <DESCRIPTION>Trellis Trough</DESCRIPTION>
    <COLOR></COLOR>
    <QUANTITY>447</QUANTITY>
    <UNITPRICE>229.95</UNITPRICE>
  </ITEM>
  <ITEM>
    <ITEMNO>AN04332-00</ITEMNO>
    <DESCRIPTION>Square Planter 15"</DESCRIPTION>
    <COLOR></COLOR>
    <QUANTITY>48</QUANTITY>
    <UNITPRICE>109.95</UNITPRICE>
  </ITEM>
</INVENTORY>
```

FIGURE C1HO.1
Notepad Window with text describing the inventory document.

3. Use the Save As command to save the document with the filename **Inventory.xml** in a new folder.

Step 2: Display XML File

1. Open Internet Explorer offline.
2. Expose the Address Bar by selecting the Address option in the Toolbars submenu of the View menu. Type in the full path name of the Inventory.xml file.
3. Click Go to open the file in Internet Explorer. The document is displayed as shown below. Alternately, the file could have been opened in Internet Explorer by double-clicking the file in Windows Explorer or Windows NT Explorer.

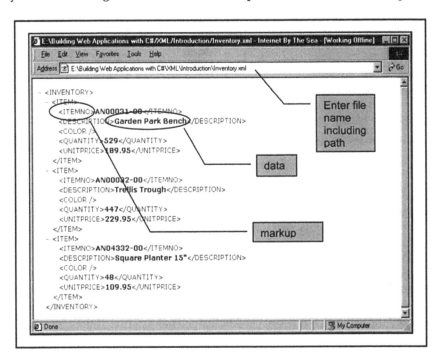

FIGURE C1HO.2
Inventory.xml opened in Internet Explorer.

The XML file is displayed as a text file. Internet Explorer contains an XML Processor and thus is able to break down a *well-formed* XML document into its constituent parts. Additionally, the processor is able to use color to distinguish between the parts — for example, display markup characters in color and the data characters as bold black type.

Step 3: Change the Detail Level

The detail level of the XML Document's components can be contracted by toggling the minus sign (–) to the left of the component. The detail level of a component can be expanded by toggling the plus sign (+) to its left.

1. Open the file Inventory.xml in Internet Explorer if it is not already open.

2. Click the minus sign to the left of the top line. Note that the XML file is displayed at the lowest level of detail and that the minus sign is replaced with a plus sign.

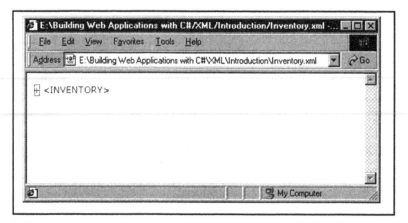

FIGURE C1HO.3
Inventory.xml opened in Internet Explorer.

3. Expand the listing by clicking the plus sign.
4. Click a different minus sign and observe the contraction of the resultant display.

Step 4: Debugging XML Files with Internet Explorer

The processor in Internet Explorer will display error reports when an XML error is detected. For example, XML is strict about the spelling (even distinguishing case) of the names used to identify the various data components in a file. For example, the name "ITEM" is not the same as "Item." Similarly, "item" differs from "ITEM" and from "Item."

In the XML document Inventory, the name "ITEM" is used to start the identification of an item's description. The name "ITEM" preceded by a slash, as in "/ITEM," is used to identify the end of an item's description. The name used at the end of an item's identification must be exactly the same as the name used at the start of it. Thus, if the identification starts with the name "ITEM" and ends with the name "Item," the names are not the same, resulting in a syntax error. XML processors cannot process documents with syntax errors and will express their frustration with an error message. Remember how your English teacher complained about missing punctuation? The XML processor is just as strict, if not stricter.

1. Open the file Inventory.xml in Notepad.
2. Change the name at the end of the first item's description from "ITEM" to ":item" as shown below.
3. Save the file as BadInventory.xml.
4. Open the file BadInventory in Internet Explorer.

Internet Explorer displays a message indicating that the XML page cannot be displayed. Additionally, a message indicating the specific syntax error detected is displayed. In the above example, the browser displays the message that the name beginning at position 5 on line 8 does not match the name it expects, i.e., "ITEM." This is possible because the browser contains a processor that implements the XML specification regarding what will come to be known as "well formed."

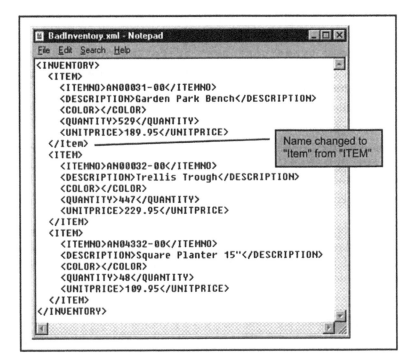

FIGURE C1HO.4
Inventory.xml opened for editing in Notepad.

Internet Explorer can be used to debug XML documents.

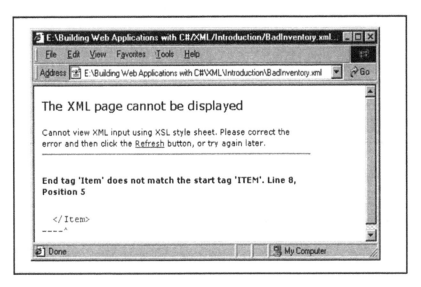

FIGURE C1HO.5
Syntax error detected by Internet Explorer.

Step 5: Displaying an XML File with Cascading Style Sheet

1. Open the file Inventory.xml in Notepad.

2. Add the following style sheet reference as the first line. (See Figure C1.6. Inventory.xml with style sheet reference.)

```
<?xml-stylesheet type="text/css" href="Inventory.css"?>
```

3. Using the Save As... option in the File menu, Save the revised file as **Inventory-WithStyleSheetRef.xml**.

4. Open a new file in Notepad.

5. Type in the style sheet shown in Figure C1.5. Inventory.css.

6. Using the Save As... option in the File menu, save the file as **Inventory.css**. Make sure that the style sheet file, **Inventory.css**, is saved in the same folder as the file **InventoryWithStyleSheetRef.xml.**

7. Open the **InventoryWithStyleSheetRef.xml** in Internet Explorer.

Internet Explorer opens and displays information relevant to a user interested in the inventory. The display is not burdened with the "XML markup" used to describe the inventory items and the inventory item's characteristics such as item number, name, quantity on hand, color and price.

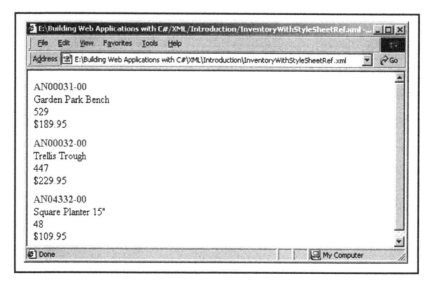

FIGURE C1HO.6
Inventory.xml displayed with style applied.

Note that the item number is displayed in bold red type and that each item is separated from the preceding item by a 10-point space.

Appendix C.2

Document Object Model: An Introduction

Modeling a Document as a Node Tree

A typical XML document representing an inventory is shown in Figure C2.1.

The hierarchical, tree-like organization of the document in the file Inventory.xml is shown in Figure C2.2. The figure illustrates the type of node used to represent the various components of the document. The document, as a whole, is represented by the Document type node. Similarly, the processing instruction and comment are represented by a ProcessingInstruction node and Comment node, respectively. In the same fashion, elements of the document are represented by Element nodes. Note that some of the elements, for example, INVENTORY and ITEM elements, have child nodes and that the topmost element, representing the document's root element, is a child of the Document element.

```
<?xml version="1.0" ?>

<!-- File: Inventory.xml -->

<INVENTORY>
  <ITEM>
    <ITEMNO>AN00031-00</ITEMNO>
    <DESCRIPTION>Garden Park Bench</DESCRIPTION>
    <COLOR></COLOR>
    <QUANTITY>529</QUANTITY>
    <UNITPRICE>$189.95</UNITPRICE>
  </ITEM>
  <ITEM>
    <ITEMNO>AN00032-00</ITEMNO>
    <DESCRIPTION>Trellis Trough</DESCRIPTION>
    <COLOR></COLOR>
    <QUANTITY>447</QUANTITY>
    <UNITPRICE>$229.95</UNITPRICE>
  </ITEM>
  <ITEM>
    <ITEMNO>AN04332-00</ITEMNO>
    <DESCRIPTION>Square Planter 15"</DESCRIPTION>
    <COLOR></COLOR>
    <QUANTITY>48</QUANTITY>
    <UNITPRICE>$109.95</UNITPRICE>
  </ITEM>
</INVENTORY>
```

FIGURE C2.1
XML document representing an inventory (Inventory.xml).

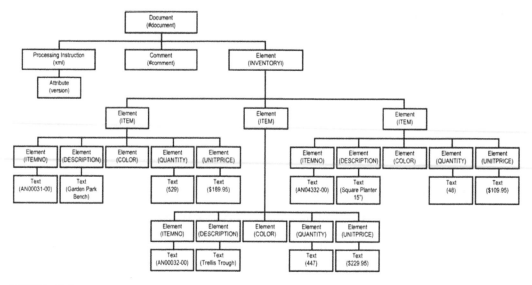

FIGURE C2.2
Hierarchical Organization of Data Described in Inventory.xml.

Document Object Model

The **Documents Object Model (DOM)** creates an interpretation of a document as an object node tree. Documents interpreted in the DOM model are manageable by Microsoft's MSXML parser, including the following:

- Loading or creating a document
- Accessing and manipulating including adding, changing and deleting components
- Saving the document as an XML file

The parser is contained in the MSXML Library. Classes, interfaces and enumerations used to implement the DOM are contained in the System.Xml namespace. Selected classes implementing the DOM are summarized in Figure C2.3.

The **XmlNode** class provides the basic class used to represent the document object model's nodes. The class hierarchy of selected classes is shown in Figure C2.4.

The XmlNode class represents a single document node. The class is derived directly from the Object class. The formal reference is:

```
public abstract class XmlNode: Icloneable, IEnumerable
```

Note that the XmlNode class is an abstract class, i.e., it cannot be instantiated and it provides the base for other classes. The namespace is System.Xml. Selected properties illustrating the capability of the XmlNode are listed in Figure C2.5.

XmlNode methods provide for management of the document including the addition and deletion of document nodes. Methods of the XmlNode class are summarized in Figure C2.6.

The **XmlDocument** class provides for representation of an entire XML document; it inherits the properties of the XmlNode class with its declaration:

```
public class XmlDocument : XmlNode
```

Name	Representation
XmlAttribute	Attribute with schema-defined values and default.
XmlComment	Content of an XML comment.
XmlDeclaration	XML declaration.
XmlDocument	Entire XML document.
XmlElement	XML element.
XmlLinkedNode	Gets the node immediately preceding or following the current node.
XmlNode	Single node in an XML document.
XmlNodeList	An ordered collection of a child nodes.
XmlProcessingInstruction	A processing instruction.
XmlSignificantWhitespace	White space between markup in a mixed content mode.
XmlText	Text content of an element or attribute.
XmlWhitespace	White space in element content.

FIGURE C2.3
Classes implementing the DOM nodes.

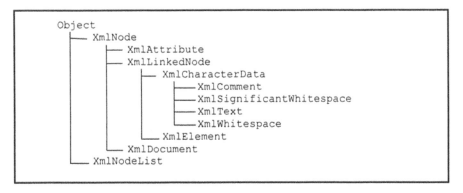

```
Object
   └── XmlNode
          ├── XmlAttribute
          ├── XmlLinkedNode
          │        └── XmlCharacterData
          │                 ├── XmlComment
          │                 ├── XmlSignificantWhitespace
          │                 ├── XmlText
          │                 └── XmlWhitespace
          │        └── XmlElement
          └── XmlDocument
   └── XmlNodeList
```

FIGURE C2.4
Hierarchy of selected DOM implementation classes.

Name	Value	Description
FirstChild	XmlNode	The FirstChild property gets the first child node of the current node. A null reference is returned if there is no node.
NodeType	XmlNodeType	Gets the type of the node as an XmlNodeType value.
Name	string	Gets the name of the node.
Value	string	Gets or sets the value of the node.
InnerText	string	Gets or sets the concatenated values of the node and all its child nodes.
ChildNodes	XmlNodeList	The XmlNodeList object returned contains all the node's children. The XmlNodeList is empty if there are no children.

FIGURE C2.5
Selected properties of XmlNode class.

Definition	Description

`public virtual XmlNode AppendChild(`
`    XmlNode newChild`
`);`
	The method adds a new child node at the end of the list of the node's children. The method has a single parameter, `newChild` object, which represents the node to add. If the new node is already in the list it is first removed.

`public virtual XmlNode InsertAfter(`
`    XmlNode newChild`
`    XmlNode refChild`
`);`
	The method inserts the specified new child node immediately after the specified reference node.
	The method has two parameters:
	• `newChild`, which represents the node to insert.
	• `refChild`, which represents the node after which the new child node is added. When the `refChild` is null the `newChild` is added at the beginning of the list of the node's children.
	If the new node is already in the list it is first removed.

`public virtual XmlNode InsertBefore(`
`    XmlNode newChild`
`    XmlNode refChild`
`);`
	The method inserts the specified new child node immediately before the specified reference node.
	The method has two parameters:
	• `newChild`, which represents the node to insert.
	• `refChild`, which represents the node before which the new child node is added. When the `refChild` is null the `newChild` is added at the end of the list of the node's children.
	If the new node is already in the node tree it is first removed.

`public virtual void RemoveAll( );`	The method removes all of the child nodes and attributes of the current node.

`public virtual XmlNode RemoveChild(`
`    XmlNode oldChild`
`);`
	The method removes the specified old child node. The method has a single parameter:
	`OldChild`, which represents the node to be removed. The method returns the node removed.

`public virtual XmlNode ReplaceChild(`
`    XmlNode newChild`
`    XmlNode oldChild`
`);`
	The method replaces the specified old child node with the specified new child node. The method has two parameters:
	• `newChild`, which represents the node to put in the list to replace the `oldChild` node.
	• `oldChild`, which represents the node which is replaced by the new child node.
	If the new node is already in the node tree it is first removed.

FIGURE C2.6
Selected methods of XmlNode class.

Objects of the XmlDocument class can be instantiated and initialized with the class constructors, as illustrated in Figure C2.7. Another constructor creates and initializes a new instance of the XmlDocument class with a specified XmlNameTable. Properties, summarized in Figure C2.8, provide the class with the ability to represent a node including the node representing the entire document.

The XmlDocument class methods shown in Figure C2.9 include provisions for loading and saving XML documents.

```
public XmlDocument( );          Initializes a new instance of an
                                XmlDocument class.
public XmlDocument(             Initializes a new instance of an
   string name                  XmlDocument class with DocumentName
);                              property value name.
```

FIGURE C2.7
XmlDocument class constructor.

public XmlElement **DocumentElement** {get;}	Gets the root XmlElement of the document, that is, the root of the XML document tree. A null reference is returned if a root node does not exist.
public string **Name** {override get;}	Gets the name of the node. For XmlDocuments the name is "#document".

FIGURE C2.8
Selected properties of the XmlDocument class.

```
public virtual void Load(       Loads the XML document from the
string fileurl                  specified URL. The method takes a
);                              single parameter fileurl which is
                                the URL of the file containing the
                                XML document. Other versions of the
                                load method enable loading documents
                                referenced by TextReader and
                                XmlReader objects.
public virtual void LoadXml(    Loads the XML document represented
      string xmldoc             as a string. The method takes a single
);                              string parameter, xmldoc, containing
                                the XML document.
public virtual void Save(       Saves the XML document from the
      string fileurl            specified URL. The method takes a
);                              single parameter fileurl which is
                                the URL of the file where the XML
                                document is saved. Other versions of
                                the load method enable loading
                                documents referenced by
                                TextReader and XmlReader
                                objects.
```

FIGURE C2.9
Selected methods of the XmlDocument class.

The members of the **XmlNodeType** enumeration specify the types of DOM nodes. The formal reference is:

```
public enum XMLNodeType
```

Members of the enumeration are listed in Figure C2.10.

Consider the simple document shown in Figure C2.11, which is typical of a document that might contain the results of a query pertaining to a single item in an inventory. The node tree model of the document illustrating the class used to represent the various nodes is shown in Figure C2.12.

Member Name	Value	Description
All	19	All node types.
Attribute	2	An attribute.
CDATA	4	A CDATA section.
Comment	6	A comment.
Document	9	A document object which provides access to other objects.
DocumentFragment	11	A document fragment.
DocumentType	10	The document type declaration.
Element	1	An element.
EndEntity	16	Returned by XmlReader at end of entity replacement.
EndTag	15	Returned by XmlReader at end of element.
Entity	6	An entity declaration.
EntityReference	5	A reference to an entity.
None	0	XmlNavigator cursor is not positioned on a node.
Notation	12	A notation. Example: `<! NOTATION ... >`
ProcessingInstruction	7	A processing instruction. Example: `<?pi sample?>`
SignificantWhitespace	14	White space.
Text	3	Text content of an element.
Whitespace	13	White space.
XmlDeclaration	18	Xml declaration.

FIGURE C2.10
XmlNodeType enumeration members.

```
<?xml version="1.0"?>

<!-- File Name: SingleItem.xml -->

<ITEM>
    <ITEMNO>AN00031-00</ITEMNO>
    <DESCRIPTION>Garden Park Bench</DESCRIPTION>
    <UNITPRICE>$189.95</UNITPRICE>
</ITEM>
```

FIGURE C2.11
SingleItem.xml representing a query result document.

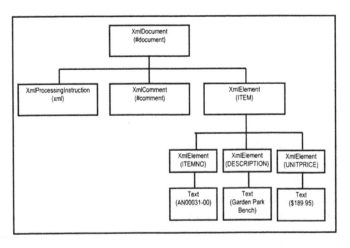

FIGURE C2.12
DOM of SingleItem.xml document.

```
<%@ Page Language="C#" %>

<%@ Import Namespace="System.Xml" %>

<HTML>
  <HEAD>
    <TITLE>Document Node Properties</TITLE>
    <script language="C#" runat=server>
      void Page_Load(Object Src, EventArgs E)
      {
         XmlDocument xmlDoc = new XmlDocument( );
         xmlDoc.Load("C:\\Inetpub\\wwwroot\\DOM\\SingleItem.xml");

         name.Text = xmlDoc.Name;
         type.Text = xmlDoc.NodeType.ToString() + " " +
            Enum.GetName(xmlDoc.NodeType.GetType(),
                  xmlDoc.NodeType);
         innertext.Text = xmlDoc.InnerText;
         value.Text = xmlDoc.Value;
      }
    </script>
  </HEAD>
  <BODY>
    <h3>Document Node Property Values:</h3>
    Name:
    <asp:label id="name" text=" " runat="server"/><br
    Type:
    <asp:label id="type" text=" " runat="server"/><br>
    InnerText:
    <asp:label id="innertext" text=" " runat="server"/><br>
    Value:
    <asp:label id="value" text=" " runat="server"/><br>
  </BODY>
</HTML>
```

FIGURE C2.13A
ASP creating DOM of SingleItem.xml (DocumentNode.aspx).

Creating, Loading and Saving an XML Document

An XmlDocument object represents an XML document. An XmlDocument object, xmlDoc, for example, is created with the statement

```
XmlDocument xmlDoc = new XmlDocument();
```

The document's content can be loaded into the XmlDocument object, xmlDoc, with the Load method.

```
xmlDoc.Load("C:\\Inetpub\\wwwroot\\DOM\\SingleItem.xml");
```

The single parameter of the Load method specifies the URL of the file containing the XML document. An XlmDocument object is a node, i.e., an XmlNode, and has the properties of a node including Name, NodeType, InnerText and Value. The ASP page (Figure C2.13A) illustrates the creation of a DOM of the SingleItem.xml file.

The following statement computes the Name, Type, InnerText and Value properties of the node representing the entire document:

```
name.Text = xmlDoc.Name;
type.Text = xmlDoc.NodeType.ToString() + " " +
    Enum.GetName( xmlDoc.NodeType.GetType(), xmlDoc.NodeType);
innertext.Text = xmlDoc.InnerText;
value.Text = xmlDoc.Value;
```

The property values are assigned to asp.label elements and displayed when the page is loaded.

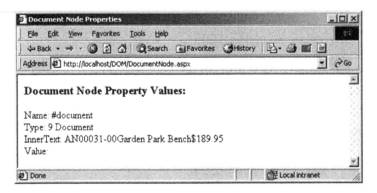

FIGURE C2.13B
Display of ASP showing properties of SingleItem.xml DOM document node.

Note that the Type property of the node is "Document," the Name property is "#document" and the Value property is null. The Name and Value property values returned depend on the type of node and are summarized in Figure C2.14.

Node Type	Name	Value
Attribute	Name of attribute	Value of attribute
CDATA	"#cdata-section"	Content of the CDATA section
Comment	"#comment"	Content of the comment
Document	"#document"	null
DocumentFragment	"#document-fragment"	null
DocumentType	Document type name	null
Element	Tag name	null
Entity	Entity name	null
EntityReference	Name of entity referenced	null
Notation	Notation name	null
ProcessingInstruction	Target	Content excluding the target
Text	"#text"	Content of the text node

FIGURE C2.14
Name and Value property values of selected node types.

The InnerText property of a node returns the concatenated value of all the element child nodes. Thus, the InnerText property of the node representing the entire document returns the concatenated text of all the SingleItem.xml document elements:

```
AN00031-00Garden Park Bench$189.95
```

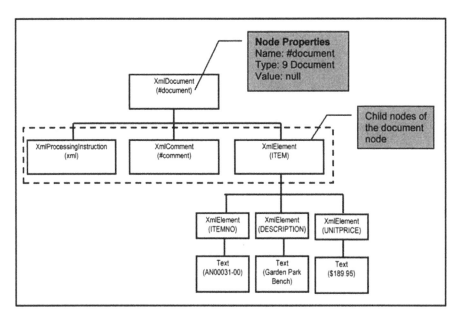

FIGURE C2.15
DOM of SingleItem.xml showing the child nodes of the document node.

Accessing the Document's Nodes

The document node represents the entire document. The document node of the Single-Item.xml DOM has three child nodes, as shown in Figure C2.15. The ChildNodes property of an XmlNode class object gets an ordered collection of the child nodes of the current node. The ChildNodes property returns an XmlNodeList class object.

The XmlNodeList class represents the ordered collection of child nodes of the node object from which it is created. For example, an XmlNodeList object is returned by the ChildNodes property of the XmlNode class. The class is derived directly from the Object class. Selected XmlNodeList properties are summarized in Figure C2.16. XmlNodeList class methods, depicted in Figure C2.17, include provisions accessing the nodes in the list.

The listing in Figure C2.18A illustrates the creation of a list of child nodes and their access. The entire document is represented by the XmlDocument class object xmlDoc:

```
XmlDocument xmlDoc = new XmlDocument( );

xmlDoc.Load("C:\\Inetpub\\wwwroot\\DOM\\SingleItem.xml");
```

`public int ` **`Count`** ` {abstract get;}`	Gets the number of nodes in the list.
`public XmlNode ` **`this[ int i ]`** ` {virtual get;}`	Gets the node at the specified index. The single parameter *i* is a zero-based index into the list. A null is returned when the index is greater than or equal to the number of nodes in the list.

FIGURE C2.16
Selected properties of the XmlNodeList class.

`public abstract XmlNode Item(int i);`	Retrieves the node at the specified index. The single parameter *i* is a zero-based index into the list. An XmlNode object, representative of the node at the specified index, is returned. A null is returned when the index is greater than or equal to the number of nodes in the list.
`public abstract IEnumerator` `    GetEnumerator();`	Returns a ForEach-style iteration over the collection of nodes in the XmlNodeList.

FIGURE C2.17
Selected methods of the XmlNodeList class.

```
<%@ Page Language="C#" %>

<%@ Import Namespace="System.Xml" %>

<HTML>
  <HEAD>
    <TITLE>Document Child Nodes Properties</TITLE>
    <script language="C#" runat=server>
      void Page_Load(Object Src, EventArgs E)
      {
         XmlDocument xmlDoc = new XmlDocument( );
         xmlDoc.Load("C:\\Inetpub\\wwwroot\\DOM\\SingleItem.xml");

         XmlNodeList docChildNodeList = xmlDoc.ChildNodes;
         noChildNodes.Text = docChildNodeList.Count.ToString();

                XmlNode node0 = docChildNodeList[0];
         node0Name.Text = node0.Name;
         node0Type.Text = node0.NodeType.ToString() + " " +
         Enum.GetName(node0.NodeType.GetType(), node0.NodeType);
         node0InnerText.Text = node0.InnerText;
         node0Value.Text = node0.Value;
         XmlNodeList node0List = node0.ChildNodes;
         noNode0Nodes.Text = node0List.Count.ToString();

                XmlNode node1 = docChildNodeList[1];
         node1Name.Text = node1.Name;
         node1Type.Text = node1.NodeType.ToString() + " " +
         Enum.GetName(node1.NodeType.GetType(), node1.NodeType);
         node1InnerText.Text = node1.InnerText;
         node1Value.Text = node1.Value;
         XmlNodeList node1List = node1.ChildNodes;
         noNode1Nodes.Text = node1List.Count.ToString();

                XmlNode node2 = docChildNodeList[2];
         node2Name.Text = node2.Name;
         node2Type.Text = node2.NodeType.ToString() + " " +
         Enum.GetName(node2.NodeType.GetType(), node2.NodeType);
         node2InnerText.Text = node2.InnerText;
         node2Value.Text = node2.Value;
         XmlNodeList node2List = node2.ChildNodes;
         noNode2Nodes.Text = node2List.Count.ToString();
      }
    </script>
  </HEAD>
```

FIGURE C2.18A
Accessing child nodes of the SingleItem.xml's document node.

```
  <BODY>
    <h4>Document Node :</h4>
    No. of Child Nodes:
    <asp:label id="noChildNodes" text=" " runat="server"/><br>

    <h4>Document Child Node 0 Properties</h4><br>
    Name:
    <asp:label id="node0Name" text=" " runat="server"/><br>
    Type:
    <asp:label id="node0Type" text=" " runat="server"/><br>
    InnerText:
    <asp:label id="node0InnerText" text=" " runat="server"/><br>
    Value:
    <asp:label id="node0Value" text=" " runat="server"/><br>
    No Child Nodes:
    <asp:label id="noNode0Nodes" text=" " runat="server"/><br>

    <h4>Document Child Node 1 Properties</h4><br>
    Name:
    <asp:label id="node1Name" text=" " runat="server"/><br>
    Type:
    <asp:label id="node1Type" text=" " runat="server"/><br>
    InnerText:
    <asp:label id="node1InnerText" text=" " runat="server"/><br>
    Value:
    <asp:label id="node1Value" text=" " runat="server"/><br>
    No Child Nodes:
    <asp:label id="noNode1Nodes" text=" " runat="server"/><br>

    <h4>Document Child Node 2 Properties</h4><br>
    Name:
    <asp:label id="node2Name" text=" " runat="server"/><br>
    Type:
    <asp:label id="node2Type" text=" " runat="server"/><br>
    InnerText:
    <asp:label id="node2InnerText" text=" " runat="server"/><br>
    Value:
    <asp:label id="node2Value" text=" " runat="server"/><br>
    No Child Nodes:
    <asp:label id="noNode2Nodes" text=" " runat="server"/><br>
  </BODY>
</HTML>
```

FIGURE C2.18A (CONTINUED)
Accessing child nodes of the SingleItem.xml's document node.

The ChildNodes property of the xmlDoc object gets an XmlNodeList object containing a collection of XmlNode objects representing the child nodes of the xmlDoc node:

```
XmlNodeList docChildNodeList = xmlDoc.ChildNodes;
```

In this case, the returned XmlNodeList object is assigned to the XmlNodeList variable docChildNodeList.

The Count property of the XmlNodeList class gets the number of nodes in the node list. For example, the expression

```
docChildNodeList.Count
```

returns the number of nodes in the node list object docChildNodeList. The expression

```
docChildNodeList.Count
```

evaluates to the number of child nodes in the list.

The first node in the list is accessed with the statement

```
XmlNode node0 = docChildNodeList[0];
```

The node's Name, NodeType, InnerText and Value properties are accessed with the expressions node0.Name, node0.NodeType, node0.InnerText and node0.Value, respectively.

The list of child nodes of the first node is determined by the statement

```
XmlNodeList node0List = node0.ChildNodes;
```

The number of nodes in the list is computed by the expression

```
node0List.Count
```

Other nodes in the document are similarly accessed. The program's output is shown in Figure C2.18B.

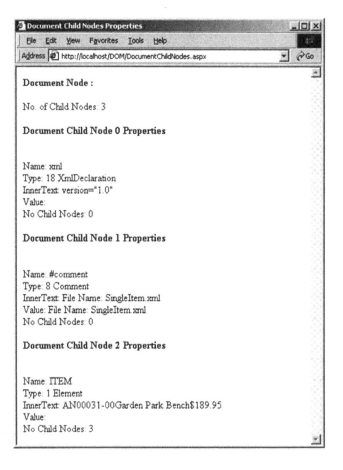

FIGURE C2.18B
Output of program accessing child nodes of the SingleItem.xml's document node.

Note the number of child nodes associated with the third node in the document. Compare the results of the analysis performed in the program with the document object model shown in Figure C2.15. Note that the third node of the document node has three child nodes.

Appendix D

SOAP

Simple Object Access Protocol (SOAP) is an XML-based protocol that enables software components and applications to communicate across the Web using HTTP.

Simple Object Access Protocol (SOAP) 1.2

Simple Object Access Protocol (SOAP) enables communication between distributed components and applications over the Internet using HTTP.

SOAP, an idea fostered by Dave Winer at Userland Software, was formalized by the combined efforts of Dave Winer, Don Box at DevelopMentor, and Microsoft. The current version represents the thinking of a wider group, including IBM, Sun Microsystems and Canon. At first, the reaction of the development community was cool. However, SOAP has emerged as the industry's "standard."

W3C stewardship of SOAP is the responsibility of the XML Protocol Working Group, which is part of the XML Protocol Activity. The XML Protocol Working Group's charter is described in the *XML Protocol Activity Statement* as:

1. An envelope to encapsulate XML data for transfer in an interoperable manner that allows for distributed extensibility, evolvability, as well as intermediaries like proxies, caches, and gateways

2. In cooperation with the IETF (Internet Engineering Task Force), an operating system-neutral convention for the content of the envelope when used for RPC (Remote Procedure Call) applications

3. A mechanism to serialize data based on XML Schema datatypes

4. In cooperation with the IETF, a non-exclusive mechanism layered on HTTP transport

Information regarding the Simple Object Access Protocol (SOAP) is available at http://www.w3.org/TR/soap12-part1/ and http://www.w3.org/TR/soap12-part2/.

SOAP consists of four parts:

1. An envelope that defines the overall framework for expressing what is in the message and how the message is to be handled

2. A binding framework that defines an abstract framework for exchanging SOAP messages using a transport protocol such as HTTP

3. Encoding rules that define how instances of application-defined datatypes can be serialized for exchange

4. A convention for representing remote procedure calls (RPC)

SOAP is simple and extensible and is not tied to any component technology or programming language. It is hoped that SOAP will become a W3C standard. The SOAP fundamentals presented are based on the SOAP Version 1.2 Part 1: Messaging Framework and SOAP and Version 1.2 Part 2: Adjuncts, a W3C Working Draft, dated October 2, 2001. The following exposition is intended to provide the SOAP insight required to develop Web Services, but not to develop the knowledge required to develop SOAP Tools.

Example and Basic Syntax

A SOAP message is an XML document containing the following XML elements:

- An envelope defining the content of the message, which is the outermost or root element that contains all other elements
- An optional header containing information regarding the message that can be targeted to receivers along the message path
- A body containing the actual message — typically, call and response information

An example of a SOAP XML document message requesting the amount of a service fee, based on provided account amount and type parameters, is shown in Figure D.1. This example illustrates the envelope and body elements.

```
<?xml version="1.0" encoding="utf-8"?>
<soap:Envelope
  xmlns:xsi="http://www.w3.org/2001/XMLSchema-instance"
  xmlns:xsd="http://www.w3.org/2001/XMLSchema"
  xmlns:soap="http://schemas.xmlsoap.org/soap/envelope/">
  <soap:Body>
    <ServiceFee xmlns="http://tempuri.org/">
      <amount>321.58</amount>
      <type>R</type>
    </ServiceFee>
  </soap:Body>
</soap:Envelope>
```

body element

envelope element

FIGURE D.1
SOAP request example.

The choice of namespace prefix is arbitrary. Figure D.2 summarizes Namespace prefixes. Included in the summary are prefixes and namespaces used in the example. The summary also presents the prefixes used in the SOAP Working Draft. Elements and attributes must be correctly namespaced.

Example	Working Draft	Namespace
xsi	xsi	"http://www.w3.org/2001/XMLSchema-instance"
xsd	xs	"http://www.w3.org/2001/XMLSchema"
soap		"http://schemas.xmlsoap.org/soap/envelope"
	env	"http://www.w3.org/2001/09/soap-envelope"
	enc	"http://www.w3.org/2001/09/soap-encoding"

FIGURE D.2
Namespaces prefix summary.

Note that a SOAP message must not contain a Document Type Declaration and it must not contain processing instruction information items.

SOAP Envelope: The Overall Framework

A **SOAP node** processes a SOAP message according to the SOAP principles. A **SOAP message** is the entity of communication between SOAP nodes. Components of a SOAP message are summarized in Figure D.3.

Component	Description
Envelope	Outermost construct of a SOAP message. A message has only one envelope that encloses all other components.
Block	A syntactical structure that delimits a logical entity that is to be treated as a whole by a SOAP node. Blocks encapsulated within the SOAP header and the SOAP body are referred to as a header block and a body block, respectively.
Body	Zero or more body blocks targeted at the ultimate or final node.
Fault	A special SOAP block that contains information regarding faults raised at a SOAP node.

FIGURE D.3
SOAP message components.

SOAP Envelope Element

The SOAP **envelope element** is the topmost element of the XML document representing the message. Figure D.4 summarizes the envelope element syntax.

> The Envelope element has the following:
> - The name envelope.
> - Namespace "http://www.w3.org/2001/09/soap-envelope ".
> - Zero or more namespace-qualified attribute information items.
> - An optional Header child element that precedes the Body element.
> - A required Body child element.

FIGURE D.4
Envelope element syntax summary.

An **encodingStyle** attribute provides for describing encoding rules used to serialize the SOAP message. The encodingStyle is a white-space-separated list where each item in the list is a namespace name and identifies a set of rules used to deserialize the SOAP message. The items should be ordered listing the most specific first and the least specific last. Note that a zero-length URI, i.e., "", specifically states that no specification is made regarding the encoding style. An example of the encodingStyle attribute is the following:

```
EncodingStyle="http://company.com/encodingrule"
```

Note that the SOAP versioning is nontraditional. Versioning is simply handled by ensuring, first, that the received message must have a topmost element of envelope and, second, that the namespace must be "http://www.w3.org/2001/09/soap-envelope". Messages not meeting these requirements are viewed as having a version error and generate a VersionMismatch SOAP fault.

The envelope tag can include namespace prefix declarations. Three prefix declarations are in the example:

```
xmlns:xsi="http://www.w3.org/2001/XMLSchema-instance"
xmlns:xsd="http://www.w3.org/2001/XMLSchemac"
xmlns:soap="http://schemas.xmlsoap.org/soap/envelope/"
```

SOAP Header Element

The SOAP **header element** provides for extending a SOAP message outside the content of the actual message. Typically, the header provides for providing information regarding authorization and authentication. Note that the actual information in this instance would be the account number, transaction type and amount. The header element syntax is summarized in Figure D.5. Header element attributes are summarized in Figure D.6. The namespace of the header element attributes is "http://www.w3.org/2001/09/soap-envelope."

> The Header element has the following:
> - The name header.
> - Namespace "http://www.w3.org/2001/09/soap-envelope ".
> - Zero or more namespace-qualified attribute information items.
> - Zero or more namespace-qualified child element information items.

FIGURE D.5
Header element syntax summary.

Attribute	Description
encodingStyle	Used to specify encoding rules used to serialize a SOAP message. (See Envelope Element.)
actor	Used to indicate the SOAP node at which the SOAP header is targeted. The value is a URI that names the role the node can assume. When omitted, the SOAP header block is targeted at the ultimate SOAP receiver. A receiver is a SOAP node that accepts a SOAP message. The ultimate receiver is the receiver specified by the initial sender as the final destination of the SOAP message.
mustUnderstand	Indicates that the header processing is mandatory or optional if true. Omission of the attribute is the same as including the attribute with the value false.

FIGURE D.6
Header attribute summary.

SOAP Body Element

The Soap **body element** contains the information intended for the ultimate SOAP receiver; its syntax is summarized in Figure D.7.

> The Envelope element has the following:
> - Name: body.
> - Namespace: "http://www.w3.org/2001/09/soap-envelope ".
> - Zero or more child elements, called SOAP body blocks. Each body block may be namespace qualified and may have an encodingStyle attribute.

FIGURE D.7
Body element syntax summary.

The example body element is shown in Figure D.8. The body element contains three child elements: <ServiceFee>, <amount> and <type>. Note that namespace qualification of the child elements is not mandatory and that the body child elements carry the message information, in this case, parameters for the method ServiceFee. The first parameter is the amount and its value is 321.58. The second parameter is account type and its value is R.

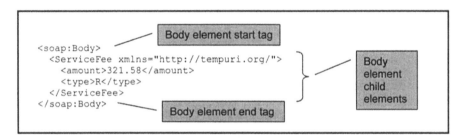

FIGURE D.8
Body element example.

SOAP Fault Element

SOAP also defines a special SOAP body block, the SOAP fault. The Soap **fault element** is used for reporting errors detected by SOAP nodes. One and only one SOAP fault can appear in a SOAP body and must be contained in a body block. The SOAP fault element syntax is summarized in Figure D.9.

> The Fault element has the following:
> - Name: fault.
> - Namespace: "http://www.w3.org/2001/09/soap-envelope ".
> - Two or more child elements in order as follows:
>   1. A mandatory faultcode element.
>   2. A mandatory faultstring element.
>   3. An optional faultactor element.
>   4. An optional detail element.

FIGURE D.9
Fault element syntax summary.

The **faultcode element** provides means for specifying faults in a program friendly manner. Unique codes are used to specify specific faults. Faultcode element grammar is summarized in Figure D.10. The SOAP codes are XML-qualified names. The member selection operator, i.e., the dot character, is used to separate SOAP faultcode values where the more general code is to the left of the dot and the more specific code is to the right of it. The *Working Draft* provides an example of an authentication fault:

```
Client.Authentication
```

> The Faultcode element has the following:
> - Name: faultcode.
> - Valid faultcode values are the following:
>   - VersionMismatch   Invalid envelope element namespace.
>   - MustUnderstand   An immediate header element child element was not understood.
>   - DataEncodingUnknown   Header or body encoding specified is not supported.
>   - Client   Improperly formed message or inappropriate information supplied.
>   - Server   Processing fault raised at server.

FIGURE D.10
Faultcode element syntax summary.

The **faultstring element** is intended to provide a readable interpretation of the fault. This element is also intended to complement the faultcode element, which is intended to be programmatically processable, whereas the faultstring element is not.

The **faultactor element** is intended to provide information about the node at which the fault was raised. If the node is the ultimate SOAP receiver, the faultactor element may be included, whereas if the node is not, the faultactor element must be included.

The **faultdetail** element is intended to provide specific error information regarding the SOAP body and must be included when the SOAP body cannot be processed successfully. Figure D.11 summarizes the faultdetail element syntax.

> The Faultdetail element has the following:
> - Name: faultdetail.
> - Zero or more attributes.
> - Zero or more child elements. The child elements may be namespace qualified and may have an encodingStyle attribute. Note: The encodingStyle attribute is used to specify encoding rules used to serialize a SOAP message. (See Envelope Element.)

FIGURE D.11
Faultdetail element syntax summary.

SOAP Encoding: Data Serialization

SOAP encoding provides the rules for serialization of a graph of typed objects. Encoding is performed on two levels. First, a schema for an XML grammar is constructed based on the type schemas typically used in programming languages and databases. Second, an XML instance of a graph of values conforming to the schema is constructed. The following examples illustrate the serialization produced by the SOAP encoding rules.

Simple Types

The simple types include all the "built-in datatypes" of the XML schema. Examples include int and float datatypes. These types might be used in a schema describing a customer account. Consider, for example, the schema shown in Figure D.12A.

```
<!-- schema document -->
<xs:schema xmlns:xs=http://www.w3.org/2001/XMLSchema>

  <xs:element name="id" type="xs:int" />
  <xs:element name="amount" type="xs:float" />
</xs:schema>
```

FIGURE D.12A
Example of a customer account schema with simple types int and float.

A message illustrating an instance of data conforming to the schema is shown in Figure D.12B.

```
<!--Instance example -->
<id>711</id>
<amount>1001.101</amount>
```

FIGURE D.12B
Message illustrating serialization of simple data types.

Simple types are encoded as the content of elements. Encoding rules provide for the serialization of strings, arrays and enumerations.

Compound Types

SOAP provides for serialization of compound data types. Included are "struct" types in which the members are accessed by name and each member of the "struct" has a unique name. Also included are "array" types in which the members are accessed by their ordinal value. A C# struct data type, modeling a business customer, is shown in Figure D.13A. The struct is identified as Customer and contains members representing the customer's unique identification, name and balance amount. The schema fragment shown in Figure D.13B describes the Customer struct. An instance message fragment is shown in Figure D.13C.

```
public struct Customer
{
  public int id,
  public string name;
  public float amount;
}
```

FIGURE D.13A
Example of a customer struct.

```
<!-- Customer schema document -->
  <xs:element name="customer"
              xmlns:xs=http://www.w3.org/2001/XMLSchema>
    <xs:complexType>
      <xs:sequence>
        <xs:element name="id" type="xs:int" />
        <xs:element name="name" type="xs:string" />
        <xs:element name="amount" type="xs:float" />
      </xs:sequence>
    </xs:complextype>
  </xs:element name="amount" type="xs:float" />
```

FIGURE D.13B
Example of a Customer schema fragment.

```
<!-Instance example -->
<customer>
  <id>711</id>
  <name>Any Customer</name>
  <amount>1001.101</amount>
</customer>
```

FIGURE D.13C
Message illustrating serialization of a customer instance.

SOAP Binding: Message Exchange Framework

SOAP provides for using SOAP with HTTP. SOAP is consistent with the HTTP request/response model in that SOAP provides for a SOAP request message in an HTTP request and a SOAP response method in an HTTP response. This section provides examples illustrating SOAP HTTP examples.

SOAP HTTP Request

An example of a SOAP HTTP Request is shown in Figure D.14. Use of SOAP within HTTP Request is only defined for HTTP POST requests.

The SOAP document is the body of an HTTP request. Note the inclusion of the SOAP-Action header. Additionally, the SOAP document specifies two parameters: an amount parameter with value 321.58 and a type parameter with value R.

```
POST /FeeServices/Fees.asmx HTTP/1.1                    [SOAP message]
Host: lajolla
Content-Type: text/xml; charset=utf-8
Content-Length: 334
SOAPAction: "http://tempuri.org/ServiceFee"  —  [soapaction header]

<?xml version="1.0" encoding="utf-8"?>
<soap:Envelope xmlns:xsi="http://www.w3.org/2001/XMLSchema-instance"
  xmlns:xsd="http://www.w3.org/2001/XMLSchema"
  xmlns:soap="http://schemas.xmlsoap.org/soap/envelope/">
  <soap:Body>
    <ServiceFee xmlns="http://tempuri.org/">
      <amount>321.58</amount>
      <type>R</type>
    </ServiceFee>
  </soap:Body>
</soap:Envelope>
```

FIGURE D.14
Example of a SOAP HTTP Request using POST.

The **soapaction** HTTP header provides information needed by some SOAP receivers. The value of the soapaction header can be any URI reference, including both absolute and relative. A **req-soapaction** header is provided for cases in which the SOAP receiver requires information in order to perform.

SOAP HTTP Response

A SOAP HTTP response is shown in Figure D.15. Note that the SOAP document describes a result with value 5.5.

```
HTTP/1.1 200 OK
Content-Type: text/xml; charset=utf-8          SOAP response body
Content-Length: 355

<?xml version="1.0" encoding="utf-8"?>
<soap:Envelope xmlns:xsi=http://www.w3.org/2001/XMLSchema-instance
  xmlns:xsd="http://www.w3.org/2001/XMLSchema"
  xmlns:soap="http://schemas.xmlsoap.org/soap/envelope/">
  <soap:Body>
    <ServiceFeeResponse xmlns="http://tempuri.org/">
      <ServiceFeeResult>5.5</ServiceFeeResult>
    </ServiceFeeResponse>
  </soap:Body>
</soap:Envelope>
```

FIGURE D.15
Example of SOAP HTTP response.

Appendix E

WSDL

Web Services Description Language (WSDL) is an XML grammar for describing network services as a collection of communication end points, or ports, capable of exchanging messages. A WSDL document describes these services.

Web Services Description Language (WSDL) 1.1

The document describing the language represents the collective thinking of more than a dozen companies regarding recommended suggestions for describing network services as a set of end points operating on messages. Although the messages and operations are described abstractly, they are bound to a concrete network protocol and message format to define concrete end points. Related end points are combined to describe the service. Information regarding WSDL is available at www.w3.org/TR/wsdl.html.

Overview

A WSDL document defines services using sections that correspond to grammatical elements, as summarized in Figure E.1.

Abstract Definitions	
Types	A container for machine- and language-independent data type definitions.
Message	A definition of the data transmitted, the input parameters and output response.
Operation	A description of the action performed by an end point.
Port Type	A set of operations supported by an end point.
Concrete Descriptions	
Binding	A concrete protocol and data format for a specific port type.
Port	A single end point defined as a network address and binding.
Service	A collection of end points.

FIGURE E.1
WSDL document elements summary.

The abstract definitions provide for describing messages in a machine- and language-independent manner. As such, the messages are applicable to the diversity encountered throughout the Web, i.e., different operating systems, different machines and different programming languages. The concrete definitions enable realization of the description with site-specific factors such as serialization and network address.

The Types section provides for abstractly describing the message data, while the Message section uses the definition of the Types elements to define the data exchanged. The PortType elements use the Message definitions and contain the Operations describing the actions performed by the service. The PortType is an abstract definition.

The Binding section refers to definition in the PortTypes section. Operation elements contained in the Port type section are modified by the operation definitions in the Bindings section. The Service section refers to the Binding section and contains the Port elements.

Note that the Binding, Port and Service sections and elements are concrete, i.e., site specific.

A WSDL document defines services as a collection of endpoints or ports.

A class Fees, shown in Figure E.2, contains a ServiceFee method that is exposed as a Web Service method. The method declares two parameters: a type decimal and type char. The method returns a type decimal value. A WSDL document, automatically generated by the WSDL authoring tool contained in Visual Studio.NET, is shown in Figure E.3.

```
public class Fees
{
        [WebMethod]
        public decimal ServiceFee(decimal amount, char type)
        {
                if (type == 'G')
                        return 0m;
                else
                        if (amount > 500m)
                                return 0m;
                        else
                                return 5.5m;
        }
}
```

FIGURE E.2
Web Service.

The WSDL document describes the Web Service Fees with an operation ServiceFee. Note the verbosity of the WSDL document. Fortunately, developers of Web Services need not write the WSDL document because tools that will generate it are available. The following description of WSDL is intended to provide an introductory understanding of the language.

Definitions

The **<definitions>** element is the root element of the WSDL document. An example is shown in Figure E.4.

Namespaces pertaining to the entire document are declared in the <definition> element. This allows references to the namespace later in the document by simply qualifying a

```
<?xml version="1.0" encoding="utf-8"?>
<definitions
  xmlns:s="http://www.w3.org/2001/XMLSchema"
  xmlns:http="http: //schemas.xmlsoap.org/wsdl/http/"
  xmlns:mime=" http: //schemas.xmlsoap.org/wsdl/mine/"
  xmlns:tm="http://microsoft.com/wsdl/mime/textMatching/"
  xmlns:soap="http://schemas.xmlsoap.org/wsdl/soap/"
  xmlns:soapenc="http://schemas.xmlsoap.org/soap/encoding/"
  xmlns:s0="http://tempuri.org/"
  xmlns:s1="http://microsoft.com/wsdl/types/"
  targetNamespace="http://tempuri.org/"
  xmlns="http://schemas.xmlsoap.org/wsdl/">
  <types>
    <s:schema attributeFormDefault="qualified"
        elementFormDefault="qualified"
        targetNamespace="http://tempuri.org/">
      <s:import namespace="http://microsoft.com/wsdl/types/" />
      <s:element name="ServiceFee">
        <s:complexType>
          <s:sequence>
            <s:element minOccurs="1" maxOccurs="1" name="amount"
                type="s:decimal" />
            <s:element minOccurs="1" maxOccurs="1" name="type"
                type="s1:char" />
          </s:sequence>
        </s:complexType>
      </s:element>
      <s:element name="ServiceFeeResponse">
        <s:complexType>
          <s:sequence>
            <s:element minOccurs="1" maxOccurs="1"
                name="ServiceFeeResult" type="s:decimal" />
          </s:sequence>
        </s:complexType>
      </s:element>
      <s:element name="decimal" type="s:decimal" />
    </s:schema>
    <s:schema attributeFormDefault="qualified"
        elementFormDefault="qualified"
        targetNamespace="http://microsoft.com/wsdl/types/">
      <s:simpleType name="char">
        <s:restriction base="s:unsignedShort" />
      </s:simpleType>
    </s:schema>
  </types>
```

FIGURE E.3
WSDL document describing a Web Service Fees.

name with the appropriate prefix. Note that the WSDL namespace is declared as the default namespace for the document; thus, all elements belong to this namespace unless another namespace is explicitly stated. Included are namespaces for SOAP, SOAP Encoding, HTTP, MINE and Microsoft WSDL Types.

Note that URIs are used for namespaces to guarantee uniqueness. The URI does not have to point to a real Web location; it simply uses the unique character of domain names that are unique across the Web. In the example, the default namespace is declared with the line

```
xmlns="http://schemas.xmlsoap.org/wsdl/"
```

All unqualified names in the document belong to this namespace.

Namespace prefixes are summarized in Figure E.5. The summary lists the prefixes declared in the example and similar prefixes declared in the *Web Services Description Language (WSDL)*.

```
<message name="ServiceFeeSoapIn">
  <part name="parameters" element="s0:ServiceFee" />
</message>
<message name="ServiceFeeSoapOut">
  <part name="parameters" element="s0:ServiceFeeResponse" />
</message>
<message name="ServiceFeeHttpGetIn">
  <part name="amount" type="s:string" />
  <part name="type" type="s:string" />
</message>
<message name="ServiceFeeHttpGetOut">
  <part name="Body" element="s0:decimal" />
</message>
<message name="ServiceFeeHttpPostIn">
  <part name="amount" type="s:string" />
  <part name="type" type="s:string" />
</message>
<message name="ServiceFeeHttpPostOut">
  <part name="Body" element="s0:decimal" />
</message>
<portType name="FeesSoap">
  <operation name="ServiceFee">
    <input message="s0:ServiceFeeSoapIn" />
    <output message="s0:ServiceFeeSoapOut" />
  </operation>
</portType>
<portType name="FeesHttpGet">
  <operation name="ServiceFee">
    <input message="s0:ServiceFeeHttpGetIn" />
    <output message="s0:ServiceFeeHttpGetOut" />
  </operation>
</portType>
<portType name="FeesHttpPost">
  <operation name="ServiceFee">
    <input message="s0:ServiceFeeHttpPostIn" />
    <output message="s0:ServiceFeeHttpPostOut" />
  </operation>
</portType>
<binding name="FeesSoap" type="s0:FeesSoap">
  <soap:binding transport="http: //schemas.xmlsoap.org/soap/http"
          style="document" />
  <operation name="ServiceFee">
    <soap:operation soapAction="http: //tempuri.org/ServiceFee"
            style="document" />
    <input>
      <soap:body use="literal" />
    </input>
    <output>
      <soap:body use="literal" />
    </output>
  </operation>
</binding>
```

FIGURE E.3 (CONTINUED)
WSDL document describing a Web Service Fees.

The **targetNamespace** attribute declares a namespace in which all the names declared in the element belong. In the example, the targetNamespace for <definitions> is declared with the line

```
targetNamespace="http://tempuri.org/"
```

Thus, names declared in the WSDL document belong to this namespace.

A description of the service is defined with five elements within the description element. These five elements are summarized in Figure E.6.

```
   <binding name="FeesHttpGet" type="s0:FeesHttpGet">
     <http:binding verb="GET" />
     <operation name="ServiceFee">
       <http:operation location="/ServiceFee" />
       <input>
         <http:urlEncoded />
       </input>
       <output>
         <mime:mimeXml part="Body" />
       </output>
     </operation>
   </binding>
   <binding name="FeesHttpPost" type="s0:FeesHttpPost">
     <http:binding verb="POST" />
     <operation name="ServiceFee">
       <http:operation location="/ServiceFee" />
       <input>
         <mime:content type="application/x-www-form-urlencoded" />
       </input>
       <output>
         <mime:mimeXml part="Body" />
       </output>
     </operation>
   </binding>
   <service name="Fees">
     <port name="FeesSoap" binding="s0:FeesSoap">
       <soap:address location="http://localhost/FeeServices/Fees.asmx" />
     </port>
     <port name="FeesHttpGet" binding="s0:FeesHttpGet">
       <http:address location="http://localhost/FeeServices/Fees.asmx" />
     </port>
     <port name="FeesHttpPost" binding="s0:FeesHttpPost">
       <http:address location="http://localhost/FeeServices/Fees.asmx" />
     </port>
   </service>
</definitions>
```

FIGURE E.3 (CONTINUED)
WSDL document describing a Web Service Fees.

```
<definitions
  xmlns:s="http://www.w3.org/2001/XMLSchema"
  xmlns:http="http: // schemas.xmlsoap.org/wsdl/http/"
  xmlns:mime="http: // schemas.xmlsoap.org/wsdl/mime/"
  xmlns:tm="http://microsoft.com/wsdl/mime/textMatching/"
  xmlns:soap="http://schemas.xmlsoap.org/wsdl/soap/"
  xmlns:soapenc="http://schemas.xmlsoap.org/soap/encoding/"
  xmlns:s0="http://tempuri.org/"
  xmlns:s1="http://microsoft.com/wsdl/types/"
  targetNamespace="http://tempuri.org/"                    ┌──────────┐
  xmlns="http://schemas.xmlsoap.org/wsdl/">                │ default  │
                                                           │ namespace│
                                                           └──────────┘
        ┌──────────────────────────────────────────────────────────┐
      / │ Elements comprising the content, for example <types>, <messages>, │
        │ <portType>, <binding> and <service>, are placed here       │
        └──────────────────────────────────────────────────────────┘

</definitions>
```

FIGURE E.4
FeesService Web Service WSDL <definitions> element.

Visual Studio	Description	WSDL Document
s	Schema namespace as defined by XSD	xsd
http	WSDL namespace for WSDL HTTP GET & POST binding	http
mine	WSDL namespace for WSDL MINE binding	mine
tm	microsoft.com/wsdl/mime/textMatching	
soap	WSDL namespace for WSDL SOAP binding	soap
soapenc	Encoding namespace as defined by SOAP	soapenc
s0	http :// tempuri.org/	
s1	http :// microsoft.com/wsdl/types/	
	WSDL namespace for WSDL framework (*Default*)	wsdl
	Envelope namespace as defined by SOAP 1.1	soapenv
	Schema namespace as defined by XSD	xsi

FIGURE E.5
Summary of namespace prefixes.

Element	Description
types	A container for data type definitions.
message	An abstract definition of the data being transmitted.
portType	An abstract set of operations performed by an end point.
binding	A concrete protocol and data format for a specific port type.
service	A collection of related end points.

FIGURE E.6
Description content elements describing the service.

Types

The **<types>** element encloses definitions of data types relevant to the message. An example of a type element is shown in Figure E.7. A WSDL document can have, at most, one types element. If the message does not refer to data, a types element is omitted.

The types element contains a **<schema>** element that declares its own namespace. Thus, all names defined in the schema element belong to that namespace and not the main namespace declared in the definitions element.

The **<import>** element provides for importing an independent document that allows for the separate definition of elements that can be imported as needed. The advantage is the ability to separate definitions, based on level of abstraction, that are easier to maintain and to use.

The message parts types of the ServiceFee message are defined:

```
<s:element name="ServiceFee">
  <s:complexType>
    <s:sequence>
      <s:element minOccurs="1" maxOccurs="1" name="amount"
          type="s:decimal" />
      <s:element minOccurs="1" maxOccurs="1" name="type"
          type="s1:char" />
    </s:sequence>
  </s:complexType>
</s:element>
```

```
<types>
  <s:schema attributeFormDefault="qualified"              Import element
      elementFormDefault="qualified"
      targetNamespace="http://tempuri.org/">
    <s:import namespace="http://microsoft.com/wsdl/types/" />

    <s:element name="ServiceFee">
      <s:complexType>
        <s:sequence>
          <s:element minOccurs="1" maxOccurs="1" name="amount"
              type="s:decimal" />
            <s:element minOccurs="1" maxOccurs="1" name="type"
              type="s1:char" />
        </s:sequence>
      </s:complexType>
    </s:element>
                              Description of types relevant to the
                              service request

    <s:element name="ServiceFeeResponse">
      <s:complexType>
        <s:sequence>
          <s:element minOccurs="1" maxOccurs="1"
              name="ServiceFeeResult" type="s:decimal" />
        </s:sequence>
      </s:complexType>
    </s:element>
                          Description of types relevant to the
                          service response

    <s:element name="decimal" type="s:decimal" />
  </s:schema>

  <s:schema attributeFormDefault="qualified"
      elementFormDefault="qualified"
      targetNamespace="http://microsoft.com/wsdl/types/">
    <s:simpleType name="char">
      <s:restriction base="s:unsignedShort" />
    </s:simpleType>
  </s:schema>
</types>
```

FIGURE E.7
<types> element defining types used in the Fees Web Service.

Note the definition of the decimal type named amount and the char type named type.
Similarly, the message parts types of the ServiceFeeResponse message are defined:

```
<s:element name="ServiceFeeResponse">

  <s:complexType>

    <s:sequence>

      <s:element minOccurs="1" maxOccurs="1"

          name="ServiceFeeResult" type="s:decimal" />

    </s:sequence>

  </s:complexType>

</s:element>
```

In this case, a single decimal type named ServiceFeeResult is defined.

Messages and Parts

The message is the payload. Typically there are two messages: an input or request message sent for the client to the service and an output or response message sent from the service to the client. The message is protocol neutral in that it may be used with SOAP, HTTP GET or any other protocol.

A message is described with the WSDL **<message>** element, shown in Figure E.8. The **name** attribute provides a unique name among the messages defined in the WSDL document. The WSDL tools have naming conventions that provide for uniqueness.

```
<message name="ServiceFeeHttpGetIn">
  <part name="amount" type="s:string" />
  <part name="type" type="s:string" />
</message>
<message name="ServiceFeeHttpGetOut">
  <part name="Body" element="s0:decimal" />
</message>
```

FIGURE E.8
Messages in the WSDL document.

In the example, the message associated with the request is named "ServiceFeeHttpGetIn." Similarly, the name associated with the response is "ServiceFeeHttpGetOut."

The message element contains one or more **<part>** elements. The part element **name** provides a unique name among all the parts in the message. Again, the WSDL tools have naming conventions that provide the uniqueness. Each part describes a type using a message-typing attribute:

- **element**   An XSD element
- **type**   An XSD simpleType or complexType

For example, the message

```
<message name="ServiceFeeHttpGetIn">
  <part name="amount" type="s:string" />
  <part name="type" type="s:string" />
</message>
```

is associated with the HttpGet input protocol. The parts correspond to the request parameters. Note that the type attribute values prefix refers to the namespace http://www.w3.org/2001/XMLSchema.

The message

```
<message name="ServiceFeeHttpGetOut">
  <part name="Body" element="s0:decimal" />
</message>
```

is associated with the HttpGet output protocol. The part corresponds to the return value. The type attribute value prefix refers to the namespace http://tempuri.org/, a temporary development namespace. The HTTP POST protocol message elements are similarly defined; the SOAP protocol message elements are shown in Figure E.9.

```
<message name="ServiceFeeSoapIn">
  <part name="parameters" element="s0:ServiceFee" />
</message>
<message name="ServiceFeeSoapOut">
  <part name="parameters" element="s0:ServiceFeeResponse" />
</message>
```

FIGURE E.9
SOAP protocol message elements.

In this case, the element attribute is used to associate the message with types defined in the schema:

```
element="s0:ServiceFee"
```

and

```
element="s0:ServiceFeeResponse"
```

Note!

Parts enable the logical abstract definition of message content.

Port Types and Operations

The collection of methods, formally called operations, are represented with the **<port-Type>** element. For example, the port type element relating the HttpGet protocol operation is shown in Figure E.10. The name attribute provides a unique name among all the port types within the document.

```
<portType name="FeesHttpGet">
  <operation name="ServiceFee">
    <input message="s0:ServiceFeeHttpGetIn" />
    <output message="s0:ServiceFeeHttpGetOut" />
  </operation>
</portType>
```

FIGURE E.10
Port type element relating HttpGet request and response messages.

The **<operation>** element contains input and output elements that name a message by its fully qualified name. The **<input>** element specifies abstract request messages and the **<output>** element specifies abstract response messages. For example,

```
<input message="s0:ServiceFeeHttpGetIn" />
```

specifies the abstract input message s0:ServiceFeeHttpGetIn. Similarly,

```
<output message="s0:ServiceFeeHttpGetOut" />
```

specifies the abstract output message s0:ServiceFeeHttpGetOut. The HTTP POST protocol portType element is similarly defined. The SOAP protocol portType element is shown in Figure E.11.

```
<portType name="FeesSoap">
  <operation name="ServiceFee">
    <input message="s0:ServiceFeeSoapIn" />
    <output message="s0:ServiceFeeSoapOut" />
  </operation>
</portType>
```

FIGURE E.11
SOAP protocol portType element.

Note!

A port type abstractly represents the methods, formally called operations, exposed by the service.

Binding

Bindings define the concrete aspects of operations and are effected by the **<binding>** element. The **name** attribute is unique among all the bindings in the document. The **type** attribute references the portType that it binds. For example, the binding in Figure E.12 binds the portType FeesHttpGet.

```
<binding name="FeesHttpGet" type="s0:FeesHttpGet">
  <http:binding verb="GET" />
  <operation name="ServiceFee">
    <http:operation location="/ServiceFee" />
    <input>
      <http:urlEncoded />
    </input>
    <output>
      <mime:mimeXml part="Body" />
    </output>
  </operation>
</binding>
```

FIGURE E.12
Binding for the HttpGet protocol.

Binding information is specified by the element

```
<http:binding verb="GET" />
```

The <http:binding> element indicates that the binding uses HTTP and its verb, in this case, GET. Valid verb values are GET and POST.

Operation binding information is specified by the element

```
<operation name="ServiceFee">

</operation>
```

The location attribute in the <http:operation> element specifies a relative URI for the operation. For example, the relative address "/ServiceFee" is specified in the element

```
<http:operation location="/ServiceFee" />
```

Concrete grammar for input and output operations is specified by the input and output elements. The **<http:urlEncoded>** element indicates that the message parts are encoded using the URI-encoding. Similarly, the **<mime:mimeXml>** element indicates that the message parts are encoded in a MIME (multipurpose Internet mail extensions) format.

Note!

MIME (multipurpose Internet mail extensions) is an encoding standard promulgated by the Internet Engineering Task Force (IETF).

The HTTP POST protocol binding element is similarly defined. The SOAP protocol binding element is shown in Figure E.13.

```
<binding name="FeesSoap" type="s0:FeesSoap">
  <soap:binding transport="http: //schemas.xmlsoap.org/soap/http"
          style="document" />
  <operation name="ServiceFee">
   <soap:operation soapAction="http: //tempuri.org/ServiceFee"
          style="document" />
   <input>
     <soap:body use="literal" />
   </input>
   <output>
     <soap:body use="literal" />
   </output>
  </operation>
</binding>
```

FIGURE E.13
SOAP protocol portType element.

Service

A **<service>** element aggregates the ports. The **name** attribute is unique among the services defined in the document. The service with name attribute Fees is shown in Figure E.14.

```
<service name="Fees">
  <port name="FeesSoap" binding="s0:FeesSoap">
    <soap:address location="http://localhost/FeeServices/Fees.asmx" />
  </port>
  <port name="FeesHttpGet" binding="s0:FeesHttpGet">
    <http:address location="http://localhost/FeeServices/Fees.asmx" />
  </port>
  <port name="FeesHttpPost" binding="s0:FeesHttpPost">
    <http:address location="http://localhost/FeeServices/Fees.asmx" />
  </port>
</service>
```

FIGURE E.14
Service element aggregates the service's ports.

The ports are specified with the **<port>** element. For example,

```
<port name="FeesHttpGet" binding="s0:FeesHttpGet">
<http:address location=
    "http://localhost/FeeServices/Fees.asmx" />
</port>
```

The **name** attribute uniquely identifies the port and the **binding** attribute specifies the applicable binding. The **<http:address>** element specifies the actual service address with a **location** attribute, in this case, http://localhost/FeeServices/Fees.asmx. The file Fees.asmx shown in Figure E.15 is located in the FeeServices directory of the server.

```
<%@ WebService Language="c#"
               Codebehind="Fees.asmx.cs"
               Class="FeeServices.Fees"
%>
```

FIGURE E.15
File Fees.asmx.

The Web Service directive Class attribute references the class Fees, declared in the code-behind file Fees.asmx.cs. Figure E.2 shows the class Fees.

Appendix F

Relational Database Fundamentals

Databases are the primary medium of information storage; the relational database is the most widely used type of database. Software used to store and manage data in these databases are referred to as **relational database management systems (RDMSs)**. Commonly used RDMSs are described below:

- Microsoft Access is a widely used RDMS for departmental and intranet applications. A major advantage is that it can be administered by clerical and administrative staff.
- Oracle is the most widely used RDMS and is a robust, full-feature RDBM suitable for enterprise and distributed applications. Administration of Oracle databases is best left to certified Oracle database administrators.
- Microsoft SQLServer is an increasingly used RDMS. SQLServer is full featured and robust and suitable for enterprise and distributed applications. Administration of SQLServer databases is best left to certified SQLServer database administrators.

Underlying relational databases are the concepts of tables and table relationships. Tables provide for the structured storage of data. The ability to relate tables provides for the efficient and effective management of data stored in tables.

Table Basics

Tables are widely used to store data. For example, Figure F.1 illustrates the type of chart that might be used by a school secretary or administrator to quickly reference the school's students. Note that the chart is tabular in character. Each row of the chart contains data regarding a specific student — specifically, the student's last name, first name, social security number, emergency contact name and emergency contact telephone number. Note also that the data are arranged as columns; for example, last name is in the first column and emergency contact is in the fifth column.

			Students		
Last Name	First Name	Grade	SSI	Contact	Telephone
Care	Helen	6	202 46 8759	Care, Joan	973 762 5465
Dash	Thomas	6	202 77 8392	Dash, Thomas, Sr.	973 330 9161
Smart	Harry	5	201 18 8101	Wilma Smart	973 239 4751
Williams	Mary	5	202 30 1782	Ronda Williams	973 775 4802
Wilson	William	6	201 73 2820	Annette Blue	973 445 1826

FIGURE F.1
Chart used to quickly reference students.

Tables provide a natural means of arranging data for easy use. A more formal structure, illustrating naming practices and terminology used in the industry, is shown in Figure F.2.

The table consists of rows and columns or attributes. It is essential that each table row pertain to a specific student and that a student be uniquely represented by a single row. Imagine the consequences if a single student were to be represented by more than one row and the data pertaining to the student were different in each row. Characteristics describing the students (often referred to as attributes) are arranged in columns. These attributes are referred to by name. Note that the attribute names do not contain spaces and the first letter of each word is capitalized, a common naming convention.

A new column, named StudentID, which assigns each row a unique identifier, has been added. This unique identifier enables a specific row to be referenced simply by specifying the value of the StudentID. Note also that the StudentID has integral values. Although any data type can be used as long as each row has a unique value, integral values are used as the unique identifier for performance values.

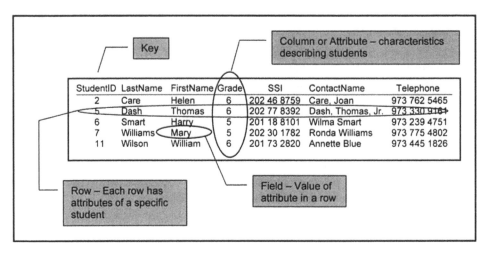

FIGURE F.2
Formalized version of student information table.

The unique attribute used to reference a specific row is known as the key. Although the SSI is unique to each student and could be used as a key, the SSI is generally expressed with spaces, as shown, or dashes as in 202–46–8759, neither of which can be represented as an integral value. Most RDMSs provide for the automatic assignment of unique values to the attribute used as a key when a new entity, in this case, student, is added to the table.

Typically, the table would contain many more attributes, such as street address, city, county, state, postal code, English proficiency, migratory status, birth date, race and sex. A student table at a state institution could easily contain more than 50,000 rows. A table with 50 attributes for 50,000 rows (containing 2,500,000 values) is common. Larger tables are not unusual.

A database administrator or designer would specify the table with a table schema, which specifies the table's fields, as shown in Figure F.3. The field, StudentID, is specified as the table's key. Note that integral values are assigned automatically. The LastName, First-Name, ContactName and Telephone fields have string data type. The Grade field has Integer data type. Other data types that can be used include date, time, currency, hyperlink and memo.

```
┌─────────────────────────────────────────────────────────────────────────────┐
│ Name: Student                                                                 │
│                                                                               │
│ Field Name      Data Type                 Indexed  Caption            Key     │
│ StudentID       Long Integer, Automatic   Y        Student ID         X       │
│ LastName        String                    Y        Last Name                  │
│ FirstName       String                    Y        First Name                 │
│ Grade           Integer                   Y        Grade                      │
│ SSI             String                    N        S S I                      │
│ ContactName     String                    N        Contact Name               │
│ Telephone       String                    N        Contact Telephone          │
└─────────────────────────────────────────────────────────────────────────────┘
```

FIGURE F.3
Student table schema.

The RDMS builds indexes for some attributes. Use of the index tables provides for efficient lookup, and subsequent retrieval, of rows with a specific value. For example, assume that the RDMS has been directed to reference all of the students in grade 5. The Grade field of the Student table is defined indexed in the table schema.

As a result, the RDMS builds and maintains the index described in Figure F.4. When required to reference students in grade 5, the RDMS first reviews the index, which is a small table, and quickly identifies the unique identifiers of the applicable students, i.e., students with ID values 6 and 7.

Grade	StudentID
5	6
5	7
6	2
6	5
6	11

FIGURE F.4
Grade index for Student Table.

As such, the entire Student table need not be reviewed to identify those students in grade 5. This is not important for the sample table, but reviewing all of the entries in a table of more than 50,000 rows to find those rows with a specific attribute value is no little task, even for an advanced computer. Consequently, indexing is an important performance consideration. On the other hand, maintenance of the indexes is a performance-robbing overhead. The proper balance is one of the trade-offs made by experienced database designers and administrators.

The schema provides for the specification of captions for each attribute that are typically displayed in place of the field names in reports. Although field names should be self-explanatory, some database designers prefer short abbreviated names, which can prove to be cryptic when displayed on a report.

An abbreviated form of the schema is often used to illustrate the key elements of a table in design diagrams, as shown in Figure F.5.

Selecting Data For Retrieval

Structured Query Language (SQL) is the standard language for relational databases, providing for expressing statements that can insert, delete, update and retrieve data stored

```
          Student
        StudentID
        LastName
        FirstName
        Grade
        SSI
        ContactName
        Telephone
```

FIGURE F.5
Abreviated Student table schema used in design diagrams

in a relational database. High-level languages, such as C# and Visual Basic, provide for embedding SQL statements in programs written in these languages. SQL is declarative in that a simple sentence is used in place of procedural code to affect database management.

The basic SQL construct is the SQL SELECT statement. The SELECT statement defines rows that are to be retrieved, that is, rows returned from a table. An elementary form of the SELECT statement is shown in Figure F.6.

> **SELECT** *attributes returned*
> **FROM** *tables containing the attributes to be returned*
> **WHERE** *conditions satisfied by rows selected*
> :

FIGURE F.6
Elementary form of SELECT statement.

The SELECT part of the statement defines the attributes that are to be returned. The FROM part of the statement defines the tables from which the data for the specified attributes are to be retrieved. The WHERE part of the statement defines the conditions that the retrieved rows must meet. An example of a SELECT statement defining selection of last name and first name attribute values for students in the fifth grade is the following:

```
SELECT LastName, FirstName
FROM Student
WHERE Grade = 5;
```

Basically, the rows of the table specified in the FROM part are examined one at a time. The Student table is specified in the FROM part. Those rows are selected for which the conditions of the WHERE part, in this case Grade = 5, are satisfied; the third and fourth rows meet the conditions. Those attributes, in the selected rows specified in the SELECT part, are returned. The specified attributes are LastName and FirstName. Figure F.7 shows the returned data stored as a table in memory.

```
Smart        Harry
Williams     Mary
```

FIGURE F.7
Data returned by example SELECT statement.

The selected data stored in memory, can be accessed programmatically using constructs in the programming language. The asterisk (*) can be used in the SELECT part to specify that all attributes be returned. For example,

```
SELECT *
FROM Student
WHERE Grade = 5;
```

returns the information shown in Figure F.8.

| 6 | Smart | Harry | 5 | 201 18 8101 | Wilma Smart | 973 239 4751 |
| 7 | Williams | Mary | 5 | 202 30 1782 | Ronda Williams | 973 775 4802 |

FIGURE F.8
Data returned by example SELECT statement with *.

Note that all attributes for the selected rows are returned. Note that arithmetic expressions can also be used in the SELECT statement. For example,

```
SELECT LastName, FirstName, ContactName, Telephone FROM Student
WHERE Grade > (7 - 6)*5;
```

returns the information found in Figure F.9.

Care	Helen	Care, Joan	973 762 5465
Dash	Thomas	Dash, Thomas, Jr.	973 330 9164
Wilson	William	Annette Blue	973 445 1826

FIGURE F.9
Data returned by example SELECT statement with arithmetic expression.

Logical AND and OR keywords can be used to return data rows meeting more than one condition. For example,

```
SELECT LastName, FirstName, ContactName, Telephone
FROM Student
WHERE ((LastName>"W*") AND (Grade = 5));
```

returns rows in the table where the student is in grade 5 and the first name begins with the letter W. Note use of the string literal "W*" that specifies a string with first letter W and following characters. The asterisk stands for all possible character strings. The table returned is shown in Figure F.9.

| Williams | Mary | Ronda, Williams | 973 775 4802 |

FIGURE F.10
Data returned by example SELECT statement with compound condition.

The dot operator can be used to fully qualify names. For example, the attributes are fully qualified by prefixing the attribute with the table name:

```
SELECT Student.LastName, Student.FirstName, Student.ContactName,
Student.Telephone
FROM Student
WHERE (((Student.LastName)>"W*") AND ((Student.Grade) = 5));
```

Related Tables

Related tables can be used to store related data efficiently. For example, consider the need to record the students' English proficiency. A suitable classification of English proficiency is the following:

- Native speaker
- Fluent speaker
- Limited proficiency/language learner
- Non-English speaking
- Redesignated as fluent/proficient
- Status unknown

A simple approach is to add another column to the Student table to store English proficiency classification. This requires addition of a column capable of storing the longest classification caption, in this case, "Limited proficiency/language learner." This approach has two major drawbacks. First, the addition of a field to store the caption requires a storage space for each character in the caption, in this case 36. In a large database with 50,000 students, this amounts to almost 2 million storage spaces — a costly solution in terms of cost of storage and performance degradation due to increased size.

Second, the entry of a classification such as "Redesignated as fluent/proficient" each time that it is required is highly unlikely. An entry such as "Redesignated as fluent" or "Redesignated proficient" means the same thing and in all likelihood would be interpreted correctly by a user; however, this represents a small sample of the possible variations. Imagine the WHERE clause in a SELECT statement required to return all of the students with English proficiency of "Redesignated as fluent/proficient."

A better approach is provided by the entry of a code in the Student table that relates to a classification in an EnglishProficiency table. This requires the addition of a column to the Student table capable of storing a numeric code and the creation of an English Proficiency table that relates the numeric code to the classification captions, as shown in Figure F.11. The diagram shows the relationship between the database's tables and is called a **relationship diagram**. A line is drawn between the fields, providing the basis of the relationship between the two tables. Symbols at each end of the line are used to describe the relationship further. In this case, the symbols indicate that many rows in the Student table relate to a single row in the EnglishProficiency table. Similar notations are used by database designers to indicate other relationships. A revised Student table and new English Proficiency table are shown in Figures F.12 and F.13.

As shown, students Helen Care, Thomas Dash and William Wilson are classified in terms of English proficiency as "Native speaker." Harry Smart and Mary Williams are classified as "Fluent speaker" and "Redesignated as fluent/proficient," respectively.

Note the advantages of this solution:

- A number is used to classify English proficiency in the Student table, resulting in a minimal size increase in the Student table size.
- The entry of the codes provides for unambiguous identification of English proficiency classification in the Student table. Typically, the available classifications are presented to the user entering the classification as a list from which one must be selected.

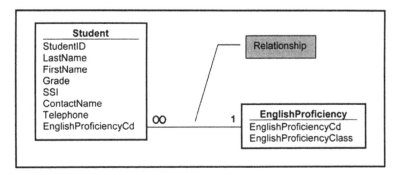

FIGURE F.11
Database design with related tables

StudentID	LastName	FirstName	Grade	SSI	ContactName	Telephone	EnglishProficiencyCd
2	Care	Helen	6	202 46 8759	Care, Joan	973 762 5465	01
5	Dash	Thomas	6	202 77 8392	Dash, Thomas, Jr.	973 330 9161	01
6	Smart	Harry	5	201 18 8101	Wilma Smart	973 239 4751	02
7	Williams	Mary	5	202 30 1782	Ronda Williams	973 775 4802	05
11	Wilson	William	6	201 73 2820	Annette Blue	973 445 1826	01

FIGURE F.12
Revised Student table with English proficiency code added.

EnglishProficiencyCd	EnglishProficiencyClass
01	Native speaker
02	Fluent speaker
03	Limited proficiency/language learner
04	Non-English speaking
05	Redesignated as fluent/proficient
99	Status unknown

FIGURE F.13
EnglishProficiency table.

Name: Student

Field Name	Data Type	Indexed	Caption	Key
StudentID	Long Integer, Automatic	Y	Student ID	X
LastName	String	Y	Last Name	
FirstName	String	Y	First Name	
Grade	Integer	Y	Grade	
SSI	String	N	S S I	
ContactName	String	N	Contact Name	
Telephone	String	N	Contact Telephone	
EnglishProficiencyCd	Long Integer	Y	English Proficiency Code	

FIGURE F.14
Student table schema revised to include EnglishProficiencyCd.

The downside is that two tables must be accessed when the caption associated with the English classification caption must be returned. Schemas for the revised Student table and the EnglishProficiency table are shown in Figures F.14 and F.15, respectively.

Note that, although the key field in the EnglishProficiency table is integral, it is not automatically inserted by the RDMS. This is because the RDMS assigns the number in order and the numbers used in the table are not in order: they skip form 5 to 99. This is not a problem because entries to the table will generally be made once and thus care can be taken to ensure the key code is unique. Tables of this type are said to be **static**.

Name: EnglishProficiency				
Field Name	Data Type	Indexed	Caption	Key
EnglishProficiencyCd	Long Integer	Y	Code	X
EnglishProficiencyClass	String	Y	English Proficiency	

FIGURE F.15
EnglishProficiency table schema.

The EnglishProficiencyCd in the Student table is called a **foreign key**, which is an attribute in one table that is not a key of that table but in another table. The English-ProficiencyCd is not a key in the Student table, but it is a key in the EnglishProficiency table and thus is said to be a foreign key in the Student table. Note that a foreign key can be a set of attributes.

The EnglishProficiencyCd can be used in SELECT statements. For example, the following statement returns students with an English proficiency classification of "Redesignated as fluent/proficient":

```
SELECT LastName, FirstName, ContactName, Telephone FROM Student
    WHERE EnglishProficiencyCd = 5;
```

The data returned are shown in Figure F.16.

Williams	Mary	Ronda, Williams	973 775 4802

FIGURE F.16
Data returned by SELECT statement with English proficiency condition.

Data can be returned from more than one table. For example, the statement

```
SELECT Student.LastName, Student.FirstName,

EnglishProficiency.EnglishProficiencyClass

FROM EnglishProficiency

INNER JOIN Student

ON EnglishProficiency. EnglishProficiencyCd =

Student.EnglishProficiencyCd;
```

returns the LastName and FirstName from the Student table and EnglishProficiencyClass from the EnglishProficiency table. Rows in the two tables are joined; specifically, rows in the Student table are joined to a row in the EnglishProficiency table when the English-ProficiencyCd is the same in both tables. Note that the fully qualified names of the English-ProficiencyCd are required in order to make the reference unambiguous. For example, which reference refers to the Student table and which to the EnglishProficiency table?

The statement returns the information shown in Figure F.17.

Care	Helen	Native Speaker
Dash	Thomas	Native Speaker
Smart	Harry	Fluent Speaker
Williams	Mary	Redesignated as fluent/proficient
Wilson	William	Native Speaker

FIGURE F.17
Data returned by example SELECT statement joining Student and EnglishProficiency tables.

Note!

Many types of joins are available to the database designer to describe various methods of joining related tables.

A common problem in database design is providing for multiple instances of an attribute. For example, assume that provisions must be made for recording several contact instances, such as Mother, Father and After-School Care. One approach is provision of multiple contact columns in the Student table, as shown in Figure F.18.

```
Name: Student

Field Name           Data Type                 Indexed   Caption                     Key
StudentID            Long Integer, Automatic    Y        Student ID                  X
LastName             String                     Y        Last Name
FirstName            String                     Y        First Name
Grade                Integer                    Y        Grade
SSI                  String                     N        S S I
ContactName1         String                     N        Contact Name
Telephone1           String                     N        Contact Telephone
ContactName2         String                     N        Contact Name
Telephone2           String                     N        Contact Telephone
ContactName3         String                     N        Contact Name
Telephone3           String                     N        Contact Telephone
EnglishProficiencyCd Long Integer               Y        English Proficiency Code
```

FIGURE F.18
Student table schema revised to include columns for multiple contact entries.

Problems with this approach abound. First, the space not used for contacts is wasted. Second, what is to be done when there are more than three contacts? Fortunately, a viable approach exists: create a second table called "contact" with rows related to a specific row in the Student table. Figure F.19 shows an example of the Contact table.

ContactID	StudentID	Name	Telephone
1	1	Care, Joan	973 762 5465
2	5	Dash, Thomas, Jr	973 330 9101
3	5	Dash, Evelyn	973 330 9101
4	6	Smart, Wilma	973 239 4751
5	7	Williams, Neville	414 539 6249
6	7	Williams, Ronda	973 775 4802
7	11	Blue, Annette	973 445 1826

FIGURE F.19
Contact table.

The ContactID attribute provides for the unique identification of each row of the table. The StudentID attribute relates rows in the Contact table to a single row in the Student table. For example, the fifth and sixth rows of the Contact table relate to the fourth row of the Student table. That is, Neville Williams and Ronda Williams are contacts for Mary Williams. Note that, in this approach, all of the contact information is removed from the Student table. Because records are added to the Contact table only when needed, the database does not have wasted space.

A revised database relationship diagram is shown in Figure F.20. The diagram indicates that multiple records in the Contact table relate to a single record in the Student table. The rows in the two tables are related by the StudentID attribute. In this arrangement,

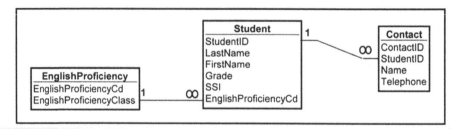

FIGURE F.20
Database design with related tables.

the rows in the contact are referred to as the **child** rows and the related row in the Student table is referred to as the **parent** row.

Data can be returned from both tables. The following SELECT statement returns the LastName and FirstName attribute values from the Student table. The related Name and Telephone attribute values from the Contact table are also returned:

```
SELECT Student.LastName, Student.FirstName, Student.StudentID,
Contact.StudentID, SContact.Name, Contact.Telephone,
Contact.ContactID
FROM Contact
INNER JOIN Student
ON Contact.StudentID = Student.StudentID;
```

Note that the attributes, or fields, are fully qualified, thereby eliminating ambiguity. For example, Contact.StudentID refers to the StudentID attribute in the Contact table and Student.StudentID refers to the StudentID attribute in the Student table. Data returned are shown in Figure F.21. The StudentId attribute values from both tables are returned to further illustrate the concept underlying the joining of related records.

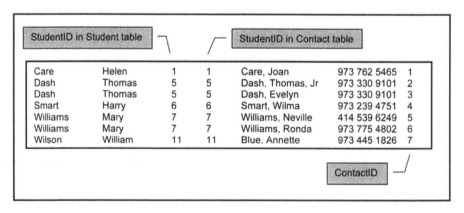

FIGURE F.21
Data returned by SELECT statement joining Student and Contact tables.

Note!

Database designers have a process, known as **normalization,** that is used to develop efficient and effective databases. An accepted classification provides for five levels of normalization. Typically, databases should be normalized to the third level.

Updating Tables

Appending a Record to the Contact Table

The INSERT INTO statement appends a row in a specified table. Figure F.22 shows the INSERT INTO statement syntax.

```
INSERT INTO table ( list of attributes )
VALUES ( values inserted into corresponding attributes )
;
```

FIGURE F.22
Elementary form of INSERT INTO statement.

The INSERT INTO part of the statement defines the *table* to which the row will be appended and *lists the attributes* for which values will be specified. The list is enclosed in parentheses. The VALUES part of the statement defines the *values that will be inserted* into the corresponding attributes listed in the INSERT INTO part of the statement. The values are also enclosed in parentheses. An example of an INSERT INTO statement defining the values for the StudentID, Name and Telephone attributes of a new row appended to the Contact table is the following:

```
INSERT INTO Contact (StudentID, Name, Telephone)
Values (5,"A Name","Telephone No.");
```

In this case, the table contains the ContactID field whose value is automatically assigned when a new row is added to the table. Consequently, this field is not included in the list of attributes specified in the INSERT INTO part of the statement. The list of attributes specifies the following fields: StudentID, Name and Telephone. Values inserted into these fields, specified in the VALUES part of the statement, are the following: 5, "A Name" and "Telephone No." Note that the text data type values are expressed in quotation marks.

Note!

Characters used to enclose selected data types such as text and date/time vary from RDMS to RDMS.

When executed, the statement results in the appending of a row to the Contact table with the specified values. The Contact table with the added row is shown in Figure F.23.

Updating a Record in the Contact Table

The UPDATE statement enables modification of specified rows in a specified table; the syntax of the UPDATE statement is shown in Figure F.24.

The UPDATE part of the statement specifies the *table* to be modified. The SET part of the statement consists of a comma-separated *list of attributes = value pairs* specifying the values to be assigned to the attributes in the affected rows. The WHERE part of the

FIGURE F.23
Contact table after row added by example INSERT INTO statement.

```
UPDATE table
SET list of attribute=value pairs
WHERE conditions specifying row to be updated
    :
```

FIGURE F.24
Elementary form of UPDATE statement.

statement defines the *conditions specifying the rows to be updated*. An example of an UPDATE statement changing the value of the Telephone attribute in the Contact table for rows where the ContactID value is 10 is shown below:

```
UPDATE Contact SET Contact.Telephone = "973 988 2172" WHERE
    (((Contact.ContactID) = 10));
```

The updated Contact table is shown in Figure F.25.

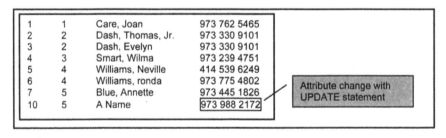

FIGURE F.25
Contact table after telephone attribute changed with UPDATE statement.

Delete a Record in the Contact Table

The DELETE statement removes specified rows from a specified table; its syntax is shown in Figure F.26.

```
DELETE *
FROM table
WHERE conditions specifying row to be deleted
    :
```

FIGURE F.26
Elementary form of DELETE statement.

The *table* from which the rows are to de deleted is specified in the FROM part of the statement. The rows to be removed are specified with the *conditions* in the WHERE part of the statement. An example of a DELETE statement is shown below:

```
DELETE  *
FROM Contact
WHERE ContactID = 10;
```

Rows in the table Contact in which the ContactID value is 10 are deleted. Note that ContactID is a primary key, and thus a single row is deleted. Figure F.27 shows the Contact table after the row where ContactID = 10 is deleted.

1	1	Care, Joan	973 762 5465
2	2	Dash, Thomas, Jr.	973 330 9101
3	2	Dash, Evelyn	973 330 9101
4	3	Smart, Wilma	973 239 4751
5	4	Williams, Neville	414 539 6249
6	4	Williams, Ronda	973 775 4802
7	5	Blue, Annette	973 445 1826

FIGURE F.27
Contact table after deletion of row where ContactID = 10.

Note!

The unique character of the primary key enables unambiguous table access.

Hands-On Exercise: Creating a Student Administration Database

Step 1: Create the StudentAdministrator Database

1. Open Access.
2. Start → Microsoft Access. The Microsoft Access dialog box presents database creation options.
3. Select the Blank Access database radio button option.
4. Click the OK button.
5. The File New Database dialog box opens.
6. Navigate to the C:\Inetpub\wwwroot folder.
7. Click the Create New Folder icon. The New Folder dialog box opens.
8. Enter "StudentAdministrator" in the Name textbox.
9. Click the OK button.
10. The File New Database dialog box regains focus at the StudentAdministrator folder.
11. Create a new database file. Enter "StudentAdministratorDB" in the File Name textbox.
12. Accept the default Save as Type value: Microsoft Access Databases.

FIGURE F.HO.1
Microsoft Access dialog box with creation options.

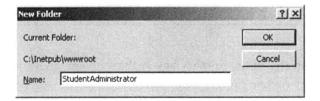

FIGURE F.HO.2
New Folder dialog box.

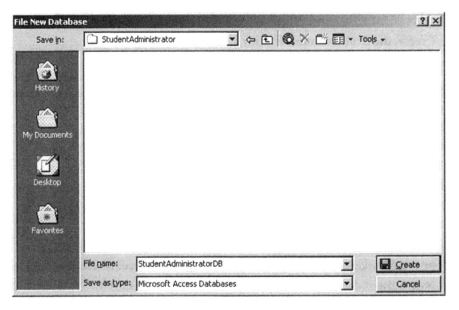

FIGURE F.HO.3
File New Data dialog box.

13. Click the Create button. Microsoft Access creates the new database. The Database window is displayed. The database objects are shown at the left side of the window.

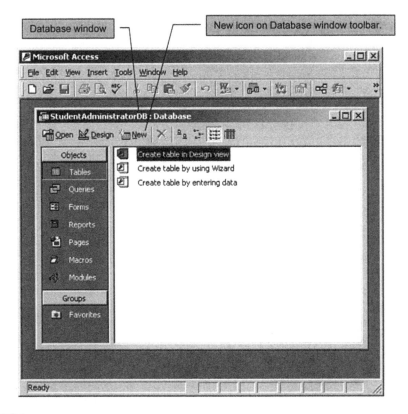

FIGURE F.HO.4
Database Window.

Step 2: Create Student Table

1. Select the Tables object option.
2. Click the New icon on the Database window toolbar. The New Table dialog box opens.

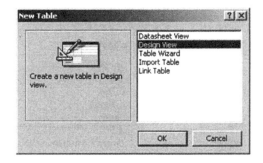

FIGURE F.HO.5
New Table dialog box.

3. Select the Design View option. Click the OK button. Alternately, double-click the Design View option.

4. Define the table fields. Enter the field name in the Field Name column. In the Data Type column, click the down arrow at the left side of the column and select the desired data type. A description of the field is optional and is entered in the Description column.

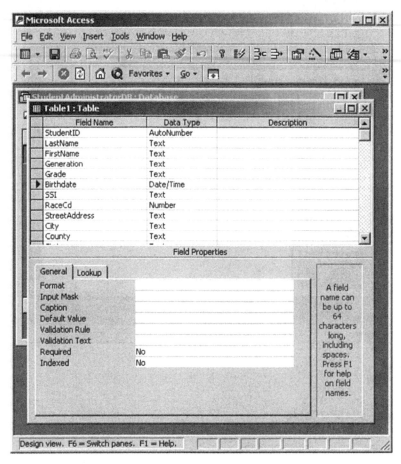

FIGURE F.HO.6
Table Design View window.

5. Enter the following:

Field Name	Data Type	Field Name	Data Type
StudentID	AutoNumber	RaceCd	Number
LastName	Text	StreetAddress	Text
FirstName	Text	City	Text
Generation	Text	Country	Text
Grade	Text	State	Text
Birthdate	Date/Time	ZIP	Text
Sex	Text	EnglishProficiencyCd	Text
SSI	Text		

6. Right-click the StudentID Field Name entry. Select Primary key from the submenu.

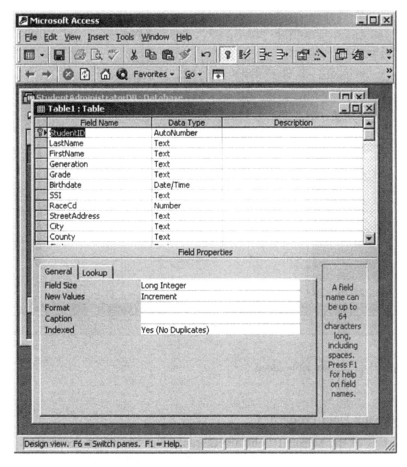

FIGURE F.HO.7
Table Design View window with Primary Key field designated

7. Alternately, select the table schema row containing the StudentID Field Name. Click the primary key icon on the toolbar.
8. In the File menu, select the Save As... option. Alternately, save the table by clicking the Save icon on the Toolbar. The Save As dialog box opens.

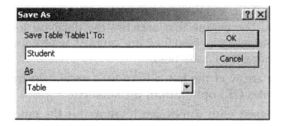

FIGURE F.HO.8
Save As dialog box.

9. Enter the name of the table in the first textbox, in this case "Student."
10. Click the OK button. The Student table is created.
11. Close the Table object design window.

FIGURE F.HO.9
Database Window with Student table added.

Step 3: Modifying Field Properties

Field properties of the selected field are displayed in the Field Properties panel at the bottom of the Table object design window. Often the default properties associated with a data type can be changed to provide for a more efficient database.

1. Select the Generation field. This field is intended to record name suffixes such as Jr., Sr. and III. The default field size is 50 characters. Most generation titles can fit in a field of 5 characters.

2. Change the field size to 5. The field reduction saves 45 spaces, a very large amount in a database with 50,000 rows.

3. Select the Grade field. It is expected that many information queries will refer to a specific grade. The engine that searches the database to satisfy queries will utilize applicable indexes. Searches are quicker where an index is available; consequently, index the Grade field.

4. Click the down arrow at the left side of the Grade field Index property. Select the Yes (Duplicates OK) option from the submenu.

5. The field is indexed with duplicates to allow for the entry of more than one student with the same grade value. The default field size of the Grade field is 50 characters or memory spaces. Typically, the grades will be 1 through 12. In some cases, the grade classification provides for sections of a grade, for example, 1A or 7B.

6. Change the field size property value to 3. Again, storage space is saved.

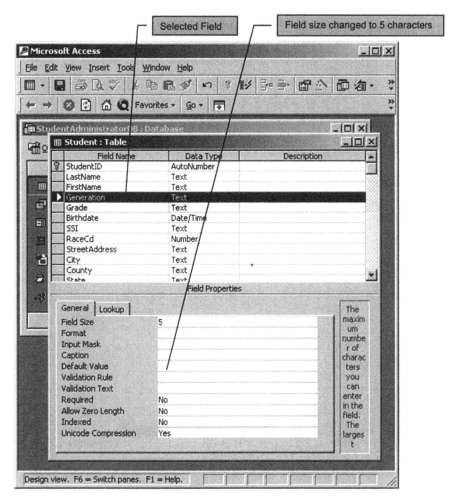

FIGURE F.HO.10
Student Table Design View field property assignment.

7. Modify the Student table's field properties to conform to the following:

Field	Property	Value
LastName	Field Size	30
	Indexed	Yes (Duplicates)
FirstName	Field Size	20
	Indexed	Yes (Duplicates)
SSI	Field Size	11
StreetAddress	Field Size	30
City	Field Size	20
County	Field Size	20
State	Field Size	2
ZIP	Field Size	5

8. Save the changes. Click the Save icon on the toolbar. Alternately, in the File menu select the Save option.

9. Close the Table object design window.

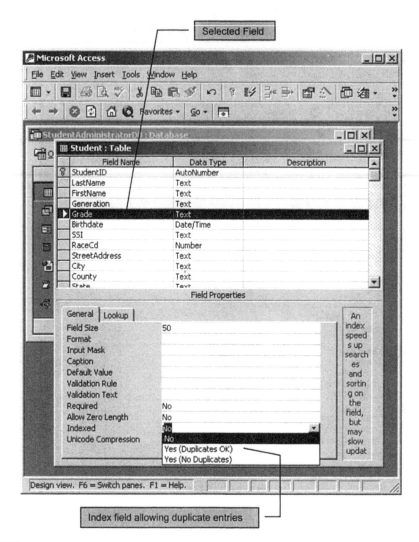

FIGURE F.HO.11
Student Table Design View field index property assignment.

Step 4: Create the English Proficiency Table

1. Select the Tables in the Objects pane of the Database window.
2. Double-click the Create table in Design View icon in the Database window. The Table design window opens.
3. Enter the following:

Field Name	Data Type
EnglishProficiencyCd	Number
EnglishProficiencyClass	Text

4. Click the margin to the left of the EnglishProficiencyCd to select the row.
5. Click the primary key icon. Care must be taken to ensure that the EnglishProficiencyCd values are unique.

6. In the Field Properties window, set the Indexed field property value:
   Yes (No Duplicates).

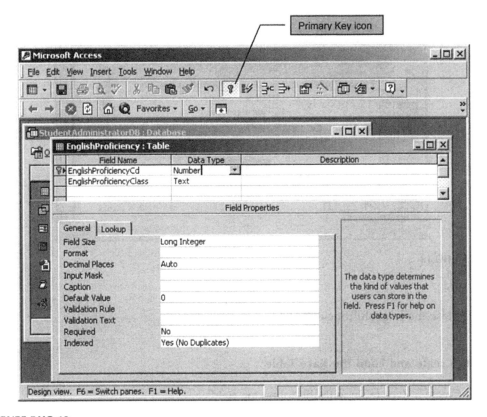

FIGURE F.HO.12
Primary Key icon in Database Window.

7. Save the table with the name "EnglishProficiency."
8. Close the Table object design window.

Step 5: Load EnglishProficiency Table with Data

1. In the Database window, double-click the EnglishProficiency table, which will open in the data mode. Note that the column names appear across the top of the table. The first data row appears under the column titles.
2. Click the EnglishProficiencyCd field in the first data row. Enter "1."
3. Click the EnglishProficiencyClass field in the first data row. Enter "Native speaker."
4. Complete the table with the following entries:

EnglishProficiencyCd	EnglishProficiencyClass
2	Fluent speaker
3	Limited proficiency/language learner
4	Non-English speaking
5	Redesignated as fluent/proficient
99	Status unknown

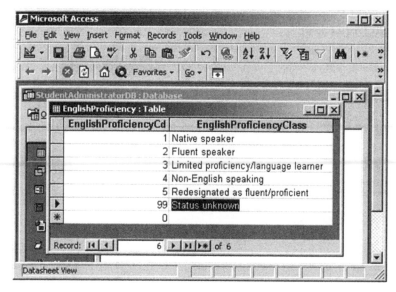

FIGURE F.HO.13
Table View.

5. Close the EnglishProficiency table.

Step 6: Create and Load the Race Table

1. Create a Race table with the following fields:

FieldName	DataType
RaceCd	Number
RaceClass	Text

2. In the Field Properties window for the RaceCd field, set the Indexed property value to Yes (No Duplicates).
3. Set the RaceCd field as the Primary Key.
4. Save the table with the name "Race."
5. Load the table with the following data:

RaceCd	RaceClass
1	American Indian/Alaskan Native
2	Asian
3	Black/African American
4	Native Hawaiian/Pacific Islander
5	White

6. Save the table.

Step 7: Create Contact Table

1. Create a Contact table with the following fields:

FieldName	DataType
ContactID	AutoNumber
StudentId	Number
Name	Text
Telephone	Text

2. In the Field Properties window for the StudentID field, set the Indexed property value to Yes (Duplicates OK).
3. In the Field Properties window for the Telephone field, set the Field Size property value to 12.
4. Set the ContactID field as the Primary Key.
5. Save the table with the name "Contact."
6. Load the table with the following data:

ContactID	StudentID	Name	Telephone
1	1	Care, Joan	973 762 5465
2	2	Dash, Thomas, Jr.	973 330 9101
3	2	Dash, Evelyn	973 330 9101
4	3	Smart, Wilma	973 239 4751
5	4	Williams, Neville	414 539 6249
6	4	Williams, Ronda	973 775 4802
7	5	Blue, Annette	973 445 1826

7. Save and Close the table.

Step 8: Load Student Table with Data

1. In the Database window, select the Student table.
2. Click the Open icon in the toolbar to open the table in the data mode. Alternately, right-click the Student table and select the Open option in the submenu. The Student table opens in the data mode.
3. Click the LastName field in the first data row. Enter the student's last name — in this case, "Care." The first column contains the StudentID field, which is AutoNumber data type. Values of the StudentID for a row are added automatically when data are added to any field in the row.
4. Click the FirstName field in the first data row. Enter the student's first name: "Helen."
5. Skip the Generation field.
6. Click the Grade field in the first data row. Enter the student's grade: "6."
7. Click the Birthdate field in the first data row. Enter the student's birthdate: "11/04/1990."
8. Click the SSI field in the first data row. Enter "202 46 8759."
9. Click the RaceCd field in the first data row. Enter "1."

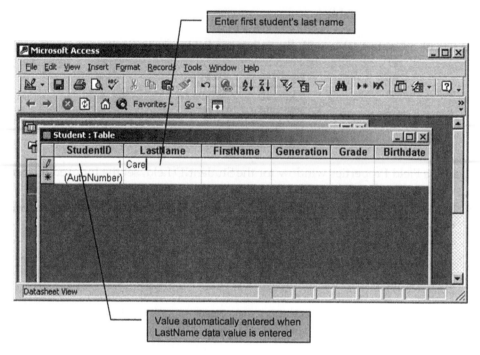

FIGURE F.HO.14
Student table ready for data entry.

10. Click the StreetAddress field in the first data row. Enter "510 Sixteenth Ave."
11. Click the City field in the first data row. Enter "Belmar."
12. Click the County field in the first data row. Enter "Monmouth."
13. Click the State field in the first data row. Enter "NJ."
14. Click the ZIP field in the first data row. Enter "07719."
15. Click the EnglishProficiency field in the first data row. Enter "1." The first row, describing the student Helen Care, is complete.
16. Click the Save icon to save the table.
17. Continue to load the Student table rows with the following data:

Field Name	Row 2	Row 3	Row 4	Row 5
LastName	Dash	Smart	Williams	Wilson
FirstName	Thomas	Harry	Mary	William
Generation				
Grade	6	5	5	6
Birthdate	9/4/1990	2/1/1989	10/4/1988	3/25/1990
SSI	202 77 8392	201 18 8101	202 30 1782	201 73 2820
RaceCd	2	3	4	5
StreetAddress	1729 Federal St.	1432 Annin St.	742 Ocean Blvd.	1104 Belmar Blvd.
City	Belmar	South Belmar	Spring Lake	Wall Township
County	Monmouth	Monmouth	Monmouth	Monmouth
State	NJ	NJ	NJ	NJ
ZIP	07719	07718	07722	07717
EnglishProficiency	1	2	5	1

18. Save and Close the table.

Step 9: Create a Select Query: Student Contacts

1. Click Queries in the Object pane of the Database window.
2. Double-click the Create query in Design view in the Database window. The Show Table dialog box opens.

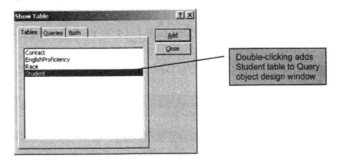

FIGURE F.HO.15
Show Table dialog box.

3. Double-click the Student table option. The Student table is added to the Query object design window.
4. Select the Contact table. Click the Add button. The Contact table is added to the Query object design window.
5. Click the Close button to close the Show Table dialog box. The tables selected are displayed in the Query object design window. Note that the possible relationship is recognized by Access.

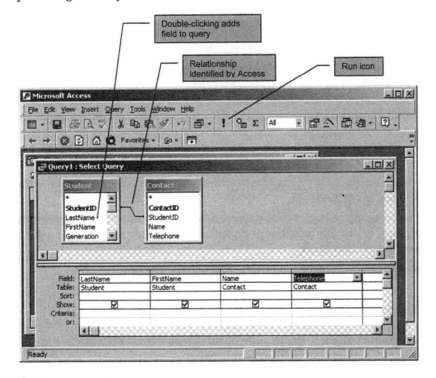

FIGURE F.HO.16
Query Design View.

6. Double-click the Student table FirstName field in the Query design window to add the field to the query.

7. Double-click the Student table LastName field in the Query design window to add the field to the query.

8. Double-click the Contact table Name field in the Query design window to add the field to the query.

9. Double-click the Contact table Telephone field in the Query design window to add the field to the query.

10. Click the Run icon to run the query. The query results are displayed.

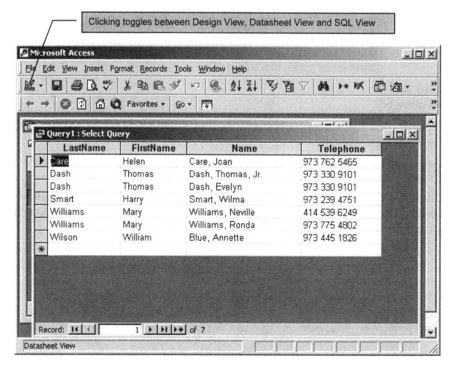

FIGURE F.HO.17
View toggle.

11. Click the arrow next to the View option icon. Select the SQL View option. The SQL View is opened.

12. Close the Query design window. Note that the user is prompted regarding saving the query. If No, the window is closed and the query is lost. If Yes, the Save As dialog box is displayed.

13. Enter Student Contacts. Click OK. The window closes.

Step 10: Run Existing Query

1. Click Queries in the Objects pane of the Database window.

2. Double-click Student Contacts in the Database window.

3. The Query design window opens with the Datasheet View of the Student Contacts query.

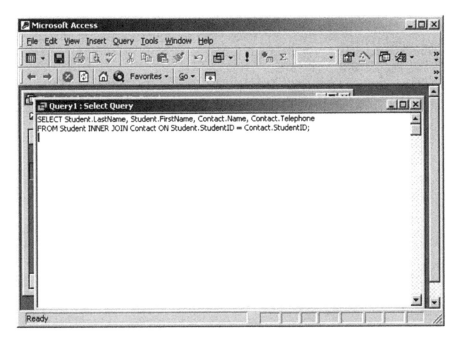

FIGURE F.HO.18
Select Query Editor Window.

Index

Acronyms

Symbols

Text

A

B

C